Architecture and Society | Selected Essays of Henry Van Brunt

Architecture and Society

Selected Essays of Henry Van Brunt

Edited with an Introductory Monograph by William A. Coles

The Belknap Press of Harvard University Press

Cambridge, Massachusetts 1969

For Elsa

The essays in this edition have been selected to give adequate representation of the range of Henry Van Brunt's writings and also to illustrate most fully his concern with architecture as it was developing in America and with the forces that were affecting that development. I have printed the earlier periodical text of a few pieces later reprinted in *Greek Lines* because they are less easily available to readers and show Van Brunt's concerns closer to the time at which they were first thought out and expressed. References, in my Introduction, to Van Brunt's writings are without page references when the essays are reprinted in this edition; otherwise the place of original publication is indicated in the bibliography of Van Brunt's works. Since that bibliography is chronologically arranged, I have given dates of publication in references to essays not reprinted so that the reader can more easily identify them.

I would like to thank Mr. John B. Bayley, Mr. Alan Burnham, Mr. Christopher Tunnard, Mr. Walter Muir Whitehill, and especially Mr. Henry Hope Reed for giving help and information. I am grateful for assistance to Mr. Jack Jackson, Mr. Bainbridge Bunting, Mr. Henry Sorenson, Mrs. Paul M. Rhymer, Curator of Prints, the Chicago Historical Society, Mr. Albert K. Baragwanath, Senior Curator, the Museum of the City of New York, Miss Eleanor Pearson and Mr. Robert Bell Rettig of the Cambridge Historical Commission, Mr. Arthur Ziegler, Executive Director of the Pittsburgh History and Landmarks Foundation, Miss Eleanor Collins, Mr. Donald Hoffman of *The Kansas City Star*, Mrs. J. E. Ledden, Rare Books Librarian of the New York State Library, Mr. Pierce Rice, Mr. James T. Maher, Professor Charles K. Warner, Mr. Neil Beacham, Librarian of the National Monuments Record, Dr. James Heslin, Director, New-York Historical Society,

Preface

and Mr. Robert Kennard, Senior Warden of Trinity Church, Boston. The Rackham Publication Fund of the University of Michigan has kindly made a grant to cover some of the cost of assembling the photographs for this edition.

I also owe a deep debt of gratitude to members of the Van Brunt family who have kindly lent me materials and information. They are the late Mrs. Helen Van Brunt Washburn and the late Bradlee Van Brunt. But to Mr. Henry Van Brunt, Jr., my obligations for advice, the loan of materials, and information are beyond calculation. I can only acknowledge them and gratefully thank him.

William A. Coles

Ann Arbor, Michigan
June 1968

Contents

The Essays of Henry Van Brunt

107. Austin Hall, Mrs. Schuyler Van Rensselaer, *Henry Hobson Richardson and His Works*, Boston, 1888.

108. Quincy Library, courtesy Boston Athenaeum.

109. Auburndale Station, Mrs. Schuyler Van Rensselaer, *Henry Hobson Richardson and His Works*, Boston, 1888.

110, 110a, 110b. Allegheny County Buildings, photographs by Charles W. Shane, courtesy Pittsburgh History and Landmarks Foundation.

111. Washington Monument, Mills design, *American Art and American Art Collections*, ed. Walter Montgomery (Boston, 1889), I, 354.

112. Washington Monument, Searle design, *American Architect and Building News*, V (1879), No. 166.

113. Washington Monument, Frazer design, *American Art and American Art Collections*, ed. Walter Montgomery (Boston, 1889), I, 360.

114. Washington Monument, Story design, *American Architect and Building News*, V (1879), No. 162.

115. Washington Monument, Hapgood design, *American Architect and Building News*, V (1879), No. 168.

116. Washington Monument, Schulze design, *American Art and American Art Collections*, ed. Walter Montgomery (Boston, 1889), I, 364.

117. Washington Monument, anonymous design, *American Architect and Building News*, VI (1879), No. 202.

118. Crosby's Opera House, courtesy Chicago Historical Society.

119. Nickerson house, *American Architect and Building News*, IX (1881), No. 270.

120. Calumet Building, courtesy Chicago Historical Society.

121. Chicago Opera House Block, courtesy Chicago Historical Society.

122. Union Club, courtesy Chicago Historical Society.

123. Potter Palmer house, courtesy Chicago Historical Society.

124. Home Insurance Building, courtesy Chicago Historical Society.

125. Insurance Exchange, courtesy Chicago Historical Society.

126. Rookery Building, courtesy Chicago Historical Society.

127. Phoenix Building, courtesy Chicago Historical Society.

128. Kansas City Board of Trade Building, *Architectural Record*, XV (1904), 137.

129. Marshall Field Wholesale Store, courtesy Chicago Historical Society.

130. Owings Building, courtesy Chicago Historical Society.

131. Buffington office building, *American Architect and Building News*, XXIV (1888), No. 673.

132, 133. Auditorium Building and Art Institute, courtesy Chicago Historical Society.

134. Tacoma Building, courtesy Chicago Historical Society.

135. Monadnock Building, courtesy Chicago Historical Society.

136. Masonic Temple, courtesy Chicago Historical Society.

137. Woman's Temple, courtesy Chicago Historical Society.

138. Schiller Building, courtesy Chicago Historical Society.

138a. Schiller Building, detail, photograph by Clarence W. Hines, courtesy Chicago Historical Society.

Illustrations

Architecture and Society | Selected Essays of Henry Van Brunt

Introduction

I. Life and Career

At the time of his death in 1903, Henry Van Brunt was one of the acknowledged founders and leaders of the architectural profession in America. In noticing his death it was, therefore, quite appropriate that the *Architectural Review* remind its readers what the condition of architecture had been at the start of his career in the decade before the Civil War. There was then, it said, no standard of architecture in this country. Apart from some few of the larger buildings of colonial and postcolonial days, there were only dwellings to serve as precedent. The period when builders could be trusted to use intelligently the textbooks of Sir Christopher Wren's pupils was long past, and it was customary for men of culture either to copy some building they had seen abroad, in whole or in part, or to buy a set of plans from an English architect. The United States was dismissed in any history of architecture with a few justifiable and derogatory lines. If the *Review* errs on the side of pessimism, it does not do so by much. Its résumé of the profession is closer to day-by-day practice than the summary in the history book which leaps from one conspicuous monument to another. During this period the comforting supports and restraints of colonial and provincial status were falling away, while the more substantial ones of imaginative artistry were yet to be.

"It is much," said the *Review*, with reference to Van Brunt's efforts, "in a desert of drought to believe in the oasis . . . It was much when there was no architecture to try bravely to make one." [1] By the end of the century Van Brunt's belief in the oasis was no longer a mere mirage of thirst. He could look back on half a century during which the practice of architecture had been established in America along rigorously professional lines. The American Institute of Architects had been organized to uphold high standards of ethical conduct and design. A system of ateliers and schools was helping to ensure thorough and competent architectural training for students. Journals were providing necessary means of communication to a profession that was much better informed and more thoughtful. It was with evident sober pride that Van Brunt, as president of the A.I.A., in his address to the annual convention of 1899, offered his professional colleagues a view of the significance, achievements, and responsibilities of architecture in America considerably altered from the mid-century condition: "You may be sure that the civilized world will receive with peculiar interest all that we may have to give forth in the elucidation of the strange and unprecedented condition under which a rich and prosperous nation, unembarrassed by patriotic traditions of art, is developing style; that it will eagerly hear all that we may have to say on the practical application of science to architecture, on the progress of invention in respect to building, on the discovery of new materials and new methods and their effect upon our art, and on the incidents of our unimaginable progress in the future. We alone are in position to influence the expression of the immense energies of our nation in architecture. Let us endeavor adequately to fulfil these duties." [2] Within the half-century span of Van Brunt's career American architecture had come of age and was shaping its own courses.

Van Brunt's contributions to the development of American architecture were not limited to his own practice nor to the duties of guidance and teaching that he undertook within the profession. By temperament and talent he was inclined to literature and scholarship and by principle he was concerned about the relationship between art and society. Therefore throughout his professional life Van Brunt addressed to the public a series of articles on art, architecture, and allied subjects intended to heighten awareness and intelligent understanding of the nature of architecture and the peculiar conditions of its growth in America. Though he could have considered his task to be primarily missionary, and accordingly have adopted an emotional tone in his writings (with even more justification than Ruskin, whose audience was generally more sophisticated than American readers), Van Brunt nevertheless avoided argumentation that was excessively literary or theoretical. He always distrusted unenlightened zeal or unguided energy, preferring to rely, like Dr. Johnson or Edmund Burke, on common sense, reason, and principles derived from experience. He was more concerned to set the foundation of a liberal culture that might endure and prosper than to inaugurate a movement or champion a cause. When there was no developed architectural taste, he had to try to make one, and he wisely understood that true taste was a cultivated habit of thought and feeling rather than a succession of fashionable enthusiasms.

Henry Van Brunt was born in Boston on September 5, 1832. His father, Gershom Jacques Van Brunt (Fig. 1) of the United States Navy, was at one time commandant of the Portsmouth Navy Yard and was retired from service with the rank of Commodore. His mother was Elizabeth Price Bradlee of Boston. He was educated at Boston Latin School and at Harvard College, from which he was graduated in 1854. During his freshman year at college Van Brunt received a football injury which left him lame for the rest of his life and required periodic surgical treatment. In spite of the great pain he endured during this period and absences from school of about a term's time in all, he applied himself diligently to his studies and with the aid of a tutor was able to keep pace with his class and attain high honors in his college work.

Van Brunt kept diaries during his college years (1851–1854) which reveal much of his early scholarly bent, his wide reading, and his liking for literature.[3] They also record his turn toward architecture as a profession and are of special interest in establishing the mood of his entire later career. The diaries are in several volumes, written in beautiful penmanship, with the capital letters of each day's entry elaborately illuminated. In the first volume (1851, when Van Brunt was 19) the style of writing is at its most florid, and the diary is frequently illustrated by pen sketches that suggest that the young writer early acquired the discipline of constant sketching, which he was to continue all his life.

The writing in the volumes is always carefully wrought and correct in grammar, syntax, and spelling. It offers abundant evidence of wide reading and a literary cast of mind — though some of its flights of reflective fancy barely rise above the ground. What gives the writing special interest is the evidence it provides of a naïve self-consciousness groping toward the gravity and balance which characterize Van Brunt's mature prose style. Passages spiced with wit or irony — often directed at himself — vary, if they do not altogether relieve the formality. They are frequently linked to many quotations and allusions which, especially in the early years, are often in Latin.

Van Brunt's wide and constant reading can not only be deduced from its impact on his writing, but is also apparent from the many books mentioned throughout the diaries. He seems to have gone through a period of religious groping when he read widely in, and speculated frequently upon, the New Testament. He writes in 1854 that he has "read every evening in the New Testament" and begins to see something behind the words of which he was "not before conscious." There is also a good deal of reading in Latin and Greek texts, Aristophanes, Herodotus, Sophocles, and Cicero, for instance, though he seems to have kept on with Greek merely as a lesser evil than higher mathematics. When President Sparks of Harvard wrote him in September, 1852, that his examination in Latin, Greek, and mathematics was "satisfactory," in fact, "highly creditable," he immediately wrote back requesting the President to send books for Greek studies and rejecting the "muddy fen of Curves and Functions." He had earlier referred to mathematics as a "nauseous potion." German also seemed too harsh a fate for the convalescing young gentleman.

His reading in modern English literature was guided by inclination rather than academic responsibility. In 1852, for instance, he noted that he had "finished the perusal of the 'New Timon' and I must say that I never read a modern poem which pleased me more. It purports to be a 'Romance of London' and teems with passages of great beauty, imagination and depth of thought. The roll of the opening line — to use the words of another — stirs the heart like a bugle at midnight

'O'er royal London, in luxuriant May,
While lamps yet twinkled, dawning crept today.' " [4]

One might not guess from his comment that the poem is a satire. Equally cryptic is his statement that the author is, he believes, unknown, "although the style and general train of thought are similar to those of Bulwer in his better moments," since the poem had been published as Bulwer's. In the same year he is much taken with Washington Irving's *Sketch Book*. In its tales, he says, "is betrayed such a diversity of talent and such a refined and delicate taste that I confess myself guilty of transgressing the tenth commandment and of sincerely coveting the genius and pen of Washington Irving." Two years later he was reading Pope's *Dunciad* and discovering "a very beautiful poem" by Frederick Tennyson, Alfred's brother, called "The Bridal." He remarks that it reminds him of Spenser's "Epithalamium." As for Milton, he found that *Paradise Regained* "loses very much from its proximity to the great epic of which it is a sequel . . . only a poetical amplification of Our Lord's temptation in the wilderness." But *Samson Agonistes* is "a splendid creation full of majesty and dignity."

Some indication of the extent as well as the range of Van Brunt's reading is given by an entry on Sunday, February 26, 1854: "I have been employing the day (rainy) reading Coleridge's 'Religious Musings' and Cowper's 'Task,' also John Ruskin's 'Modern Painters.' " His choice of reading seems both substantial and discriminating. Van Brunt's lifelong study of Shakespeare (evident from numerous quotations in his writings) also deserves mention here. His freshman diary contains a careful analysis of Hamlet's character, and Van Brunt's son, Henry, Jr., remembers that years later Julia Marlowe, the Shakespearean actress, who was a friend of the family, used to come to the house in Kansas City when she was on tour and admired his father's profound knowledge of Shakespeare. On several occasions she asked for his interpretations of scenes and situations.[5]

In spite of Van Brunt's evident learning, precocious even by nineteenth-century educational standards, the total impression of the diaries is by no means that of the cloister. There is frequent mention of a wide circle of friends of both sexes (his tutor's certificate to President Sparks speaks of his pursuit of studies "despite . . . the allurements of a very agreeable circle of friends"), and every indication of a keen interest in life and a relish for experience.

During this period the family lived in a house built by the Commodore in Kittery, Maine, where the Portsmouth Navy Yard is actually situated. Van Brunt speaks many times of long trips by train or carriage — or by sleigh in winter — and of trips back and forth to Cambridge by boat. His diaries have much local color: observations of town idlers, descriptions of events such as the launching of the U.S.S. *Merrimac* (which was to achieve fame in the Civil War), or ventures into local history, as in a lengthy account of the Pepperell family, induced by a visit to their Kittery mansion. There is mention of arguments with friends on almost every conceivable subject and, of course "the alienation existing between the North and the South" is already a topic for long and serious conversation.

Van Brunt's recorded envy of Washington Irving was not merely a humorous hyperbole. The journal sequences seem to show that, although from the first he had a professional career clearly in view, he had some doubt as to his precise direction, but leaned definitely toward art or letters, perhaps more strongly toward the latter. He was never to make a full division between the two careers, not merely because of his conception of the proper relationship between the architectural profession and the public, but because writing was for him an early and enduring love. The *Architectural Review* at the time of his death spoke of him as "belonging to that disappearing type of readers and writers to whom style means often as much as matter," [6] and the *American Architect and Building News* considered him "more estimable as a writer and critic than as a creating artist," offering the opinion that "his lasting reputation will rest rather on his writings than on the architectural worth of the buildings he designed." [7]

The diaries show that Van Brunt's literary efforts were not confined to prose, though they surely reveal his wisdom in not pursuing a poetic career. His verse is struck in the eighteenth- and early-nineteenth-century descriptive and didactic mold; abstractions and conventional poetic diction abound. The medium is generally, though not always, the rhymed iambic couplet, still the popular verse form in spite of Wordsworth's *Lyrical Ballads*. As far as I know, Van Brunt's only venture into print in verse is the poem "The Church Door. A Study in Romanesque," which closes his article on "Architecture among the Poets" in the *Atlantic Monthly* of April, 1893.[8] In this article he examines the problem of why poets have generally failed to do justice to the real meaning of architecture in their descriptive and lyric passages. His own poem is introduced, with deserved modesty, as an exploration of possibilities to be realized, he hopes, by more gifted followers.

Van Brunt's career, however, was not to be in poetry. From his sophomore year there is apparent, first a lively interest in architecture, and then a dedication to that field. His account of the Pepperell family on July 29, 1852, has architectural as well as historical interest. He describes the family mansion in some detail and evidences a concern for what we now call historic preservation:

The old mansion has just been vacated by a set of unprincipled vandals who have marred its antiquated beauties sadly. Not content with tearing down the old family portraits in the galleries, destroying and otherwise disposing of them, they have impiously cut up the gallery itself into three apartments, removing the heavy cornices and Corinthian columns. In short, desecrating hands have been indiscriminately laid on everything which one would suppose would command the respect and veneration of the merest savage. There formerly was a magnificent approach to the mansion — a fine carriageway embowered by rows of majestic elms, most of which have been ruthlessly cut down for firewood . . . Of these ancient trees a few still remain, and through their wild, untrimmed branches the evening

5

breeze moaned dolefully, as if complaining of their loneliness. Two fine twin Linden trees, brought from England, are on either side of the door. To those accustomed to the pent up and limited proportions of modern dwellings the entrance hall appears truly grand and there is a certain sturdy, venerable appearance about it that is really charming; throughout the house panelling is very abundant; the staircase is square, spacious, and of easy ascent and the bannisters are very massive and imposing with the heavily carved balustrade still in an excellent state of preservation. On the right, as you enter, is the mutilated picture gallery and on the left a queer old reception room whose walls still display a rich, dark paper which has hung there since the house was built; the chimney-pieces are wide and tiled in the old style. Mrs. Newell (the present occupant) is busily engaged in the herculean task of restoring the old mansion, as far as possible, to its pristine grandeur — a task, indeed, quite equal to that of cleaning the Augean stables.

There is already in evidence here a careful attention to architectural detail and to its effects. Furthermore Van Brunt was not only busy sketching, but he also went to look at paintings. On June 16, 1852, for instance, he was at the Boston Athenaeum to see a portion of the "much talked of" Dusseldorf collection of pictures. He says he was "particularly attracted by 'The Adoration of the Magi' (Steinbruck) and the pictures of a student (his departure from home, his examination at the university and his return) betray a vast deal of humour, as is also the case with 'Falstaff Mustering His Recruits.' 'Othello and Desdemona' both pleased and disgusted me; the Moor is erroneously represented as a curly-headed Negro who is relating his adventures to Desdemona whose beautiful and eager face and graceful form are truly admirable." [9] On the same day he was also at Faneuil Hall to see an exhibition of G. P. A. Healy's colossal painting of Webster delivering his reply to Hayne in the United States Senate. Van Brunt and his father on this occasion were guests of the artist, who some years earlier had painted the Commodore's portrait.[10]

Van Brunt's deepened interest in architecture is most strikingly evident in his entry for February 15, 1854 (age 21). He had taken a trip to New York to visit a relation and he spent a good deal of his time viewing the offerings of the city. He noted that the houses on Fifth Avenue have "too little uniformity of beauty . . . These buildings stand in contiguity, separately not without merit, but together each destroying and cancelling the effect of the others." He also missed in them "the great essential of beauty, deep strongly-marked shadows . . . Fronts are too flat and staring and without those deep embrasures, heavy cornices and prominent bold features, which, by creating shadows, give grandeur and character." His observations show by now a wider reading in the criticism and theory of architecture. The same is true of his vocabulary. A close description of Trinity Church reveals a familiarity with the detailed terminology of Gothic architecture. He remarks on the absence of transepts in that building and goes on to write, "I always regret the necessity of pews. Were the pavements of Trinity unobstructed . . . I am persuaded that the tout ensemble would be much grander. They necessarily hide . . . the bases of the columns." He was probably already aware of the English ecclesiologists' attacks on pews as a Protestant corruption of medieval Gothic architecture.

He visited the new Astor Library, on Lafayette Place, designed by Alexander Saeltzer.[11] With a collection of 100,000 volumes it was then the largest library in the country, surpassing Harvard's collection of 72,000 volumes. Oddly enough he describes its style as Byzantine; we would call it Anglo-Italian or Italianate today. Of the brownstone house fronts, which he liked, he notes that "the facings of the windows, the tympana above doors, the cornices and basements are very frequently adorned with elaborately sculptured ornaments." One or two of these brownstones on Fifth Avenue below Twenty-Third Street were the work of Detlef Lienau, with whom Van Brunt was later to work. He was sufficiently motivated to walk on up to the Spingler Institute[12] to look at Thomas Cole's series of four paintings "The Voyage of Life," which he described in some detail. These well-known works by the Hudson River School painter later went to St. Luke's Hospital in New York and are now in the Munson-Williams-Procter Institute in Utica. One of the most interesting diversions of the city was the exhibition in the Crystal Palace, which had opened the preceding summer on the site that is now Bryant Park. The building, of glass and iron, was modelled on Paxton's London Crystal Palace, constructed to house the Exhibition of 1851. The New York exhibition was the first international fair held in the United States. Van Brunt was later to be actively involved in three other American fairs: the Philadelphia Centennial Exposition of 1876,[13] the great World's Columbian Exhibition of 1893 at Chicago, for which Van Brunt and Howe did the Electricity Building on the Court of Honor (Fig. 150) and the Wyoming State Building, and the Louisiana Purchase Exposition of 1904 in St. Louis, for which his firm designed the Varied Industries Building, finished after his death (Fig. 75). The engineering style of the Crystal Palace, through which the young Van Brunt roamed, did not even remotely anticipate the grandeur and monumentality of the 1893 Chicago Fair, but he took particular interest in the paintings there, which he viewed through "an instrument called the 'stereoscope.'"

Back in Cambridge on March 4 he was preoccupied with getting his degree on schedule with his class. The president reassured him because of his uniformly excellent grades, but suggested the possibility of additional examinations, which he did not like. He was not concerned over the threat of difficulties, but was by now firmly committed to his professional training and writes that he was "averse to having (his) architectural studies encroached upon." Several items of his reading underscore the intensity of his studies during that year. He says that "at Little and Brown's in Boston I saw Gwilt's abridgement of Sir William Chambers' work an architecture. This is decidedly the most complete work on architecture I have seen . . . It is the only copy for sale in the city and, inasmuch as the binding is plain and, indeed, a little defective, I got it for only $9." The Commodore advanced him the money for this rather expensive volume. The book was Joseph Gwilt's edition of the *Civil Architecture of Sir William Chambers*, which he probably read in the

1825 edition. Originally published in 1759 as *A Treatise on Civil Architecture*, Chambers' work is one of the principal English examinations of the classical orders and a pillar of American Colonial and Federal styles. Fortunately we have a clue to the way in which Van Brunt must have approached his study of the volume — in a fashion that was by no means desultory. In an article on "The Education of the Architect" in the *Technology Architectural Review* of October 31, 1890, he maps out a course of self-instruction for young students who are unable to attend an architectural school. His first stage is a program of reading in the history of architecture, to be followed by one on theory, and then finally, or coincidentally, he recommends a thorough and exhaustive study of the classical orders:

I found Gwilt's edition of the "Civil Architecture of Sir William Chambers" a very convenient introduction to this study. Any good edition of Vitruvius, however, or the works of Vignola or of any of the Italian masters would perform the same service . . . These orders should be carefully drawn and committed to memory with precision, that is, without fanciful variations. The test to which the student should subject his knowledge of the classic proportions is in free-hand memory sketches of the correct orders and of their combinations at large and small scales without measuring. This exercise will begin to bear fruit when these sketches shall have been found to retain the traditional proportions and details, and when the respective characteristics of the orders, according to the Romans, shall have been fully mastered. The attainment of absolute knowledge with regard to these venerable formulas will at once place the student far in advance of those of his fellows who remain ignorant of the classics, and content themselves with such specious nourishment as they can obtain from dalliance with the picturesque and the romantic. He will have been taught to regard architecture seriously and sincerely, while they still look upon it as a sort of amusement, which gives opportunity for the display of a shallow facility, easily acquired, and affording no discipline to the habit of mind in designing.[14]

We may assume, then, that memorizing and sketching the orders from Chambers was part of the architectural study he did not want encroached upon, and that he acquired the formal repertory of classical architecture early and valued it long.

But he was also at work on the more practical side of his profession during this period. Goaded by his interest in architecture he apparently recovered from his loathing of the "muddy fens" of mathematics, for on March 8, 1854, he notes that he is halfway through William Minifie's *Geometrics and Drawing* and says that he has obtained much valuable information from the book.[15] Further on he writes, "All Saturday morning I drew diagrams, etc. from Minifie's excellent geometric textbook. I feel that I am obtaining much knowledge of practice from this book . . . having already got through the part devoted to linear perspective." It is significant, though, that this aspect of architecture was not his first or strongest love, and it is perhaps for this reason that he could later easily perceive the excesses of the structural theorists, who, for the sake of dogma, would throw aside so much of the art that was visually satisfying. He realized, of course, the necessity of mathematical studies and pursued them with diligence, but his increased proficiency further intensified his visual interests. On April 1 he writes, "The constructive part of architecture, although it does not have so attractive an appeal in my eyes (as does the decorative part) obtains from me much study and attention. My progress in this department is necessarily slow and tedious . . . I desire very much to become acclimated to the architect's office, and the further I proceed the more I see the necessity to examine with my own eyes the architectural monuments of Europe." His longing was increased by his reading of George Stillman Hillard's *Six Months in Italy* at this time.[16] Unfortunately, however, he was not to visit Europe until 1900, when his life and career were nearly ended. With reference to that European trip the writer of Van Brunt's memorial in the *American Architect* speculates that "those who had had the fortune to visit Europe in their earlier years could not but be envious of the impressions which were sure to overwhelm a man so thoroughly prepared to appreciate and analyze them." [17] It is ironical that Van Brunt, surely one of the most learned men of his profession, should have been denied this essential stage of his education, the importance of which he himself fully recognized, until it came too late to affect his work. The *American Architect* observes that if he "could have had a few years of travel he would unquestionably have so broadened his powers of design that his work as an architect would have been fairly comparable with his work as a writer." [18] That written work can at least afford his readers considerable consolation.

In 1855, the year after Van Brunt's graduation from Harvard, the family moved from Kittery to a new house built by the Commodore in Dedham, Massachusetts. Soon after his graduation Van Brunt had entered the office of the Boston architect George Snell, where, he said later in his Harvard College classbook,[19] he familiarized himself with the English school of architecture. Snell, who is little remembered today, is credited by Walter Kilham with the design of the old Music Hall in Boston (1852), long the home of the Symphony Orchestra.[20] One can surmise that Van Brunt's apprenticeship under Snell was not altogether satisfactory. Years later, in his eulogy of Richard Morris Hunt, delivered at the twenty-ninth annual convention of the American Institute of Architects, on October 16, 1895, he described the "discouraging conditions" under which the study of architecture was pursued at the time of his youth — with little respect, no schools, few books, and an atmosphere thick with prejudice and controversy. "Community of thought," he says, "mutual friendship hardly existed among architects. The hand of each was turned with jealousy and suspicion against his brother. His processes of design and his business methods were personal secrets. Each concealed his drawings from the rest as if they were pages of a private diary. Even books and prints were carefully secluded from inspection by any rival. Pupils were apprentices, and as in my own case, often looked with eager and unsatisfied eyes through the glass of their master's locked bookcases." [21] For a sensitive and lively student, accustomed to an atmosphere of humanistic encouragement, Snell's office could hardly have been a Palace of Art. There he found mercantilism rather than comradeship and ardor, and he was cast in the uncongenial role of the hungry apprentice calling for more nourishment. He was to find the much heartier fare he craved in New York.

The immediate motivation for Van Brunt's move to New York and its precise date are not altogether clear. Talbot Hamlin, writing in the *Dictionary of American Biography*, puts the move in 1856, but this seems too early. Van Brunt himself in his Harvard classbook says he was in Snell's office for nearly three years and then went to New York in the fall of 1857 to study the French systems of architecture with Richard Morris Hunt. This statement is also puzzling, since in his eulogy of Hunt Van Brunt says that in the autumn of 1858 he and Charles Dexter Gambrill (his college classmate, who later entered into partnership successively with George B. Post and Henry Hobson Richardson) and Post applied to Hunt, "who had then just completed the Tenth Street Studio Building in New York, to take one of the studios himself and install them there as his pupils." [22] The Richard Morris Hunt Papers, a biographical account put together by the architect's wife, Catherine Howland Hunt, more or less agree with Van Brunt, by saying that the three students joined forces after Post's graduation from the Engineering School of New York University in the spring of 1858.[23] The date there given for Post's graduation is correct.

The inauguration date of Hunt's atelier is of considerable importance since from it we can date the founding of serious architectural training in the United States. The first trio of students was joined early in the following year by William Robert Ware, Frank Furness of Philadelphia, Edmund Quincy, and E. L. Hyde (the latter two men never practiced as architects). It was in Furness' office that Louis Sullivan was later to take a year's training. Ware's contributions to education were immensely more substantial, for in 1868, after he had entered into partnership with Van Brunt, he was to set up the first school of architecture in the United States at the Massachusetts Institute of Technology. Later he was to found yet another at the Columbia School of Mines. In both office and university Hunt's seeds of training were resown and his architectural progeny were multiplied. Even those who departed from his canons of design were still deeply indebted to his influence as a teacher.

Hunt was the first American-born architect to receive thorough professional training. Born into comfortable circumstances in Vermont in 1828, he was taken to Europe by his widowed mother at the age of 15. After preliminary training under Samuel Darier in Geneva and Hector-Martin Lefuel in Paris, he entered the Ecole des Beaux Arts as a pupil in Lefuel's atelier. At the time of his return to the United States in 1855 he had had years of training and extensive travel on the Continent and in Egypt and had assisted his master Lefuel on the design of the Pavillon de la Bibliothèque du Louvre. His return to his native country, interrupting what was already the beginning of a brilliant career in France, was sparked by an ambition to help forward the lingering cause of art in America. In a letter to his mother shortly before his return he expressed his hopeful purpose: "It has been represented to me that

America was not ready for the Fine Arts, but I think they are mistaken. There is no place in the world where they are more needed, or where they should be more encouraged." [24] Hunt was not merely seeking encouragement himself; he was willing to give it to others too.

Soon after his return, in March, 1856, Hunt accepted an offer to become the assistant of Thomas U. Walter, the architect in charge of the extension of the Capitol in Washington. The desire to participate in important public works was a significant legacy of Beaux Arts training and professional ideals, but for Hunt the contrast in civic munificence between Imperial Paris and mid-nineteenth-century republican Washington must have been somewhat discouraging. He stayed in Washington through the winter, returning to New York in May of 1857. He was also working at the same time on the Rossiter house in New York (Fig. 166), which was finished late in 1857,[25] and on the Tenth Street Studio Building of the same year (Fig. 168). We know that Hunt was in New York on February 23, 1857, for the meeting which inaugurated the American Institute of Architects, at which time he was appointed Secretary of the group.[26] Van Brunt, who was also an early member, attributes to Hunt the most potent influence toward the founding of the Institute. Its purpose reflected Hunt's beliefs, being in large measure educational; for as Henry Saylor says, "from the moment of its birth the organization laid great stress upon the library of books and drawings it should assemble." [27]

Hunt was the ideal director for Van Brunt's studies, yet we do not know precisely how the two men came together. It seems unlikely that Van Brunt and Gambrill (who surely must have been acquainted in Cambridge) and George Post in New York would have converged on Hunt without first knowing one another — and knowing Hunt, or at least his work, his qualifications, and his habits. To enter into the plan Van Brunt must already have been in New York. If his ultimate destination was study with Hunt, that was not necessarily the initial motive for his trip.

The reasons for a move to New York at this time cannot be far to seek. Boston was thriving in the 1850's, but New York's growth was considerably more brisk. In 1855 the population of Boston was over 160,000; New York's three years earlier had been nearing 700,000. If the quality of New York architecture at this period was not necessarily higher than Boston's, it was certainly more ambitious and more responsive to current fashion. Furthermore the livelier pace of the city would have promised more excitement than the sober Athens of America could afford. Van Brunt may even have first learned of Hunt in New York and of the recent founding of the Institute from George Snell, who was one of a dozen outsiders asked to join the original group.[28] In any case we can probably accept his recollection that he went to New York in the fall of 1857. Soon afterward he must have met Hunt, whose library, art collection, and buoyant personality were already celebrated in the New York world of art.

Additional information on Van Brunt's activities can be gleaned from five small sketchbooks of this period which are now in the possession of his son, Henry Van Brunt, Jr.[29] Two of the books are signed on the first leaf and bear the address of the Studio Building on Tenth Street in New York; one of these books has a date, October 23, 1858, under the signature. One of the sketchbooks gives further evidence that Van Brunt was in New York before this date. On one leaf of the book there are two delicate drawings of rosaces from Scipio's tomb, the first of which is marked "Drawn from cast, Dec. 17, '57" and the other, "Jan 9th. '58." On the preceding leaf there are sketches of panels under windows from houses on Fifth Avenue at Eighth and Tenth Streets. This is the most substantial evidence that Van Brunt's New York period extends back into 1857. A later sketch in the book is labeled "Chimney Piece at our Studio. 15 10th Street N. Y. Apr. 1858"[30] (Fig. 4). The scene pictured contains a decorated chimney piece surmounted by vases, objects, and, in the center, a large baroque cabinet with glass doors. The walls above and on the sides are covered with sconces, casts, and framed drawings. The scene pictured is identical with that described by Van Brunt in his eulogy of Hunt and shown in a photograph in Mr. Alan Burnham's article on Hunt[31] (Fig. 167). Since neither Van Brunt himself nor any one else but Hunt had such possessions in profusion, the phrase "our Studio" supports the thesis that Van Brunt was already working under Hunt before autumn (the time designated in his article) and presumably even before Post would have been graduated from New York University. The sketch also contradicts Mrs. Hunt's assertion that her husband did not transfer his pupils to the Studio Building until 1859.[32]

Van Brunt has eloquently described the atmosphere of Hunt's atelier, and the ardor of his description coupled with the profound significance of the undertaking for the history of the architectural profession in America, make especially curious the historian's general lack of awareness of the event.[33] It was without doubt a turning point in America's artistic history and Van Brunt recognized and described it as such: "Thus we together entered upon an era so rich, so full of surprise and delight, that it seems, as we look back upon it, as if once more in the world the joy of the Renaissance, the white light of knowledge had broken in upon the superstition of romance. To us it was a revelation and an enlargement of vision so sudden and complete that the few years spent by us in that stimulating atmosphere were the most memorable and eventful in life." We have already observed the dampening conditions of apprenticeship which prevailed in American offices. But Hunt, says Van Brunt, was "generous to teach." He could successfully combine the most stringent technical standards, the most exacting criticism, with a contagious enthusiasm for every aspect of the life of art. Not much older than his pupils, though years ahead in knowledge and experience, he nourished them with warm and lively comradeship and provided for them a sense of the significance of their pursuits which was everywhere lacking in the American scene of the day.

Hunt's own studio and apartment were in the New York University Building,[34] which stood on the northeast corner of Washington Square (Fig. 16).

"Here he lived [Van Brunt tells us] as bachelor in spacious and lofty apartments, filled with the spoils of foreign travel. Here were carved antique cabinets, filled with bronzes, medallions, precious glass of Venice and curiosities of fine handiwork in all the arts. The walls were rich with hangings, old panels, sculptured or painted, and modern studies from the studios of Paris. These, together with mediaeval missals and embroideries, instruments of music, masterpieces of forged and wrought metal work and of Faience, strange and costly toys of every era of civilization brought into the great chamber the mellow atmosphere of the old world."

The surroundings provided for his students were equally rich: "Our own workshop in the Studio Building was hung with cartoons in colors, and furnished with casts of architectural and decorative detail. Even that working place was not without its ancient carved chimney piece and its cabinets of tarnished gilding [shown in Van Brunt's sketch]" (Fig. 4). But even more important than this was Hunt's impressive library, "by far the richest, most comprehensive, and most curious collection of books on architecture and the other fine arts which at that time had been brought together in the new world." Nor were these volumes, like Snell's, under lock and key: "To these treasures the fortunate pupils were welcomed with boundless hospitality. Indeed, Hunt's attitude sometimes made us feel that he considered the labor and cost of bringing them together justified in the light which they shed upon us. For myself I can truly say that the hours spent in the gracious seclusion of that dim chamber were the most fruitful in my life. The aspect of every page, the emotions of every revelation of the world of art come back to my memory clear and distinct as I speak in gratitude and affection."

Not merely the riches, but some of the spirit of the artists' quarter of Paris (as romanticized only a decade earlier by Henri Murger) seemed to be miraculously transplanted to the sidewalks of New York. "Here," says Van Brunt, "we lived in the midst of a congenial and sympathetic brotherhood of painters and sculptors from the neighboring studios, happy Bohemians, free to come and go as we pleased." To the Bostonian the phenomenon must have been as unusual as the descent of "the Europeans" in Henry James's novel — but Van Brunt found his taste of Bohemia more congenial than the Cambridge Wentworths in the novel did: "In such a place the most imaginative mind could not fail to be kindled. Whatever latent powers of expression in art we might have were aroused to vigorous action. In that beautiful chamber where he lived we traversed every corner of the world of art and filled our sketch books with the fruits of enchanted travel."

Hunt constantly exhorted his pupils to practice drawing whenever possible in order to increase their facility to express thoughts on paper.[35] This advice is repeated by Van Brunt in his articles on the education of the architect, where the methods and style of the "greatest graphic delineator of our time, Viollet-le-Duc," [36] are offered as a model. Van Brunt also tells us that by making copious notes and sketches of the volumes he read he made them more his own than if they had belonged to him.[37] His sketchbooks bear out the truth of his words and suggest that the vistas that opened out from Hunt's library were astonishingly varied. We know of the historical-mindedness of the nineteenth century and also of its eclecticism, but we are often insufficiently mindful of the amount of learning that went into the really conscientious training of the time. The basis of study in the atelier was strictly academic, according to the method of the French school. This was so in order that the substructure of the students' knowledge might be "serious, sane and solid" and the "romantic license which at that time tended to turn the practice of architecture into the hands of amateurs and virtuosos" might be curbed. (It is well to remember, in this connection, that the Ecole des Beaux Arts, at the time of Hunt's study there, was itself strongly tinged with neo-Grèc and rationalist Gothic doctrines which were threatening to overthrow its traditional French-Italian academic discipline. Hunt himself was influenced by both movements in his early career.) But if the classical formulas were preserved for the sake of training the hand and mind and inculcating such a sensitivity to form that no detail in a composition could be altered without altering the whole balance of the work, Hunt also "heartily encouraged the study of every style in which the thought of man had expressed itself in beauty or power." Academic prejudices, Van Brunt tells us, never affected the large catholicity of Hunt's mind.

Van Brunt's sketchbooks reveal this catholicity and in addition are a useful index to the contents of Hunt's library.[38] Most of his architectural sketches have on the page a name or an abbreviated title from which we can usually identify the particular volumes he was using. The sketches vary from Pompeian mouldings to cast iron structures; from medieval German construction in wood to the palaces of Louis XIV; from a sketch of minor detail to a comprehensive outline of Rickman's study of Gothic architecture, with copious drawings of the characteristics of every period (Figs. 6–15). Learning in this form was supplemented by assigned problems of design to be turned in by a specific time for analysis and criticism by Hunt and the other students.

The devotion that existed between Hunt and his pupils never waned; it was increased by continued kindnesses in later life. Van Brunt's own affection for his teacher was particularly strong, and of it Mrs. Hunt has written: "It has always seemed to me that Mr. Van Brunt's appreciation for his old master was deeper than that of any of his other pupils." [39] It was to this "ideal relationship of mutual interest and affection" between master and pupils that Van Brunt attributed the unity of the Court of Honor at the 1893 Chicago Fair. Louis Sullivan's charge that Hunt's autocratic nature was the cause[40] springs from (among other things) a failure to understand Hunt and the bonds of affection and gratitude that linked him and his students.

Van Brunt writes in his college classbook that he studied with Hunt for one year and afterwards practiced the profession in partial connection with him and subsequently with Detlef Lienau. We do not know exactly what work he was doing at this time. Hunt's practice was not yet as distinguished as it was subsequently to be, but Lienau (1818–1877) was already one of the principal architects of the city. Born in Germany, he had studied in Munich and in Paris under Henri Labrouste, the leader of the neo-Grèc movement. He came to New York in 1848 and after a brief partnership with Henri Marcotte set up in practice alone. Among his most significant works up to this time were the Hart Shiff house (1850) on Fifth Avenue and Tenth Street and the William Schermerhorn house on West Twenty-Third Street. He was well known for his sound knowledge of the technique of construction, and most of his work is more restrained than that of his contemporaries because of the simplifying influence of neo-Grèc ideas of style.

Van Brunt would undoubtedly have been more than a mere draftsman by this time — around 1860 — for in that year he was elected Secretary of the A.I.A., succeeding Hunt in the office. He was also becoming known about town as a young man of promise. A letter of January 20, 1860, written by the sculptor John Rogers (1829–1904) to his mother, says that he has been "introduced to a Mr. Van Brunt of Dedham who is an architect in N. Y. I could not help feeling how grateful I ought to be for the honor of his acquaintance and how proud N. Yor[k] should be that it possessed an architect of such wonderful acquirements." [41] By the following year, though, his enthusiasm had waned, for he complained that Van Brunt was always intending to come and see him, but never did. The sketchbooks also reveal that Van Brunt took a trip up the Hudson with Sanford Robinson Gifford (1823–1880), the landscape painter and a neighbor in the Studio Building. One of the books contains a sketch of the river labeled "from West Point." On another leaf is an amusing patriarchal drawing of Gifford entitled "SRG in character of Wandering Jew by Henry Van Brunt, G.A." It is answered by a jaunty picture of Van Brunt with pince-nez (he was always nearsighted) and broad-brimmed straw hat entitled "VB in character of Verdant Green. West Point June 24 1860. by S. R. Gifford NA" (Fig. 3). [42]

It was at this time that Van Brunt published his first essays on architecture, "About Spires" in the *Atlantic Monthly* of January, 1860, and "Greek Lines" in the June and July, 1861, issues of the same magazine. These must have considerably enhanced his professional standing. [43] In its notice of Van Brunt's death the *American Architect and Building News* said that "Greek Lines" "created a great sensation, not only in the artistic world, but among cultivated people generally, and ought still to be read by every young architect." [44] Today's reader would probably find both early pieces too ornate and effusive. Later in his life Van Brunt may have thought so too, for when he reprinted "Greek Lines" as the title essay in a small collection of 1893 he revised it, excising some of the most offending passages. The style and glorification of medieval spirituality in "About Spires" owes much to Ruskin, while "Greek Lines" is a romantic panegyric to the neo-Grèc values that Van Brunt probably had first absorbed from Hunt. The modern works of Labrouste, Constant-Dufeux, and Duban, which are celebrated in the essay, also appear in his sketchbooks (Fig. 10). Nevertheless, some of the ideas in these earliest works were, as we shall see, to develop into the central pre-occupations of his subsequent writings.

This first phase of Van Brunt's professional life was brought to a close by the Civil War. The family of Bradlee Van Brunt, the architect's son, have memoranda in his father's handwriting indicating that he was on naval duties from May, 1861, to August, 1862. He served for the most part as a secretary to Admirals L. M. Goldsborough and Samuel Phillips Lee, who were successively in command of the naval squadron blockading the Carolinas and Virginia. He also served at times in the same capacity for his father, the Commodore, who was in command of the frigate *Minnesota*. He held a temporary commission as Lieutenant, J.G., and after the war was a member of the Loyal Legion, an organization of Union officers of all services. Van Brunt consistently understated his duties, in which monotony was, perhaps characteristically, the greatest hazard, but he did serve in the *Monitor-Merrimac* battle at Hampton Roads on March 8 and 9, 1862. Henry Van Brunt, Jr., remembers his father telling on one occasion that he was placed in command of a small boat from the *Minnesota*, sent out to identify a floating object at a time when the command was nervous about the presence of the *Merrimac* offshore. The object turned out to be a "very dangerous empty beer keg." However, Van Brunt brought his sketchbooks along with him to help while away the hours. One of them contains a drawing of ships at anchor, labeled "Hatteras Inlet Jan 20. 1862." In the same book there are also drawings of several Union gunboats, the *Louisiana*, the *Hetzel*, the *Brinker*, the *Whitehead*, and the *Underwriter* (Fig. 5).

In 1863, after his return from war duty, Van Brunt entered into practice in Boston in partnership with William R. Ware (1832–1915), a fellow pupil in Hunt's studio. They immediately set up an atelier in their own office, in imitation of Hunt's. As a result of this teaching, when Massachusetts Institute of Technology two years later decided to establish a school of architecture, Ware was approached to direct it. He accepted the offer, and then went to Europe for an extended tour to study the various systems of architectural instruction. In 1868, the year the first class was enrolled at the M.I.T. school, Frank Howe became an assistant in the firm. Ware continued on as an active partner until 1881, the year of his departure for Columbia University. The original partnership was still not formally dissolved, however, until 1883, although Frank Howe had been made a full partner in the preceding year.

Ware and Van Brunt soon became one of the most distinguished architectural firms in Boston. Perhaps because of the scholarly leanings of both partners their work was more institutional, ecclesiastical, and domestic than mercantile (Figs. 18–43b). For Harvard College they (or their successor firm, Van Brunt and Howe) designed Memorial Hall (Fig. 28); Weld Hall (Fig. 25); the old Harvard Medical School on Boylston Street (Fig. 48), until recently part of Boston University; and the east wing of the old college library (Fig. 30), where they first introduced Labrouste's principles of stack

16

construction to the United States. Other institutional work included Episcopal Theological School in Cambridge (Figs. 22–22b) and the library of the University of Michigan, where some of the original bookstacks are still in use (Fig. 46). Among the many churches of their design in New England, the finest and best known is the First Church in Boston (Unitarian) on Berkeley and Marlborough Streets recently destroyed by fire (Fig. 18); others are St. John's Chapel in Cambridge (Fig. 22) and St. Stephen's in Lynn (Figs. 43–43b). The firm also designed the Union Station in Worcester (Fig. 26). Of their domestic architecture the *Architectural Review* has written, "There are houses on Beacon St., Boston, quiet brown houses, unassertive but with mouldings so well adjusted, openings and walls so well proportioned that they are grateful to the eye, and they are Mr. Van Brunt's work; and upon entering those houses it will be found that there is a distinction both of plan and attack." [45]

Van Brunt seems to have taken special interest in the architectural problem of the monument. His sketchbooks record many examples of sepulchral monuments and late in life, during his European tour, he gave much thought to the question of a memorial for Queen Victoria, comparing plans proposed with the Siegesallee in Berlin. Two of his articles, one on Grant's Tomb (1885) and another on the Washington Monument (1887) deal with this subject. A letter to John Quincy Adams Ward, the sculptor, on May 21, 1867, discusses in detail the project for a statue to the Civil War General George Henry Thomas.[46] The statue was finally unveiled in 1878. Ware and Van Brunt are also credited with the Ether Monument in Boston's Public Garden (Fig. 20), which contains another Ward statue. In addition Van Brunt also collaborated with Hunt and Ward on the Cornwallis Surrender Monument at Yorktown (1881–1883) (Fig. 41).[47]

Harvard's Memorial Hall (Figs. 28, 29), however, is certainly the firm's most conspicuous building, though time, fire, and official neglect are rapidly doing for it what the Reformation did to the abbeys of England. Its Victorian Gothic design is permanently identified with the firm, though it was an early work and though Van Brunt, with the characteristic eclecticism of the times, also designed in other styles.[48] If Marcel Breuer and Charles Eliot Norton have been among its critics (Norton disparaged most Harvard buildings — most American buildings, for that matter), it has found its defenders in Henry James, Montgomery Schuyler, Walter Kilham, and a French professor of architecture, Duquesne, who, just prior to the First World War, found it the only Harvard building worthy of exclamation.[49]

Ware and Van Brunt won the competition for the building in 1865, at which time they looked upon the project as an "opportunity for elevating the tone of architecture in this country," [50] much as Ruskin had viewed the construction of the Oxford University Museum (Fig. 81). However, by the time the building was completed, in 1878, countless changes had been made, many being compromises for the sake of economy. Though the building may have fallen short of the architects' ideal conception (as any building will,

17

where cost imposes restrictions), Van Brunt took care on at least three occasions to demonstrate the thoughtfulness of the design within and without.[51] He maintained, somewhat surprisingly, that the cathedral plan of the building was purely accidental, derived, not from romantic sentiment, but from the three-fold requirements of the building (war memorial, dining hall, and academic theater). "The tower," he wrote, "rises from the central division, partly as a conspicuous and solemn exterior expression of its memorial function, and partly to dominate the building at the point where such a culmination and emphasis are demanded by the conditions of line and mass in the rest of the composition." His explanation effectively demonstrates that concern for function does not operate indeterminately, but in a context of more or less received stylistic and aesthetic notions.

When Charles Eliot Norton criticized the later-nineteenth-century architecture at Harvard, Van Brunt as the architect of the largest and some of the most important of those buildings, was moved to reply to his critic's "Rhadamanthine judgments, which condemn or approve and give no reason." [52] He himself was on principle an advocate of close formal analysis of architecture in support of concretely based judgments, and many of his points of defense are fundamental to his whole critical thought. It is interesting to observe, however, that his central argument — that the later buildings, like their eighteenth-century neighbors, also emanate from the spirit of the times in which they were built and add other chapters to the visual record of American civilization within the Harvard Yard — is the argument still used by the college to justify new buildings in any style or material. Van Brunt, himself, however, later modified this position, as can be seen from a letter to W. C. Sabine of 1899, accompanying the drawings of the building.[53] On that occasion he explained that the Gothic style thirty years earlier had been "a universal cult among all English-speaking people, and had reached the dignity of an intellectual if not a moral movement." It was the only style felt to have "life and progressive power," and to build in any other would have seemed anachronistic. However, he concluded, if he were now called upon to build a similar building, it would "assume other characteristics, recognizing possibly classic and academical influences, which not only would make it a more accurate exponent of the spirit of contemporary civilization, as we understand it at this moment, but would perhaps give it a better chance for permanent recognition as a work of art, and would bring it into some relations of consanguinity with the older college buildings." The strong pull of historicity and the concept of the organic evolution of styles had by then somewhat relaxed.

On October 6, 1869, Van Brunt married Alice Sterritt Osborn of Baltimore. They settled in the handsome Fayerweather house on Brattle Street (Fig. 2), formerly occupied by the British colonial governor of the area. The house was rented from the Newell family, which then lived abroad. On the return of the family, in 1883, Van Brunt purchased a parcel of their property at 167 Brattle Street and built his own house there (Fig. 45). In the Newell's house were born their first four children: Charles Gershom (1870–1951), Alice Mathews (1872–1956), Osborn (1875–1939), and Helen Bartlett (1878–1967). The last three children, Marion Bradlee (1885–1963) and the twins, Henry, Jr. (1886–   ) and Courtlandt (1886–1961), were born in the second house.

The years in Cambridge and Boston were not only satisfying in terms of architectural practice, but were intellectually stimulating too. Van Brunt continued to publish occasional articles and reviews in such magazines as the *Atlantic Monthly*, the *Nation*, and *American Architect and Building News*, though in the early years of establishing a practice he did not write as frequently as he did later on. In 1875 he brought out the first volume of his translation of Viollet-le-Duc's extremely influential *Entretiens sur l'architecture* (1863–1872), having already announced the work in the *Nation* as early as 1866.[54] The second volume was not to appear until 1881.

For the scholar there was also the pleasure and profit of familiar intercourse with men of letters in the period when Boston was still the literary and intellectual capital of America. Van Brunt was on friendly terms with Longfellow and James Russell Lowell, both of whom lived close by, with Thomas Bailey Aldrich, and with John Bartlett, the Little, Brown editor and compiler of *Familiar Quotations* and the *Concordance to Shakespeare*. The latter was a next-door neighbor and his wife was godmother to Helen Van Brunt. In addition he had many friends among the Harvard faculty. Henry Van Brunt, Jr., recalls an incident which gives a glimpse both of his father's personality and of his social activities at this time:

An anecdote involving my father, characteristic of his sense of humor, is recalled by a note in his autograph in a copy of Carlyle's "French Revolution." Father was particularly interested in Carlyle because of that writer's long association with Ralph Waldo Emerson, but detested his prolixity, particularly exemplified in "The French Revolution."

The Cambridge group of which my father was a member established at one period a reading and discussion club which met at intervals at the houses of members. One summer the meeting was at Bar Harbor in the summer retreat of Henry James (not the novelist, but his father, the theologian). The members at that time had started wading through Carlyle's opus and, at Bar Harbor, it was Father's turn to read. Aware of this in advance, he had composed a paragraph of sheer nonsense in Carlyle's style which he slipped into the book and, in the course of his reading, interpolated as part of the text. It read:

"Word-splitting organisms, of whatever shape — not, as now, with Plutarchian apologies; nay, rather without any such apologies — antiphonal, too — in the main — born into the world to say the thought that was in them — butchers, bakers, candlestick makers, men, women, pedants — for you, too, it is now or never!"

Having read this passage, he broke off with an exclamation of frustration and bewilderment, scornfully challenging anyone to explain it. Highly indignant, old Mr. James took up the cudgels for the author, asserted that it was easily interpreted and spent the next several minutes gallantly attempting to do so. The others gave him respectful attention and the warmest compliments.

Father said nothing, but continued to read. He told the family rather sheepishly many years later that he cast about in his mind for some way in which he could confess his duplicity to members of the group, but the longer he waited the more difficult it became, and, as far as I know, he never revealed his trick — and I'm quite sure, not as long as Mr. James lived.

The second phase of Van Brunt's professional career was brought to an end by his move to Kansas City. The *American Architect and Building News* attributed this move to the stagnation that followed the rebuilding of Boston after the Great Fire of 1872. The journal commented that for a man of his years and temperament the step seemed singularly rash.[55] But there was an added reason. In 1884 his friend Charles Francis Adams had become president of the Union Pacific Railroad and Van Brunt was asked to design a large number of stations in the West. In the following year he sent Frank Howe to Kansas City to open an office and he himself followed soon afterward, though he did not move permanently with the family until 1887. Kansas City was then still a booming "cow-town," and the intellectual and social climate there, as well as the architectural work, were very different from what Van Brunt had been accustomed to in the East. He must at first have particularly missed the company of men of learning. There has survived a copy of a letter he wrote on December 4, 1894, to about a dozen male friends in the city, in an attempt to reproduce some of the atmosphere of Cambridge. In view of Van Brunt's nature and intellectual attainments the letter has a pathetic ring:

It has often occurred to me that a dozen intelligent and more or less representative men might obtain from life in Kansas City a sort of pleasure and profit which the present conditions do not seem to furnish, if they could meet socially at stated times at one another's houses for rational discussion after a simple repast. I greatly miss here the stimulus which I obtained in Cambridge from a small club of a dozen members representing various professions, several of them professors in the university, who for many years have been accustomed to meet on alternate Saturdays in this way, the host for the time being furnishing the theme for discussion, generally by reading a paper or by the recital of some interesting fact or argument relating to his personal or professional experience. All this was very informal, but the results were always satisfactory to men of thought.[56]

It is ironic to think of Van Brunt, one of the leaders of his profession and, of all American architects of his day, probably the one most sensitive to the whole fabric of culture, trying to weave together an intellectual community in what was then the far Southwest. In this respect, however, he was carrying on the work of Hunt, though in much more extreme circumstances. The letter was productive, and a group of men met according to the suggested plan until 1899. In addition to Van Brunt there were two lawyers, a professor from the University of Kansas, a civil engineer, an industrialist, a circuit judge, two distinguished clergymen of different faiths (Henry Hopkins and Cameron Mann), a representative of Boston financial interests who made heavy loans in the city, and a physician. In time, however, as he grew established and Van Brunt and Howe became the leading architectural firm in the region, his homesickness was swallowed up in the activity of his new life and it gradually diminished.

The new work in Kansas City, reflecting the conditions of society there, was primarily concerned with commerce and industry (Figs. 56, 62, 73). The firm designed stations for the Union Pacific Railroad at Sioux City, Iowa; Omaha, Nebraska (Fig. 68); Ogden, Utah (Fig. 57); and Portland, Oregon (Fig. 67). Among their larger works in Kansas City were the store of the Emery, Bird, and Thayer Dry Goods Company (Fig. 66) and the Coates House hotel (Fig. 65). In domestic work they designed houses for the Armour and Griffiths families and for August R. Meyer (Figs. 71, 72). The Meyer house has since been converted for use by the Kansas City Art Institute. The firm also worked together with McKim, Mead and White on the New York Life Insurance Building in Kansas City (Fig. 76). In recognition of their importance, Van Brunt and Howe were commissioned to design one of the buildings on the Court of Honor at the Chicago Fair of 1893 (Fig. 150). Though their Electricity Building was the least successful component of that majestic complex, the commission did give Van Brunt the opportunity to participate closely in what was undoubtedly the most significant architectural event of the close of the century. Perhaps the finest fruit of that experience was the series of articles he wrote interpreting the most important buildings of the Fair and its implications for American civilization.[57]

If the years in Kansas City decreased Van Brunt's opportunities for learned discourse, they increased his publication. It is tempting to surmise that communication with the nation at large expanded as talk in the study dwindled. But whatever the cause, during the nineties Van Brunt wrote his most suggestive essays, ripened by over thirty years of study and active practice in his profession. Rooted in a habitual desire to see the conditions of architecture and the culture of his own time in a perspective of the thought and experience of the ages, they rose above both transient enthusiasm and enduring dogmatism. It is certain that Van Brunt's practice in Kansas City increased his concern with the phenomenon of American architecture, its nature and prospects. He was there confronted with that architecture in its most doggedly practical and frankly commercial domains and had to make his way competitively in that world.

His own experience was markedly different from that of Charles Eliot Norton who, for instance, from the repose of his study in the East, could offer enthusiastic consolation to the fretful "pioneer," George Woodberry, out in Nebraska: "What a chance it affords to study Primitive Institutions! I wish I had as clear a concept as you are getting of the first rough stage of a modern civic community. It is all elucidation of history." [58] Van Brunt, in contrast, had experienced the actual West and had the advantage of a pivotal position as ambassador between the East with its European ties and the West where those allegiances were dimmer. He could interpret the needs of one area in terms of the other, but could also evaluate the distinctive achievements of both regions from the larger perspective of continental American architecture. From these special opportunities emerged a contemporary commentary on some of the most significant chapters in our architectural history by probably the one man who was doubly equipped — both by capacity and by situation — for the task.

Throughout the years in Boston and Kansas City Van Brunt had been actively concerned with the affairs of the A.I.A. (of which he was a fellow), both nationally and regionally. He figures frequently in the discussions on various topics which are recorded in the annual *Proceedings* of the Institute conventions and he participated often in committee work and as a judge of competitions. The architectural periodicals of the day, especially the *American Architect and Building News*, add to this picture with accounts of his many activities at local meetings.[59] These services were recognized and honored when in 1898 he was elected president of the Institute. In that capacity he presided over the annual convention of 1899 in Pittsburgh and delivered the opening address to the members. In his address, however, he forestalled the customary renomination for the office by announcing his intention to leave on an extended tour of Europe early in the following year. The trip had been made possible by a substantial bequest from his younger brother Charles, who had died that year.[60]

The tour was a considerable, and doubtless a very costly, undertaking. Van Brunt, together with his wife and daughters, Alice and Helen, sailed from New York on January 25, 1900, and did not return until mid-April of the following year. They began their journey on a cruise ship which took them through the Mediterranean to Egypt, the Middle East, and Greece. At Sicily they separated from the ship and proceeded on their own to tour the countries of Western Europe. During the summer of 1900 the party was joined by the three youngest boys of the family, Bradlee, Henry, Jr., and Courtlandt, who accompanied their parents on a tour of England and Scotland and then returned to America in mid-September together with their sister Helen. Long as it was, the trip was originally to be even longer; it was cut short because of Helen's impending marriage. For Van Brunt it was the culmination of a fifty-year old ambition and had to be planned on a scale sufficient to satisfy accumulated desires. It was undertaken not merely to visit foreign lands, but to examine the important cities and buildings, the architectural record of Western civilization. It was Van Brunt's opportunity at last to flesh out with three-dimensional experience a lifetime's detailed study of books, prints, and photographs. The undertaking was even by moderate estimate thorough, for hardly a day went by without the close examination of one or more monuments.

Fortunately Van Brunt recorded his experiences and impressions in a journal which was subsequently transcribed by his son, Courtlandt.[61] He made entries daily and in all filled eleven volumes during the trip. The length of the project affords some indication of its scope. The journal was intended as more than a record of places visited and significant occurrences along the way. It was a conscientiously kept account of impressions and, like Van Brunt's explicatory essays in criticism, an attempt to analyze the formal qualities of the monuments he was seeing. In all it is an impressive performance. Years of considered thought are brought to bear on most of the principal buildings of Europe; impressions are modified in particular and in the aggregate; the impact of one building or culture jostles against that of another to call forth fresh insights. The diary parallels the later nineteenth-century novel of the "International Theme," though Van Brunt, unlike Henry James's innocent hero, Christopher Newman, for example, had explored the culture of the Old World and participated fully in that of the New. His mind was fertile and receptive, critical but appreciative. Like James himself, Van Brunt was a cosmopolitan spokesman for American maturity. Though his trip came too late to affect his professional practice, it at least found expression, characteristically, in his other medium, prose.

There is good reason to believe that Van Brunt himself intended to extract a book from his European diaries. A clue is given in the *American Architect and Building News*, which says — obviously from personal knowledge — that the letters and notebooks from the trip should enable his literary executor to produce "a book of rare worth." [62] The format of the diaries, moreover, testifies to Van Brunt's intentions. Entries are not random jottings; each analysis of an important building is a brief essay in itself. Often he must have made extended notes on the spot, since his descriptions are precise and detailed. The sights of each day's trip were written up every evening in clear, faultless prose. Though he writes in some places that he wants his notes to act as a stimulus for future recollection, the journal can nevertheless be read as it stands, without emendation or expansion. It would be even now an illuminating and thorough guide for the traveller. I quote in full the following excerpt from the diary, the observations which result from a day's trip to Peterborough Cathedral (Figs. 17–17b). Though all entries are not this long, the passage gives a fair indication of the scope of the project and of Van Brunt's characteristic analyses when he has time for a careful examination of an important monument.

Peterborough.

Wednesday, September 19 [1900].

A fair day invites us to make our projected visit to Peterborough which we reach by a half hour's railroad ride to Ely, northward from Cambridge, and by an hour's ride thence westward. The immense grey mass of Ely Cathedral, with its imposing octagon and lantern in the centre and its tall western tower, is a most impressive object as we pass it in the train, dominating the town with a mountainous majesty and overlooking the vast plain stretching for miles on every side.

The splendid mass had hardly faded from sight in the distance when ahead of us we see the aspiring towers of Peterborough. We watch this changing grouping as we approach with eager interest until they are shut out from view by the present buildings of the railway station.

The Approach.

Fifteen minutes' walk through the streets of the little provincial town brings us to the market-place surrounded by picturesque old houses with a market cross in the centre. A few steps thence at the end of a narrow street we see the dark mass of the gateway to the minster precincts.

This is a Norman structure and the fine round archway with its ancient vaulting is clearly of that period, but the superstructure has been faced with detail of the Decorated period. In fact it is an epitome of the cathedral itself whose vast west frontage as we enter the close presents itself suddenly to view with a colossal dignity, astonishing us with a strangeness of outline and detail for which no familiarity with its image in prints and drawings could give us adequate preparation.

The Cathedral Exterior.

Like Bishop Hugh's front at Lincoln, it is a vast early English screen or mask set against a Norman structure, with which it has no affinity whatever. But it is a far bolder composition than the Lincoln example.

The original Norman front was in plan like a western transept. But the early English front which is set against it hardly recognizes a single feature of the original design. In fact it is a most hardy 'parti-pris', independently conceived, presenting what the English are fond of calling a colossal Gothic portico, quite unlike anything which has been executed before.

But the three tall gaping niches with their black shadows, which are the principal features of the composition, are not doorways or portals in any sense, and, as regards window openings, are quite meaningless, the narrower central niche being the only one which coincides with any of the west windows.

There is a horizontal gallery over the points of the three arches, and over each arch is a gable with pinnacles between, for which there is no preparation of architecture in the piers of this vast screen. This strange design is flanked on each side by a tall, narrow tower with spire and beyond it rises incongruously the upper part of the bell tower which formed the northern feature of the old Norman front.

A bigger or more elaborate architectural mistake or aberration has never been committed. The huge frontispiece stands stilted upon long legs and has no body for the legs to uphold. The whole composition being such as it is, I cannot commend too highly the architectural importance of the central parvise or gabled porch, which was added in the latter part of the 14th century (judging from its style); for it adequately fills the lower part of the central niche, gives it a proper base and strengthens the thin piers at the point where their apparent weakness most demands assistance.

This real porch is moreover an excellent design of its time, and it unquestionably saves the great early English front of Peterborough from the greatest disaster as a piece of merely ornamental screenwork. As an architectural design, I cannot agree either with Fergusson, who says it is the grandest and finest portico in Europe, or with Freeman, who lauds it as the translation of a great Greek conception into Gothic language.[63]

I admit that much of the detail is interesting and correct; but as a whole it is neither a portico or a triumphal arch; it surprises but does not please, and I had a greater admiration for the patriotism than the artistic judgement of the English critics who have persuaded themselves that it embodies a great architectural thought.

The desire for originality, which seems to have been a powerful motive in the minds of the English mediaeval architects or amateurs, apparently betrayed them into gross aberrations, like the western screen fronts of Lincoln and Peterborough, as often at least as it inspired them to such conspicuous successes as the octagon of Alan de Walsingham at Ely, which we plan to see next Sunday.

Certainly the desire prevented them from always uniting harmoniously in the development of style, sacrificing individuality, as was the case with their contemporaries in France. On the other hand they exhibited a most effective union in the beautiful development of the Tudor Gothic.

The Norman feeling, which is exhibited in its earlier phases in the exterior of the choir and transepts of Peterborough, and in its later phases in the nave and what can be seen of the west end, is very fine indeed. And it is very curious to see how little injury has been done to the artistic effect of the Norman exterior where the Norman window openings have been filled with the tracery of the 16th century.

Indeed I am disposed to think that the finer vertical elements in this tracery afford an agreeable and entirely harmonious offset to the stern round-arched Norman. But where the superimpositions of the Perpendicular period have effected the form of the window arches, as is frequently the case in the nave, the result is more interesting from a historical than from an artistic point of view.

The central tower is a finely restrained expression of the Decorated period rising with a noble promise, which is not fulfilled in the uncompromising and unbroken squareness and simplicity of its skylines at the summit.

The cathedral has undergone and is undergoing extensive and most necessary repairs and restorations, and these for the most part have been done judiciously. But at several points the exterior is sadly dilapidated and in some places threatens to fall unless soon protected.

The magnificent activity of the Tudor Gothic period, to which I have had occasion to refer in so many places, finds expression in Peterborough in the square eastern extension enveloping the apse of the Norman choir. This extension is very skilfully done and its fan vaulting is ingeniously adapted; but the glass is all white, and, as I have elsewhere intimated, these vast expanses of mullioned and traceried windows are conspicuously incomplete until obscured by the charms of color.

The Cathedral Interior.

The interior of the great fabric has all the magnificent and ponderous unity of the round-arched Norman and makes an impression even more overwhelming than that which we experienced at Durham. The triforium is larger and more spacious than any yet seen by us, and it has its own range of windows; it has thus the character of a high gallery.

The interposition of the dark triforium between the light clerestory and the illuminated openings of the nave arches is to my mind a much more artistic disposition than we see at Peterborough, where the triforium and the clerestory have too nearly equal value.

Moreover the rough carpentry of the aisle roofs is disagreeably evident as one looks up from the nave. I could not help contrasting the beautiful carpentry of the roof of King's College Chapel above the stone vaulting, which of course is invisible from below.

The aisles of Peterborough have a fine early quadripartite vaulting and afford an exceedingly beautiful perspective, unbroken, for a length of at least four hundred feet; but the ribs are so massive as to deprive it of lightness and spring.

The nave has a wooden ceiling; but the choir has a beautiful illuminated fan-vaulting of wood. The nave piers are all alike and are composed of heavy grouped shafts, but the choir has noble round columns. There is but little stained glass and this is not good. The lower range of windows in the apse, as they now open into the Tudor Gothic eastern extension, are unglazed.

The modern Gothic oak stalls are exceedingly beautiful and have some very fine carving with small exquisite portrait figures. The screen between nave and choir is as yet unfinished. The latter has the best inlaid marble pavement that I have seen in England, except, perhaps, that in the Albert Chapel at Windsor. The nave is bare and but a few shattered monuments have been spared by the commissioners whom Cromwell sent to superintend the systematic spoliation of the building in 1643.

All the interior stonework has been cleaned and the yellow of it fills the long perspective with an effect of smoothness and cleanliness which give the space a somewhat modern appearance. There is no effective mystery of gloom about the whole interior. It is flooded with light.

The Cathedral Surroundings.

The surroundings of the cathedral are interesting and, indeed, beautiful. The Dean's house and garden are exquisite specimens of English comfort and scholastic repose. They lie north of the church. On the other side, to the southeast, is a mass of old buildings constructed largely in the early English arches of the ancient Infirmary of the monastery. These arches are lovely in their ruin.

I have not time to detail the incidents of old and new architecture throughout the picturesque close, nor to do more than refer to the "laurel cloisters" on the south side of the nave which are now ruinous and show interesting superimpositions of work of several eras. In short, this has been a very full and interesting day—one of the most fruitful and most enjoyable we have had in England. We reach Cambridge at 5:00 pm.

In some areas the taste of today will part company with Van Brunt's. He tended, for instance, to be impatient with the more exaggerated elaborations of the baroque and rococo styles, particularly when they were carried out with plaster or stucco surface ornamentation, "posturing and fluttering" figures, and "garish, theatrical" coloring. In this attitude the combined influences of nineteenth-century constructive rationalism, neo-Grèc simplicity, and Ruskinian Puritanism — all opposed to dramatic movement, "worldly" sumptuousness, and any attempt to conceal the line and materials of construction — are manifest. Thus in the nave of St. John Lateran he writes: "The terrible spirit of the 17th century, the spirit of Bernini and Borromini, prevails . . . with that bumptious pomp and magnificent pretence which have taken possession of so many of the churches of Rome.

"The splendid columns of verde antique which formerly decorated the nave are now embedded and lost in vast brick and plaster piers with two colossal Corinthian pilasters in each and a big canopied niche between. In these niches the twelve apostles are posturing in heroic attitudes, after the manner of the school of Bernini, as the prophets and fathers are posturing in the high winds on top of the facade outside." On the other hand he could respond fully to the power of Bernini's colonnade at St. Peter's, and at least in part could admire Santa Maria del Popolo, "rebuilt by Bernini in the 17th [century] after the pompous impure fashion to which the genius of the master ministered with a magnificently fatal effect."

Even in a realm where he shows limited sympathy the reader still has something to gain from Van Brunt's remarks since they are usually delivered in a context of close observation, which is instructive; and, unlike some of Ruskin's, they never fall into mere rhetoric, however superb. The grounds of his disapproval are almost without exception aesthetic, so that if we disagree with him, we know at least the basis of our dissent. The influence of moral and literary attitudes, so disastrously widespread in nineteenth-century architectural criticism, as in the celebrated condemnation of Renaissance pride and worldliness which concludes *The Stones of Venice*, is in general carefully controlled. But Van Brunt is always sensitive to, and respectful of, the *legitimate* dimension of external associations which color our response to architecture. He praises, for instance, modern Scottish Gothic work, which testifies to the influence of Sir Walter Scott, and at one point even observes that the wild extravagances of Borromini have "unexpected dignity" in Rome, where they are a venerable and genuine growth of the traditions and genius of the Italian race.

His use of the biological analogy for the cycle of styles, their rise and decay, is also less rigid than we find in many of his contemporaries. He did not, for instance, share the widespread scorn for Tudor or Flamboyant Gothic. When he calls the chapel of King's College, Cambridge, "impure" or decadent he uses the terms historically, for he is highly appreciative of the technical and decorative richness of the style. He means that in such work the Gothic principle of the decoration of construction has come to an end or has been transformed into the construction of decoration. But particularly in the late adaptation of Gothic forms to domestic and civil architecture, as in the house of Jacques Cœur at Bourges, he seems to discern a new vitality, an inner renaissance, which might have yielded a disciplined development had not the revival of classical forms superseded it.

Van Brunt's heightened sensitivity to architecture derived from his double perspective as a critic. He looked upon a building both as an integrated aesthetic object and as the "exponent" of a phase of culture. Hence his strict judgment of the way a particular building to a greater or lesser degree realized the potentialities of its style was modulated by his interest in its expressive and, in a broad sense, its "historical" qualities. St. Mark's, in spite of flaws, was for him an overwhelming emotional experience:

No photograph and no pictorial art can adequately express its charm. The front on the Piazza violates every academical principle of design. It is weak at the corners where it ought to express strength and rigidity; the arch of its central doorway interrupts the horizontal line of the gallery without any evident effort of design to correct or cover so manifest a defect.
Its skyline with its wild crockets is fantastic and almost barbaric in its defiance of all the conventionalities of architectural composition; the great central window asks in vain for the tracery which should carry across this gaping void some decorative continuation of the wall screen; and yet the modern architect, versed in his rules of aesthetics and hidebound in his principles of academic design, who does not, in this presence, forget them all and find himself carried away by the charm of this beautiful monument, has indeed no poetry in his soul.

Architectural "hard facts" are here chastened and premises of judgment are elevated by an imaginative sympathy for the pervasive aura of an individual artistic entity.

Elsewhere he notes that the drums upon which the domes of Santa Maria della Salute are set are connected with the facades by immense marble consoles which have no other function than to establish a fine outline. "We can almost excuse their costly absurdity," writes Van Brunt, "for the sake of the success with which they accomplish this object." At York he says that he is grateful for the expressions of early English, Tudor, Renaissance, Jacobean, Stuart, and other styles in the tombs and monuments of the choir. He thinks that "every demonstration of historic style, wherever it occurs, should be respected." Even the "want of conformity or purity of style" or the "absence of unity of conception in the structural design or in the subordinate detail" of the churches and houses he has seen in England and Scotland concern him less than "their genuineness, their authenticity, their unaffectedness as demonstrations of history through architecture." Finally, it was architecture's capacity and need to express the quality of a civilization that could condone such an act as the eighteenth-century destruction of the principal features of San Pietro in Vincoli: "As the venerable work of the first years of the Christian church in these historic basilicas was probably falling into sad decay through neglect and age, it may be a question whether the rehabilitation of them to fit them for the more splendid service of the far richer and more worldly churches of the 17th and 18th centuries was not after all better done by the frank masking of the ancient features in the pompous taste of these eras of active and ambitious reconstruction and repairs than by any attempt to restore them with archaeological correctness, as would have been done in our own day."

Van Brunt's critical rigor was thus delivered from narrow pedantry by a humanistic respect for the associations and evidences of civilization, while this respect was in turn restrained from degeneration into mere sentimentality or aesthetic relativism. He was aware that the attitude embraced in the phrase "savoir c'est pardonner" was more an archaeological than an architectural instinct, and that by an excess of respect, the artistic consciousness could be "charmed into atrophy." Critical response was, therefore, for Van Brunt an elaborate counterpoise or tension of feelings and judgments, any of which might predominate, but not to the extent of submerging the others. It was for this reason that he so greatly regretted both archaeological and academic tendencies in architecture. Each, he felt, moved toward a cold authoritative perfection of style at the expense of expressive qualities, except in the limited sense that such tendencies were themselves expressions of the thought of an age. Cologne Cathedral, in the scientific precision of its design, is pervaded with a "cold aestheticism": "Everywhere there is perfect repetition and exact correspondence of parts and an extraordinary display of architectural cleverness; no errors animate it, and the poetry of the art is frozen into a fine mechanical conformity. . . . Doubtless it is all very elegant, very magnificent in its tremendous scale, very correct in its way and enormously costly, but I infinitely prefer the comparatively little facade of Freiburg." And St. Mary's Cathedral in Edinburgh, by Sir Gilbert Scott, which was then much praised, he considered betrayed by its own perfections into lifelessness. In such ways architects lost sight of the elastic possibilities of design and were too timid to "snatch a grace beyond the reach of art."

But if the artist should on occasion offend against the rules, he ought never to transgress the ends toward which they are directed. In admiring imaginative liberties Van Brunt never ran to the extreme of expressive licence. The term he employs over and over again to describe the quality he most approves of in a building is "reserved force." This is what he greatly admires in works of the early, as opposed to the later, Italian Renaissance. The Certosa di Pavia has preeminently "joyous liberality of thought and labor and . . . elegance of line and detail. This richness of detail is not riotous but restrained and refined; there is no touch of barbarism or licence about it, it is all disciplined and correct." An essential element of this achievement is the proper subordination of the components of an architectural scheme to its total conception. Van Brunt praises the Certosa particularly because "the redundance of ornamentation is not only most beautiful and precious in itself, but is so subordinated to a calm and distinctly defined architectural scheme that it is not in evidence till one is near enough to study and appreciate it." In contrast, the Duomo of Milan in its exterior design squanders art without apparent order or discipline. As a result its architectural scheme is "effeminate and almost petulant"; it lacks "repose of mass." These observations apply to interior work also. After careful study of the Maggiore Consiglio in the Ducal Palace at Venice and the upper hall of the Scuola di San Rocco, the two most beautiful and majestic rooms he had ever seen, Van Brunt discovered the secret of their success "in their splendid unity of conception and in the subjection of the largest amount of thought in design of detail to the controlling idea." The rooms are easily understood as a whole; they hold nothing in reserve except the preciousness of details which makes them worthy of careful study.

The ideal end of architecture for Van Brunt was the construction of a perfected organism, which, in the world of art as in the world of nature, ought to have an expression of completeness. In the journals he italicizes the maxim that "an architectural design cannot be perfect if it is not so accurately and visibly balanced that nothing can be added to or taken away from it without a shock to the whole system." Therefore, though he gives high praise to the Farnese, the most monumental of the palaces of Rome, he feels the want of a natural stopping place at the two ends. French architects of the seventeenth century, by inventing the pavilion to emphasize the structural completeness of the facades and hence to perfect the aesthetic unity of the whole, made one of the most important contributions to Renaissance architecture.

Van Brunt's conception of the organic in architecture is both freer and larger than some modern naturalistic theories. He did not naïvely confuse the provinces of art and nature by maintaining that a building had to rise out of the ground like a trunk, branching into rooms or sections. But he thought it ought to have clear form in the Aristotelian sense, with a beginning, a middle, and an end, and its parts ought to be subordinated to the effect of the whole. Furthermore, he did not even feel that structure *had* to be the sole determinant of decoration or receive *direct* expression in an architectural scheme. This, too, was to his mind a narrow view of organicism; sometimes the application of a decorative-structural system would better express the divisions of the building. For this reason he gives high praise to the Roman treatment of the amphitheater, in which the buttresses were expressed by pilasters and columns and the floors of the great outer corridors by the lines of the entablatures. Romanesque builders, by the plain superimposition of arches, as in the naves of their great basilicas, could have exhibited the same general arrangement of decorative lines as was adopted by the Romans, but they could not have attained to such an expression of force and majesty as the Romans achieved by the use of the classical orders to the same end. "Under the conditions of a Roman amphitheater," he concludes, "I am entirely persuaded that the union of the Greek orders with arcuated construction, which it has been the universal custom of modern critics to condemn in measured terms, is logical and architectural. I certainly, in the presence of such majestic architectural compositions as the amphitheaters of Arles and Nimes, can imagine no decorative treatment, whether Romanesque or Gothic, so beautiful and so effective. The monotonous repetition of these alternate arches and columns, as they gradually recede and vanish around the magnificent curve of the ellipse, constitutes one of the most imposing and entirely satisfactory architectural effects that I can conceive."

The word which best expresses the implicit values of the observations on architecture in Van Brunt's European journals is "life." Architecture worthy of the name has life. Goethe had once called architecture "frozen music," implying that it had a temporal as well as a spatial dimension. Its form reconciles in a vibrant stasis the dynamic interrelationships of its parts, like T. S. Eliot's Chinese jar in "Burnt Norton" which "still/Moves perpetually in its stillness." Van Brunt, too, felt this metaphysical dimension of form, but he saw in addition that architecture was instinct with the actual life — spiritual as well as material — of the time and place which created it and with the life of a style. A building, therefore, was precious because of this cultural vitality, even though it might have flaws, which are to some extent inevitable in an actively developing style. Vulgar and tasteless experimentation or the illiterate quest for originality were paradoxically antithetical to life, since they were ephemeral. They would not affect future work; they could not grow or advance style. Furthermore, this life within architecture was not only important for historical reasons, but it served to underscore the scope and significance of the artist's mission in the present, which was to achieve again a living architecture.

In keeping with his convictions about art's responsiveness to culture, Van Brunt paid particular attention to the national tendencies of architecture as he observed them in each country. He noted the Englishman's fondness for domestic privacy, which stretched out his cities with suburbs of private houses instead of the large apartment buildings which were characteristic on the continent. He especially appreciated their sympathy for rural architecture and their ability to adjust their houses to the soil and the surroundings. The French, on the other hand, seemed cockneyish. When they tried to be rural and irregular, they were affected and ridiculous; more commonly they priggishly mimicked the formalities of chateaux. He also felt that English architecture was much more parochial and conservative than American, which was bolder in adapting to modern conditions of living. But he valued this expression of the Englishman's innate reverence for tradition, just as he admired their preservation of the early Renaissance style of Wren and his followers. It was not very elastic or fluent, but it was "at home" in England, just as the "old Colonial" was in America.

He was predictably conscious of the French genius for art as manifested in the nation's quick and sensitive development of style. He also noted the respect that France had for its historical monuments, understanding their immense value in refreshing modern art and keeping alive a healthy modern spirit. He questioned, however, the effects of the restrictive building ordinances in Paris, which destroy some of the animation that comes from contrasts and variety. While occasionally they produced magnificent general effects, they often gave streets a stately and uninteresting monotony. Architects were then constrained to seek for individuality in a profusion of *rocaille* ornament, with which he was not always in sympathy. But he did find that the persistent regularity of the architecture was "the best possible running accompaniment to the splendid boulevards, the magnificent vistas, the monumental squares, the superb public buildings, which confer upon this city of cities its wondrous charm." Paris was for Van Brunt the triumph of artistic munificence, rivalled elsewhere in the journals only by the splendid terraces and vistas of Rome, and he rises to eloquence in its praise: "The Seine, with its quays and bridges, the public gardens and squares with their statues and balustrades and monuments, the obelisks and fountains, the triumphal arches, the sculpturesque groups, the great public buildings which may be seen at the end of the long vistas, the crowded streets, the elegance and brilliancy of the shops, the magnificent avenues of trees, all these constitute the Paris we have come to see. It has no disappointments. The place seems to be in a continuous fete, and the people sit at their tables on the sidewalks in front of the cafes as if they had nothing to do except to form a picture in a wonderful civic 'mise-en-scène.' "

Naturally Van Brunt was interested in making comparisons between the conditions of architectural practice in Europe and America. For instance, with his intimate experience of the limited opportunities for school building in this country, he was especially struck at Cambridge by the dignity with which collegiate benefactors invested their gifts in the cause of learning. Buildings were to be like palaces in their structure and equipment. "Statues and ornament, monumental gateways and bridges, terraces and balustrades, towers and pinnacles, oriels and tracery, stained glass, vaulting and carved timber roofs, courts, cloisters and magnificent gardens seem to be as essential as financial foundations upon which the permanent maintenance and the practical usefulness of the whole institution must rest. It is a splendid exhibition of the pride and power and the respect in which the cause of learning is held." Perhaps it was architecturally symbolic, then, that Emmanuel College, the alma mater of John Harvard, was "one of the lesser and least prosperous of all the houses" and "far less splendid than the others in its appointments."

Berlin particularly impressed him by its monumentality and cosmopolitan elegance. Even a department store, like Julius Wertheim's, was willing to sacrifice practical space and to subordinate display of goods for architectural richness. Evidently, he observed, much more money had been spent for purely decorative purposes than in Emery, Bird and Thayer's, which he had designed in Kansas City (Fig. 66). The contrast seemed to him significant, and when he saw the abundance of statues which adorned the squares and the solid substantial quality of the institutional buildings, he was moved to recall "with mortification and regret our own rigid economies and puritan plainness in our building of corresponding class in American cities. The Germans seem to aim not only to build well, but to build beautifully and luxuriously as if beauty and richness of decorating were an essential part of all their scheme of education."

It would be senseless to look in the journals for dramatic alterations of attitude or a persistent developing theme. They were, after all, the day-to-day observations of a man of age and experience, making his way through territory long familiar, at least in the study. Apocalyptic conversions and sweeping theories are more common in youth. There was, however, an increase in the length of entries as the pace of travel became more leisurely; there were more comparisons as more experiences were absorbed; and there was a further loosening of already liberal judgment, resulting from prolonged exposure to new sights. What is recorded throughout the volume is a profound respect for the generous use of architecture to enrich life in all great societies. The impact of this feeling is still fresh; its relevance for us is more than ever urgent.

The *Dictionary of American Biography* says that Van Brunt's European tour signalled his retirement from active practice. This is not true. According to his family, he returned to his professional work in Kansas City, and we know that he was among the architectural planners of the Louisiana Purchase Exhibition of 1904. Van Brunt had severely censured the frivolous and decadent spirit of the architecture at the Paris Exhibition of 1900 (Figs. 100, 100a), and he would doubtless have urged the architects at St. Louis to follow the example of high artistry and monumentality provided by Chicago in 1893. However, he did not live to see the exhibition open. Early in 1903, while in Boston on a professional trip he suffered a recurrence of his hip ailment and entered the hospital for a bone operation.[64] Mrs. Van Brunt and his daughter Alice came East from Kansas City to be with him, taking an apartment in the Back Bay. On his release from the hospital he was brought to his sister-in-law's house, Overmead, in Milton, supposedly to convalesce; but complications had developed, and he died shortly thereafter, on the eighth of April. He was buried in the family lot in Cambridge.

The severe pain which Van Brunt suffered throughout his life and the heavy mental and physical strain which resulted from it was responsible, according to one writer for an "unconscious air of impatient arrogance that first and last cost him many friends." [65] About the pain itself there can be no doubt, but there seems to be no real indication of any alienating effects because of it. Intellectual and sincerely religious (Episcopalian) by nature, his physical affliction probably increased his tendency to reflection and introspection, but he was fond of society and was revered by the many friends he made and kept during his life. The grace and measure of his prose amply express his manner, which was formal, courteous, and courtly to all. He seems to have disliked the business side of his profession, avoiding it whenever possible to concentrate on design, though he was, of course, aware that architecture in a commercial society must take account of commercial needs. His impeccable dignity was far removed from priggishness. He had a quick wit, an unfailing sense of humor, and a hearty resonant laugh. His family remembers him as a singularly lovable man of impressive tenderness. His son Henry tells that the youngest sons, when they were children, always went to his study to kiss him goodnight: "We called him 'pa-*pa*' with the accent on the second syllable in the old Bostonian style — as we called our mother 'ma-*ma*' — and he always held each of us by the ears to study our faces, kissing us tenderly on each cheek; he called us 'boy-dee' indiscriminately — probably because he never could tell the twins apart, although he found a distinguishing feature in the way my hair grew from the crown, the only obstacle being that he couldn't remember which one of us was so distinguished. In fact he had difficulty remembering the names of all of us, including my mother, whom he called 'dear' to distinguish her from her elder daughter, Alice. We all remembered the time when he was winding the grandfather clock on the stairs and, for some reason, found it necessary to summon mother. In an exasperated way he ran through all the family names in succession and finally, when mother appeared at the foot of the stairs, laughing, demanded sternly: 'Woman, what *is* your name?' "

His photographs present him tall and lean, with frock coat, cane, and pincenez, twisted mustaches and goatee. His face is scholarly and sensitive; his eyes keen, sometimes with a slight twinkle. The pictures reveal a nineteenth-century gentleman, of a school that we recognize from the fiction of the period, and that we can once again freely admire.

II. The Writings

Van Brunt's critical essays claim our attention for a number of reasons. First of all, they are an unexpectedly large and intellectually coherent inheritance from one of the founders of American architecture and the molders of American taste. They comprise the first large collection of essays by a prominent American architect, giving continuous comment on our architectural development for half a century. Secondly, they are suggestive and illuminating on basic problems of continuing interest in modern aesthetic thought, such as the relationship of art to society and the significance of art as cultural evidence. Thirdly, owing to Van Brunt's wide reading and intellectual curiosity, they are a valuable reflection of, and introduction to, many of the key ideas in nineteenth-century thinking about art and architecture, especially as they appear to the American mind. For this reason it is important that we explore some of the origins, interrelationships, and ramifications of these ideas, the better to understand the attitudes of Van Brunt and his contemporaries, to whom we owe many of our own habits of thought on such matters. We should also observe where a concept which still affects us today, such as the notion that art must express its age, can be destructive as a conscious aesthetic aim, whatever its validity as an abstract historical truth. Fourthly, because the later nineteenth century was so crucial for our own intellectual development, it is especially necessary that we be able to comprehend and properly evaluate its art and thought. Many of the principal ideas that lie behind the profound changes in art during the nineteenth and twentieth centuries we now increasingly perceive are the outgrowth of the intellectual revolution of the eighteenth and early nineteenth centuries that is associated with the Romantic Movement and its precursors. But it was in the later nineteenth century that these ideas came to a head and produced their largest effects of change. As we move farther and farther away from a period of transition we tend to forget the full context of its thought, the problems with which it wrestled, the innovations it made, and the traditions it hoped to preserve. Van Brunt can serve to recall these things from the days before our own age and thus afford us a valuable perspective on today.

In almost every area of his critical writings Van Brunt shows the pervasive historical orientation of his thought. He observed the profound impact of historical awareness on his age and noted its effects; he studied the history of architecture and the role of architecture as historical evidence; he pondered the relationship between architecture and history, looking for a key to interpret the processes and the significance of architectural development; he sought to interpret the historical development of architecture in his own time; and, finally, he examined, in the manner of a historian, the forces that were influencing and molding those architectural changes. In this respect he mirrors the central preoccupation of his age. Drawing on hints from its predecessors and on aspirations for a universal compendium of knowledge, the nineteenth century developed the methods of modern historical study. Its scholars opened archives and catalogued their contents. They scrutinized historical evidence, inventing modern techniques of documentation. They parceled out history into subjects, nations, and periods in the attempt to bore deep into the intricacies of a special field where minute study might reveal truth. They constructed philosophies of historical developments. They explored the individual, social, political, intellectual, religious, economic, material, and technical forces which influenced historical change and they even perceived the complex interrelationships of these factors. Small wonder, considering the vastness of their undertakings, that ignorance could grow in Malthusian proportions to their researches and that incoherence was often the reward of an excess of illumination.

Such was the lamentable result of architectural scholarship. The Renaissance translations of Vitruvius, which had authorized Roman precedent, were followed in the eighteenth century by measurements of Greek monuments. Then came the researches of antiquaries into Gothic architecture, and finally the profusion of studies on every available style which created what Van Brunt called a "new Babel in modern architecture . . . a confusion of tongues worse than that which interrupted the building of that famous architectural unity on the plains of Shinar." [1] What was necessary documentation for the historian became dangerous precedent for the architect, who either felt called upon to be "correct" in his reproduction of the minutest details of a style or took refuge in eclecticism[2] and "embarrassed by precedent, impeded by . . . knowledge of the past . . . produced an unintelligible polyglot made up of Greek, Roman, Saracenic, Byzantine mediaeval types, mixed together in various proportions, which we must distinguish as the architecture of the nineteenth century." [3]

With curious irony a movement supposedly begun in scientific objectivity of scholarship betrayed its relationship to quixotic fashion by rapidly encouraging capricious subjectivity in both architect and client. By putting the architect in possession of his whole patrimony of historic styles and hence showing by an apparent multiplicity of standards that architecture was no longer one thing — no longer the classical system of proportion and its vocabularly of ornament, for instance — archaeology seemingly recognized no authority but taste in architectural design. Without any way of meaningfully organizing the materials put before him, or of grading them by a systematic scale of values, the architect stood bemused before his knowledge and found it "not power, but a snare." [4]

The picture just drawn, a distillation of Van Brunt's view of the condition of architecture in the second half of the nineteenth century, is no doubt exaggerated to the extent that no architect confronted with a specific job was likely to have been stranded between styles, like a donkey between bales of hay. Views of function and suitability, we tend to forget, are various, and many different styles could be found suitable for individual needs. For instance, Gothic, according to a line of argument German in its origins, was considered appropriate to the Christian spirit of modern life,[5] or, on other grounds, as fitted by its picturesque informality to the elastic needs of modern living. Other styles could also be rationalized by their adherents. At an early meeting of the A.I.A. Van Brunt himself, for instance, countered the Gothicists by arguing that, however suitable for religious architecture, the Gothic style was not in accord with modern domestic feeling. He suggested the modified Greek style of the Pompeian villa as expressive of the "intellectual refinement and luxurious elegance" wanted in the contemporary home.[6]

Furthermore the phenomenon of eclecticism, which was the outcome of the flood of history, instead of being rejected as a burden, could be justified for its appropriateness to modern thought. In an article on Henry Hobson Richardson Van Brunt noted that the era of research and experiment, which put an end to the progress of the renaissance of classical architecture and inaugurated eclecticism, had also launched science, under the same influences, on "its phenomenal career of successful discovery." "Eclecticism," said Van Brunt, "is entirely consonant with the spirit of the times." [7] His remark was itself indicative of a considerable body of mid-nineteenth-century opinion. Louis Hautecœur, for instance, has illustrated the impact of eclecticism on the philosophical, political, and artistic thought of France:

> Cousin s'efforçait dans ses cours et ses livres de concilier Platon et Aristote, Descartes et Kant et prétendait unir les vérités successives établies par tous ces penseurs. Hegel érigeait l'éclectisme en système, lorsqu'il conciliait la thèse et l'antithèse en la synthèse et l'idée des arts symboliques de l'Orient avec la forme plastique des arts classiques. Considérant que le cycle des expériences était désormais fermé, il recommandait à ses contemporains l'éclectisme. Fichte reprochait à la France de croire au fini, à l'immuable, au limité et lui opposait la conception allemande du devenir. Son panthéisme le conduisait à accepter le Tout sous ses divers aspects, sous ses formes apparentes. Jouffroy se faisait le théoricien de l'éclectisme et, dans un article publié en 1825 sur l'éclectisme en morale, il définissait l'esprit historique "conciliant, étendu, qui sort de chez lui, visite les croyances de tous les pays et de tous les âges . . . admet comme observation tous les systèmes, glane partout sans se fixer nulle part, parce que la vérité est partout un peu, mais toute en aucun pays, en aucun temps, chez aucun homme." Lorsque Pierre Leroux réfute, en 1839, l'éclectisme de Cousin, il aboutit en fait, comme l'a noté Lasserre à un syncrétisme.
>
> Les écrivains politiques estimaient que le libéralisme était la seule doctrine susceptible de concilier les éléments stables du passé et les conquêtes raisonnables de la Révolution, le conservatisme et le "mouvement." Pour Rémusat "l'esprit libéral est l'esprit dont le principe est la liberté de la raison humaine, principe qui suppose nécessairement qu'aucune tradition n'a une autorité absolue, définitive et qu'en toute manière un progrès est toujours possible."
>
> Le gouvernement de Juillet, qui semblait, après les désordres de la Révolution et l'intransigeance de la Restauration, unir les avantages de la monarchie et de la démocratie, encouragea ces tendances. Le "juste milieu" ne fut pas seulement un parti politique, mais une attitude de l'esprit, qui explique les tendances de littérateurs, comme Casimir Delavigne ou Ponsard, de peintres, comme Delaroche, Scheffer, Vernet, soucieux d'unir le Romantisme et la tradition.
>
> Des architects à leur tour crurent possible de réaliser un semblable compromis entre les formes de tous les temps et de tous les pays.[8]

In a similar spirit Sainte-Beuve had objected to the too rigid definition of a classic in the 1835 Dictionary of the Academy. "A true classic," he said, "as I should like to hear it defined, is an author who has enriched the human mind, increased its treasure, and caused it to advance a step; who has discovered some moral and not equivocal truth, or revealed some eternal passion in that heart where all seemed known and discovered; who has expressed his thought, observation, or invention, in no matter what form, only provided it be broad and great, refined and sensible, sane and beautiful in itself; who has spoken to all in his own peculiar style, a style which is found to be also that of the whole world, a style new without neologism, new and old, easily contemporary with all time." [9]

There were, then, many different classics, each with its own peculiarities, yet each relevant to contemporary experience. Accordingly, Sainte-Beuve would have had the temple of taste rebuilt. But its reconstruction, he said, was "merely a matter of enlargement, so that it may become the home of all noble human beings, of all who have permanently increased the sum of the mind's delights and possessions." [10] The idea that there are many mansions in the house of our Father he would apply to the kingdom of the beautiful as well as to the kingdom of Heaven.

Matthew Arnold was saying much the same thing when he defined criticism as "a disinterested endeavour to learn and propagate the best that is known and thought in the world." [11] For his English audience he laid particular stress upon the last phrase of his definition: "By the very nature of things, as England is not all the world, much of the best that is known and thought in the world cannot be of English growth, must be foreign." [12] Since what was foreign was the element that was most likely to lie outside one's knowledge, it was the element he felt especially obligated to stress.

The eclectic point of view, though generally characteristic of Western thought as a whole during this period, had a peculiarly forceful relevance to the American situation. In his Introduction to Viollet-le-Duc's *Discourses*, Van Brunt argued that Americans, occupying a new country and having no inheritance of ruins and no embarrassment of traditions in matters of architecture, were absolutely free from historical prejudice. This, of course, was not strictly true. We had a classical tradition of architecture and civic design, stretching back to our early Colonial days, which was to be revived in the last quarter of the century, especially after the Philadelphia Centennial Exhibition of 1876. Van Brunt was aware of this tradition, but the spirit of eclecticism had so dissipated its force that by the middle of the century it was swallowed up by the eclectic idea that, as Van Brunt phrased it, "we . . . are a people made up of diverse elements, which have been gradually moulded into a national unity," and that all the past was ours.[13] That the melting pot of nations was also a melting pot of styles and traditions was a concept too obvious to be overlooked. Moreover, we were not only a nation, but a continent, geographically distinct from the "compact art-producing communities of the Old World," driven by our very scope as well as our diversity to an eclectic experience. We may remember that the endless cataloguing in Whitman's poems testifies as much to a view of the American experience as large, diverse, and eclectic as to the desire for stylistic innovation. The expansive novels of John Dos Passos and Thomas Wolfe — to cite only two later writers — reveal the fundamental continuity of this nineteenth-century American point of view.

Van Brunt felt that the American's freedom from a national tradition could give him a distinct opportunity in the history of art. Accordingly, he entitled his review of Charles Moore's *Development and Character of Gothic Architecture* "An American Definition of Gothic Architecture," stressing the uniquely American quality of its point of view. Americans, he felt, if they used their advantages correctly, were the only people in the world to occupy an unprejudiced judicial position. Hitherto the history of art had been in the hands of the descendants of those who made it. "They have been surrounded and overshadowed," he wrote, "by the monuments of their ancestors. It has been impossible for them to study these monuments with a mind clear of patriotic partisanship. Thus an English, a French, or a German history of the same era of art will present it from an English, a French, or a German standpoint of prejudice. It seems evident that an American authority, treating the same subject with equal knowledge, should present it in a manner different from all these writers, occupying, as he does, a point of view uninterrupted by a single national tradition of art." [14] Though Van Brunt did not think that Moore had fully exploited his opportunities, he nevertheless applauded the direction taken and grasped the idea that the American condition of alienation from a single cultural tradition in the Old World — so distressing to some — was not without its potential compensations for the eclectic and critical mind. In a paper delivered at the A.I.A. convention of 1892, entitled "The Growth of Characteristic Architectural Style in the United States," Van Brunt quoted with evident agreement an observation made in the London *Times* about Henry James, "that he possesses 'an advantage which a cultivated American often enjoys as compared with an equally cultivated Englishman, in that he sees the whole culture of others in Europe in a common perspective, and assimilates all its elements indifferently.' " [15] Van Brunt went on to apply the concept to the American architect. The *Times*'s remark testifies to the currency of Van Brunt's idea and also links it with a finely cultivated sensibility. It may be observed that, as the quest for national style developed, this eclectic objectivity would diminish.

Nevertheless, however much it could be defended theoretically, eclecticism on the streets was, as we have already noticed, a less attractive matter. Houses designed in different styles, drawing on a huge reservoir of motifs, jostled one another in endless argumentation. The American tradition of freehold lots, discouraging as it did the building of residential squares and uniform blocks, only intensified this anarchy. Furthermore, the sheer volume of building in the nineteenth century, as cities doubled and quadrupled in size within decades, new towns and suburbs grew up to accommodate new industries, and new industrial and commercial needs demanded new accommodation, was bound to magnify a discord which slower growth might more easily have contained. This was especially true in America where the cities of the East were rebuilt several times over during the century and the cities of the West shot up in a few decades from bare ground to metropolitan proportions. The spread of wealth in America also provided enormous opportunities to compound the anarchy of styles by a desire for architectural display. Such display is not in itself new; it is probably as old as architecture itself and is an entirely legitimate human motivation. But in America, where an unparalleled opportunity for individual rather than institutional display was developing side by side with architectural eclecticism, a new peril was added to an old situation. An architect might not only offer, and a client might not only demand, what was "different" and bizarre in a building, but both could use novelty as a means of surpassing competitors in a race for public attention and status. In the absence of any systematic aesthetic or aims, no more substantial motive guided taste. Fashions in architecture changed as quickly as fashions in dress — but unhappily they were less easy to relegate to the attic.

When Van Brunt had observed in an essay on Richardson, that eclecticism and modern science had developed under the same influences, he had been by no means sanguine in the conclusion that he drew from the parallelism. "The same impulse," he went on to say, "which made science productive has made architecture unproductive." [16] Though the collection, analysis, arrangement, and study of all the historical forms of art had made architects learned and reflective, it had "dissipated their inventive power, and rendered impossible that unity of effort without which characteristic progress in style is impossible." Van Brunt would have agreed with the English Comtist, Frederic Harrison, that "to collect facts about the past and to leave the social application of this information for anyone or no one to give it a philosophic meaning, is merely to encumber the future with useless rubbish." [17] In the realm of architecture the rubbish was all too immediately present. Clearly what was wanted by the thinking critic was some kind of theory which could clarify and interpret architectural knowledge, some principles that would organize an embarrassment of very dubious riches. Therefore, Van Brunt called for a theory of architecture which would be "capable of application to the most common uses of the art among us" and which would enable the public to understand what the architect was about in his design. "At present," he lamented, "popular opinion, where there is any at all, is based upon the merest caprice or prejudice, patronage is woefully misbestowed, quacks flourish, and the true architect is misunderstood and neglected." [18]

The spectacle of architecture, after eroding the principles of classical tradition, now deploring the very lack of such principles, of the libertarian uneasy in his strenuous liberty, is not without its irony for the student of intellectual history. Van Brunt correctly saw the connection between architecture's mid-century state of disarray and the scientific researches of historical scholarship. Yet he could look for a remedy only deeper within the provinces of scientific historicism. What was wanted was some "theory" (the scientific ring of the word is significant) which could pull together all the data of historical scholarship. It would explain the diversity of architectural forms, find a pattern in them, perhaps even help to evaluate them, and hopefully clarify their relationship to modern man with his own peculiar building needs and problems. Van Brunt and his contemporaries never fully understood that their continued preoccupation with theory signified an increasing tendency toward abstraction in architectural thought. Their concern to explain and interpret architecture only distracted attention from its highest function as an art, the design of beautiful forms. Gradually the "significance" of a building — its relationship to time, place, and society — blurred the question of its objective value as a formal composition, and the "spirit" of a building became more important than the harmony of its proportions or the beauty of its detail. Oddly enough, in the name of scientific objectivity one looked less at the building as *object* and more at the *idea* of how it satisfied a preconceived theory of what architecture was supposed to be.

The idea that Van Brunt hoped would clarify and direct the development of architecture was the concept that it was the "exponent" of a civilization or culture. He meant that architecture expressed not merely the individual taste of its designer or client, but that it mirrored the condition of life of a society, its needs, its climate, its materials, its technology. Furthermore, he says, it "has really taken shape and style coincidentally with the progress of mankind . . . it is an essential part of that progress, and has been closely dependent on it for all those qualities which give it value in art. It is therefore an art of humanity, and may be read like an open book." [19] Architecture was, therefore, the profoundest kind of historical evidence, though it was as yet unavailable to the historian because its subjective qualities had not been properly analyzed. Its characteristics were "the clearest, the most naive, unaffected, and deliberate expressions which humanity has uttered in any stage of its career." [20] One who has carefully observed the growth of styles, Van Brunt felt, has obtained an "insight into the sources of history denied to those who have obtained their knowledge from literature. He has a wider and more unprejudiced view of the growth of civilization, — a view unimpeded by the personal equation of historians, by their false deductions and literary moods; a view undazzled by personalities, and undisturbed by the immaterial accidents and incidents of the foreground." While "he thought he was merely learning the value of lines, colors, and combinations of beautiful or effective detail . . . he was also familiarizing himself with the distinctive attitudes of the human mind which gave birth to them." [21]

The style of a building, from this point of view, was seen to be the unique historical expression of the social, political, and religious values of the civilization which produced it. It only needed one more step — one which the nineteenth century was quite willing to take — to turn a historical insight into a criterion of value by maintaining that what was most precious and most desirable in a building was its capacity to offer historical evidence, its relevance to the life of its time, that is, to the time when it was built. This concept had vast implications for nineteenth-century architecture, whose history had been marked by a succession of revivals of past styles, such as Greek, Gothic, and Romanesque. Van Brunt seems to have stumbled upon the curious paradox that by being retrospective and historical, in the sense of reproducing forms of the past, architecture was being unhistorical, not merely because it was failing to give testimony about its own time, but also because it was borrowing the mere external shell of a building without the reality of the historical spirit which animated it. The Petit Trianon, so the argument goes, tells us about the reign of Louis XV. Place a copy of it in an American suburb and it is irrelevant or "unauthentic" — to use the word which bespeaks the nineteenth-century preoccupation with truth.

40

The whole idea of eclecticism and revivalism, which had seemed appropriate to the data-gathering dimension of historicism, now became totally deficient from the perspective of the *theory* of historical evidence, which considered the relationship of that evidence to the culture producing it. Hence Van Brunt could write by the end of the century that the concept of architecture as an exponent of civilization, though now familiar to all, is really one of the latest revelations of the century, and "is doing more to make architecture intelligible, to restore to it its proper and peculiar function among the fine arts, and to rehabilitate it than any other influence whatever. Indeed, among the architects of today, the necessity of such rehabilitation and the way to secure it were not made clearly apparent until the true relationship of the art which they studied and practiced to the time in which they lived had been thus revealed. They discovered that if it was to be once more a living art, they must work in the spirit of their environment; must cease to be merely archaeological or eclectic, and learn how to free themselves from their own memories." [22] The idea of the exponent or historical expression was the crucial intellectual weapon which destroyed eclecticism and indeed all reliance upon established styles.

An inability properly to dim the lamp of memory was the cause of the failure of the Gothic revival, according to Van Brunt. He did allow that it was a much more serious movement than any of the many other styles that paraded in and out of fashion during the century. It rested on principle, not taste and prejudice: "The polemics of Pugin, Ruskin, Eastlake, Street, and a score of inferior essayists on the part of the English, and of Victor Hugo and Viollet-le-Duc, on the part of the French, conferred upon the movement the dignity of a reform, of which the watchword was truth. But," he concluded, "it was mediaeval truth, not abstract truth, which they virtually taught, and the architectural disciples of these literary masters did not succeed in separating the principle from the form, the spirit from the letter. They were, in fact, more concerned with the preservation of the integrity of a style, than with the attempt to elevate modern architecture so that it might fitly express the modern spirit by the application of the principles which had guided the Greeks and the lay architects of the Middle Ages to their distinctive triumphs." [23]

Shifting his logic, however, Van Brunt defended the later-nineteenth-century architecture of Harvard University, which was an amalgamation of the various styles of the period — Gothic, Old English Renaissance, and Southern Romanesque. He was, of course, personally involved in Charles Eliot Norton's attack on the buildings. Norton, writing in *Harper's Magazine* in 1890, had stated that if a great benefactor wished to do service to the University, he would pull down all the buildings of the last half century and reconstruct them "with simple and beautiful design, in mutually helpful, harmonious and effective relation to each other." [24] The wish is occasionally echoed today, and Van Brunt's reply is still the standard defense. He argued that later buildings deserve our respect as monuments to the development of architecture, or, in other words, of architectural history, in the same way that the modest colonial and federal buildings do. Though they show some incongruity and tumult, they make at least an "advance." To design in the colonial style, and so secure a relationship with the older buildings would be merely to affect a "masquerade." [25]

A single Gothic Revival building, so the reasoning would seem to go, conveys only its medieval truth; whereas fifty years of Harvard revivalism makes the Yard a historical textbook of the rapid alteration and development of American architecture. History, then, will not be silent. But, we might ask, would it be silent if ten "colonial" buildings had been built in place of all the variously styled ones? Or would history then speak of a continued reverence for old traditions and forms or of a tacit agreement to move along harmonious lines of architectural development? Moreover, Van Brunt asked, turning the argument, if an architect were to rebuild Harvard's buildings, who would judge in what style the simple, beautiful buildings should be built? "Who shall decide what is best suited to the age and most in harmony with its spirit? Is there not a danger that the harmony thus obtained would be merely the expression of an individual taste, and not that of an age of artistic and intellectual progress?" [26]

The meaning of history, it may be observed, is indeed difficult to ascertain, especially if one is attempting to write it contemporaneously. History, after all, does not begin until it is past. The nineteenth century decided that it was an age of transition above all else,[27] and Van Brunt thought of transition as a period of hesitation between two styles. He could, then, accept a changing, transitory architecture as historically representative of the period, at the same time that he and his age kept an ideal of a new style constantly before them as the goal of their development and also — somewhat unhistorically, because it was an abstraction — as the "real" expression of modern civilization, once it would have found itself. One uniform design for a number of buildings was thought less likely to incorporate the spirit of the age (though the uniform design of a "new" style would) than various designs in conflicting styles, largely, one must surmise, on the basis of statistical odds. If one man designed a series of buildings in a single style, he *might* be expressing merely his personal taste. If ten men did the same, they would be expressing an age of transitory searching taste. But the *one* man, of course, always could have been the lucky man (or "genius," to use the Romantic term) who coincided with the "spirit of the age" and hit on the style that would develop into the ideal "new" style. How was one to know? History was not merely writ on sand, but on treacherous quicksand! Meanwhile, consideration of the forms of buildings and how they related to one another as an ensemble had gone by the board: it had no place in the discussion. The abstraction of historical expression and association had replaced the concreteness of a visual environment.

In his earliest published essay, in 1859, Van Brunt wrote that architects became antiquaries when they copied traditional shapes *"however beautiful"* without reanimating them with the breath and spirit of the present.[28] It is obvious from those words that the leading question of architectural criticism had become "What does the building mean?" not "How beautiful is it?" We ought to bear this in mind when we examine some of the monuments of the mid-nineteenth century and wonder about the taste of the period, or when, with another sort of uncritical interest, we dote on its charming "curiosities" and "eccentricities." The nineteenth century, as we shall see, did think deeply about architecture, but often in ways that carried it far away from a concern for visual beauty.

When Van Brunt referred to colonial designs as a "masquerade," he was suggesting by his metaphor that beneath the dress of the style there was a reality of expression that was being hidden or disguised. The notion appears also in a phrase that he borrowed from an English review of Arabian poetry and applied to architecture. The review drew a distinction between the art of a people who have preserved their own natural character and simplicity and that of a nation open to influences from other styles that "*teach them to affect impressions which they did not feel.*" [29] Once again the focus is on the difference between reality of feeling and the posture of a Style. At first glance the underlying theme of the passage seems to be the familiar Romantic concept of art as self-expression, so intimately related to the cult of originality and uniqueness of personality. In the quotation expression of the true self is seen to be thwarted by modern life and its learning processes. Wordworth's celebrated definition of poetry as the "spontaneous overflow of powerful feelings" [30] is a *locus classicus* of the idea on which the quotation seems to rest. However, the full context of Van Brunt's remarks makes it clear that the very thing he is protesting against is a desperate searching after originality and striking new motifs of design. He is advocating, with something of an apparent contradiction, an architecture that is at once impersonal and authentically expressive. The contradiction is resolved, however, if we remember that for Van Brunt, as indeed for most of his contemporaries, authentic feeling consisted, not in unrestrained abandonment to individual impulse, but in high seriousness and moral earnestness. The faculty that would put one in touch with truth was not the uncensored unconscious but the strict, self-regulating conscience. It was this latter agency that was enlisted to promote the true historic expression of the age.

In an essay in the *Atlantic Monthly* for August, 1878, Van Brunt defined conscientiousness in design as the practice of regarding "art not as a business, or an amusement, or an accomplishment merely, but as a duty, carrying with it certain moral responsibilities like any other duty." [31] As it is gradually being applied to art in modern times, it consists in the "desire to establish some consistent and conscious standard, by the observance of which, in the midst of the enormous and complicated demands made upon the decorative arts in our day, in the midst of the embarrassing accumulation of available and conflicting precedents, in the midst of the new materials, new inventions, new creeds, new manners, and customs, constantly presenting themselves, a new art made up of many arts may be formed and kept from anarchy and confusion." It is evident that conscientiousness is concerned, not with taste or merely aesthetic judgment, but with the establishment of principles of historical action that will produce an authentic historical expression of a new culture with its new technology and patterns of behavior. This culture would naturally have produced such an expression had it not been prevented from doing so by conscious historical awareness which retards and complicates the unconscious development of style. "Conscience" has become the faculty to solve the riddle of the relationship between history and design, to understand what principles all historic styles have in common so that beneath their surface differences of form they are similar and equal as process.

Later on in the essay Van Brunt illustrates the kind of self-scrutiny the architect must undergo before he can be satisfied that his work is "right": "I have reasoned about it," he says, "and can explain it by an appeal to your intellect. It belongs in its place and accomplishes its object with a directness which could not be reached by mere intuition. It is not a mere matter of taste concerning which there is no disputing. I cannot do otherwise than I have done and remain true to the conditions of my art. My forms are developed out of the necessities of my problem; they are not chosen because they are beautiful only, but because they are fit. Indeed, they would not be beautiful for my use if they were not fit. I have been taught by experience to distrust my own intuitive fancies and predilections for this or that form, for this or that style; they seduce me from the truth. I have been taught to discipline my resources; to subject them to critical analysis and discussion within my own mind before using them; to lop off what is irrelevant to my theme; to give greater emphasis here; to distract attention there; to harmonize the whole with the especial demands of my subject." The words "necessity" and "fit" are a clue to the dominance here of function, economy, and practicality, apart from which beauty has ceased to have an independent existence. It shines only in use. What now demands the allegiance of the designer is the utilitarian condition of art.

The emphasis upon "experience" as the antithesis to "intuitive fancies" also suggests the hostility of utilitarianism and empiricism to supposedly vague and groundless fancy — the idle shapings of the mind. But in addition it further defines the quality of reason that enters into this process of conscience. Reason is no longer the so-called theoretical reason that required the harmonious balance of forms in a classical composition. It is now busy "reasoning the needs." Those that can most readily be explained factually to the utilitarian mind are needs of function — so much support here, so many feet for such a purpose there. Yet in spite of the play of reason in this process of design, it fundamentally rests on a far less objective basis of value or attitude. If certain details are judged right because they can be reasoned in a certain way, it is only our individual values, after all, that tell us that such a way *is* *right*. The argument is really circular. In value judgments, a thing is so because we think it is so. Given other expectations, we would value other things.

Furthermore, the fact that conscience is the agency that conducts such reasoning, or at least the fact that the process is analogous to the operation of conscience, implies that imperatives of a different sort than those of reason are being called upon. Van Brunt seems to acknowledge this when he says that because it designs with conscience "modern art thus allies itself more closely with humanity than ever; it must appeal not to the senses alone, but to the mind and heart. Indeed, so saturated is it with humanity that we apply to it moral terms: we say that it is sincere or insincere, true or false, self-denying or self-indulgent, proud or debased. Or we speak of it as a thing of the intellect: it is learned or ignorant, profound or superficial, closely-reasoned and logical, or shallow and discursive." [32] At this point he dwells only on the benefits which accrue from art's close association with human feelings and moral judgments. He does not consider the subjectivity of judgments of the heart and the way in which such judgments and their rhetoric of moral attitudes can become confused with judgments of the mind. Judgments of the heart were most compelling, but also most treacherous, when they became so confused, for the reality of the senses was often likely to be passed over with only a negative phrase and a belittling attitude. During this same period, Alfred Tennyson was at work on the *Idylls of the King*, a poem in which traditional myths were being rewoven to fit the most urgent modern theme which he described as "sense at war with soul." Tennyson came down firmly on the side of soul or conscience. The growth of conscience in the decorative arts provoked the very same conflict — with, however, disastrous consequences for those arts whose primary level of appeal, as distinct from morality, is, after all, sensuous.

Van Brunt's observation that conscience drew the arts closer to humanity is one clue to its influence upon the age. "Self-examination," as he said at the beginning of his essay, "has become one of the characteristic instincts of modern civilization." An age so preoccupied in finding an exponent of itself in art could hardly forbear to incorporate in its works one of its dominant qualities. Self-examination prevailed in every major area of human concern, religious, moral, and intellectual, thence spilling over into aesthetic judgments. In *Culture and Anarchy*, for instance, Matthew Arnold had said that the ruling force of the Victorian world was, and long had been, "a Puritan force . . . strictness of conscience, Hebraism." [33] This attitude had its roots in the Wesleyan revival of the eighteenth century and the Evangelicalism that developed out of it and brought together in feeling men as diverse in creed as Thomas Arnold, the Broad-Churchman, and John Henry Newman, the Anglo-Catholic convert to Rome, both of whom reacted against slack belief and a feeble moral life. In an age when religion was threatened by science and skepticism, and when believers and nonbelievers alike were concerned to defend the shaky bulwarks of morality, no passive faith or unquestioned principle could be relied upon for strength and durability.[34] For Thomas Arnold, only when the conscience was awake could one be in earnest, and for Newman constant self-examination was essential for moral self-discipline. The latter called on his parishioners to let no day pass without its self-denial in innocent pleasure and tastes. "Let your very rising from your bed," he exhorted, "be a self-denial; let your meals be self-denials." If a man would wish to know whether he be in earnest, Newman counseled him to "make some sacrifice, do some distasteful thing, which you are not actually obliged to do." [35] This same word "self-denial" figures prominently in Van Brunt's vocabulary of conscientious architectural scrutiny, and sacrifice was, of course, one of Ruskin's seven lamps of architecture. For him beautiful churches were important principally for the sake of the moral spirit of sacrifice that would build them.

In secular matters too (and often in the nineteenth century the distinction between religious and secular issues is hard to make, so much were issues felt to have repercussions in both spheres and so similar was the language used in both kinds of writing) conscientiousness was held to be essential if the crises of the time were to be faced and solved. The strains of rapid social change and industrialization made necessary a reexamination of fundamental ideas and social prophets of varying and conflicting persuasions, united in calling for a bold reconstruction of human thought. In such an atmosphere of engagement the worst offender was the dilettante, the aimless, unquestioning drifter who refused to subscribe conscientiously to a cause and a course. Carlyle cried out that "the time for levity, insincerity, and idle babble and play-acting, in all kinds, is gone by; it is a serious, grave time." His words carried the same message that Van Brunt and others, under the strain of rapid architectural change, were preaching apropos of the "masquerade" of styles. For Carlyle, "honest scepticism, honest atheism . . . [was] better than the withered lifeless Dilettantism and amateur Eclecticism which merely toys with all opinions." And drawing a moral for his own times he warned, "We find it written, 'Woe to them that are at ease in Zion'; but surely it is a double woe to them that are at ease in Babel." [36]

In architecture, too, the absence of all attempts at style soon came to seem preferable in the eyes of some critics to a pastiche of styles, the eclectic "confusion of tongues" which Van Brunt, paralleling Carlyle, likened to Babel. Also significant, with reference to the functionalist element in Van Brunt's description of architectural conscientiousness, is John Stuart Mill's remark, first made in his *Autobiography*, that it was because the Benthemites [the Utilitarian functionalists] wrote with an "air of strong conviction . . . when scarcely any one else seemed to have an equally strong faith in as definite a creed" that they dominated the thought of the early part of the century.[37] The intellectually atheistic warriors of the head derived benefit from their conscientious pursuit of principles, just as did the more passionate warriors of the heart. Both bands were also to be found among adherents of conscience in architecture.

The arts can mirror the social prophet's call for conscious thought and moral scrutiny by becoming directly didactic and *illustrating* issues. Literature, of course, can and did do this, and its didactic dimensions notoriously soared during the Victorian period. Tennyson was only one of many writers of the mid-nineteenth century who was made to learn the force of the injunction that "man cannot live by art alone," that the artist must abandon the aesthetic isolation of his Palace of Art and join the workers and doers in the world. Painting can also follow the same course of overt moral and social exhortation. A painter can paint a scene that clearly conveys a social message; he can even underscore its meaning with a title, if he wishes. The architect, however, cannot make such a direct illustration. He can only preoccupy himself with the problems of serious social inquiry, such as factories or workers' housing, and illustrate these problems frankly in his designs. But, in addition, he can immerse himself in theory, in the search for principles of design, such as Van Brunt called for, and thus manifest his unanimity with the deeply questioning trend of the times.

In this tendency literature preceded and stimulated architecture. At the beginning of the century the Romantic poets had had recourse to critical theory in order to counter what they felt was a chaos of critical standards and ignorance of the true nature of poetry in the reviews which viciously attacked their own works. Their battle against the concept of Taste was a major element in the reaction against the notion of passive acceptance of style as opposed to active creation of new form. In the "Essay Supplementary to the Preface" of the 1815 edition of his works Wordsworth attacked the idea that taste was the paramount faculty of artistic judgment.[38] The very word, he said, implied passivity since it suggested a faculty merely responding to or registering simple sensory impressions, just as our taste buds register bitter and sweet sensations. For Wordsworth, the faculty which creates and responds to poetry was not merely dependent upon external stimuli, not just a slave of the material world, but a "power" of vision which could intuit a truth beyond what logic alone, reasoning from sense data, could determine. The emphasis upon this faculty, called Imagination, answered the empirical philosopher's disparagement of poetic creation as a mere fabrication of the unreal out of details stored and grouped in the mind. But it did so at the cost, first, of overemphasizing the role of inquiry and questing in art, and, second, of elaborating a theory of the imagination to replace lifeless taste. Taste became associated with accepted style and the pulling together by rote of things devoid of conviction and real feeling. It is interesting to observe that Wordsworth included harmony and proportion as subjects upon which taste was competent to judge. These were qualities that eventually came to be seen as lifeless and unauthentic when the reaction to this new concept of taste spread and honest atheism seemed preferable to passive dilettantism.

But if real style in art and real understanding of it had to be *creatively* achieved, if a man could no longer passively accept another's concept of style, how was he to discern *true* creative achievement? Certainly more was wanted than his own possibly capricious taste. Here Coleridge explored the critical problem much more fully and systematically than Wordsworth. In his *Biographia Literaria*, probably the most important single book of modern English literary criticism, he pronounced that "till reviews are conducted on far other principles, and with far other motives; till in the place of arbitrary dictation

47

and petulant sneers, the reviewers support their decisions by reference to fixed canons of criticism, previously established and deduced from the nature of man; reflecting minds will pronounce it arrogance in them thus to announce themselves to men of letters, as the guides of their taste and judgment." [39] Coleridge's emphasis, then, is on the search for principles to deliver criticism from arbitrary taste. By saying that he wanted them deduced from the nature of man he meant that principles of judgment in poetry depended on an understanding of the nature of poetry, which, in turn, depended upon an understanding of the nature of the human mind and, more specifically, of the imagination, the authentic poetry-making faculty in the mind.

It is not necessary here to follow Coleridge through the devious course of his subsequent argument and analysis. The points to be emphasized are, first, his insistence upon principle to guide the standard of taste which had previously been shattered by a shift in taste and, second, the philosophic orientation of his criticism. In his hands poetry was detached from established forms and genres and became a process of mind eventuating in a particular and definitive *way of using language*. Architecture, too, in the course of its search for principle and its preoccupation with theory became, as we shall see, a process of building, a way of using forms, not a system of forms. When Coleridge wrote, "To admire on principle, is the only way to imitate without loss of originality," [40] he foreshadowed the idea that Van Brunt would voice as a call for the "establishment of principles, and not forms, as standards of excellent work." [41] The words "principle," "conscience," "authentic," "duty," and "originality" in such nineteenth-century criticism cluster together to do battle with "style," "forms," "lifeless," and "taste" with some of the same intellectual and moral rigidity to be found in the melodrama of the period.

Such ethical simplicities, which are an outgrowth of architectural conscientiousness, also betray another aspect of its origins, its oblique relationship to cultural primitivism, that is, the longing for the simpler and purer conditions of an idealized past age. One of the commonplaces of nineteenth-century thought was the belief that the age differed radically from its predecessors. The eighteenth century had already engineered a shift in attitudes toward the medieval past whereby the notion of "Gothic" barbarity was replaced by a new myth of Gothic grandeur and sublimity. By the next century the Middle Ages were plainly idealized as a period, variously, of "faith," "unity," "belief," or "organic wholeness." These qualities, of course, were felt to be lacking in modern times. But not only the Middle Ages were idealized in this way. Attitudes toward this period, which so dominated the thought of the century, tended to color the view of *all* other times. Historical awareness saw that the very quality of such awareness itself set modern times off from *every* previous age of man's history by altering his mental climate. Hence his uniqueness and total isolation from the past. Ironically the sense of history seemed to separate him from the *natural* operation of history.

Therefore, since art is the exponent of the intellectual condition of a people, Van Brunt could say that "the modern process of design . . . must be a complicated one, and must differ fundamentally from all which have preceded it." [42] The distinctive characteristic of modern art which differentiated it from the art of all previous periods was the absence of fixed standards of form, the result of a new historical awareness of multiple standards. In contrast, the Greek architect had taken the dim traditions which he inherited and developed from them a "hieratic system." "He had no choice," said Van Brunt, "his strength was not wasted among various ideals; that which he inherited was a religion to him." Because he was undiverted by choice of forms he was able to concentrate upon perfection of details, harmony of proportion, and purity of line. So, too, with the builders of the Middle Ages, whose art was "kept in the track of consistent development." So it continued, even after the Renaissance, "wherever there grew a pure style."

The image of a primitive Paradise of style haunted the nineteenth-century mind and can be glimpsed in adjectives like "pure" and "innocent" that were applied to the art of the past. Modern man, by contrast, had tasted the fruit of the tree of knowledge and had fallen from this innocence. His Fall was irrevocable: he "can never do a *good* thing by accident." [43] But he *could* now consciously choose between good and evil, between architectural salvation and damnation, by strictly obeying "conscience," which would guide him to the "principles" of true faith. His new self-conscious convictions would then paradoxically restore the unconscious faith of primitive style and perhaps even make his Fall, like Adam's, ultimately fortunate by bringing about a new, if more complex, unity.

The new conscientious architectural faith of the nineteenth century had much, besides language, in common with the newer liberal religious faiths of the age. Both were attempts to extract a rationalistic core of truth from a collapsing body of belief. As developments in the linguistic and physical sciences increasingly called into question the literal truth, or at least the traditional readings, of scripture, humanists like Matthew Arnold sought a quasi-divine moral faith beneath the fragile fabric of institutional religion. What now mattered were the *principles* symbolized or allegorized in Biblical narrative, not the precise details of historical truth. [44] So too with architecture. As the authority of the classical style waned, architects like Van Brunt, no longer able to give absolute belief to its forms, or those of any other historical style, searched for "principles" which would reveal the common architectural truth of every great style. These principles would abide beneath all fluctuations of form and, more important, they could take a modern form in keeping with modern conditions. By finding them, then, the conscientious modern architect would have the key to historic expression. For by discovering the principles by which every major period has expressed its environment, and by recognizing the dominant characteristics of his own civilization, the architect could once more achieve historical truth, that is, an adequate exponent of his age.

The universal principles of architecture, to which Van Brunt alludes, are the rationalist and functionalist dicta which were postulated in the eighteenth century by such men as Marc-Antoine Laugier and Carlo Lodoli and became the commonplaces of architectural theory in the following century. They can all be grouped under the heading "truth of expression." This includes truth of construction, that is, forms developed out of the necessities of the problem and expressing the devices of construction; truth of materials, that is, the use of materials according to their natural capacities, with ornament suited to and invented for the quality and grain of the substance, and in general the favoring of native materials given their "proper" development; and truth of color, that is, the refusal to use color to imitate material other than what is actually being employed. The whole concept can be conveniently summed up in the phrase, the "honest" expression of function, structure, and materials. The last two items were given their widest currency in English in the writings of John Ruskin, for whom they were central postulates of the Lamp of Truth.[45] From him they were taken up by disciples like Charles Eastlake who applied them to furniture and interior design, thus bringing them into the heart of the household and the domestic consciousness. Both men saw in Gothic, as opposed to classical, architecture, the noteworthy merit that "the origin of every decorative feature may be traced to a constructive purpose." [46]

Though Van Brunt considered Ruskin the "most prominent among those who have created the present tendency among English architects to design and build more according to reason and less according to prejudice and fashion," [47] he recognized in the Frenchman Eugène-Emmanuel Viollet-le-Duc a more important influence upon the architectural profession because he was "less visionary, less poetic, and less dogmatic." [48] The term Van Brunt applies to Ruskin is "literary," a somewhat ambiguous word which implies an awareness of the poetic and rhetorical dimension in his writings, the realm of feeling, but in addition an insistence upon extra-aesthetic moral and religious values in architecture. Ruskin wished to establish principles, but he could never have pursued a logical premise to its abstract conclusion. Furthermore, he would have despised the activities of contemporary structural expression and the cold, mechanical materials it flaunts. He loathed the machine and its handiwork above all else. But Viollet-le-Duc, as Van Brunt perceived, was solid, practical, and concrete where Ruskin tended to be most vague. Both men shared the same aims (at least at the start): the desire to overthrow classical architecture and the academic system of education by which it was propagated and to replace it with values derived from their understanding of the Gothic. But their methods and temperaments were very different. Viollet-le-Duc wrote as the cool and impartial inheritor of the Cartesian rationalist tradition who hoped to impose logic and order on the morass of prejudice which was modern architectural thought. "My aim in writing on architecture," he said, "is to investigate the reason, the cause, for every form of the art, for no historical form or style is merely capricious; I propose to indicate the origin of the different principles of the art and their logical consequences." [49] His energy in pursuing this goal and in construing causation structurally, as in the case of Gothic architecture, was immense and ruthless. "Any form," he proclaimed, "whose raison d'être cannot be explained, cannot

50

be beautiful; and in architecture any form that is not suggested by the structure should be cast aside." [50]

But Viollet-le-Duc was also a practicing architect, well-versed in the techniques and crafts of his profession, not merely the inspired amateur or critic. As such he spoke with peculiar authority to an age which expected utopian transformation from technology and industry. This outlook, it must be stressed, though in some respects a repudiation of Ruskinism, was a reincarnation of one of its essential components, the Puritan revulsion from what was considered the useless sensuousness, decorativeness, and worldly monumentality of the classical. The twin Puritan gospels of work and hatred of display, which underlay Ruskin's dogma, could not long be estranged from the machine, the century's chief instrument of practicality and productivity. Eventually they poured with religious fervor into the utilitarian and positivistic cults of science and industry as twin avenues to a New Jerusalem of light and order. Hence a frame of mind was produced which was hospitable to Viollet-le-Duc's astringent interest in applying the developments of modern science to the arts of construction and giving them architectural expression. Hence also the rapid appreciation of his stress upon function or programme, "to fulfill exactly, scrupulously, the conditions imposed by the requirements of the case," together with construction, as the two "indispensable" and primary truths of architecture.[51]

To this practical element, so dear to the factory-minded, Ruskin had given very little attention. Attempting to distinguish between Architecture and Building he had written, "Let us, therefore, at once confine the name [Architecture] to that which, taking up and admitting, as conditions of its working, the necessities and common uses of the building, impresses on its form certain characters, venerable or beautiful, but otherwise unnecessary . . . It may not be always easy to draw the line so sharply and simply; because there are few buildings which have not some pretence or colour of being architectural; neither can there be any architecture which is not based on building; but it is perfectly easy, and very necessary, to keep the ideas distinct, and to understand fully that Architecture concerns itself only with those characters of an edifice which are above and beyond its common use." [52] For Ruskin, art was still above function, but for Viollet-le-Duc this sort of hierarchy was untrue. "What are regarded as questions purely belonging to art, symmetry and external form, are only secondary conditions [of architecture]," [53] he affirmed, thus carrying his readers and his age much further than Ruskin along the strict path of architectural "principles."

Another, and for Van Brunt, a more important, area in which Viollet-le-Duc passed beyond Ruskin was in his concern with architecture as an exponent of civilization. It would have been impossible, of course, for a man of the nineteenth century to be oblivious to the historical dimension of art, its relationship to the age in which it was created. But Ruskin's interest was merely general and spiritual. Though in the *Seven Lamps* he spoke of the "uncorrupted marble" as the brightest Lamp of Memory[54] and declared that it had been his endeavor "to show . . . how every form of noble architecture is in some sort the embodiment of the Polity, Life, History, and Religious Faith of nations," [55] he made no attempt to explore the physical conditions of life or the complex events of history that exerted their influence on the Art. He was principally convinced that Art reflected the religious and moral values of a society, and though his insistence that Art was not detached from human concerns and responsibilities was valuable, his reading of historical epochs tended to be simplistic. His antithesis of Middle-Ages/Gothic versus Renaissance/Classical was painted in bold strokes of Faith in opposition to Corruption. His reading of history was romantic rather than scholarly, and he was concerned with the vague general spirit rather than the specific events which made it up. By temperament more a reformer than a critic, he wanted a renovation of men more than of architecture. Characteristically, one of his seven lamps of architecture is the moral lamp of sacrifice. In preaching the theme Ruskin declares that he does "not want marble churches at all for their own sake, but for the sake of the spirit that would build them." [56] He was not interested in *expressing* the material concerns of his own, or of any other age; he wanted to *convert* those concerns.

To Van Brunt, however, Viollet-le-Duc was "the only man who has ever written history from an architect's point of view." [57] He cites as illustrations Viollet-le-Duc's articles on Cathedrals and Monastic Architecture in the vast and influential *Dictionnaire raisonné de l'architecture française du xie au xvie siècle.*[58] The former can serve as a model of his historical method. His outlook is more secular than Ruskin's and his view of the spirit of an age more sophisticated in its awareness of cultural forces, if not of aesthetic motives. He sees the building of the great cathedrals of the twelfth and thirteenth centuries as the outcome of a large movement to overthrow feudalism and found the French nation through an alliance of church and monarchy. The buildings are monuments of religion, he admits, but people were just as religious in France at the beginning of the twelfth century as at the end. What interests him is not (as with Ruskin) that a deep religious feeling has brought the cathedrals into being, but why they have taken this particular form at this time; why the *change* in religious architecture. He argues that vast quantities of money would not have been forthcoming for the cathedrals had the bishops not espoused the cause of the people; that a new architecture was needed, and was found, to differentiate the cathedrals of the people from the feudal monasteries; and that their preservation over the centuries signifies their closeness to the heart of the people. That Viollet-le-Duc's avenue of inquiry was a matter of conscious intellectual program is apparent from his introductory remarks in the *Discourses on Architecture*: "in my view a course of lectures in Architecture must embrace a wide field of studies — research into the history of Nations, an examination of their Institutions and Customs, and a proper estimate of the various influences that have raised them to distinction or effected their decay." [59]

Nevertheless, Viollet-le-Duc's view of history cannot escape the prejudices of his age, especially in its preeminent concern with nationalism, the obsession of the century. Van Brunt correctly pointed out his treatment of history "not as a mere story of the movements of parties and rulers . . . but as an exhibition of the *genius of the nations,* to which the facts of traditionary or written history are in every sense subordinate." [60] The trouble with this point of view is that the "genius of nations" is a large abstraction which is very susceptible of being interpreted according to the observer's own preoccupations. Viollet-le-Duc's interpretation of Roman architecture as an expression of Roman civilization is a case in point. It was influenced by his hostility to classical architecture, his primary interest in structure, and his insistence upon structural expression. For him the fundamental Roman characteristics were organizational skill and engineering abilities. The reality of Rome lay in its vast public works which held together and symbolized the Empire. Its achievement was truly expressed only in the vast concrete shells of vaults and domes. To Viollet-le-Duc the Roman use of the Greek classical orders was just a vulgar borrowing of foreign forms for "artistic" embellishment. He could not see that the Romans' command of structure could free them from being limited by structure in decoration or that they might find in the orders forms of ideal beauty which they could interpret according to their own criteria of design. The "genius of nations," according to Viollet-le-Duc, resided in structure, and, accordingly, he tailored his readings of history to suit his views.

The same bias is also evident in his treatment of Gothic cathedrals. His real aim is to establish Gothic architecture, which he admires and interprets structurally, as the one authentic expression of the French spirit; so he uses history to tie it firmly to French nationalism. Classical architecture, hitherto considered the exponent of French taste and glory, now becomes the foreign intruder, subserviently borrowed from Italy, just as the Italians had earlier taken its forms from the Greeks. Divorced from structure, it is for him an academic exercise, cut off from the life of the nation. Once again one feels that history is being made to do some special pleading and that the "genius of the nation" omits much of the real taste of the country throughout the ages. In his actual treatment of the cultural influences upon, and the implications of, architecture Viollet-le-Duc does not probe with sufficient depth and imaginative sympathy to pass beyond what we can today recognize as the large social myths of his century.

His limited view of historical expression in architecture derives chiefly from his attempt to link it with structural expression. We may well ask why a building which expresses the manners and customs or the spirit of a society should of necessity also directly express structure in its design. The two premises actually pull in opposite directions. The notion that architecture — and the society which produces it — is in decline if it does not obey the laws of truthful expression is a uniformitarian concept which derives from the Enlightenment's rationalist search for a single universal standard underlying all diversity. Instead of universal forms or orders, we now have a universal *principle* of architecture. Styles which do not conform to this standard, such as Roman or Renaissance classical, are viewed as degenerate. *They* must yield to the principle, rather than the principle expand to fit them. In spite of abundant evidence to demonstrate that the so-called degenerate styles were consciously following very different aesthetic aims, in spite of the fact that the energy and versatility of the cultures producing these works seem beyond question and the merit of the works themselves has for so long never been questioned, we are now asked to find them wanting according to an alien system of values. But this attitude is in direct contradiction to the notion that underlies the concept of historical expression, which can only make sense if one believes that every age and culture has a unique essence which is communicated in its art. The implications of this idea are pluralistic or diversitarian; it rests on the premise of multiple standards, all equally valuable.

This notion of cultural diversity was itself a product of Enlightenment cosmopolitanism in such men as Montesquieu, but its principal funnel to the nineteenth century was the German philosopher J. G. Herder. "What lies at the heart of the whole of his thought," Isaiah Berlin has said, ". . . is the theme to which he constantly returns: that one must not judge one culture by the criteria of another; that differing civilizations are different growths, pursue different goals, embody different ways of living, are dominated by different attitudes to life, so that to understand them one must perform an imaginative act of 'empathy' into their essence." [61] This act, at least as far as classical architecture is concerned, Viollet-le-Duc cannot make, notwithstanding his protestations to the contrary. He will not recognize that art is, by its very nature, a *symbolic* expression of the manners and customs of a people; and although architecture has, of all the fine arts, the closest connection with the practical requirements of life, it is distinguished from mere building by the extent to which it goes beyond those needs to give expression to aesthetic impulses. A cinder-block garage tells us something of the customs and usages of a people, just as a prehistoric arrowhead or a mud hut does. But it does not tell us in addition — except negatively — about the emotional, aesthetic, intellectual, and spiritual temper of the age, as a design for stables by Vanbrugh, for instance, will. Viollet-le-Duc confused architectural thought by associating through a faulty leap of logic the ideas of truth of expression in structure and historical expression. In this confusion, Van Brunt followed him, especially in his early years. His first article on Viollet-le-Duc, "Architectural Reform," opens with the subject of architecture as exponent, suggesting that "it is of the first importance that we should understand how it is that history has expressed itself so plainly and so intelligibly in the architecture of the past." Solving this question, he tells us, "involves a theory of architecture capable of application to the most common uses of the art among us." Yet as he proceeds to the realm of "theory" he takes up Ruskin's concept of truth of expression in structure without ever attempting to scrutinize the assumptions of his line of reasoning. For the moment the two ideas are so deeply rooted in the thought of the age that they come together unchallenged. The word "involves" is the unspecific — and suspicious — term which implies a relationship that cannot be more closely defined because it does not really exist.

Yet it is through his deep attachment to the concept of historical expression, or the exponential character of architecture, that Van Brunt comes to see the limitations of Viollet-le-Duc's theories and the unique value of the classical tradition. His early articles, "About Spires" (1860) and "Greek Lines" (1861), come before Viollet-le-Duc's *Discourses* and show the heavy influence of Ruskin in their ornateness of expression and sentiment. They also follow Ruskin in a very spiritual view of architectural expressiveness. Gothic spires and Greek decoration are seen as the exponents of religious yearning and the spirit of love, respectively. Both take a highly idealistic and idealized view of great art and of the cultures that produce it. Yet in spite of its patently romanticized view of Greece and the Middle Ages, the two ages that the nineteenth century worshipped to idolatry, this attitude later enabled Van Brunt to withstand the excessive materialism in Viollet-le-Duc's reading of architectural expression. His earliest sympathies led him to see more demonstrated in great architecture than just the satisfaction of structural and planning needs. Moreover his aesthetic sensibility allowed him to praise, however reluctantly, the expressive capacities of Renaissance architecture, scorned by Ruskin and Viollet-le-Duc alike.[62] "When we examine the works of the Renaissance," he wrote, "after the system [that is, the Roman orders] had become more manageable and acclimated under later Italian and French hands, we cannot but admire the skill with which the lightest fancies and the most various expressions of human contrivance were reconciled to the formal rules and proportions of the Roman orders. The Renaissance palaces and civil buildings of the South and West of Europe are so full of ingenuity, and the irrepressible inventive power of the artist moves with so much freedom and grace among the stubborn lines of that revived architecture, that we cannot but regard the results with a sort of scholastic pride and pleasure."[63] Furthermore Van Brunt's admiration for the expressive qualities of Greek architecture enabled him to see, without hostility, that Greek forms were not primarily constructional or material in their inspiration. "No natural form," he wrote, "was ever made use of by a Greek artist merely because suggested by a constructive exigency. It was the inward life of the thing itself which he saw, and it was his love for it which made him adopt it."[64] Great architecture has other values and motivations to express than structure, and classical forms, from the start, have been a supple vehicle for such feelings.[65]

A review of Leopold Eidlitz' *The Nature and Function of Art* (1881) gave Van Brunt his first occasion to refute doctrinaire attacks on the expressive capacities of classical architecture. Eidlitz, a disciple of Viollet-le-Duc and Ruskin, defined architecture antiseptically as "the expression of an idea through the just modelling of construction."[66] Since the Roman orders depart from this structuralist definition, they are corrupt and empty of meaning. He maintained that because of the influence of classicism, architecture "has been silent since the thirteenth century." This notion, Van Brunt declared, was not true. "It needs but a glance," he said, "to show that the function of architecture as a recorder of history has never been exhibited with greater success than in setting forth the spirit of the successive reigns in France and England, for example, from the thirteenth century to the present time. There is a characteristic modification of forms in the architecture respectively of the Stuarts, of Queen Anne, of the Georges, and of Victoria, as in that of the successive Louises of France and in that of the Empire. The historian will one day recognize these as the most significant exponents of the spirit of these modern civilizations." [67] Van Brunt is here implying that the exponential dimension of architecture is not limited to the material and practical sides of a structure, or, in other words, he is abandoning Viollet-le-Duc's insistence on the identity of the two dimensions. Furthermore, he turns the claims of scientific objectivity upon those like Viollet-le-Duc, who in the name of scientific theory, totally disregard the taste of the past. "*A priori*," he argues, "it is not scientific to assume that the experiments and studies of successive generations of artists, through nearly five centuries since the Renaissance, are a mere waste of human endeavor, unworthy to be counted by the student among the treasures of experience." [68]

At this point Van Brunt wants to assert that classical architecture can be, and has been, as reasonable as any other style, that the "formula of pilasters and entablature" can be "an expression of structure as direct as the buttress and pinnacle." He is still essentially keeping to the rationalist values, while expanding their application to include other styles. But in attacking the non-historicism of those who have neglected the actual experience of history, he is moving closer to the traditional classical point of view, stated with massive common sense by such a spokesman as Dr. Johnson, that time is a determinant of value, and that what educated taste has long admired is our surest standard of excellence. Moreover, his praise of Renaissance artists for their "boundless wealth of beautiful invention" and "preponderance of brilliant work" gives evidence of a steadily deepening preoccupation with the unique achievements of classical art. The severities of abstract conscience are being moderated by concrete sensuous response to architectural form.

The alteration of Van Brunt's attitude toward classical architecture becomes fully apparent a few years later in an essay entitled "The Personal Equation in Renaissance Architecture." Implicit in this article is a rethinking of the relationship between architecture and the spirit of the age. Van Brunt now explicitly states that writers who have confined their studies to what he calls the "external and technical manifestations" — that is, the functional and structural sides — of architecture have missed its real historical dimension. A great cathedral will tell us about the spirit of the age that produced it, "not so much because it is a great municipal and ecclesiastical monument, but because it is a work of art." [69] That is to say, its fullest meaning derives rather from the human motives that are expressed in the composition and arrangement of its forms than from the practical uses it satisfied. This being so, judged by the criterion of its capacity to give historical evidence, architecture can be divided into two broad classes: that in which the design of form and ornament is primary, and that in which it is of secondary importance. Gothic architecture is an example of the latter, since it is "an art of construction more or less ornamental." [70] The successive developments in the style were the result of steadily increased capacity in vault construction: "The decoration of these structures was not an essential incident in this scheme of general development. No single monastic or lay builder could impress his individuality upon this mighty advancing tide. Its progress was made up of forces far too great to be turned this way or that at his bidding. He was the servant of evolution, and not its master; he made the evolution consistent, grammatical and beautiful, and in this disinterested service his name and character were lost." [71] Ornament in this art did not call for the highest effort of invention since the craftsmen involved were basically touching up or adorning a structure that was essentially independent of their efforts.

But in classical architecture, runs Van Brunt's argument, a scheme of decoration was devised based on a system of proportion in the relationships of isolated columns or attached pilasters supporting entablatures, each element having its various subdivisions. With the refinement of civilization and artistic experience, this system, known as the classical orders, developed to perfection of adjustment and proportion. Since perfection cannot be perfected, the orders were freed from further evolution. Desirable variation in their use came about rather through the composition and application of ornament which called forth "a new and higher quality of invention and imagination, because ornamentation had become a far more important function in architecture." [72] Ornament, like poetry, depends upon and reflects the personality and qualities of its author. It is either composed of sculpture and painting, which is infused with the personal genius of the artist, or, where it is conventional, it reflects the choice, training, and discretion of the architect in the subtle variation of its proportions and disposition of its details. Therefore classical architecture becomes the most accurate exponent of the civilization that produced it, since it is necessarily and immediately responsive to qualities exoteric to building needs — to the taste and feeling of the artist and the civilization he serves. In the emphasis and scope it gives to the use of ornament it surpasses the Gothic cathedral as an exponent of civilization. In the truest sense it is saturated with humanity. This is why, although every classical architect aims to be correct, "the result has been not monotony, not cold and colorless uniformity, but a variety of expression, hitherto unknown in art." [73] Every country, every age, every reign finds its unique reflection in the ever-changing mirror of classical forms. In the use of convention lies the paradox of freedom. For the student of history and the historical significance of architecture, the classical orders, for so long the repository of the profoundest thoughts of mankind, could not remain forever still. It is through the medium of history that Van Brunt comes to the fullest recognition of their significance.

Van Brunt brings all his philosophical, historical, and social preoccupations to bear on the subject of American architecture. From the beginning to the end of his career he was absorbed in watching the developments of American practice and charting its progress. He is always asking what it reveals about American life and the quality of American civilization. Even more, he asks how adequate it is as an exponent of the loftiest aspirations and achievements of American society. His curiosity is wide and his tastes are catholic. He is interested in the problems of American monuments, like the Washington Monument or Grant's Tomb, and developments in American mural painting (as in Trinity Church, Boston, and the Assembly Chamber, Albany), interior decoration, and architectural scholarship. He is concerned to assess the achievements of such important architects as Richard Morris Hunt, Henry Hobson Richardson, Louis Sullivan, and John Wellborn Root. He writes, not as an outsider or an aesthete, remote from the iron and brick of construction, but as a close participant in all the developments of American practice — in building, education, literature, and thought. As a result Van Brunt offers a unique, central perspective on American architecture during its most crucial and some of its most productive years. To read his essays is to share as a contemporary the excitement and the sense of purpose of America's artistic coming of age.

Nowadays we are so accustomed to national pulse-taking that we forget how interesting the American condition must have appeared to speculative temperaments of the nineteenth century. An age which had just learned to think in terms of distinct national characteristics had, in the American experience, a powerful example for contemplation of a large and rich nation coming into its own identity. Van Brunt's interest in the problem was not merely sociological. He wanted not only to observe the direction that American architecture, as an aspect of American culture, was taking, but to note the forces that were influencing its growth and "if possible, correct it and give it proper development." [74] He writes, then, as an enlightened educator. In 1875, before America's architectural maturity, he lists as the three principal elements of American practice, "*first*, practical local necessities and conditions; *second*, a dangerous superficiality of thought and work, arising from a deficient education in art and from a want of leisure, — from the spirit of haste and impatience which prevails in all new communities; and, *third*, indifference or absence of sympathy in the public for the just expression of beauty or fitness in buildings."

Under the first element Van Brunt mainly considers the businesslike habits of Americans who want practical requirements fulfilled in a straightforward and commonsense manner. The merchant requires that the first-floor front of his shop be of glass, irrespective of the traditions of architecture; the building committee insists that all the congregation of its church see and hear the speaker and that all the social and educational needs of the congregation be comfortably housed. Streets must have narrow facades and be built to the skies and crowded with windows. There are no precedents for such things, but the architect must accept the conditions and design accordingly. Van Brunt would here seem to be acquiescing resignedly to the coarser aspects of

American materialism and forgetting that the practical conditions of a society can be altered by altering its frame of mind. We may remember that just a few decades later shops like Altman's on Fifth Avenue would be demanding something more than just plate-glass facades, and railroads would satisfy their needs in some of the most sumptuous palaces of business ever constructed. What had happened was, of course, that client and public both had been taught to want monumentality and splendor in their architecture, and architects were called upon to satisfy new and aesthetically more exalted necessities. However, Van Brunt has not really forgotten the transformation of taste which must be made in the cause of better architecture. America may remain a commercial civilization, but the conditions and attitudes of its commerce can change. Elements two and three of his list relate to these needs in our society.

On the matter of education Van Brunt can point to present and projected accomplishments like the founding of the American Institute of Architects and schools of architecture. But the conditions of life in the country are still not hospitable to the highest production of art. They encourage the architect, he says, "to habits rather of rapid composition than of study and reflection, and tend to make of his occupation rather a business than a fine art." [75] He does not have the leisure and tranquillity to build with care and deliberation. Instead "the modern Ictinus must supply the design for the new Parthenon, 'ready for estimates,' in three weeks at furthest," and then watch his sins and errors turned into stone. The enormous pressures of growth and expansion have given unparalleled opportunities for building in America, but at the same time they have prevented the highest use of these opportunities. With his acute awareness of the relationship between architecture and the society that produces it, Van Brunt knows that a sympathetic and exacting public must be developed before achievements of the highest order will be forthcoming. "Professional culture and professional genius," he maintains, "will eagerly arise under the impulse of appreciation." [76] His essays, of course, are an attempt to induce this proper appreciation. He is aware that Venice and Genoa, for instance, were bustling commercial societies, but they asked their architects to satisfy more than just "practical local necessities and conditions." America too had to learn how properly to use and adorn its material wealth.

A decade later, writing on the present condition and prospects of architecture, Van Brunt sees in the art a reflection of the national life. Unbound by any official prejudice, American architecture is in a condition of freedom. This has both advantages and disadvantages. On the positive side, we can give a proper degree of respect to the formulas and traditions of the Old World and can use them without bias and with a freedom which is characteristic of American work. We can "profit by conventionalities without being bound by them." [77] But contrarily, "our national offense has been license and insolent disrespect of venerable things, arising from want of appreciation and ignorance." The extremes are then liberty and license, and Van Brunt, like Jefferson and others, sees true liberty as involving more, not less, care and intelligence for the individual. Aided by mechanical genius in building, the architect is called on to erect buildings for a bewildering variety of novel purposes. But only the finest intelligence, guided by wise and thorough training, can really achieve what is new, yet enduring. Without it, there are, "confusion of types, illiterate combinations, an evident breathlessness of effort and striving for effect, with the inevitable loss of repose, dignity, and style. The practitioner becomes reckless of rules, and, despairing of being able to please, he aims to astonish." [78] The vision evoked is of the restless and insatiable pursuit of originality, already familiar to Ruskin[79] and common coinage in art today.

His praiseworthy example of discipline is to Van Brunt the reason for Henry Hobson Richardson's achievement in architecture and for his great popularity. He did, of course, introduce a new revival style based on southern French and Spanish Romanesque motifs. And it was, moreover, the first revival inaugurated in America. But according to Van Brunt one more revival added to the potpourri of nineteenth-century styles could hardly account for the reception of Richardson's work. "It is because of the almost unexampled proof of the potency of breadth, unity, and simplicity of style," writes Van Brunt, "that we are chiefly indebted to our friend [Richardson]. These are the qualities which, irrespective of the especial forms which he affected, constitute his greatest claim to recognition as a leader." [80] Resisting the temptation of extravagance and novelty, he sought clarity and masculine strength. He could be betrayed into brutality and rudeness, and in this direction his imitators often travestied his style; but, according to Van Brunt, his works show "a steady process of development from savage and brutal strength to strength refined by study, enriched by experience, and controlled by indomitable will." [81] Richardson makes a kind of reverse evolution in American architecture from picturesque Gothic gingerbread to classical order and repose by way of the Romanesque. The most original architect of the post-Civil War period is the learned Beaux-Arts graduate who is willing to accept restraint and express his personality by subjecting it to control. It is in following Richardson's principles that Van Brunt sees hope for the development of American style in architecture.

Van Brunt's concern for the growth of American style naturally focused on the productions of the West, whose characteristics he observed at closer hand after his own move to Kansas City in the late eighties. Writing in 1889, he saw that in the past decade architects trained in the best schools and offices of the East had put to flight the crude and vulgar vernacular architecture of pretense that had grown up in the new towns and cities of the West in the absence of any training. Chicago, with its great wealth and ambition, was the center of this reform. At the same time, however, the new architects took on the qualities of Western civilization — its independence, energy, and enterprise, and the breadth of view inspired by its boundless opportunities. They created a school, said Van Brunt, whose best work is based "not on elegant dilettanteism [sic], which is appreciated only by the elect, but by the frank conversion of practical building into architectural building without affectation or mannerisms; . . . on a sleepless inventiveness in structure; on an honest and vigorous recognition of the part which structure should play in making a building fitting and beautiful; on an intelligent adaptation of form to the available building materials of the West; upon the active encouragement of every invention and manufacture which can conduce to the economy or perfecting of structure and the embellishment of structure; upon an absolute freedom from the trammels of custom, so that it shall not interpose any obstacles of professional prejudice to the artistic expression of materials or methods; and, finally, upon knowing how to produce interesting work without an evident straining for effect." [82]

The Chicago School is obviously functionalist (Van Brunt's word is "practical") and structuralist in its emphasis. Of the two concerns, the structural, he feels, is the more revolutionary in its effects and it consumes more of the architect's energies. Van Brunt is eloquent in his admiration of the palace of commerce with its intricate machinery of elevators, heating, ventilation, fireproofing, and steel construction, all in nice adjustment. "Whether one compares a modern building of this sort," he writes, "with a cathedral of the first class, with one of the imperial baths or villas of Rome, or with the Flavian amphitheatre itself, it must hold equal rank as a production of human genius and energy, not only in the skillful economy of its structure and in its defiance of time, but as a work of fine art developed among practical considerations which seem fundamentally opposed to expressions of architectural beauty." [83]

Van Brunt's eulogy of the tall office building — so prophetic of Louis Sullivan and twentieth-century theorists — nevertheless forgets the hierarchy of types. There can be good essays and good epic poems, but a good essay is not the equivalent of a good epic poem because it cannot mobilize the same emotional, intellectual, and imaginative resources from the skilled reader as the poem. There is a similar distinction between office buildings and cathedrals. Van Brunt's statement is also of its epoch in its implied worship of the machine, which is often, as indeed here, in reality a wistful longing to compete with science and technology on its own terms. [84] But though he sees the architecture of the West as making some of the boldest stylistic advances of the century, it would be wrong to assume that he favors unimpeded development in this direction. He posits, and indeed seems to condone, a dialectical struggle between the conservative and traditional forces of the East, which look more to the Old World, and the reformative forces of the West. The palefaces are as essential as the redskins, for the traditions of art must constantly nurture, refine, and control advance. [85] The attempt to do without them only ends in the failure of the vulgar vernacular style.

What Van Brunt seems to want is an architecture of dynamic tension, analogous perhaps to the Hegelian synthesis of opposing forces. As we contemplate the flat, monotonous glass boxes of today we are more in a position to realize the loss that occurred when the guardians of tradition abandoned their functions and rushed to join the forces of innovation. The result was the destruction of tradition and the impoverishment of innovation, which is only meaningful within a defined and established context of knowledge and skill. Removed from this context it preys upon itself and becomes emptier and emptier. The reformers of the nineteenth century were nourished by tradition, and according to men like Van Brunt it was essential that this be so. With the abrogation of this inheritance our gruel has grown steadily weaker.

Van Brunt's assessment of the advantages of American and particularly Western architecture reaches a climax in a group of essays which center on the works and effects of the Chicago Fair of 1893. For too many years our view of the Fair has been dominated by the disparagements of Louis Sullivan, the unreliable utterances of a neglected and understandably embittered old man. According to Sullivan, the classical buildings of the White City were bogus academicism snobbishly imposed by domineering architects from the East who sensed its future commercial possibilities. Their alien sophistication destroyed free, native, living architecture.[86] Sullivan's views attracted the generation of the thirties, who subscribed to a conspiratorial view of history and saw the spectre of vicious Eastern bankers and their like behind every social phenomenon. However, Van Brunt, who was extremely appreciative of Sullivan's own nonclassical contribution to the Fair,[87] helps us to redress the balance of opinion. His personal experience as one of the participating architects and his knowledge of all the artists at work on the project make him an especially learned observer. His essays form by far the most thorough analysis of the Fair to date. He tells us of the thoughts and intentions of the architects, the reasoning behind individual buildings, the impact of the Fair, and its implications for the future of American architecture. Van Brunt is our indispensable guide to what Henry Adams was to call "the first expression of American thought as a unity."[88] He helps us to see how this architectural unity came about and, perhaps even more important, why it was not to last.

Van Brunt makes the suggestive point that previous international exhibitions, which were held in less impressionable, established centers of civilization like London, Paris, or Vienna, were mainly emulative in nature, whereas the Chicago Fair was largely instructive.[89] In a region like the West, without well-founded institutions of higher culture, the Fair was a vast university where the most significant attainments of modern culture might be absorbed by an eager populace which had never before been exposed to examples of the highest art on a monumental scale. Therefore, much to the surprise of foreigners, the Fair was not the "greatest show on earth," with the most audacious structural novelties, but the most carefully studied, refined, and scholarly of expositions. Its aim was to compete in terms of quality, or, rather, to offer the nation a demonstration of the supreme effects of quality. The Fair carried on the work of Richardson in the direction of greater discipline, refinement, and unity of style. This is the context of Van Brunt's statement that the architects of the Fair intended it to serve as "a timely corrective to the national tendency to experiments in design."[90] He meant that the influence of the Fair, like that of Richardson, would help to eradicate the illiterate American vernacular style with its cheap and pretentious decoration of vulgar gewgaws. The Fair would "prove such a revelation that they [uneducated and untrained architects] will learn at last that true architecture cannot be based on undisciplined invention, illiterate originality, or, indeed, upon any audacity of ignorance."

The movement from the severe, utilitarian Roman arches of Richardson's Marshall Field Wholesale Store in Chicago (Fig. 129) to the Roman civic grandeur and sumptuousness of the Court of Honor at the Chicago Fair (Figs. 141, 142), was a natural step in the reform and educated growth of American architecture. More, however, was involved in the step than just a sobering and maturing of American art. By the last decade of the century America had amassed great wealth and power, together with the necessary training, craftsmanship, and incentive to employ these resources to adorn its civilization. The Chicago Fair was the public proclamation or exponent of its desire to get on with the job. Notice of intention was served, and the way was shown, for American cities to join the company of sophisticated metropolises of the Western world. Henceforth would be built the great public buildings, libraries, universities, museums, boulevards, parks, monuments, railroad stations, concert halls, banks, stores, and exchanges which suited not only the nation's needs but its lofty aspirations (Figs. 188–194). Hence Van Brunt's feeling, shared by Henry Adams, that the Fair, commemorative of Columbus' discovery, was itself symbolic of a new departure for the nation and, indeed, for modern civilization. It marked America's discovery of a new world, a world of style as well as prominence. The nation formally declared itself ready to enter the cosmopolitan company of the leading nations of the world. It left behind the provincialism and irresolution of the mid-century decades and stepped forward with an assured and confident stride to its new urban and urbane destiny. The exhibits of the Fair showed the material productiveness and technological achievements which supported American prosperity. But the buildings in which they were housed proclaimed the nation's recognition that, in the words of Van Brunt, "it is the high function of architecture not only to adorn this triumph of materialism, but to condone, explain, and supplement it, so that some elements of 'sweetness and light' may be brought forward to counterbalance the boastful Philistinism of our times," and furnish "that 'rest, grace, and harmony,' which are needed as a compensation for materialism." [91] Such an awareness marks the greatest of civilizations at their finest pitch of life.

Henry Adams' somewhat stunned observation that Chicago had given a look of unity to her taste derived from the overwhelming impact of the *plan d'ensemble* of the Court of Honor. As Van Brunt makes clear, Louis Sullivan's assertion that "make it big" was the cry of the Fair's builders is quite simply not true. In contrast to the streets of every American town, where each building rudely shouldered aside its neighbors, unlike the pavilions of the States at the Fair itself, where the same competitiveness held true, the Court of Honor was a rare and unparalleled example of unity of effort among the designers. Any motif or detail in the composition of an individual build-ing which threatened to mar the impact of the whole group was cheerfully altered by the architect. This courtesy and cooperation, this willingness to curb individual ambition or whim for the sake of a larger ideal, was the prin-cipal lesson of the Fair. And the unity manifested itself in a variety of sig-nificant ways. Perhaps the most important was the cooperation of the several branches of the Fine Arts in the work of the Fair. No longer was architecture stripped of its proper and necessary adornments. "For the first time in our country," wrote Van Brunt, "architects have enjoyed the inestimable advan-tage of completing their works by sculpture and painting of a high order adjusted to the exigencies of the original design." [92]

Van Brunt paints a stirring picture of the friendly cooperation that prevailed among the artists working at the Fair. The scene is rare in the history of art and unique in American experience, though it does recall Van Brunt's de-scription of the magic chamber of art in Richard Morris Hunt's atelier on Washington Square where he had taken part of his training.[93] He describes how "at the midday rest painters and sculptors would assemble around their table at the commissariat, compare notes, exchange advice and chaff over the social pipe, after the manner of the studios; and then, with new zeal, each would take his electric boat, and, over the waters of the canals or the Lagoon, find his way to his distant field of operations, disembark at the broad water-stairs of his palace, as if he had been in Venice, climb his rough scaffolding, and resume his difficult and dangerous labors upon the panels of his particular dome or wall surface. In this way they have all lavished their efforts, cheered by the consciousness that they were doing their honest part in this great con-cert of the arts." [94] For Louis Sullivan the scene may have been an alien vision artificially conjured up on the shores of our continent, but the American ex-perience need be no different from that of Venice or Florence, Rome or Paris. The same ideals inspire the same concord. Van Brunt helps us to understand why we can call the period launched by the Chicago Fair the American Renaissance. If we are tempted to dismiss his description as romantic scene-painting, we ought to ask ourselves if it seems so to us because our imagina-tions are poorer, our experience and goals the less.

Hardly less important an instance of unity afforded by the Fair was the relationship established between the design of the grounds and the principal exhibition buildings. Under Frederick Law Olmsted, America's greatest land-scape architect, the flat sand dunes of the lake shore were transformed into a series of low, broad terraces, intersected by a basin, canals, and a lagoon. The sense of orderly arrangement of space, the monumental vistas, the sublime effects of water — the attention everywhere to visual delight as well as to physical comfort — were all a revelation to a country where monotonous speculator-inspired plans were the common diet of urban design. The at-tempts to alter this stale fare with civic centers, boulevards, plazas, and other sorts of city planning were one of the most needed and welcome effects of the Fair. And, as Van Brunt wisely pointed out, the lesson for architects and other artists all to work together for grand effects gave a special fillip to the movement to develop national style.[95] Indeed, the Fair itself was a kind of national venture of unity. Though the chief buildings of the Court of Honor were given to Eastern architects, much of the planning was in the hands of the Chicagoans, D. H. Burnham and John Wellborn Root. Even more important, the Fair joined together the energy and aspiration of the West with the knowledge and refinement of the East to produce a worthy symbol of the nation's finest qualities. Divisive influences of sectionalism were given no play by the organizers of the Fair. Knowing that their city would be on show to the world, they were only concerned to patronize the finest architecture that could be secured. Their action testifies to the enlightened cosmopolitanism of their judgment and to the high quality of their civic pride.

Van Brunt also makes it clear that the desire for unity was the principal reason for selecting the classical style for the buildings of the Court of Honor. The formal character of the Court as a ceremonial entrance to the Fair and the mutual dependence of its buildings on each other required a perfect harmony of feeling in the architecture. In no other style would it have been possible to achieve this goal, to minimize personal fancy or caprice, to have a common module of proportion and an open portico along the entire frontage, and yet to avoid tedious monotony and secure the greatest possible variety in unity. Only the classical style was sufficiently flexible as a language of design, yet capable of variation, as Van Brunt pointed out, according to the "personal equation" of the architect.[96] Any other style or mixture of styles would have produced a disorderly masquerade. Furthermore, by narrowing their language of form and general outline, "the architects have necessarily been invited to a study of detail and expression far more fastidious than would be easily practicable in dealing with a style less accurately formulated. In somewhat similar manner a dozen trained writers, expressing their thoughts on a similar range of subjects in an established literary form, — in that of the sonnet for example, — would commit themselves by their differences in treatment to a comparison more subtle and sensitive than would be possible had they been at liberty to handle their common theme without definite and arbitrary restrictions of form. Whether the test is one of architecture or poetry (and the two are closely analogous), it seems to compel the architect or poet to enter a region, if not of higher thought, then of more delicate study and of fine discrimination in method."[97] The chains of stylistic bondage are in reality superficial; they goad the artist to higher accomplishment, whereas in absolute freedom he flutters around, dispersing his energies in vain.

Nevertheless, though Van Brunt's notion of the "personal equation" in classical architecture, its sensitivity as an exponent of feeling, ought to have allowed him to see the Fair as a reflection of national taste and aspiration, his attitude toward its style was ultimately ambiguous. Like most men of his age, he could not fully get past the notion that style *grew out of* physical and material conditions. He could not see that style might be *applied to* the exigencies of modern life — might even direct them, as least to the extent that it gave them aims and ideals. Hence his insistence that the Fair buildings were a kind of pageant, a display of form, while real architecture lay outside the fair grounds on the city streets:

> The highest claim which can be made for modern architecture must rest on those characteristics of ornamented or ordered structure which have grown out of the unprecedented exigencies of modern buildings. Wherever these exigencies have been met in such a spirit that a corresponding development of style has been produced, justly differentiated from all other historic or contemporary styles not by caprice, but by growth, there exists a living and progressive art, which, like all other living arts in history, will stand as the exponent of the civilization under which it obtained its definite form. Probably the largest, the most deliberate, and the most conspicuous expression of the present condition of architecture in this country will be looked for by foreign critics on the grounds of the World's Columbian Exposition; but they will find it rather in the latest commercial, educational, and domestic structures in and near our larger cities. By these our architecture should be judged.[98]

Van Brunt underestimated the extent to which the style of the Fair buildings could be a language to express and clothe the complex needs of modern life. Therefore, when he insisted that it was neither desired nor expected that the Fair buildings, however successful they might be, make a new revival or school of architecture in America,[99] he was miscalculating the course of architectural development during the next few decades. For the classical was taken up and was applied successfully to "commercial, educational and domestic structures" across the land. America, the last great classical nation, thus experienced the last flowering of that Renaissance that had begun in the fifteenth century.

The concept that underlies Van Brunt's reservations about the Fair as representative of American architecture is the idea that architecture is a living and growing thing — an organism, as it were. We have seen that Van Brunt, in common with his age, too completely equated "life" in architecture with functional and structural expression, as though function and structure *had to be* the key determinants in form. There was also a large element of fallacy in the notion of growth in architecture. The whole of the nineteenth century, and especially the second half, following the publication of Darwin's *Origin of Species*, was obsessed with the idea of growth or evolution in all areas of life. All arts and institutions were interpreted by analogy with human life. But an art form is really not a living thing, and it does not follow the relatively unimpeded and necessary development of an organism. The area in which it is most likely ever to behave *like* an organism is in its structural development, where a structural innovation can undergo a process of technological development toward greater and greater competence or mastery of constructive technique. Accordingly, the nineteenth century, led by Viollet-le-Duc, rewrote architectural history in these terms, holding up Gothic architecture as the prototype of architectural life. As builders developed greater and greater capacity to handle the pointed arch and to bridge over larger and larger spaces, Gothic architecture grew from simpler to more complex forms, that is, from primitive ultimately to decadent types. The very notion of decadent types is likely to be very subjective and fallacious, as Geoffrey Scott has pointed out,[100] and as Van Brunt himself saw in his analysis of the Louis XII wing of Blois;[101] but even more important, the idea that architectural style followed structural development applied very little outside Gothic architecture, if indeed even there. Van Brunt himself, as we have observed, noted that it did not apply to classical architecture, where changes of style responded to the taste, feeling, intelligence, and quality of life of the society. Capacity for varied expression was, indeed, the "life" behind classical architecture. Once the system of classical forms was mastered, this architecture underwent change, but not growth.

Yet Van Brunt seemed to fear for the capacity of classical architecture to serve as an exponent of modern life and for its ability to undergo change. Referring to recent American experiments in Byzantine, Romanesque, and Saracenic art, he speaks of their ability "to infuse new blood into an art which, in the hands of the graduates of our schools of design, may be in danger of becoming scholastic or exotic, and of developing forms far removed from the uses and sympathies of modern life." [102] That the forms of classical architecture *could* adapt to such "uses and sympathies" is demonstrated by their ability to clothe nobly and beautifully such varied products of modern life as skyscraper office buildings, apartment houses, and railroad stations. His charge of exoticism has a subtler significance and probably refers to remoteness from public sympathy. The subject of the relationship between architecture and the society which it serves is for Van Brunt a matter of abiding and crucial concern and therefore deserves treatment at length.

It follows inevitably that if architecture is viewed as an exponent of a civilization, its relationship to society must be in some way very intimate. Since the former tenet was the keystone of Van Brunt's critical theory, he was especially concerned about the lines of communication between architecture and society. At the end of his introduction to Viollet-le-Duc's *Discourses* he had written that a work of architecture is "the outgrowth, to a great extent, of a prevailing sentiment. It cannot exist without the sympathy of the people." Accordingly he had listed among the elements which were molding American architecture the condition of "indifference or absence of sympathy in the public for the just expression of beauty or fitness in buildings." [103] Later, in his survey of the present condition and prospects of architecture, he observed that the artistic instinct which prevailed in Athens, in Ravenna, and in the Isle de France did not exist in Manchester or New York.[104] Architects lived as a caste apart, misunderstood, neither praised for their good points, nor blamed for their bad: "Not having the correction, the stimulus, and assistance of public knowledge and interest to keep them in a straight path of fruitful development, they make devious excursions in new fields, 'they affect impressions which they do not feel,' they masquerade in various capricious disguises, all with the hope of astonishing the ignorant and arousing the indifferent." All Van Brunt's essays were, of course, an attempt to remedy this condition by exciting intelligent public interest in architecture, thus putting the architect back into communication with his society.

It would be difficult to prove that the man in the street in Athens or Ravenna was a more intelligent critic of architecture than his modern counterpart. The sense of alienation is surely in part one of the self-conscious myths of the nineteenth century, which bred its primitivistic countermyth of the "togetherness" of past ages and cultures. If anything had shattered a preexisting harmony, it was more than likely not the remoteness of classical architecture, but the eclectic and alien researches of the antiquarians. Furthermore, Van Brunt undoubtedly overestimated the extent to which classical architecture had become a "court language," unintelligible to the vast mass of people.[105] If in its most refined details, its subtlest proportions, and its learned quotations it is an art of knowledge and high culture, it can also be appreciated on a far humbler and more immediate level for such qualities as harmony, grandeur, monumentality, or noble serenity. By these means it makes its primary appeal to the layman who knows nothing of the orders. Also its human scale and decoration are readily understood and sensuously apprehended by the common man. In the same way, a work of literature such as *Hamlet* can interest on a primary level through plot, suspense, and the unfolding of character. Beyond this lies the region of rich poetry — of image, symbol, allusion, and structural design — which the sophisticated reader explores through repeated study and thought. Most works of art of the highest order are similarly complex in their levels of meaning and stimulus. As the Fair itself proved, and as the American Renaissance which followed substantiated, classical architecture was once again capable of eliciting a profound popular response. Against the reservations and fears of the cultivated Van Brunt, we might place Hamlin Garland's moving description of the Fair's impact on his own provincial family. He describes how "the wonder and the beauty of it all moved these dwellers of the level lands to tears of joy which was almost as poignant as pain . . . Stunned by the majesty of the vision, my mother sat in her chair, visioning it all yet comprehending little of its meaning. Her life had been spent among homely small things, and these gorgeous scenes dazzled her, overwhelmed her, letting in upon her in one mighty flood a thousand stupefying suggestions of the art and history and poetry of the world." [106]

It is also difficult to believe that functional or structural architecture has been more popular with, or more readily understood by, the public than classical architecture. When Van Brunt tried to account for the encouraging phenomenon of Richardson's great popularity, he found the reasons to lie, as we have seen, in his "subjective" or stylistic, not his functional, qualities. And although Van Brunt seems to imply that Louis Sullivan's freer, more functional architecture in the Transportation Building (Figs. 152, 153) at the Fair carried his work closer to public sympathy,[107] the evidence of history surely does not bear out the claim. The Transportation Building was certainly not the most popular building at the Fair, and Sullivan's work in general never commanded wide and enduring public enthusiasm. Like most Romantic Secessionist ventures, it has quickly dated once its novelty has worn off. As for function, as time alters functions, it renders functional architecture especially vulnerable to obsolescence. Moreover, function is but one of the conditions of architecture and is by no means the principal source of pleasure to be derived from it. Also the modernist concept of mechanical function is itself only one, and that a rather narrow aspect of function.

As to Van Brunt's fear that classical architecture was in danger of becoming scholastic, he himself seems curiously to have contributed to the tendency. He divided the historic styles into two classes, the classic and the romantic, and his conceptions, like many applications of those terms, were based on polarities.[108] The Romantic styles, such as Gothic or Romanesque, if treated with strict archaeological fidelity, could neither be an exponent of modern life nor express its structural techniques or functions. They could only be useful if they were used with the greatest liberty, following the spirit, not the forms of the original, provided, of course, that an educated sensibility was controlling the design. Romantic architecture, therefore, so treated, was flexible to modern structure, and hence became the vehicle of growth and progress or evolution in style. Classical architecture, on the other hand, was for Van Brunt "a perfected language of form." It performed for the architect "a constant service of refinement and purification." It was "the repository of the highest and most beautiful thoughts of mankind which can be expressed in form." Classical architecture was, therefore, fundamentally an art of stasis. It admitted of variations, but no essential change. In countering those who had branded it as immoral, in providing a defense for it which also recognized its peculiar authority, Van Brunt turned it into a dead academic art, lofty but rather cold and aloof. Once again we may be reminded of Matthew Arnold, who in his defense of the classical tradition could sometimes make it seem curiously unappetizing. In Van Brunt's defense of classical architecture there is a touch of the Victorian schoolmaster's view of the classics as a brisk tonic for character building and discipline. He and his generation could not see that classical architecture could incorporate the highest thoughts and aims of society and still be far more flexible and lively than they imagined. But then we must remember that they generally dismissed the Baroque as a bizarre and tasteless aberration.

Van Brunt's concept of the polarities of American architecture at the end of the century is most aptly illustrated by two architects he knew and admired, Richard Morris Hunt and John Wellborn Root. Both worked on the Chicago Fair; both died in the last decade of the century. One was the leading traditional architect of the East; the other, one of the most progressive architects of the West. Van Brunt had trained in Hunt's atelier, but he eventually came to the tumultuous West, like Root, to practice his art. He was, therefore, well placed to appreciate the excellence of each man. Hunt was the epitome, according to Van Brunt, of aristocratic reserve: "He did not pretend to be inventive, or desire to be original, and the impulsive individuality, so prompt to assert itself under all other conditions, nearly disappeared behind the historic types which he used in design." [109] His was an imagination that was disciplined and controlled; not given to ingenious speculation about modern art, but painstaking in its perfecting of detail. Root, on the other hand, was the experimenter and stylistic innovator, the theorist and seeker after new architectural forms. Of Hunt, Van Brunt wrote that no one could follow him and go far afield. But Root, who was volatile by nature, could be led astray, as he himself recognized, by his own brilliance: "throughout his life the absence of a systematic grounding in the classics left him too free and unrestrained, too much at the mercy of his own moods. The delicate feeling for proportion and for refinement and precision of detail, which, as he himself acknowledged, can be obtained only from a study of Greek and Roman architecture in the schools, could not come to him as an instinct or as an inspiration." [110]

Nowadays, when we are likely to welcome originality or so-called creativity at any price, it is well to be reminded that there are other qualities which are necessary in architecture. Mistakes embodied in monumental form are not easily expunged. We also tend to judge the art of the past wholly in terms of the way it foreshadows that of the present, as though evolution were necessarily a matter of the survival of the fittest and the best. It is naïve to think so, and blind not to count the cost of artistic change. Van Brunt could not, of course, have predicted the future development of twentieth-century architecture, but he was aware of complex and even contradictory qualities which ought to have been represented in it if it was to be a suitably rich expression of modern civilization. For him the qualities of both Hunt and Root were still necessary. Surely it is time for us to consider whether we have achieved a unified movement toward a modern style at the price of a radical and unfortunate oversimplification of the ends, aims, and values of architecture. The great merit of a writer like Van Brunt is that he carries us back to one of the most crucial moments in the history of architecture. He enables us to see the ambitions and intentions of that period, as well as the unquestioned assumptions that underlie its thought. To illuminate the immediate past is to shed light on the forces that have made us what we are. Proper understanding of the past achieves its richest reward in a more balanced evaluation of the present and an informed freedom of choice for the future.

Van Brunt's connection with the Chicago Fair called forth his richest vein of architectural criticism. It also provided him, in the series of articles he wrote for the *Century Magazine*[111] on the main buildings of the Fair, with an impressive occasion to demonstrate his large capacities as a formal critic of architecture. Like Matthew Arnold in literature and Ruskin in art and architecture, Van Brunt was a social critic. He was interested, that is, to explore the relationship between art and the society which produced it.

In this preoccupation, he was, as we have seen, following one of the main tendencies of his age. The difficulty with social criticism, however, is that it distracts attention from the work of art as a formal object and concentrates it upon external relationships. One sometimes feels, with such criticism, that the argument is being carried out on a theoretical or emotional plane, at great remove from the specific experience of how a work of art produces its effect. Also, in the cases both of Ruskin and of Arnold, the critic eventually verges on the reformer, determined to change society in order to alter art. Here, more or less consciously, art takes over some of the functions of religion. Van Brunt, however, never crossed over this line. He felt that the way to improve art was to increase public understanding of, and sympathy for, it. Above all he wanted the public to take art seriously, to see it as an activity of mind. Therefore he can describe his purpose in his analyses of the Fair buildings as an attempt "to show how a work of architecture, like any other work of art, is the result of logical processes studiously followed, and not a mere matter of taste, a following of fashion, or an accident of invention more or less fortuitous." [112]

What underlies this statement is the concept of a work of art as a total organism whose parts are related by an essential unity, the outgrowth of a central germinal idea. This concept of art as an organism, so fundamental to Romantic critical theory, is the common denominator of two other cardinal tenets in Van Brunt's aesthetic thinking, his idea of art as exponent and of style as a vitally evolving sequence of form. For the three main features of a biological organism — which supplies the analogy for art — are that its parts are a growth from a central unifying germ, that it is in process of evolution as a species, and that its evolution is conditioned by environmental features, which it thus reflects. It is owing to his organic view of art, then, that Van Brunt undertakes the close analysis of architecture. He wants his readers to understand the process of thought which lies behind the composition of a building, which unfolds as the design takes shape, and which can be read in the finished form. Through such understanding he believes the public will become more sensitive, critical, and demanding about architecture. Van Brunt's social criticism, accordingly, leads *to*, not *away from*, precise formal analysis of the artistic object.

As attempts to show the reasoning behind the design of buildings, Van Brunt's analyses are achievements of a very high order. He enables us to see what motives participate in the composition of a building and what effects are produced by its design. Since so much architectural criticism is opinionative or merely descriptive, it is particularly valuable to have his articles as models for an understanding of the *working* of a design, that is, of the reason why the architect chose his forms and arranged them as he did. Van Brunt provides us with a "practical criticism" of architecture, similar to the so-called New Criticism of the twentieth century which probes the formal structure of a work of literature, the choice and arrangement of its language and figures of speech. It is based upon the premise that a poem, or a work of creative literature in the highest sense, is a subtle and careful ordering of language to communicate a complex organization of thought and feeling. Figurative language is, then, not decorative, but the organic expression of an imaginative construct which is the poem.

This notion of the organic unity of poetic language is the outgrowth of the criticism of such Romantic writers as Coleridge, who explored with great sensitivity the rich and complex unities of the poetic imagination. Coleridge showed, for instance, that a writer like Shakespeare was not an untutored, irregular primitive genius, but a man of profound penetration and insight who grasped, not arbitrary dramatic rules, but the authentic unities of human character, action, and expression.[113] What is especially interesting about Van Brunt's analyses of the Fair buildings is that he too, like Coleridge, rescues from misinterpretation works that were likely to be dismissed as inorganic and merely mechanical in their unity. He, however, extends a Romantic concept to embrace classical architecture, just as he had done with the idea of the exponent. The unity of form and function or of decoration and construction is not the only or, indeed, the highest kind of unity. There is in classical architecture a symmetrical unity and adjustment of detail, which is a far cry from the slapdash pastiche of traditional motifs depicted by hostile and uncomprehending critics. Since the nature of composition in the high classical language of architecture was so much misunderstood and its rigors underestimated, Van Brunt felt the need to explain for his readers the workings of organic unity in a classical design.

It would be well to state, once for all, [he writes] that in monumental designs based upon pure classic formulas, the principle of symmetry — that is, of a balanced correspondence of parts on each side of a center line — must govern the disposition of the masses into which, in order to form an articulate composition, each façade should be divided. The greater the dignity and importance of the building, the more absolute and uncompromising must be the application of this principle. The monument must be evident as the orderly result of forethought, and not as a growth from a succession of unexpected contingencies. It must embody the idea of a harmonious development of structure from beginning to end, so exactly adjusted, and so carefully proportioned in respect to its elements, that nothing can be added to or taken from it without sensibly affecting the composite organism as a whole. The test of the completeness of a classic design resides in its sensitiveness to change — a sensitiveness which becomes more delicate as the design approaches perfection. In fact, symmetry is the visible expression of unity. The moment the correspondence of balanced parts on each side of a center line is disturbed by the introduction on one side of a mass or detail which does not appear on the other, at that moment the design begins to lose somewhat of its unity and to enter the domain of the picturesque, in which ceremony and state become secondary to considerations of comfort and convenience.[114]

The *Century Magazine* articles themselves realize the principle which Van Brunt interprets. They grasp the leading idea of each building and follow its development both as a single organic form and as a participant in the total harmonious structure of the Fair.

For the student of American civilization, Van Brunt will be of value not only as a vivid reflection of the period when our national art came to its maturity, but for the quality of his intelligence and — its external reflection — the weight, texture, and polish of his prose style. He belonged to an age in which the architect had not yet been subsumed by the engineer. He would not have liked a world, or a profession, where this was no longer true. For all his responsiveness to modern technology and its influence on architecture, he was no worshipper of the machine. He did not confuse the bridge and the cathedral. In a letter on the architectural qualities of bridges, solicited for J. A. L. Waddell's *De Pontibus: A Pocket-Book for Bridge Engineers*,[115] he claimed that bridge engineering was in an immature condition until beauty was recognized, not as an accident but as an aim of development. Recalling an observation of Henry James, he said that the French speak of those who see *en beau* and those who see *en laid*. The modern steel-bridge designer, he felt, still belonged in the latter category. For all his responsibilities to modern society, the architect, according to Van Brunt, must strive to see *en beau*. But the quotation from James itself reveals one of the ways by which the architect maintained his connection with the beautiful. He was still an artist, a man of culture; a humanist, not a technologist. He still believed it the job of the artist to transform the products of science and technology into the harmonies of art. He still felt and maintained his kinship with the poet and the painter.

The tie is to be seen in the allusive density of his prose, as well as in the rhythm of his cadences. Phrases from the major English writers come readily to his pen, and he is constantly taking up an idea or a point of departure from the leading writers or reviews of the day. Van Brunt is even interested in the way poets treat architecture in their works, as well as in the analogies between poetic and architectural composition. Architecture thus becomes less a technical field of specialization and enters more fully into the main currents of human thought. Whatever disadvantages its involvement in history had for creative designers, this condition at least warded off mechanical disinvolvement from human concerns. By contrast, architects writing today seem almost culturally disinherited and, as sociology has replaced history in the architect's thought, human beings are relegated to the role of arid statistics.[116] In part the writings of Ruskin offered Van Brunt the precedent and example of a man of poetic imagination and vivid powers of rhetoric applying himself to architectural matters. But he became quickly aware of the dangers of a too literary and emotional approach to architecture, and he welcomed Viollet-le-Duc for his more dispassionate, analytical treatment of the subject. Van Brunt's later work successfully combined both methods. He had to evoke the interest of the layman, yet at the same time guide him to an understanding of the cultural climate of architecture and architectural thought in the later nineteenth century and also provide him with specific principles and a critical method for a more enlightened judgment of value.

What is likely to strike the reader today is Van Brunt's high-mindedness

Introduction

combined with liberality and tolerance of view. He insists upon an architecture of conviction, and yet he constantly appeals from the petty tyrant and doctrinaire to the common sense of human nature. This generousness is the hallmark of a fine critical intelligence. Far too often we ransack the past looking in the margins of history for pale anticipations of the fashionable opinions of today. The price of such narcissism is intellectual stagnation and an inability to recognize and appreciate truths we may have forgotten. Van Brunt can give us a perspective on values we hold today, but he can also remind us of those which have been displaced, and not always intentionally. The generation which produces a revolution is always nourished by the very values it reacts against. However, the intellectual framework of succeeding generations can get weaker and weaker: they are familiar with only the fruits of change; they forget the full context of thought in which change first occurred. Van Brunt is one of the writers who can restore us to the full context of later nineteenth-century thinking about art. He carries us into a period full of profound implications for the art and thought of the Western world. It was even more crucial for art in America. For with us art cast off its provincial bondage and became mature in the midst of this change and tension. The pride and power of the nation's commercial and industrial growth demanded a cosmopolitan exponent which could resolve tensions into an art that was poised and self-confident, uniting learning with vitality, individuality with self-discipline, tradition with innovation. That this could be achieved by the end of the century is owing, in no small measure, to the work of men like Van Brunt, one of the first and foremost of those who undertook the arduous labor of developing in America a cultivated and conscientious taste in architecture. It is fitting today that we should be restored through his work to a key part of our intellectual patrimony. It is also appropriate, when we are setting about to reclaim our urban wastelands, to hear once again Van Brunt's reminder that the supreme test of architecture is to develop out of practical things demonstrations of art which will furnish "that 'rest, grace, and harmony' which are needed as a compensation for materialism."

Selected Essays of Henry Van Brunt

Cast Iron in Decorative Architecture

(1859)

It cannot be doubted that the purest eras of architecture have been those in which building material has been used with the most honest regard for its nature, attributes and capacities. On the other hand, the histories of the decline of every pure style and the rise of every impure style, have been but illustrations of improper uses of the constructive means which nature everywhere yields for the comfort of mankind. She offers to enter into a fair alliance with us; to combine her innate powers with our adaptive skill in the production of objects of beautiful utility. But when those natural powers are misused — when, forgetting that we are their allies, we act as their lords, a virtue has gone out of our works which no human cunning can supply. We admire the Pointed buildings of the 13th century, because instinctively we recognize in them the complete presence of this alliance. Nature yields somewhat of her wild rudeness to man, and man stops wisely short of the full scope of his power for the sake of nature, and the result is a perfect stone architecture. There is nothing in it which makes us forget the quarry. The skill of the workman does not attempt to conceal or contradict the skill of God. But when this stone becomes unnaturally twisted and frittered away into the lacework of the Mechlin tower, or the pendant roof of Henry VII's chapel;[2] when it is violently contorted into the wild vagaries of the Cinque-Cento, however much we may wonder at the cunning workmanship, we cannot but lament the conquest of nature in those bewildered mazes and empty fantasies. The moment when the holy alliance was broken, the moment when the stone was taught to forget its native frown of power, its preadamite sternness, and was made to smile and flutter under the chisel, the life of that style departed. For the aim of true art is not conquest over material, but rather a fine compromise with material. Thus it is evident that there is much more true architecture in the carving of an early English capital, where, while all the sentiment of the leaf is retained, the obstinate hardness of the stone is not denied — or even in the rude monolithic dome of Theodoric's Mausoleum at Ravenna,[3] so conscious of its marble quarry at Istria — than in any of the wonderful tabernacle-work of Germany in the 14th and 15th centuries.

But if nature is thus revenged for conquest over her by misapplied skill, the results of simple *neglect* of her are hardly less disastrous. The aggregate growth of the human mind constantly develops out of nature new means and appliances, new mechanical resources and constructive materials. These are her progressive steps, and she asks of us, her allies in art, a corresponding activity.

In neglect of this activity lies a principle fatal to architecture as a fine art; and this, touching as it does the inventive pride of the artist, is perhaps especially deserving our attention. No fine art is so dependent as this on scientific invention, and consequently to none are the principles of conservation and conventionalism so dangerous. Architects become antiquaries when they feed exclusively upon the past, and are content to reproduce archaeological curiosities and copy shapes, however beautiful, of a fossil art, without re-animating them with the breath and spirit of the present. And when, through this respect and love for old things and old ways of doing them, the powers of architectural invention are suffered to lie dormant, amid intense intellectual activity as regards the arts of utility, the result is necessarily that architecture exists merely as a cold respectful reminiscence, a lifeless system of imitation and eclecticism. Such a system, destitute as it must be of that inspiration which is the life of all fine arts, cannot be exponential of any age of scientific activity. If we should transplant the sphinx of Egypt into the square of a modern city, its cold stony stare would not have less sympathy than this with the life surging around its base.

It becomes *us* then to look around us, and to ask ourselves with special solicitude if in our architectural works we are expressing the character of the age in which we live. Are we properly exercising our high and peculiar prerogatives of monumentalists? Is ours a *representative architecture*?

In this era of great discoveries of new things and of new applications of old things, the rapid advancement of mechanical and constructive science has opened an immense field for all the imaginative activity and inventive skill which can be brought to bear on architecture. And many of the requirements of modern buildings are such as cannot fairly be met without constructive devices and corresponding architectural features, for which precedent cannot be found in mediaeval or classic times. This is true not only of commercial, but of domestic and, in a measure, of ecclesiastical buildings. With all these facilities and incentives about us, Art should be a living and growing reality; and as such, though subject to the faults of excessive vitality, it would contain a hundred fold more elements of happiness for the people, than if taken pure and unsullied from the fountains of antiquity. For men have a right to expect new expressions from esthetics, as fast as they get new revelations from the sciences. Our tendency, instead of being eclectic and conservative, should be inventive and reformative. A new method of decorative construction should arise with each new mechanical or constructive means placed in our hands. It is obviously not proper or just to reject contemptuously new building materials and new constructive devices, because they were unknown to Phidias, to Palladio or William of Wyckham,[4] and are unsuited to their styles. Is it not noble rather to weigh seriously their advantages and disadvantages, and suffer no formal rule of scholiast or warning of pedant, no refined deduction of the theorist to scare us from adopting them, if worthy the immortality of art? The conviction forces itself upon us that true architecture does not exist where innovation and novelty of any kind are dreaded.

If we examine into the history of any period of the world when the art of building was in reality a fine art, we will find that ample and characteristic use was made of every fitting material and mechanical appliance then known, even though principles perfected by the study of previous generations had to be sacrificed to the innovation. Wood and brick were as readily received and as fairly and tenderly treated as stone. The glorified lintel of Greece gave place to the rude arch of Rome, and this, though sanctified by Byzantium and Lombardy and the Norman, though made venerable by the accumulated art of centuries, yielded to the novelty and superior constructiveness of the pointed arch. Thus was the progress of beauty coincident with the advance of science. Thus, like the fabled lovers of the "Day Dream," they walked together with mingling garments through the nations. Happy would it be for us could we pursue the analogy and say with the poet:

> And far beyond the hills they went
> To that *new world* which is the old! [5]

But *is* the presence of this union known to us? Does the beauty of art still keep pace with the advance of science? Or rather are there not among us antique prejudices against such an association — are there not tender sensibilities shrinking from the shock of accustomed things?

This is called an *iron* age — for no other material is so omnipresent in all the arts of utility. Whether moulded from the furnace, battered on the anvil, or rolled in the mill, it is daily developed for new forms and new uses. Its strength, its elasticity, its ductility, its malleability, its toughness and its endurance render it applicable to a thousand exigencies of manufactures; and it has arrived at last to be the exponent of the noblest physical qualities of manhood. With all these wonderful facilities, it has been again and again offered to the fine arts. But architecture, sitting haughtily on her acropolis, has indignantly refused to receive it, or receiving it, has done so stealthily and unworthily, enslaving it to basest uses and denying honor and grace to its toil. None can have failed to remark with what a storm of anathema and abuse the use of iron in decorative construction has been welcomed by every writer on the fine arts and by nearly all architects; yet they will avail themselves of it in trusses, they will use it in concealed construction, in anchors and ties, secretly to strengthen walls and relieve arches. They have *authority* too for making ornamental hinges of it for their Gothic doors. But as for making an honest system of architecture out of a material which is found so invaluable in the gravest exigencies of construction, this is quite out of the question. For how degrading and pernicious, they will cry, are its decorative uses! As it comes from the mould, where is the finish and elegance of our carving, where is the noble expression of free labor, of individual sacrifice, of personal thought and exertion in it? And as it comes from the anvil, what aspiration or solemn purpose can there be in it? How shall we sweeten its laborious curves or enrich its wire-drawn construction? Where, in short, are all those qualities by which our ancestors have rendered architecture an ennobling and sanctified art to us? It is in this spirit that critics on art have been accustomed to speak of this material as applied to decorative architecture, singing to us meanwhile the same song of labor which the lodges in old times raised among the scaffoldings of Strasbourg, as if the grand master could square his emblematic ashlar in the stone yards of New York, and the companion exercise his "Liberty of the workmen," in the new works on Broadway! They have called this in derision "a cast iron age." What if it is? Let us then make a cast iron architecture to express it; and if we set about it earnestly and thoughtfully, it is certainly within the bounds of possibility to ennoble that much reviled material.

The prejudice among men of taste against this new style of building has doubtless been much increased by the many crude attempts already made to adopt it as the legitimate offspring of true art. Architects have too readily set their faces against this adoption, believing it subversive of their professional reputation, and utterly antagonistic to their studies of the antique, whose forms of art are naturally so sacred and oracular to them. But the public, not so influenced by the power of old habit and classic association, and believing it expedient and proper to build in iron, have done so, notwithstanding the opposition of professional men. Thus, the first training of this child of art has fallen into incapable hands, and the result has been what I have been led to believe all true artists deplore. A whole Olympus-full of immortal gods had to constitute themselves a college of tutors to the infant Hercules, to give finesse and strategy and skill to his heroic strength, ere he could accomplish his twelve labors. And so this new child, Hercules, with powers a thousand times more heroic, which the spirit of the age has so earnestly offered for our nourishment and guidance, needs all the care and thoughtful tuition we can bestow. Else, misdirected, out of the very abundance of those powers will grow imitations more base, and monstrosities more hateful than they have even yet exhibited. For, instead of such a modification of old forms as to accommodate them in every respect to the peculiar conditions of the new material, so that at length a new style might be created expressive of its before unapplied attributes — instead of this, we behold those old forms expressed in iron without the slightest alteration, ashlar joints and all the ordinary necessities of masonry, imitated with careful nicety, while all the devices of iron construction are concealed with peculiar cunning.

Of all the arguments which have been urged against the decorative use of iron in architecture, perhaps the most specious have been those with reference to *machine ornament* and cast iron work generally, as entirely at variance with all preconceived notions of what ornament should express, viz.: the happiness or the sacrificial spirit of the workman, his individual thought and personal presence, as it were, in his work. Hence, as men do not often think or act the same thing twice, comes the precept so earnestly enunciated by Ruskin: "All noble ornamentation is perpetually varied ornamentation, and the moment you find ornamentation unchanging, you may know that it is of a degraded kind or a degraded school." [6] And monotony, he continues, should only be used subordinately, as in some architectural mouldings, and merely as a contrast to variation in more important members. This is certainly a lovely and precious principle in its application to a stone architecture in a mediaeval age. For the greatest peculiarity of Gothic times was personal labor and enterprise. Whether in the arts of war or peace, it was with the *hands* that all work was done; and so all industrial arts were, in the most proper use of the word, *handicrafts.* The Gothic spirit then was a *handicraft spirit,* and, to be expressed in a noble architecture, demanded the sacrifice and thought of a varied ornamentation. Now the age which we are called upon to express is not one of individualities, but of aggregates. It is not one of barbarous sacrifice either of time, labor, money or material, but of wise economy. Science has nearly destroyed personal labor, and has substituted the labor of machinery, and almost all the industrial arts are carried on not by hands but by machines. In fact, we have mechanics now, not handicraftsmen, who work not so much out of devotion to any craft, as for the homely necessities of life. Labor now is the means and not the end of life. Therefore the architecture, to express our spirit best, is not one of personal thought and aspiration in the workman; it is not one where the individual irregularities of genius or enthusiasm may find scope in tender or grotesque idiosyncrasies of detail; but rather one of system, and, as regards the workman one of organized subordination; it is essentially an architecture of strict mechanical obedience. The gargoyle, the corbel and the boss, as vehicles of personal thought in the sculptor, would be acts of rebellion with us. The principle of the "Liberty of the Workman" no more belongs to our age than feudality. However lovely it may be with all its poetic and romantic associations in cathedral architecture, it is of another age, and we cannot and should not hope to revive it. When from amid the great bustle and activity of our times, we look back upon the Gothic age, and contemplate its serenity and statuesque repose, its deliberate and dreamy thoughtfulness, as it were, in all those matters of science and art embodied in architecture; when we behold how slightly time and labor were considered in questions of high art, how years passed by as days, and all effort was patient, simple, earnest and slow, we at once comprehend the secret of the success of Gothic art. Yet may not our own spirit, though apparently prosaic and leaning too much towards mere utilities, though rejoicing in clamor and hurry, may it not have its own peculiar high capacities for artistic expression? May there not out of its sternest necessities and most practical exigencies be born new principles of beauty to adorn our own age as those old ones were adorned? Let us not then despair because, when measured by antique standards and principles, our art seems ill-grown

81

and awkward. Our new conditions demand new standards and new principles. If, as it affected practical art, the Greek spirit was an intellectual spirit, — the Roman, an ostentatious spirit — the Mediaeval, a sacrificial and handiwork spirit, so ours should be eminently a mechanical spirit. It is absurd to mourn over our degeneration, when some of this spirit, instinctively and in spite of ourselves, gets into our reproductions of old forms and seeks to acclimate them to our atmosphere. For to this spirit we owe most for which our age is honorable above all others, and why should it not move the wings of art as well as the wheels of science? Thus it is not just to consider and criticise the architectural decoration of the present day *objectively*, as we do with Gothic details, but *subjectively*, or as it relates to and harmonizes with the general design. We should not in our judgment have thought for the immediate and mechanical producer of the effect, as an intelligent being, but simply for the effect produced, and criticise that effect abstractedly as it appeals to our sentiments of the beautiful and fitting. If this argument be admitted, no objection remains against ornamentation in cast iron, or any other material, provided that ornamentation offends not against any abstract rules of taste and propriety, and provided also there is no inconsistency between the ornamentation and the material in which it is wrought.

Now a mechanical architecture is evidently one of strict unities and formal repetitions, as expressive of the mechanical means by which it is produced. And these qualities, under the skillful treatment of the architect, are peculiarly exponential of an age which seeks not for instruction or emotional impulse in a building, as the Greeks did from their friezes and pediments, the Romans from their panelled bas-reliefs, and more especially the mediaeval Catholics from the sculpture of their porches, but rather of a period which, having ample instructional and emotional resources in other directions, expects in an edifice little more than the pure architectural expression of fitness for its peculiar purposes. How in instinctive obedience to this demand there has gradually crept into our present architecture those strict uniformities and formal repetitions, which have laid it open to the charge of thoughtlessness, it is useless here to recapitulate, nor is it necessary to prove that these qualities are much more natural in a moulded architecture than in a sculptured one, where they are suggestive of a weary servility of workmanship and a painfully laborious reproduction of one idea. Now inasmuch as nature, when she urges upon us the use of iron, actually demands from us a mechanical treatment of it with the mould, we may fairly expect that the principle of monotony, usually so repugnant to a stone architecture, may under these more favorable circumstances be elevated to a beauty and an honor (Fig. 94a). For as regards truth of material, monotony is as noble in iron as variety is in stone. And even when we look upon monotony abstractedly in all architectures, we will find that, in a purely aesthetical point of view, and without reference to any external conditions of mere execution, it is by no means a despicable quality. In general the more earnestly an edifice appeals to the sentiment of human pride, the more powerful we will find is the influence exerted over the design by this very principle of monotony. For architectural repetition, besides being expressive of an "artificial infinity," is the quality which most distinguishes the works of man from the works of God, *which never are repeated*, and the farther man gets from nature in his creations, without denying the instructive beauty of her forms, the more boldly he asserts his intellectual freedom and the creative powers of his mind. It is unquestionable that a certain degree of artful repetition, both in primary and subordinate positions, exercises much fascination over the mind of the beholder, provided there is not implied by it any poverty of thought or servility of workmanship. But there is certainly a triumph of human art when man in his works reconciles *repetition*, which, as it expresses his creative competition with nature, is Godlike, with *variety*, which, as it expresses the versatility of his genius and his admiration for nature, is lovely. Every observing man can recall how pleasantly he has been affected by such diapered surfaces as are not unfrequent in some of the later developments of Gothic, and this too, notwithstanding the implication in it of human machine work. How much more charming it is, therefore, in its frequent occurrence in the terra-cotta architecture of Lombardy, where it is the legitimate expression of the mould! But, it may be asked, how can the principles of monotony be so wedded to those of variety as not mutually to destroy each other?

In the west front of the cathedral at Monza (S. Maria in Strata) the great rose window is flanked on either side by a pointed window of the same height, and all the spandrels being occupied by appropriate decoration, the whole group is divided and framed in by a system of small square panels or quarries, seventy-four in number, each containing a minute foliated design. At first sight, it is doubtless the principle of repetition which pleases in this group; but the pleasure and value of the whole is infinitely increased on discovering that in all these seventy-four quarries there are twelve different foliated designs or symbols, so subtly arranged that it needs the closest inspection to detect any recurrence, though each pattern is repeated about six times. There is a perfect expression of variety, but the latter so subordinated, that the whole at once satisfies every requisite that the laws of artistic beauty can demand. This example is quoted the more readily because it is an example in moulded brick and fitted constructively and aesthetically for use in cast iron.

The oft-repeated objections to this material, on the ground that it forms merely a superficial system of decoration, arise, I presume, from the assumed premises that, as such systems do not illustrate, but rather effectually conceal all constructive expressions, they are consequently untrue and inadmissible. Now as regards such veneering processes as the Italians were often guilty of, out of love for their sumptuous and costly marbles, that they might thus display the variety and richness of their natural colors — and as regards the same processes which we make use of out of no such love, but rather for the sake of the vacant ostentation of a white marble front, this objection is valid in the fullest degree. For inasmuch as there is no acknowledgment of the superficiality in any of these decorative systems, but rather a studious attempt to force upon the mind the conviction that they are constructive, and that the richness of the material extends deep into the mass of the wall, they are deceitful. But as regards iron, such deceit is scarcely possible, for no one could for a moment suppose that this material would be used in solid blocks like masonry, and therefore its very texture confesses its superficiality. Besides this, every fair and well-conceived cast-iron decoration, avoiding base imitation of all classic or other solid architectures, would take especial pains to acknowledge this its peculiar quality, either by drawing attention to the constructive expedients which this quality demands, such as rivets and anchors, or by permitting the *backing* material (the use of which has been found to be absolutely essential to comfort in this climate) to be honestly apparent in solid buttresses or through open work in the iron. Here are presented means for an entirely new architectural expression, arising directly out of that only pure fount for all such expressions — constructive necessity. This peculiar character of superficiality seems as legitimate a source for architectural expression, as thickness of wall was made by the Lombards, when they emphasized it so successfully in their broad, flat piers and panels and in the artificial perspective of their window and door splays; or as thinness of wall was made by Gothic artists when the necessity of buttresses and pinnacles to withstand the thrusts of vaultings was so fairly acknowledged and signally honored by them. So let the cast iron decoration of our own age not only confess but boast its superficiality; and if architecture is not a dead art among us, if some of the enterprise and inventive genius of our age may be made to inspire this the most practical of the fine arts, it is hardly a frivolous speculation to assert that out of this necessity may grow a new system of architectural decoration, in which will be as readily acknowledged the peculiar expression of our cultivation as the Greeks confessed in the friezes of the Parthenon.

The cheapness of iron, its rapidity and ease of workmanship, the readiness with which it may be made to assume almost any known form, instead of being, as Ruskin asserts, "so many new obstacles on our already encumbered road," [7] are qualities which, in the present state of society, render that metal especially precious as a means of popular architecture. For costliness, difficulty, and laboriousness, so confine the uses of architecture to the monopoly of the wealthy, that this magnificent art in its domestic applications, becomes expressive merely of distinctions of social rank, merely a means of ostentation, instead of standing as the exponent of the highest refinement and cultivation of the people — the universal handwriting, as it were, on our walls, which shall speak eloquently the character of our age. Let us not, then, shrink from cast iron as too base and cheap to be translated into a noble architecture, as too common for such elegant uses; but as this art is our symbolic and monumental language, let us rather consider that the more common and available its elements are, the more truthful and just will it be in this high capacity. The elements of a spoken language, *words*, are common; yet while in the mouths of the vulgar they are slang, on the lips of the wise they are oracles and epics. So an architecture which, by facilities of material, is made applicable to all the grades and conditions of society, from which is banished all quaint restraints of ancient laws, and which suffers no effete precedent or formalism to stand in the way of its boundless pliability and exhaustlessness — such an architecture truly deserves the name of language.

This is not, of course, intended to imply that precedent should be neglected, for architecture is essentially inductive, and its progress is made, not so much in the invention of new forms as in the gradual and almost imperceptible growth and development of new things out of old things. Thus, should we desire to express the stately and formal in cast iron architecture, we might take, perhaps, the Florentine Gothic of Arnolfo da Lapo in the cathedral, and of Giotto in the Campanile, as a starting point, and from the peculiar surface architecture of this style, with its distinctly defined panels, so suggestive of metallic plates, might easily be elaborated an honest system for cast iron, full of repose and dignity. Even the rivets or boltheads and the anchors might be made to bear an appropriate part in the decoration. The brick or stone constituting the *backing* of the wall could appear as piers, perhaps, dividing the composition into large and noble bays, or it could show in its working capacity in discharging arches severe and undecorated. The terra-cotta architecture of the valley of the Po has already been suggested as full of hints which would render valuable assistance to the artist in this new labor; for it is not only a legitimate moulded style, but one peculiarly expressive of the variation which ornament undergoes in its transferrence from one material to another — a variation which we, in similar contingencies, have been so little sensitive to. The mechanical repetitions of Gothic panels, which form so exclusively the surface decoration of the English perpendicular style, and the frequent recurrence of formal vertical lines in the piers and mullions of that style, together with the height and slenderness of shafts — all these are *motives* which one who would compose a stately edifice of iron would scarcely neglect.

Or would we desire to build in a more sportive and fantastic mood? What material better fitted architecturally to express such attributes than this? Adam Kraft and Peter Vischer recognized this fact so early as the fourteenth century, when they cast in bronze the delicate font and shrine of St. Sebaldus (Fig. 93) and the beautiful fountains of Nuremburg.[8] It would have been well for their German contemporaries, from Bruges to Freiburg, had they acknowledged bronze or iron, rather than stone, as the fitting material for the elaborate fretwork of their tabernacles, domes, and spires. For when these works began to call for the pride of the workman, rather than the spirit of the artist, to accomplish them; when their difficulty began to be their only honor, it was high time for them to be transferred to a plastic material like iron; and then the true artist might once more have resumed his studies, and elevated the old forms into new and wonderful expressions of beauty. Are not these old forms *ours now* to work upon? They say that Bruges laughs in the playfulness of her belfries and pinnacles. Is there not an element of happiness among us which requires some such expression, and may not the means of that expression come from the mine as well as the quarry, the mould as well as the chisel? This seems scarcely visionary, for the discreetest economy of our times does not so much overshadow our enthusiasm and joyfulness as to forbid their being expressed in so *cheap* a material as cast iron. In fact, for our comfort it may justly be said, that even in the happiest days of that "quaint old town of toil and traffic, quaint old town of art and song," [9] had labor been as costly as it is with us, not all their enthusiasm and joyfulness would have built up those pinnacles and gables, so pleasant to see, but so beautifully useless! In the latter part of the thirteenth and beginning of the fourteenth century, a feature appeared in German Gothic which, though according to many critics highly objectionable in a stone architecture, appears peculiarly adapted to iron. I refer to those lines of tracery which were sometimes spread over window and wall, in the manner of open screens, distinct and separate systems from those incorporated into the body of the building, as in the west front of Strasbourg and in Cologne, and in one instance only, I believe, in England, the easternmost part of the clerestory wall of the choir of York minster. As a *motive* for composition in iron in its more fantastic moods, this seems especially valuable, inasmuch as it is suggestive of a distinction between the ornament and the construction of a building sufficiently broad to separate the playful from the serious, without disturbing their architectural affinities. How appropriate to the peculiar conditions of our material, that the solid wall which does the serious work behind, should be plainly seen and acknowledged, and that decorative openwork should beguile its surface with everchanging shadows, and half veil the painful arch of brick or stone with fancies that make sport of its frowning labor! Such a parasitical use of iron, it must be admitted, is not its noblest use, nor do we fairly test its decorative capacities till it is made to illustrate its own constructive properties. Yet it is evident that in all cases this peculiar interstitial feature could be made one of the most important characteristics of the style. It is understood that architecture is in a great measure the art of shadows, and hitherto the *chiaro-oscuro*, as it were, of architectural design has been limited to contrasts of masses and lines of shade with masses and lines of light. It has been considered the peculiar privilege of the painter to break lights into the mass of his shadows, and by these quick and sparkling touches to enhance its repose and depth, and give brilliancy and life to his subject. Now, the use of interstitial decoration would at once place this power in the hands of the architect, and open to him a large field for new and delicate effects in his designs. Take the simplest instance, a pierced trefoil in the spandrel of an arcade; the sun, finding thus an unencumbered pathway through the thin ironwork, would paint the trefoil in light against the dark wall behind. The open pattern, stencilled in shadow, would be repeated in light. The sun, in his progress, would delight in it, would sport with it, and make grotesque and changeful mockery of it all the day long; he would make anagrams of our ornamentation, and sprinkle unexpected interpretations of it among the shadows. No masonry could yield a negative copy of its tracery with such readiness, its ponderous and serious nature admitting only the "sleep" of broad sunshine or shadow upon its surface. The Saracenic styles, with their profuse geometrical open-surface ornament, their pierced arabesques, and the lily patterns that fringe their level skylines, are full of *motives* for cast iron. And there is something very suggestive of the exceeding pliability of iron in that fantastic tendency of the Saracens ostentatiously to conceal or defy all constructive necessities, in the hollow intrados, the piercing and fretting of the apparent archivolt, the wild overhanging cusps, the horse-shoe arch, the square reticulated framing-in of their pointed and ogival apertures, the honey-combed pendentive, and all the savage but beautiful conceits with which they loved to beguile and deny their labor and science. In short, it will at once be perceived by all who have sought for instructive precedent and for authorities among ancient buildings, how many lovely and noble features there are which have hitherto been considered too costly for our use, how many quaint individualities which considerations of economy have forbidden our expressing, all of which the facilities of moulded iron not only place within our reach, but offer to us the flattering prospect of excelling, in the same proportion as we excel the ancient builders in opportunities and scope of study.

It is not to be forgotten, that in transferring these old forms to iron, we are met in the outset by the difficulty of imitating with the mould those high reliefs so frequent in rich architectures. But such imitations, presenting this material in an unfair light, as the carvings of masonry are unsuited to its primary condition of inability to be undercut, should be carefully avoided. Indeed, it may well admit a doubt whether the low relief, which the mould so imperatively requires, when assisted in its expression by the contrasts of color, as in the sculpture of the Greek metopes, or the tracery of the Arabs; whether low relief, under such circumstances, does not present quite as many charms as that extreme high relief which some have considered indicative of decline, in its purely architectural uses, because requiring too much masonic cunning to accomplish it. If, for instance, we take an iron capital, none will doubt that this capital would be nobler, both as a constructive feature and as an expression of material, if its ornamentation were *incised* in the manner of Byzantium and the Alhambra, rather than *applied* as with the acanthus leaves in the Corinthian capital; and if depth of shadow is lost in our low relief, we shall find in another of the necessities of cast iron an ample compensation. I refer to *color*. The natural color of iron, besides being unsuited to decorative uses, is liable to the disagreeable changes of oxidation and rust, which also impair its strength and durability. The application of external color, therefore, is very essential to its preservation, and as such, may be used with all the license which art may desire. It is needless here to dwell upon how such an architecture as we have been endeavoring to set forth would be illustrated in all its parts by the judicious application of color; how the unspeakable charm of contrasted tints would add to the value of all its aspects, and how by this a still higher demand would be made upon that inventive genius and that artistic cultivation in the architect, which the present practice of his profession gives him so few opportunities of exercising. Color, in these uses of it, would afford a sensitive test to distinguish the artist from the pretender, and present to all an evident proof of the refinement of the one and the vulgarity of the other.

Nor is it to be forgotten, while taking old models for our guides, that if the constructive properties of our material are to be fairly exercised, very many old axioms and laws of architecture must undergo a fundamental change. The old principles of mural construction, requiring a piling of masses perpendicularly upon each other, requiring a careful economy and division of weight upon its arches, requiring moderation in the width of all openings, especially lintelled ones, and requiring a very strict observance of the necessity of placing the light and airy upon the heavy and massive — these have created in decorative architecture those exact laws of superimposition, intercolumniation, proportion by module, and the like, which have hitherto held tyrannical sway over all our composition. But it is evident that an iron construction does not call so imperatively for a strict observance of these laws, as its properties are such as to admit masses over voids as well as voids over masses, to admit downward thrusts of almost any force upon any point of its arches without fear of fracture, to admit almost any width of aperture, and almost any slenderness of supports; so that in our iron façades we are not so limited to solid basements, to the open upon the massive, to the inviolability of piers from the foundation through all the stories up to the cornice, to the exact perpendicular centre-lines of apertures and columns, and to a discreet moderation in the width of our openings. On the contrary, the utmost latitude is allowable in these respects, provided there be not too great an offence against those finer aesthetical rules, which, though derived in great measure from old necessities, could scarcely be disregarded at once without danger. When we reflect upon what violations of ancient laws and possibilities we are daily called upon to commit in our street architecture, especially in shop-fronts, the capacities of a real iron architecture to violate these laws and possibilities with complete artistic propriety, and to meet all the strange exigencies of modern buildings, cannot be justly neglected.

It is evident that an architecture so *new* as this would be, if fairly studied, besides hanging out, as it were, our banners on the outward walls, to denote the hearty presence of our inventive spirit and enthusiasm in it, would exercise a direct active influence over the minds of men. For what charm so potent, to break through the weariness of life, as novelty? A new object or a new thought, if it appeals to any of the higher sentiments of humanity, strikes deep into our being, and opens new channels for the escape of many affections which in the monotony of daily experience become stagnant and useless within us. How grateful then the task thus opened to the artist, of creating new things for the surprise of men; of writing a new chapter in the history of architecture, and thereby adding to the happiness and comfort of mankind!

Architectural Reform[1]

(1866)

Of all the fine arts architecture is that which has the closest connection with the practical requirements of life. Its very existence is based upon necessity, and therefore wherever men live some form of it must appear, varying in quality according to the conditions of the society in the midst of which it has grown. Its characteristics have been governed by those conditions to such an extent that when we are engaged in archæological research regarding any people, their architectural remains form an important and sometimes the only basis of judgment by which we can arrive at a definite opinion touching the nature of their civilization. A deduction by reason from these primitive types of art to the circumstances of their peculiar development is natural and easy, and the result, in our minds, is intelligible and distinct. We recognize the ancient Egyptian in the temples of the Nile; we know the Greek when we have studied the fragments at Athens and the Greek colonies; the most eloquent type of Roman empire is in the shattered temples, baths, arches, aqueducts, and basilicas of antiquity; and the mediæval mind is present to us intact in the churches, monasteries, castles, and town-halls built from the eleventh to the fourteenth centuries. These impressions are, to a certain extent, spontaneous, but are developed and deepened, not changed, by deliberate analysis.

Now, in the entire absence of a standard of architectural criticism in this country, as applied to our own daily use, it is of the first importance that we should understand how it is that history has expressed itself so plainly and so intelligibly in the architecture of the past. It is evident that the solving of this question involves a theory of architecture capable of application to the most common uses of the art among us — a theory which, when once understood, will enable the public to sympathize with the architect, to relieve him from his isolation, and restore that mutual confidence and interest between them and him without which there can be no real and national art. At present, popular opinion, where there is any at all, is based upon the merest caprice or prejudice; patronage is wofully misbestowed; quacks flourish, and the true architect is misunderstood and neglected. Without the intelligent sympathy of the public this art cannot live and progress; the architect needs to be sustained, protected, encouraged, chastened by the consciousness that the people understand what he is doing. Caprice and fashion, with their infinite and childish vagaries, must give place to a public appreciation of the architectural problem not as a mere matter of taste or even as a question of art — this would be expecting too much for the present — but as a matter of reason and common sense.

One of the first results of a revival of interest in architecture in the Old World, particularly during the last century, was the multiplication of archæological works illustrating certain local or temporary phases of the architecture of the past. Thus, the great architectural writer of Roman antiquity, Vitruvius, was translated, edited, and illustrated by almost innumerable architects from the fifteenth to the nineteenth century; the result was the reproduction throughout Europe during this period of forms borrowed from Rome; it was the period of the Renaissance, a period when all architecture was governed by Vitruvian rules variously interpreted, when nothing was done without a Roman precedent to support it, and everything in art was judged according to Roman authority. Then came writers on Greek art, led by Stuart and Revett, who, on their return from Athens in the last century, gave to the world the results of their accurate admeasurements of the temples and monuments of Greece.[2] In this manner a certain Greek element was introduced into modern architecture. Later the German antiquary, Boiserée, published, at Cologne, his works on mediæval architecture hitherto despised.[3] He was followed by numberless others, copying, editing, and restoring the details of nearly every cathedral in Europe. Thus arose modern mediævalism, and with it an interminable controversy between those who yet clung to the principles of antique architecture, and designed according to Vitruvius and his followers, the Italian masters of the fifteenth century, and those who embraced the new architectural religion revived from the Middle Ages, and built churches and chapels after the manner, but not according to the principles, of the freemasons of feudalism.

This controversy has created a new Babel in modern architecture. There is a confusion of tongues worse than that which interrupted the building of that famous architectural unity on the plains of Shinar. Eclecticism has arisen. Architects, embarrassed by precedent, impeded by their knowledge of the past, have produced an unintelligible polyglot made up of Egyptian, Greek, Roman, Saracenic, Byzantine mediæval types, mixed together in various proportions, which we must distinguish as the architecture of the nineteenth century. It has found its way in a diluted form to the New World, where it has been uttered in town and country with increasing bewilderment to the people.

In the midst of this embarrassing complexity, and in the pressing need to

repair once more to the primitive fountains of art for refreshment and inspiration, and for that new knowledge which discusses, analyzes, and compares, a
purely literary element has been introduced into modern architecture, with
the intention of instituting a careful and philosophical examination into the
whole question of the proper use of precedent, of eliminating all the perplexing points of controversy, and thus of arriving at some theory of architecture
from which may proceed a new and more wholesome progress, a style peculiar
to our time, not an imitation nor a conglomerate, but a logical deduction. This
literary element is represented in England by John Ruskin, who, with all his
faults, may almost claim to have accomplished, in that country, with his pen
that which hitherto in the history of architecture has only been accomplished
by the great organic movements or changes of society, a revolution. He, at
least, is the most prominent among those who have created the present tendency among English architects to design and build more according to reason
and less according to prejudice or fashion. Whatever the result may have been
so far, it cannot be justly doubted that for the first time in five centuries there
exists in the mother country a theory of architecture which can be applied by
architects to practice, and by the intelligent public to criticism. And this is a
state of things which is full of promise for the future. However much we may
differ from Ruskin in detail, and however much we may distrust his glittering
and seductive eloquence, this fact is undeniable — that he has created an
atmosphere which is wholesome for art. The mysterious agencies established
by the freemasons in Europe during the Middle Ages, by which their various
phases of progress from good to better were made simultaneous throughout a
continent, is more than equalled by the modern diffusion of books. So we
have already experienced in this country somewhat of this new feeling in architecture. We read Ruskin and his followers, and people here begin to take an
interest in the subject of which these writers are the ministers. The fundamental result of their teachings, as regards the actual practice of art, is the
application of the idea of *truth of expression* to design in the place of that
mere correctness of imitation, that servile adherence to archæological precedent and authority, that reproduction of styles which, until now, has held
sway in all modern architecture. The most advanced of these teachers hold
that architectural precedents are not mere formulæ on which all design must
be strictly and correctly modelled, but that they constitute, as it were, a dictionary of phrases, a grammar of form, to be referred to not for its own sake,
but to give scope and freedom to the language of art. The problem presented
to the architect is simply this: Given a subject, to develop it with all the grace
and elegance which a perfect command of language and a complete knowledge of grammar can confer upon the art of composition. This problem accepted, a national path of progress is open to art. Then it is for genius to render
the incident of this progress illustrious by great works. Individual genius cannot take all progress upon its shoulders and achieve an era of art. In architecture, as in the other arts, it can only accomplish illustrious results when surrounded by a prevailing atmosphere of intelligent criticism, which sym-

pathizes, encourages, and applauds. The analogy between literature and the fine arts is, in all these respects, complete.

The English mind is not sensitive to the appeals of art; it moves sluggishly in grooves of conventionalism and custom, and is extremely jealous of change or innovations. Mr. Matthew Arnold's charge of Philistinism against the English people is sustained by a study of the development of their arts.[4] No nation has exhibited such a profound respect for the archæological side of architecture, or has transferred precedent to modern uses with such pedantic and unimaginative precision. Foreign influences have been rigorously excluded, save those derived through Italy and Greece from classic antiquity; and even these, before becoming current, have had to pass through the alembic of Sir Christopher Wren or Sir William Chambers. Their modern Gothic has been a bold and unpoetical imitation of their mediæval Gothic, which, for the sake of mechanical convenience, has been artificially divided in their books into Norman, early English, decorated, and perpendicular periods. In short, their architecture has been antiquarianism — nothing more or less; and yet, by the establishment of new schools of architecture, based upon the common-sense principles to which we have referred, there has arisen among them a prevailing sentiment of healthy criticism, the practical results of which we already see in the abandonment, to a great extent, of their late narrow rules and formulæ of design. This new era has already been elegantly illustrated by such buildings as the Oxford Museum (Fig. 81) and the Assize Courts at Manchester (Fig. 84),[5] — buildings the design of which has been controlled not by archæology so much as by fundamental principles. Regarding these as types of British progress in architecture, and comparing them with the perpendicular pedantry of the new Houses of Parliament (Fig. 77), English architects may at length fairly claim that they at least are no Philistines; that they are discovering other precedents besides English precedents, and, underlying them all, controlling them all, more important than all, a vital principle of art.

The English are instructing us in architecture to this extent. Let us continue to read their new books and watch their new works. Let us profit by their labors and their experience. But there is another field of instruction no less fertile than this, no less fruitful in ideas and examples, though far less familiar. There is an important rational movement in France on this question, into the causes and progress of which it is becoming we should examine with scrupulous care, and which we shall discuss in our next number.

SECOND NOTICE

Unlike England, France is essentially artistic. The imagination of her people has ever been bold, enterprising, and indomitable, even under the organized restraints of a National Academy. The last of the chivalry of France became *dilettante* in the Italian wars of Louis XII. and Francis I. With other *spolia opima* of their conquests they brought back the art and artists of Italy. They planted the Renaissance on French soil. But with all their imported artists, with all their Primaticcios, their Berninis, their Da Vincis, they never built an Italian palace in France.[6] The artistic instinct was too strong to yield to foreign dictation in matters of art. The new forms and ideas were received from Italy, but there was at once mingled with them a national sentiment. The chateaux of Blois, Chambord, Amboise, Chenonceau, Madrid, Fontainebleau, arose not in imitation of the palaces of the Farnesi or the Medici, but as new expressions of French art in harmony with the new taste which had arisen for classic learning. The formulæ of classic architecture, the exact proportions of the orders, as laid down by the Italian masters of the fifteenth century after Vitruvius, which were received submissively, and used with scrupulous bigotry, by all such unimaginative nations as the English, never had much authority in France until Louis XIV. established the School of Fine Arts, for the purpose of doing for art what the French Academy was intended to do for literature, viz., to organize, chasten, and keep it respectable. The Academy kept the language pure by concerning itself with verbal niceties of expression, by chasing panting syllables back to Noah, by eliminating from the dictionary all words without a pedigree, lopping off all those concretions of time which made language picturesque but rude. It did a good work; but its business was less with the matter than the manner of composition.

Such was the case, also, with the professors of the School of Fine Arts. Their tendency was to create standards of authority in art, to become a learned and exclusive areopagus, to foster and establish such formulæ of expression in design as they could find concrete in the ruins of Rome, to pride themselves upon the exactness of their knowledge, and to keep architecture pure from contact with the vulgar. Indeed, their aim was to talk unsullied Latin in the midst of modern France. So far as this went they did far better than the English. They built the Hôtel des Invalides and the Madeleine and the Louvre, while the English uttered their best architecture in St. Paul's and Somerset House. This advantage the French obtained less from the fact that their architectural learning had become organized under royal patronage than from their natural freedom and grace of imagination, which, though under the most oppressive of all restraints, could not but assert itself. The results of the French Renaissance are beautiful. All recognize this; but many have lately arisen in France who question whether this beauty, which they find recommends itself only to the cultivated, and is understood only by the initiated, should not be an inspiring presence in the midst of the nation; whether this lovely Franco-Latin, if made pure French, so as to be understood by all, might not touch more hearts, and thereby accomplish the higher purposes of art. This question has been urged by certain men who have been rejected by the Academy because they believed that the indigenous mediæval art of France should be revived, and that into this channel exclusively all architectural thought and effort should be turned. The warfare of words between these two parties has been all the more bitter because the School of Fine Arts has become grey in a traditionary creed, and can point to a long historical record full of triumphs, while the new mediæval school is regarded as schismatic in the highest degree. But heresy begets heresy. Other schools have lately arisen, such as the Greek school and the Romantique; they have most of them beat themselves to death against the solid fabric of the national school. But this school has not been insensible to these various shocks. It has gradually enlarged the borders of its phylactery, and become more catholic; but in the year 1863 it received from the hands of one man a blow far more effective than any yet administered. It was a veritable *coup d'état*. On the 13th of November, in the year above named, an Imperial decree, inspired by M. Viollet-le-Duc, Government Architect and Inspector of Diocesan Buildings, was issued, making fundamental changes in the School of Fine Arts, turning out all the professors, and establishing a system by which the professors instead of being a self-electing body were to be appointed by an officer of the Imperial household, thus virtually breaking up that exclusiveness which was the peculiar characteristic of the academical faculty. The *coup* was autocratic and ill-judged. M. Viollet-le-Duc was made professor, but soon found it expedient to resign, the active and incessant opposition of the old school rendering his position uncomfortable and practically useless; and finally, for various reasons, the school relapsed silently into nearly the former condition of things. The seed of judicious reform has, however, been planted in good ground, and will bear fruit.

M. Viollet-le-Duc has long been known as a profound scholar in mediæval architecture and a man of indomitable activity and enterprise. He is an architect of extensive practice and influence and a profuse author of archæological works, chief among which is his "Dictionnaire Raisonné de l'Architecture Française du XIe au XVIe Siècle," now in process of publication. But in his "Entretiens sur l'Architecture" he has, in our opinion, asserted his claim to a far higher position than any other work of his can give him — that of the leading architectural reformer of France.

It is difficult for any work touching the higher occupations of human thought to be other than controversial in a city like Paris, which is an intellectual arena thronged with combatants and partizans, each ready to assert his creed against any opposition. These "Entretiens" have been thrown out, like a weapon, in the midst of a ceaseless warfare of books, pamphlets, and articles concerning art. They were intended to strike mortal blows against old abuses and against prejudices which have become venerable. The tone of the work is, therefore, necessarily polemic and, to a certain extent, local. Without the singular literary ability of the "Stones of Venice" or the "Seven Lamps," it is a deliberate declaration of opinion, uttered by a practical architect, thoroughly versed in all the technical points of his profession and conscious that he is speaking in the midst of an audience severely critical. Though he writes with the same aim and intentions as Ruskin, he is far more valuable to art, because less visionary, less poetic, and less dogmatic. He has a palpable, concentrated enemy before him, inspiring him to directness and animation of thought. He has no cause, like Nero, vaguely to wish that the Roman people had but one head, that he might strike it off; for all the elements of opposition are incarnate in the School of Fine Arts. Yet he is no radical; his work is in no sense that of an intemperate fanatic. It may be described in general terms as an appeal to reason against prejudice. In this is its strength, and in this is its immeasurable value to the cause of art throughout the world. We are glad to know that it has been translated into English by an architect of this country with a view to its publication here at an early day.[7] We shall hail it as a promise of better things.

Though it has been generally understood in France that M. Viollet-le-Duc is a warm partizan of the revival of mediæval architecture, this work exhibits him as a philosophical investigator of the whole field of architectural precedent, building up his conclusions from a broader basis of study than any of his predecessors. He earnestly denies that his views are confined within the narrow limits of a specialty. On the contrary, he undertakes to develop the great principles of architecture by a thorough, searching, and appreciative investigation of all the great eras of art, by a comparative analysis of Greek, Roman, Byzantine, Mediæval, and Renaissance architectures. He contends that merely to describe and illustrate in turn these various styles, without indicating the process of their growth and their relations with the genius of nations, without seeking in the history, institutions, and manners of every country the primary causes of its peculiarities of form in art, is to make a sterile compilation of numerous antiquarian works which are available to any one who searches the public libraries. "Should I confine myself," says he, on the other hand, "to treating of one style to the prejudice of all others, I should regard myself as doing that which is dangerous to the true interests of education in architecture, and I shall never cease to condemn all who profess to teach with any such narrow aim." [8]

M. Viollet-le-Duc professes to enter upon a task so new and so difficult with great diffidence, but he proceeds to say in his preface:

"One thing alone sustains and encourages me — my respect for truth, my love for an art which, in all its forms and styles, has never in my life ceased to be an object of careful and, I think, unprejudiced study. I should be content if my efforts had no other result than the inculcation of this principle: to judge the architecture of the past not by prejudice but by reason, to neglect no lesson which it can give, and to combine the results with method and discrimination. I feel that the new generations of architects are eager for knowledge, that they have no taste for the sterile disputes of rival schools, and that they are filled with the practical spirit of our age, which demands liberal and unprejudiced education. My aim in writing on architecture is to investigate the reason, the cause, for every form of the art, for no historical form or style is merely capricious; I propose to indicate the origin of the different principles of the art and their logical consequences; to analyze such styles as are the most logical results of these principles, and to explain their process of development; I propose more especially to explain how all these ancient arts can and should be applied to modern use; for the everlasting principles of truth underlie them all. Man, though his manners and customs may undergo modifications in the course of history, remains in spirit the same, with the same reason, instincts, desires, passions; he has employed various languages, various forms, but these have been inspired by the same humanity, have served to express the same ideas, and satisfy the same necessities of life. No expression of this many-sided life should be despised. I declare distinctly if any of my readers are disposed to believe that I profess doctrines profitable or agreeable to one school rather than another, he will find himself in error, as these discourses will prove. I have taken up my pen with no intention of propagating systems or refuting theories to gratify passion or party. I have another aim: to know the truth, to develop the immutable principles of our art, applied, as they have been, variously by various civilizations. I shall express no preference for one style or form of architecture rather than another; neither shall I say, You have heard — now choose; but I shall endeavor to give to the architectural studies of my readers definite direction and method. In no other way can such studies be made profitable in practice or criticism. The professor who indicates to his pupils all the paths of knowledge alike, without pointing out the best and showing why it is the best, is a bad professor; he creates in the minds of his pupils obscurity and confusion instead of order and distinctness. But this path should be no narrow, beaten track of habit or prejudice; it should be wide, large, and free to all, so that each one can follow it according to his inspirations, his natural leanings, his peculiar genius. This path is the only true and profitable one, the only one which does not lead astray, the only one by which human reason has reached its highest and best results. This is the path which, though in many very different ways, has been followed by all the artists of the most glorious epochs of antiquity and modern times." [9]

No architectural writer has professed a creed more liberal and rational than this, or developed from it a theory of architecture more in harmony with the progress of civilization. We are sorely in need of such a philosophical analysis of the art and a judicious elimination of all those accidental and merely capricious features of it which are conventionally accepted as models of design. M. Viollet-le-Duc has entered upon his task with the highest inspirations. He betrays, of course, certain very human traits of prejudice; but, it must be admitted, nowhere else on the whole has the subject been treated so philosophically and so fairly, or with a basis of knowledge so thorough and so comprehensive. Thus, his critical analysis of the architecture of Greece and of Rome exhibits the forms of Greek and Roman art not merely as certain æsthetic results, to be studied for their own sake, but as expressions of the two civilizations respectively, as deliberate but unconscious records of history. It enables us to contemplate that history not as a mere story of the movements of parties and rulers, not as we behold it from the familiar stand-points of literature, but as an exhibition of the *genius of the nations,*[10] to which the facts of traditionary or written history are in every sense subordinate. M. Viollet-le-Duc's "Entretiens," in this respect, are a signal and singular contribution to the sum of human knowledge. In these and in all the other eras of architectural history on which he touches, he concerns himself with the process of the development of styles and with the sources, the main springs, of this process in the character of peoples. This is the philosophy of the history of architecture, which is valuable not only for what it adds to our knowledge of general history, but, more especially, for the information it affords regarding our own relations with the architecture which we are creating around us.

We earnestly recommend this remarkable work to all who would seek for a satisfactory reply to the popular and frequent demand for *a new style,* an architecture of the nineteenth century.

Translator's Introduction to the Discourses on Architecture of Eugène-Emmanuel Viollet-le-Duc

(1875)

Eugène-Emmanuel Viollet-le-Duc, born in Paris in the year 1814, a diligent student of art, a learned archæologist, and an architect of experience, published in the year 1863 a work entitled *Entretiens sur l'Architecture*. In the year 1872 a second and concluding volume appeared. The first volume, relating more especially to the theory of architecture, is now presented to the public of this country in an English dress. Its peculiar claim to attention consists in the fact that its argument is an appeal to philosophical analysis against the tyranny of tradition and usage in matters of architectural design. "I am convinced," the author says, "that we can bring the taste of this generation to perfection by making it reason." [1]

It would seem that such an argument would be most properly addressed to some nation possessing the desire and means to build monumentally, but destitute of that natural love and appreciation of art which would develop ideas of especial grace and fitness in its works, and enable it to take due rank in the history of civilization. To publish such an appeal in the very capital of civilization, where, ever since the Renaissance, the public mind has been constantly occupied by questions of art, and has diligently searched for the ideal of beauty by every path of practice and theory, would seem to be a most superfluous return to first principles. But the author begs the chief architects of the Latin race and the students who crowd their *ateliers* to review their knowledge of the architecture of the past, to ascertain if they have not lost their way in the midst of dogmas, commonplaces, and formulas, and if it is not worth while to begin to think again. He professes to attack ancient abuses and professional errors made academical in the instructions of the great art schools of the capital and perpetuated in the modern architecture of France. In the midst of his polemic, the eagerness of his appeals to reason, his constant return to the practical conditions of structure as the true basis of design, may well attract attention. If the characteristic and deliberate architectural expression of French civilization, which is admired and imitated in every city of Christendom, is open to criticism such as this, it is high time for us to analyze the sources of our admiration, to enter upon a logical examination of architecture, and to learn at last whether there is an absolute right and an absolute wrong in this region of æsthetics, and whether taste or artistic feeling, or whatever the quality may be called which concerns itself with this expression of the human mind, can discriminate between them. Such an inquiry is not for architects alone, but for every man who is interested in questions affecting the uses of art in life. If architecture, in its good estate, is an art amenable to laws, and not a mere body of arbitrary formulas, — if all the phases of its proper development can be analyzed and explained by whatever process of reasoning, — every layman should be capable of an intelligent appreciation and enjoyment of it without a course of technical study, and the architect could no longer cover his errors of ignorance, carelessness, or haste behind his specious shield of conventionality.

In order as nearly as possible to give the American reader an impartial standpoint from which he may intelligently survey this field, it is important to glance briefly at the present state of architecture, — more especially in France, — and to ascertain, if possible, under what impulse or inspiration it has developed in the direction of the Louvre, the Hôtel de Ville, the New Opera, and the other familiar and characteristic monuments of French taste (Figs. 95, 99, 98). Thus we may see in what an atmosphere and under what especial conditions these Discourses were prepared, and make due allowance for their peculiarities of temper and tone.

M. Viollet-le-Duc in the following pages has sufficiently set forth the historical conditions under which, in the time of Louis XII. and Francis I., classic forms supplanted mediæval forms on the soil of France. The question with which we are immediately concerned is how this fruitful derivative of Roman art has maintained its footing, and how it has continued its consistent development, in the midst of enormous social and political revolutions, and notwithstanding the love of change and fashion which is certainly a leading peculiarity of this people.

The French Academy of Painting and Sculpture was founded in 1648; that of Architecture, in 1671. The modern *Ecole des Beaux Arts* is a direct descendant from these official schools; it has inherited all their collections, and in it are merged all their traditions of theory and practice. It is in the department of the Minister of Fine Arts, and is governed by a director appointed by the minister for five years; the administration includes a secretary, a treasurer, a librarian, and a custodian of the museum. This bureau is assisted by a council of instruction, composed of certain officials of state, two painters, two sculptors, two architects, an engraver or medallist, and five others. New members are elected to this council every year, replacing old members, who retire in turn. But old members are eligible for re-election, and practically the council has the power of filling its own vacancies. This important council has thus for a century been adapted naturally to the preservation of whatever inheritance of style and practice should be perpetuated for use in the great monuments of state, according to the traditions and prejudices of the school. The curriculum undertakes to embrace all branches of theory and practice. The theoretical studies comprehend æsthetics, the history of art, the elements of anatomy, perspective, geometry, mathematics, geology, physics, chemistry, archæology, construction, and the administration of works. Practical instruction in drawing and design is given in the seven official *ateliers* of the school, three of these being devoted to architecture, and each being under the charge of a director. The whole is enshrined in a superb Palace, constructed for the accommodation of the school, and filled with precious objects of art and every appliance which can inform and inspire the mind.

Public interest is periodically attracted to the school by the annual competition for the "grand prize of Rome." This is open to any Frenchman under twenty-five years of age, whether a member of the school or not, who shall have been successful in two preliminary and stated competitions. For architects, sculptors, and painters, the grand competition is annual; for engravers on copper, every second year; for engravers on precious stones, every third year. One grand prize is given to each branch of art. The successful competitors (*lauréats*) are maintained at the public expense for four years, at least two of which must be spent at the Academy of France at Rome (in the Villa Medici, purchased for the purpose by Louis XIV.), under the control of a director, who is responsible to government for the progress of their studies. In witness of this progress, each *lauréat*, during his stay at Rome, sends to the school at Paris a work of sculpture, painting, or an architectural composition. The remaining two years may be spent in travel, at the discretion of each *lauréat*, he previously having reported his intentions to the authorities. At Rome the architectural student usually devotes himself to measuring and restoring the antique.

Outside of the school proper, the principal architects of Paris, assuming functions as *patrons*, have their *ateliers* filled with students, who, with more or less regularity, attend the lectures of the school, but have their greatest interest engaged in a series of stated competitions (*concours*) based upon programmes officially prepared and announced. These competitions are decided by juries largely composed of architects not officially connected with the faculty of instruction, and culminate in the two great annual competitions preliminary to the final struggle for the grand prize of Rome.

All this machinery tends directly to the creation and prevalence of a style of architecture peculiarly academical, and which, considering the atmosphere of emulation in which it has grown and its extraordinary fidelity to a comparatively narrow range of precedent and study, must necessarily be carried to the highest degree of technical perfection. This style, first made national by the châteaux of Pierre Lescot, Philibert Delorme, Jean Bullant, and the other French architects of the sixteenth and seventeenth centuries,[2] and afterwards giving expression, with peculiar felicity, to the pomp of that great builder, Louis XIV., is of course a form of the Renaissance.

The council of the school, loyal to the exclusive traditions of the place, is content to keep this national inheritance pure from foreign alloy and free from any rivalry or distractions of mediævalism. The architects of Paris, who desire official patronage and decoration; the students, who rejoice in the superb emulation and national distinction of the grand prize; the multitude, who are proud of their great historical monuments, — all, under these inspirations, cling to the academic style, and recognize no other. Within the shadow of Notre Dame and of the Sainte Chapelle, they are intolerant of any nearer approach to the pointed arch than the conventional use in their ecclesiastical buildings of the round-arched Romanesque of the twelfth century and of such other Byzantine elements as can be adapted to modern means and necessities.

Until lately even Greek influences have been admitted with jealousy. M. Henri Labrouste, a *lauréat* of Rome in the year 1824, studied the monuments of the Greek colonies, and sent home, as his official contribution to the school, a correct restoration of a Greek Doric temple. M. Joseph Louis Duc, a *lauréat* of the following year, and immediately afterwards M. Duban and M. Vaudoyer, pursued their studies in Italy in the same direction with intelligent enthusiasm, and brought back to France prolific seeds of Greek sentiment.[3] This sentiment afterwards took form in what was known a few years ago in Paris as "the Romantic School," which consisted in the admission of a larger scope of invention and in the refinement of architectural forms by somewhat of the Greek feeling for purity and elegance of line. It was rather a Renaissance of Greek *expressions* than of Greek *principles*, and, owing to the facility with which even caprices could assume an air of studious elegance under this treatment, it became so popular and so well suited to French taste, that, after the construction of the Library of St. Genevieve (Fig. 94) by M. Labrouste, the prejudices of the Academy were overcome, and it became an essential element of French architecture.

Meanwhile, in this uncongenial atmosphere, the Gothic or mediæval school received its chief encouragement from the archæological spirit; and M. Lassus[4] and M. Viollet-le-Duc became engaged, not in the legitimate and practical development of their theories of art, but in the restoration of the Gothic monuments of France.

The academic style of Paris has thus enjoyed the unprecedented advantage of an undisturbed growth of four hundred years in the hands of the wealthiest and most artistic people in the world. They have lavished upon the Roman orders and upon their Italian derivatives of the fifteenth century — a basis of a few simple architectural *motifs* — all the decoration and refinement of nearly four centuries of industrious and consistent culture. What wonder if the civilized world accepts the extraordinary result with admiration? Elsewhere, it may be said, architecture has suffered from anarchy; here is what may be accomplished by the vigorous administration of art. Why ask for it the blessing of perfect freedom, when discipline can achieve such triumphs?

If all this is wrong, where shall we look for the right? Who shall tell us how we can develop good architecture? Who, in short, shall interpret for us the architectural myth?

There has hitherto been such a mystery about the practice of architecture, such an unexplained accumulation of formulas and rules, such peremptory exclusions on the one part, such affectations of lawlessness and caprice on the other, such a warfare between the picturesque and the symmetrical, that the theory of architecture has gone begging for a rational exposition. Literary enterprise both in France and England has occupied this tempting field of speculation with more or less of dogmatic assertion. In France the æsthetic faculty is by birth and growth so diffused, that criticism in the hands of Quatrèmere de Quincy[5] and other men of letters has been kept in a workmanlike track, and has done its work with comparative modesty and efficiency. But in England, to use the words of a late writer in the "North American Review," "since Mr. Ruskin set the example of a literary man erecting himself into a dictator on questions of art, we have been subjected to a fearful tyranny in æsthetics. It is true that no one else has carried matters so far nor with so high a hand, but there are innumerable petty despots laying down the laws of the sublime and beautiful, who only lack the ability to be as peremptory, as arbitrary, and as paradoxical as he." Thus, in the absence of a natural appreciation in regard to art and taste, the literary view of the theory of architecture has with us absorbed popular attention and moulded popular opinion. As for the architects, they have, with few exceptions, addressed no word of explanation to the public, and the speculators have had the field to themselves; indeed, in this country and in England certainly, the art itself for the last twenty years has been affected rather by prejudices based upon the literary exposition of the question than by convictions founded upon practical knowledge, — rather, in short, by sentiment than by reason. Since the publication of the "Seven Lamps of Architecture" and the "Stones of Venice," the characteristic expression of English architecture has been obviously colored by the mediæval monuments of Northern Italy. Many conspicuous structures have been directly inspired by these examples. The Manchester Assize Courts (Fig. 84), the new Town Halls (Fig. 85), most of the designs for the new Law Courts in London (Figs. 89, 90), would scarcely have existed in their present form but for this predominance of letters in art.[6] It is premature to declare, perhaps, that these phenomena are evidences of more than an ephemeral fashion. M. Viollet-le-Duc maintains in the text (without reference, however, to this phase of actual experience) that the architecture of Northern Italy developed biographies and not history, and that it can accordingly afford but little profitable instruction. He also elsewhere very justly remarks that a true Renaissance has never arisen from corrupted types: "Only primitive sources can furnish the energy for a long career." [7] But if, as has been asserted in some quarters, this adaptation of Southern *motifs* in a Northern architecture contains the elements of a just and reasonable progress towards a national style, this new English Renaissance exhibits curious and instructive contrasts with that of the sixteenth century in France; while the latter was the result of warlike conquests, and followed in the footsteps of French armies returning with captives and spoils from Italian cities, the former has come in this nineteenth century from the same fountain of art through the peaceful medium of literature and critical exegesis. However, we are witnesses of a rebellion taking place at this moment in the very strongholds of these English mediævalists, in the revival here and there throughout England of the long square windows, the brick panels, the attenuated orders, the fretted and ornamented gable lines of the reign of Queen Anne (Fig. 92). Is this an indication of anarchy, or is it a healthy reaction from a mere artificial excitement? We have noted the results of the discipline of the schools in France, in the scholastic elegance and finish of their monuments. Is this picturesque and uneasy groping after a type in England likely to result in something nobler than the façades of the Hôtel de Ville of Paris and of the New Opera?

In this condition of doubt we may welcome any man of trained observation and large professional experience, acquainted with the technicalities and manipulations of the various crafts whose labors enter into the construction of a building, — any architect, who is willing and able to explain the sources of his convictions. And here at last is a man who has studied, measured, analyzed, and drawn Greek and Roman monuments in Italy and the Greek colonies, certainly with singular fidelity and intelligence; who has rebuilt and completed the great Gothic château of Pierrefonds, built the town-halls of Narbonne and St. Antonin, restored numerous churches, constructed the flèche and sacristy of the Cathedral of Paris; repaired the fortifications of Carcassonne; architect of the works on the cathedrals of Laon, Sens, and Amiens, and the abbeys of St. Denis and Vézelay; author of the exhaustive *Dictionnaire Raisonné de l'Architecture Française, du Xe au XVIe Siècles*, and other works of large research. Thus equipped, M. Viollet-le-Duc appears upon the scene, and endeavors to set forth the true sources of design; how best to analyze, classify, and use the enormous accumulation of precedents in all styles, by which we are so seriously embarrassed; how to receive the developments of modern science in the arts of construction, and how to give them place and due expression in our modern architecture; how to subject all our fancies, impressions, and prejudices to rigid philosophical investigation, and how thus to create new things fairly representative of the spirit of modern civilization, if not the new style for which literary criticism is constantly clamoring. We do not mean to assert that M. Viollet-le-Duc has succeeded in all these things, but we think it important to give a new publicity to this honest and earnest effort, and to place it side by side with similar essays of literary men and amateurs, that it may do its work with theirs.

It will be observed, as a characteristic of his argument, and as a reassuring fact to the professional reader, that at every step the allurements of mere sentiment, so irresistible to the layman, are distrusted, and that the premises of every conclusion claim to be practical facts in the arts of building. It is admitted, of course, that he starts with a strong professional bias in opposition to the practice of architecture as carried on under the inspiration of the School of Fine Arts, and with a zealous admiration of the principles both of Greek and of mediæval art; but if his argument is logical, his appreciation of the great historical and contrasting styles reasonably discriminating and just, and his field of observation large and well occupied, we may well pardon the bias for the sake of his contributions to knowledge and the picturesque contrasts of his historical retrospect. Convictions based upon practical knowledge, gained from experience and observation, even if involving some professional bias or one-sidedness, are at least worthy of comparison with theories evolved in the literary manner and subject to the literary temptations of arbitrary statement and sweeping generalizations.

We Americans occupy a new country, having no inheritance of ruins and no embarrassments of tradition in matters of architecture; we are absolutely free from historical prejudice; and yet with our great future we have a constant and growing necessity to make of architecture a living and growing art; we may therefore be in a position peculiarly well adapted to appreciate at its just value any honest and earnest effort to give this art true development according to modern necessities. The great range of architectural precedents at no point touches our local domain or concerns our national pride. We are so far removed from such entanglements, that we alone of all civilized people may be said to occupy a position of judicial impartiality, and perhaps to us, therefore, with our obviously great material resources, may be intrusted the duty of finding a new solution of the architectural problem. If this be our great function, let us be worthy of it; let us prepare ourselves, whether as architects or critics, by understanding our duties.

But why, it may be asked, being so free and untrammelled, may we not break off from the past entirely and create a new American architecture, — why not begin afresh? To this, of course, there can be but one intelligent reply. All the past is ours; books, engravings, photographs, have so multiplied, that at any moment we can turn to and examine the architectural achievements of any age or nation. These suggestions of beauty and use are always with us. It must not be forgotten that the most essential distinction between the arts of primitive barbarism and those of civilization is that, while the former are original and independent, and consequently simple, the latter must be retrospective, naturally turning to tradition and precedent, and are therefore complex. A beginning once made by primitive discovery and experiment, art, like nature, must thenceforward proceed by derivation and development; and where architectural monuments and traditions have accumulated to the vast extent that they have in modern times, the question is not whether we shall use them at all, but how shall we choose among them, and to what extent shall such choice be allowed to influence our modern practice.

It is not to be inferred that the "hope of modern architecture" — to use the imposing phraseology of the latest petty tyrant of art[8] — resides in the library of the antiquary. His researches among the architectural characteristics of nations are made in an entirely different spirit from those of the architect.

The former seeks among the monuments of the past for illustrations and vouchers in his historical studies, and, by curious analysis and patient comparison, to place before us in all their minute details such restorations as shall enable those monuments to play the part of authentic archives of human progress. His function is to make out of these the complement and completion of the political story and of the records of princes and parties. He aims to discover in tombs, temples, cathedrals, abbeys, and palaces, in all religious and civic structures, whether of pomp or necessity, deliberate and unconscious expressions of the prevailing sentiments, the social and political condition of the people in any given time. But such studies do not make architects nor affect architecture further than to create such a spirit of imitation, and, with it, such a mania for absolute "correctness" and such an abject fear of anachronism, as in England, during the early part of this century and up to within twenty years perhaps, bound the art hand and foot, and proved a stumbling-block in the path of its progress. The architect has felt himself called upon to make arbitrary selection of the "style" in which he would design his building, and to be "correct" in his archæological reproduction of its minutest details, leaving little room for the free spirit of invention, and no opportunity for the honest adaptation of his work to the new social and material conditions constantly pressed upon him in the advance of knowledge. If his work was in "Early English," he must anxiously consult his authorities, lest some characteristic detail of an earlier or later period should find its way into his design and ruin his reputation. Under the pressure of this widely prevailing spirit of antiquarianism, Sir Charles Barry was constrained to meet the exceedingly complicated requirements of the new Houses of Parliament with a masquerade of obsolete architecture of the time of Henry VII (Fig. 77).[9]

Are we then, on the other hand, to find the true architect in "the master-workman," as the Quarterly Reviewer would have it, — in the man who knows nothing of archæology and who cares less? In the beginning of things, when the needs of mankind were simple and their resources of knowledge and experience comparatively small, the master-workman had his day. He developed his primitive forms directly and honestly from practical necessity;

> He builded better than he knew,
> The conscious stone to beauty grew.[10]

His successors, unembarrassed by knowledge of other styles, avoided his obvious errors, profited by his experience, learned economy of materials, and, in a succession of tentative structures, gradually and innocently evolved monuments exhibiting the results of well-concentrated thought and of fidelity to a few simple conditions. The master-workman, however, laid aside his functions as an originator, and the architect was born, when precedent began so to accumulate, when civilization became so complex and exacting, the wants of mankind so various and conflicting, that, to meet the more elaborate emergencies of building, there came to be needed a larger and more exact knowledge, a more careful study of plans and details, and a more deliberate and scientific method of construction. These conditions began to render essential the organization of some processes and appliances, by means of which the system of structure in each case, embracing all the details of the building, could be more exactly and completely set forth long before the first stone was laid. They implied, in short, draughtsmen, instruments of mathematical precision, a library of reference, and all the other appointments and conveniences of an office, that is, both of a studio and of a place of business. They implied, moreover, not only the unwritten experience of the builder, but the training and observation of the scholar, by means of which the most remote results could be foreseen and provided for; and more especially, they called for the feeling, the inspiration, the patience, self-denial, and tempered zeal of the artist. Uncultured genius may be eloquent, but its eloquence is ungrammatical; and although in architecture as in literature we may sometimes pardon the awkwardness of the phrase for the sake of the preciousness of the thought, in neither — and more especially in architecture, whose highest duty it is to embody history and civilization in durable monuments, and whose processes are so artificial and scientific — can the preciousness of the thought render less necessary purity of language, elegance of expression, and exactness of knowledge. Uncultured genius may in a moment of heaven-sent inspiration invent a great architectural thought, but plodding culture is needed to give it such expression as to render it worthy of place in the records of time and capable of doing duty as a new starting-point of architectural style. This is the plain *raison d'être* of the architect. He exists because civilization demands him. It is our present duty to see that he is worthy of his mission.

The architectural work of our own country indicates clearly enough that we have made the largest and most catholic use of European precedent, and endeavored to repeat European forms with all the fidelity in our power. But it is important to note that these forms have in each locality insensibly submitted in a greater or less degree to practical and social conditions. They have, however reluctantly, yielded some of their characteristics to the exactions of absolute local necessity and convenience, and, in so yielding, have created to a certain extent local peculiarities of form or style. Municipal regulations, characteristics of the local building materials, difference of climate, habits of building and living, the greater or less degree of culture, — all these conditions have contributed to create distinctions of style between the various cities and districts of our country. There is a recognizable difference between the architecture of New York and that of Boston, between that of Washington and that of Baltimore, between that of Philadelphia and that of Chicago. Our close proximity to these scenes of activity prevent us from seeing these processes in true perspective; but it is a fact that we are living in the midst of the development of styles, such as they are. If methods of intercommunication were as difficult now as they were several centuries ago, we should doubtless see very much stronger contrasts between the works of different localities; and if, added to this, it were possible to conceive that these localities existed without the means for the diffusion of knowledge given by the graver, the printing-press, and the photographic camera, we should in all probability exhibit variations of style as marked and characteristic, if not as picturesque, as those in the cities of Belgium, France, and England in the thirteenth and fourteenth centuries. But even under our present conditions the intelligent eye can detect the gradual development of local characteristics, not only in the subdivisions of our country, but, in a larger sense, in the nation itself as a whole and as distinguished from the other nations of Christendom, — characteristics not so marked, indeed, as those which made English work contrast with that of the Scotch in the thirteenth century, or that of Central France with that of Southern France in the twelfth century, but sufficient to indicate the existence of some influence insensibly and unconsciously working against our intentions to imitate foreign styles. This is illustrated most conspicuously by the large use of wood which is imposed upon us by our obvious necessities; and although the master-builders of a few years ago tried very hard to imitate with this material Grecian temples of marble according to Stuart and Revett,[11] or the mansions of brick and stone of the Georgian era according to the traditions brought over from the old country and loyally followed by our ancestors, yet, with due acknowledgment for certain suggestions from Swiss art, we have, under the pressure of necessity, produced at length certain forms in our wooden houses peculiar to ourselves, and capable under proper treatment of a high degree of artistic development.

Now, inasmuch as all history may be read by an intelligent observation of the monuments of the past, as the following pages show with sufficient distinctness, it is certainly important for us to see to it that *our* civilization is having a proper exponent in our monuments. We cannot remain indifferent to the operations of this mysterious influence which is building history for us. It is the part of intelligent beings to examine, and, if possible, correct it and give it proper direction. If we analyze it in this spirit, we shall discover that its principal elements are, *first*, practical local necessities and conditions; *second*, a dangerous superficiality of thought and work, arising from a deficient education in art and from a want of leisure, — from the spirit of haste and impatience which prevails in all new communities; and, *third*, indifference or absence of sympathy in the public for the just expression of beauty or fitness in buildings.

The natural local conditions, material and social, constitute a legitimate and controlling element of this influence. It is self-evident, that, to the formation of good style in architecture, the study of convenience and economy is the first duty, to which everything else must be subordinate. A public like ours, trained in habits of business, is positive and exacting, and at least has the virtue of compelling the architect to fulfill all such practical requirements in a straightforward and common-sense manner. Doubtless to this quality in our people we are indebted for the most characteristic expressions in our work. It is not a common occurrence for a man to incommode himself nowadays for the sake of an architectural idea. The merchant requires that the first story of the front of his shop or warehouse shall be of glass; the formulas of Vitruvius, Vignola, Palladio, and all the most venerable traditions and usages of the art, must yield to this inexorable demand; the building committee insists that their church must be a place where all may see and hear the speaker, and that accommodation must be provided on the first floor for vestry, Sunday school, class-rooms, kitchen, and all the social and religious exigencies of their style of worship and service, although Pugin (Fig. 78) would faint with horror at the result.[12] Yet it is out of just such prosaic exactions as these that our architecture must be developed. We must have narrow façades on our streets, and these must be built to the skies and crowded with windows. We can find no historic precedent for such things. We must accept the conditions as they are given to us, and create our architecture accordingly.

But the second element of the influence which is at work on our buildings is one which we can and ought to control, namely, superficiality of thought and work, whether arising from want of education or from the atmosphere of bustle and haste in which we live. American architects, as a rule, have not hitherto been men of high training; the standard has been low, and access to the recognized ranks of the profession has not been denied to the most ignorant and audacious pretenders. In order to counteract this great evil, a few architects who happened to live, practise, and study their art in the city of New York in the year 1857, — men who either in the schools abroad or in offices at home had been educated to the point of feeling the necessity of greater professional comity and of more intelligent rules of practice, — embodied themselves in a society known as the American Institute of Architects. The second article of its constitution sets forth that its objects are "to unite in fellowship the architects of this continent, and to combine their efforts so as to promote the artistic, scientific, and practical efficiency of the profession." The Institute, reorganized in 1866, has chapters or branches in every principal city of the Union, each of which has stated monthly meetings, and there is an annual convention of the national body. There is a steady increase of membership throughout the country, and the organization has already tended directly and indirectly to raise the standard of the profession, to prompt a large amount of active and fruitful work, to create an important *esprit du corps*, and to encourage a higher culture. It has been the means in several cities of obtaining important legislation for improvement in the arts of building, and its members in New York and Boston have established monthly publications, containing drawings and architectural projects, — which, without such a vehicle, would remain concealed and unproductive in the architects' portfolios, — together with studies and designs for buildings actually erected, thus facilitating the comparison of competitive designs, encouraging more careful work, and diffusing a knowledge of the general progress of the art. In Boston the members of the local society have also delivered a course of lectures for the benefit of students, established prizes to encourage progress in their studies, and have inaugurated a series of exhibitions of industrial art. A body like the Institute, composed largely of young men, and recruited to a considerable extent in late years from graduates of colleges, bringing to it an important contribution of liberal training and general culture, and all fired with a certain degree of emulative and generous enthusiasm, — a body so composed can hardly fail in a young and impressionable country to do much towards diminishing the anarchy which has hitherto distinguished the practice of architecture here. Much has been projected, and somewhat has been accomplished, in the direction of the founding of architectural schools and the establishment of architectural departments in educational institutions. But, *from a national point of view*, the work of organized education is but begun, and a basis of cultivated conviction, not only on the part of those who preach and criticise, but on the part of those who practise and produce tangible results, is yet to be attained.

The atmosphere of haste in which we live is another element distinctly detrimental to the development of good style. Unlike the French, we have no such prevailing academical restrictions as are attributed to the influence of the School of Fine Arts, concentrating all architectural effort on the development of a few strictly defined ideas such as constitute French Renaissance; but, like the Greeks, we are in this respect free, and our appeal, like theirs, is directly to the people, not to any body of professors. But the Greek democracy, says our author, "had the inestimable advantage of leisure." [13] The Greek temple therefore is an expression of utter tranquillity. The very essence of that great art was deliberation. The architect was never hurried; his inspiration proceeded, not from impulse, but from conviction. He built slowly. But with us he is pressed to the completion of his work amidst bustle and confusion. The public is impatient of delay; it must have promptness and despatch, at all hazards. The modern Ictinus must supply the design for the new Parthenon, "ready for estimates," in three weeks at furthest; and the unfinished study is perpetuated in a workmanlike manner, with all its sins of omission and commission made permanent and monumental. Indeed, all the conditions of life in this country encourage the architect to habits rather of rapid composition than of study and reflection, and tend to make of his occupation rather a business than a fine art. The "strenuous liberty" which we have inherited involves a constant and often harassing struggle for existence. Therefore the aim of the architect is to multiply his opportunities of professional work to the utmost extent, having in view, first, his pecuniary emoluments of course, and, second, his art. Under these circumstances he has no time to review his studies; he cannot afford, after his first sketches are made and his work in progress of routine development in his office, to distrust and chasten his favorite *motifs*, with the solicitude and patience of an artist aiming at perfection like the Greek; much less, having discovered on reflection a new condition in his problem which would enable him perhaps to raise to a higher plane of artistic excellence or fitness the whole sentiment of his work, to throw aside his old labors and begin anew. This costs too much. If the products of routine and of conventionality will satisfy his impatient public, he has the strongest impulse under the circumstances to content himself with the superficial appearance, and let the substance of art go for those who can afford it. Art is a mistress who is won by no such partial service.

Notwithstanding the narrow path which they have chosen for themselves and their peremptory exclusions, even if their efforts are misdirected in the manner and to the extent which M. Viollet-le-Duc maintains, there pervades the schools of Paris an atmosphere of noble devotion to art. Whether this comes from the inspiration of venerable traditions and monuments, or whether it arises from a condition of society which enables respectability to be maintained at less expense and thus makes money less indispensable there than here, — whether it is the result of any or all of these causes, the spectacle of lives given up to art — sacrificed, from the mercantile point of view — is much more common with the French than with us. It would be impossible of course, even if it were desirable, to make a Paris — even a Paris of art — in this country. Our young architects may go to Paris, but they cannot bring Paris here. *Cœlum non animam mutant.*[14] Yet, to compare our conditions of life as they affect the growth of artistic feeling with those of the French or English is useful and indeed indispensable, not only to bring us to our bearings, and, by comparison of results, to save us from the common sin of complacency, but to enable us to understand the philosophy of the development of distinctive styles, and to what extent these distinctions are due to natural and necessary premises on the one hand and to artificial and remediable causes on the other. It is impossible for us to enter upon any such comparison, without discovering at an early stage that our state of society is not such as necessarily to inspire the architect with high thoughts, or to exact from him that serious study and self-denial without which there can be no really great results. Civilization has no exponent more sensitive than architecture; for it is an art not only absolutely indispensable, but one which adapts itself practically and æsthetically to the condition of things amongst which it grows. Of course individual genius, caprice, or invention finds expression in it, but no individuality can control it. We may conceive of the production of a perfect work of sculpture, painting, or music, or a great achievement of literature, in the midst of a community which cannot appreciate it and who had nothing whatever to do with giving it existence; but an architectural work, unless it is avowedly an imitation of some monument which has received the stamp of historical approval, notwithstanding all the original invention which the architect may bestow upon it, is the outgrowth, to a great extent, of a prevailing sentiment. It cannot exist without the sympathy of the people. It is an archive of history, having its birth in necessity, and its peculiar characteristics in the conditions of life. The Renaissance of Italy, France, and England may have exhibited individualities more than the ancient or mediæval styles, but it was created respectively neither by Arnolfo da Lapo,[15] by Philibert Delorme, nor by Sir Christopher Wren, nor yet by their followers, however illustrious. Their works were the unconscious expression of their eras. They were the instruments, and not the authors, of styles.

To the sympathy of generous culture then we must mainly look to encourage the development of a fitting architectural expression of our time and place in history; professional culture and professional genius will eagerly arise under the impulse of appreciation to meet the great emergency and to give it grammatical utterance. To the creation of this spirit of sympathy therefore this reproduction of the earnest work of an illustrious Frenchman is humbly commended and dedicated.

Growth of Conscience in the Decorative Arts

(1878)

Self-examination has become one of the characteristic instincts of modern civilization. It was not long ago that Carlyle described this instinct as a sort of moral dyspepsia prevailing more or less absolutely in all the grades of society.[1] However this may be, it is true that, unlike our forefathers, we take nothing for granted. The religious passions, the social traits, the manners and customs, which we may have inherited from them, are subjected to analysis and discussion. Reason modifies them, and establishes certain types with which, in the conduct of life, according to our several lights, we seek to establish a conscientious conformity. Concerning art, however, for various reasons which we shall presently consider, there has been, until lately, a reluctance to bring to bear upon it any such reorganizing and revolutionary tendencies.

Hitherto, when those of us who have been engaged in works of design have undertaken, in the modern spirit, to analyze our motives in any succession of cases, we have found that the standard of excellence by which we would measure our work, the ideal which we would approach, has been, so far as the form at least was concerned, inconstant, and for the most part capricious. These variations of style have not occurred according to any known law. Our art seems to have been in great degree controlled by some power outside of ourselves. We have found it convenient and comfortable to accept the dictates of this power without questioning, and our standard has been set up indifferently in ancient Greece or Rome, in mediæval France, England, or Italy. At one time it has held to some phase of the Renaissance; at another it has been absolute as to its Gothic; "all these by turns and nothing long."[2] Its caprice has been curious and unaccountable, and not at all in accordance with the modern spirit in other walks of intelligence.

This vacillation of the type which has prevented modern art from developing a style, in the accepted sense of the word, is the natural result of the increase of our knowledge of form and the growth of the archæological spirit.

Unlike any of our predecessors in art, we have been seriously embarrassed by the unbounded range and variety of precedent at our command. There is no phase of historical art which we have not studied; wheresoever and howsoever humanity has expressed itself in forms of art, these forms are at our fingers' ends, and are ready to seduce us this way or that according to our mood. The mind of the designer is preoccupied by innumerable favorite *motifs* derived from every side and every era, each associated with some phase of ancient life, and sanctified or sweetened by ancient traditions; each with a value aside from intrinsic picturesqueness, beauty, or quaintness; and all contending for new expression. Whether he has been engaged upon a composition of architecture or upon a composition of decoration, — which also is architecture, or the completion and fulfillment of it, — his energy has been concerned, first, perhaps, with the choice of types agreeably to the caprice or fashion of the moment; next, with the degree of precision with which he is to follow them when chosen; and, finally, — by such reserve of force as might be at his disposal after these exhausting processes, — with the adjustment of his chosen forms to his needs according to his best ingenuity and skill. Under these circumstances, the modern process of design, whether this exact order of proceeding has been followed or not, must be a complicated one, and must differ fundamentally from all which have preceded it. The exact character of this difference it is important for us to understand at the outset, to the end that we may the better comprehend the new and strange conditions under which art is developed in these modern days.

The Greek architect of the time of Pericles had before him a fixed and sacred standard of form. There were probably dim traditions from his Pelasgic ancestors, and from Syria and Egypt. These were the only styles or forms that he knew, and his own had been developed from them into a hieratic system. He had no choice; his strength was not wasted among various ideals; that which he had inherited was a religion to him. The simple cella with a portico or peristyle, — this was all; he had no wants or ambitions beyond this; it satisfied all his conditions of art. But he shared in the intense intellectual activity of his fellow-citizens; his art had been developed in the same atmosphere as the philosophy of Plato and Aristotle, the drama of Æschylus, Sophocles, and Aristophanes. He was content with nothing but absolute perfection. Undiverted by side issues as to the general form of his temple, undisturbed by any of the complicated conditions of modern life, he was able to concentrate his clear intellect upon the perfection of his details; his sensitiveness to harmony of proportion was refined to the last limits; his feeling for purity of line reached the point of a religion. Hence the subtle swell or entasis in the shaft of his column; hence the eloquence and fitness of the echinus molding by which the supporting and supported members of this order were united. This molding was the gesture of Attic civilization. It coincides with no geometrical form; it is the symbol of strength and sweetness. In each temple it obtained a new form, adjusted to its new conditions, but still in harmony with the pure ideal. It was drawn in the midst of a deep silence, like an act of worship.

112

In like manner, many centuries subsequent the monkish builders developed the Christian temple in the cloisters of Cluny. All that they knew of style had been developed in a direct line of descent from Gallo-Roman traditions, and they, like the Greek, were undisturbed by any knowledge of conflicting forms. Their art was thus kept in the track of consistent progress, and developed with purity and irresistible force.

So it was with all the intermediate builders. So it was when the Taj Mahal was built in Agra. So it was wherever there grew a pure style. So it was even after the period of the Renaissance. The development of styles continued strong and steady until archæology began to revive, classify, and make known to the world, as a contribution to history, the various methods and forms which were pursued and invented by old civilizations in the erection of their temples, tombs, and palaces. Then there followed a confusion of tongues which has lasted until our day.

From all this it necessarily follows that the distinctive characteristic of our modern art is the absence of a fixed standard of forms. It is eclectic, and apparently has not encouraged us to reach convictions as to forms or styles. At all events, there are few architects or designers, in this country at least, who are content to confine themselves to the exclusive development of any one particular set of forms, as Gothic, or Romanesque, or Renaissance, and voluntarily to shut themselves off from the rest of their inheritance of beautiful things; and wherever any such exist their neighbors are not so confined. In this particular we do not work together with any characteristic unity of sentiment. All the decorative arts are subjected to the same dissipation of forces. At the same moment we are designing and painting Greek vases; decorating Japanese screens; constructing furniture according to our reminiscences of the Gothic of the Edwards, or of the Renaissance of the Jameses, of Queen Anne, or of the Georges; covering our walls with designs suggested by the stuffs of Florence and of the inexhaustible East, by the brocades of France, by the stamped leather of Venice, with arabesques and conceits from all the styles; and with these we decorate the interiors of houses which on the outside have been inspired originally from traditions of every era of art, as set forth in books, prints, and photographs innumerable.

It is therefore a common reproach against the arts of to-day that they are discursive, without convictions or enthusiasm; that our depth is shallowed in many channels; that we produce many and not great things; that in painting we have no masterpieces like those of Italy in the fifteenth century, or of Flanders in the sixteenth; that in sculpture the ideal of the Greek marbles, though shattered and defiled, is to us absolutely unapproachable, not in execution only, but in comprehension; that in architecture we cannot reproduce the perfection, the purity, and perfect fitness of the Greek forms, the grandeur and extent of those of the Roman empire, the idealism, the enthusiasm, the consistent and powerful development, of the religious works of the thirteenth century, the elegance and refinement and self-control of the Italian masters of the fifteenth century; that in the fictile arts we cannot approach the

French and Italian potters of the sixteenth; that in fabrics we are still far excelled by the Orientals, and by the products of mediæval looms; that in furniture, for fertility of design, for perfection of execution, for richness of carving, we are surpassed by the Philibert de l'Ormes, the Le Pautres, the Boules, of France, in the fifteenth and sixteenth centuries, by the Gibbons and the Chippendales of England in the eighteenth.[3] In like manner we know that antique gems and intaglios, Etruscan jewels, boxes, fans, and bronzes of Japan, ironmongery of Nuremberg, — these, in their several departments of art, are the despair of modern workmen; that in no respect of art do we exceed our progenitors. It would seem, in fact, as if our knowledge, our ingenuity, our industry, had swamped our art, — as if our art were in a condition, if not of eclipse, certainly of hopeless anarchy, and this while its patrons were apparently never so rich, never so numerous, never so ready.

But over these accumulating and incongruous elements presides the self-conscious spirit of the modern artist. The innocence and *naïveté* of the older day have gone by, never to return. Our ancestors perhaps "builded better than they knew."[4] But we can never do a good thing by accident. Each of us, in whatever style he may work, must necessarily impress himself upon his design. We can never be quite lost in the style which we have chosen. A new subjective, personal element has thus been born into art. This self-conscious spirit began to be felt when the necessity of making choice among several types or styles was first imposed upon the artist; this choice implying the idea of self-justification, and giving an added sense of personal responsibility, which has naturally grown with the increase of our knowledge. During the existence of a prevailing or exclusive style, as in any time previous to the middle of the last century, there was far less scope for individuality of expression than now, when the necessity of making choice among many styles and among innumerable motifs constantly recalls the designer to a consciousness of his own resources, and in the new labor imposed upon him of rejecting with discretion compels him to an expression of his own peculiarities of thought and habits of mind, which would have been impossible to a Greek of the time of Pericles, or to a Frenchman of the time of St. Bernard.

Hermogenes and Callicrates, Apollodorus and Vitruvius, Viellard de Honcourt, Robert de Luzarches and William of Wyckham,[5] — each of these concerned himself with the development of a type of form, and carried it on one step further toward perfection. In this type their individuality was lost. They and their brethren are therefore but the shadows of names. Erostratus, the fool, who burnt the temple of Diana at Ephesus, is far better remembered in history than Ctesiphon, the architect, who built it.[6] Ctesiphon, though a great artist, was but the agent of a process of development in style; his work was rather a growth than a creation. But Sir Charles Barry, Alfred Waterhouse, Charles Garnier, Karl Friedrich Schinkel, of our time, built their monuments in the Houses of Parliament at London, the Law Courts at Manchester, the New Opera at Paris, and the Royal Theatre at Berlin (Figs. 77, 84, 85, 98); these buildings, and all other conspicuous monuments of modern times, are full of the personality of their authors, because they are rather creations than growths. Even so late as the fifteenth century the Renaissance palaces of Italy, built by Vignola, Scamozzi, Serlio, and Palladio, do not betray the personal characteristics of their designers to the same extent and in the same manner as do the Neo-Grec works of Henri Labrouste in Paris (Figs. 94, 94a), the modern Gothic of Scott, Burgess, and Street respectively (Figs. 86–90), the modern Greek of the Scotch Thompson in Edinburgh (Figs. 82, 83), the "Queen Anne" revival of Norman Shaw (Fig. 92), and so on through a host of more or less illustrious contemporaries, most of them changing their styles from time to time according to their moods.[7]

Confused amongst a multiplicity of types, we impress upon our work a certain effect of breathless effort, and overcrowd it with details; our greatest and most difficult virtue, therefore, is reserve of force, self-denial, simplicity, repose. The artists of antiquity found simplicity and repose in mere fidelity to a rigid standard, — a fidelity untempted by the discoveries of archæology, and easy because of the purity and perfection of the type. Their ideal was a divinity; their service to this divinity was worship and obedience. Our ideal is a museum of heterogeneous and beautiful forms, and our service to it is selection, rejection, analysis, discussion, classification, self-denial. Indeed, the modern artist is not the servant of his ideal; he properly seeks to be its master. Whenever, like a mediæval artist, he tries to render obedience to the ideal, the very perfection of his knowledge betrays him. However faithful he would be to his selected type of forms, he must needs breathe into it a spirit quite his own. If he would reproduce in his modern work the strong Gothic of the early Cistercian abbeys, he remembers also the refinements of Giotto in the Campanile of Florence. If he would imitate the elegant exuberance of the Ionic in the Treasury of St. Mark, he cannot forget the fine chastisement of invention in the Ionic of the portico of Minerva Pallas. Thus his work is sophisticated by his knowledge. He is like an actor playing a part. He cannot conceal his effort. He is self-conscious.

Thus the modern spirit of self-examination, of which I have spoken, is gradually applied to art. The application of a rule of morality to the arts of design follows naturally, and is in exact harmony with the modern spirit of culture. I desire to treat of this growth of conscientiousness as the quality most characteristic of the art of to-day, — a quality which until now has never made its appearance in the decorative arts, and from which the most happy results may be reasonably anticipated; without which, in fact, these arts will become mere antiquarianism, destitute of soul or inspiration.

Conscientiousness, — this arises from regarding art not as a business, or an amusement, or an accomplishment merely, but as a duty, carrying with it certain moral responsibilities like any other duty. This is a modern idea; it consists in the desire to establish some constant and conscious standard, by the observance of which, in the midst of the enormous and complicated demands made upon the decorative arts in our day, in the midst of the embarrassing accumulation of available and conflicting precedents, in the midst of the new materials, new inventions, new creeds, new manners and customs, constantly presenting themselves, a new art made up of many arts may be formed and kept from anarchy and confusion.

It has been discovered that in every great era of art material has been used according to its natural capacities: by the consistent use of such natural capacities the arts have approached perfection; by their abuse they have inevitably declined. Thus, as regards architecture, in a district which produced granite alone the prevailing style would submit to certain modifications to suit the conditions of the material: the moldings would be few and large, the sculpture broad and simple, depending rather upon outline than upon detail for its effect; in places where the stone was easily worked, the moldings would be more frequent and the carvings more detailed; where the stone was capable of fine finish, there would be a corresponding characteristic of refinement of treatment. Where clay only prevailed, there would arise an architecture distinctively of brick and terra cotta. If the stone of the district was coarse and friable, it would be used in rough walls, covered with a finish of cement or plaster, which in its turn would create a modification of style priding itself upon its smoothness of surface, its decoration by incisions and fine molding and color. Thus, Egyptian art was an art of granite; the mediæval arts of France and England were mostly arts of limestones and sandstones of various qualities; the art of Greece was an art of fine marbles; that of North Italy was an art of baked clay; that of Rome, as her monuments were a part of her political system, and were erected all over the Roman world as invariable types of her dominion, was an art of coarse masonry, in whatever material, covered with molded plaster or with thin veneers of marble. In like manner, forms executed in lead were different from forms executed in forged iron. Forms cast in molds were different from forms wrought with the chisel. Forms suggested by the functions and capacity of wood were quite different from any other.

It is no less true, however, as is well known, that in their origins the Greek styles bore reminiscences of the primitive arts. The granite pylons of Egypt recalled the structures of mud and reeds which preceded them; the temples of Greece remembered the wooden frames of the primeval buildings; and the early Gothic of France received its first decorations from hints in Oriental fabrics displayed by the Venetian merchants in the markets of Limoges. But when these styles reached perfection, the materials and their capacity for legitimate expression had been fully developed in each case: granite no longer resembled mud; marble no longer was fashioned into wooden forms; and limestones and sandstones were decorated, not like stuffs, but in such a manner that from a drawing of an ornament one could almost predicate the quality and grain of the material for which it was designed and in which it was executed.

This quality is called truth of material. There is also truth of construction and truth of color. They all are arrayed against imitations, against producing in one material forms invented for another, against concealment of devices of construction; in short, against sham work of any kind. Thus a certain master lays down this dogma: "A form which admits of no explanation, or which is a mere caprice, cannot be beautiful; and in architecture, certainly, every form which is not inspired by the structure ought therefore to be neglected." [8]

Such doctrines as these have been so often preached in the literature of the times that they have become commonplace. They sufficiently indicate the conscientious tone of public sentiment as regards art, and the designers silently but diligently endeavor to meet the demand for a moral art with all the accepted devices of truthful work. Thus, for example, we have had an era of furniture made according to a dogma of which, for this country, Mr. Eastlake has been fortunate enough to be the prophet;[9] but as the conclusions of the dogma have been too rigid, its requirements too exacting, its illustrations of the principle of truth of material and truth of construction too literal and narrow, its productive power is already exhausted. The designers, failing to produce new effects, retrace their steps and repeat themselves, and finally take refuge in variations and modifications of the style, which are the certain premonitions of transition and change. There are *doctrinaires*, precisionists, *petit maîtres*, formalists, in this conscientious movement in the arts as in every other new intellectual activity; they are ready to push the newly discovered principles to conclusions too absolute and mechanical, and to expose our arts to the danger of a recoil. Thus the "Eastlake furniture," which excludes curved lines on principle; which makes the manner of construction, the joiners' part of it, more important than the designers'; which elevates the mortise and tenon to the dignity of art, must in time, by very reason of its great show of honesty, like any other ostentation of morality, pall upon the senses (Fig. 91). With our inexhaustible inheritance of forms, in which curved lines do appear, in which the idea of the designer is of more importance than the device of the cabinet maker, we cannot remain long content with such pious exclusions.

But with all this, the conscientious spirit once aroused in art is not likely to be put to sleep again until a great work has been done. The designer would not quiet it if he could, for it gives to his work a new significance and power; it enables him to defend it by saying, "This composition of lines or of colors I am satisfied with, not merely because it gives me a sensuous gratification; not merely because it recalls this or that motif in some of the *chefs-d'œuvre* of art; not because it reminds me of certain historic forms rendered precious by traditions and long use; not because it copies nature exactly; but because I know it is right. And why? I have reasoned about it, and can explain it by an appeal to your intellect. It belongs in its place, and accomplishes its object with a directness which could not be reached by mere intuition. It is not a mere matter of taste, concerning which there is no disputing. I cannot do otherwise than I have done and remain true to the conditions of my art. My forms are developed out of the necessities of my problem; they are not chosen because they are beautiful only, but because they are fit. Indeed, they would not be beautiful for my use if they were not fit. I have been taught by experience to distrust my own intuitive fancies and predilections for this or that form, for this or that style; they seduce me from the truth. I have been taught to discipline my resources; to subject them to critical analysis and discussion within my own mind before using them; to lop off what is irrelevant to my theme; to give greater emphasis here; to distract attention there; to harmonize the whole with the especial demands of my subject. I find that these conscientious processes, so far from weakening my fancy, so far from diminishing the interest of my work, in reality make my resources of design more available for my use, and render my compositions far more beautiful than any that I did before I had taught myself to reason. I now know how to be simple; I now know the value of self-denial in art."

Before the latter half of the nineteenth century such language as this would have been impossible, but now it simply illustrates a common thought of the modern designer undertaking to create works of art; it illustrates a growing spirit in all the decorative arts. The distinctive characteristic of the arts of to-day has been, as I have intimated, vacillation among innumerable and incongruous types. It is evident that no one can invent a new set of forms, conceived on new principles, which shall obliterate the memory of all that archæology has given us, and therefore that we shall never create that new style which dreamers and idiots have been so long asking for, but never will find. It is equally evident that our resources of precedent will increase with the progress of time. Where, then, are we to look for a remedy for the increasing embarrassment of our knowledge? What can relieve us from an anarchy of forms on the one hand, or from the ignoble domination of a series of unreasonable and capricious fashions on the other?

It seems logical to infer that as in the sciences the accumulation of knowledge never has been regarded as an affliction, so in art the accumulation of precedents from Greece, Rome, and Byzantium, from Egypt and Syria, from the Orientals and Spanish Moors, from mediæval Christendom, from the masters of the fifteenth century, from the châteaux and palaces of the Renaissance, from the revivals and rehabilitation of all those forms by our many-sided contemporaries, — this abounding wealth should hardly prove an embarrassment to us unless we are unfit to use so precious a heritage.

With this heritage we have tried all sorts of experiments. We have, for example, tried the effect of arbitrary exclusions. The time is not far distant when the world of art was divided into hostile camps, some holding to one set of precedents and regarding all others as misleading and pernicious, the rest considering that safety resided only in the very forms rejected by their competitors, — some for Gothic and some for classic. Twenty years ago two architects could not meet without a quarrel. It was the "battle of the styles." We have tried this in architecture and in the other decorative arts, but have found that under such division we have made no progress. We have also, in turn, tried indifference as to the quality of the precedent, and masqueraded now in one dress and now in another, curious only in the perfection and accuracy of our copying; in other words, we have tried pure archæology, and found that it could not satisfy the cravings of the artist to create.

We are now at last beginning to learn that this great inheritance of forms is in fact the legitimate language of our art, copious, rich, suggestive, sufficient to all our moods; valuable to us not for the sake of its own words and expressions and phrases, but because of its usefulness in enabling us the more fully and elegantly to express our own thoughts and the ideas which belong to our time.

To obtain success in the decorative arts, according to this new light, there must now be added to the qualification of the artist a new and hitherto unknown element, that of research and learning. We are compelled to processes of reasoning in design; we are obliged to have thoughts to express, and, in expressing them, not to misuse an old language, not to confine ourselves to this or that dialect, to the peculiar idioms and tricks of expression in this or that author or set of authors, — much less to invent a new language. We design at last with a conscience. Modern art thus allies itself more closely with humanity than ever; it must appeal not to the senses alone, but to the mind and heart. Indeed, so saturated is it with humanity that we apply to it moral terms: we say that it is sincere or insincere, true or false, self-denying or self-indulgent, proud or debased. Or we speak of it as a thing of the intellect: it is learned or ignorant, profound or superficial, closely-reasoned and logical, or shallow and discursive. Such should be the modern decorative arts, according to the high standard set up by the new culture. In this way, apparently, we are to create an art of the nineteenth century. It is evidently not to continue a mere art of correct revivals, now of this or now of that school, according to an inexplicable fashion. Beneath these superficial excitements there is growing this new sense of responsibility as to the real duties of art.

Thus, in building a modern church, the problem is not satisfied by accommodating a given number of worshipers for a given cost, with due regard for the decent setting forth of given rites in an edifice which is merely an accurate quotation from a given style, a correct reproduction of forms recognized by antiquarians as peculiar to a certain distinctive era of art. It is no longer sufficient that it is good Romanesque or good Gothic of any age or place. This is practical archæology, perhaps, but not architecture. The matter of accommodation, cost, and rites being the same, the question is, first, as to the most available material; then, what forms are best suited to give this material the most honest and elegant expression possible under the circumstances, adapting these forms to the local conditions of fenestration, exit and entrance, aspect and surroundings. The artist seeks not to invent new forms to meet those conditions; they will come soon enough if needed. There is a venerable and inexhaustible language of old forms; there are innumerable traditionary details developed out of the experience of mankind in former ages; there are devices of construction developed into shapes associated with the triumphs and trials of Christianity everywhere. With the fullness of this language he utters his thought completely, having in mind only the fairest and aptest expression of his idea. To these processes there are essential, as we have discovered, not learning and research merely, not inventive skill and genius merely, not poetic feeling and fine sympathies merely, but all these combined, together with the usual technical qualities which must form a necessary part of the equipment of the architect. The result is inevitably a work of art, — not a correct reproduction, but essentially a thing unknown before, a veritable contribution to the pleasure and profit of mankind, a step onward. It is of course dependent upon the genius or skill of the artist whether, in using the old forms of expression, he avoids incongruities; and, while it is not of the least consequence whether he commits anachronisms or not, he must see to it that they are not offensive. He may put Greek and Gothic together if he can, but it is necessary to the perfection of his expression that all the details shall be reconciled one to another and made one whole.

The decorative arts, from the highest to the lowest, are decorative in that they are fitted for a fixed place, and in that place related, in either subordination or command, to the effect of other pieces of art. "All the greatest art in the world," says Ruskin, "is fitted for a place and subordinated to a purpose. There is no existing highest-order art but is decorative. The best sculpture yet produced has been the decoration of a temple front; the best painting, the decoration of a room. Raphael's best doing is merely the wall-coloring of a suite of apartments in the Vatican, and his cartoons were made for tapestries; Correggio's best doing is the decoration of two small church cupolas at Parma; Michael Angelo's, of a ceiling in the Pope's private chapel; Tintoret's, of a ceiling and side wall belonging to a charitable society at Venice; while Titian and Veronese threw out their noblest thoughts not even on the inside, but on the outside of the common brick and plaster walls of Venice." [10] So also with the minor decorative arts. Their essential condition of existence is their subordination to a purpose, and therefore the modern standard requires in their design complicated processes of development, similar, though of course in a less absolute degree, to those by which, as we have seen, the most monumental and important results are to be reached.

In the completion of a room for use by the application of color, of fabrics, and of cabinet-work, it would be easy to prove that a perfect result, or rather a result of perfect fitness, the ideal, is obtained, not by masquerading in a foreign dress, or by adopting a prevailing fashion of forms or tints, or by any arbitrary inclusions or exclusions whatsoever, but by a study of the peculiar needs and uses of the room, its aspect, its shape, and its surroundings; by the discovery of the key of color necessary to the case; by the survey of available precedents for motifs and suggestions of form; by the conscientious and intelligent rejection of every fancy which, however dear to us, however fashionable, however picturesque, or original, or graceful, is not essential to the realization of this ideal. We know of innumerable rooms, decorated in innumerable ways, by innumerable devices, under all degrees and varieties of civilizations, ancient and modern, and according to all conditions of living. These are importunate in suggesting ideas to the modern designer. Without the exercise of the virtue of self-denial he is at the mercy of these thronging fancies, and becomes a mere superficial eclectic. This virtue must be a leading characteristic of the new discipline which we are approaching, both in the greater and lesser arts of decoration. The obvious necessity of exercising it, if we would create works of art, is another proof of the intense self-consciousness which we must inject into our work. We cannot decorate a panel in these modern days in any spirit but that of self-consciousness. If this takes the form of complacency in our own skill or knack, confidence in tricks of color or form which we have picked up, imitations of what has constituted other people's success, we can have no real success of our own. If the self-consciousness is conscientious; if it rejects the temptations of its own genius and knowledge; if it considers first the function of this especial panel, its position and surroundings, treating it according to the natural capacity of the material, — if of metal, adjusting the form of the decoration so that it may be beaten, chiseled, engraved, or cast into shape; if of clay or plaster, so that the form may be developed by modeling; if of wood, so that it may be carved or painted, — and, whether the composition is executed in form or color according to these conditions, if this form or color is kept properly subordinate to the rest of the composition, and is content simply to illustrate or decorate the function of the panel as an essential part of a greater whole, we may hope to create a work of art.

Moreover, how has the human mind in previous conditions of life met similar requirements? Let us take a long, upright panel and consider this point. An Egyptian would have formulated his work according to his religion, and filled his panel with a composition of reeds and lotus flowers, dead with straightness, rigid, precise, hieratic. A Greek would have contented himself with a wild honeysuckle, but would have extracted from it the very essence of beauty, grave, sweet, corrected, and chastened to the last limit of refined expression. A Roman would have chosen the acanthus and the olive, and would have given to them exuberance, vigor, sensuousness, abundance of life and motion, pride, and vainglory. A monastic designer of the twelfth century would have chosen the common leaves and flowers of the wayside, and with worshipful soul and obedient hand would have interpreted nature so that his panel would have been made beautiful with the spirit of the plant. A lay architect of the fourteenth century would have given a consummate image of what such leaves and flowers should be if they had been created for the sake of his panel; their shapes and their motions would have been adjusted to the form of his panel, conventionalized and crowded. A century later, he would have crumpled, twisted, and undercut the leaves with dangerous perfection of craftsmanship, and they would have wandered wanton outside the limits of the panel; strange animals would have been seen chasing one another among the leafage. An architect of the Renaissance would have remembered the Roman work; but the Roman acanthus and olive, under his hands, would have been quickened and refined with new detail, new motion, finer inspiration

121

and invention. They would have received a new impulse of life, a new creation, in the self-conscious spirit of the artist. He would have breathed into them his own personality, so that they would have been, as it were, the signature of his genius. But the art would still have been pagan art; not necessarily exuberant and ostentatious, but subdued to a strict relationship with the borders of the panel, observant of the centre line, illustrated with pedantic conceits of birds, masks, animals, boys, garlands, and pendants. For it was the era of the Renaissance of learning, the era of *concetti* in literature as well as art. The decorator of the Elizabethan era would have frankly left nature, and covered his panel with armorial bearings and grotesque emblazonments, with accessories of strapwork curled and slashed capriciously. The Saracen would have filled it with his arabesque tangles and pious texts. The Japanese, following immemorial traditions of art, perfected by successive generations working loyally, consummate interpreters of natural forms, would have disregarded any considerations of symmetry, and projected into the field of the panel a spray of natural leafage from some accidental point in the boundary, cutting across a background of irregular horizontal or zigzag bars; a quick flight of birds would stretch their wings across the disk of a white moon, or a stork would stand contemplative upon one leg in the midst of his water reeds, with the sacred Fusiami in the distance, barred with its conventional clouds; and yet the composition would be suited to no other shape or size than that of the long panel for which it was composed.

In the presence of all these crowding images, the modern designer stands asking, "Which shall I choose, what shall I reject, and why?" They are all his; they are his rightful inheritance, the legitimate language of his art. He not only has all the beautiful things in nature at his command, but he also knows how they have been used by his predecessors; how they have been interpreted and transformed in the service of humanity; how they have been sanctified by old religions, conventionalized and revitalized according to the knowledge, the inspiration, the needs, the opportunities, the emotions of mankind. They have become an expression of humanity, and thus, as we have said, a language of art.

Mr. Ruskin, in a lecture at the Kensington Museum, asserts, with his usual dogmatic force and confidence, "that no great school of art ever yet existed which had not for primal aim the representation of some natural fact as truly as possible." [11] Accordingly, he directs his disciples to the minute study of leaf and flower, grasses and pebbles, shells and mosses. He tells them to look into the rock for its crystals, and to look up at the sky for its clouds; to draw them all with delicate care, to carve or paint them with absolute fidelity; for by such processes alone can the secret of decorative art be revealed. All this experience doubtless is excellent, and to a degree indispensable. But how this drawing and carving have been done by our predecessors; how they have interpreted nature according to all the moods and emotions of the human soul, and under all the conditions of life; how they have made it a part of the history of mankind, conventionalized it, in fact, for the uses of art, — this is no less important. The artists who practice design and the theorists who dream of it naturally disagree. What! cry the latter, must we go to art when we have infinite nature all around us? When the clover and the daisy grow in the clod beneath our feet; when the sagittaria, with its pointed leaves, the water-cress, and the long reeds wave by the river's brim, and the white lily floats upon its bosom; when the oak leaf and the acorn help to form the shade in which we repose, — must we go afar to learn how these things were carved by forgotten hands upon the capitals and corbels, in the spandrels and panels and friezes, of sacred buildings, six hundred years ago; or to discover in what way they made beautiful the oaken screens and cabinets in the châteaux of the sixteenth century; or how they were beaten and twisted out of ductile iron in the balconies of Venice, or molded, baked, and colored in the potteries of Palissy and of Sèvres; how they were painted upon the fans or cast on the bronze vases of Japan? On the other hand, the artist says, What are we to do with our heritage of forms? Are we to leave them to the antiquaries to label and classify and set up in museums, or are we to abandon them to quacks and pretenders, the spendthrifts of art, to be worn by them as savages wear the costumes of civilization? In any event, they cannot be forgotten. Every day they are made more accessible. The instinct of mankind is to use them, and we must see to it that they are used in a manner consistent with the dignity of art, with far-reaching research, but with self-control, self-denial, and conscience.

Thus there are two great books of reference for the artist: the book of nature and the book of art, that is, the book of the interpretation of nature by mankind. If we could close the latter and forget it, and if nature were our only resource, the best of us would perhaps become pre-Raphaelite, and we would peep and botanize in a manner commendable to this great prophet. Much of a certain class of errors might be obliterated from modern art; but our imagination, untrained, undisciplined, without food of immemorial experience, would run into unreasonable excesses. The opportunity and the desire to ornament would not be less, but the available resources would be infinitely impoverished. Our observation of nature would doubtless become quickened, but the element of conscience in art would be deadened, if not destroyed. The decorator would soon perceive that the natural form could not be sculptured upon his capital, or painted upon his ceiling, or woven in his fabric, or burned into his porcelain, for a thousand obvious reasons, without undergoing some process of transformation. The work of conventionalizing these forms would at once begin; but in the absence of instruction and inspiration from all precedent art it would develop slowly, painfully, with barbarous imperfections and childish crudities. Our art would be a strange mixture: there would be, on the one hand, an absolute fidelity to natural forms, interpreted with the skill which would result from concentration of thought; and on the other, a more prevalent element of barbarous and illiterate invention, covering the surfaces of things with thoughtless repetitions of detail, like an Indian paddle. We would be relieved from our embarrassments of precedent, indeed, but we would suffer from a new and greater embarrassment of poverty. The embarrassments of our wealth we are now learning to correct by cultivating the ennobling qualities of self-denial and conscientiousness. The embarrassments of poverty could only engender an overworking, and consequently a debasement, of the powers of imagination. Man, with an infinity of thought to express, — for no fate but death could stop the activity of the mind, — would have no competent language with which to express it. He could only utter inarticulate cries, like a child.

Therefore, to say that nature is the only fountain of art is incorrect. Ruskin, illustrating this principle, says, "If the designer of furniture, of cups and vases, of dress patterns and the like, exercises himself continually in the imitation of natural form in some leading division of his work, then, holding by this stem of life, he may pass down into all kinds of merely geometrical or formal design with perfect safety and with noble results . . . But once quit hold of this living stem, and set yourself to the designing of ornamentation, either in the ignorant play of your own heartless fancy, as the Indian does, or according to received application of heartless laws, as the modern European does, and there is but one word for you, — death; death of every healthy faculty and of every noble intelligence; incapacity of understanding one great work that man has ever done, or of doing anything that it shall be helpful for him to behold." [12] There is much more of this very beautiful language, but when we get away from the spell of it and return to facts it seems as if we had been listening to a sort of pantheistic hymn. To go to nature for refreshment and inspiration is always wise; but there is refreshment and inspiration also in the works of man. After God had made the green things of earth and all the animals, the creeping and swimming creatures, he made man, and endowed him with faculties to appreciate, enjoy, and command the rest of the creation. The result was that man immediately began a creation of his own, — a creation of the second order. His materials were not chaos and darkness, but light and nature. The result of this secondary creation is art. To us of the nineteenth century, for whom have been preserved most of the productions of this secondary creation, not by dim tradition but by scientific researches above and beneath the ground far and near, accurately collated, analyzed, and published, — to us, richly endowed as none of our predecessors have been (for literature has only discovered the true art of Greece and Syria, of Japan and India, for example, within the last twenty-five years), this secondary creation stands as the image of the primary creation in the human mind; and the human mind, doubtless, is the masterpiece of the supreme creator. By this agency nature has undergone wonderful transformations; and although the water-lily of Egypt, the acanthus and honeysuckle of Attica, the olive and laurel of Rome, the trefoil, the ivy, the oak, of the Christian builders, the inexhaustible flora of later times, and all the animal creation, from man to insects, by the processes of art have taken new shapes, — although they have been often modeled in "the light that never was on sea or land," [13] it is not wise to stigmatize these "old things made new" as the product of heartless laws, and as a conspiracy against nature. There is, in fact, as much nature in the minds which have thus idealized and conventionalized natural forms as there is in the natural forms themselves; and those minds and all the forms of art in which their thoughts have been embodied can no more be neglected by the modern designer than can the primary creation itself.

This is the thought which I would enforce. Our present conditions of life must give to art in all its forms certain distinctive characteristics. These conditions require the establishment of principles, and not forms, as standards of excellent work. They make forms the language and not the end of art; and they inculcate the enlargement and enrichment of this language by the study of nature and of all the antecedent arts, to the end that we may express our thought in art as we would in literature, with an elegance, precision, and completeness commensurate with our larger opportunities and our greater resources. Modern design, especially in architecture, has hitherto concerned itself with the parts of speech, and given us exercises in grammar. Now we are prepared to give to art its true function; to instruct as well as to delight; to appeal to the intellect and heart as well as to the taste; to have larger scope and fuller meaning in all its expressions.

The New Architecture at Albany

(1879)

To the Editor of the American Architect:

Sir, — The provisional occupation of the Court of Appeals Room at the Capitol at Albany, by the State Senate, and the permanent occupation by the Assembly of their magnificent Chamber, on Wednesday, the 8th instant, were preceded on Tuesday evening by a grand reception, at which the new architecture of the great building was for the first time displayed to the public. As the evening was distinctly architectural, rather than social or political, it seems eminently proper to accept the challenge suggested by the occasion, and seriously to discuss this latest, most imposing, and perhaps most significant manifestation of the national progress in art. As a contribution to this discussion, the writer, who was fortunate enough to be present at these opening scenes, ventures to accept your invitation, Mr. Editor, and to give the result of his impressions, with the frankness which befits a theme so interesting and important.

The history of this undertaking is too well known to be again rehearsed, and much of it would not be germane to a purely architectural discussion. It is sufficient to say that two architects of high reputation have, in this building, undertaken the very serious task of completing and correcting a work begun by another professional brother, and carried on by him, at vast expense, to a point which must necessarily commit all subsequent work to the realization in great part of an architectural scheme defective in certain fundamental points. A *résumé* of the report of Messrs. Eidlitz, Richardson, and Olmstead,[1] with respect to the original design, when they were acting as a professional Advisory Board to the Capitol Commission, was published in this journal March 11, 1876, together with reproductions of the first studies of their proposed alterations. The violent contrasts between the original and this modified design, the sudden and phenomenal transition in the latter from the well-defined Renaissance of the two lower orders to the equally well-defined new

Romanesque in the upper orders, and the fundamental change in the character of the skylines (Fig. 103), elicited, it will be remembered, a very formal expression of dissatisfaction from one or more chapters of the Institute, followed by a resolution of the legislature, requiring that the building should be completed in the style in which it had been begun. After Messrs. Eidlitz and Richardson, the professional members of the Advisory Board, had been constituted the architects of the building, and they had assumed the actual responsibilities of construction, their more deliberate studies and their more serious reflections were, it may be supposed, sufficient in themselves, without any extraneous impulses, to cause an essential modification of the most objectionable parts of their original scheme of alteration which was evidently merely a preparatory study (Fig. 103a). The fruits of this sober second thought are very evident in that portion of the exterior which is advanced towards completion, namely, the new north front, which, it may be remembered, according to the original conception, that has not been fundamentally changed in the plan, is composed of two square flanking pavilions, the curtain wall between them being broken by two comparatively slender towers enclosing the main central division of the façade. This curtain wall has been, throughout this front, reduced from the original in height by one story, and the central division between the two towers is now crowned by a vast steep roof, of severe and effective outline, covering the new Assembly Chamber, and broken by well-designed, tall chimney-shafts, the whole recalling the French civic architecture of the fifteenth century, of which the Château of Blois may be considered the type (Fig. 103d). These curtain walls are crowned with balustrades and tall gabled dormers, also conceived with the feeling of early French Renaissance, and certainly well composed. The Romanesque arcade of windows, which in the published design audaciously surmounted the Corinthian order of pilaters below, and arrogantly disregarded its centre lines, is now adjusted to the order upon which it rests in this latter respect, is increased in height, and its Romanesque quality seems to have been modified by certain late Roman characteristics, such perhaps as might have been seen rather in the palace of Diocletian at Spalatro than in that of Frederick Barbarossa at Gelnhausen (Fig. 103c).

The corresponding window in each of the two towers which flank this arcade is still, however, distinctly Romanesque, its jamb shafts being Lombardic or Norman, and the audacious spirit which controlled the first condemned study of alteration has left its trace upon the cornice of the Corinthian order below, which has been very frankly changed in outline to the profile of a vigorous Gothic string-course. If in the portico, which is to project from the lower order of this curtain wall, the architects can manage to carry out a corresponding freedom of design without too boldly challenging the order with which it will be continuous, it will be possible to leaven the mass, and obtain a certain degree of unity in the result. Even as it is, the whole composition up to this point is certainly more interesting by far than if developed in a coldly classic spirit, with no inspiration higher than mechanical correctness. Although such amalgamations as this must needs offend from the technical and academical point of view, they have in them certain elements which must commend themselves to him who has at heart the rehabilitation of architecture, to the end that it may express rather the boldness than the timidity of knowledge. In the presence of this especial experiment the spectator who knows and venerates his orders will be pleased at the general result so long as he allows himself to be led by his first emotions, but when he has time to bring his learning to bear on the subject, and spies out the anachronisms of detail, he will be apt to recoil in astonishment from his first impulse of approval, and say, "Is this indeed the architecture which is promised, or are we to look for another?" Evidently the combination so far is not the result of mere vulgar audacity nor of ignorance, for there is a unity of spirit about it, if not of letter, which could not have been fortuitous. The new ornamentation is bestowed with a spirit of elegant reserve. Above the cornice of the second order appears the decorated belt, which was a feature of the original study of the present architects; the two Romanesque windows in the towers are made especial points of enrichment.

The pediments of the dormers are also embellished with sculpture, and under the cornice of the high central division is a rich shell frieze, the effeminate delicacy of which is judiciously corrected where the same feature occurs on the unfinished north façade (Fig. 103c). This statement comprises, so far as I remember, substantially all the decoration.

Of course, Mr. Richardson, to whom the work on the exterior has been assigned, will know how to make use of the picturesque skylines of the French châteaux on the corner pavilions of this north front, as he has done on its central division over the Assembly Chamber; and with his peaked roofs, high dormers, and lofty chimneys, he will be enabled to create a very effective façade, especially when viewed in the somewhat violent perspective compelled by the comparatively narrow street on which it stands. The same remark is true of the south façade. But Chambord itself will scarcely give us a prevision of the effect of the main east façade when the towering dome is united to the other aspiring features of the composition (Fig. 103b). Mr. Richardson has not signified in what manner this difficult feat of design is to be accomplished. Certainly, the heavy German Romanesque of the dome in the original study of the Advisory Board, before it can in any respect be affiliated with this new work, must undergo a fundamental change (Fig. 103).

The only portions of the interior which are at all complete are the Hall for the Court of Appeals in the first story above the high basement, the great Assembly Chamber occupying the two stories above, one grand staircase giving access to these, a great entrance hall, and various surrounding corridors and offices; all these occupying the main part of the south wing, and comprising apparently less than one quarter of the whole building. For this part of the work Mr. Eidlitz is responsible, and to it he has brought the resources of a trained intellect, great experience and boldness in design and construction, and an inventive power which has already been exhibited in many important works. These qualities have served him well, especially in the lower parts of the building, where the work had been already so far advanced when it fell into his hands that his task was confined to the adjustment and extenuation of existing features. But in the newer parts, where he was less embarrassed, he has given us an example of honest and elegant workmanship, of careful design and profuse invention, which cannot fail to exercise a great influence upon contemporary art in this country, but which, in its present application, exhibits also such a contemptuous disregard for the style to which he was called upon to adapt his ideas that one hardly knows whether to admire him for the boldness of his convictions, or to be amazed at his want of sympathy for what we have been accustomed to regard as the obvious proprieties of design.

His interior is unrelenting Gothic, without any touch of affiliation with the mask of orders which encloses it. It is possible to imagine a mediævalism so adapted even to classic conditions that the line of demarcation would be hard to find, — a reconciled mediævalism and classicism which would impress the beholder with the idea that the learned and accomplished architect of the nineteenth century knows how to use his great inheritance of architectural forms so as to create a harmony even among the most discordant elements of design. But no such harmony is here attempted, and Mr. Eidlitz has allowed himself frankly and openly to make an absolute and sudden change in the fundamental idea of the composition. According to this new dispensation, the lion and the lamb lie not down together. The function of the modern architect among his books is indeed liberty, but it is not license; he should be in the largest sense cosmopolitan, not partisan, in his use of knowledge; this perpetuation of the battle of the styles in a monumental building, which should be a standard of progress, is therefore an ill-timed offence to the spirit of architecture, and implies a presumption of popular ignorance or indifference upon the subject which should not be allowed to pass without notice.

If an architect of the thirteenth century had built a vaulted hall in his own fashion, within the shell of the Roman amphitheatre at Pola, we can imagine that he would have done the very same sort of thing that we see at Albany. But an architect of the nineteenth century in America should be held to a very different account in a similar emergency, for obvious reasons.

Forgetting, however, for the moment this confusion of tongues, we may study Mr. Eidlitz's Gothic with pleasure and profit. It is, as we have said, solid and monumental work which he has given us, thoroughly studied, and, within the arbitrary limitations of the style which he has chosen to set for himself, there is no better or bolder modern composition to be found anywhere, none with more refinement and elaboration of execution, and none with more ingenious and beautiful detail. The great staircase is in two flights, and is a grammatical example of modern Gothic in the English sense (Fig. 103e). It is built in light and dark sandstones around a square well, which is enclosed in an open screen of columns and pointed arches carried up to the highest runs of the stairs, and there stopped. These arches on the ranges are stilted on the lower side in each case, the higher impost being marked on the lower side by the capital of a jamb shaft, which starts from the abacus of the next capital below. The rail is supported by a die elegantly pierced with open Gothic panels repeated in blank on the dado against the wall. The screen, however, considering its functions, seems quite too heavy, and its details are coarse enough for exterior work. It is to be regretted that a constructor so skilful should not have availed himself of the opportunity for a lighter and bolder treatment, and given us perhaps a single ramping or flying arch for each run. The vaulted corridor by which the main entrance to the Court of Appeals is reached is lighted by a glazed arcade, opening on the court, and affords us our first salutation of color, — an ingenious symphony (shall we say) in red patterns upon a gold ground, the naturally varying nature of the gold in different aspects admirably illustrating the different inclinations of the vaulted surfaces, which are further separated at the angles of the vault by small gilded heads, a temperate but very effective enrichment (Fig. 103f). It is to be noted, as a fair example of the intellectual as opposed to the sensuous spirit, which has made its way into the best modern design, that the functions of each member of this simple architectural ordinance are recognized by some difference of treatment. Thus, as regards the walls, the eye is balked of its natural, or perhaps inherited, desire to see certain of the belts of decoration upon the piers continued along the wall surfaces between, so as to bind the whole together. All such lines stop without ceremony at the internal angles, where also the belts of the wall surface experience a sensation of discontinuance; but if the senses are cheated of their birthright in this manner, the intellect, which recognizes that the pier has a different service from the wall-veil, is expected to be moved by an emotion of gentle approval.

The Court of Appeals is a parallellogram in plan, divided by a screen of stone arches, with a flat ceiling arranged in coffers of oak elaborately carved; the room is wainscotted some ten or twelve feet high in the same manner, with richly carved oak, having a wall treatment of red above (Fig. 103g). The light sandstone of construction appears in the window jambs and doorways, and the wainscotting is set flush with it. The color of the oak, with the red walls, makes a beautiful harmony of subdued richness. The carving is very abundant, very beautiful, and very real, and the draperies are large, rich, and ornamental in character. The carpet is crimson. The Gothic element, as a contrast to the classic, offends less here than elsewhere, but one inclined to criticise might object to the elaborate affectation of honesty in the truss-work by which the oak-encased iron girders are to the eye supported at their bearings. In the neighboring office of the Attorney General the corresponding iron girder, which by the bye is in every case a part of the original construction, is frankly gilded, with all its bolts and rough angle irons, and the floor arches which it supports are confessed in the decoration, which is simple and effective, although the portion of the wall surface above the impost line is too nearly equal in width to that between the impost and the dado, and too heavy in color. Perhaps the intellectual sensitiveness of the modern architect would have been better content if, in the case of the oak ceiling of the Court of Appeals, which in reality forms an impervious screen under the floor arches, it had been designed in open-work, to show that it was a screen, and not a piece of construction. The grosser professional sense, however, which loves it knows not why, may well be content with the show as it is.

The testimony of the countless throngs of ladies and gentlemen, on the night of reception, wandering through the solemn Gothic corridors, so monumental both to the eye and to the understanding, and entering these apartments so rich but so serious and comfortable, for all their color, was a testimony of undoubting delight and surprise. And well it might be, for so rare a feast has never been set before them on this side of the water. The greater, therefore, the offence of the wise but cunning Aladdin who rubbed his wonderful lamp with such bewildering effect. If it had indeed been a lamp of truth, these pointed arches, would they not have been changed to round, and these beautiful details, would they not have yielded somewhat of their mediævalism for the sake of the harmony which should prevail in a great monument of architecture?

I propose in another letter to treat of the Assembly Chamber, which of course was the main object of interest.   H. V. B.

II.

To the Editor of the American Architect:

Sir, — In the letter which you printed last week I ventured to give my impressions of the exterior architecture, and the interior decorations and constructions, of the new capitol at Albany. In this letter I propose to devote myself to a description and study of the essential points of the Assembly Chamber.

This room has already achieved a reputation as presenting the most monumental interior in the country; it certainly has the primary advantage of size, without which element no contrivance or skill of the architect can avail to produce an effect of grandeur, although of course it is a very common thing for architectural effort to be so ill bestowed as to diminish the apparent area. In this case the full value of the available space as an element of effect has been retained by the judicious simplicity of the leading features as contrasted with the complication and delicacy of the subordinate parts. Four great polished red granite columns with marble capitals sustain a vast quadripartite vault of stone over the central space; this vault is surrounded by four narrow lateral vaults with four square vaults in the corners, all having their outer bearings upon wall piers, as shown upon the accompanying plan (Fig. 103j). This simple disposition at once fills and satisfies the mind and leaves no essential point to be explained. The square compartments C and D are enclosed upon the floor with open stone screens supporting galleries about two thirds of the way up the height of the shaft; on a level with the capitals of the shafts is a higher gallery, extending across the end of the hall over the lobby G; a disposition of features nearly similar occurs at the other end of the hall, back of the Speaker's desk, so that the longitudinal dimensions of the upper regions are extended to the outer limits of this plan. This arrangement of galleries is very noble and impressive. The screen surfaces beneath them are highly enriched in the spandrels and over the arches with incised diapers, giving to them, with their filling of positive color distributed in small quantities, an effect almost Saracenic in profusion of surface enrichment. The lower galleries are furnished with stone railings pierced with patterns in geometrical Gothic; those of the upper galleries are flamboyant in character and broken around the piers at H and K, thus forming great corbelled capitals (Fig. 103i). The wall-surface B B is in the centre of the north front, while A A opens on the central court. These two wall-surfaces include the two upper orders of the central division of the façades, which I have already described. On each side we have thus two stages of windows, the lower stage showing three great round-arched windows on the main floor level, the upper showing six small divisions of the famous so-called Romanesque arcade, all glazed; two other continuous divisions of the arcade flank this range over the square compartments on either side. Between these two stages is a frieze or belt of panels to be occupied by Mr. Ward's bas-reliefs,[2] and in the tympanum, formed on each side of the hall by the pointed lateral vault impinging against the wall-surface over the archivolts of the arcade, appears Mr. Hunt's decorative painting,[3] too high to be easily seen from the floor, occupying a space too small by comparison to be conspicuous, and too much bedazzled by the windows beneath to assert itself as an indispensable element of the decorative scheme. The conditions of Mr. Hunt's work are seriously complicated also; first, by the large, positive, incised decoration, enforced with black and primary colors, with which many courses of the stone *remplissage* of the vault are embellished, and, second, by the absence of a wall-rib which should prevent these decorative ranges from coming into absolute contact with the edges of the painting (Figs. 104a, 104b). With such unsympathetic surroundings it would seem that the only way by which Mr. Hunt could secure to himself the necessary freedom in his composition, both as regards form and color, was to isolate his pictures, after the fashion of the Venetian and Roman masters of fresco, by a surrounding frame, or to make a conventional background of black or gold against which his subject should be projected. I cannot but think that the manner in which he has carried his picture out to the perilous edges of the spaces at his disposal, and his preference for the natural rather than for the conventional treatment of his subjects, are, under the circumstances, not justified by the results. No artist, however subtle, could secure in such a place the preëminence which is due to a work of higher art unless he frankly started with the determination to vanquish these surroundings by a *tour de force*, and create rather a pictorial decoration than a decorative picture. The decision and firmness of the conventional forms by which the neighboring vaulting surfaces are enriched, the general character of the architectural features by which these tympana are beset, and the blaze of light which penetrates the arcade beneath them, all these appear to demand of the artist not so much measures of compromise, as measures of absolute conquest. Mr. Hunt's vigor of drawing and boldness of color have hardly proved sufficient to this task. There are, however, vacant wall-surfaces under the vaults at the ends of the hall, far better lighted, which offer a much better field for such work as Mr. Hunt has given, and which we understand he will be invited to occupy. But the immediate results are unimportant as compared with the fact that an attempt is here made on a great scale to give to Architecture and to Painting their proper relations in respect to each other. No one interested in the progress of better art can be indifferent to a beginning so noble in its intentions and so fruitful in its promise.

There are several vital points of design with respect to this magnificent ceiling which the careful critic cannot fail to notice. Mr. Eidlitz, true to his *parti pris*, exhibits in this part of the work his characteristic indifference, even to those external conditions of the façade which he might himself have controlled and adapted to his interior if he had so chosen. His vaulting at the wall-piers A A and B B starts below the level of the upper arcade of windows, which was designed and executed under the present administration of the work, and *cuts across* those openings of the arcade which adjoin the piers in a manner which in France would be called brutal, but which we should prefer to characterize as audacious and defiant. Moreover, one looks in vain for an abutment to the thrusts of these vaults at the points named; there is no such appliance to be seen within or without, nor is the honesty of the Italian builders imitated by any visible tie at the springing line. But even this magician cannot conjure up a vault which will hold itself, and we must seek in the dark recesses above the vaulting for the hidden contrivances of iron which must bind the construction together.

All this work is Gothic, and Gothic which is at the same time vigorous and delicate. The lower parts of the wall-surfaces are profusely decorated with countersunk arabesque, defining the masonry of the wall, and filled in with strong color, well contrived to unite with the stone and relieve it from coldness and monotony. The scale of the corresponding decorations in the filling-in of the vaulting surfaces is so much larger than that of the diapers below, and occupies so much more of the space, that the effect of masonry, at the point where it is most desirable to show the solidity and reality of the work, is in part lost. The vaulting is so noble that to treat it thus seems almost like a painful excess, and it has certainly, as I have intimated, increased the difficulty of an artistic treatment of the wall-surfaces. The furniture is in all cases carefully designed and of course very richly decorated, and the drapery of the lower windows is sumptuous in fabric and large and noble in detail. The chimney-pieces under the square galleries and in the neighboring offices are of sculptured stone, and in some cases very elegant; but they seem in scale somewhat too domestic and hardly adequate in size of opening (Fig. 103h). The obvious difficulty of arranging the screen-work under the square galleries, so that it may adjust itself against the four great, round shafts, is frankly acknowledged, but the solution here attempted is not in all respects satisfactory. In

133

short, in the innumerable details of an architecture so vast and complicated as this, a critic might find a boundless field for objections more or less petty if he chose to hunt for them. Yet, setting aside, for the moment, my objections to Mr. Eidlitz's contemptuous indifference for the casket in which his jewel is enshrined, I am prepared to believe that there is no modern work recalling the mediæval spirit of design, conceived with greater intelligence and learning or executed in a manner more thorough and, on the whole, sincere.

Mr. Richardson will, it is to be hoped, remember his academic training in the schools of Paris, and respect the exterior enough to continue at least the sentiment of it into the portion of the interior assigned to him. But as to the qualities of design and workmanship, he will find in the parts already done within the north wing a competition of the most stimulating kind.

H. V. B.

The New Dispensation of Monumental Art

The Decoration of Trinity Church in Boston, and of the New Assembly Chamber at Albany

(1879)

The industrious Signor Brumidi[1] at Washington has grown gray in the service of art while covering the walls of the National Capitol with Italian decorations, carried to a point of manual perfection which leaves nothing to be desired as regards technical qualities, but which has proved itself absolutely barren of results (Figs. 105, 105a). The art of the country is no better for it, and possibly no worse. When we are told that the aged artist is now crowning his long labors by painting upon the frieze or belt which encircles the rotunda, under the dome, the history of American civilization, in an imitation of bas-relief so admirable as to deceive even the elect, we can comprehend the mechanical spirit which underlies his work; we can understand why the excellent conventionalities which occupy the walls and vaults of the corridors and committee-rooms, — here in one style, there in another, and all correctly set forth, — have not served as fruitful examples of high inspiration. They were born of a cold artisan spirit, which has not in it any principle of life. Each example of strong, original artistic convictions in history has given direction more or less sensibly to the currents of contemporary art. But such work as this is not inspired by such convictions; it has therefore furnished to the art of mural decoration in this country no impulse and kindled no enthusiasms.

Our opportunities for heroic work in this department of art have been frequent enough, but few intelligent efforts have been made to improve them until within the last two years, when Mr. John La Farge, at Trinity Church in Boston, and Mr. William Hunt, in the Assembly Chamber of the State Capitol of New York, have for the first time given to the country examples which may prove to be the seed planted upon good ground. It is a duty of civilization to subject such examples as these to serious critical examination. The results of good examples of mural decoration are so beautiful and so profuse, and bad examples, if they are inspired with any strength of enthusiasm, are so fruitful in errors, that to suffer them to fructify in either direction without a word of thoughtful praise or blame would be the loss of a golden opportunity. Indifference is a quality of barbarism.

We propose, therefore, to study these examples of mural decoration candidly, to the end that we may awaken a spirit of inquiry, that we may know in what direction they are apt to lead us, and that we may be duly forewarned if they have in them any element of danger.

The architecture of Trinity Church is particularly hospitable to high decorations in color, because it affords large interior surfaces, and because its features of construction, unlike the conventional Gothic of the churches, do not make too large a demand upon the decorative scheme (Figs. 101a, 101b). When the architect was permitted to call Mr. La Farge to his assistance in completing this work, the latter found at his disposal, in the first place, ample dimensions and broad, suggestive spaces; and, in the second, he had the intelligent sympathy of those for whom and with whom he worked. He undertook, however, a heroic task, with limitations of time and means, — such perhaps as no painter of monumental art had ever subjected himself to in previous works. He brought to this labor a genuine artist's spirit, strong in its convictions and brave in its hopes, but unused either to the study or to the production of architectural effects.

Let us now consider the architectural conditions of his work; for without a thorough comprehension of the theme as affected by the spirit of the place, we can arrive at no just conclusion regarding the result. The church is cruciform, nave, transepts, and chancel being each about fifty feet wide within the walls, and the interior dimensions being about one hundred and forty feet in extreme length and one hundred and fifteen feet in extreme width. The interior height is somewhat more than sixty feet. The tower which arises over the crossing of the nave and transepts is nearly fifty feet square within, and its ceiling, which is open to view from the interior, is one hundred feet from the floor. The ceilings of the auditorium are of light furrings and plaster in the form of a continuous barrel vault of trefoil section, abutting against the great arches of the crossing, which are furred down to a similar shape, with wooden tie-beams encasing iron rods carried across on a level with the cusp of the arches. The four great granite piers which sustain the weight of the tower are encased with furring and plastering, finished in the shape of grouped shafts with grouped capitals and bases. The whole apparent interior is thus, contrary to the convictions of the modern architectural moralist, a mask of the construction. We do not propose here to enter upon the question as to whether or to what extent the architect was justified in thus frankly denying his responsibility to the ethics of design as practiced and expounded by the greatest masters, ancient and modern; it suffices for our immediate purpose to note that the material of actual construction being nowhere visible in the interior, to afford a key of color to the decorator, or to affect his designs in any way, he had before him a field peculiarly unembarrassed by conditions.

The exterior architecture of the church is a very vigorous and masculine form of round-arched Romanesque, affected by traditions from Auvergne and

Salamanca, and with a good deal of later mediæval detail, the whole well amalgamated and a proper work for an architect of the nineteenth century (Fig. 101). Thus, even in respect to style, the painter had no reason to yield anything of his freedom to archæological conventions; he was left at liberty to follow the same spirit of intelligent eclecticism which had guided the architect.

The tone of the interior, as regards color, being thus left open to some arbitrary solution, the desire of the architect for a red effect was accepted as a starting-point, and this color was adopted for the walls throughout, its quality being solemn and neutral. Either in fact, or by effect of light, or by variation of surface, this color submits to variations in tone, so that it really has different values in different parts of the church; and thus, in the very beginning, we seem to be spared the homely virtue of mechanical correctness and equality of workmanship. The vaulted surfaces of the ceiling are divided into narrow cross-sections by small moldings of black walnut or black walnut color, and these sections very properly receive the complementary color of red, namely, a greenish blue, with the value of bottle green. These sections or strips are cut up by transverse lines into quarries or squares, each of which is occupied with a form or device of conventional character, appealing rather to the imagination than to the intellect, rather to the material than to the moral sense. There are perhaps a dozen of these devices, some of them apparently cabalistic or vaguely mysterious in character, distributed among the quarries with a certain Oriental irregularity, and carefully avoiding geometrical recurrences. These forms are in various shades of olive, brown, and buff, here and there accentuated capriciously with gold. Out of this complication results a very rich, quiet, and original effect, — an effect cunningly conceived and artfully executed, but legitimate and worthy of study by all decorators who know not how to be sober without being wearisome. It is really surprising to see with how many elements of color and form this serious result is achieved. It indicates a very intelligent study of Oriental methods. The same colors are used in the decoration of the four arches of the tower, so that their important representative function of support is not defined and recognized with that force and dignity which the circumstances require; but the four great grouped piers at the angles of the intersection of nave, transepts, and chancel have received a treatment in dark bronze-green, — very broad and simple, with gilded capitals and bases, — an arrangement remarkable alike for its reserve and its strength, and for its harmony with the prevailing tones around. The cornice which forms the important line of demarcation between the dull red of the walls and the dark green of the ceiling is weak and insufficient, and it encounters the moldings of the capitals of the great piers in a manner which would be called artless and innocent if this were the work of an architect of the twelfth century, but which under the present circumstances must be considered careless or defiant. As regards color, which might have been so bestowed as to condone these faults of weakness and insufficiency in the cornice, it rather enhances them by emphasizing and separating its unfortunate details.

The decoration of the walls of the nave, so far as it has been developed, is conceived in an independent and original spirit, with the result of a very rich surface effect. It is mostly confined to the clere-story wall over the aisle arches, and is composed of a belt under the cornice and on a line with the impost of the windows, with painted pilasters of various device between the windows, inclosing spaces which in two cases are occupied by pictorial subjects, and in others by an enrichment of diapers. The architectural *motifs* of this decoration are Italian in character, very freely treated, and the belts and pilasters are embellished with Raphaelesque scrolls and foliage, conventionalized in the Italian manner, with variations of green and rose colors. Portions of the backgrounds behind the pilasters are treated with patterns and colors borrowed from Oriental carpets. The amount of design lavished upon the detail of this part of the work, the absence of repetitions and stencil-work, the disregard of the non-essentials of symmetry, the multiplicity of parts, with the general effect, however, of sober richness and repose, — all these characteristics combine to render this work a remarkable departure from the perfunctory and more or less mechanical styles of surface enrichment to which we have been accustomed. The very imperfections of execution and design, — such, especially, as are shown in a want of decision in the treatment of the architectural motifs employed, — and the numerous offenses against the conventionalities of decoration, give to these walls a certain charm of individuality, for the prime result of a harmonious and jeweled enrichment of color is obtained, and the quality of this harmony of color is just such as could have been obtained by no mechanical methods. As compared with the best sort of modern conventional surface decoration, with its accuracy of craftsmanship and its precision of method, this is remarkable for the evidence it contains not only of the personality of the artist, as exhibited in his manner of thought and study, but of his characteristics of manipulation, such as never could have been delegated to artisans or handicraftsmen, however skilled and sympathetic, unless under his immediate supervision.

The two pictorial subjects — one our Saviour and the Woman of Samaria at the Well, and the other our Saviour with Mary Magdalene (Fig. 102), — are treated in an academical manner, with great solemnity of feeling in line and color, and with all the restraint and reserve which comes of respect for consecrated types. In this regard they exhibit a curious contrast to the *naïveté* and independence of precedent exhibited in their more conventional surroundings. These compositions have light, shade, shadows, and perspective, and as such are an offense to the higher æsthetics which do not recognize as correct any wall decorations which are not flat. But the purist could hardly find it in his heart to blame a fault which is condoned by the fact that there is no distance to the pictures, the figures being defined against a screen surface or wall in each case, — by the fact that they make no marked spot on the wall, and that they form an integral and not an exceptional part of the general scheme of color.

The details of the decorations in the tower, which, as we have said, is open from the area of the auditorium to the height of one hundred feet, where it has a flat, green ceiling divided into caissons or panels by crossing beams, are on a much larger scale, as is befitting their greater distance from the eye. There are three round-arched windows in each wall of this tower resting upon a molded string-course, perhaps ten feet above the crowns of the four supporting arches. It is thus, as it were, a box filled with light. It is pervaded by the dull red tone of the walls, and upon this background has been placed a profuse enrichment, which in line and color borrows much from the works of the pupils of Raphael, belts and panels being disposed according to the architectural opportunities very much as they would have disposed them (Fig. 102b). But in parts, notably above the crown of the great arches, there is a certain boldness of contradiction between the lines of the square panels and those of the archivolt which recalls the decorative methods of the Japanese. But if there are parts which remind one of the work of Giotto at Assisi, of the altar screens of Fra Angelico, of the Stanze of the Vatican, or the panels of the Villa Madama, there is still more which could have been thought and done only by a scholarly painter of the nineteenth century. Much of the detail is invisible from below, especially the studied Raphaelesques in the tympana of the tower windows; but one can see that the panels in the corner piers of the window-stage are filled with the emblematical creatures of the evangelists, — the lion of St. Mark, the eagle of St. John, and so on, ramping or perching upon curious conventional frets, scrolls, or diapers; and one can read written upon the belt of gold under the windows the solemn inscription: "Blessing, and Honour, and Glory, and Power, be unto Him that sitteth upon the Throne, and unto the Lamb forever and ever." The archivolt of the great arches is also marked by a broad golden belt, and the spandrels between are occupied in the upper parts by adoring angels leaning out of square windows, as it were, and by gigantic figures of apostles and prophets (Fig. 102c). The arrangement, as a whole, is not according to any old master exactly, as we have said; still less does it imitate any pagan or Oriental manner. But it has absorbed enough of all pertinent precedent to create an effect which belongs to the times in which we live. The red *fond* is never quite obliterated, and against it is projected a system of decoration which, though complex in motive and abounding in various color, is harmonious in general result.

The six great figures of prophets and apostles, although conceived with learning and with a marked degree of religious feeling, although suggesting a certain grandeur of sentiment, such as one who knows the prophets and sibyls on the pendentives of the Sixtine Chapel must needs have in mind when undertaking any similar scheme, are wanting in vigor and correctness of drawing (Fig. 102a). Their outlines are hesitating and indecisive, the hands are badly drawn, there is no human structure under the robes, they have no clearness or freshness of color, and in execution they seem crude and hasty; but they are by no means conventional or commonplace, as works much more correct than these might well be, and as decorative accessories they are large, bold, and effective. They are in harmony with the general scheme of color, and they add to the total effect a human interest of the very highest kind. But technically they furnish another and a very significant instance of the timidity and irresolution which the learned and conscientious artist of modern days is apt to exhibit in the presence of the august ideals which, by careful study, he has compacted out of the achievements of all the old masters. The execution lags far behind the intent. But better the serious aspiration and noble thought, though imperfectly set forth, than the dull perfection of the disciplined hand, otherwise uninformed and uninspired. "What we are all attempting to do with great labor," said Sir Joshua Reynolds, "Velasquez does *at once.*" [2] This remark is pregnant with suggestions of the inadequacy of modern art, under its common conditions, when called upon to do really great work. It explains not only the indirectness and indecision of the productions of the most thoughtful modern artists, but also the state of incompleteness in which they are compelled to leave much of their most ambitious work. Their process of composition, especially in work conceived upon a heroic scale, seems to be challenged at every step by a spirit out of the past. They are deprived of the virtue of simplicity, and the joy of their initiative is tempered with doubts.

As to the significance and interest of this remarkable example of interior decoration as a whole, there cannot be a moment's question. When the vacant red fields in the transept walls have been completed like the nave (Fig. 102d), when the empty hemicycle of the apse has been filled with its processional glories, and the whole interior thus brought to a condition of unity, it will be found that the experiment of bringing to bear upon our public monuments a higher form of art, such as that which made illustrious the Italian walls in the sixteenth century, is fully justified. But even in its present state of incompleteness, even as a record of curious tentative processes, more or less successful, in the art of decorating wall spaces, this effort, like every other bit of true art, is a point of departure for a new series of developments. It has in it a principle of life capable of indefinite expansion. It breaks away from traditions of mere craftsmanship, and opens a new field for the artist of learning, experience, and poetic feeling. It shows to what noble uses he may put the resources of his memory and invention. It encourages the study of great examples. It suggests, moreover, how the decoration of the simpler wall surfaces in domestic work may be rescued from the hands of the mechanical painter, and how, by a judicious bestowal of thought upon details, a more subtle adjustment of colors, a more intelligent recognition of its capacities, it may be developed into a work of art.

The work of Mr. William Hunt at Albany is conceived upon a very different scale, and is adjusted to architectural conditions far less fortunate. We have observed that Mr. La Farge's work at Boston was especially free from embarrassments or conventional limitations. The whole scheme of color in the interior was at his command; the place and the opportunity were in every way favorable to the greatest liberty of design in color and form; and this liberty, as we have seen, notwithstanding the artistic and perhaps constitutional timidity or reserve of which we have spoken, and notwithstanding his abridged conditions of time and means, he has used with great discretion and religious

140

respect, — qualities which were not violated when he was bold enough to mingle so much of Orientalism, so much that was at least not ecclesiastical, in the very substance and fibre of his work.

The Assembly Chamber at Albany is a monumental hall of vast proportions, walled and vaulted with yellowish stone, very bold in its general design, and charged with a great abundance of incised decoration colored with red, blue, black, and gold. This decoration, though uninteresting in detail, is rich, and indeed almost Moorish, in general effect. The constructive features are Gothic, the carving is conventional and coarse, but the whole design is carried out with great boldness and intelligence, and the whole result is bright, large, noble, and, though wanting in sentiment of detail, is eminently fitting for a great civic hall. Two opposite walls of this chamber are occupied by round-arched windows in two stages, the lower stage having three openings, and the upper being a continuous arcade of six openings. Between the arches of this arcade and the broad, pointed ceiling vault which abuts against the wall above is a triangular space or tympanum forty feet wide and perhaps half as high, and, we should suppose, about forty feet from the floor of the chamber (Fig. 103i). In this high space, on either side of the hall, Mr. Hunt has painted two decorative and pictorial compositions, — the most important of the kind yet executed in this country. We propose to consider these pictures from a purely decorative point of view, not as independent easel pictures, but as monumental accessories to a great architectural composition.

When the artist undertook this important work, the conditions of *entourage* had already been fixed. The style of the work was uncompromising Gothic; the lower boundary of each tympanum was an arcade of bright windows; the upper boundary was the outline of the great inclosing vaulting arch. This vaulting surface was decorated with a series of ornamental belts with sunk patterns of coarse design enforced with the crude colors of which we have spoken. These belts abutted against the field of the proposed picture at right angles, and there was no vaulting rib or molding to mark the line between the wall and ceiling. To meet these conditions of light and color, Mr. Hunt was compelled to paint his pictures on a very high key, and to give to his outlines an accent of exceptional vigor. We cannot but think, however, that he was deceived as to the amount of light which these surfaces would receive from the opposite windows, and that the mass of the staging upon which he painted made a twilight to which he adapted his work; for the broad light of the morning betrays a coarseness of outline and color which is veiled in the waning light of the afternoon, when apparently the pictures are in their most favorable aspect. But even then there is a fatal rawness in the decorative effect, which is readily accounted for by the absence of a distinct line of demarcation, or frame, to separate the aerial spaces of his compositions from the hard colored lines of the belts in the vaulting, which attack the very edges of his clouds. The pictorial character of the designs is another reason for their isolation by some such device from this unsympathetic neighborhood. The greatest masters of decoration fully understood this principle, and always used an inclosing frame wherever their work ceased to be continuous. The loggie of the Farnesina and the Vatican, the ceiling of the gallery of Apollo at Paris, of the council chamber at Venice, of the Sixtine Chapel at Rome, and innumerable other examples, clearly prove that the masters were not content with a mere angle as a boundary for the separate compositions of which their decorations were composed. The only example of high art which we can recall in which this principle has not been observed is that of the Last Judgment of Michael Angelo, which occupies the whole end of the chapel; and the failure of this great work *as a decoration* is to be attributed almost entirely to the rawness of its boundary lines. But in Roman work, as at Pompeii, in Romanesque work, as at Byzantium and St. Mark's, and in the art of the early Christian painters, the same effect of isolation is obtained by placing the composition upon a background of gold, or of flat conventional color, sufficiently contrasting with the surrounding colors to establish a separate area.

"Artistic races," says Eugène Véron, "have regarded monumental painting as illuminated and but slightly modeled drawing; when it gives us good design wedded to harmonious colors, it has done all that we should expect." "In the decorative painting both of ancient times and of the Middle Ages," he elsewhere observes, "the greatest care was taken to avoid everything which seemed to be an attempt at impossible illusion." [3] This principle was observed up to the time of the magnificent apostasy of Michael Angelo, who admitted into his wall decorations effects of perspective and realism of treatment. These great examples have seduced nearly all subsequent art from a fair recognition of the flat surfaces which it occupies, and have tempted it to feats of illusion which are not in harmony with the principles of decorative as opposed to pictorial design. The mediæval setting of Mr. Hunt's compositions, instinctively suggesting the flat treatment which the mediæval decorators invariably used, and the shape and position of the tympana which they occupy, seem to render their free pictorial treatment even more incongruous. The conditions not only suggest a return to antique and mediæval principles, which require illuminated and but slightly modeled drawing, such indeed as Mr. Hunt has very properly confined himself to in this work, but compositions of figures grouped with a certain regard to formal symmetry, even to the extent of a central figure or mass with supporters. The emergency is one of architecture, which is better suited by a treatment of conventionalities than by one of romantic illusion in color, modeling, and movement. We do not mean to say that such pictorial illusion as Mr. Hunt has attempted is absolutely inadmissible; that there are not unoccupied surfaces still left in this chamber which are less architectural, that is, less beset by structural conditions, and less inaccessible to the eye, and which therefore would be much more hospitable to compositions of this kind.

We have hitherto discussed these compositions purely in their function as architectural decorations, for such in their highest artistic uses they should be. We cannot but consider that the opportunity has been misunderstood in a fundamental point, and that work of a far lower grade than that of Mr. Hunt would have better served the purpose. With all his strength of will, with all

his skill in the adaptation of his tones, and all his fiery determination of drawing, he has been unable to conquer a right to fill such spaces with such work.
It is a waste of great resources.

The consideration of these works of art simply as pictures calls into play a
different set of critical faculties from those required in the consideration of
them as decorations. The artist has symbolized the simultaneous occurrence of
the revival of letters and the discovery of America by the allegories of the
Flight of Night and the Discoverer (Figs. 104a, 104b). The former has in its
elements long been familiar to those who frequented Mr. Hunt's studio (Fig.
104). It is in fact a flying cloud, the substance and movement of which is
figured by the suggestion of an aerial chariot drawn by three plunging steeds,
to the mane of one of which clings a torch-bearing groom, rather guiding than
restraining the downward flight. High upon the cloudy seat sits a female
figure, directing the vision with a gesture of her hand; and below, enveloped
in a shadowy fold of fleecy drapery, dimly portrayed, is a sleeping woman with
a child, and over her hovers a little protecting spirit. The visionary character
of the composition is unencumbered by any material appliance; there are no
reins, no harness, no chariot, no wheels. It is a precipitous movement of vapor
poetically set forth with a superb flight of horses, and enough of human interest in the figure to suggest a meaning which each can interpret in his own way.
It is a very fine point in the sentiment of the picture that the allegory is not
forced upon the spectator by the insistence of vulgar accessories. The horses
are drawn with magnificent spirit and with the confidence and *élan* of a
master. The human figures are little more than suggestive; they are fleeting
visions, — a part of a cloudy pageant. When illuminated by bright sunlight,
or by the artificial lighting of the chamber at night, the vigorous mechanism
of outline and color which are contrived to produce an effect are somewhat
unpleasantly betrayed. In the half-light of the afternoon, as we have said, the
very qualities which are crudities at other times contribute to make up a pictorial harmony of the most effective and poetic kind. The same may be said
with even greater force of the Discoverer. A Hamlet-like man, in armor and
cloak, stands conspicuous in a boat, riding half disclosed upon a billowy swell
of the ocean. Behind him, at the helm and holding a bellying sail of drapery,
stands a winged female figure in an attitude of dignity somewhat like that
suggested by the Venus of Milo; and upon the prow, with her outlines defined
against a bright rift in the western sky, leans a spirit of the water, with a frank,
onward look and a gesture significant of confident hope. This figure seems to
us the best in the group; it is beautifully drawn, and plays a happy part in the
composition. Two other female figures float upon the waves. We have thus
Fortune at the helm and Hope at the prow. The guide-books shall interpret
the rest of the allegory, which, to us, as compared with that portrayed on the
opposite wall, is wanting in significance, and made up of too many elements
and of too much of materialism to leave upon the mind a concrete poetic image. The composition is wanting in simplicity, and the effect of the whole depends upon a momentary incident; the next instant of time beyond that de-

picted, the next wash of the uncertain billows, will evidently throw the whole group into confusion. This impending catastrophe seems in some way to detract from the dignity of the allegory. The masters of the Renaissance, when they chose a sea-pomp for their subjects, such as the Triumph of Galatea, the Rape of Europa, and the Venus Anadyomene, managed to spare us from doubts of this kind by a more multitudinous grouping of figures capable of falling into new combinations without loss of harmony. But Mr. Hunt's allegory is disjointed, and appears to need some harmonizing element to give us that feeling of security which accompanies the floating and flying groups of Guido, Rubens, and Annibale Caracci. The idea of the Flight of Night is in this respect admirable; in a moment the cloudy vision will have departed, leaving a serene sky, and space for all the succeeding pageants of civilization.

These remarks are made with a constant reservation of confidence that the vigor and truth of this master's artistic convictions and his practiced hand and eye will bear him on with safety into regions of "high emprise;" that in qualities of technique, even in this last essay, there are few modern painters who can surpass him. He has proved his capacity for great achievement in far wider fields than those bounded by the gold frame of an easel picture. The confident boldness and enthusiasm with which he has entered into those fields, and the masculine breadth of comprehension which he has exhibited there, are an admirable forecast of still greater triumphs. We sincerely trust that his genius may have better scope in his next trial, and may not again be condemned to a "pent-up Utica" [4] under a high vault, with a blaze of windows beneath and a semi-barbarous pomp of crude color above, — a place which should only be treated with an artifice of conventionalities too strict in their limitations for the endurance and self-denial of a spirit so bold and a hand so free.

144

Eidlitz's Nature of Art [1]

(1881)

The Nature and Function of Art, more especially of Architecture. By Leopold Eidlitz. New York: A. C. Armstrong & Son. 1881.

"At the present time," says Mr. Eidlitz, "it becomes a serious question whether the rapid progress of thought, and the more general acceptability of new ideas, does not demand a philosophic development of art expression of ideas which will keep pace with general progress, in order to afford to the masses that instruction which can by them be derived only from works of fine art." [2]

With this proposition in view, Mr. Eidlitz has been bold enough to enter upon the difficult field of æsthetics, and to survey the relations between art and modern civilization not merely as a speculator, but as a reformer. The five hundred pages of his book bear witness to his own consciousness of the serious nature of his task, and he has brought to it a vigorous and uncompromising spirit and the courage of strong convictions. His argument is that art should resume its ancient functions as an instructor of the people, and, to this end, that it should lay aside its accumulated wealth of traditions, should virtually cease to be scholarly, and start from a basis of pure reason. He follows in the main the lines laid down by the greatest writer of the century on the theory of architecture, M. Viollet-le-Duc, and he accepts without hesitation and with all their consequences the purist dogmas of Pugin, Ruskin, and the other modern literary reformers of art, so far as they rest upon the practice of developing forms of art out of structural necessities, as in mediæval monuments. But he does not fail, on occasion, to differ rigorously even from those in his own camp. He exalts the function of art as a practical method of ennobling life and of educating the masses through their emotions, not only in painting, sculpture, and architecture, but in dress, manners, ceremonies, and rituals. He candidly declares that in this service taste is a blind and dangerous guide; that archæology misleads; that the artistic instinct or feeling is to be distrusted, and that enthusiasm is seriously detrimental in the pursuit of fine arts; moreover, that the expression and embodiment of ideas in matter, through certain conscientious and intellectual processes of analysis and development, constitute the sort of art which alone is fitted to instruct mankind and to adorn the civilization of the nineteenth century.

The true interest of this volume, however, arises not from its essays in the domain of pure æsthetics, but from the fact that its author, not a mere bookman and theorist, but an architect of established repute, held in high esteem by the profession and entrusted with important work, desires to look beneath the specious and prosperous surface of things, and, with a mind sharpened by professional observation and practice, to dig deep among the roots of art. This spirit of investigation is in full accord with the genius of our time, and, whatever heresies may thereby be evolved, however our convictions or prejudices may be assailed by new and uncompromising deductions of philosophy, there is health in the attempt to get at the truth, if only it compels architects — as this work assuredly must, if they will read it — to a serious work of self-examination.

The portions of the book by which their interest would be most naturally attracted are such as deal with architecture pure and simple, with monuments, form and construction, proportion, style, analysis, criticism, and professional education. These constitute two-thirds of the volume, and bear the marks, always interesting, of a mind practised in habits of design; but they are overweighted by the ponderous logic of the other third, dealing with definitions of art, beauty, ideas, and the ideal — speculative themes, which, however ingeniously discussed, disturb the balance of the work, and distract the mind from that part of it which is the natural and proper function of the author. If these incongruous portions could be eliminated, and if the essential part of the text could be purged of its unnecessary involutions, and of its tendency to abstract speculation, which perplex the student and often make the argument too transcendental in thought and statement for the service of practical and busy men, the work would doubtless have its due effect on a profession which, whatever may be said to the contrary, we believe to be at this moment eager to be guided by convictions instead of prejudices.

Mr. Eidlitz's attitude toward his brethren in the craft is by no means conciliatory. He follows the prevailing fashion among theorists and doctrinaires, and has no extenuation to offer for the condition into which modern architecture has been brought by their efforts. He arraigns them because they are led by taste, which is shallow, and fashion, which is superficial; because they have constituted themselves the conservators of barren traditions which have no essential relationships with modern necessities and modern methods of construction; because they suffer the engineer to lead them in progress, and are willing to embarrass themselves with the guardianship of antiquated formulas. He is never weary of accusing the classic orders of being a fruitful source of architectural corruption, and he even speaks disrespectfully of "the poor Co-

146

rinthian capital." [3] But when the profession, thus betrayed by one of its own members, and asked to surrender its inheritance of beautiful things, looks into these pages for a compensation, it finds a bare philosophic dogma — viz., a work of architecture is the expression of an idea through the just modelling of construction; it is a thought expressed in matter by logical development; and so on. Although this proposition has an ascetic tinge, which at first may repel the student, he will probably find that essentially it is a truth which lies at the basis of constructive expression in architecture as he is accustomed to regard it, and that the substance of it has been taught him in the schools. Indeed, any conscientious practitioner of architecture is ready to explain, when any one asks, why it is that he has chosen a formula of pilasters and entablature, or of buttress and arch, to express the nature and quality of his structure; why it is that he has concealed his iron and wooden construction with an uninflammable envelope, and why he has used or failed to use pinnacles, balustrades, or any other feature of utility or decoration. You will often find him a reasonable creature, and his works upon the street, whether expressed in terms of Gothic or Renaissance, not infrequently capable of logical defence. But Mr. Ruskin, Mr. Pugin, Mr. Eidlitz, and a score of literary amateurs besides, assure the modern architect that there is no health in him unless he turn his back upon all the other architectural expressions of history, and, by following the logical methods of the mediæval cathedrals, develop in his work "an idea in matter." None of these earnest thinkers have undertaken to enforce this doctrine of exclusion and of philosophic design by the only method which can be appreciated by the architect and bear fruit — viz., by graphic statements illustrating to the eye their processes of composition. The essays of the brilliant Viollet-le-Duc in this direction are of exceeding interest to the architect, are very brave and ingenious and marvellously presented, but they have proved to be impracticable, and they have had no appreciable influence upon the practice of architecture. If Mr. Eidlitz should set forth his own logical processes in the same manner, he would commend his theories to the profession he addresses, and perhaps clearly illustrate that the development of construction is the only safe guide to architectural design; but we do not believe that he could in this or in any other manner logically exclude from the repertory of the modern architect any part of the precious inheritance of beautiful forms, whether classic, mediæval, Saracenic, Indian, Japanese, or other, which are his peculiar property, which cannot be concealed from him, which enrich him far beyond the wildest dreams of any of his predecessors, which constitute alike his greatest privilege and his greatest danger. By the vastness of his inheritance, he is compelled to a labor of comparison and selection, which if he is wise will enrich his legitimate resources of design, but which if he is foolish will embarrass him and make him a spendthrift. As he cannot turn his back upon his wealth, modern architecture must inevitably be eclectic. This constitutes the fundamental distinction between old and new work. By this intelligent catholicity, under the guidance of just laws, and recognizing all new developments in mechanical forces, and all new discoveries in material, the complicated conditions of modern buildings can receive the most characteristic development — a result impossible to be obtained by any system of exclusion, however philosophic.

Mr. Eidlitz very happily says that "architecture tells us as much of Greece as Homer did, and of the Middle Ages more than has been expressed in literature; yet," he adds, "it has been silent since the thirteenth century." [4] The latter proposition is picturesque, but it is not true. It is a statement frequently repeated in other forms in this book. It needs but a glance to show that the function of architecture as a recorder of history has never been exhibited with greater success than in setting forth the spirit of the successive reigns in France and England, for example, from the thirteenth century to the present time. There is a characteristic modification of forms in the architecture respectively of the Stuarts, of Queen Anne, of the Georges, and of Victoria, as in that of the successive Louises of France and in that of the Empire. The historian will one day recognize these as the most significant exponents of the spirit of these modern civilizations. Nay, he will find, even in the much depreciated work of the present century, no doubtful indication of the sort of people we are. Certainly the indication would be clearer if the practitioners of the present time had been taught to eliminate the personal element from their work; they would be better performing their function as educators if they were more prone to observe principles than fashions, and they would produce better art if, in their use of historical forms, they better understood how to make them the expression of the structural conditions. Still, we have an art of the nineteenth century, and it is not entirely despicable.

Mr. Eidlitz frequently insists that a proper use in art of old forms under new conditions is a practical impossibility. But it is evident enough that old forms are applicable to new work to the extent that new constructions are similar to old constructions; as the construction is modified the form is modified with it, and the old type is thus gradually merged into a series of new expressions. The process is perfectly legitimate. No philological purist would venture to say that the only language fit for poetical expression is the pure Anglo-Saxon, and that the polyglot inheritance out of which is compacted the modern English tongue has only served to render it useless as the clothing of lofty thought. All human knowledge advances from the work of the past by processes of deduction, growth, and assimilation. Architecture is no exception to this rule, and, *a priori*, it is not scientific to assume that the experiments and studies of successive generations of artists, through nearly five centuries since the Renaissance, are a mere waste of human endeavor, unworthy to be counted by the student among the treasures of experience. It is more in accordance with the thoughtless prejudice of the doctrinaire than with the prudent and educated conservatism of the professional student to assert that the formula of pilasters and entablature, which is the basis upon which the artists of the Renaissance lavished such boundless wealth of beautiful invention, is not an expression of structure as direct as the buttress and pinnacle; that a window frame may be decorated by mouldings in chamfer and not by mouldings in relief; that it may be covered by a drip moulding or by a canopy, but never by a cornice or a pediment. It must be admitted that the architects of certain periods of the Renaissance, like those of the decadence of the Gothic, have made serious errors; have often made ornament more important than construction, often quoted the classic orders too literally or distorted them too capriciously; that they have misused their elements and misunderstood the essential principles of design; but surely their preponderance of brilliant work is not to be obliterated from the memory of the student because of such offences.

In short, what the modern student of architecture needs is a grammar, not an *index expurgatorius*. To the extent that this prominent architect has, in the work before us, lent his powerful assistance to the fundamental fallacy of exclusion, his book is harmful, unphilosophic, and misleading. But there yet remains enough of sound reasoning and vigorous statement to make it worthy of respectful consideration and a notable addition to the literature of art. Mr. Eidlitz's views of the status of the architect in relation to competitions, of the use and abuse of drawings in architectural education and experience, of proportion and modelling, are wise and well stated, and need to be formulated in just that vigorous, not to say aggressive, style which makes Mr. Eidlitz an unpleasant opponent in argument, but a tower of strength when he is on the right side.

The Personal Equation in Renaissance Architecture [1]

(1885)

It is a truism to say that the qualities of Gothic and of Renaissance civilization are graphically expressed in their respective arts, and that the characteristic differences between these two arts constitute the most suggestive evidence of the conditions of the societies out of which they grew. Referring to architecture in especial, I ask you to consider with me some of these differences, with a view to ascertaining the true functions of the men who were more immediately concerned in producing them. Writers of general history collect and analyze traditions, documents, and archives with infinite patience and industry, but the evidences of architecture are inaccessible to them, because those who have written upon this subject have confined their studies rather to its external and technical manifestations, as to a development of natural forces, than to the human interests, from which they proceeded; the human wants, to which they were adjusted; the human skill, which gave to them character and direction. Behind every apparent form in architecture is a human motive, and a great monument, therefore, which is a concert of innumerable forms, must, as I conceive, constitute an invaluable record of the civilization which produced it. It is not merely an incident in the history of architecture, but an incident in the history of mankind. I am persuaded that the time is not far distant when it will be possible to predicate from the internal evidence contained in such a work, the true genius of the times, the bases of contemporaneous history. Thus the Cathedral of Paris, to take a familiar example, if it could be properly analyzed, would be found to contain not only all that it is essential to know of the spirit of the Middle Ages in general, of the fall of the monastic orders, of the decay of feudalism, of the birth of civil liberty, but in specific detail all the religious, social, and political life of the time; and this not so much because it is a great municipal and ecclesiastical monument, but because it is a work of art.

Mediaeval architecture was a gradual and steady evolution of structural forms, with but little influence from external traditions, and under exceptional conditions of enthusiastic devotion and religious zeal. It was saved from barbarism and savagery, first, by the learning of the cloisters, and afterwards by the coherence of the lay architects or masonic guilds, which preserved, developed, and transmitted a compact and consistent body of building traditions. The process of evolution progressed with amazing rapidity; it pushed Gothic art to its highest expression in the thirteenth century, and in the fifteenth, this art had said all that it had to say; it had become an architecture of *tours de force* of conceits and grotesques; as its strength failed, it became attenuated and affected, and at the end, the skill of the craftsman triumphed over the inspiration of the artist. It was, I say, an architecture of structural evolution; and so long as the evolution continued in a healthy condition, it was as free from abnormal examples as the evolution of any animal or vegetable type in natural history. The successive buildings of the style were links in a continuous chain, each one essential to the development of the type. By this series of tentative processes the art of constructing roofs with small stones, progressed from the simplest and most timid vault to the most complex and daring, each step in the progress involving changes more or less fundamental in the supporting walls, piers, and buttresses, and hence affecting the entire structural and architectural character of the buildings.

But it should be understood that a mere evolution of structure cannot in itself constitute a style of architecture. We have in modern times, an evolution of structure, which, like the Gothic art, consistently "broadens from precedent to precedent;"² absorbing into itself all the inventions and discoveries of science in the art of building; but this evolution is in the hands of engineers; it appears in the steady and admirable progress of achievement in monumental works of severe utility, bridges, aqueducts, sewers, canals, embankments, factories. But this is not art, because unlike the Gothic evolution, it is not in the hands of artists. The function of the modern engineers, and that of the lay builder of the Middle Ages differ in this important respect: the one develops a theory of construction with a view to obtaining perfect fitness and stability in the most direct and economic way possible; the other, in like manner, aims at fitness and stability by the use of scientific and technical methods, but he confers upon his work beauty as well as fitness, grace as well as stability; he decorates his construction. A Cistercian abbey, in its austere, unornamented construction, shows how a work of engineering may be made a work of art. A Clunisian abbey is no more a work of art, because of its superadded luxury of sculpture and splendor of color. The modern engineer gives us prose, the Mediaeval builder gives us poetry.

In the beginning of the period of the Renaissance—the Gothic tree having exhausted itself with blossoms — there was grafted into its enfeebled stock a new shoot, which, with the advancement of learning, and the growth of the human mind, gradually, but surely changed the character of the Mediaeval forms, until at length they disappeared entirely. Indeed, so completely did this new influence take possession of the human mind, that after hardly a century of transition, the vast poetic monuments of Mediaeval art became in the midst of the new civilization not only barbaric enigmas, but objects of insult and contumely. Even the antiquary neglected them, until the middle of the seventeenth century, while Inigo Jones was building a Corinthian portico on the west front of the Gothic St. Paul's, of London.

This new principle of art was based upon an architectural formula, the Classic orders. This formula was the standard by which architecture henceforth was to be measured and corrected. If Mediaeval architecture was a system based upon the free development of structural forms, that of the Renaissance was based upon authority and discipline. The Classic formula was recognized as the embodiment of the spirit of the antique world, by means of which alone, it was thought redemption from Mediaeval barbarism, and revival of civilization were possible. The essence of this formula was an arbitrary system of proportion composed of isolated columns or attached pilasters supporting entablatures. The former were composed of bases, shafts, and capitals; the latter, of architraves, friezes, and cornices. Each of these divisions was further subdivided into mouldings, and as all these parts had developed together, and got their shape by mutual adjustment after many trials, as with the advancement of refinement artists became curious in respect to the shape and relative disposition of these subordinate parts, the result was finally the highest expression of architectural style known to mankind. Though this delicate and precise mutual adjustment might have been reached in other styles, as in Gothic, it has only been reached in the Classic, and the examples of it are the so-called orders of architecture. It is their advantage that they were developed in actual use — not by theory, but by practice — and that they grew into shape, embodying in their modifications the experience and feeling of successive generations of Greek and Roman architects. As they were received in the fifteenth century, they had undergone the final revision of the great Italian masters of the Renaissance, who studied their proportions with the last degree of refinement, and recorded them exactly. They conferred upon the coarse Roman orders a degree of perfection rivalling the perfection of the Greek orders. The ancient Romans, in taking their forms from the Greeks, had vulgarized them; but the Italian masters nearly restored the purity of the original type. So developed, these Classic orders are the key to almost all that has been done in architecture to our day.

Now the Classic formula thus revived and rehabilitated, because it represented perfection of proportion, could have no career of evolution in the Gothic sense. Perfection cannot be perfected; it can only be adorned. In fact, the essential principle of the architecture of the Renaissance is a scheme of decoration based upon a dogma of proportion.

To our present purposes it is important to observe that the invention and application of ornament to structure in process of evolution is a very different thing from the invention and application of ornament to a rigid formula of proportion. The consideration of this difference brings us at once to the point to which I would draw your attention.

"Architecture," says M. Veron, "even when considered from the aesthetic point of view, remains so dependent upon geometry, upon mechanics, and upon logic, that it is difficult to discover accurately the share our sentiment and imagination have in it." [3] This is certainly true of Gothic art, because its character rests upon geometry, mechanics and logic, applied to the harmonious and consistent evolution of structure. But M. Charles Blanc observes of this architecture that "every structural necessity became a pretext for ornament, and the most capricious conceptions were in reality nothing more than contrivances for embellishing the work, forced upon the artist by the inexorable law of gravitation." [4] This is equivalent to saying that Gothic art was an art of construction more or less ornamental. Now ornament is the product of sentiment and imagination, but the invention of ornament in such a service as Gothic art did not call for the highest artistic effort in this domain. The grouping of pinnacles upon buttresses, the filling of apertures with rich tracery, the fretting of sky-lines with crockets and finials, the decoration of wall surfaces with an embroidery of cusped arches and canopied niches — this sort of work was not the labor of illustrious masters, but of nameless trained craftsmen; nay, even the iconography and symbolism which crowded the porches were part of a hieratic system to which the men who produced it were in the position rather of humble catechumens or neophytes, than of independent artists. Their labors were didactic, like the labors of writers and printers. The composition of ornament for its own sake did not become a leading principle until a new style arose, based upon a rigid formula which was itself perfection, and therefore, as I have intimated, incapable of progression. Under these circumstances, the variety demanded of art by the newly awakened civilization was only obtainable either by distorting or degrading the formula itself, as was actually done in the eras of the Baroque, the Rococo, the Churrigueresque, or by overlaying it with ornaments not necessary to constructive effects — with constructive ornament, in fact.

It is evident that this process of decorating without degrading the unalterable Classic type could not have been effected by tradition, or by any such anonymous body of trained artisans as kept the Gothic evolution in a workmanlike track. The contingency called into existence the modern architect, with his books and prints and his archaeological equipment. The composition and application of ornament demanded a new and higher quality of invention and imagination, because ornamentation had become a far more important function in architecture. In short, the Gothic method resulted in an impersonal art; the Renaissance method necessarily led to a personal art. If Gothic art was the development of principles of construction applied to meet similar requirements, each experimental abbey or cathedral differed from its predecessor in exact proportion to the progress in the art of building vaults with small stones, not in proportion to the genius of the master-builder. The decoration of these structures was not an essential incident in this scheme of general development. No single monastic or lay builder could impress his individuality upon this mighty advancing tide. Its progress was made up of forces far too great to be turned this way or that at his bidding. He was the servant of evolution, and not its master; he made the evolution consistent, grammatical and beautiful, and in this disinterested service his name and character were lost. In like manner, if the earliest artists of the Renaissance had discovered in the Flavian amphitheatre, (as the first Romanesque builders did at Spalatro), a new principle of construction, capable of indefinite expansion in the wider fields of the new civilization, instead of an order of architecture, and if Francis I had carried that principle back to France with the spoils of his first Italian conquest instead of a crowd of Italian artists, the guardians of the ancient formula, we might have witnessed the phenomenon of another impersonal art, to the development of which, in the course of time, the genius of Philibert de Lorme, Pierre Lescot, and the Mansarts[5] would have done loyal but anonymous service. If on the other hand, in the twelfth century, it had been possible to invest a certain form and proportion of vaulting and abutment with such peculiar sanctity that it would have been impious to vary from it henceforth in any essential particular, decoration would have at once assumed the first, instead of the subordinate place in the architecture of the thirteenth and fourteenth centuries, and, instead of a series of nameless masons and master-builders, we would have had a catalogue of individualities as illustrious and specific as that which confers its peculiar personal interest on the history of the Renaissance.

Now as to the evidences of the personal character of Renaissance art. Although the Classic formula was set up and accepted as absolute authority in the fifteenth century, although it has been used with veneration for four centuries up to the present time, and although every architect designing in the style of the Renaissance intends above all things to be *correct* in his use of this simple type, the result has been not monotony, not cold and colorless uniformity, but a variety of expression, hitherto unknown in art. Now in studying these variations as they are exhibited in the buildings of the Renaissance up to the present day, we shall find that they are not capricious or accidental; there was one class of variations in France, one in England, one in Germany, one in Spain, one in Holland, one in Italy. These distinctions of class are easily recognizable: they follow natural laws, they interpret national temperament or genius by a visible demonstration. Thus the French Renaissance abounds in elegant variety; it is nearly always refined, delicate in detail, and full of feeling and animation. The English Renaissance is for the most part unimaginative and heavy, feeble in invention, prosaic and dull; but it was not without its single era of great and original development, at the hands of Wren, after the London fire. The German follows the French at a great distance; where it has not been merely imitative, its principal characteristic has been cold correctness and pedantry. The Spaniard handles the orders with great freedom, and overlays them with a sort of barbaric but ungrammatical splendor, which is almost Oriental in its profusion and color. The Dutch variation was homely and honest, like the people. But in Italy the natural birthplace of the Renaissance, Vignola, Serlio, Palladio, Bramanti, Scamozzi first taught the world how true artists, holding alike to a rigid formula, could invest it with purity and delicacy; how they could be correct without dullness, precise without pedantry, poetic without license. These were the earlier Italian development; the later masters, betrayed by the contortions of Borromini, the undisciplined inventions of Bernini, the coarse magnificence of Michael Angelo, lost their purity in profusion, and vulgarized the type in their passion for grandeur. Still the Italians were always the true masters of the Renaissance, and the rest of Europe went to school to them. But we have seen that though the architects of France, England and Germany tried to imitate the Italian manner, they were always French, English and German; the national spirit betrayed them. All the forces of art were united in the desire to make the revised Classic forms cosmopolitan. They studied the same authorities, learned by heart the same formulas of proportion, copied the same monuments, but failed in their efforts to make a universal architecture. Indeed, there was not only a national impress left upon their works, but no two architects of the same nation could produce similar work. Each interpretation had a character of individuality; the phenomenon remains true to this day.

A late writer very happily said that "architecture tells us as much of Greece as Homer did, and of the Middle Ages more than has been expressed in literature. Yet," he adds, "it has been silent since the thirteenth century." [6] This latter proposition is after the dogmatic fashion prevalent in modern English criticism. It is equivalent to saying that the personal equation in modern architecture, rendered necessary by the adoption of a formula as the basis of design, has prevented the art from exercising its natural function as an evidence of contemporary history, as it did when design was confined to the development of a theory of construction, in the series of Greek temples and mediaeval cathedrals. The fact is that architecture, whether personal or impersonal, cannot be forced away from this function, even by the most determined exercise of the modern privilege of masquerading in the trappings of old forms of art. Indeed it is sufficiently evident that this very personal character imposed upon architecture by the conditions of the Renaissance, in rendering it more sensitive to exoteric impressions, has made it a more accurate exponent of the quality of the civilization which produced it than has been the case with any form of impersonal art, the characteristics of which must be largely due to internal forces. It is not so much its structural as its decorative character which makes the metropolitan cathedral a reflection of the life which swarmed about the market-place under its shadows, or entered its porches with banners. But if we survey the progress of mediaeval French architecture from the time of Philip Augustus, in 1180, to that of Charles VII, in 1422 — from St. Bernard of Clairvaux to Joan of Arc; though in this era more than sixty cathedrals of the first class were built, involving an expenditure of more than $500,000,000 in our money (an activity in building operations unsurpassed in history), we shall find that no monarch and no court was able to impress upon it any characteristic which should enable us to distinguish any one phase of its progress as the style of Louis VIII, the Lion; or Louis IX, the Saint; of Philip III, the Hardy; or Philip IV, the Fair; of Charles V, VI, or VII. There are no such styles; the art of these reigns was an evolution of forces, and, as such, it was an impersonal art. If any phase of this evolution is identified by the name of a sovereign, this is purely a matter of convenience in nomenclature; it is not significant of cause and effect, for the art refused to submit to the caprices of any court.

On the other hand, when architecture had ceased to be a structural evolution, and was based upon a formula of pilasters and entablatures, enclosing imposts and arches, decoration, ornament assumed a function until then unknown, and there was a distinctive style corresponding to the character of each reign, often contrasting with curious abruptness. Thus we recognize a style of Francis I, free, elastic, poetic, romantic; of Henry IV, bold, coarse, grotesque; of Louis XIV, full of grandeur without, of pomp and splendor within (Viollet-le-Duc has called it "the new Renaissance"); of Louis XV, frivolous, licentious, ostentatious, Rococo; of Louis XVI, decent, orderly, pure to prudishness; of the first empire, a theatrical display of imperial Roman properties, meagre and tarnished; of the second empire, elegant, but profuse and luxurious, drawing its *motifs* from every historical source, but harmonizing them with a fastidious academical spirit; a style of to-day, too near to us to be recognized now in just perspective, but for which we will be held responsible in the next century. So there is a style of Elizabeth, of the Stuarts and Tudors, of bloody Mary, of Queen Anne, and of Victoria. So also in Spain, as Fergusson says, the enthusiasm and exultation and pride of Ferdinand and Isabella, and of Charles I are well expressed in the architecture of their times, until Philip II substituted, for the joyous and sunny exuberance of his predecessors, a cold, academical formalism, in full sympathy with his iron rule.[7]

This scenic display is rendered possible by the fact, that the architecture of these eras must necessarily be saturated with the subjective personality of the architects, in order to [achieve?] its proper adjustment to the spirit of the times. In fact, the composition of ornament is like the composition of poetry; neither can be evolved from theory alone; neither can exist in definite shape save by virtue of the individual character, attributes and mental equipment of the author. It is his genius which confers upon it all its specific quality. It is his knowledge, his training, his convictions, his taste, which so adjust ornament to a formula of proportion as to confer upon it especial character and interest. It is true that a large part of Renaissance ornament, as of all architectural ornament is conventional. The enrichment of the order is obtained not only by the imaginative arts of sculpture and painting, which must necessarily be infused with personal genius like a poem, but by ornament of convention, which is common property, *i.e.*, certain types of ornament applied by general acceptance to the decoration of the mouldings, and other details of the order; but it is also obtained by a certain hardihood in varying its proportions. But the use of conventional ornament implies choice, discretion on the part of the architect, and these are surely personal qualities, and the variation of the proportions is an appeal to his academical training, to his knowledge of precedent, to his artistic feeling. If an ignorant man plays with proportions, the result is inevitably disgrace and vulgarity. He can produce successful results, only by an abnegation of himself, and is only acceptable when he follows the Classic formula with unimaginative fidelity. The advancement of archaeological learning, the accumulation and accessibility of architectural precedent, in making it impractiable to the modern architect to build better than he knows, have inevitably forced him into an increasing degree of self-consciousness in his work, and in depriving his work of the grace of innocence and naïveté, have made it a more sensitive index of his individuality. The picturesque and romantic days of an impersonal architecture will return no more.

On the Present Condition and Prospects of Architecture

(1886)

In a recent number of the London Athenæum there appeared a review of a new translation of Arabian poetry. A passage in this review is worth quoting, because, in commenting on the conditions of civilization which affect that form of art called poetry, it uses language equally applicable to that other form of art called architecture, and is thus unconsciously significant of the close analogy existing between the various forms of art in which man has expressed his higher emotions. The passage, with a few verbal changes, mainly in substituting the word "architecture" and its derivatives for the word "poetry" and its derivatives, is as follows: —

"The architecture of a people, who have preserved their natural character and simplicity, and have so far learnt nothing from other civilizations, must always possess a strong fascination. As soon as the period of study and learning arrives we obtain, indeed, forms of architecture and poetry beautiful in themselves, and full of the thoughts and inventions, the spirit and characteristics, of the best works of many nations, but we lose the simplicity, the unaffected naturalness, the fresh outlook upon life and nature, which belong to primitive races. The freshness and sincerity which are exhibited in the architectural works of such races arise from the fact that they formed their styles for themselves, with no assistance from other nations, and developed form naturally and out of necessity, with no admixture of preconceptions derived from books and study. They did not suffer from the difficulties which beset the modern architect; they had no models in other styles *to teach them to affect impressions which they did not feel*; there was no searching after originality with them, since the native and instinctive ideas and forms of art had not been exhausted in their time; and though they spared no pains to attain the utmost degree of artistic finish in their work, they were not ever striving after the discovery of new *motifs*, or rare combinations and tricks of design, to render their work original and interesting." [1]

This quotation may fairly introduce what I have to say on the present condition of architecture. It is impossible justly to study this theme without constant comparison of the attitude, functions, and methods of the architects, who produced what we now recognize as the historical styles, with those of the modern architects, who, far more learned and versatile, far better equipped, are contending with projects of building far more complex, in an atmosphere infinitely less favorable to purely artistic achievement.

We may follow the development of architectural form from the hypostyle temple of Karnac to the Parthenon, from the Parthenon to the Pantheon, from the Pantheon to St. Sophia, from St. Sophia to St. Mark's, from St. Mark's to the cathedral of Cologne, and thence to the basilica of St. Peter in Rome and of St. Paul in London, and can see in these a very frank and undistorted series of reflections of the progress of the human mind through consecutive civilizations. They are monuments of a succession of well-defined styles, one following the other in logical sequence, and, in a large degree, according to the laws of structural evolution. But after St. Paul came the era of books, prints, and photographs. Since then we have gathered, assimilated, and classified the fruits of all previous civilizations; we have invented a science of æsthetics, which pretends to analyze the very germs of art, to reveal the secret of the spirit of architecture, to discover the mental processes which were unconsciously followed by our less instructed but more fortunate predecessors; we have, in short, become learned, and the architectural result is chaos, — or, at least, what seems chaos to us, who view the results of modern architecture in the distorted and violent perspective of proximity. Possibly, — nay, probably, — to our successors this inchoate, nebulous mass may resolve itself, not into a style in the historical sense, but into a sort of architectural constellation, in which may be seen, in a manner, some reflection of the spirit of the times in which we live.

The profession of architecture is now reproached because it has failed to establish "a style," because it has not agreed upon a system, because its followers do not move in parallel lines onward towards a consummation of art commensurate with our civilization, in the same way that contemporaneous science has moved towards the development of the electric telegraph, of electric lighting, of the telephone; because at our annual conventions the president of the British or American Institute of Architects is not able, like the president of the National or International Academy of Sciences, to report in his address a definite and orderly progress of achievement.

But architecture is a fine art upon a basis of science; if it were a pure science, we could emulate the electrician, the geologist, the political economist, the naturalist, the civil engineer, and report, like them, an annual record of consistent advance in all that relates to questions of construction and practical building methods. Modern architecture, as a fine art, cannot make its annual boast of improvement, for reasons which are well worth investigating. But, on the other hand, Callicrates in his day could have reported to Pericles, if required, a definite progress in the development of the Doric order within any twelvemonth of his career; Apollodorus, in like manner, might have reported to Trajan a corresponding progress in the architectural use of the arch; Anthemius, of Tralles, could easily have described to Justinian a clear advance in domical architecture in any successive half dozen years of the reign; the Abbé Suger could have traced distinct stages of growth in all the details of Gothic art from year to year, if St. Louis had needed any such statement; and Marie de Médicis would not in vain have ordered from Philibert de Lorme a report of annual progress in French Renaissance, nor would Charles II. have been without response if he had thought it worth while to summon Sir Christopher to give account of the conversion of the orders in English hands.[2] Those were days when styles were visibly unfolding towards perfection; when the practice of architecture broadened from precedent to precedent without distraction or bias; when temple followed temple, church followed church, château followed château, in a reasonable development and natural growth of architectural forms, confined within practicable limits. The study of the architect was limited to a type which all understood, and there was an orderly, intelligible, and harmonious evolution of styles. The forms in vogue, by means of a series of practical experiments in a succession of structures of the same sort, adapted to a comparatively simple condition of civilization, underwent a process of purification and natural enrichment. They gradually approached, and finally achieved, technical perfection and consistent harmony. At length, when the inherent capacities of the style were exhausted by use (the human mind declining to rest upon, or, indeed, to recognize, the attainment of perfection, but demanding ever new things, fresh surprises), it was by degrees overlaid and overwrought with invention, it declined with laborious splendor, and, in due time, gave place to a new set of forms, which were introduced in a political conquest, perhaps, like that of the Normans in England; in a religious revolution, like that of St. Bernard in France; in an intellectual revival, like that of the Renaissance in Italy; or by the influence of a brilliant court, like that of Elizabeth or Louis XIV., demanding an especial expression of splendor or triumph. And these new forms, in their turn, were developed to completion by the same processes of consecutive experiment in a narrow field of enterprise, and constituted in each case a style, an exponent of manners and customs, with a beginning, a middle, and an end, between two brief eras of doubt, called, in the history of art, eras of transition.

Now in the modern architectural chaos there appears to be a notable exception in the work of the French people. In Paris, archæology and the theory of architecture are taught in an official school of fine arts, which is the guardian of the national traditions. In this school the basis of study is the classic formula or dogma of the orders received in the fifteenth century from Italy, and since then adorned and vivified so as to form a great body of national precedent, reflecting the advance and character of French civilization through all its stages. Architecture is in this way officially organized and kept in a steady line of academic development. Thus confined, French genius is not, as elsewhere, exhausted in experiments, or spread thin over fields of enterprise too extensive for a display of effective progress; nor is it distracted by capricious archæological revivals. This concentration of energy expresses itself in a degree of refinement in detail, a degree of clearness and directness of thought, a degree of self-restraint and repose, which are quite unapproached in the practice of any other nation. Under this dispensation technical qualities of design are naturally carried to the highest perfection. Refinement is often pressed to the verge of effeminacy. The highest results obtained under this system are, on the one hand, extreme dignity and repose, as in the Palace of Justice (Figs. 96, 96a); and, on the other, a poetic and florid, but always a correct, brilliancy, as in the Hôtel de Ville, of Paris, and the New Opera (Figs. 98, 99). If the architectural conventionalism which it fosters is sometimes commonplace, it is always correct, never illiterate, and often scholarly. If it disciplines individuality of thought, so that the style, in the hands of inferior artists, becomes unduly uniform and uninteresting, it protects common work from the dangerous vagaries of invention, and keeps it pure. Originality is not sought after with the feverish eagerness which must be the prevailing characteristic of work done under a condition of liberty. The school, in fact, is a Propaganda of faith in an arbitrary type of art. While it narrows the range of expression, it encourages academic precision, fosters beautiful invention in detail, and leads to a study of ornament far more delicate and precious in its results than is elsewhere possible. As a school for practice and education, it maintains a conspicuous advantage. Viollet-le-Duc, with all his knowledge and all his convictions, eloquently urged in favor of a return to Greek and mediæval methods in design, was unable to create a successful revolt from the national styles as established under this official system. On the whole, modern French Renaissance, with its vast accumulation of motifs, resulting from five centuries of constant use in the hands of a naturally inventive and imaginative race, constitutes a language of art, at once homogeneous and copious. If its essential paganism makes it less fit for the expression of romantic, picturesque, or religious thought, and perhaps, by reason of its academical character, less adaptable for domestic purposes, this quality renders it more elastic than any other for monumental and civic uses. It can be gay or grave, profuse or severe, stately or poetic, without straining its resources of expression, and it still continues to reflect the spirit of the times with the same fidelity that has characterized it in all its historic phases from the style of Francis I. to that of Napoleon III.; yet, when used out of France, it becomes an unfruitful exotic, and degenerates into cold conventionalism. Its blossoms invariably die in crossing the English Channel, and when imported to this side of the Atlantic there is nothing left of it but branches and withered leaves.

English architecture, on the other hand, is still groping after a fit type of national expression. If in France, under the patronage of government, there is a living style consistent with national traditions, a style still to a certain extent receiving accretions from the spirit of the times, thus serving as an index of national character, in England, without official guidance, liberty of thought is unrestrained except by the unrecognized influence of custom. The result is that the elements of design, which are repressed by the tyranny of a refined scholasticism on the other side of the channel, find the fullest expression, while the study of detail and ornament, to which French genius has been compelled to confine itself, is essentially wanting. Thus, English architecture abounds in picturesque, romantic, and religious thought. Indeed, through these sentiments alone, it has occasionally succeeded in entering into the difficult regions of noble architecture; but, with certain exceptions quite rare enough to prove the rule, as in the Banqueting House at Whitehall, in St. George's Hall at Liverpool (Fig. 79), in some of the earlier work of Barry in the club houses of London (Fig. 80),[3] and in some of Thompson's Greek work in Edinburgh and Glasgow (Figs. 82, 83), English essays in classic types of architecture have hitherto proved cold and colorless, if not absolutely incorrect and vulgar. The orders have been used rather as an inflexible geometrical expression than as a language of art. In fact, the English have failed where the French have succeeded; they have succeeded where the French have failed. But the English failure is the more disastrous to the rank of English architecture because its vain attempts to vitalize and nationalize the classic formula have been frequent enough to constitute a characteristic feature. On the other hand, the severe academic training of the French architects has preserved them from conspicuous error in any branch of picturesque or romantic effects which they have attempted. The French, in short, cannot be ungrammatical; but there is no street in a modern English town which is not full of offenses against correctness. Notwithstanding this, the history of modern architecture in England, though its condition of artistic liberty has never given it its Augustan era, to correspond with that of Shakespeare or Addison in literature, attracts our interest and claims our sympathies to a greater degree than that of any other nation. It abounds in episodes of ingenuous and gallant effort. Twenty years ago it became necessary, in the interest of peace and quiet, to exclude by formal by-laws the discussion of the relative merits of classic and of Gothic art in the societies. The profession in England was divided into hostile camps by an irrepressible conflict of architectural principles. The Gothicists, by the chance of war, gained the day, and held the field undisputed for some fifteen years. This warfare, however grotesque it may now appear to us, who, by conviction and not by indifference, have become catholic, bears witness to a sincerity and zeal on pure questions of principle in art which are unparalleled in history. Indeed, these are among the best fruits of liberty.

The main characteristic of modern English architecture consists in its series of revivals. In the absence of academic taste, guided by official schools, the architect is under the dominion of a prevailing fashion, which, while it lasts, is as powerful as if promulgated by an edict of government. He aims less to please with old forms than to astonish with new. Any strong mind or hand in the profession which is fortunate enough to make a happy revival of a style or phase of architecture, which had until then been laid aside and forgotten, establishes a starting point for a host of young imitators, who at length constitute a school, numerously and enthusiastically followed: and thus a fashion in design takes possession of contemporary art and has its run through a course of years, until some other guiding spirit awakens a new revival and makes a new fashion, which succeeds until its capacity for producing novelty has been exhausted. The movements which have had the most enduring effect are the Gothic revival (Figs. 84–90), the Queen Anne revival (Fig. 92), the free classic revival; and now, under the impulse of the new war office competition, we shall see, perhaps, another attempt to acclimate the French Renaissance in England, to do service for a succession of years wherever English thought and English speech prevail.

It is a peculiarity of these successive experiments that they are revivals of completed systems, of forms incapable of further progression. Viollet-le-Duc justly observed that a prosperous career in art can start only from primitive types, of which the powers of development are unexhausted by use.[4] The practical effect of the revival of a style, which has had its era of glory and its associations of history, is to give to the architect an opportunity to exhibit his ingenuity in adapting old forms to new uses, and to display a facility of quotation which is often mistaken for genius, but which is really little more than memory, cultivated and effective indeed, leading him "to affect impressions which he does not feel," but not touching the springs of life in art. Meanwhile, the public are interested in it simply as they are interested in any other new fashion: not because it has in it the healthy breath of life, but because it is in vogue, and has been made reputable by architectural usage. Few practitioners have courage or force enough not to follow this usage. They are bound by it hand and foot while it lasts, and its powers are tested and strained to the uttermost limits by being forced into service often uncongenial to its natural capacity.

It is very noteworthy that the first and greatest of the English revivals, that of mediæval art, had its basis in an awakened conscience. Pugin (Fig. 78) and Ruskin preached the gospel of this revival; they asked for a return to the era of truth in art; they asked that architectural expression should be controlled by structure, and that decoration should follow the methods of nature. The Gothic revival is the only instance in history of a moral revolution in art. On the other hand, the revival of the style, called of Queen Anne, was a revolution effected under the influence of a literary sentiment. If the genius of Norman Shaw struck the first blow, the genius of Thackeray gave the movement inspiration and character.[5] Both revivals were patriotic, and would have been impossible if not associated with phases of English history. But neither conscience, nor historic sentiment, nor patriotism, can make art; they can give character and variety, they can supply motifs, they can minister to emotions and inspire poetry, but they cannot make a style. Hence these English fashions, which have had loud and sometimes effective imitations in the practice of American architects, have apparently had no permanent influence in improving the practice of architecture either in England or here. They have made *dilettanti* among the public and *virtuosi* among the architects, but they have not created artists. There is plenty of archæology, but no inspiration, in an architectural fashion which is hampered by the necessity of strict conformity. The Gothic revival gave opportunity for innumerable experiments; for many years it preoccupied the minds of the Anglo-Saxon people, and was ingeniously and sedulously adapted to every possible habit of modern life which could be ministered to by architectural forms. But this adaptation, though the writers have called its results "Victorian Gothic," did not advance Gothic art one step towards the creation of a modern English style, because it did not develop any capacity for expansion in this new service. Its potency for new expressions was speedily exhausted without satisfying the requirements of common sense or meeting the practical conditions to which it was applied. It was replaced — not, it is important to note, through any process of logical succession, by the accident of the Jacobean, or Queen Anne, or free classic revival, which at every point was an offense to the architectural morality engendered by the preachments of Pugin and Ruskin, and possibly a result of them, as the license of Charles II. naturally followed the rigid Puritanism of the Commonwealth. This revival also is proving unsuccessful, because the capacities of the type had been already exhausted before the revivalist made his first quotation. Neither of these types permitted expansion or progress; and the rehabilitations of them have proved to be merely sterile incidents in the history of modern architecture. They have not, so far as we can see, furnished to the English civilization of the nineteenth century any fitting and adequate architectural expositions.

These revivals, as I have said, have found a large and by no means an unintelligent expression in the United States. But the national genius of our architects and their freedom from the tyranny of historic precedent have encouraged them to a far wider range of experiment in architectural forms. Out of these experiments hitherto there have as yet come no definite promises for art. But the higher education of the practitioner and the more exacting demand for studied and grammatical expression have in these latter days, especially in those parts of the country where the better civilization obtains, already practically supplanted the illiterate products of our earlier condition with better work. They have succeeded in establishing a higher technical standard of performance without loss of that quality of intelligent liberty in which lie our greatest hopes and our largest promise. The service of our architectural schools is already amply justified by their results. Their graduates have spread abroad in Western as well as Eastern States, and wherever they have had opportunity of practice they have sown good seed, and are steadily rendering obsolete the normal American types of raw and undisciplined invention, of audacious exaggeration and caprice (Fig. 118). This is the first and most wholesome step towards rational reform. We have had good practice and experience in following the English fashions, but here their reign has never been undisputed. By the entire absence of local traditions; by the entire absence of monuments more ancient than those which we call "old colonial" (which we are recognizing for a little while in our practice to the extent of its limited but respectable capacity); by the entire absence of any official

164

prejudice, of any venerable conventionalities, of any national system of instruction in architecture, we are left in a condition of freedom which is fatal
to art while we are ignorant, but capable of great developments when we are
educated. In regard to the use of precedent we are essentially eclectic and
cosmopolitan. But education is enabling us to accord a proper degree of respect
to the formulas and traditions of the Old World, to avail ourselves of them
without bias, and to use them with a freedom which is becoming characteristic
of our work. We are in position to profit by conventionalities without being
bound by them. If our heritage of liberty has made us impatient of academical
discipline, it has made us peculiarly hospitable to unprejudiced impressions
of beauty and fitness. Our national offense has been license and insolent disrespect of venerable things, arising from want of appreciation and ignorance.
We have carried experiment and invention in matters of design further than
any other people. We are, as a new nation, a nation of builders. No part of
the history of civilization is so abounding in architectural expressions, good,
bad, and indifferent, as that of the American people. In quantity, certainly,
we have in a given time accomplished more in this field than any other people.
Our distinctive practical necessities, our mechanical genius in the matter of
building appliances, the nature of our building materials, the exigencies of
climate, and the characteristics of social life have created certain corresponding
distinctive qualities in our architecture; but they have not established as yet
anything approaching that coherent body of architectural forms which constitutes a style.

The architect, in the course of his career, is called upon to erect buildings
for every conceivable purpose, most of them adapted to requirements which
have never before arisen in history. Practical considerations of structure, economy, and convenience preoccupy his mind, and his purely and conventionally
architectural acquirements are subject to frequent eclipse in practice. His great
architectural models give him no hint, and stand too far apart from modern
sympathies and use to serve him for inspiration and guidance. Railway buildings of all sorts; churches with parlors, kitchens, and society rooms; hotels
on a scale never before dreamt of; public libraries, the service of which is
fundamentally different from any of their predecessors; office and mercantile
structures, such as no preëxisting conditions of professional and commercial
life have ever required; school-houses and college buildings, whose necessary
equipment removes them far from the venerable examples of Oxford and Cambridge; skating-rinks, theatres, exhibition buildings of vast extent, casinos, jails,
prisons, municipal buildings, music halls, apartment houses, and all the other
structures which must be accommodated to the complicated conditions of
modern society, — these force the architect to branches of study to which his
books, photographs, and sketches give him no direct aid. Out of these eminently practical considerations of planning must grow elevations, of which the
essential character, if they are honestly composed, can have no precedent in
architectural history.

Even though a prevailing fashion or revival may give a color of unity to contemporary buildings erected under such conditions, what wonder if there is the most perplexing variety of architectural expression? What wonder if the superficial critic, seeking for a characteristic type and finding none, cries out that art is dead, that there is no American style? What wonder if he decries the American architect as a creature without convictions? In fact, the canons of criticism which guided the opinions of our forefathers under narrower conditions, and which led them to pronounce judgment with the formulas "correct" or "not correct," are no longer applicable. The art which of all the fine arts is the only one dependent on practical considerations must be a free art, from the nature of the case. It cannot be confined within the bounds of any historic styles and remain true to its functions; it cannot meet the requirements of modern life in a strait-jacket of antiquarian knowledge and archæological forms. The functions of the critic have become far more difficult, and require a far more catholic, unprejudiced, and judicial mind, a far wider range of knowledge and sympathy, than could possibly grow up under the teachings or examples of Vitruvius or Palladio, Philibert de Lorme or Sir William Chambers, Sir Christopher Wren or the brothers Adam, Pugin or Ruskin, or any other prophet or expounder of ancient principles, with their rigid doctrines of exclusions and their exact formulas of practice in design. It is an era of experiment and invention, of boldness and courage. Conscientious fidelity to style in the merely archæological sense no longer leads to great and successful achievements, because the requirements of modern buildings are far beyond its capacity. The narrow city façade, crowded with necessary windows, elbowed by uncongenial neighbors, restricted by municipal regulations, with story piled upon story, and the whole hanging over a void filled with enormous sheets of glass, the *bête noir* of architectural composition, is a defiance to all rule and precedent in art. Iron construction can be adjusted neither according to the elegant precepts of Vitruvius nor the more elastic principles of mediæval art. At every step the architect is confronted with problems which cannot be solved by the suggestions of his library and sketch-book. He is compelled to employ new devices, to invent, to reconcile incongruous conditions, to strain the conventionalities of architectural design beyond their capacity, to produce new things. The result, in the absence of a wise and thorough architectural training in the fundamental principles of art, is confusion of types, illiterate combinations, an evident breathlessness of effort and striving for effect, with the inevitable loss of repose, dignity, and style. The practitioner becomes reckless of rules, and, despairing of being able to please, he aims to astonish.

Under these conditions, a new style of architecture — a style in the sense of the great historical styles, as those of Greek, Roman, Byzantine, Romanesque, mediæval Saracenic, and early Renaissance periods — is impossible. But good architecture *is* possible. The progress of architectural knowledge has already begun to enable us to have our own revivals, and the experiments we are trying in this respect, being free from the prejudices of patriotic sentiment which I believe to be a serious hindrance to the advance of English art, are curious and not without promise. Among these minor revivals, that of the Romanesque forms of Auvergne, in which the vigorous round arches, the robust columns, the strong capitals, and the rich but semi-barbaric sculpture are tempered with reminiscences of the finer Roman art, is at the moment the most interesting and perhaps the most promising. Mr. H. H. Richardson deserves great credit for his persistency in pressing this style towards the limits of its possibilities (Figs. 101, 106–110b, 129). It has the advantage of being an early and uncorrupted type, and it will be interesting to see in what direction and to what end its apparently unexhausted capacities will lead us, by the course of constant and intelligent experiment to which it is now subjected. But these experiments are often open to the charge of an affectation of barbarism and heaviness inconsistent with our civilization. They have hardly broken loose from the bonds of precedent in the style, or shown signs of acquiring new elements with any tendency to that delicacy and refinement which are necessary to satisfy modern culture, or to that elasticity essential to modern requirements. This revival will cease to be a masquerade, and will be in the healthy path of natural development, as soon as it begins to show a capacity for adjustment to our material and moral conditions. Whether it will succeed in reaching this stage, or whether it will presently begin to fatigue by monotony and so fall into disuse, there is no question that the experiment is based upon sounder principles than that of any other now under study. To take a larger view of the present attitude of American architecture, there is no doubt in my own mind that all the conditions are favorable to developments of the greatest interest. With thorough education, the future of our architectural practice is secure, and though "the American style" may never be realized, *style* will undoubtedly be a feature in our work, and will give it high rank in the history of art. Indeed, our best achievements are already showing how a certain unconventional art of the highest sort may be an essential part of the science of good building, and are not surpassed, in respect to genuine promise, by any contemporary work whatever in any part of the world.

This essay began with a quotation explaining how the necessary equipment of the modern architect, his organized business appliances, his library, his prints, his photographs, his familiarity with the historic styles in all their phases of development, glory, and decline, his conscious æsthetics, — his study, in short, has predisposed him to insincerity and affectation, and prevented him from competing on equal terms with the creators of the great styles. There is another element of difficulty which it is important to note. Our predecessors, before the era of learning, had the good fortune to be sustained by public sympathy. Criticism they felt to be an active, incessant, and intelligent force. There could be no such thing among them as pedantry. The language of art was a common language which all understood; it was therefore used with force, correctness, and discretion, and broke naturally into poetry and songs. The result was that the builder designed, not better than he knew, but under correction, and with the knowledge that his efforts would be appreciated at their full value; he was encouraged, surrounded, sustained, admonished, and taught by public opinion. If, in this atmosphere, he was a leader, it was solely by force of genius working in familiar paths. The people were all handiworkers. Fingers, brains, and heart wrought together at the forge, in the stone-cutter's yard, with the weaver's shuttle, at the jeweler's bench, with the carver's chisel, in the armorer's shop. The mind of every artisan was prompt to conceive, and his hand was quick to execute variations of form in his own craft, to give new interest and individuality to his work, however humble. It was natural

> Dass er im innern Hertzen spüret
> Was er ershafft mit seiner Hand.[6]

This constant exercise of intelligent invention made him sensitive to every expression of art, and he was not indifferent when his brethren, the stone-carvers, or painters, or workers in wood or metal or glass, united their best individual handiwork in an architectural symphony. Under this pressure, with this powerful correlation of forces behind, the growth of definite architectural styles was inevitable.

It was no less inevitable, in the progress of civilization, that labor-saving machinery should take the place of handiwork; that artisans should become mechanics or tenders of machinery, in whose product their best qualities of mind and heart could have no concern whatever. Thus the common artistic instinct, which, in the aggregate, constituted intelligent public sympathy in Athens, in Ravenna, in the Isle de France, does not exist in Manchester and New York. The architect is left to work out his problems alone, "with difficulty and labor hard," [7] unsustained by appreciative recognition and criticism, buried in the study of ancient precedent and in the contemplation of theories of design. The fundamental motive of his work is changed, and the best results of his labors, more or less affected by the pale cast of thought, are set up in the public places in complete silence. Criticism, if any, has become indifferent and careless. The architect is neither praised for his good points, nor blamed for his bad. Few care whether they are good or bad. They are not understood. In this emergency the architects unite in societies, for the sake of professional fellowship and mutual encouragement. They form a caste apart; they are no longer the leaders and exponents of public sentiment and thought in questions of art; no longer agents in the development of a style. Not having the correction, the stimulus, and assistance of public knowledge and interest to keep them in a straight path of fruitful development, they make devious excursions in new fields, they "affect impressions which they do not feel," they masquerade in various capricious disguises, all with the hope of astonishing the ignorant and arousing the indifferent.

Under these circumstances, it is much to be feared that the advance of the profession in these modern days is, to a large extent, a progress of architecture into regions inaccessible to the public. The most intelligent laymen do not pretend to appreciate its motives or to comprehend its results. But without their aid architecture cannot advance.

The members of the profession have begun to say one to the other, Let us cease this process of fruitless sophistication; let us study how we can excite intelligent interest. This point once gained, we shall at length have established a standard of performance which, if advanced by us in our practice with wise persistency and honest, straightforward endeavor, may at length give us a public whose good opinion will be worth earning. We have discovered that mere caprice, mere novelty, will not answer. This may amuse the vulgar for a while, but it makes the judicious grieve. When in our schools and in our practice we can succeed in cultivating a fine artistic feeling and in establishing really catholic ideals in design without falling into dilettanteism or into habits of mere imitation; when we can use our knowledge of good examples, modern and ancient, so that it will not betray us into quotations for the sake of quotations, into correctness for the sake of correctness; when we can work without caprice and design *reasonably*, so that every detail shall be capable of logical explanation and defense, without detriment to a pervading spirit of unity; when we can be refined without weakness, bold without brutality, learned without pedantry; when, above all, we can content ourselves with simplicity and purity, and refrain from affectations; we shall have conquered the indifference of the people, and shall have accomplished more than has yet been done in modern England with all its archæology, or in modern France with all its academical discipline, but we shall have done no more than should result from an intelligent use of our precious and unparalleled condition of liberty in art.

Henry Hobson Richardson, Architect

(1886)

It is recognized that since the beginning of this century architecture has not kept pace with the general advance of the other arts of civilization. Science has made steady progress all along the line, and often has astonished the world by leaps and bounds; its torch has flooded vast regions of doubt and darkness with triumphant illuminations. But while there is undeniably a style of the nineteenth century, and while England, France, Germany, and America have impressed certain national characteristics upon the architecture of the period, no definite advances have been made corresponding with those which occurred in every decade in Europe from the twelfth to the fourteenth century, when most of the other arts were asleep, or with those from the fourteenth to the seventeenth, when the artistic invention of the world found ample scope for expression and development in the renaissance of classic forms. The architects of this latter period were content with the language of the four orders, and with the coördination of arch, pilaster, and entablature, according to established formulas of proportion.

The modern era of research and experiment, which began with the encyclopædists in the eighteenth century, put an end to the progress of the renaissance of classic architecture, and inaugurated eclecticism. Under the same influence, science began its phenomenal career of successful discovery. Eclecticism in architecture is entirely consonant with the spirit of the times; it implies the collection, analysis, arrangement, and study of all the historical forms of art. This process, while it has made architects learned and reflective, has dissipated their inventive powers, and rendered impossible that unity of effort without which characteristic progress in style is impossible. The same impulse which made science productive has made architecture unproductive. In rendering this art more scholarly and correct, it has gradually removed it from the stimulus of public sympathy and correction. The history of modern architecture has thus become rather a history of study and experiment than of accomplishment and progress.

The question now is, When will this long discipline of probation bear its natural fruit, and furnish us with the elements of a true progress in art, consistent with our civilization, and competent to express it with the same sort and degree of precision with which the civilizations of the Middle Ages, of the Spanish Saracens, of the Italians of the fifteenth century, of the English of the Tudor times, for example, were respectively symbolized in their buildings and works of decorative art?

The Greek revival of the last century, the Gothic revival of the first half of the present century, the late revival, improperly called, of the Queen Anne style, and all the various subordinate revivals which, meanwhile, have arisen and fallen apparently as illogically as fashions in costume, have failed, because they were revivals of perfected styles, incapable of further progression; they were quotations, admirable for their archæological correctness, and for the skill with which they were adapted to modern uses. But they infused no new life into modern architecture, and failed to arouse public attention.

In our own country there have been corresponding movements, with corresponding results.

The constant desire for new things has made architecture extremely sensitive to impressions and hints. Every successful building is the parent of a score of imitations, not in its neighborhood only, but in distant places, sporadically all over the Union. For the publication of designs is prompt, and every architect has in his hands duly every new expression of form. Thus we have had and are having a succession of little fashions, contemporaneous, overlapping, intermingling, dying out, and coming into vogue, the duration of each being in proportion to the strength of the original impulse. We have imitations of imitations, the quality of each varying according to the training of the practitioner, and, as a general rule, deteriorating according to its distance from the original revival or invention.

At the present moment we are under the dominion of an impulse so vigorous, healthy, and stimulating, so different from any which has preceded it, so elastic to practical uses, that, in the hands of a profession far more accomplished and far better trained than ever before, it gives us the right to hope for results of the first importance in the development of style.

If there are any prevailing characteristics in the best architectural work of the present day in this country, they consist in the free use of heavy Romanesque forms from the south of France, low-browed round arches, stone mullions and transoms, wide-spreading gables, severe sky-lines, apsidal projections, rounded angles, and towers with low, pointed domical roofs; great wealth of carving, where the work is rich; a general aspect of heaviness and strength, frequently degenerating into an affectation of rudeness. Columns are short and stumpy, and capitals show Byzantine influence. Colonnades and arcades of windows are frequent, and all are free from the trammels of classicism (Figs. 101, 106–110b, 129). The new fashion has, for the moment, driven

171

aspiration and lightness as well as precision and correctness out of the market. Important buildings with such features have lately been completed, or are under construction, in nearly all the large cities of the Union, from Boston to San Francisco. No modern buildings of this sort are to be seen either in France, Germany, or England. For the Romanesque of to-day in Europe is derived mostly from Norman traditions, and is more or less stiffened by pedantry and straightened by monastic formulas. In fact, we apparently have at last, and for the first time, a purely American revival of certain ancient forms. There is scarcely a trained architect in this country who is not at the moment more or less attracted towards this especial phase of Romance art (Figs. 57, 59–61, 125, 126, 128, 130, 131, 133). There are, however, none who have not been, from their days of pupilage, as familiar with these forms as with that variety of them which the Normans introduced into England in the eleventh century; or with those derivatives of them which the monastic orders in the twelfth and the lay-builders in the thirteenth successively developed and brought to perfection; or with those forms which Francis I. brought from Italy to France in the fifteenth century; or, in fact, with any of the historic styles which have formed the basis of design for the last fifty years. Yet, until now, the front of Poictiers, the porches of St. Trophime at Arles, and the apses of St. Julian at Brioude have remained neglected in their portfolios, — a sort of antique rubbish, archæologically interesting, perhaps, but practically useless. Barbaric and rude, they have seemed in no respect germane to modern thought and modern practice.

It is observed also that, unlike any of the experiments in style which we have adopted from our English brethren, unlike our correct classic, our irreproachable Gothic, our Dutch reform, with its fretted gables, its sash windows, and its brick carving, this new revival has something about it which interests the public. Educated people of the laity are at last taking notice; and this is a most remarkable and encouraging sign.

Under what impulse has this change taken place among architects and laymen? What is its significance? Has the new movement a future before it? Has it come to stay?

It is a peculiarity of every change of style in modern practice that it must start from an archæological revival of some sort. Indeed, archæology is the necessary basis of every style; for it cannot be too often repeated that a style is a growth, and not an invention; and yet, as Sergeant Troy said, "Creation and preservation don't do well together, and a million antiquarians can't invent a style." [1] Thus at the beginning of every revival there must stand one or more architects of exceptional force and ability, to give to the new movement its first impetus, — to show how it can be adapted to modern usage, to establish its respectability and success.

The personality which has performed this function in America with reference to the Romanesque of Auvergne is certainly one of the most interesting, and perhaps one of the most remarkable, in the history of modern architects. Other contemporaries in his profession have exhibited at least equal professional attainments. Others have surpassed him in the amount of work accomplished. But none have had a professional career so fortunate, so exceptional in its characteristics, and so brilliant in its results as that of Henry Hobson Richardson, of Brookline, Mass. It would not be difficult to point out single works by some of his professional friends which, in respect of artistic and technical merit, would occupy a rank at least as high as anything from his hand. But it would not be possible to show a succession of works from any other hands exhibiting an individuality so strong, a personal force so imposing, a progress of achievement so steady, a development of genius so harmonious and consistent. Certainly we shall find no career which has made upon the public an impression so marked, none which has had an influence upon the profession so powerful and so widely spread.

Dr. Johnson said that every human life, however humble, must have something of interest in it for all mankind.[2] No biography can fail, at some point, to touch the sympathies and awaken profitable thought. Above all, a career of consistent progress in any walk of experience, a career which developed from good to better and from better to best, deserves to be studied and analyzed in all its phases, for the benefit of those who are still in the midst of the labors of production. Such a career should ultimately belong to the public, with all the incidents and accidents which helped to make it possible. That, however, with which we are now especially concerned is too recent and too near to us to be spread before the world in all its details. Its results are not yet sufficiently ascertained, its value is as yet too much a matter of question, to justify a premature invasion of its privacy. But, even at this stage, an outline of its purely professional part may be permitted, because it had qualities which have visibly affected the taste of to-day, and which therefore claim serious consideration.

Henry Hobson Richardson was born at Priestley's Point, St. James' Parish, Louisiana, September 29, 1838. His father, Henry D. Richardson, was a planter of ample means, born in America, but whose ancestors were originally Scotch, and afterwards took up their abode in England. His mother, Catherine Caroline Priestley, was a daughter of the famous Dr. Priestley, of England. Their son received an appointment as cadet at West Point from Judah P. Benjamin, who was then Senator. He passed his examinations, but, his father dying at that time, he gave up the appointment and entered Harvard College, whence he graduated with the class of 1859. In July of the same year he went abroad with two of his classmates, traveled extensively, and finally settled in Paris, where he began the study of architecture in the School of Fine Arts, entering, in 1860, the *atelier* of M. André. Meanwhile, his family, in the vicissitudes of the war for the Union, lost their fortune, and Richardson was for the first time thrown upon his own resources. But he pursued his studies in Paris until October, 1865, when he returned to this country, and in the following year began the active practice of his profession as a member of the firm of Gambrill and Richardson, in New York. In 1867 he married Julia Gorham Hayden, daughter of Dr. Hayden, of Boston, and took up his residence at

Clifton, Staten Island, N. Y., where he remained until May, 1875. The professional partnership having been previously dissolved, he moved to Brookline, Mass., in 1875. Here he established his studio, and here he lived until his death, April 27, 1886.

In 1866 he was made a Fellow of the American Institute of Architects; in 1879 he became a member of the American Academy of Arts and Sciences, and in 1881 of the Archæological Institute of America.

The incidents of his professional career may be most briefly stated in a chronological list of his works, which is approximately correct: —

1. Grace Church, Medford, Mass.
2. Boston and Albany Railroad Offices, Springfield, Mass.
3. Church of the Unity, Springfield, Mass.
4. The Agawam Bank, Springfield, Mass.
5. House for William Dorsheimer, Esq., Buffalo, N. Y.
6. The State Asylum for the Insane, Buffalo, N. Y.
7. Exhibition Building, Cordova, Argentine Republic.
8. American Express Co. Building, Chicago, Ill.
9. Brattle Street Church, Boston, Mass.
10. Worcester High School.
11. The Hampden County Court-House, Springfield, Mass.
12. Trinity Church, Boston, Mass.
13. Cheney Buildings, Hartford, Conn.
14. Phœnix Insurance Building, Hartford, Conn.
15. House for B. W. Crowninshield, Boston, Mass.
16. The North Church, Springfield, Mass.
17. William Watt Sherman's house, Newport, R. I.
18. Portions of the New York State Capitol, Albany, N. Y.
19. Public Library, Woburn, Mass.
20. Ames Memorial Library, North Easton, Mass.
21. Sever Hall, Cambridge, Mass.
22. Ames Memorial Town Hall, North Easton, Mass.
23. Trinity Church Rectory, Boston, Mass.
24. Monument to Oliver and Oakes Ames, Sherman, Wyoming.
25. Gate lodge for F. L. Ames, North Easton, Mass.
26. Crane Memorial Library, Quincy, Mass.
27. Bridges for the Back Bay Park, Boston, Mass.
28. City Hall, Albany, N. Y.
29. Depot for the Boston and Albany R. R., Auburndale, Mass.
30. New Law School, Cambridge, Mass.
31. House for F. L. Higginson, Esq., Beacon Street, Boston, Mass.
32. House for General N. L. Anderson, Washington, D. C.
33. Railroad depot, Holyoke, Mass., for Connecticut River R. R.
34. Depot, Palmer, Mass., for Boston and Albany R. R.
35. Depot, North Easton, Mass., Boston and Albany R. R.
36. Dairy Building, North Easton, Mass.
37. House for Grange Sard, Esq., Albany, N. Y.
38. Store on Kingston and Bedford Sts., Boston, for F. L. Ames, Esq.; also store on Washington Street.
39. Billings Library for University of Vermont, Burlington, Vt.
40. Depot, Chestnut Hill, Mass., Boston and Albany R. R.
41. Converse Memorial Library, Malden, Mass.
42. Baptist Church, Newton, Mass.
43. House for Henry Adams, Esq., Washington, D. C.
44. House for John Hay, Esq., Washington, D. C.
45. Alleghany County Buildings, consisting of Court-House and Jail, Pittsburgh, Penn.
46. Wholesale warehouse for Marshall Field & Co., Chicago, Ill.
47. Armory, Detroit, Mich.
48. Chamber of Commerce, Cincinnati, Ohio.

49. Dwelling-house for Franklin Mac-Veagh, Esq., Chicago, Ill.

50. Dwelling-house for B. H. Warder, Esq., Washington, D. C.

51. Dwelling-house for J. J. Glessner, Esq., Chicago, Ill.

52. Dwelling-house for Robert Treat Paine, Esq., Waltham, Mass.

53. Dwelling-house for Professor E. W. Gurney, Beverly, Mass.

54. Dwelling-house for J. R. Lionberger, Esq., St. Louis, Mo.

55. Dwelling-house for William H. Gratwick, Esq., Buffalo, N. Y.

56. Store on Harrison Avenue, Boston, for F. L. Ames, Esq.

57. Railroad depot, New London, Conn.

58. House for Professor Hubert Herkomer, A.R.A., England.

Of these buildings, the fourteen last named were incomplete at the time of his death, though practically developed in design.

The mere number of his works does not necessarily imply an exceptionally successful career; but in the character of all of them, in the importance of many of them, in their logical succession in point of merit, in their consistency to an ideal established as firmly as the foundations of his most massive buildings, in the impression which they bear of the unrelenting vigor of his mind, they are unique.

It is the fate of most modern buildings — not less of the most scholarly and correct among them than of the most vernacular and commonplace — that they have failed to excite public interest. They are not discussed or criticised, as are the latest works in sculpture or painting. They seem to have no word to say which is intelligible to the passers-by. They may give pleasure in some sort, but the pleasure is undefined, and no layman seeks to analyze the cause of these unconscious impressions. This great art, therefore, seems to live a life quite apart from public sympathy, and the genius of the architect becomes introverted and sophisticated without the continual spur and admonition of common appreciation.

But Richardson's works, wherever placed, have in some way made an impression upon the public mind. They have always surprised, and generally pleased, all who looked upon them. They have aroused discussion outside the closed areopagus of the profession. To discover the cause of such a phenomenon and rightly to profit by this unusual experience would make architecture at length a living art in our land. Its professors have but to gain their public by their works, and the *reform* has begun. Reform is better than any revival, however learned or picturesque.

It is therefore eminently desirable to discover the nature of these potent qualities in Richardson's works. They are not likely to reside in the characteristics which first attract the architect, certainly not in the cleverness with which this skillful student has adapted to modern uses certain devices of construction and decoration which were developed by a few unknown builders in the south of France, in the tenth or eleventh century; they are not in his archæological correctness, nor in the light which he has thrown upon the spirit of certain phases of historical art, nor in his technique. But we may find them among the more obvious characteristics of his work, namely, in its subjective qualities, — in the weight and breadth of his touch, in the remarkable simplicity of his architectural conceptions, in their large, manly vigor, in their clear and powerful accentuation, in the plainness of their sky-lines, and in their freedom from the conventionalities of design. The general idea of each of his buildings is patent to all. The beholder is flattered to find that here, at last, is a fine building which he can understand. His eye is not distracted by detail; that is to say, the detail remains subordinated to the general conception, and only presents itself to the mind subsequently as a confirmation of the first impression. He may like or dislike the design, but he does not forget it.

It would seem an obvious conclusion from this experience that a theory of composition based upon general principles of simplicity and breadth or strength is a better starting-point for a school of reform than any revival, the greatest virtue of which must be correctness of reproduction and skill of adaptation. This, in fact, is the most important bequest left by Richardson to his professional brothers. The natural tendency of modern architecture is to complexity and pedantry, born of familiarity with the whole history of art; its appeal is rather to the profession through technical qualities and displays of science than to the public through the larger and more robust virtues which all can comprehend. I am referring to the best work of the best men in the profession, who disdain to sacrifice their convictions for the sake of astonishing the vulgar with extravagances, or of attracting them with novelties. To such, a career like that of Richardson is a welcome refreshment. Its influence upon contemporary work is altogether wholesome, and seems not unlikely to prepare the way for a reform of the best sort. The Rev. J. L. Pettie, in the preface of his admirable Architectural Studies in France (1854),[3] said, "I would look forward to an architectural style that shall appeal to a deeper sense than a critical taste for correctness, and display a power beyond that of mere science. That such a style will spring up sooner or later I have little doubt. But I cannot venture to pronounce what will be its constructive or decorative character . . . It may prove to be something as little within the contemplation of our present architects and architectural writers as the richest Gothic was in the imagination of the first builders of the Roman basilica."

The lesson of Richardson's career is conveyed to us mostly in the language of the Romanesque of Auvergne, but with reminiscences from the neighboring provinces of Anjou, Aquitaine, and Provence. He was fortunate enough to hit upon an undeveloped style, full of capacity, picturesque, romantic; its half-savage strength beguiled by traces of refinement inherited from the luxury of the later Roman Empire. It was a style quite in harmony with the natural habits of his mind, and he was wise enough to resist the temptation to experiment in other styles. He forced his Romanesque to uses the most various, — from Trinity Church to the Pittsburgh Court-House (Figs. 101, 110), from dwelling-houses at Washington to railway stations in Massachusetts (Fig. 109), from warehouses in Boston and Chicago to the State House at Albany (Figs. 129, 103–103d). In all these the influence of his chosen style was dominant in various degrees, colored more or less, as occasion required, by influences of later styles. It must not be inferred that he was an archæological architect, like Sir Gilbert Scott, whose works were always correct and learned but dry and prosaic (Figs. 86, 87); or like Burgess, whose whole life was a beautiful early Gothic masquerade (Figs. 88, 89); or even like Vaudremer, who, in his famous church at Montrouge, showed how a refined artist could evolve an ideal Romanesque out of the traditions of the Paris studios.[4] And yet no architect ever made a more thorough and conscientious study of his chosen style; he collected all the books, prints, and photographs which bore upon the subject, and personally ransacked all the forgotten by-ways among the springs of the Loire for examples and details. He saturated himself with the spirit of the unsophisticated builders and stone carvers of southern France who preceded the builder-monks of Cluny and Citeaux; and yet he never permitted his antiquarianism to swamp his individuality. The success of his revival must be attributed far less to this sympathy with the spirit of these Romanesque designers than to the powerful personality which was everywhere infused in his work. It is this element which distinguished his performances above those of any of his contemporaries on either side of the Atlantic, and has given to them their peculiar attractiveness. They were never mere adapted quotations, like the works of the Gothic and Queen Anne revivalists; they constituted a living art, for, as has been intimated, the succession of his works, from the Boston and Albany Railroad offices and the Agawam Bank at Springfield to his competitive designs for the Cathedral at Albany, shows a steady process of development from savage and brutal strength to strength refined by study, enriched by experience, and controlled by indomitable will. His artistic biography may be clearly read in his buildings taken in the order of their date. The most casual observer recognizes in each his big, plain, unmistakable sign-manual. His range of favorite architectural *motifs* is exceptionally small for an architect of his accomplishments. The predominant horizontal string course, the low arch, the heavy stone transom, the frieze of windows, separated by grouped shafts, the apsidal projection, the accentuation of points by profuse semi-barbaric sculpture, the coarse mosaic, the large, unbroken wall surface, the depressed gable, the severe sky-line, the general tendency to a sort of grandiose archaism, — these features are incidents in every work of masonry which came from his hand. His invention was active, but it found ample scope for variety of expression with this simple language of form. Every problem of design, whether large or small, — especially in a few little wooden country houses, — was developed in a broad, strong way; with mannerism, indeed, but without sophistications of detail. Evidences of recklessness and carelessness in matters of technique are not unfrequent. In some of his earlier work, notably in Trinity Church, he seemed impatient of the study of detail (Fig. 101). He never made a sacrifice for the sake of symmetry; very few of his *facades* are controlled by a centre line, none are overladen or overstudied; some, on the other hand, are bald and vacant. But he always obtained an effect of repose, and sometimes of a reserved force unusual in modern work. He knew how to decorate without weakening, and no modern designer ever more thoroughly understood the value and true function of sculpture in a work of architecture. He rarely placed an ornament where it was not duly subordinated to and illustrative of the architectural frame-work. Much of his earlier work was abandoned to a display of bigness and force which betrayed him into grotesqueness and extravagance. This tendency never entirely deserted him, and even in the later part of his career made possible that extraordinary piece of architectural athleticism, the gate lodge on the estate of F. L. Ames at North Easton, which might have been piled up by a Cyclops. This specimen of boisterous Titanic gamboling was nearly coincident with some of the most refined and most patiently studied work of his hand, as, for example, the Town Hall at North Easton and the New Law School at Cambridge (Fig. 107).

Richardson poured into the antique mould such a stream of vital energy and personal force that the old types seemed transformed in his hands. The productions of such a man must necessarily be open occasionally to adverse criticism in matters of technical detail. It is not the object of this paper to review his works in any such spirit. It is sufficient that there are qualities in them which interest the public, and which have made an almost unexampled impression upon contemporary architects. There are few of his countrymen in the profession who, at this moment, among the influences which affect their hands in designing, will not recognize the distinct enrichment and enlargement of their resources by a new range of architectural motifs first made current by Richardson's practice.

On general principles, every addition to our means of expression in an art, the language of which is a language of forms, appealing to the imagination through the eye, would be accepted as a benefit, were it not that this *copia verborum* is already so overcrowded with contributions out of the inexhaustible past that the architect is apt to overlay the fundamental idea of his work with favorite expressions and phrases, so that its intention becomes "caviare to the general."[5] He is somewhat like the Chinese poets, who, when they would write a sonnet to their mistress' eyebrows, make a mere compound of quotations from their classics, ingeniously dovetailed, and intelligible only to Chinese scholarship. But we have to thank Richardson for something more than an interesting addition to our architectural vocabulary. This has been done before him by many architects of genius, who did not leave their successors practically any richer, nor advance their art a single step towards reform or the development of a style.

It is because of the almost unexampled proof of the potency of breadth, unity, and simplicity of style that we are chiefly indebted to our friend. These are the qualities which, irrespective of the especial forms which he affected, constitute his greatest claim to recognition as a leader. The benefits of this example may be detected not only in the work of his immediate school of young followers, but in the practice of older men in the profession. It is rather from this influence that we have a right to anticipate beneficent results than from his peculiar mannerism in handling his favorite phases of

Romanesque. One has but to glance at the innumerable wooden country houses of the cheaper sort which have arisen during the last two or three years, to see, even in this homely branch of the art of building, that the day of fatal facility in jig-sawing, machine-made mouldings, and "gingerbread work" has gone by, and given place not to antiquarianism or old colonial masquerading, but to a careful simplicity of outline, to a reserve in matters of detail, which, while they make possible any desirable degree of quaintness or picturesqueness of expression, are entirely consistent with convenience, economy, and a display of the best sort of architectural power. We venture the opinion that this wholesome phase in the building art is the direct result of Richardson's example.

As might be expected, he has imitators, who travesty his peculiarities of style and affront the civilization of our times with elaborate affectations of savagery and archaic rudeness. These brutalities, fortunately, find no general acceptance, and will soon be forgotten. Evidence of refinement and study is essential to any work of the nineteenth century; and when these qualities are made consistent with those nobler qualities which work for strength, simplicity, and life, as we may see in the Chamber of Commerce at Cincinnati, in the Library at Woburn, and in the unexecuted studies for the Cathedral at Albany, we seem to approach the highest architectural achievements of our time, and to catch a glimpse of the dawning of a new era, having its foundations in principles, and not in imitations and conventionalities. Perhaps the hope of architecture resides largely in a continuation of Richardson's experiments with the Romanesque of Auvergne. The resources of the style and its capacities for development are evidently not exhausted. If it is treated merely as a revival, there is no health in it, and it will presently fail, like the other revivals which have preceded it. If it is treated as a basis for true progress, it will be found more fruitful than any other style now available, and the movement may have before it a future entirely beneficial for American art, — a future which will differentiate that art from contemporary work on the other side of the Atlantic, and give us at last, perhaps, a definite American style.

Architecture in the West

The various stages in the slow developments of civilization from barbarism are marked by a corresponding series of visible monuments, in which may plainly be read the character and quality of the social conditions out of which they grew. The true value and significance of these almost ineffaceable records have never been duly recognized. The industry of the archæologist in classifying them, the ingenuity of the modern architect in quoting from them, the instinct of poet and novelist in using them darkly as the background of romance, have made their external aspects more or less familiar to all; but their subjective qualities have never been so analyzed as to make them accessible to the historian. They have never been used by him like traditions, documents, and chronicles, though their characteristics are the clearest, the most naive, unaffected, and deliberate expressions which humanity has uttered in any stage of its career. Since the Renaissance this contemporaneous record has been sophisticated by revivals, imitations, adaptations, combinations, and other affectations of the modern architect, so that it has apparently become more difficult to be deciphered; yet its relation to the spirit and essential quality of the human life about us cannot be entirely obliterated, even by the most cleverly planned masquerading in the trappings of Greek or Roman, Romanesque, Mediæval, or Renaissance art.

Having in view this unconscious function of architecture, whether ancient or modern, skilled or unskilled, as a chronicle of mankind, there should be no manifestation of it without some interest to every intelligent observer, whatever qualities of art may be involved in it.

I propose to attempt a brief descriptive sketch of a modern phase of this architectural chronicle, which, by reason of the exceptional social conditions under which it is produced, presents some unprecedented features.

Civilization is advancing into the wilderness of the great West like a brimming and irresistible tide which knows no ebb. Its first waves of occupation bear upon their crests a human element of astonishing energy and force. No conquest or crusade of history has been accomplished with a greater display of hardy intelligence. It has planted cities and established civil order upon virgin soil in less than thirty days. The external aspects of these first occupations are remarkable for the skill, directness, and economy with which means are adapted to ends. The first settlers are comfortably housed in a week, so that all the processes of simple domestic life are made possible without delay. Structures to accommodate the land office, the saloon, the variety store, the railway station, the bank, the school, and the church arise to meet the emergencies of border life, and the visible town is begun. These structures, of course, have value only as temporary makeshifts; but as material prosperity increases, and with it the ambition for permanent investments, the way is open for a much more definite expression of thought in building. At this stage of development the natural desire of every citizen to own property of the best possible appearance at the lowest possible cost leads to what may be called an architecture of pretense, — an architecture intended to appear better than it is (Fig. 118). This architecture, or, more properly, this method of building, has, without essential local characteristics, spread over the entire occupied territory of the West. It has met for many years, and will meet probably for many more, all the practical requirements, and has flattered the crude artistic aspirations of millions of intelligent and exceptionally ingenious and prosperous people. It must, therefore, be respectfully considered as, at present, the vernacular art of the country, though, when judged by the most liberal and catholic canons of educated taste, it fails to satisfy *in esse* if not *in posse*. Nowhere else in the civilized world can be found anything resembling it. It is peculiar; it is ours.

I have called this characteristic and almost universal expression of Western civilization an architecture of pretense, because of its ambition and of its desire to make a vain show with small means. No people in the world understands cheap construction and economical methods of building so well, and is so inventive in providing for it. But, unwilling to let it appear what it is and to let it grow into a legitimate expression of art by natural processes of development, it has been forced to assume forms which do not belong to it, which contradict its proper functions, and which are devised to satisfy false and unsettled ideals of beauty and fitness. The facility with which wood and galvanized iron may be moulded, painted, and sanded to imitate stone or other nobler materials makes this baleful process possible, and tempts the builder to mask his honest work with crude travesties of conventional art.

It must be admitted that this method of architectural masquerading had its origin in the eastern part of our country; but there, under the influence of better examples and higher education, it soon fell into disrepute, because, theoretically, it is an offense against fundamental principles of art, so gross that it cannot survive the first touch of intelligent criticism; and, practically, because this architecture of pretense cannot stand the test of time. Like all other experiments in the evolution of forms, only the fittest remain. But the

West, eager to anticipate the fruits of success, too impatient to wait for a natural growth of art, ambitious to emulate the older civilizations, is, for the moment, contenting itself with an appearance. The vernacular style in the remoter districts has still undisputed sway, and, in the hands of uneducated builders, plays with these dangerously facile materials such fantastic tricks before high Heaven as make the angels weep, and give no true and permanent satisfaction even to those whom they are intended to surprise and delight. It serves, for the time, to confer upon the newly built streets of the West a delusive aspect of metropolitan completeness and finish, until, after a few years, the paint wears off, the wooden sham begins to decay, and the galvanized iron to betray its hollow mockeries. "A thing of beauty is a joy forever,"[1] but a thing of cheap and vulgar ostentation, by a happy accident of fate, finds speedy oblivion. It is a piece of singular good fortune that the vernacular style has thus within itself the seeds of its own dissolution.

The present building methods and architectural character maintained in the rural districts in France, England, Germany, Italy, Spain, Switzerland, Russia, etc., differ from those of five centuries ago only in proportion to the advance of civilization and progress of knowledge; and they differ contemporaneously, one from another, as much now as they did in the Middle Ages. Even the cities which are planted along the highways of the world, subject to the cosmopolitan influences, such as are afforded by rapid and constant intercommunication, by the interchange of books, prints, and photographs, by technical schools and schools of art, remain almost as distinct in their architectural character as they were when they were the strongholds of civil liberty against the feudal system. Their frank attempts to imitate the street façade of Paris are betrayed by the unconscious instinct of localism. The foreign accent is readily detected. The common and distinctive architectural forms in these older communities of the world are the results of established customs and ancient traditions, which have their roots not only in characteristics of politics, race, and religion, but in the soil itself, which has furnished the materials of building, and, through these, has dictated the forms by which they are most readily adapted to meet the wants of mankind. The arts of civilization, thus significantly grouped and ordered in the progress of history, rise slowly

> By stepping-stones of their dead selves
> To higher things.[2]

The deliberateness of these changes, their independence of permanent influence from individual vagaries and experiments, are an assurance that they are developed unconsciously out of the essence of the time. Architecture, under these conditions, must be recognized as a true exponent of the quality of contemporary civilization.

By contrast with these established, slowly growing, indigenous styles, it cannot be doubted that the fantastic vernacular of the West, where there are absolutely no inherited traditions, no customs rooted to the soil to keep the architecture in a reasonable path of development, is merely provisional, a feverish expression of transition, a groping after a natural expression in art. It is carelessly compounded of exoteric and heterogeneous elements, and, so far as its decorative or architectural character is concerned, it has no basis in the essential conditions of the people. The very fecundity of undisciplined and misapplied invention which makes it what it is; the distortion and exaggeration of conventional forms of architecture, which convert some of its productions into a grotesque travesty of art; the fact that none of these experiments give such permanent satisfaction as to cause their repetition, but that they are succeeded by new experiments of illiterate fancy, — these things indicate very clearly to my mind that the necessity for a more orderly system of forms, capable of natural growth and expansion, is unconsciously felt. A reign of caprice in architecture, with frequent new departures, may be accepted *prima facie* as proof of the need of such a system, in order that the civilization of the time may express itself in a copious language of its own, instead of using dumb signs and gestures, or trying to find quotations from other tongues and adapting them to its use.

In the absence of such a natural language, by which all the ideas which are to be expressed in building may be expressed at least grammatically without the need of especial training in art, architecture is completely at the mercy of architects. When they happen to be men of education, as we shall presently see, there is an astonishing activity in the development of legitimate style. When, as is usually the case, they are not educated, this process of natural evolution is very much embarrassed, if not entirely interrupted. It is pathetic to see towns of thirty to fifty thousand energetic, public-spirited, intelligent, enterprising inhabitants, with factories, school-houses, churches, public halls, convenient dwellings, and all the external signs of prosperity, but without a single building really good, grammatically constructed, or conceived in a spirit of subordination to any type of art. The people are not indifferent to this state of things. They are intelligent enough to recognize a work of architecture when they see it; and, as a general rule, their judgment encourages good things. Never has the missionary of art had such a fruitful field for his labors. A fair building, planted in such a town, is like the preaching of a gospel of truth among an eager and sympathetic people. It bears its legitimate fruit with amazing promptness. In a twelvemonth there will be fifty imitations. It gives a distinct stimulus to architectural life. Details of design taken from the new model may be seen, copied with various degrees of fidelity, on every hand. It proves to be not only a source of pride to the citizens and a most grateful enlargement of the resources of the builder, but, to a great extent, a correction and rebuke of prevailing errors. Of course not one or two or even a dozen good models are sufficient to obliterate all the evils of architectural illiteracy and inexperience in a given locality. A free and unrestricted foraging by undisciplined practitioners among the commonplaces of architecture has made them bad disciples of reform. It has created a singular disrespect for all the safe and conservative elements in design, an unwholesome

183

ambition to inject an undue amount of their own personality into architectural work; and when they instinctively recognize a piece of sound construction expressed in an artistic manner, they are prepared only to imitate some of its exterior aspects, not its essential spirit, which alone can fructify.

Thus the progress of the transition, though it receives in an indirect way a slight impetus in the right direction, is not logical and steady, as it was when, by a series of experimental buildings, each an improvement on its predecessor, rising by "stepping-stones of their dead selves," the debased Roman was gradually developed into Byzantine art in the East, and into the various forms of Romanesque art in the West; or when these, in turn, grew inevitably, by changing social conditions, into the arts of the Middle Ages. If the ministers of these great historical transitions, unconsciously interpreting and giving visible form to the spirit of their respective eras, "builded better than they knew," [3] it was because, unlike the multitudinous architects of the West, they were familiar only with a certain accepted method of construction and a certain limited set of architectural forms connected with it. Undistracted by a more or less exact knowledge of other methods and other sets of forms; knowing only what their fathers and grandfathers did before them; seeing no journals illustrating what contemporary builders were doing elsewhere within and without the boundaries of Christendom; reading no books and studying no prints in which the achievements of classic times were measured and analyzed for their instruction; attending no schools of art save those which were established under the builder's scaffolds, or in the cloisters where the religious traditions were preserved, they were the servants of a single style, and happily could concentrate all their energies upon it. Changes came about by natural growth and by logical processes of induction, not by caprice or by reviving old forms according to individual taste.

It is to be observed that the scene of transition in the West is enacted on so broad a stage, with so many distracting incidents and episodes, and, withal, we are so near to it and so much a part of it, that it is difficult for us to appreciate its progress and to understand its ends. We do not realize that the great transitions of history are made clear to us by the fact that there remain to us only a comparatively few isolated monuments in which we can read readily the progress of the civilizations. The great multitude of inferior contemporary structures which lay between these monuments, and in which were tried the experiments, do not remain to distract and complicate our views. Moreover, in the perspective, compelled by our distant point of observation, the great spaces of time which stretched between them are abbreviated. And though the advance of the great transition now going on in the West is far more rapid than any known to history, we must remember that this transition is governed by far more complicated conditions of life, and is illustrated by a perplexing infinity of ephemeral buildings. The prejudices and desires of the most impartial observer must necessarily color his deductions. It is scarcely for us to separate the wheat from the chaff in the products of these mills of God. I venture to believe, however, that the forward movement has gone far enough to enable us to appreciate the spirit of it, if not to comprehend the general direction of its progress.

I believe I am justified in stating that what, for the want of a more convenient name, I have called the vernacular art of the West — that which accompanies the first advances of civilization into the new lands, and lingers long after the successful establishment of all the institutions of civil order and prosperity — will not be recognized in the future history of American architecture; much less, that it will be stigmatized as a reproach. In fact, it is merely preliminary to architecture, though for the moment it pretends to be the real thing. It is evidently a hasty growth out of the immediate necessities of an enterprising people, too busy with the practical problems of life and the absorbing question of daily bread to have established ideals of art, or to have deliberately formulated in building an adequate expression of their civilization. It is an art whose essential characteristics have been derived from expediency, — an art which has been mainly concerned with mechanical devices for quick and economical building. These devices have been invented by practical men to meet practical wants in a practical way. When freed from the misleading adornments imposed upon them by ignorance and pretense; from shams of wood, galvanized iron, machine-made mouldings, and all the other delusive rubbish of cheap deceit, which have no connection whatever with the structure, these practical devices will develop style. Until these quips and cranks of undisciplined imaginations shall have shabbily descended into their inevitable oblivion, and have been replaced by methods of decoration developed out of the construction according to the spirit of precedents furnished by the best eras of art which remain to us for our delight and instruction, deliberate and permanent architecture will not come into existence.

Upon this simple proposition rests the hope of architecture in the West.

Chicago seems to have fairly won the distinction of being the fountainhead of architectural reform in the West. The healthy impulses from this active and intelligent centre are felt in the remotest towns as soon as opportunities have occurred for permanent improvements. The dangerous liberty which the entire absence of schools, traditions, precedents, and consequently of discipline in art has conferred upon the architects of the New World, and more especially of the West, and which has given rise to all the crudeness and vulgarity of our vernacular building, has proved, in the hands of a few well-trained young men in Chicago a professional privilege of the most conspicuous importance, — a privilege, indeed, which has not been enjoyed to the same extent in any other city in the world. The resistless enterprise and public spirit of the Western metropolis, its great accumulations of capital, the phenomenal growth of its commercial and social institutions, and the intelligent ambition of its people to achieve a distinctive position in all the arts of civilization have given abundant opportunity for monumental expressions in architecture. The manner in which these opportunities have been used during the past eight or ten years gives encouragement to the hope so long cherished that we may at last have an American architecture, the un-forced and natural growth of our independent position in art.

It is not to be understood that these fortunate men have deliberately set to work to invent a new architecture. They have been too well trained in the best schools and offices of the East, and often by travel and study abroad, not to respect the great achievements of the past, and not to make the fullest use of their rich inheritance of architectural forms. But their merit consists in the fact that some quality in the civilization of the West — its independ-ence of spirit, perhaps, its energy, enterprise, and courage, or a certain breadth of view inspired by its boundless opportunities — has, happily, ena-bled them to use this inheritance without being enslaved by it. It would have been easiest for them to quote with accuracy and adapt with grace the styles of the Old World, to be scholarly, correct, academical, and thus to stand apart from the sympathies of the people, and to constitute themselves an aristocratic guild of art. They preferred to play the more arduous and nobler part; to become, unconsciously, ministers of an architectural reform so potent and fruitful, so well fitted to the natural conditions of the strenuous liberty of the West, that one may already predicate from it the speedy over-throw of the temporary, experimental, transitional vernacular art of the coun-try, and the establishment of a school which may be recognized in history as the proper exponent of this marvelous civilization. The hope that we are entering upon such an era rests mainly upon the fact that the characteristics of the best new work of the West are based, not on the elegant dilettanteism, which is appreciated only by the elect, but by the frank conversion of prac-tical building into architectural building without affectations or mannerisms; thus appealing directly to the common sense of the people, and creating a standard which they may be capable of comprehending. It is based on a sleepless inventiveness in structure; on an honest and vigorous recognition of the part which structure should play in making a building fitting and beau-tiful; on an intelligent adaptation of form to the available building materials of the West; upon the active encouragement of every invention and manu-facture which can conduce to the economy or perfecting of structure and the embellishment of structure; upon an absolute freedom from the trammels of custom, so that it shall not interpose any obstacles of professional prejudice to the artistic expression of materials or methods; and, finally, upon knowing how to produce interesting work without an evident straining for effect. These are the qualities of true artists who accept the natural conditions of their en-vironment, and can adapt themselves to those conditions without surrender of any essential principles of building as a fine art. Any architect of education and accomplishments is fortunate who finds himself a part of a young com-munity so ambitious, enterprising, and resistless in the pursuit of wealth and power, — doubly fortunate if he can make his art keep step with a progress so vigorous without losing the finer and more delicate artistic sense.

I am conscious of the extreme inadequacy of words, unaccompanied by a series of graphic illustrations, to make clear to the laity in art the characteristics of this interesting architectural situation. If one can imagine how a plain, concrete idea may, by an unskillful writer, be overlaid with conceits, affectations, and verbiage, not growing out of it or inspired by it, frequently expressed in bad grammar, and generally offending against the simplest rules of rhetoric, he may have a fair type of the protean vernacular. If it is elegantly set forth in correct Greek, Latin, or Old French, or paraded in the language of the Elizabethan era, or imitates the style of Browning, or Tennyson, or Carlyle, with ingenious quotations of their characteristic phraseology or methods of expression, he may understand by the obvious analogy how the educated architect is tempted by his learning, misses his opportunities, and appeals over the heads of the people to the few who are versed in the history and æsthetics of architecture. If one can distinguish the subtle essence which, infused into a concrete idea expressed in plain and straightforward prose, elevates it into the region of poetry, he may be enabled, without the technical training which analyzes and dissects, to comprehend how a sound construction in building may be converted into architecture. To this task inspiration alone is inadequate. The conditions of modern architecture are so complex that without a thorough training in construction and design, based upon a familiar appreciation of the history of art, inspiration is speechless.

The opportunities afforded by the West to architecture on the high plane which I have endeavored to describe are mainly commercial. It is in making the wisest use of these that the leading architects of Chicago have achieved their characteristic successes. A ten-story office and bank building, fireproof throughout; with swift elevators for passengers and freight, a battery of boilers in the deep sub-basement, giving summer heat throughout, and supplying energy for pumps, ventilating fans, and electric dynamos; equipped like a palace with marbles, bronze, and glass; flooded with light in every part; with no superfluous weight of steel beam, fire-clay arch, or terra-cotta partition, no unnecessary mass of masonry or column; the whole structure nicely adjusted to sustain the calculated strains and to bear with equal stress upon every pier of the deep foundations, so that no one shall yield more than another as it transfers its accumulated burden to the unstable soil beneath, — such a problem does not call for the same sort of architectural inspiration as the building of a vaulted cathedral in the Middle Ages, but, surely, for no less of courage and science, and, in providing for the safe, swift, and harmonious adjustment of every part of its complicated organism, for a far wider range of knowledge. The one required a century of deliberate and patient toil to complete it; the other must be finished, equipped, and occupied in a year of strenuous and carefully ordered labor; no part of its complex being overlooked, all the details of its manifold functions being provided for in the laying of the first foundation stone, and the whole satisfying the eye as a work of art as well as a work of convenience and strength. Whether one compares a modern building of this sort with a cathedral of the first class, with one of the imperial baths or villas of Rome, or with the Flavian amphitheatre itself, it must hold equal rank as a production of human genius and energy, not only in the skillful economy of its structure and in its defiance of fire and the other vicissitudes of time, but as a work of fine art developed among practical considerations which seem fundamentally opposed to expressions of architectural beauty.

A problem of this sort cannot be satisfactorily solved by academical formulas. The education derived from venerable traditions, from the teachings of the schools, from the examples and models furnished by the masters, from the admirable monuments of history, when confronted by the inexorable requirements of modern commercial civilization, is confounded. Between the practical question and the discipline of the schools there seems sometimes to be an irrepressible conflict. If the prejudices of the schools are permitted to prevail, a correct and scholarly result may be achieved, but practical interests are apt to be sacrificed in important particulars; if practical interests are faithfully provided for, there is likely to be a palpable offense against some of the most accepted formulas of art. But there is a conflict still more apparent and still more incessant between these formulas and the methods of structure imposed upon building by the application of modern science to all its details. The progress of invention is so rapid and constant that it is almost impossible for the architect to keep abreast of it with his work. It is in constant warfare with the precepts of Vitruvius, which guided our grandfathers in a safe but uneventful path; with all the consecrated traditions of mediæval masonry, which were followed by our fathers with religious awe; with all the wealth of precedent available to us in the history of architecture. If the office of the architect is hospitable to these modern influences, there must be a revolution. The results of this revolution must constitute the ultimate style of the nineteenth century.

Indeed, the history of modern architecture during the last ten years is a chronicle of the various fortunes of this struggle between the conservatism, which separated architecture from the people, and reform, which brings them into sympathy with it. The Old World is the natural stronghold of the former; the New World is the natural theatre whereon the latter is making its most hazardous and successful advances.

When a mighty political leader was required to carry our country through the mortal perils of the civil war, a new man, modeled on a new plan out of

> Sweet clay from the breast
> Of the unexhausted West,[4]

was raised for this heroic service. I am tempted to believe that we may look to the same virgin and prolific source for the spirit which may give us, in due time, a national art. This would be logical, and, if I do not read too hopefully the signs of the times, the fulfillment is not far removed.

It is proper that the centres of culture in the East should, in a large degree, sympathize with the conservative tendencies of the Old World, and that Boston and New York, like the monastic cloisters, should be to the New World the guardians of the precious traditions of art, as the latter were to the

Middle Ages. This lamp of memory is kept trimmed and burning, also, in the professional schools of the colleges and universities of the North. From these schools, where they learn the theory, and from the principal offices, where they are taught the practice of architecture, goes forth every year a crowd of young men, whose business it is to replace the provisional vernacular of our country with an architecture which, while it preserves the mellow traditions of art, shall, in proportion to the various capacities and opportunities of the architect, represent the especial conditions of our civilization. The effort to make an architecture without these traditions has been tried for the first time in our country, and it has failed, as we have seen. We have been trying to write essays and poems without a knowledge of grammar or of the structure of language. The result has been a vulgar vernacular, made up of commonplaces, catch-words, and slang. The graduates of the schools are steadily purifying the language, enlarging the vocabulary, and endeavoring to reconcile what often seems the almost irreconcilable interests of practice and theory.

It has been said that the fundamental ideal of domestic architecture in France is a monument of art, while in England it is comfort and fitness. Certainly the former is characteristically symmetrical, and the latter characteristically picturesque, save for a brief period when it was under the dominion of an Italian revival, in the latter part of the eighteenth century. The social conditions of our own country have been the first influence to affect the character of our own domestic architecture, and it has yielded to this influence with a frankness which has had the most satisfactory results. The sentiment of domesticity has presided over the development of the dwelling-house in this country, so unrestricted by the affectations of fashion and style; and the methods of wood construction which have been almost universally applied to it have been brought to such mechanical perfection that it may safely be asserted that no people in the world are so comfortably and decently housed as our own. Under these circumstances, the domestic branch of architecture has been the first to take upon itself definite characteristics of style. Of course, as a matter of art, the facility and cheapness of the materials used have given us in dwelling-houses the most grotesque and fantastic forms of the vernacular. On the other hand, the builders have shown themselves very sensitive to good impulses, and the first architecture which we see in a Western town is invariably exhibited in buildings of this class. They are, in fact, playing no inconsiderable part in the great movement of reform. They prepare the way, as it were, for demonstrations of a more permanent and monumental character.

The attitude of the West towards architecture, as distinguished from that of the more cultivated parts of the East, may, I think, best be illustrated by the fact that a graduate of the best schools and practice of the East, who, finding himself in one of the rapidly growing Western cities, should insist on being scholastic, and should confine himself to the correct use of strictly classic or mediæval motifs, would soon have no opportunities for the exercise of his proclivities; because, in the first place, he would not be understood, and because, in the second, he could not effect a reconciliation between his academical convictions and the modern methods of structure which he is compelled to adopt, at whatever cost of purity of style. Indeed, his most anxious study must be bestowed on the structural part of the problem. If the artistic is one part, the structural is nine parts, of his endeavor. The question which must preoccupy his mind is how he can meet the practical conditions with the greatest economy of material and labor; how he may adjust the dimensions, forms, and connections of every girder, beam, column, pier, and other parts of his structure, so that each shall be adapted to the service which it has to perform, with no superfluity of weight and strength, on the one hand, and so that, on the other, all considerations of stability shall be duly provided for within the limit of safety. His inventive zeal must be constantly on the alert to improve on the known methods, for there are none which are not subject to improvement more or less fundamental. Fireproof structure, in especial, makes a never-ceasing demand upon his resources. An envelope of fire-clay, porous terra cotta, plaster, or some other material impervious to fiercest heat must cover every piece of structural iron or wood. There must be no brute masses of material, such as formed the basis of Roman structure. None of these devices and methods were dreamed of when the old masters of architecture perfected their forms and proportions; so that the decoration or artistic expression of this complicated and, in each case, to a certain extent, unprecedented organism, and the conversion of it into an object of architecture, as contrasted with one of engineering, must demand of the architect such a freedom from academical restraint, such a command of the resources of design, as to make his task at once inspiring and perilous. Under these conditions, error is far easier than success: the grooves of custom, if indolently followed, will sooner or later lead him astray from the opportunities of original expression which are lying in wait for his use. The silent growth of the building on the drawing-boards must be attended by a constant strain of doubt and anxiety. The spirit of a recognized historical style must be followed, in any case, but these new practical conditions of construction and service compel him to various and perplexing degrees of divergence from the consecrated types. To meet these difficult emergencies with adequate spirit, he must possess the thorough knowledge of the scholar, the exact training of the engineer, the enthusiastic zeal and inventive courage of the artist, and the prompt decision of the man of business. The stimulus of enterprise and the incitements of emulation are in the air which he breathes. The qualities which I have named have certainly been exhibited in some of the best buildings of the West to a degree and in a manner which distinctly differentiate them from any contemporary work of the Old World, which challenge the best endeavors of the East to emulate them, and are already giving cheering evidence of the establishment of a vigorous architecture characteristic of the West.

Architecture has not kept pace with the advance of science and invention during the present century. This has been one of its gravest reproaches. But an architecture which, like this of the West, is frankly based upon science and invention must keep fairly abreast with them, and thus redeem the waning influence of this noblest of the arts. If it can thus be made a living art instead of a studio art, it will not be long before it will be justifying its function as an expression of our civilization.

We are too near to these developments to judge of them without prejudice, but it is certainly true that the architectural publications of the Old World which illustrate the current work of our era in that quarter have ceased to have that same degree of interest with and authority over the profession which they exercised three or four years ago. Previous to that time all the movements of the modern schools in Europe, all the changing fashions of design, and all the characteristic revivals of England in especial were marked and closely followed in our own country. Now, our own publications, setting forth our own achievements, are studied with equal if not greater interest. They certainly show that, in fundamental respects, we have broken loose from the old bondage, and are entering upon developments of style which seem to be actuated by our own local conditions. If we still (as we must always of necessity) send our students to the ancient and exhaustless fountain-heads of art in Europe, to draw from them inspiration, refinement, and culture, we have the satisfaction of receiving in our own country diligent scholars, who come to us from England and the Continent for the refreshment to be obtained from our own methods of structure and design. If they come expecting to patronize and criticise, they remain to study and to acquire a broader professional vision. This is a pilgrimage full of significance and promise.

I do not mean to assert that, even in some of the most successful examples of new work in the West, there are not evidences of crudeness and caprice as well as the usual sophistications apt to result from high training in art, though I might name a dozen characteristic buildings in Chicago and some of the larger cities of the West which combine extreme boldness and ingenuity of design with scholarly reserve and refinement. But, on the whole, the errors seem to me rather errors of force than of weakness; they are such as we are accustomed to see in the earlier expressions of every healthy and vigorous style which proved to possess the elements of life and the capacity for a long career. I certainly can assert that none of the work which, by happy instinct, commends itself to builders and is copied and travestied with various degrees of success, according to the degree of education in the practitioners, is characterized by that fastidiousness and elegant dilettanteism which belong to styles which have said all that they have to say, and have lost their reproductive power.

I think I can discern in this architecture of promise just such points of difference from the more finished, elegant, and scholarly contemporaneous work of Boston and New York (Figs. 173, 184–187) as should grow naturally out of the peculiarities of Western life. The best Eastern architects frequently have some practice in the West, and have set up in Chicago, St. Louis, Kansas City, Omaha, Denver, San Francisco, and elsewhere examples of refined work of high artistic quality, full of inspiration and suggestiveness to local practice. All of them are doing good missionary work, putting out of countenance the buildings of coarse and florid pretense and cheap ostentation about them, and rendering more and more improbable the baleful repetition of them in the future. But by far the most effective missionary work in the West is done by the few structures which have risen "like an exhalation" [5] from its own spirit.

It is difficult to specify in words the details or characteristics of composition which constitute this difference between the works of the East and the West.

In the latter, however, one can certainly detect a greater freedom from the restraints of the European schools. Qualities of material and the nature of the peculiar constructive methods evolved by practical experience are allowed to appear in the decorative scheme to an extent which, I fancy, the conservatism of the East has not encouraged. I have seen Western work wherein the capacities of terra cotta, for instance, have been recognized in the architectural design with a boldness and ingenuity, and a resultant success, which the East has not yet equaled. It is properly treated like a part of the face-brick structure, and the terra-cotta forms are not merely substituted for stone forms without change, as is customary in the East. Ornaments are contrived for the baked moulded clay suited to its capacities and without regard to precedents in stone, and they are built into the brickwork in a manner which shows that they are made of the same material. The same independence of the conventionality which keeps architecture in safe but unprogressive and comparatively uninteresting grooves may be seen in the decorative treatment of metal, both on the inside and the outside of the best buildings, and its fireproof envelope is treated often with a distinction which is at once bold and felicitous. The diminished importance of the exterior cornice, in cases where that member has lost its characteristic function as a gutter, is frequently accepted in the design, and its form is changed to that of a mere wall coping. Buildings of ten or twelve stories are treated with a different expression from that made conventional by buildings of four or five stories, and the usual procrustean processes are not admitted. No accepted formulas are permitted to interfere with the primary necessity of abundant interior light. The first consideration is that windows shall be large enough and frequent enough for this exacting service, without regard to any studio predilections, furnished by the noble wall surfaces of Italian palaces and mediæval monasteries, or by any of the buttressed or pilastered symmetries of the Old World. There is no attempt to avoid the enormous difficulty forced by the requirements of modern shop fronts, and by the priceless invention through which they can be occupied with vast single sheets of polished plate glass set under girders of iron and steel, — a condition important enough in itself to set at defiance nearly all the precepts of all the academies, and, if frankly accepted by the architect, to create, perhaps, out of this nettle, the flower of a new art. It is the disposition to meet these unavoidable and increasing obstacles of structure and practice with hospitality instead of hostility, and the ability to provide for them in a manner at once fitting and distinguished, that mark the work of the best trained architects of the West.

If the attitude of the government of the United States in regard to its public buildings were one of fostering care, as is the case with all other civilized nations, instead of crass indifference, we should look to these for examples of the most characteristic and advanced monumental work. The profession of architecture is not recognized by the general government, and for many years it has petitioned in vain for employment upon work which should be the greatest prizes of the profession and the most representative of our highest aspirations in art. The architect of the Treasury Department, to whom, against his own annual remonstrances, has been committed this great trust, has been constrained to adopt an official style in the public buildings, — one so ordained as to be capable of convenient and almost mechanical adaptation to the various and complicated service of the government with the least practicable expenditure of thought and study, so that no official time may be wasted in conferring upon them especial character. Generally, this work has been done according to the most conventional formulas, making it easiest to design and most costly to execute; consequently, it is absolutely without interest and has had no influence whatever upon the development of architecture in the West or elsewhere, even in places where there is the most manifest eagerness for good instruction. The same is true, though perhaps in a less degree, of most of the state capitols. They have usually been erected under conditions which have afforded little or no scope for the same sort or quality of architectural thought which is bestowed upon private work of much less conspicuous character. Therefore, whatever advance is making in this great art is to be attributed entirely to the people as individuals or corporations; never to the State.

The buildings of the general government, and those of the States, counties, and cities, are usually well constructed and frequently quite correct in the academic sense, though the vernacular has expressed in them some of its most vicious fancies; but foreigners seek in vain among them for an exposition of national character. In Chicago, where one might expect at least to find a type of the energy and sound common sense of the people, the county, city, and national buildings are monuments not only of civic corruption and barbaric extravagance, but of a total eclipse of art. But alongside of them are private structures, erected with judicious economy of means and a lavish expenditure of well-directed study, betraying at all points the spirit which has made Chicago, and surpassing in ingenuity and felicity of design any other commercial buildings in the world.

To name names is a guaranty of good faith, but at the same time it commits the writer of an essay, intended to be very general in its statements, to a certain definiteness which subjects him to the danger of serious omissions. It is obviously impossible to make an exhaustive list of the men and works most potent in the national transition which I have endeavored to describe. But I venture to think that my argument will be strengthened as well as illustrated by distinct reference to the Rookery office building, the Phœnix, the Insurance Exchange, the Art Institute, and other buildings in Chicago, by Burnham and Root, of that city (Figs. 125–127, 132, 133), who also built the beautiful Board of Trade building and others in Kansas City (Fig. 128); to several of the best theatres of Chicago, notably to the new auditorium building, which promises to be one of the most scientifically constructed and perhaps the best appointed large hall in existence, by Adler and Sullivan, of that city (Figs. 132, 138, 138a); to the Union Club, the Chicago Opera House, the Owens building, and many fine dwellings, by Cobb and Frost, also of Chicago (Figs. 121–123, 130); to certain excellent ecclesiastical and domestic work by Burling and Whitehouse, of the same city (Fig. 119); to some miscellaneous work of high merit by W. L. B. Jenny (Fig. 124), Edbrook and Burnham, Holabird and Roche (Fig. 134), and other young men who promise to become distinguished in the active work of reform. I cannot refrain from referring also to Buffington's work in Minneapolis, where the transition is receiving some of its most notable impulses (Fig. 131).[6]

I do not believe there are as yet a dozen men really conspicuous for a capacity to express their art in those indigenous terms which take root and fructify in the great West. But the work to be done is so great and the field so vast that, if these were the only effective missionaries of art in the West, we might well despair of seeing the establishment and confirmation of a national art there within the century. Fortunately, they are closely followed by a crowd of trained workers, earnest and honest, doing yeoman's service in the great towns; all of them tending, I think, to unity of effort in the right direction. If they can be held together long enough by the influence of powerful examples, the result is assured.

I cannot properly close this essay without referring to the work of the lamented Richardson, whose genius was large enough and robust enough to belong to the whole country, and whose influence for reform has been greater for his day and generation than that of any other architect of the century. I can almost say that the direct results of his powerful example may be seen in the principal streets of nearly every city of the West, not unfrequently, indeed, with "a damnable iteration." [7] These results are often rude and undisciplined caricatures of the phase of Romanesque, which he was great enough to make peculiarly his own; on the other hand, there are sufficient evidences that the strong style, of which he was the chosen heir, is being acclimatized and developed under Western influences beyond the point to which he was able to carry it in his brilliant but brief career, until it promises to become one of the most effective agencies in establishing the architecture of the West (Figs. 129, 132). With varying fortunes it has been adapted to buildings of every kind and degree. Sometimes it is merely the sentiment or spirit of it which can be detected, indicating, perhaps, that it is being unconsciously merged with the other fructifying forces, in that great amalgam of precedents which constitutes historical architecture. Any architecture deserving this name must be compounded of too many elements to be the work of any one man or set of men, however illustrious. It must emanate by slow and indistinguishable processes from the essential spirit of the times. Individuals and schools must presently be lost in a movement so large.

The Washington Monument

(1889)

First Article.

By an act of hardy rebellion against the authority of a mighty nation unjustly exercised, a certain people, after a long and bloody war, were once set aside from the rest of the world to form a true republic; and, because of the wisdom and prudence of its founders, this republic eventually became one of the greatest nations of the earth. There was one, the leader in this rebellion, and chief among these founders by the greatness of his services, the dignity of his character, and the pre-eminence of his virtues, upon whom has been conferred by the common voice of mankind a singular title, — "The Father of his Country."

The sentiment of nations with respect to their greatest benefactors, whether it has contented itself with natural emotions of gratitude and admiration, or found more satisfactory expression in acts of adoration, has always been among the most fruitful inspirations of art; indeed, its only adequate utterance has been in visible monuments. Thus all ancient civilizations commemorated their heroes by inscriptions carved upon tablets, or incised upon hieroglyphic shafts; by statues and sculptured history upon arches of triumph, columns, or mausoleums; or they worshipped them as demigods in votive temples. They found in their resources of art a natural and sufficient means of speaking to posterity by tangible and durable shapes in marble, granite, or bronze, — a direct, unmistakable, and unaffected language. Whether Egyptian, Assyrian or Indian, Greek or Roman, Romanesque or Mediæval, each had distinctive and characteristic forms of memorial, which we recognize as unconsciously appropriate, and as significant, not only of the monarch or hero commemorated, but of the people who would honor him and of the times in which he lived. The peculiar value of the service of art to history, as contrasted with the service of literature, seems to reside in the fact that, though, from the nature of things, it is less diffuse and descriptive, it is less liable to be colored by the individuality and prejudice of authorship, and is thus more expressive of a general average of emotion. It visibly sets forth a common ideal of life, and is singularly indicative of the attitude and quality of contemporary civilization. But, in the midst of the complicated civilization of modern times, the visible memorial has in great part lost this expressive power; for architectural utterance has been distracted by archæology, it has lost the divine virtue of simplicity, and is oppressed by the accumulation of knowledge; so that, by reason of the very completeness of its appreciation of the monumental expressions of antiquity, architecture cannot speak without a consciousness of itself, — a condition under which great and simple achievements of art have become extremely difficult. Architects who are learned must needs quote from the past, thus losing some of the initial force of inspiration, and becoming more or less pedantic; those who are unlearned, not being kept in the safe track by a prevailing style, as was the case with their predecessors before the Renaissance, are utterly lost in mazes of ungrammatical originality. Nevertheless, modern times have known a very few cases of straightforward and really poetic monumental expressions, as in Thorwaldsen's Lion of Lucerne, Kranner's monument of the Emperor Franz I. at Prague, the memorial of Frederick the Great at Berlin by Rauch, Von Klenze's Bavaria, the Arc de l'Etoile at Paris by Chalgrin, the Scott monument at Edinburgh, Rochead's monument to Wallace on the Abbey Craig of Stirling, and in some recent projects of the French School, remarkable alike for elegant reserve and studious refinement.[1] These, not with the *naivete* and innocence of the antique, but with more or less of directness and force, show the sort of service even modern art can render in giving utterance to a certain range of national emotions otherwise unexpressed, and indeed inexpressible.

A great nation, such as we have described, recognizing a single august figure as its father, its greatest and most characteristic expression of humanity, the prototype of national character, possesses the highest inspiration of civic monumental art which could be given to any people. No theme other than a religious one has ever been presented more worthy of treatment by a form of art. This fact has been recognized, with more or less of intelligence, from the beginning of our history as a nation. Even at the conclusion of the War of Independence, and before Washington's election as President, when his personality had not yet been removed into the heroic region by lapse of time, an equestrian statue was resolved on by the Continental Congress; but the resolve was not fulfilled. Fifty years later, an Association was formed, with a view to redeem the plighted faith of the nation by invoking contributions. After a lapse of twelve years, in 1845, the public conscience was once more awakened; and, by the efforts of this Association, a design was obtained from Robert Mills,[2] which was recognized by the signature of the President of the United States as a fitting monumental expression (Fig. 111). This composition of architecture became familiar to the public, and by reason of its official indorsement, rather than through any especial technical excellence or appropriateness of sentiment, it was for a long time instinctively acknowledged, in the absence of any other published design, as the natural exponent of public sentiment. It was a vast circular colonnade, of the Greek Doric order, two hundred and fifty feet in diameter and one hundred feet high, surrounding a central shaft in the form of an obelisk, fifty-five feet square at the base, and six hundred feet high. The estimate of cost was within a million and a quarter of dollars. The corner-stone was laid on the 4th of July, 1848. Seven years later, when the bare shaft had been raised to the height of one hundred and seventy-four feet, the funds of the Association were exhausted. In 1878 the Government undertook the completion of the monument, assisted by the National Monument Society. A large sum of money was appropriated, and the work was resumed January 28, 1879. In 1883 the money again came to an end, and Congress once more devoted a sum to the work sufficient to finish the monument; and in December, 1884, the last stone was set.

In erecting the obelisk there were many engineering difficulties to encounter. As it now stands the top of the monument is five hundred and fifty-five feet above its base, which, exclusive of its concrete foundations, is about fifty-five feet square. The original height designed by Robert Mills was six hundred feet; but upon careful investigation of the foundation by the engineers in charge, it was found there was not sufficient area at the base to support the shaft with any positive security. The question then arose as to whether it would be better to underpin the monument, or to build a solid wall of earth around and under the base. The plan of underpinning was finally adopted, and was carried out principally by a large supply of concrete, which was extended under and around the old foundation. The original depth of eight feet was increased to thirty-six feet, partly by raising the level of the surface of the earth so as to cover the concrete buttresses, and partly by lowering the new foundation. This part of the work was successfully completed in 1880; and then the remainder of the work, that of erecting the shaft, was pushed rapidly forward. The weight of the obelisk at this time was about thirty-one thousand tons. The present foundation is one hundred and twenty-six feet square, and covers sixteen thousand square feet of ground, against sixty-four hundred square feet of the original plan. The walls of the obelisk are about fifteen feet thick at the lower parts, and they taper to one and one half feet at the top. The exterior is of white marble from a quarry in Maryland, and the backing is of gneiss and granite. The shaft is thirty-four and a half feet square at the top, and the pyramidoid which surmounts the walls is fifty-five feet in height. A vast amount of thought and skill was expended in the planning of this apex. At first it was intended that the top should be roofed over with an iron frame-work inserted with glass, to light the well in the centre, but it was finished finally so that this part of the obelisk consists of a series of twelve light-arched buttresses of marble, the inside of which springs from a point in the wall eight-five feet below the apex. These buttresses, about seven inches in thickness, support slabs of marble on the outside, which form a smooth covering. Above the point, four hundred and fifty-two feet from the base, the veneering of marble runs through the walls to the well, — which place contains an elevator and a staircase. The total weight of the obelisk, including the foundations and the earthwork, is one thousand tons; the weight of the shaft alone is about half this amount. Even with a strong wind blowing against it on one side, it is estimated that the final pressure on the earth under the foundations will in no place exceed nine tons per square foot. The following figures, taken from Haswell, show the highest monuments in the world; and it will be seen that the Washington monument, for height, stands first:

Washington Monument	555	feet
Pyramid of Cheops	520	"
St. Peter's	518	"
Cologne Cathedral	501	"
Balbec	500	"
Strasburg	486	"

Evidently the leading technical motive of the design of Mr. Robert Mills was that it should assert itself as the loftiest structure yet built by the hands of man. Its principal competitor in this respect was the ambitious tower projected four thousand years ago upon the plains of Shinar, whose top should reach unto heaven, in order to symbolize and obtain a more complete union among the people of the earth. The confusion of tongues which followed upon this vain attempt perhaps foreshadowed the Neo-Græco-Egyptian jumble which was the æsthetic characteristic of the proposed modern symbol of national unity and greatness. The element of height is by no means an ignoble one in an architectural conception; but if it is the sole motive, the result cannot be otherwise than ignoble. The true test of quality in a structure started with such pretensions is to be obtained in considering the amount of thought which enters into it. The claim of superiority in height was set forth by a popular print, in which the highest monuments of the world, drawn to equal scale, were grouped together around the proposed monument to Washington, and the inferiority of Michael Angelo's St. Peter's at Rome, of Erwin von Steinbach's spire of Strasbourg,[3] and the other masterpieces of lofty building, was thus made sufficiently obvious. The question of the relative quality of the art employed in these several conceptions was not insisted on. It is requisite in a work of art, in which height is to be the leading motive, that it should be made up of details all of which are essential to the expression of loftiness, and are arranged to set it forth in the most effective manner by contrasts of proportions, and by emphasizing the idea of ascension. The degree and quality of the height resides in its essential composition from the beginning, and is foreshadowed even in the lowest stages of the monument, as in the Giralda at Seville, — which, though begun by the Moors in the Saracenic style and completed by the Christians some two centuries later in the style of the Renaissance, is still remarkable for unity of effect, — in the brick tower of Saragossa, the Campanile of Santa Maria del Fiore at Florence and that of St. Mark at Venice, and in all the later mediæval spires without exception. In these each part is essential to the whole. Once begun, they could not be curtailed or lengthened without a painful breach of the laws of harmony. The western towers of Notre Dame of Paris have remained in their present state of incompleteness for five centuries; yet, by the preparation suggested in the arrangement of their masses, the disposition of their lines, and the quality of their proportions, the height of the spires which should surmount them and the character of their lines and details can be foretold with inevitable accuracy; so that, though the original design has been lost, a competition of designs among trained architects for the completion of these structures would vary only with respect to minute details. But the modifications of height in the completion of the Washington shaft, which had been arbitrarily proposed by the successive committees and commissions in charge, varied one from the other through a range of two hundred and seventy-five feet, without offence to any artistic condition essential to the Monument as it then existed. The degree of sensitiveness to modifications of this sort which must reside in any structure is in direct proportion to its rank as a work of art. If it exhibits no sensitiveness, it is a mere brute mass, which may have an expression of bigness, but not of grandeur. This shaft is called an obelisk; but the Egyptian prototype has fixed proportions, is essentially a monolith, was intended to convey a concrete idea by the hieroglyphics which filled its four polished sides, with reliefs against a background of brilliant colors, and the pyramidion at the summit was covered with bronze or bright gold. It was conspicuously an historic record. The American invention fulfilled none of these conditions, and its pyramidion was so ignorantly debased in the geometrical elevation as to be entirely invisible from any near point of view in perspective. In fact it was not an obelisk; it was a chimney without an outlet. But in order to give to this structure, so cheap to design but so costly to build, conceived in a day and executed in half a century, — in order to give to it some show of excuse for existing, the original designer proposed to build around its square and expressionless base a vast circular porch in the form of a colonnade of the Græco-Doric order. The result was, that this peristyle — though in actual size more gigantic than the order of the Temple of Diana at Ephesus, the greatest temple of antiquity, or than the order of St. Peter's at Rome, the greatest temple of modern times — was so dwarfed by the prodigious mass of masonry around which it was placed, that no one can possibly realize its true proportions. No work of art would suffer one part so to degrade and neutralize the other. Never was there a waste of treasure and material so barbaric. A central dome might have been so arranged as to excuse the circular portico; a grouping of mighty pylons about the base of the shaft might have tended to justify its enormous blankness. But no attempt was made either in the colonnade or in the shaft to reconcile the perpetual and fundamental incompatibility which must have prevailed between them in every respect of line, detail, and proportion.

In the eloquent eulogy of Washington delivered by Mr. Winthrop on the laying of the corner-stone of this pile, he said: "Build it to the skies, — you cannot outreach the loftiness of his principles; found it upon the massive and eternal rock, — you cannot make it more enduring than his fame; construct it of the purest Parian marble, — you cannot make it purer than his life." [4] He might have added, Build it as you propose, and you cannot make it in any respect significant of Washington, or in any way worthy of the great civilization which he founded, — you cannot make it other than a misquotation barbarously misapplied.

The quality of simplicity and plainness is not undervalued as an element of grandeur in a monumental composition of this sort. Repose and size are essential to such an expression. But if a mountain cliff, or even a work of engineering, is sublime because of its vast unoccupied spaces, a monument which is expressly devised to convey such a sentiment as this must be something better than a colossal cairn or a mighty chimney. Its composition should betray a certain amount of human thought and intention. Its proportions should be so delicately adjusted as to give to it an expression of unity and wholeness, to which nothing can be added, from which nothing can be subtracted, without detriment to its essential quality. Its sentiment of repose must be obtained from its completeness, from its evident reserve of power, and from the contrast between its great spaces of stillness and its occasional spaces of careful detail adjusted to the scale of a man, so as to force upon the spectator a true idea of its size. Its great areas of rest must have a *raison d'être*; they should not exist merely for their own sake; mere courses of masonry, however multiplied, do not constitute a work of art; they must have an especial object to fulfil which is not merely prosaic. The lofty pilasters of the tower of St. Mark would be meaningless and absurd, if they did not support the delicate order of the belfry. The great wall veils of the Romanesque churches would be expressionless and without true majesty if they were not bounded by battlements and buttresses, crowned by arcades and machicolations, and broken, however rarely, by windows and doorways decorated with the most exquisite sculpture and the most graceful tracery. Nay, even the triumphal arches of Rome, if they did not bear aloft mighty inscriptions, would lose half of their significance as monuments.

Therefore a bare unfigured tapering shaft of masonry, magnifying the Egyptian monolith, but drawn out far beyond the proportions fixed in the prototype, and set upon a level platform, which furnishes the principal novelty of composition in the modified design which was then actually in process of erection, though brutally, from its mere size, it must force itself upon the attention of the beholder and awaken a certain sense of amazement, is not capable of suggesting any emotion such as should be conveyed by a monument erected to express a national sentiment. We can conceive that as a permanent landmark erected to fix a definite point of territory, like a term, or perhaps to mark the starting-point of an initial base-line in some great geographic survey, as a mathematical point, it might have had a certain fitness, as it was tall, durable, and singular. But if it was intended for any higher service, — to emphasize a point in the history of a nation, or to symbolize the character and services of its greatest citizen, — it was dumb. Imagination was starved, and memory slept in its presence. It can hardly be too earnestly insisted that such higher service demands a work of art, and that mere hugeness and smoothness do not meet the conditions; therefore, even if carried to the height of a thousand feet, a mere shaft is no more than an expression of geometry, grossly inadequate to an occasion so great, and unworthy of a nation so liberal, prosperous, and enlightened.

The monument on Bunker Hill is of the same kind. It has but one merit, — it speaks from afar, and stands like a mighty beacon. But until the story which it is intended to commemorate has been told by bas-reliefs or historical inscriptions, engraved upon its now vacant and expressionless sides, until it bears the names of the patriots who served or fell upon that pathetic field, set forth with letters which cannot perish, the stranger can only wonder, as he approaches it, why so vast a pile makes no sign and utters no oracle.

We have now to consider various of the suggestions which were volunteered from time to time, with a view to develop, for architectural expression, the possible capacities of the shaft while unfinished, and to render it more worthy of its function as a national monument.

Concluding Article.

Mr. H. R. Searle's design for the completion of the Washington Monument is published with a descriptive pamphlet by the author (Fig. 112).[5] Its principal claim to notice resided in the treatment of the lower stage, which was composed of three terraces with battering walls, from the uppermost of which the main shaft arose with a greater propriety and dignity of effect than was attained in most of the other designs. The transition from the sloping walls of the base to those of the shaft was not without a character of originality, and the treatment of the three terraces, following the principle of the Mexican teocallis, exhibited a commendable spirit of hardihood in substituting for the more familiar types of form one which perhaps is rarely recognized by the architect among his resources of design. The three successive truncated pyramids of the base, and the massive quality of their structure, were acceptable features in combination with a plain treatment of the shaft, and prepared the eye for its final grave ascent much more effectually than any composition of classical detail or feeling then offered. This was the strong point of Mr. Searle's study, and if it had been carried out with a commensurate breadth of treatment in all its parts, if its vigor of outline had been combined with that refinement and thoughtfulness of detail which is absolutely essential to the national monument of a great civilized people, and with a due feeling for proportion and scale, which are necessary elements in any work of art, it would have fairly entered into the domain of high composition.

The main opportunity of the design was its capacity for breadth and severity of treatment; but by the division of the faces of the terraces into panels by a series of strongly-marked piers of massive masonry, the full effect of repose which would have been attained by leaving the long horizontal lines of the terraces unbroken save at the corners, was lost; and there was substituted an unnecessary and fatal contrast of vertical features which disturbed and distracted the eye, broke up the surfaces, and destroyed their due relations of harmony with the shaft above. The important effect of repose was still further disturbed by the ascending lines of the steps, which, except perhaps in the first terrace, would have been more happily bestowed in the interior. The whole effect of the base was thus rendered far too busy for the superstructure, and the subdivision into panels was contrived with an affectation of rudeness and with an absolute want of study and feeling for the value of detail, which conferred upon the whole composition an aspect of barbarism. The opportunity offered by the faces of the terrace walls for a continuous frieze of sculpture, historical or emblematical, was very precious, and the arbitrary division of these faces into panels was thus, in respect to sculpture, also a distinct loss; for separate pictures or compositions of figures, could never leave upon the mind of the spectator an impression of grandeur so deep and lasting.

The obelisk which surmounted this basement of terraces received in this design a modification of treatment, which neither reconciled it with the terraces, nor in any respect enhanced its effect. Whatever majesty resided in the original unbroken shaft was quite lost by the addition of capricious features, which added no element of interest to the design, and increased its unfortunate resemblance to a chimney. We can conceive that the theme of the obelisk might have been so developed as to obtain an actual effect of harmony with the lines of the terraces below; thus a repetition of numerous vigorous horizontal mouldings about the lower quarter of the shaft, such as the Hindu architect so well understood how to use in his topes, pagodas, and temples, would have echoed the characteristic lines of the terraces below, and established a natural conformity between the two features, and at the same time would have acted as a foil to the peaceful and solemn vertical development of the obelisk in the upper three quarters of its height towards its natural completion in the pyramidion at the summit. The lines of the obelisk have become so sanctified by ancient usage, and so commend themselves by propriety of proportion, that they cannot submit to modification without imminent danger of detriment. Any modifications which cannot be explained and defended on high principles of design are to be distrusted; thus, the two widely separated horizontal cornices at the bottom of the shaft in the design were conceived with a mind too light, and were executed with a hand too heavy, to be extenuated by any theory of art. In like manner, the long vertical divisions of the upper part of the shaft, and the treatment of its summit in the form of a colossal Egyptian capital or cornice, were audacious but illiterate innovations, which established no relationship with the terraces below, added no new significance to the shaft, had no intrinsic value or interest in themselves, and were utterly destructive of scale, having served rather to diminish than to increase the apparent dimensions. It would certainly have been wiser in this case, if less original, not to meddle with the consecrated form of the obelisk, except to fill its sides with the names of all the heroes and worthies of the Republic, and to depend for architectural effect upon a strong contrast of crowded horizontal mouldings at its base "with bossy sculptures graven," [6] and upon the series of terraces which we cannot but consider on the whole the most valuable suggestion that was offered for a base to the obelisk.

The study of Mr. John Frazer was more conventional in character (Fig. 113). His composition was sufficiently correct in its essential parts to stand as a bell-tower for a convent of the twelfth century in North Italy. As a work of architectural, or rather of archæological design, apart from its scale and from its immediate purpose as a memorial, it was careful, timid, precise. But it retained the worst of the characteristics of the Romanesque campaniles, — the recurrence of similar heights of stories, the monotonous round-arched openings, one at the bottom, two in the middle, and three at the top, the bald and unstudied outlines, — and it added to these characteristics the unfortunate invention of four miniature campaniles of the same sort, attached to the angles of the base, with gabled curtain-walls between, which were pierced on one side with a great niche forming the portal, but how treated on the other three sides did not appear. From behind this strange mask of gables and pyramidal roofs the enormous mass of the central tower rose with a curious sort of surprise, and without any diminution or relief of outline from bottom to top, proceeded upward *ad infinitum*, repeating its unimaginative details and offering no preparation for its final completion; until at last, by an act of arbitrary choice, it was cut off at a prodigious height, and finished with a very proper machicolated cornice and a low pyramidal roof.

The manifest difficulty of adjusting a scale of details fit for such enormous dimensions meet in this design even with a less satisfactory solution than in any of its competitors. The four corner towers attached to the foot of the great pile, with the gables between, were in their details adapted to the scale of a man with reasonable precision; but the details of the colossal central tower belong to a race of giants, and it contained no feature to give a just idea of its size. A tower of less than half the dimensions would properly receive the same amount, character, and proportion of details. From an archæological point of view this design was mechanically correct, but the composition was uninformed with any touch of poetic feeling. As a monument to Washington, the founder of a great Republic, based upon modern ideas of political liberty, this vast monastic bell-tower was curiously anachronistic and inapplicable. The introduction of the colossal equestrian statue of the Father of his Country, in the niche over the portal, after the fashion of that of Louis XI. at Blois, although furnishing a sufficiently secular element, was not enough to redeem it and render it fit for these new uses. Perhaps its designer had in mind the notion expressed by the late Robert Dale Owen in speaking of the architecture of the Smithsonian Institute, that the masculine energy and rude strength of its Romanesque prototypes are appropriate to a new departure in civilization, because of their proved vitality and productive force.[7] But even this analogy was destroyed by the precise modern character of the masonry, by its whiteness and smoothness, and by the very delicacy of workmanship which was suggested by the drawing. It told no story, struck no chord, awakened no emotions, save of astonishment at its vast proportions, at its gloomy waste of spaces within and without, and its absolute silence.

The most conspicuous of the projects volunteered for the completion of the Monument in a manner commensurate with the great occasion and with our position as a civilized nation was embodied in the design of the sculptor Story, sent to us from his studio in Italy (Fig. 114).[8] He proposed to encase the stump of the shaft with a marble envelope profusely enriched with panelling, after the manner of the Florentine Gothic of the Campanile of Giotto, and to extend the composition thus encased to a height about double that of the statue as it then was, and to crown it with a pyramid of marble surmounted by a little figure of Fame, at a height of about three hundred and fifty feet from the ground. The podium more nearly recalled classic forms, and was one hundred feet high with vast projecting porches on each side of the four faces, one of which contained enshrined a colossal statue of Washington set in a niche more than sixty feet high. This podium finished with a cornice of sharp projection and an overhanging balustrade, which, being six feet high instead of three, gave to the whole a false scale. From this gallery the Gothic shaft, with a sudden change of *motif*, rose abruptly. In its design it adhered quite closely to the suggestions presented by the Florentine masterpiece; but in the absence of the marble inlays, of the abundant fine sculpture, and of the rich and various details which were the real *raison d'être* of the original, and gave to it all its interest and value, the modern example seemed bald and mechanical, — the identity of its parts was absolute. Its division into four stages of irregular heights was managed not without feeling for harmony of proportion, and went far to correct the effect of effeminacy occasioned by the superabundance of slender vertical lines in the shafting and panelling which covered the surface; but the lower story of the shaft proper was concealed at every accidental point of view by the projection of the gallery from which it ascended, and as no architectural features have been furnished in this story to soften the transition from the podium to the shaft, the composition at this point suffered an incurable dislocation. The same sort of multiplication of horizontal features which characterized the treatment of the basement of Giotto, if applied to this lower stage, would have contributed to redeem the design as a composition of architecture. But, still judging this interesting design from a purely architectural standpoint, and without regard to its fitness as a memorial to Washington, it was to be noted that in the composition of the shaft proper the prevalence of vertical lines should have been counterbalanced, for the sake of repose, by a more judicious use of interrupting horizontal belts, such indeed as seem to give repose and massiveness to the great original. If the design had been drawn so as to expose two of its sides at once, the absence of the technical devices which we have named, and more especially of that variety of detail which alone can excuse and give a character of art to a composition of this sort, would have been more keenly felt. Moreover, from an æsthetic point of view, what was to be said of an envelope so enormous and so costly as this, which depended for its character entirely upon the disposition of forty-four blank windows, each divided by the same attenuated shaft into two parts, and each having its head filled with the same form of round-arched tracery, and that of the most conventional and uninteresting kind? Like all the other designs to which we have referred, if this had been reduced to one half its present dimensions, it would have lost nothing essential to its architectural character. As judged by this test, its treatment in respect to scale was fundamentally defective; and here again the rare opportunity of using vast dimensions in a manner to enhance rather than to belittle them had been lost. Considering that this design was furnished by a sculptor of distinguished merit and a poet of recognized inspiration, and that he has chosen an architectural form which was invented for an inlay of rich marbles, the absence of any suggestion of such an inlay, and more especially the paucity of carved decoration and of imaginative detail, are very remarkable.

With proper modifications, doubtless, this design would be capable of assuming shape much more grammatical and correct as an academical study, and, with proper additions, much more poetic and significant as a work of art. Most of these modifications would have had to be addressed to the justification of its scale and to the reconciliation between the podium and the shaft. But no study could have made this appropriate as a memorial to Washington. The very process of perfecting the architectural design would have removed it still farther from its purpose. A monument so effeminate and dainty in its character, and inspired, as originally invented, by ideas so essentially at variance with those that pervaded the era of the Revolution, or which underlie our own character as a nation, could not satisfy the primary conditions of the theme. The Florentine Gothic of the fourteenth century seems to imply exuberance of youth, love of splendor, luxury of life, ostentation of manners, pride of art, fastidious refinement carried to the point of effeminacy. If we might venture to name the qualities which should inspire the especial work which we have in hand, we should rather think of repose, strength, virility, dignity, simplicity, as the leading characteristics of such a shrine; but these qualities should be set forth with every available resource of learning and poetic feeling, tempered, however, with that evident reserve of power which is the most difficult expression to confer upon a composition of architecture.

The study by Mr. M. P. Hapgood, of Boston, an architectural student, made apparently rather as an exercise in design than with competitive intent, was a much more grammatical example of the use of an accepted type of form than any of the compositions to which we have referred, with a better appreciation of scale, and was fairly representative of the sort of work to be expected from students trained in the theory and practice of design (Fig. 115). It had grace and sentiment modestly expressed, and with a wholesome sense of discipline; it had the obvious advantage of a distinct place for a central statue on one side, without suggestions of competition on the other three; it had a good play of outline, and on the whole indicated the beginning, at least, of a workmanlike achievement in monumental design. Its faults were mainly faults of detail. Thus, at the base, the horizontal line should have had a fuller and more vigorous expression, especially in the offsets of the water-table, and some of the vertical lines of the buttresses on the sides of the monument should have been lost in these offsets before they reached the platform; all the gable copings were far too heavy, and detracted from the size of the building; the corbelled stage of the corner buttresses at the top of the tower was overweighted; the cornices of the pinnacles were clumsy, and interfered with the sense of ascent which should have prevailed in these features; the lantern which sat upon the platform of the tower should have been considerably higher, so that it might be disengaged from the parapet, and unite more effectually with the four pinnacles; and the crowning spire would have had much more dignity, and appeared more in scale, if it had arisen more simply from the mass below, and with less fretting of outline. A perspective study would have betrayed the necessity of many other ameliorations of detail. But the question whether English Gothic, however modernized and however secularized, was a proper medium for the expression of such sentiments as should have been conveyed in a monument to Washington, was one which admitted of discussion. Certainly, as here treated, it was too conventional for a use so august and exceptional. If this design had been adopted as the central feature for a great town-hall, it would have had to submit to no essential change. Such a consideration should have made us hesitate before we accorded to it even a guarded approval, when proposed as a national memorial. We ask for greater repose of surface, for less of the florid and more of the serious in expression; we would make the architecture for the sculpture, and not the sculpture for the architecture; we would rather have an architectural enshrinement of inscriptions and bas-reliefs than a mere conventionality of windows, balustrades, and buttresses. In short, a style which has been so *ordained* as the "Victorian Gothic" must yield its easy conventionalities and its too facile elegance, — some of its more remote and unused sources of expression, if any it has, must be called into play, before we can fitly commit to it such solemn duties.

All these designs accepted the embarrassing condition of the then existing stump of the obelisk, and in various ways aimed to give it an architectural development; but in none of them was this condition accepted so frankly as in that of Mr. Paul Schulze, of Washington, and none of them so promptly or so directly evolved out of the unpromising materials an architectural idea (Fig. 116). Upon the summit of the unfinished shaft he placed a well-composed belvedere, massive enough in its proportions to establish harmonious relations with the heavy masonry below; upon the roof of the belvedere he dared to erect a low circular tower, covered by a dome, and surmounted by a bronze figure of Washington thirty-five feet high; at the base he established two terraces, the faces of which were occupied by the ascent of vast monumental steps; and upon the upper platform, against the four corners of the shaft, he erected four mighty buttresses, upon which were seated four emblematical figures, also in bronze, thus having secured an outline which with some nobility of effect connected the structure with the surrounding plain. Against the sides of the shaft, between the buttresses and the emblematical figures, were affixed enormous tablets of bronze which bore inscriptions and bas-reliefs; and at the top of the shaft, under the belvedere, was a frieze of garlands or festoons, also in bronze. The whole composition was simple to bareness, and the two cornices were dangerously equal in value, but it betrayed a practised hand in the management of great architectural masses, and an intelligent professional appreciation of the technical conditions of the problem. It was a workmanlike academical study, without high inspirations, but also without any straining for originality. It had repose, dignity, and strength. But the attempt to make a satisfactory combination of bronze and white marble in such relative quantities could scarcely succeed; the two materials will not blend, and the effect of them together is really that of black against white, unless the contrast of the metal is mitigated by gilding; and even with this mitigation, the quantity of the metal, almost encircling the base, would be too great. Gilded or bright metal against marble seems acceptable only in small quantities, as in the shields of metopes, or in capitals, and dark bronze against marble, only in subordinate positions. Moreover, the composition of the great tablets, forty by twenty feet at least in dimensions, was wanting in dignity and consciousness of scale, and they were treated like after-thoughts. One would be compelled also to object to the staircases at the base, as having been much too vast for their uses, and as having had a tendency to destroy the repose which should have prevailed about the foundations of so great a pile. It was a serious work, however, and although it was by no means inspired or poetic, it was perhaps the nearest approach then made to a practical, business-like solution of the problem.

In strong contrast to all the other suggestions for the completion of the Monument, an interesting project from California, published anonymously in an old number of the *American Architect*,[9] and here reproduced by permission, afforded abundant and satisfactory recognition of the scale of the structure and made an adequate use of sculpture as a decorative accessory (Fig. 117). It was a spirited and poetic composition, correctly set forth in the style of the modern French Renaissance, and might have been submitted in the latest architectural *concours* of the Ecole des Beaux-Arts. It would seem that a style which has been so consistently and so consecutively developed from Roman types, which has been so refined by the study of a race of artists through successive centuries of civilization, and which in this progress has received such abundant accretions, such a boundless wealth of phraseology, and has thus become so pliable to the expression of modern ideas, — that such a style might have had resources peculiarly applicable to the interpretation of the theme which has been held in contemplation. The present essay draws upon these resources perhaps with a too liberal hand, but it presents on the whole a conception which might have been accepted as the expression of a nation advanced in the higher arts of life.

The monument had its roots firmly planted in the ground by means of successive stages or stories with battering walls; it stood, as Browning says, "four-square," [10] and finished at the top with a sudden upward leap, which presented in general outline and in its multiplicity of detail strong points of affinity with some of the better Hindu pagodas. Indeed, in respect to detail it was enthusiastically overloaded, although this fault was largely condoned by the severity of its sky lines. If the designer had judiciously held his hand and spared his somewhat profuse invention, the dignity and repose of his design would have been increased. We feel this want of reserved force mainly in the central stage or die of the shaft below the well-conceived frieze of processional sculpture. This die was occupied by a great central aperture in each face, divided vertically by columns, and horizontally by a belt of mouldings, which was superfluously continued around the shaft; and the shaft was further subdivided at this place by long vertical channels, apparently with a view to counteract the too great prevalence of horizontal lines below. We venture to assert that this central die, which had been heralded by such a vast preparation of bases, and which was crowned with such ceremonial splendor, demanded an especial distinction of treatment; and that if the horizontal belt and the channelling had been omitted here, and possibly if the columnar order dividing the aperture had been extended in long piers without the interruption of the belt, and if the masonry had been left unfretted by details, the proper contrast and balance of parts would have been more completely and more satisfactorily maintained.

This is the substance of the description which accompanied the design: The panels on the face of the first terrace are stones presented by the various States of the Union; those presented by foreign States find a place in the battering plinth of the monument. The statue of Washington is seated in front of a niche, and the pedestal of the statue is supported by figures of Truth and Industry. The niche is flanked on either hand by groups representing Peace and War. Against the die of the pedestal of the monument are placed busts of the Revolutionary worthies, and under the corner of the pedestal is a frieze enriched with a procession of Industry; above, on the four angles of the cornice of the pedestal, are figures of Liberty, Justice, Education, and Suffrage. Against the next stage are the emblematical statues of the original States, and the gables which decorate the centres of the third stage bear statues typifying the North, the South, the East, and the West. The frieze under the main cornice is filled with a warlike procession, and the figure of America surmounts the whole, at a height of three hundred and thirty feet.

The iconology of this design might have been improved. This, however, was not an essential point. Evidently the design was but a study; it was the outline of an heroic poem, crowded with incidents, set forth with a degree of rhetorical elegance which is full of promise. It had the merit of being distinctly monumental and entirely appreciative of the colossal scale of its masses.

Having in mind the lesson conveyed by these voluntary and patriotic contributions, which we have referred to because of the importance of the theme, and because they serve to suggest the boundless field of design which it opens to professional study, we heartily congratulate the Monument Commission for having so cleverly completed the original shaft. As it now stands, it not only is a fit and just tribute to the skill and enterprise of the American people, but a noble tribute to the name which it perpetuates.

The Architecture at Harvard

(*1890*)

To the Editor of the Nation:

Sir: I venture to call your attention to the following passage in Mr. Norton's interesting paper in *Harper's Monthly* for September on the condition, functions, and prospects of Harvard University:

The value of the influence of noble architecture, simple as it may be, at a great seat of education, especially in our country, is hardly to be overestimated; and yet it has been either absolutely disregarded at Harvard, or, if recognized, the attempt to secure buildings that should exert this influence has been little short of total failure. If some great benefactor of the University should arise, ready to do a work that should hand down his name in ever-increasing honor with posterity, he might require the destruction of all the buildings erected in the last half-century, and their reconstruction with simple and beautiful design, in mutually helpful, harmonious, and effective relation to each other, so that the outward aspect of the University should better consist with its object as a place for the best education of the youth of the nation.[1]

The object of this communication is less to question the justice of the very severe animadversions of the Professor of Fine Arts regarding those buildings erected for the service of the University during the last fifty years, than to ask whether the drastic remedy which he would apply — admitting for the moment that it is possible — would be consistent with the highest duties of the University towards its students.

In your notice of this paper (September 4), you summarize it as presenting "less a description of the University as it is than a general view of its lines of development in the last twenty years in connection with the collateral development of the nation." [2] Now, if the older halls of the University, such as Massachusetts (Fig. 159), Harvard, Stoughton, Hollis, and Holworthy, and Holden Chapel, which, as they are excluded from Mr. Norton's censure, may be supposed (in some degree, at least) to meet with his approval, represent without affectation or pretence the modest condition of art and civilization in the last century, and for this reason deserve our respect and veneration, do not the later buildings also emanate from the spirit of the times in which they were built? Are not they also records of contemporary history? Do they not present to the physical eye a general view of the lines of development of architecture, parallel with those of the University itself during the last twenty years "in connection with the collateral development of the nation"? And are they not for this reason deserving of a measure of respect as monumental?

Memorial Hall, the Hemenway Gymnasium, Sever and Hastings Halls, the Law School, the museums, and the other modern buildings of the University, not including Appleton Chapel (Figs. 25, 28, 106, 107, 165), could not have existed in their present forms but for the exacting nature of certain practical requirements, for the condition of building materials and methods, and for the dominance of certain theories and fashions of design, at the times when respectively they were built. Some of these theories and fashions have been more or less superseded in the rapid and wholesome progress of the art by newer methods, which at present seem better adapted to prepare the way for the architecture of the future. It results, therefore, that the later modern buildings are better than the earlier; but all of them are the work of conscientious and loyal graduates of Harvard, over whose minds, it may be presumed, the vagaries of personal caprice and invention have had less influence than with many contemporary builders less fortunate in their opportunities for general and special training. It may fairly be assumed that these architects have presented in the later monuments of Harvard unusually just architectural expressions of the civilization of their times. Certainly, as regards practical construction and adaptation to the more complex uses and the more exacting conditions in the life of the modern university, these modern buildings are immeasurably in advance of all which preceded them.

Modern methods and conveniences are in continual warfare with the conservative instincts of architecture, but modern architects are compelled to adjust their methods of construction and design to these methods and conveniences, hoping and expecting that out of those adjustments there will be presently developed an adequate architecture for the close of the century. It is true that those modern buildings of the University are, from the point of view of art, merely a succession of hazardous experiments — so, indeed, were the temples of the Greeks and the cathedrals of the thirteenth century; but the accumulation and organization of precedents have in modern times imposed upon the architects a certain self-consciousness which has rendered the lines of progress in their art less consistent and regular than was the case with the ancients. Our advance is tumultuous, many-colored, and disorderly, but *it is an advance*, although none of us seem able to secure a point of vantage whence the scene may be viewed in just perspective, and the accidents and incidents of this progress may take each its proper place. May we not assume that to posterity these accidents and incidents of the art of today may become as venerable and significant as those of the last century are to us as we walk through the college yard? It would not have been difficult in the modern buildings to affect a spurious relationship with the older buildings by masquerading in "the colonial style," thus securing a uniformity which would be agreeable to the taste of many. But is there not a better lesson for the youth of the University in the honester method which has been adopted? May they not more clearly discern the character of the civilization of these latter years of the century by such methods, even if those methods have rendered it impossible to avoid incongruity in the styles of neighboring buildings?

Five years of the latter quarter of this century are more prolific of healthful change in all the arts than fifty years of the eighteenth century, and architecture, now at last, we hope, in sympathy with this material advance, is subjected to a series of quick transitions. The building of 1880 is different in style from the building of 1870 for the same reason that the building of the year 1250 is different from one of the year 1350. If in some of the later examples of those incongruities of style in the college yard we may not see, as some of us think we see, a hopeful sign that the true line of consistent and direct progress has been in them discovered, our children, at least, when they look upon Sever Hall and the Law School (Figs. 106, 107) will recognize that among all the sons of Harvard none have done more distinguished honor to their *alma mater* than the lamented Richardson. The destruction of these monuments would obliterate one of the brightest pages in the history of her achievement.

How are we to be assured that the substitution which Mr. Norton proposes will be an improvement? Who is to judge in what style the new buildings, "of simple and beautiful design," are to be built? What pilot is to guide the new composition of art safely between the Scylla and Charybdis of mere archaeological correctness, ideal academic conformity, and safe scholastic purity on the one side, and on the other picturesqueness, romanticism, and an undue infusion of personal habit and taste? Who shall decide what is best suited to the age and most in harmony with its spirit? Is there not a danger that the harmony thus obtained would be merely the expression of an individual taste, and not that of an age of artistic and intellectual progress? Would it not be far less interesting and significant as a matter of history than even the juxtaposition of modernized Gothic, Old English Renaissance, Southern Romanesque, and what not, which at present so offends the eye of the critic, but so fairly represents the irregularity and indecision of the lines upon which the art of our time has been working its way to some sort of triumphant finality? It is our fate to live in the midst of a period of transition and eager development. If architecture contented itself with falling back upon fixed and approved academic types of form, it would be immediately placed out of reach of the sympathy of the public, without which there can be no true architecture for one time. If the critics will be patient with the experiments through which the architects are trying to keep step with the material progress of the time; if, better still, they will give us specific criticisms instead of Rhadamanthine judgments, which condemn or approve and give no reason; if the new architecture, as it is produced, should awake a clamor of intelligent discussion instead of being received in dead silence, the elimination of the unfruitful or merely exotic elements and the growth of those which have in them the seeds of life would be much more promptly secured.

Henry Van Brunt.

Manitou, Colorado, September 9, 1890.[3]

John Wellborn Root

(1891)

It is difficult, while yet our hearts are sore with a sense of bereavement, to review with eyes of cool judgment the unfinished life of a man professionally so conspicuous and personally so well beloved as John Wellborn Root. The stroke, which has deprived us suddenly of the gracious bodily presence and the active human sympathy forever, seems to throw over our memory a spell, through which the story of the bright career now closed is changed to poetry, and the voice now silent becomes a song. This pathos of death converts a memorial into a panegyric, unless the impulse of affection to gild and of admiration to extenuate is carefully corrected and chastened.

> For it so falls out,
> That what we have we prize not to its worth,
> Whiles we enjoy it; but being lack'd and lost,
> Why, then we rack the value; then we find
> The virtue that possession would not shew us
> Whiles it was ours.   *   *   *   *   *
> The idea of his life shall sweetly creep
> Into our study of imagination,
> And every lovely organ of his life
> Shall come apparalled in more precious habit,
> More moving, delicate and full of life
> Into the eye and prospect of the soul
> Than when he liv'd indeed.[1]

It is the fortune of every true artist to have the best, the essential part of himself made visible in his works. His mental development has a concrete, tangible expression, which can be studied and analyzed in the light of his achievements. He who would know Root as he really was — a man of genius and accomplishments, of generous impulse, of quick invention, of inexhaustible zeal — must look for him rather in what he accomplished professionally than in the accidents and incidents of his external career. Sir Christopher's epitaph referred not to his monument alone, but to his whole life.[2] I tell the brief story therefore of the events which occurred between the birth and death of our friend, merely to introduce and explain, so far as they may, the man himself, as he more fully revealed himself in the best architecture of the West, upon which his example has undoubtedly conferred many of its most marked characteristics. To interpret the part which he played in that architecture is to give to the world the portrait of his restless and indomitable genius, and it is with this that I am mainly concerned.

His father, Sidney Root, a native of New England, was a wealthy merchant in Georgia before the war, and his mother was a native of that state. John, the eldest son, was born at her southern home January 10, 1850; but, while he was yet an infant, his parents moved to Atlanta, where he spent his boyhood. When the army of Sherman occupied that city the family, by military necessity, in common with other non-combatants of the place, was compelled to leave, taking refuge in the southwestern part of the state, whence presently the boy was sent to England by a blockade runner from Wilmington, N. C., so that he might secure an education more thorough than the conditions of the South at that time permitted. He attended school for three years at Claremont, near Liverpool, and in 1867 passed the preliminary examinations for entrance to the University of Oxford.

Meanwhile his father, still in good circumstances, had moved, after the close of the war, to New York, to which place John was recalled from abroad in 1867. He entered the university of that city and graduated about 1870 with high honors. At school and at college it seems that he was noted for the ease with which he assimilated knowledge, and for the sureness with which he retained it. He was equally renowned, at this part of his career, as an athlete and a scholar. His architectural tendencies were early developed, and his studies in New York were largely directed toward engineering and other sciences allied to his chosen profession.

At the conclusion of his college course he became a student in the office of James Renwick, the architect of St. Patrick's Cathedral in New York.[3] Later he gained valuable experience in the employ of Mr. Snook, then architect for the Vanderbilts.[4]

At this time, his love for music, which throughout his career exercised a strong influence over the habits of his mind, was developed, and he was recognized as a keen critic and as a skilled performer on the piano and organ.

In the spring of 1872, strongly prepossessed in favor of the neo-gothic of the time, he went to Chicago, being attracted by the opportunity offered to the profession by the rebuilding of the city after the great fire. Here, together with his friend, Daniel H. Burnham, he spent a year in the employ of Carter, Drake & Wight,[5] and in 1873 the two young men entered into the partnership, which, beginning under the happiest auspices, continued through eighteen years of complete mutual confidence, of high achievement, brilliant enterprise and uninterrupted success.

About the year 1879 he married Mary, the daughter of the late J. M. Walker, but she died within a few weeks after the wedding day. Three years later he married the daughter of Henry S. Monroe, Esq. By this happy union he became the father of three children, and they and his widow survive him.

The peculiar alertness and openness of his mind, his hospitality to every form of intellectual appeal, his wide information, and his quick sympathy with art in all its forms, attracted to him the affectionate interest of the most advanced society of Chicago. He was an active member of its best organizations for the encouragement of literature and art. His clients became his friends, and he had the capacity of so impressing them with his force of character and with the generosity of his zeal in their service, that his work was to an unusual extent relieved from the interference of lay prejudice, and expressed, not a compromise, but the attitude of his mind at the moment of composition. He designed with marvelous rapidity and correctness of touch, reaching his conclusions at a bound. In his office he was the wise counsellor and sympathetic friend of the draftsmen. His recognition by the profession as a leader is evident in the fact that he was the second secretary of the Western Association of Architects, its third president, and for six years a member of its advisory board. Upon the consolidation of the association with the American Institute of Architects, under the latter title, he was appointed to the especially responsible office of secretary, and was reëlected for the second term at the last annual convention.

He was, with universal acceptance, appointed consulting architect of the World's Columbian Exposition of 1893, at Chicago. During the exhausting preliminary labors connected with that vast enterprise, and while the commission of his brother architects, called from distant parts of the country, was in daily personal contact with him in laying out the great buildings of the exposition at Jackson Park, he was stricken with pneumonia, and, after an illness of only four days, he died January 15, 1891, five days after he had completed his forty-first year, leaving a void which cannot be filled. His last conscious utterance called attention to strains of unearthly music which seemed to soothe his listening ears, from some sphere beyond the reach of time.

The work accomplished by the firm during the eighteen years of its existence is, numerically, of almost unprecedented magnitude, and in quality always interesting and scholarly, frequently brilliant and original, very rarely commonplace or merely conventional. It is generally understood that in the division of labor in the firm of Burnham & Root, the latter had charge of the department of design. But Burnham's influence throughout their whole joint career was undoubtedly very great and very salutary, not only as a restraint to exuberance, and as a power of especial sanity and force in the combination, but as an organizer, who made possible the efficient conduct of its large and complicated affairs, and brought its work into sympathy with the practical views of the commercial public.

A list of his works has been taken from the books of the firm, and represents, approximately, the order in which they were executed. These include forty-four structures of a public character, such as office buildings, hotels, churches, apartment buildings, schools, railway stations, etc., in Chicago; twenty-five of the same classes elsewhere; eight buildings to cost from $400,000 to $1,000,000 each, in course of erection, and one hundred and twenty residences of the first-class.

I cannot review the more important of the many works enumerated without recognizing the fact that they touch, in importance and in quality, the highest points yet attained in the characteristic architecture of the West. Clearly, they differ essentially from any contemporaneous work in other countries, and exemplify, from the earliest to the latest, in their due order, a consistent progress toward some more or less remote point of ideal perfection. But we have yet to discover whether this point is attainable on the lines which he followed. There are fewer indications in this series of the forcing of structure into archæological or academic molds than can be found in any modern European examples of corresponding buildings. Indeed, it seems evident that no architectural form has been imposed upon these monuments, but that their decorative character has, to an unusually large extent, grown out of their conditions of structure and use. At almost every point this healthy development has been protected from extravagance, affectation, caprice or vagaries of invention by a fine spirit of discipline and self-restraint, and by a delicate feeling for purity of line. Like all the other characteristic work of the West, this is based distinctly on romantic, as opposed to classic motifs, and there are few indications in these examples of any aim to conserve the formulas of the schools in the matter of design, though Root had the true spirit of the Renaissance ever in his mind and on his lips. "No lasting success," he said, "comes to an architect who is not grounded in classics. Life is not long enough for one to himself discover those laws of beauty which thousands of years have evolved for architecture." [6]

Root's mind was of studious habit, and though especially subject to artistic emotions and open to a quick appreciation of beautiful form in every style, he rarely suffered the enthusiasm of the moment to betray him into archæological masquerades. With a mind so thoroughly equipped with knowledge of the history of art, and a library so full of the most tempting precedents in other styles, he never fell into the student's error of eclecticism, but remained in all his conspicuous works loyal to that essential spirit and range of progress which had its roots in the archaic romanesque of Southern France, and may have its flower, we venture to hope, in that illimitable country of the West which was a wilderness unknown when the craftsmen of Auvergne were carving the grotesques of the porches of Arles and Trophime eight hundred years ago.

If one were asked to define what constitutes a living art, I am mistaken if he would not recite conditions of practice in design not unlike those which I have outlined in this general view of the work executed under the impulse of this bright intelligence. It had opportunity and temptation to express itself in every mood of versatility, by reason of the incessant demands made upon its resources by the exigencies of a large practice. It would be a miracle indeed if, in this public exposition of an artist's inner life, illustrated by hundreds of buildings of every grade, we did not discover occasional evidences of carelessness and haste, of momentary caprice, of indifference begotten of fatigue, when his genius was off its guard. These evidences no one was so prompt as Root himself to point out and condemn. In the recent article on the architects of Chicago, statements were printed concerning Root similar to these; his friends were indignant until they found that it was written by Root himself. A recent minister to England cleverly said, in an after-dinner speech, "The man who does not make mistakes very seldom makes anything." [7] But on the whole, Root's enjoyment of his work was so genuine, his resources of mind were so well ordered, his loyalty to his own ideals was so thorough that he was enabled to keep his record incorrupted by vagaries or disloyalties. In the numerous dwelling houses built by the firm we occasionally see excursions into free classic forms, into reminiscences of Flemish-Gothic or of the transitional era of Francis I, as illustrated in the royal chateaux of the Loire; in some of them we may discover faint reflections of the caprice of the hour, which, before the national architecture had been corrected and put in the line of national development by men of education, had tyrannized over the architectural expressions of the whole country. There is also evident in these minor buildings an occasional straining for novelty at the expense of that secure repose which is indicative of an art confirmed and established, as opposed to an art experimental and progressive. Nowhere, so far as I am aware, did Root give clear evidence of his love for the classic formulas, though the spirit of order and discipline, and the chastisement of refinement, which are the direct result of classic training and which can scarcely be obtained by any other process, are patent in all his works.

Aberrations from purity of type, expressions of personal moods, occasional absence of discipline, experiments in form and in the sentiment and application of ornament, such as I have indicated, are in themselves unavoidable incidents of a condition of vigorous progress and signs of a living art. It advances by errors. If these errors are suffered to bear fruit and to multiply, if they are permitted to create side issues, and to encourage caprices of invention so that the fundamental architectural unit is at length masked by conceits, the art is not advancing, but groping in the dark, and there is no health in it; but if they are dropped as soon as they are found to be destructive or unessential and to interfere with the purity of type, they are a part of progress.

The series of important buildings executed by Burnham & Root from 1880 to 1891, from the Calumet Club to the Temple of the Women's Christian Union at Chicago, or the Mills Building of San Francisco, show a succession of experiments in form, mainly resting on a consistent Romanesque basis (Figs. 120, 125–128, 133, 135–137). It is easy to see which of these experiments were thrown aside in subsequent buildings as contributing no desirable element to the progressive power of the style, and which of them were retained and amalgamated, so that their accretions were gradually leading the style out of its condition of mere archæological correctness into one elastic to all the new and strange conditions of structure, material and occupation. By reason of the very intelligent and spirited manner in which Root improved his vast opportunities, by reason of the serious way in which he attacked these more monumental problems, thoroughly realizing his responsibilities to art, it was his fortune to contribute to the development of this great Americo-Romanesque experiment nearly or quite as much as Richardson did. The latter introduced the revival, and, through the unexampled vigor of his personality, had already led it on to an interesting point of development, when his career was interrupted by death (Figs. 101, 106–110b, 129); the former carried it still further toward the point of its establishment as the characteristic architectural expression of American civilization. The latter conferred upon it power, the former, variety, and both, with their trained coadjutors in the profession, have already proved that the experiment is not merely a revival, barren of results, like the neo-gothic, the free classic or Queen Anne, and other numerous English trials, but the introduction and probable acclimatization of a *basis of design*, established upon Romanesque round-arched elements, which elements had never been carried to perfection, and were, consequently, capable of progression. It seems to have been nearly proved that, in the hands of such men as Root, upon this basis can be built an elastic system, capable of expressing any degree of strength or lightness, simplicity or complexity, force or refinement. It has also been proved, largely by his efforts, that the maintenance of the essential principles of the style does not depend upon the preservation of its peculiar original archaic character in structure or ornament, but that it can amalgamate elements from classic, gothic, Saracenic, or even Indian sources without being diverted from its strong natural growth, and that it is capable of a variety of expression and application which makes it adjustable to the most exacting requirements of that civilization which it is our duty to express.

A careful comparative analysis of the qualities exhibited in Root's first and last more important designs, with a glance at a few intermediate buildings, will serve to illustrate how a trained intelligence in active sympathy with the spirit of his times and loyal to a leading motive of composition, progresses with the progress of general civilization, and creates an art, which is not an exotic but ultimately a flower of our native fields. This analysis will further show that this flower is not an invention but a growth, having its roots in fundamental principles illustrated by historic forms, but varied in the process of development by new conditions of society, material and methods. To this process the persistence and force of one or two strong personalities seems to be absolutely essential. Such plants will become noxious weeds unless subjected to careful culture.

I think no such growth can be detected in any other modern phase of architectural thought either here or abroad. It is high time that it should be recognized, and that the man should be duly honored who, together with the lamented Richardson, availed himself of great opportunities to develop a definite architectural system by processes so logical and reasonable as to bring it within the range of public sympathy and appreciation. Indeed, it seems hardly too much to say that those two men have created a public for architecture.

Among the earliest important works of Burnham & Root, which attracted public attention, are the Grannis, Montauk, Calumet and Insurance Exchange office buildings (Figs. 120, 125). In the last named, which of the four seems to have had the most extensive influence over architectural thought in the West, we have a composition of ten stories forced into five for the sake of establishing a harmonic proportion of horizontal divisions. Of these five architectural stories, the first is a basement of two floors with round arched windows; the second, of two floors, is a colonnade of pilasters; the third, of only one floor, is occupied by a row of low segmentally arched windows; the fourth and most important, inclosing four floors, is an arcade with long pilasters, and the fifth, of one story, is a frieze of closely grouped arched windows. The scheme of design is simple, effective and easily understood, and the Romanesque element is plainly confessed. The distribution of ornament is temperate and its archaism is chastened with somewhat of Renaissance feeling. The skyline is accentuated with a round tourette at the two corners. The porch is composed of a low entrance arch, flanked by two round tourettes, corbelled out above the impost line, nearly detached from the wall, with conical finials, and connected by a corbelled balcony as a cornice, the whole inclosing two rows of windows continuous with the order of the second architectural story. This porch has been frequently imitated. The façades are of brick and terra-cotta construction; the spandrels of the basement story are decorated with quiet diapers of terra-cotta, and those of the upper arcade with marked horizontal lines composed of alternately recessed brick courses which are continued in the frieze above and assist the main cornice of brick corbels in adequately crowning the edifice. The vertical divisions by piers are distinctly subordinated to the horizontal divisions above described. These horizontal divisions are separated by four small string courses, which are carried around the façades continuously. The whole composition is distinguished by great reserve, and many of the experiments tried in it were repeated in subsequent buildings of the firm. To me its most pleasing feature is the interjection of the low story of single windows in the middle, by which there is obtained a strong harmonic or musical contrast with the lofty stories above and below. To the absence or presence of this agreeable feature of proportion by contrast in subsequent works is to be attributed not a little of their failure or success respectively.

The new Calumet Club House, which preceded this building, is less marked as an example of style and far more conventional in general character. We miss in it the simplicity of general outline and the reserved force which Root afterward obtained. The design is crowded and busy with detail, and the skyline is worried without obtaining a satisfactory result of picturesqueness.

The building, of course, has some good detail, but it seems to have had no apparent influence over Root's subsequent work. It is a significant mile-stone in his career.

The competitive design for the Cincinnati Chamber of Commerce and the executed design for the Art Institute of Chicago (Figs. 132, 133) belong approximately to the same era as the Insurance Exchange. The former is an emphatic break from the Romanesque succession, and indicates a mood rather than a conviction. It presents a clever study, in the contemporary English manner, of a mediæval Flemish town hall, with a lofty hipped roof, corner towers with steep conical spires, dormers fantastically crowned with capricious, flamboyant open pediments; it has the carved balconies, the original canopies, and all the other picturesque features of the Low Countries in the fifteenth century, except their chimneys, which, strangely, are not apparent in this design. The design is interesting as an exotic. Many of its features made their appearance afterward in Root's domestic work, but it had no value whatever in the work of establishing the architectural system which was the greatest result of his more serious efforts. The Art Institute, however, takes up the thread of consistent progress much more effectively, and is one of the most successful works of this period of study.

In the Rialto Building, constructed in 1886, we have a design in which the vertical elements are much more strongly accentuated than in any previous trials. Very properly, most of its characteristic features were never repeated. It was a useful lesson. It has three architectural stories, of which the first and second inclose two floors each, and the third four floors. The pilasters or piers in the last story have the expression of buttresses, and their vertical lines are somewhat coarsely interrupted at the top by heavy balconies, which serve as the main cornice, above which is a final attic story through which the pier-lines break and form clumsy pinnacles against the sky.

The office building of the Central Safety Deposit Company, otherwise known as The Rookery, built about 1886, marks another step of progress, with far more adventurous detail (Fig. 126). In this we feel the absence of subordination and repose. It was a large field for experiment in Romanesque detail used with an amount of intrepidity which commands respect. Horizontal and vertical divisions have nearly equal value — a fatal error in an architectural composition. There is an immense deal of successful and beautiful invention in these crowded façades, of which much found its way into Root's later, better and more temperate work. The position of this building in the succession shows, I think, into what a state of feverish energy his powers were then stirred, and how large were his resources. Though perhaps the least successful of his more important works, it is one of the most interesting and suggestive.

By this time the organization and training of Burnham & Root's office force must have converted it into an orchestra controlled by a powerful but not tyrannical spirit. In no other way can we account for the immense amount of studious and thoughtful work accomplished at this period. "The Rookery" is not only a noted example of great fertility of design, but there is nothing bolder, more original or more inspiring in modern civic architecture either here or elsewhere than its glass-covered court. Where the work has been committed to such a multitude of new devices in construction and to such a prodigality of invention in ornament, it is not strange that one may find reasonable objection to certain points of detail. One may admire the audacity of the double iron staircase which, supported by ingenious cantilevers, ramps with double curvature out into open space, meeting at a landing in the sky, as it were, from which the straight second run rises soberly backward to the stories above. One may admire this and wonder whether such an obvious *tours de force* is worth the study which must have been bestowed upon it. Even the imaginative prison visions in the famous etchings of Piranesi, with their aerial ladders and impossible galleries, present nothing more audacious.

The American Bank Building and the Exchange Building of Kansas City, which belonged to '87 and '88, fall into the line of steady and wholesome progress. Their fenestration is ample, but they have every desirable quality of refined repose. In these brick structures are emphasized several features which have had great influence over the style. Decorative terra-cotta is built into the brick surface, forming a part of it, with excellent and appropriate effect, and the rounding of the pier angles in brickwork is used with good judgment. The harmonious proportions of both buildings is masterly, and in the high stories the iron mullions, enveloped in brick fireproofing and forming slender colonettes, form a fine note of contrast with the corresponding massive brick pier-jambs. The flat segmental bays, which resulted from the experiment in "The Rookery" building at Chicago, are here used with infinitely greater elegance and success, and the scheme of ornament, largely infused with Saracenic spirit, shows how hospitably the growing style receives such accretions, which enlarge its resources without affecting its essential qualities of dignity and strength. These are beautiful buildings.

The Phenix Building of Chicago strikes another note of variation (Fig. 127). Its harmonic horizontal divisions would have been perfect but for the treatment of the attic story, which is placed above the balconied cornice, and overweights the building at the top. The experiment in oriels, of which the vertical members are heavy, round, decorated columns forming the angles, three to each bay, will never be tried again. There is also introduced into this building, with curious and not uninteresting effect, a certain amount of richly carved detail, which would never have been invented in America but for the copious suggestions in certain of the barbaric topes and Buddhist temples of India. The porch of this building is of noble and interesting design.

The current works of Root — momentarily interrupted by the inexplicable providence of his death, but sure to be fruitful in the future, through the spirit which he left behind him and which cannot die — show advances so distinct in all the elements of wholesome growth; they show a mind so capacious and so facile; a spirit which so happily combined conservatism with audacity; a

222

power of progression so marked, that his sudden taking off becomes doubly pathetic, and almost assumes the proportions of a disaster to our beloved art. At all events, in him we have lost a Hotspur, whose gallant example kept the Lamp of Life blazing like a beacon.

The eighteen-storied tower of the Masonic Temple of Chicago (Fig. 136), now erecting, is an extreme example of the daring quality of his genius; of his wise conservatism, the great structure now constructing under the auspices of the Woman's Christian Temperance Union of Chicago (Fig. 137), and the Mills Building of San Francisco, may stand as final and triumphant witnesses. The former is a departure so fundamental from the traditions of decorative architecture that I hardly know how to characterize it. It is a building absolutely committed to what one may call a perpendicular tyranny of pilasters, resting upon an inadequate open stylobate, and supporting two severe gables, connected by a steep roof and broken by dormers. Thirteen stories of similar use and importance, typical of an industrial hive of democratic industry, find themselves expressed here externally in an absolutely monotonous and unmitigated system of fenestration, separated by vertical piers which rise from top to bottom without incident. It is perhaps the frankest admission of a structural and economical necessity ever expressed in architectural form. Between these pilasters, 160 feet high, rise several oriels equally vertical and equally monotonous. For the interruption of these vertical lines there would be of course only the excuse of design; none are supplied either by structure or use. It is probable that in this experiment, which looks like the apotheosis of the elevator in the modern social system, it was Root's desire to permit an exceptional character of structure to have the fullest and most honest architectural expression once for all. But, as Mr. Fergusson would say,[8] one cannot but wonder why, under this conviction of duty, the stylobate was not made more massive and more evidently capable of the vast labor intrusted to it by the structural conditions above, and why, instead of connecting his pilasters together at the top by arches, he did not finish them with offsets like buttresses, treating the structure above like a group of lanterns recessed behind aerial galleries, the skyline being broken with pinnacles, dormers, gables and chimneys, following the suggestions contained in such spires as Ulm and Freiburg. Doubtless Root could have defended this composition with eloquence which would fascinate, while it might not convince; we are sure that it was not a caprice, for this would be contrary to the serious habit of his mind when engaged with problems of such magnitude. But his lips are sealed, and we must await with curiosity such revelations and condonations as may be supplied by the total effect in execution.

As for the temple erecting for the Woman's Christian Union, it is a design far more orderly and sane; a vast building in two lofty pavilions, with an open recessed court between, closed at the bottom by a curtain wall continuous with the two-storied stylobate, in which is the main entrance. Architecturally the building is committed to the style of chateaux of the Loire before they

223

had been greatly affected by the Renaissance. The group has twelve stories, two of which are in the stylobate, seven in the walls which arise thence to the machicolated cornice, and three in the battlements and dormers above.

The angles of the pavilions are mighty, round towers engaged in the corners, starting from corbels in the stylobate, finishing with an attic or battlement story above the cornice and crowned with conical roofs. Between are two-storied dormers with steep gables, grouped with noble effect, and the masses of the building behind are carried boldly to the sky with hipped roofs. There is a light and slender but adequate lantern in the center. The skylines of this design are beyond all praise. The serious and noble quality of the building is due to the underlying Romanesque sentiment, which, though not expressed technically, has to my mind clearly served to eliminate the luxury and gaity which distinguished its prototypes, the royal chateaux of France. It is true that the Romanesque roof is nearly lost in the late gothic expression into which it has flowered, while in the Masonic experiment it is much more frankly retained. Between the two one cannot but admit that the gothic device is far more architectural as the crown for a building composed of the superimposition of numerous equal stories. I think it will be generally admitted that this last adaptation of architecture to structure, or, more properly, this growth of architecture from structure on a heroic scale, is, on the whole, the finest effort of Root's genius. As an expression of strength and dignity crowned worthily by beauty and grace, no nobler example has been given in modern times.

"Great men," said Longfellow, "stand like towers in the city of God." [9] Perhaps the architectural treatment of these structures of unprecedented height, illustrating at once the loftiness of his aspirations, the delicate sensitiveness of his genius, and his high sense of professional duty in preserving for us to the last through many experiments a single consistent basis of design, may be accepted as a fitting expression of one who seems to me to have been one of the most interesting personalities in the history of modern architecture.

Architecture at the World's Columbian Exposition

(1892)

I.

The World's Columbian Exposition was organized April 9, 1890, and on the 25th of the same month Congress passed the bill giving Chicago the honor of this great enterprise. On July 1 following, Jackson Park and the lake front of Chicago were selected as the double site of the Exposition. On the 20th of August F. L. Olmsted & Co. were elected consulting landscape-architects. Between then and the following December the organization of the Department of Construction was perfected by the appointment of D. H. Burnham as chief and of J. W. Root as consulting architect, Mr. Burnham having acted as professional adviser from the beginning of the enterprise. Undoubtedly to his sagacity, energy, and breadth of view, and to his wide experience in important architectural work, the Chicago Commission is largely indebted for the great effective working capacity which it has developed; and under his organizing power the complicated machinery of administration in respect to grounds and buildings was fairly established.

For reasons which we need not state, the double site was finally abandoned; and it then became the duty of the Committee on Grounds and Buildings, under the advice of their chosen experts, to review this all-important question of locality, and to discover, if possible, within the limits of Chicago, or in its near vicinity, an area of land capable of containing, without crowding, a series of buildings which, in the aggregate, should be at least 50 per cent. larger than those of the last Paris Exposition; should be conveniently and economically accessible for visitors and for material; not divided by railroads, streets, creeks, or cemeteries; and not so encumbered with buildings or other improvements that it would be difficult to obtain possession of it and to prepare it for the reception of the structures of the Exposition.

Of the few places answering these requirements all were flat, low, and, from a horticultural point of view, unsatisfactory. The only large, agreeable, or dignified element of scenery within many miles of the town was the lake, and there was discovered only one place on the lake presenting the desired conditions. This was a tract of five hundred acres between six and seven miles south of the central part of the city, with a length of a mile and a half on the lake side and three quarters of a mile in width. Topographically the place consisted of a series of low sand-dunes which had been thrown up successively by the lake in lines nearly parallel with the shore, the most considerable of them having an average height of not more than six feet above the high stages of the water. Between these dunes there were broad, low, flat, swampy swales, subject to occasional floods, with water generally standing one or two feet below the surface. On some of these dunes groves of small, stunted oaks were growing, and the intermediate flats were more or less overgrown by sedge and water grasses (Fig. 141).

This tract belonged to the South Park Commission, having been obtained twenty years before with a view to its future improvement as a public park. Practically it was in a state of nature, as we have described, except as to a limited area at its northern end, which had been graded, planted, diversified by ponds, and made accessible by drives and walks. The disadvantages of this site were sufficiently obvious; but it was considered that they, together with the inconvenience arising from its distance from the thickly populated parts of the city, would be offset by these advantages: first, that it was unencumbered with buildings; secondly, that it could be made readily accessible, either by boats on the lake or by public land conveyances of various sorts, without numerous railroad or river crossings; and thirdly, that a number of railroads passed within a few hundred feet of the landward boundaries of the tract, extending in one direction nearly to the heart of the city, and, in the other, connecting, or easily to be connected, with lines to all parts of the continent. Indeed, to the experienced eye and instructed imagination of the landscape-architects the very qualities in this desert-like waste which presented the most formidable obstacles to the realization of anything approaching the horticultural splendors, or finished park-like aspects, of previous international expositions suggested the possibility of procuring out of these most unpromising elements effects quite unusual, yet of a wholly appropriate character. The broad expanse of the great inland lake itself, with its ever-changing surface and its oceanic horizon, its waters prospectively alive with sails, and animated by the incessant movement of steamers and craft of every sort, "ornate, be-decked, and gay,"[1] beneath the unlimited summer sky, would give to the *mise-en-scène* a peculiar character, under the influence of which the foreign visitor might forget to ask for that metropolitan opulence of shaded parkland which here could not be obtained. Steam-dredges and the railroad grading-processes of the West could readily at small expense enlarge the areas of higher land, and create level plateaus and stately terraces as sites for the great buildings of the Exposition, with material excavated from the wet and sedgy intervals, converting the latter into a system of lagoons connected with the lake by walled canals and basins. Thus might be created within the grounds an interior water-system, four miles in length, which would be navigable by omnibus-boats, conveying visitors from every quarter of the Park to landings before each of the principal buildings.

Under such circumstances the landscape-architects felt authorized to recommend to the committee the use of the grounds known as Jackson Park, which, after much negotiation with the South Park Commissioners, and much controversy with those advocating other sites, were finally obtained under the agreement that, after the Exposition and after the removal of the buildings, they should be left in a condition well adapted to be formed into a permanent public park for the city. A succession of ingenious plans was then prepared and reported to the committee by these gentlemen, in intimate connection with Messrs. Burnham and Root, illustrating the gradual development of a general scheme for the occupation of the site, Mr. Root making sketch-designs of all the buildings as the work progressed. The leading motives of composition were to obtain such a disposition of the greater buildings as should make the best and most effective use of the natural conditions of the ground, when modified and corrected by the art of the landscape-architect; should give to these buildings a proper and articulate relation, one to the other, and also to the water-system of the Park; should group them in a formal and artificial manner at those points where their great size and necessary mutual proximity invited a predominance of architectural magnificence, or picturesquely and accidentally, where the conditions of the landscape were such as to forbid a close observance of axial lines and vistas. But all these dispositions were made subordinate to the situation furnished by the wide expanse and horizon of the lake, so that this important element of composition should have its due value from all the principal points of observation.

Another fundamental condition affecting the general dispositions of the plan was the method of reaching the Park by the seven railroads, so that the difficult problem of debarking and embarking more than 60,000 people every hour by these means of transit should be solved with the least confusion, and at a point where the visitor should be introduced to the grounds through a monumental vestibule, from which a scene should open, stately, splendid, and surprising, alike in its architectural and in its natural elements. It was necessary, also, to consider every means of approach by streetcars and by water, — the latter suggesting the provision of moles and protected harbors on the lake side, — and also to provide for an additional intramural communication by some form of elevated railway.

None of the difficulties to be surmounted, however, were greater than those presented by the necessity of converting into a garden a tract of land which was almost a desert waste; so that the grounds in which the great monumental buildings of the Exposition were to be placed should be set forth with something more than formal architectural terraces, balustrades, bridges, statues, fountains, and canals, and should enjoy at least some of the advantages to be obtained from ordered or picturesque vegetation. Unlike the sites of former expositions, located in the heart of ancient civilizations, the prairies

227

of Illinois afford no imperial treasuries of trees and shrubbery, from which the modern Amphion could draw the means of establishing such vast, full-grown masses of foliage as were needed adequately to decorate these impoverished acres. When the thick ice which is formed on Lake Michigan during the winter is broken up, it is driven by prevailing north winds toward Chicago, and there lingers to prolong the tardy spring. A little later, while the first leaves are unfolding, a night gale from Canada sweeps over these five hundred miles of ice-cold water, and all forms of vegetable growth along the southern margin of the lake are discouraged and delayed. Moreover, the fluctuations which are characteristic of the waters of the lake, not only from day to day, but in its normal and average elevations during the summer, must create bare and dreary shores where the intramural water-system of the Park expands from the formal, stone-bordered canals into the broad and picturesque lagoon.

To obviate these difficulties it was determined — first, so to treat the existing groves of trees that their dwarfish character would be masked by the introduction of hardy, indigenous shrubs around the margin of each group, thus creating effects of massed foliage, as seen from a distance; secondly, to edge the water with a nearly continuous strip of reedy, aquatic plants, which would bear occasional submergence; and thirdly, to provide these with backgrounds of low foliage, chiefly shrub willows and brightly flowering local plants. Occasional stretches of well-kept lawn would also, where necessary, serve to refine the rustic aspect of the grounds.

At the outset the Committee on Grounds and Buildings, together with D. H. Burnham, Chief of Construction, were confronted by a delicate and difficult problem. How were the designs for these great buildings to be obtained? Should one architect be appointed for the whole, or, in view of the more practical alternative of appointing one architect for each building, should these be selected by general competition, by limited competition, or by direct selection? After a careful review of the subject, it was concluded by the committee, in accordance with the recommendations contained in a remarkable memorial presented to them by their professional advisers, to give to the architectural part of the Exposition, so far as possible, an appropriate national character, by making a direct selection of representative architects; thus not only avoiding the serious delays and embarrassments which would inevitably accompany any form of competition, but at the same time enlisting the services of a body of professional experts to consider the architectural questions from the beginning and as a whole, and to lay out a scheme of efficient and harmonious coöperation.*

---

* Innumerable experiments with architectural competitions have made it clear enough that, of all the methods of selecting the architect, this is the most wasteful, unscientific, tedious, costly, demoralizing, and uncertain. It is almost impossible to devise a competitive scheme which will, as its result, secure to the building the best service, or to the competitors an opportunity to express their most useful qualities as architects. It seems equally evident that the establishment of confidential professional relations in the beginning with an architect chosen because of his proved ability and experience, and not because of the accident of his success in a game of chance, is economical of time and money, and consistent with honest business principles. Therefore, the action of the Committee on Grounds and Buildings in this case is so memorable in the history of archi-

On January 12, 1891, the invited architects, Messrs. R. M. Hunt, George B. Post, and McKim, Mead, and White of New York, Peabody and Stearns of Boston, Van Brunt and Howe of Kansas City, together with Messrs. Adler and Sullivan, S. S. Beman, Henry Ives Cobb, W. L. B. Jenney, and Burling and Whitehouse of Chicago, were called together to consult with the chief of construction, the consulting architect, and with Frederick Law Olmsted and his partner, Henry Sargent Codman of Boston, regarding the architectural conditions involved in the scheme of the Exposition (Fig. 139).[2] The latest plans of the consulting architect and landscape-architects, which, as a whole, had been accepted by the National Commission and by the Chicago directors, were laid before this board of architects for consideration. After an exhaustive study of the whole problem, during which many revisions and modifications more or less fundamental were suggested and considered, it was finally resolved to recommend to the Committee on Grounds and Buildings the acceptance of the general scheme of location of buildings and waterways, as prepared by Messrs. Root, Olmsted, and Codman, with but little modification. In fact the problem had been developed by these gentlemen with so much skill and with such exact forethought for all the conditions embraced in this vast complication of interests, and the several stages of development had been so intelligently discussed by the committee and by the chief of construction, that it was evident to the board of professional experts that they could devise no better starting-point for their specific part of the work.

The sudden death of Mr. Root, after a very brief illness, during these preliminary sessions of the Architectural Board, deprived this great enterprise

---

tectural practice, that we deem it important to print here the report upon which this action was based. This report was prepared by Mr. Burnham, and, at his request, was signed by all the professional advisers of the committee.

Dec. 6, 1890.

The Honorable the Committee on Grounds and Buildings, World's Columbian Exposition.

Gentlemen: Preliminary work in locating buildings, in determining their general areas, and in other elementary directions necessary to proper progress in the design and erection of the structures of the Columbian Exposition, has now reached a point where it becomes necessary to determine the method by which designs for these buildings shall be obtained.

We recognize that your action in the matter will be of great importance, not only in its direct effect upon the artistic and commercial success of the Exposition, but scarcely less upon the aspect presented by America to the world, and also as a precedent for future procedure in the country by the Government, by corporations, and individuals. In our advisory capacity we wish to recommend such action to you as will be productive of the best results, and will at the same time be in accord with the expressed sentiments of the architectural societies of America. Whatever suggestions are here made relate to the main buildings located at Jackson Park.

That these buildings should in their designs, relationships, and arrangement be of the highest possible architectural merit is of importance scarcely less great than the variety, richness, and comprehensiveness of the various displays within them. Such success is not so much dependent upon the expenditure of money as upon the expenditure of thought, knowledge, and enthusiasm by men known to be in every way endowed with these qualities, and the results achieved by them will be the measure by which America, and especially Chicago, must expect to be judged by the world. Several methods of procedure suggest themselves:

First. The selection of one man to whom the designing of the entire work should be intrusted.

Second. Competition made free to the whole architectural profession.

Third. Competition among a selected few.

Fourth. Direct selection.

The first method would possess some advantage in the coherent and logical result which would be attained. But the objections are that time for the preparation of designs is so short that no one of services which would have been of peculiar value in perfecting the architectural work, and which already had been an essential factor in laying out the general scheme of the buildings, and in facilitating an effective, fraternal coördination of professional labor such as rarely, if ever, has occurred in the history of architecture. The strong initiative force furnished by the generous enthusiasm and bright genius of Root remained, however, with the Architectural Board, and has been an element constantly working for unity and strength in its councils.

In all projects relating to the decoration of the grounds by sculpture and monumental fountains, the large experience and eminent authority of Mr. Augustus St. Gaudens have been forces working silently for higher art, greater nobility of expression, and more effective results.[3] Unfortunately the work of his own hand will not appear in these decorations; but his advice in the selection of sculptors for them has been of permanent value, and has been followed with generous intelligence and to the manifest advantage of the Exposition.

The basis of operations is explained by the plan of the grounds herewith presented (Fig. 140), which exhibits in outline the result, not of the latest studies, but of that stage of the work reached at the time when it was necessary to prepare the map for the purpose of illustrating this paper. In a subsequent paper we hope to present a more comprehensive plan, indicating the nature of the modification to which the whole scheme has been subject from month to month. It will be observed that there are three grand divisions. Of these the northernmost, which had already been laid out as a park by the

---

man could hope to do the subject justice, even were he broad enough to avoid, in work of such varied and colossal character, monotonous repetition of ideas. And, again, such a method would evoke criticism, just or unjust, and would certainly debar the enterprise from the friendly coöperation of a diversity of talent, which can be secured only by bringing together the best architectural minds of our country. The second method named has been employed in France and other European countries with success, and would probably result in the production of a certain number of plans possessing more or less merit and novelty. But in such a competition much time, even now most valuable, would be wasted, and the result would be a mass of irrelevant and almost irreconcilable material, which would demand great and extended labor to bring into coherence. It is greatly to be feared that from such a heterogeneous competition the best men of the profession would refrain, not only because the uncertainties involved in it are too great and their time too valuable, but because the societies to which they almost universally belong have so strongly pronounced on its futility. A limited and fair competition would present fewer embarrassments, but even in this case the question of time is presented, and it is most unlikely that any result derived through this means, coming as it would from necessarily partial acquaintance with the subject, and hasty, ill-considered presentation of it, could be satisfactory, and the selection of an individual would be open to the same objections made above as to a single designer. Far better than any of the methods seems to be the last. This is to select a certain number of architects, choosing each man for such work as would be most nearly parallel with his best achievements; these architects to meet in conference, and become masters of all the elements of the problems to be solved, and agree upon some general scheme of procedure. The preliminary studies resulting from this to be compared and freely discussed in a subsequent conference, and, with the assistance of such suggestions as your advisers might make, to be brought into a harmonious whole.

The honor conferred upon those selected would create in their minds a disposition to place the artistic quality of their work in advance of the mere question of emolument; while the emulation begotten in a rivalry so dignified and friendly could not fail to be productive of a result which would stand before the world as the best fruit of American civilization.

D. H. Burnham, Chief of Construction.
John W. Root, Consulting Architect.
F. L. Olmsted & Co., Consulting Landscape-Arch'ts.
A. Gottlieb, Consulting Engineer.

city, is to be occupied centrally by the Department of Fine Arts, the State pavilions being grouped north and west of it; while the foreign government buildings will be placed east of it, toward the lake, and, if occasion requires, in the Plaisance, which is a long reserved tract 600 feet wide between 59th and 60th streets, forming a boulevard approach to Jackson Park from the west. In this tract also areas have been granted to foreign enterprise for the establishment of model villages and groups of pavilions illustrating the characteristics of domestic and industrial life in remote countries.

The middle division is formed by the lagoon, the most characteristic landscape feature of the grounds. This is an irregular, artificial water-way surrounding several islands, the largest among them being a wooded tract about 1700 feet long and from 200 to 500 feet wide, the natural conditions of which will be enhanced by aquatic shrubbery and flower-beds, with kiosks and rustic pavilions approached by bridges. A part of the northern end of this island has been applied for by, and will probably be granted to, the Japanese commissioners, who propose to lay out a considerable area in a characteristic garden, according to their ancient traditions in this art, and to embellish it with exact reproductions of several of their most venerable temples. The outer margins of the lagoon will be occupied on the west by the Transportation Building, by the Horticultural Building, with its gardens, and by the Woman's Building; on the east, toward the lake, will stand the Palace of Manufactures and Liberal Arts, and the United States Pavilion. The lagoon branches capriciously northward and eastward, giving water-fronts to the Pavilion of Fine Arts, to the Illinois State Building, and to the Fisheries and United States Government buildings. Southward this irregular quadrangle is closed by the north façades of the Mines and Electricity buildings.

The lagoon connects southward with a system of formal stone-bordered canals and basins, where will be symmetrically placed the great plaza, or *cour d'honneur*, of the Exposition, a regular quadrangle 700 by 2000 feet, about equal in size to that of the last Paris Exposition. Water-communication will be provided for at the east end of this court, and the system of railroads will debouch at the west end in a railroad terminus, masked by the Administration Building, which will be treated so as to serve as the monumental porch of the Exposition. From the railroad terminus, through the arches of this porch and beneath its lofty dome, the visitors will enter the court, which is bounded on the right hand (southward) by the Departments of Machinery and Agriculture, on the left (northward) by those devoted to Mines, Electricity, and to Manufactures and the Liberal Arts, and in front (eastward) by Lake Michigan (Figs. 142, 143, 145). The center of this court is occupied by a great artificial basin which forms a part of the water-system of the Park. Connecting with this basin, a broad canal, bordered by double terraces and crossed by arched bridges, will run southward into a minor court between the palaces of Agriculture and Machinery (Fig. 144). This minor court will be closed toward the south by an architectural screen in the form of an arcade on the first story and a colonnade on the second, with a triumphal arch in the center, through which the visitor will enter the Department of Live Stock, which constitutes the southernmost feature of the Exposition. Opposite this canal, on the same axis, is another of similar character, running northward between the Departments of Electricity and the Liberal Arts, and connecting, as we have already seen, with the waters of the lagoon.

This brief description, aided by the topographical views which we present, may serve to give in outline the general architectural scheme of the Exposition-grounds. The relative positions of the buildings being understood, we may now devote ourselves to a consideration of the architectural motives which underlie the designs of the buildings, and confer upon them character and significance as works of art. In other words, we do not attempt a description of these buildings, still less a criticism, — which would be premature, — but an analysis of the principles according to which they have been severally developed. We purpose, in fact, to put ourselves in the position of the architect when first confronted by his problem, and, as far as possible, to outline some of the processes of investigation and study through which his work gradually grew into its final form. Of course it would be impracticable to indicate the numerous false starts, the erasures, the studies tried and abandoned, and all the long tentative processes which must in every case be labored through before the scheme of a building takes its ultimate shape. The main object of these papers will have been attained if they may serve to show how a work of architecture, like any other work of art, is the result of logical processes studiously followed, and not a mere matter of taste, a following of fashion, or an accident of invention more or less fortuitous.

The highest claim which can be made for modern architecture must rest on those characteristics of ornamented or ordered structure which have grown out of the unprecedented exigencies of modern buildings. Wherever these exigencies have been met in such a spirit that a corresponding development of style has been produced, justly differentiated from all other historic or contemporary styles not by caprice, but by growth, there exists a living and progressive art, which, like all other living arts in history, will stand as the exponent of the civilization under which it obtained its definite form. Probably the largest, the most deliberate, and the most conspicuous expression of the present condition of architecture in this country will be looked for by foreign critics on the grounds of the World's Columbian Exposition; but they will find it rather in the latest commercial, educational, and domestic structures in and near our larger cities. By these our architecture should be judged. It is true that the industrial palaces of our Exposition will be larger in area than any which have preceded them, and will surpass in this respect even the imperial villas and baths of the ancient Romans. But they will be an unsubstantial pageant of which the concrete elements will be a series of vast covered inclosures, adjusted on architectural plans to the most lucid classification and the most effective arrangement of the materials of the Exposition, and faced with a decorative mask of plaster composition on frames of timber and iron, as the Romans of the Empire clothed their rough structures of cement and brick with magnificent architectural veneers of marbles, bronze, and sculpture. Mr. Burnham, the Chief of Construction, rubs his wonderful lamp of Aladdin in his office at Chicago, and the sudden result is an exhalation, a vast phantasm of architecture, glittering with domes, towers, and banners, like the vision of Norumbega, which presently will fade and leave no trace behind. But these shapes do not make themselves. There is, it is true, a creative energy, followed by an apparition of palaces and pavilions; but between the energy and the apparition are the consultations, the experiments, the studies of a very palpable board of representative architects of the nation, who have learned that this great architectural improvisation requires as much of their zeal, labor, knowledge, and professional experience as if they were planning to build with monumental stone and marble. However temporary the buildings, the formative motives behind them will be on trial before the world; for these motives, disembarrassed as they have been, to a great extent, of the usual controlling considerations of structure and cost, and concentrated upon the evolution of purely decorative forms, have made demands upon our resources of art such, perhaps, as have been required by no previous emergency in architecture.

The liberality exhibited by the management and by the architects of Chicago toward their brethren summoned from other cities has been more than generous. To the latter were assigned all the buildings around the great court, a compliment which involved the most serious responsibilities, and of which the only adequate recognition could be an especial effort to justify it. In view of the fact that these buildings had a mutual dependence much more marked than any others on the grounds, and that the formal or architectural character of the court absolutely required a perfect harmony of feeling among the five structures which inclose it, it became immediately evident to these gentlemen that they must adopt, not only a uniform and ceremonious style, — a style evolved from, and expressive of, the highest civilizations in history, — in which each one could express himself with fluency, but also a common module of dimension. These considerations seemed to forbid the use of medieval or any other form of romantic, archæological, or picturesque art. The style should be distinctly secular and pompous, restrained from license by historical authority, and organized by academical discipline. It was not difficult, therefore, to agree upon the use of Roman classic forms, correctly and loyally interpreted, but permitting variations suggested not only by the Italians, but by the other masters of the Renaissance. It was considered that a series of pure classic models, in each case contrasting in character according to the personal equation of the architect, and according to the practical conditions to be accommodated in each, but uniform in respect to scale and language of form, all set forth with the utmost amount of luxury and opulence of decoration permitted by the best usage, and on a theater of almost unprecedented magnitude, would present to the profession here an object-lesson so impressive of the practical value of architectural scholarship and of strict subordination to the formulas of the schools, that it would serve as a timely corrective to the national tendency to experiments in design. It is not desired or expected that this display, however successful it may prove to be in execution, should make a new revival or a new school in the architecture of our country, or interfere with any healthy advance on classic or romantic lines which may be evolving here. There are many uneducated and untrained men practising as architects, and still maintaining, especially in the remote regions of the country, an impure and unhealthy vernacular, incapable of progress; men who have never seen a pure classic monument executed on a great scale, and who are ignorant of the emotions which it must excite in any breast accessible to the influences of art. To such it is hoped that these great models, inspired as they have been by a profound respect for the masters of classic art, will prove such a revelation that they will learn at last that true architecture cannot be based on undisciplined invention, illiterate originality, or, indeed, upon any audacity of ignorance.

It was further agreed by the architects of the court that the module of proportion for the composition of their façades should be a bay not exceeding twenty-five feet in width and sixty feet in height to the top of the main cornice, which is about the size of a five-storied façade on an ordinary city lot. In all other respects each of these gentlemen, influenced of course by mutual criticism, and subject to the approval of the executive of the Exposition through its Committee on Grounds and Buildings, has been left perfectly free to develop, within the area prescribed in each case, the design of the building assigned to him, according to his own convictions as to general outlines and details of architectural expression. Under these circumstances, therefore, it may fairly be anticipated that the great palaces of the court will illustrate the vital principle of unity in variety on a scale never before attempted in modern times.

It must be borne in mind, however, that all this is not architecture in its highest sense, but rather a scenic display of architecture, composed (to use a theatrical term) of "practicable" models, executed on a colossal stage, and with a degree of apparent pomp and splendor which, if set forth in marbles and bronze, might recall the era of Augustus or Nero. We have not, it is true, the inexhaustible resources of the museums and schools and gardens of Paris to people this great industrial court with statues and vases, set against rich backgrounds of exotic foliage; but the opportunity will possibly enable us to prove that whatever characteristics of audacious invention or adaptation are exhibited in the best buildings of modern America, it is not because our architects are untrained in the organization of structural forms, ignorant of historical precedent, or wanting in respect for the works of the masters, nor yet because they do not know how on occasion to express themselves in the language of the most venerable traditions of art. But these great Doric, Ionic, Corinthian, and Composite orders, with their arches, porticos, pavilions, attics, domes, and campaniles, do not express actual structure in any sense, as was the case with Paxton's apotheosis of the greenhouse in the great glass and iron building of the first London Exposition,[4] they rather serve as architectural screens, of which only the main divisions and articulations have been suggested by the temporary framework of iron and timber which they mask, and which, in itself, is incapable of expression in any terms of monumental dignity. If each architect of the board had been permitted or encouraged to make his especial screen an unrestricted exhibition of his archæological knowledge or ingenuity in design, we should have had a curious, and in some respects perhaps an interesting and instructive, polyglot or confusion of tongues, such as in the early scriptural times on the plains of Shinar was so detrimental to architectural success. The show might have contained some elements of the great "American Style"; but as a whole it would have been a hazardous experiment, and it certainly would have perplexed the critics. In respect to the architecture of the great court, therefore, it seemed at least safer to proceed according to established formulas, and to let the special use and object of each building, and the personal equation of the architect employed on it, do what they properly could, within these limits, to secure variety and movement.

It is a fashion of the times, following Mr. Ruskin, to stigmatize the marvelous multiplication of mechanical appliances to life in the nineteenth century as degrading to its higher civilization and destructive of its art. Mr. Frederic Harrison agrees with these philosophers of discontent so far as to say that if machinery were really the last word of the century we should all be rushing violently down a steep place, like the herd of swine. But he says:

To decry steam and electricity, inventions and products, is hardly more foolish than to deny the price which civilization itself has to pay for the use of them. There are forces at work now, forces more unwearied than steam, and brighter than the electric arc, to rehumanize the dehumanized members of society; to assert the old, immutable truths; forces yearning for rest, grace, and harmony; rallying all that is organic in men's social nature, and proclaiming the value of spiritual life over material life.[5]

In order, therefore, to present a complete and symmetrical picture of modern civilization, it is necessary that the Columbian Exposition should not only bring together evidences of the amazing material productiveness which, within the century, has effected a complete transformation in the external aspects of life, but should force into equal prominence, if possible, corresponding evidences that the finer instincts of humanity have not suffered complete eclipse in this grosser prosperity, and that, in this headlong race, art has not been left entirely behind. The management of the Exposition is justified in placing machinery, agricultural appliances and products, manufactures and the liberal arts, the wonderful industrial results of scientific investigation, and the other evidences of practical progress, in the midst of a parallel display shaped entirely by sentiment and appealing to a fundamentally different set of emotions. It is the high function of architecture not only to adorn this triumph of materialism, but to condone, explain, and supplement it, so that some elements of "sweetness and light" may be brought forward to counterbalance the boastful Philistinism of our times. Each department of the Exposition must possess more or less capacity for architectural expression, if not by disposition of masses, by style, or by sympathetic treatment of technical detail, at least by the suggestions of sculpture and characteristic decoration. It is true that the vast preponderance of human effort in these closing years of the century has been in favor of practical things; it remains to be seen whether this supreme test of the elastic powers of architecture to develop out of these practical things demonstrations of art will result in furnishing any of that "rest, grace, and harmony" which are needed as a compensation for materialism.

By a remarkable piece of fortune, the architects to whom the five buildings on the great court were assigned constituted a family, by reason of long-established personal relations and of unusually close professional sympathies. Of this family Mr. Hunt was the natural head; two of its members, Post and Van Brunt, were his professional children; Howe, Peabody, and Stearns, having been pupils and assistants of the latter, may be considered the grandchildren of the household; while McKim, who had been brought up under the same academical influences, was, with his partners, of the same blood by right of adoption and practice. Collaboration under such circumstances, and under a species of parental discipline so inspiring, so vigorous, and so affectionate, should hardly fail to confer upon the work resulting from it some portion of the delightful harmony which prevailed in their councils.

By common consent the most monumental of these buildings — that devoted to the Administration — was undertaken by Mr. Hunt (Fig. 146). Having all the elements of an academical project of the first class, it was eminently fitting that this important structure should fall into hands so admirably equipped by learning and experience to do it full justice. It was to occupy the western or landward side of the great court, and to stand in its main central axis at the point where this axis was intersected by a transverse axis which ran north and south between the Mines and Electricity buildings. It was designed to be the loftiest and most purely monumental composition in the Park, and to serve not only for the accommodation of the various bureaus of administration, but, more conspicuously, as the great porch of the Exposition. The area assigned was a square measuring about 260 feet on each side, and it was necessary to divide it into four equal parts by two great avenues crossing at right angles on the axial lines which we have described. In fact, the building was in some way to stand on four legs astride this crossing of the ways, like one of the quadrilateral Janus-coaches of the Romans, but on a much greater scale. The whole system of railway communication was to be so connected on the west with this building, that the crowds of visitors, on arriving, should enter and cross this ceremonial vestibule; should there obtain their first impressions; and by the majesty and spacious repose of the interior, should be in a manner introduced into a new world, and forced into sympathy with the highest objects of this latest international exposition of arts. Its function, indeed, was that of an overture.

These conditions suggested to Mr. Hunt the idea of a civic temple based upon the model of the domical cathedrals of the Renaissance. Following this type, he projected, upon the crossing of the two axial lines, a hall of octagonal plan; but unlike the cathedrals, this hall was designed to form the fundamental basis, the leading motive, of the design, not only on the interior but on the exterior of the structure, there being neither nave nor transepts to interfere with the clear external development of this dominating feature from the ground to the summit. Thus, at the outset, he secured that expression of unity which is essential to the noblest monumental effect in architecture. The expression of repose, at once majestic and graceful, which is no less essential, was to be obtained, not only by a careful subordination of detail to the leading idea, but by such a disposition of masses as would impart an aspect of absolute stability. This implied the necessity of procuring a pyramidal or culminating effect; the whole composition, from bottom to top, preparing for this effect by some process of diminution by stages upward. To this end he enveloped his hall (which the conditions of area permitted him to make 120 feet in interior diameter) with two octagonal shells about 24 feet apart, the space between being occupied by galleries, elevators, vestibules, and staircases. Against the alternate or diagonal sides of the octagon he erected four pavilions in the form of wings 84 feet square, in four stories, in which he accommodated the various offices of administration; the archways, pierced through the four cardinal sides of the octagon, being externally recessed between these pavilions, thus affording two direct, broad passageways through the building at right angles. These pavilions are so treated as to be in scale with the other buildings of the great court, and are carried to the same height of 60 feet, thus securing four wide-spreading abutments with flat, terraced roofs. Above these the outer octagonal shell of the central mass detaches itself, and asserts its outline against the sky through another stage, where it stops in the form of a gallery, decorated with bronze flambeaux, and permits the inner shell in turn to become outwardly manifest in a third stage of diminished diameter, rising in an octagonal drum, the whole mass finishing with the soaring lines of the central dome; which by vertical growth, determined by conditions of proportion, reaches the height of 275 feet from the pavement. Enriched with decorated ribs and sculptured panels, and made splendid with shining gold, this noble dome rises far above the other structures of the Exposition, proclaiming afar the position of its monumental gateway.

But as the inner surface of the outer dome would form a ceiling far too lofty to serve as a proper and effective cover for the hall, it became necessary, in order to give proper proportions to this monumental chamber, to construct an inner and lower dome, 190 feet high from the pavement, with an open eye at the apex, through which from below could be seen the upper structure, like the cope of a mysterious sky beyond. This architectural device is similar to those used by Mansart in the dome of the Invalides at Paris, by Soufflot in the Panthéon, and by Wren in St. Paul's at London, which rank next to St. Peter's as the largest and most important of the great Renaissance temples of Europe. It also appears in the rotunda of the national Capitol at Washington.

But, as conceived by Hunt, the exterior dome of the vestibule of the Exposition is 42 feet higher than that of Mansart, 45 feet higher than that of Souflot, about the same height as that of St. Paul's, and 57 feet higher than that of our national Capitol, exclusive of the lantern in each case. The interior dome has a height from the pavement 15 feet higher than that of the Invalides; it has about the same height as that of the French Panthéon; is 20 feet lower than that of St. Paul's and 10 feet higher than that of the Capitol at Washington. In diameter it surpasses all these domes, being 38 feet wider than the first, 56 feet wider than the second, 12 feet wider than the third, and 26 feet wider than the Washington example. Indeed, in this regard, it is only 20 feet less than that of St. Peter's at Rome, which, however, in exterior height exceeds the American model by 90 feet, and in interior height by 143. Being thus in dimensions inferior only to the work of Michelangelo, it may be considered, in this respect, at least, an adequate vestibule to the Exposition of 1893.

The method of lighting the interior of this vast domical chamber in a proper and adequate manner was a problem so important that Mr. Hunt considered it one of the primary formative influences controlling the evolution of his architectural scheme. One of the noblest effects of interior illumination known in historical art is in the Roman Pantheon, the area of which (140 feet in diameter) is lighted only by the circular hypethral opening 25 feet wide at the apex of the dome, 140 feet from the pavement. Inspired by this majestic example, Mr. Hunt proposed in this respect to depend mainly upon such light as could be obtained from the open eye of his lower dome, 50 feet wide and 190 feet from the pavement, which should in turn borrow its light from the illumination of the space between his outer and inner domes through a glazed hypethral opening 38 feet wide, forming the summit of the building, and taking the place of the lantern or belvedere which usually forms the finial of the greater domes of the Renaissance.

In his decorative treatment of the problem thus evolved Mr. Hunt has exercised a fine spirit of scholarly reserve. The architectural language employed is simple and stately, and the composition as a whole is so free from complications, its structural articulations are so frankly accentuated, that it is easy to read, and, being read, cannot fail to surprise the most unaccustomed mind with a distinct and veritable architectural impression. But to obtain this simplicity of result a far greater knowledge of design and far more ingenuity of adaptation have been required than if the building had been sophisticated with all the consciousness and affectations of modern art. In order to bring his design into the family of which, by the adoption of a common module of proportion, the other buildings of the groups around the great court are members, Mr. Hunt's four pavilions of administration, forming the lower story of the façades, are treated externally, like them, with a single order raised upon a basement. He has preferred the Doric in his case, so as to obtain by contrast with its neighbors an effect of severe dignity and what might be called colossal repose, and to provide for a gradual increase of enrichment in the upper parts of his monument. His second story is Ionic, with an open colonnade, or loggia, on each of the cardinal faces of the octagon, showing the inner shell behind, and with domed circular staircase pavilions of the same order on the narrower alternate sides, niched between heavy corner piers, which bear groups of statuary, thus obtaining a certain degree of movement and complication in the outlines of his design, and enhancing its pyramidal effect. On all his exterior he has used conventional ornament with great reserve, depending for richness of effect upon three colossal groups of statuary on each of his administrative pavilions, upon two, flanking each of his main entrances, and upon eight, crowning the gallery below the drum of his dome.

This sculpture, the work of Mr. Karl Bitter of New York[6] is characterized by great breadth and dignity of treatment, and by that expression of heroic power and fitness which is derived from knowing how to treat colossal subjects in a colossal way, and how to model figures so that they may assist the main architectural thought and not compete with it. Thus the groups which crown the corner piers of the four wings in the lower part of the building are in repose, and are so massed that they serve properly as monumental finials, while those surmounting the gallery above are more strongly accentuated, so as to become intelligible at that great height, and are distinguished by a far greater animation of outline and lightness of movement, by means of gesture, outspread wings, and accessories, so that they may act as foils to the simple and stately architectural lines of the dome, at the base of which they stand, and so that they may aid it in its upward spring. The subjects are apparently intended to typify, in a succession of groups, beginning in the lower parts of the monument, the advance of mankind from barbarism to civilization, and the final triumph of the arts of peace and war.

Unlike the other buildings of the Exposition, Mr. Hunt's has two sets of façades, an exterior and an interior. In the latter he has not repeated his exterior orders, and the same self-denial which has chastened and purified the exterior has left these inner walls large, simple, and spacious, not even the angles of the inclosing octagon being architecturally emphasized at any point. Each of the eight sides of this interior octagon is pierced with an archway occupied by a screen of doors below and bronze grilles above; over these is a series of panels filled with sculpture and inscriptions, and upon the great interior cornice which crowns these walls is a balcony, like the whispering-gallery of St. Paul's, by means of which the scene may be viewed from above. An order of pilasters directly under the inner dome surmounts this gallery, and the dome itself is decorated with panels, the whole interior being enriched with color, so disposed as to complete and perfect the design.

We have already said that this vestibule was intended to introduce the visitors to the Exposition into a new world. As they emerge from its east archway and enter the court, they must, if possible, receive a memorable impression of architectural harmony on a vast scale. To this end the forums, basilicas, and baths of the Roman Empire, the villas and gardens of the princes of the Italian Renaissance, the royal courtyards of the palaces of France and Spain, must yield to the architects, "in that new world which is the old," [7] their rich inheritance of ordered beauty, to make possible the creation of a bright picture of civic splendor such as this great function of modern civilization would seem to require.

At the outset it was considered of the first importance that the people, in circulating around the court and entering or leaving the buildings, should so far as possible be protected from the heat of the midsummer sun. To assist in accomplishing this object the great quadrangle will be closed in by a series of sheltered ambulatories, like the Greek *stoa*, included in and forming a part of the façades of the palaces of Machinery and Agriculture on the right, and of the Liberal Arts and Electricity on the left. The vast fronts of these buildings, far exceeding in dimensions those of any other ancient or modern architectural group, with their monumental colonnaded pavilions, their sculptured enrichments, their statuary, domes, and towers, will appear in mellowed ivory marble, relieved by decorations in color in the shadowy recesses of the porticos. Immediately before him the stranger will behold the great basin 350 feet wide and 1100 feet long, stretching eastward in the middle of the court, bordered with double walled terraces, of which the lower will be decorated with shrubbery and flowers, and the upper, with balustrades, rostral columns, vases, and statuary. Broad stairs descend from the main porticos of the buildings to the water, and the canals, which enter the basin on each side, are crossed by monumental bridges (Fig. 144). On the nearer margin of the greater basin, and in the axis of the court, he will see a smaller circular basin 150 feet in diameter, on a level with the upper terrace, flanked by two lofty columns bearing eagles. In the center of this, on an antique galley of bronze 60 feet long, eight colossal rowers, portraying the Arts and Sciences, stand, four on a side, bending to their long sweeps; in the prow is poised the herald Fame, with trump and outspread wings; while aft, Time, the pilot, leans upon his helm; and, high aloft on a throne, supported by cherubs, Columbia sits, a fair, youthful figure, eager and alert, not reposing upon the past, but poised in high expectation. Eight couriers precede the barge, mounted upon marine horses ramping out of the water. The whole triumphal pageant is seen through a mist of interlacing fountain-jets, and from the brimming basin the water falls 14 feet in a series of steps into the greater sheet below, a half-circle of dolphins spouting over the cascade (Figs. 143, 144). This pompous allegory is the work of the sculptor Frederick MacMonnies.[8] At the outer end of the basin a colossus of the Republic, by the sculptor Daniel C. French,[9] rises from the water (Fig. 142). It is treated somewhat in the Greek archaic manner, with a strong accentuation of vertical lines, but with a simplicity and breadth which give to the figure an aspect of majesty and power. Beyond it, a double open colonnade, or peristyle, 60 feet high, like that of Bernini in front of St. Peter's, forming three sides of a square, closes in the great court toward the lake (Fig. 145). Of the two wings of this colonnade one is a concert-hall, and the other a casino or waiting-hall for passengers by boat. Its columns typify the States of the Union. In the center of this architectural screen is a triumphal arch thrown over the canal which connects the basin with the harbor. Through this and through the open screen of the colonnade one may see the wide-spreading lake, the watery horizon, and, still in the axis of the court and a thousand feet from the shore, a lofty pharos with an island-casino at its base. Animating the whole, banners and gonfalons flutter gaily from innumerable staffs; people of all nations walk in the shadow of the porches, linger on the bridges, crowd along the broad pavement of the terraces, and watch from the balustrades the incessant movement of many-colored boats and electric barges upon the water.

The palace of Mechanic Arts, or, as it may be better known, Machinery Hall, occupies a frontage of 842 feet on the south side of the court, and a depth of 500 feet, thus covering, with the main building of this department, 9½ acres (Fig. 147). These dimensions are nearly the same as those of the palace of Diocletian at Spalatro, and larger than the Parliament House of Great Britain in the proportion of 5 to 2. (The Capitol at Washington measures 680 feet by 280.) Attached to this building on the west is an annex 550 feet long, covering about 6¼ additional acres, for the exhibition of the rougher sorts of machinery. Messrs. Peabody and Stearns of Boston, in adjusting the constructional scheme of their main building to this fixed area, were governed by the necessity of providing large unencumbered spaces of considerable height for exhibits, so disposed as to facilitate classification and to avoid confusion; and by the fact, imposed equally upon all the other architects, that, so far as possible, the form of structure should be such that its material would be marketable after the conclusion of the Fair. These considerations led to the adoption of a typical railway-shed 130 feet wide, covered by a barrel-shaped roof 100 feet high, supported on iron arched trusses 50 feet apart, as a convenient basis for their plan. They placed three of these sheds side by side. But the site of the building was such that its main entrance had to be placed in the center of the long court-frontage, opposite the south doorway of the great vestibule of the Exposition, thus establishing a clear architectural relationship with its nearest and most important neighbor. This condition suggested the crossing of the triple hall in the center by a great transept, which, being of the same width as each of the three naves, developed a noble main hall composed of three bays 130 feet square, from each of which, to the right and left, the naves opened in long perspectives of six 50-foot bays on each side. In order still further to distinguish this main avenue, giving access to these minor naves, each of its three square divisions was covered with a conical glazed roof, giving an interior effect of a succession of domes. The architects thus secured a vast covered area composed of three parallel naves with glazed roofs, crossed by a central main transept, the combination giving a total width of 390 feet and a length of 730, affording every desirable condition of practical convenience, with structural divisions so clear, large, and simple as, in great measure, to counterbalance, with their effect of spacious harmony and noble proportion, the inevitable perplexity and confusion of a display of miscellaneous running machinery.

In this way Messrs. Peabody and Stearns proposed to satisfy the principal structural and practical requirements of their problem. But the more difficult task remained to give to the prosaic and unimaginative mass an exterior aspect of beauty and fitness, which, so far as possible, should reconcile the spirit of materialism, here, in the very central place of its power, with the spirit of organized "rest, grace, and harmony." The architectural formulas by which this new and apparently ill-assorted marriage of Hephæstus and Aphrodite was to be attempted had already been established, as we have seen, by the agreement among the architects of the court to confine themselves to a style strictly classic, and to a definite height of 60 feet to the cornice. By this limitation of effort they proposed to secure for the great quadrangle a harmonious aspect of stately ceremony; but in so doing they sacrificed invention to convention, and were constrained, in designing their exteriors, to confine themselves to the composition of a series of architectural masks or screens, as we have already explained. These, though in general arrangement suggested by the divisions of the plan in each case and by the uses of the building, were intended to be expressive rather of possible than actual structure. In fact, so far as the exterior envelop was concerned, they were to be merely plastic models of buildings, designed so as to be capable of construction in permanent materials. The whole, therefore, may be considered as little more than a pageant of practicable stage scenery on a vast scale. The architects of Machinery Hall, in studying the problem of their architectural screen, reserved for this purpose an enveloping area, about 50 feet wide, extending entirely around their central hall. This area they occupied with external and internal galleries of two stories. These galleries naturally develop pavilions 50 feet square where they intersect at the corners, and they are interrupted, in the center of the two principal façades, by main-entrance pavilions; that on the north facing the Administration Building, and that on the east facing the corresponding side porch of the Agricultural Building. It has already been noted that the architects of the court considered that it was necessary to establish sheltered ambulatories along their fronts. In accordance with this agreement, the long intermediate stretches of façade or curtain-walls of this building, between the pavilions, are faced with porticos; but in this case the porticos are arranged in two stories to correspond with the interior, treated somewhat after the manner of Claude Perrault in the east front of the Louvre, each division having Corinthian colonnades of 23 columns 27½ feet high on the long façades, and of 9 columns on the end façades, the spacing of these columns being multiples of the structural divisions of the great interior bays. Unlike the famous Paris example, however, the basement upon which these colonnades are placed is pierced with an open arcade to form the lower ambulatory, the ceiling of the latter being treated with a dome in each bay, and that of the former with richly embellished panels. To relieve the scrupulously scholastic accuracy of the main order, and to recall the days of Columbus and of Ferdinand and Isabella, the apertures in the rear walls of the upper porticos are treated with the picturesque freedom of the Spanish Renaissance, and the arms of Spain and the portrait of Columbus are frequently repeated about them.

It became evident to the architects, in the evolution of their design, that the light and open character of these long two-storied porticos needed some strongly contrasting form of relief and support, to be obtained by transition to an expression of solidity and massiveness in the corner and middle pavilions. For this reason they were led to treat the latter very boldly as plain wall-surfaces abruptly interrupting all the horizontal lines of the orders of the curtain-walls, and carried 35 feet higher, there finishing with a level cornice. On each front this plain wall-surface they divided in three pavilions, of which the outer, 29 feet wide, are treated as towers, the wider intermediate part being slightly recessed between them. Upon these towers, which contain staircases, they placed open octagonal lanterns, in three diminishing stories, rising to the height of 102 feet, like spires enriched with balustrades and finials, somewhat Romantic in character, and following suggestions contained in Spanish or Mexican examples. On the north pavilion toward the court, and opposite the south entrance of the Administration Building, the architects embedded in this central division a temple-like portico 75 feet wide and 90 feet deep, the portion developed outside the pavilion, and forming the exterior, being apsidal or semicircular in plan. This portico they treated with a colossal Corinthian order 60 feet high, crowning the apsidal projection with a low half-dome behind a balustrade, with a pedestal and statue over each column somewhat like the famous circular porch of the *calidarium* in the Baths of Caracalla. The east portico practically received the same treatment, the temple-portico, however, in this case being 75 feet square in plan, two fifths of it projecting outside the pavilion and finishing with a pediment, and the remainder being embedded, as it were, in the interior. It would be difficult to conceive of a more majestic welcome to this department of the Exposition. With the object of keeping the corner pavilions subordinate to those in the center, and to establish unity of design on the adjacent sides, the two-storied orders of the long colonnades are continued around them, but emphasized by a slightly projecting loggia on each face. The interior of each of these pavilions contains a grand double staircase inclosed in a circular cage of columns supporting a dome. This domical treatment is expressed externally by a much higher dome, raised upon a circular arcaded drum or podium supported on the corners by small circular pavilions and finishing with a lantern.

The long level sky-lines of these great façades, thus broadly accentuated at the corners by domes, and in the center by the aspiring lines of twin towers nearly 200 feet high, were devised to form an engrossing foreground to the long higher roofs of the triple naves behind, broken by masses of decorative skylights with clearstories, and by the three low conical roofs of the main central transept. On the shorter fronts these naves present their glazed circular ends behind and above the façade in the manner used in the great Roman baths. In this way every principal feature of the main structure is made to play a noble and expressive part in the decorative scheme. The details of this

243

design have been kept in rigid conformity with classical and scholarly traditions, relieved, as we have seen, in parts by motives suggested by the highly ornate Renaissance of Spain. Enriched profusely with sculpture and emblematic statues, and with effects of decorative color behind the open screen of the porticos, this composition, if it does not succeed in revealing the mysterious relationships between machinery and art, may at least stand as a beautiful model of highly organized academic design adjusted to modern uses.

The iconographic scheme of this building embraces statues representing the Sciences and the Elements, and figures bearing escutcheons inscribed with the names of famous inventors. In the great east pediment Chicago presents to America, and to the judges of the nations, various inventors and mechanics submitting their handiwork. The windows are surmounted by groups of infants bearing mechanical tools, and holding festoons composed of chains of mechanical implements instead of the conventional fruit and flowers.

Before proceeding to the consideration of the Agricultural Building, which lies east of Machinery Hall, and, with its noble façade, completes the southern closure of the great court, it is necessary to consider the treatment of the minor court, which, with the southern extension of the main canal from the basin, lies between these two buildings (Fig. 144). The terraces in front of them are connected by a bridge thrown across the canal, and the southern closure of this minor court forms a connecting link of two-storied corridors between the two buildings, solid below and open above, and repeats the orders of the curtain-walls of the Machinery Building, which, in their turn, are not unlike those of the façade of the Museo of Madrid. This light construction is flanked at each end by a solid pavilion, still of marked Spanish accent, without pilasters, and treated as a wing of the main building. One of these pavilions is designed for a restaurant, and the other for a hall of assembly. The transition from these to the delicate open peristyle of the connecting corridors is still further eased by the interposition of small towers, crowned by circular belvederes, which break the sky-line with great elegance. This screen, while making a noble connecting-link between the two buildings, serves as a frontage for the amphitheater and offices of the Live-Stock Exhibit, which will be designed by Messrs. Holabird and Roche of Chicago, and which are entered by a triumphal arch in the center of the screen. The southern end of this canal will be decorated by a fountain with spouting lions and an obelisk.

All the architectural modeling of this building is executed by John Evans & Co. of Boston, and the figures in connection with it are modeled, under their direction, by Mr. Bachmann.[10] The statues of the Sciences and the Elements, and the groups on the entrance to the Live-Stock Exhibit, are the work of the sculptor Waagen. The statues on the semicircular north porch, and the figures in the spandrels over the entrance to the Live-Stock Exhibit, are executed by Mr. Krauss.[11]

II.

It has already been stated that the main object of these papers is to secure for the great buildings of the Exposition, through an analysis of the evolution of their several designs, an intelligent if not a respectful appreciation, because of the extreme importance of the occasion in the history of American art, and also because of the exceptional circumstances under which the buildings have been produced. Without such appreciation, the work of the architect, although it may be eloquent and imposing enough to give even to the most careless observers a certain indefinite impression of order, beauty, or grandeur, fails to convey to them the most essential part of the ideas which he has in mind to set forth. He needs this popular appreciation, not only as an encouragement, but as a corrective, and that he may bring himself into fuller and more perfect sympathy with the civilization which it is his duty to express

Architecture and music alike have, in their highest developments, clearly defined qualities, which convey a delight of meaning to the capable eye or ear, but which, to the untrained mind, are nothing but inarticulate harmonies of form or sound.

In attempting, in the previous paper, to follow in outline the principles which controlled the designs of the Administration and Machinery buildings, it became evident that, before proceeding with the other buildings, it would be well to state, once for all, that in monumental designs based upon pure classic formulas, the principle of symmetry — that is, of a balanced correspondence of parts on each side of a center line — must govern the disposition of the masses into which, in order to form an articulate composition, each façade should be divided. The greater the dignity and importance of the building, the more absolute and uncompromising must be the application of this principle. The monument must be evident as the orderly result of forethought, and not as a growth from a succession of unexpected contingencies. It must embody the idea of a harmonious development of structure from beginning to end, so exactly adjusted, and so carefully proportioned in respect to its elements, that nothing can be added to or taken from it without sensibly affecting the composite organism as a whole. The test of the completeness of a classic design resides in its sensitiveness to change — a sensitiveness which becomes more delicate as the design approaches perfection. In fact, symmetry is the visible expression of unity. The moment the correspondence of balanced parts on each side of a center line is disturbed by the introduction on one side of a mass or detail which does not appear on the other, at that moment the design begins to lose somewhat of its unity and to enter the domain of the picturesque, in which ceremony and state become secondary to considerations of comfort and convenience.

With the exception of the Administration Building, which is a compact, domical composition, like the front of the Invalides, all the larger structures of the Exposition have a great extension of length in comparison to their average height, the former varying from 700 to 1700 feet, and the latter from 40 to

60. The application of the principle of symmetry to these has resulted uniformly in a central pavilion of some sort, and in a corner pavilion of varying importance on each angle of the façades. This remark does not apply to the Transportation and Fisheries buildings, which are not classic in form or intention (Figs. 152, 156). Between these pavilions there are intermediate spaces known as curtain-walls, the architectural character of which depends on a continuous repetition of bays, developed from the interior structure, and constituting the characteristic mass of the frontage, to which the three pavilions serve as points of emphasis and relief. But it will be found that this arrangement of the several buildings is not only the result of the common observance of an abstract principle of design, but follows from an obvious necessity of the plan in each case, from the mutual relations of neighboring structures, and from considerations of the most convenient ingress and egress.

It will be remembered that the architects of the five buildings surrounding the great court, which have the closest architectural relations, agreed, for the sake of securing a harmonious result, to confine themselves to pure classic forms in their designs, to fix upon 60 feet from the ground as the height of their main cornices, to provide for an open portico or shelter along their whole frontage, and to assume about 25 feet as their module or unit of dimension. We have seen also that one of the results of the fundamental conditions of the plan is the division of the façades respectively by a central pavilion and by corner pavilions, with stretches of curtain-wall between. Moreover, each of these compositions has submitted to certain compromises for the sake of harmony with its neighbors. Now this stately uniformity of design would have been too serious for an occasion of festivity, if it were not relieved by a certain luxury of conventional ornament, sculpture, painting, and decoration in metals, and by a profusion of bright and joyful accessories. We shall now see how this uniformity of scheme, apparently working for a monotony which would be fatiguing, is, by the operation of the personal equation of the architect in each case, and by the adjustment of each building to its especial use, entirely consistent with that individuality of technic, of sentiment, and of expression which constitutes the essential difference between a cold academical composition and a work of art having a definite purpose.

By this apparent identity in general outline and language of form the architects have necessarily been invited to a study of detail and expression far more fastidious than would be easily practicable in dealing with a style less accurately formulated. In somewhat similar manner a dozen trained writers, expressing their thoughts on a similar range of subjects in an established literary form, — in that of the sonnet for example, — would commit themselves by their differences in treatment to a comparison more subtle and sensitive than would be possible had they been at liberty to handle their common theme without definite and arbitrary restrictions of form. Whether the test is one of architecture or poetry (and the two are closely analogous), it seems to compel the architect or poet to enter a region, if not of higher thought, then of more delicate study and of finer discrimination in method. Freedom of style, though it is the natural and healthy condition of architecture in our country, and adapts itself more readily to our inventiveness in structure and to the practical exigencies of building, is also a temptation to crude experiments, to *tours de force*, and to surprises of design, such as form the characteristic features of an American city. Under these circumstances, personal idiosyncrasies and accidents of mood or temperament are apt to have an undue influence upon current architecture, and to perpetuate, in monumental form, the caprice of a moment or a passing fashion of design, which, in a year's time, the author himself may be the first to repudiate. It is the aim of our architectural schools not to kill but to correct this abundant vitality, and to direct it into channels of fruitful and rational progress.

A glance at the general plan of the grounds will show that the buildings are separated one from the other by avenues of water or land sufficiently wide to furnish noble vistas penetrating to the remoter regions of the Park, and to isolate each structure, so that its characteristic mass and details may not be confused by those of its neighbors, but not so wide as to prevent their mutual architectural relations from being clearly evident in a common alignment, and in a common observance of the system of axial lines which controls the location and arrangement of the group as a whole.

The general disposition of masses in these façades being thus defined, the way seems to be prepared for a more intelligent examination of the processes by which the especial architectural character of each building has been evolved.

It will be remembered that the great court of the Exposition is bounded on the south by the two palaces of Machinery and Agriculture, a minor court being provided between them. The latter building has a north frontage on the court and a south frontage toward the Live-Stock department, each 800 feet in length, while its west façade, of 500 feet, looks on the minor court, and its east on the lake. Its area, not including the annexes in the rear, thus covers nearly nine acres and a half, or a space about equal to the main building of the Machinery department, which we have already discussed. The problem was how to cover this entire area with a building which should have due regard to its relations to the grounds and neighboring buildings; by its divisions should provide for the orderly arrangement and classification of its contents, and for the most convenient and economical structure; and should secure, not only for the first floor, but for an extensive series of galleries, an effective and adequate lighting throughout. This problem must also embrace a due consideration for a division of the façades corresponding to the plan, so that its architectural character should, as far as possible, be developed from the conditions of structure.

The architects, Messrs. McKim, Mead & White of New York, solved this problem by converting their area into a hollow square surrounded continuously by buildings, and by crossing this hollow square in the center with two high naves of equal width, at right angles one to the other and open from floor to

247

roof, each being accompanied on both sides by two-storied aisles, thus forming two clearstories on each roof-slope for lighting the interior space (Fig. 148). The four long courts, 80 x 280, left by this arrangement, being needed for exhibition purposes, are severally occupied by three lower longitudinal aisles, each covered with a double-pitched roof so devised that, by a system of skylights and clearstories, abundant light should be provided for the area beneath. These three aisles are also in two stories, with an opening in the second story under the center aisle to admit light to the main floor beneath. Thus the entire space of nine acres and a half is covered and lighted, and the galleries furnish about five additional acres of floor space.

This adjustment of the plan is entirely in the interests of the agricultural exposition, with no unnecessary concessions to interior architectural effect. But this effect has nevertheless been obtained by the wide and lofty central naves, which invite the visitors to proceed on the axial lines of the building for a general survey of its contents, without distractions, and by the system of aisles on each hand, which enables them to pursue their investigations in detail with the least possible chance of confusion. The arrangement also facilitates the work of classification, and the whole presents

A mighty maze, but not without a plan.[12]

The *corps du bâtiment* inclosing the area is 96 feet wide on the long sides and 48 feet wide on the shorter sides. Where these come together at the angles of the building they naturally constitute corner pavilions, 48 feet wide on the long fronts and 96 on the short fronts; and where the naves, 95 feet wide, with their attendant aisles, 23½ feet wide, encounter the center of each façade, a central pavilion of about 118 feet results, which, from its connection with the axial line or main avenue, becomes the main porch of that side.

The architects thus found imposed upon each of their four façades the conventional arrangement of a central pavilion and corner pavilions of certain specified dimensions, with curtain-walls between. Under the agreement of the architects of the court structures, a continuous covered ambulatory or portico was required inside the building line, and there was prescribed a height of 60 feet for the main cornice. They considered that the dignity of their theme would be best expressed by the use of a colossal Corinthian order, very richly embellished, as the principal vehicle of architectural expression in their design. Accordingly they determined to occupy the whole required height with columns or pilasters 50 feet high, without pedestals, and supporting an entablature 10 feet high, the whole resting directly upon the terrace, 40 feet wide, on which their building stands. But the north front, as viewed from the opposite side of the basin, is provided with an effective and majestic stylobate in the face-walls of the two terraces which run parallel with it, the lower one being washed by the waters of the great basin, and the upper being crowned by a balustrade with vases and statues, a rostral column standing at each end.

To emphasize this relation of the terraces to the façade, a broad staircase, corresponding in width to the projecting columnar portico of the central pavilion, descends to the water's edge, after the manner of the landings in front of the palaces of Venice. Now it was evident that to extend a colossal order along the whole front, without interruption, would be monotonous and mechanical. It would force a formula — noble and majestic, indeed, but still a formula — into predominance over the more important subject matter of the composition. Therefore they concluded to group their great pilasters at points where the main divisions of the plan would be best illustrated. The central pavilion admitted eight pilasters, and each of the corner pavilions four, on the main front. But this concentration of the order at three points on the long façades, the middle and the ends, gave such long intervals between that the composition became disjointed and straggling. It was clear that the necessary unity could be obtained only by some sort of repetition of the order in these intermediate curtain-walls. The plan was devised with forethought for this emergency, for it provided for a series of subordinate transverse passages, or aisles, across the building, ending in secondary doorways, or vomitories, on the façades, occurring three times in each curtain-wall at equal intervals. These doorways furnish a motive for repetition of the order in two pilasters for each, thus forming smaller pavilions, or, more properly, piers; so that the pilasters occur discontinuously along the frontage in a manner to satisfy at once the practical and the esthetic considerations involved in the problem. This repetition is like the recurrence of a leading motive or theme in a fugue, which is set forth in full at one point and repeated at others by hints of various emphasis. In the architectural composition the main statement, with eight pilasters, occurs very properly in the center; the secondary statement, with four pilasters, at the ends; and the third, of minor importance, with two pilasters, at three intermediate points. Thus, also, the various points of ingress and egress along the façades are illustrated with a varying emphasis proportioned to their varying importance.

But the equal spaces of curtain-wall between these great pilastered pavilions and piers still constitute, in the aggregate, the larger part of the frontage. The spacing of structural interior supports generates a corresponding division of each of these wall-spaces into three equal bays; the necessity of obtaining for the interior as much light as possible suggests the piercing of each bay with a great arch, framed with bronzed grilles for windows; the two-storied division of the interior imposes a horizontal division of these arches by a subordinate entablature on a line with the gallery floors; and to provide, as agreed, for an outside ambulatory within the building lines, the space underneath must be left open, and this entablature is supported in each bay by an open screen of two subordinate columns, behind which the portico required traverses the whole length of each front. In fact, this inferior order of columns constitutes a closely set open colonnade, practically continuous between the greater order of pilasters and columns in the pavilions, giving to the vertical elements of the composition a delicate and refined contrast of harmony and scale hardly possible in a style less highly organized. But these vertical elements are always carefully subordinated to the horizontal lines of the entablatures. In this way the plans and elevations developed together with mutual concessions, and, at the same time, the whole arrangement, with its detail of buttress-like engaged columns, continuous with those of the ambulatory and supporting statues between the arches, follows the conventions of imperial Roman architecture.

Now each pier or buttress and pavilion must have its special treatment in respect to the sky-line. From an academical point of view, a fitting culmination for the center of an architectural composition so heroic in size and so full of detail is some form of dome. From a poetical standpoint, an appropriate main vestibule to a structure devoted to an exhibition of agriculture is a temple to Ceres. The conditions of the plan made it possible to realize this idea in a circular domical chamber, 78 feet in diameter and 129 feet high within, treated with the order of the exterior in eight pairs of columns, which surround and enshrine the central statue of the goddess. Her benign and beautiful presence may serve in a brief interval of unconscious influence to bring the distracted minds of the visitors, as they hurry past, into some degree of sympathy with the agricultural collections within. To this vestibule, the design of which is completed and enriched by paintings, is applied a projecting exterior portico of four detached columns, flanked by solid wings, which are treated with pilasters; the whole being surmounted by an attic order, decorated with winged figures, somewhat like those known as the "Incantada" at Salonica,[13] and a central pediment, peopled with symbolic sculpture, so disposed and grouped as to lead the eye upward to a circular podium or drum, supporting a low, spreading dome, the total effect being somewhat similar to that of the Roman Pantheon. Each buttress along the fronts is crowned with a colossal group, figurative of pastoral or agricultural life, and each of the corner pavilions is roofed with an attic or podium corresponding to that in the central pavilion, supporting a low-stepped pyramid, accompanied at its base by sculptured groups and eagles, and crowned above by a composition of figures holding aloft a globe.

The return walls on the east, toward the Lake, and on the west, toward the minor court between the Agriculture and Machinery buildings, grow without apparent effort from the conditions of the plan, as described. The corner pavilions are here made more important than those of the main front, and the central pavilion is much subordinated, while the intermediate curtain-walls are composed like those of the front, but with only one repetition of the triple-arched bay on each side of the center. The west front responds to its neighbor on the opposite side of the canal with harmonious contrast, and with a certain high-bred courtesy, in which each seems to aid and to receive aid from the other.

In its various combinations, the exterior sculpture, which is the work of Mr. Philip Martiny of New York,[14] is intended to symbolize bucolic labor: the central groups typifying human efforts in agriculture; those next the center showing the horse held in restraint by grooms; and those nearer the outward wings exhibiting the ox, urged forward, dragging the elementary beam-plow of Virgil.

The whole architectural mass may be traced rather to the Palatine Mount than to the influence of Palladio or Vignola, and it presents not only in scale and extent, but in its serious beauty, in its splendor of enrichment and refinement of detail, a model of imperial luxury and pomp, borrowed to adorn the peaceful triumph of the latest of civilizations.

That department of the Exposition classified as "Manufactures and the Liberal Arts" embraces so many and such varied industrial interests, that the building to accommodate it must be by far the most spacious in Jackson Park. The thirty acres which were assigned to it, though including an area much larger than that assigned to a single department in any previous Exposition, will need to be carefully husbanded to meet the requirements for space under this head. The site admitted of a building, in exterior dimensions, 1687 feet long, north and south, and 787 feet in width. Its southern end, forming a part of the inclosure of the great court, was necessarily subjected to the same conditions regarding architectural style and scale as were agreed upon for the other structures around the quadrangle, and these conditions were extended so as to control the other façades. The interposition of an architectural wall nearly 1700 feet long, and but little over 60 feet high, between the lake and the flat district known as the lagoon would have the effect of transforming the whole aspect of the Park as viewed from any point on land or water. The importance of an adequate treatment of this vast scheme was obvious.

Mr. George B. Post of New York, the architect of the building, in considering its general plan, promptly fell upon the scheme of converting its area into a court by surrounding it with a continuous building, and of cutting this court in twain with a central circular structure; thus recalling, but on an immensely larger scale, a much admired disposition of Philibert Delorme in his first project for the palace of the Tuileries as a residence for Catherine de Médicis (Fig. 149). But even with such subdivisions the scheme was still so heroic in dimension that no such correspondence as this could be of the slightest avail in furnishing him with types of architectural treatment. He found that he must work in regions quite removed from historical experience. With his assumed module of 25 feet, he found that he could carry around the four sides of his area of thirty acres a building composed of a nave 107 feet 9 inches wide and 114 feet high, covered with a pitched roof with clear-stories, and supported on each side by two-storied aisles, or lean-tos, 45 feet wide. This arrangement of plan permitted ready illumination, easy classification, and convenient communication. It left an interior quadrangle 1237 feet long and 337 feet wide. The domical hall in the center of this space was planned to be 260 feet in clear diameter and 160 feet high, surrounded, like the other parts of the building, with two-storied aisles, or lean-tos, 45 feet wide. These circular aisles, compared with the seating space of the Roman Colosseum, would have inclosed an area largely in excess of that great arena. The two courts thus obtained Mr. Post proposed to treat as gardens with fountains and kiosks, or, if more space should be needed for exhibition purposes, to occupy them with a series of covered sheds.

But as the practical needs of this important and comprehensive part of the Exposition became more evident, it was finally concluded to abandon the central dome, and to convert the whole interior court into the largest unencumbered hall ever constructed, by covering it with a glazed semicircular roof without columns, supported by arched steel trusses of 387 feet clear span, 50 feet apart, and with a radius of 190 feet, giving an extreme height of 210 feet. This roof was arranged to be hipped at the ends. The much admired truss of Machinery Hall in the last Paris Exposition (the largest constructed for roofing purposes up to that time) is inferior to this in span and is 58 feet lower. It has been proposed to equip this vast hall, containing nearly 500,000 square feet of clear floor-space inside the enveloping building, with seats and a stage for the ceremonies of the inauguration, before adjusting it to its legitimate objects. It was sufficiently evident that the mountainous roof which covered the hall could not fail, from the mere power and weight of its enormous structural mass, to impose upon the scheme of the building, as a work of art, an element unknown in the precedents of monumental architecture.

In studying the most effective architectural treatment of a symmetrical building more than a third of a mile long and almost a sixth of a mile wide, with a height of cornice limited to 60 feet, the architect was confronted by conditions of composition such as perhaps had not occurred before. The natural dispositions of any extended building, which is to be adapted, not to various and different services, like a royal château, with its halls of ceremony, its wings for household convenience, its chapels and galleries, its provisions for dignity and its provisions for comfort, but to a single and well-understood purpose, must be guided by the most convenient and economical structure, and show a distinct unity of thought throughout. This unity is expressed by a mutual dependence of parts. We must at least have some feature of emphasis on the corners, against which the long fronts may stop — a period, as it were, and place of rest; and there is even greater necessity for pavilions of sufficient importance to give dignity to the entrances. The natural place for these is in the middle of each front, where the visitors may be introduced most conveniently to the great interior space, and receive their first impressions of its grandeur. We have seen how the architects of the Agricultural Building on the opposite side of the court, — where it was understood that everything must be in full dress and on parade, so to speak, — in adopting this natural treatment in their façade, found it necessary, for the sake of variety and movement, to provide between the center and the ends certain regularly disposed, intermediate accentuations, which the eye, in surveying the whole façade, could readily grasp and justify by an instinctive balancing of the masses on each side of the center line. The mind of the observer is flattered by this evidence of art.

Architecture, as compared with nature, has been called a creation of the second order; but this secondary creation must be fundamentally controlled by conditions of structure which, to a greater or less degree, must impose regularity or repetition of parts, as contrasted with the irregularity or picturesqueness which results from the infinite resources and the accidental conditions in nature. Medieval art, though often picturesque in its effects, is subject to these human conditions no less than classic art.

On the one hand the author of these almost interminable façades felt that he could not treat them picturesquely or accidentally without sacrifice of truth and dignity, and, on the other hand, that to break them with frequent pavilions, however subordinate to a preëminent central feature, would fail to procure for them all the advantages of symmetry; because, in a length so great, the mind could not readily discover and, at a glance, compare that correspondence of parts on each side of the center which is essential to effects of this sort. The rule of composition which properly governs a building 500 to 800 feet long and 60 feet high cannot be applied successfully to one two or three times as long and no higher. The architect, therefore, remembering the imposing effects of certain long porticos and aqueducts of Roman structure, had the courage, in this case, to withstand the temptations furnished by the customs of the Renaissance architects in their palaces and other public monuments, and to leave his sky-line and his frontage unbroken by any competition of pavilions save the one in the center and that on each angle of each front. By this severe measure he hoped to make the unity of his design clear to the most casual observer.

The module or unit of measurement, of 25 feet, with which the architect found it convenient to lay out his plan, communicated to his elevations a corresponding division of bays, of which 29 occur on each half of the long fronts and 11 on each half of the short fronts. These bays are treated with arches, springing from piers, and each archway embraces two stories. It was anticipated that these long, monotonous, and mechanical perspectives of equal and similar arches would affect the eye like the arcades of the Campagna, and would rather increase than diminish the apparent length of the building; for repetition, even if mechanical, is, humanly speaking, a suggestion of the infinite, and the architect who has the opportunity and self-denial to adopt it frankly, and on a scale so vast, would give even to the most thoughtless and most uncritical minds a memorable impression of architectural majesty and repose.

Now the covered ambulatory, or stoa, which is made a feature of all the court fronts, should, on account of the great length of these long façades, where there is no other natural refuge from the sun, be extended all around the building, but within its lines. The lintel course or decorated belt, which is the exterior development of the floor of the second story in each bay, is supported by an open, flat, segmental arch springing from pier to pier; behind these arches this continuous ambulatory obtains spacious shade. Frequent doors open upon it from the interior. No subordinate architectural order of columns was placed under this lintel course, as was done with singularly happy results in the Agricultural Building, because it was apparent that such an order would not have been in scale with the rest of the design, and would have introduced an element which would have complicated with unnecessary details the careful simplicity of its lines and the studied breadth of its general treatment.

The adoption of a severe classical formula for the building naturally led to the adoption of a common *motif* for the four central pavilions, and another, adapted to its situation, for each of the corner pavilions. These repetitions were encouraged by the fact that all the façades were of equal importance. As these pavilions must be distinctly recognized as the main porches, they must break the monotony with emphasis, or they will not be adequate. Consequently at these points there should be a sudden change in the architectural scheme of the fronts. But the strictly classic ideal does not seem to be favorable to the absolute interruption of all the horizontal lines of frontage by the pavilions; there must be some connection by continuity of lines between them.* The Greek idea of a monumental entrance is a columned propylæum; that of the Romans, who better understood pomp and ceremony, is an arch. The former would be appropriate if the general architectural character of the façades were based upon an order of columns or pilasters; in the present case the latter would more naturally follow.

Thus the architect, by logical process, encountered the idea of inserting in the midst of his arcades the triple triumphal arches of Constantine or Septimius Severus, and of stopping his arcade at the corners with the single arch of Titus or Trajan, the *motif* in both cases being very greatly enlarged from the original in order to fit the greater scale of the building. The architectural connection of the central pavilions with the mass of the structure is established by bringing their two side arches into the same scale as those of the curtain-walls, and by causing the main cornice line to be continued across the central pavilion or pylon as a string-course over its two side arches, and as an impost, from which springs its great central arch. Over the whole is carried a horizontal entablature with a high attic, and in front of the four piers are lofty pedestaled columns, after the manner of buttresses, supporting figures against the attic, thus closely following the characteristics of the Roman prototypes. The order employed for these columns is the sumptuous Corinthian of the temple of Jupiter Stator, the columns being 65 feet high with a lower diameter of more than 6 feet. We have already intimated that the architect turned the four corners of this building with a single arch on each adjacent face of the angles; these also are decorated with magnificent coupled

* The solution of this continuity, boldly attempted by the architects of the Machinery Building in their central towers, which, as we have noted, interrupt all the lines, constitutes the most remarkable feature of their design. This, as we have said, is contrary to the strict classic idea, but in so far as this interruption does not destroy the unity of the composition, it is the successful stroke of one who dares to put his fate to the touch, "to gain or lose it all." [15]

Corinthian columns, as in some of the Roman examples. The width of the corner pavilions is adjusted to the width of the ambulatory which enters them on each side. The esthetic function of these boldly accentuated buttress-columns, which are clearly detached from the mass of the building, is sufficiently evident in the perspective views of the long fronts. They furnish the only strongly marked vertical lines in the composition, and by contrast suffice to relieve the design from the excessive predominance of its horizontal lines.

It is to be noted that as yet the architectural expression of this building, the development of which we have been following in the natural order of design, has been confined to the exterior closure of a vast interior space. Before it had been happily determined to cover the interior court with a great glazed roof, it was the professional instinct of Mr. Post to indicate externally that the area enveloped by his façades was not empty, but had a magnificent interior central feature in his original circular hall. To this end, and in order that this feature might become evident from afar as an essential element of design, it became necessary to cover it with a dome sufficiently lofty to be seen over the sky-lines of the inclosing galleries from usual points of view, and to form a crown and finish to the long, low mass of his building. This feature, if executed, would have exceeded any similar structure yet erected; but as it challenged comparison with the dome of the porch of the Exposition, the preëminence of which it was considered desirable to maintain, it was reluctantly abandoned. But the final treatment of the central court as a hall, 1287 x 387 feet in floor area, covered with a semicircular roof, whose longitudinal ridge rises far above the cornice of the façades, at once suggested an entirely different architectural aspect for the building. By the upward succession of cornice-line, 60 feet high, and clearstory-line, 108 feet high, culminating in a central ridge-line, 210 feet high, a pyramidal effect was secured; the low-lying mass at once obtained adequate height; its vast extent was condoned and explained; a dominant expression of unity was conferred upon the composition; the upper outlines of the façades were projected against a colossal roof instead of the empty sky; and the roof itself, wisely left to the majesty of its dimensions and to the simplicity of its structure for architectural effect, enhanced the refinement and purity of the architectural screens below.

Indeed, this design as a whole admirably illustrates the fact that reservation rather than expenditure of force is the secret of noble art. The modern architectural mind is an archæological chaos of ideas inherited from Egypt, from the far East, from Greece and Rome, from the middle ages, and from the Renaissance. Under these circumstances the highest virtue which can be exercised by the educated architect of to-day is self-denial in the use of his treasures. He who squanders them in his work betrays his trust, and depraves the art of his time. He who can be refined in the use of the splendid resources furnished by his knowledge of the past, who can be simple in the midst of the temptations to display his wealth, is rendering high service to a civilization which, in the midst of its complications and sophistications, needs the refreshment and chastisement of pure types.

It is evident that within his classic Roman frame Mr. Post has desired, in his detail of decoration, to bring his design into sympathy with modern civilizations; for we shall see that the luxury of Napoleon III. affects the sculpture of his spandrels and panels, and that nearly all the ornament bears traces of the influence of the latest French Renaissance and the last Paris Exposition. Moreover, in order to relieve his design from the serious expression imposed upon it by the grandeur of his leading motives, he makes a very proper concession to the festive and holiday aspect which should pervade the place by planting permanent standards and gonfalons on his triumphal arches, and by decorating his battlements with banner-staffs and bunting.

We have repeatedly stated that these papers do not embody either a description or a criticism, nor yet an apology, but constitute an attempt to explain the architectural development of the Exposition buildings. But it may be proper, before leaving the consideration of the largest of these buildings, to look back upon Mr. Post's immense façades, and to ask whether, if they had been treated with the variety, contrast, and balance of motives customary in the works of the Renaissance, if they had been broken by towers and campaniles, or tormented by gabled pavilions, they would not have presented a somewhat confused and incoherent aspect, wanting in apparent unity of thought, and resembling rather a combination of many buildings of various use than a single building of one use; and further, whether the simplicity of treatment which he has preferred (and which some, not considering its detail and the unusual difficulties of the problem, might call poverty) has not resulted in a composition having architectural qualities which, instead of confusing and puzzling the mind, can be read, understood, and remembered with pleasure. The civilization of our time owes a debt of gratitude to any architect, or to any writer, who, in the midst of the temptations which beset us to force effects of beauty by affectations and mannerisms, dares to make his work at once strong, simple, and elegant.

III.

To the building for the department of Electricity was assigned an area 350 feet on the court and 700 feet long, the major axis running north and south. Though peculiarly fortunate in its site, having an important frontage on the lagoon as well as on the court, it was the smallest building of the principal group. It thus became incumbent on its architects, Messrs. Van Brunt & Howe of Kansas City, so to design this building that it should not be overwhelmed by the superior mass of its neighbors, and that, if possible, it might have such characteristics as should at once conceal and justify its inferiority of size; which inferiority, however, is only comparative, the actual area to be occupied being considerably in excess of that covered by the Capitol at Washington (Fig. 150). Its purposes seemed to suggest a playful animation of outline, somewhat like that of the early French Renaissance in the châteaux, approaching even the fantastic joyousness of Chambord, combined with a certain delicacy or preciousness of detail, which might legitimately differentiate it from the rest in regard to expression, while, in respect to general style and feeling, and in loyalty to scholastic types, it should still belong to the same architectural family.

The area is conveniently divisible into 23-foot squares by two systems of parallel lines crossing at right angles. Upon the intersection of these lines the columns and piers of the exterior and interior are placed. This module of 23 feet, being somewhat less than that adopted for the other buildings, assists in carrying into execution that more delicate scale of design, that nervousness of movement and avoidance of massiveness, which, as we have intimated, seem to be suggested by the idea of electricity. It soon became evident that the space set aside for this department of the Exposition, though covering 4.85 acres, would be insufficient to meet the demands of exhibitors, unless the largest possible amount of floor-space which could be gained within it should be made available to them. This at once suggested a second story of flooring, covering as large a space as the necessary openings for the admission of daylight from the roof into the central parts of the first story would admit. To obtain the obvious advantages of grand central avenues in both directions, it was clear that the building should be crossed by longitudinal and transverse naves, open from floor to roof and free from columns. The module of 23 feet enters fifteen times into the width of the building. Five of these modules, or 115 feet, are taken for the width of the naves, and they are covered with pitched roofs, supported by steel arched trusses, set 23 feet on centers, and lofty enough to permit a line of clearstory windows to be elevated above the rest of the building, which, for its part, is divided into five aisles on each side of the longitudinal nave, each one module wide, and these are covered with continuous flat roofs, with a series of skylights over the central aisles corresponding with openings in the second floor. Access to these galleries is obtained by grand staircases, one on each side of each of the four main central porches.

The main exterior architectural expression depends upon these simple primary conditions. Where these high naves abut against the center of each of the four façades, an important entrance pavilion is naturally established. As for the inclosing architectural screen walls around the rest of the building, the interior module of 23 feet naturally produces a corresponding series of divisions into bays, which must be 60 feet high to the cornice for the sake of that unity of style agreed upon for all the court buildings. These screen walls are hardly long enough to permit the arrangement of the bays in groups or large divisions, without by this means drawing attention to that comparative inferiority of size which it appeared to be the obvious duty of the architects to conceal or condone; nor do the conditions of the plan suggest such groups or divisions anywhere except in the center of each front. Each bay, therefore, is made complete in itself, and is so devised as to admit of repetition all around the building, interrupted only by such slight breaks, with variations of *motif*, as are essential to illustrate the plan, to furnish bases for frequent towers, and to prevent the monotony from becoming mechanical and fatiguing, but not

257

of sufficient emphasis to clash with that expression of continuity which is recognized as an important element in noble architecture, and which, in the present case, is an echo of the plan.

Now the horizontal line, which is the predominant characteristic of all classical buildings, implies dignity and repose. But the present object is to obtain in some way an expression of brightness and movement. To this end the piers, regularly spaced, 23 feet on centers, along the façades, are treated as boldly projecting pilasters, resting upon a stylobate 8 feet high, which is made continuous to prevent the composition from becoming disjointed, but having the cornice and the paneled attic above the cornice broken around them. Each pilaster, so emphasized and detached, is finished with a pedestal upholding a staff for banners and for a constellation of electric lights, thus carrying the vertical line lightly to the sky, and securing an effect somewhat similar to that of a pinnacled buttress. This order of piers, or pilasters, is adjusted to the proportions and details of the highly enriched Corinthian of Vignola. Between each pair of pilasters the bay is divided horizontally, on the line of the gallery floor, by a subordinate Ionic entablature, supported by two jamb pilasters and by a central column of that order, the space above being treated with an arch deeply embayed. Behind this architectural screen are placed the windows, set in bronze frames. These openings occupy an unusually large proportion of the wall-veil, because of the necessity of throwing abundant light across the five ranges of aisles in both stories. Near each end of the façades this continuity of similar open bays is relieved, or punctuated as it were, by a solid bay of the same width, but of slightly increased projection, pierced with a small window in each story, the upper one having a balcony supported by sculptured brackets. The narrow pavilions thus formed are finished on the attic line with highly enriched pediments, and form the basis of a more emphatic expression of vertical energy by supporting in each case a slender open campanile of the Composite order, rising suddenly from behind the balustrade of a platform, on the corners of which are planted tall candelabra with groups of electric globes. On the long fronts, midway between each end pavilion and the central porch, the succession of similar bays is again broken by a postern doorway, set in a narrow intermediate and subordinate pavilion, crowned with a low square dome decorated with eagles.

As we have already intimated, where the transept abuts against the center of the long east and west fronts, an important central pavilion is developed. In pursuance of the scheme of this design, which is to take advantage of every opportunity to emphasize its vertical elements, this pavilion is flanked by two towers, one bay wide and three bays apart. Each of the towers supports an open belvedere, crowned with a high, round attic, decorated with festoons and vases, and roofed with a stilted dome, after the manner of Sir Christopher Wren. Each of these belvederes finishes with a girandole, 195 feet from the ground, furnished with a corona of incandescent lights under a reflecting canopy. Between these towers projects a flat-roofed portico, composed of columns 42 feet high, continuous with the order of Corinthian pilasters of which we have spoken, arranged upon a plan with rounded corners, so that, by the necessary multiplication of breaks and returns in the entablature at the angles, the seriousness of the more classic *motif* might be tempered to the lighter mood to which the architecture of this building is committed. Above is a high Composite attic with windows, set between the towers, and finishing with a balustrade, decorated with obelisks. Twenty-three feet behind this balustrade the gabled end of the transept roof may be seen.

The north front, toward the picturesque lagoon, being, by its position, relieved to a certain extent from strict conformity to the classic ideal, seemed to invite a greater freedom of treatment than was admissible elsewhere. Here, therefore, the order of the façades, after passing the point of demarcation furnished by the corner pavilions, is made to sweep around two apsidal projections, 115 feet in diameter, between which is recessed the north porch, composed of two towers, similar to those of the east and west porches, flanking a broad central pavilion, pierced with a great arched window, corresponding with the arch-lines of the steel trusses in the long nave, and divided by transoms and mullions. The sky-line between these towers is made horizontal, and the spandrel panels of the arch are occupied by gigantic reclining figures typifying Investigation and Discovery. The porch is formed by the Ionic order of the façades, which is extended between the apses in the form of an arcade of five arches supporting a wide terrace or balcony.

Up to this point, for the reasons stated, the design of the Electricity Building is characterized by an emphasis of vertical expression unusual in academical architecture, the sky-line being fretted by ten campaniles, varying in height from 154 to 190 feet, and by the four square intermediate domes, which mark the position of the posterns. But, on the south front, it was necessary to make a concession to that spirit of grandeur and ceremony which should prevail around the great court of the Exposition. Accordingly the vertical line, predominant elsewhere in the building as a foil to its long, low, horizontal mass, is here subordinate to the spirit of repose. To this end the campaniles on the corners are set back from the front, but connected with it by gabled pavilions, 23 feet wide, and the principal entrance of the building on this side is treated as a triumphal arch, 60 feet wide and 92 feet high, of which the archivolt springs from the main cornice as an impost, the jambs being formed of coupled full columns of the main order with corresponding pilasters. This arch is crowned with a classic pediment containing an escutcheon, which bears the electromagnet as a symbol of electricity, and is supported on each side by a female figure representing the two principal industries connected with this science — electric lighting and the telegraph. Above, in contrast with the somewhat fantastic movement of the sky-lines elsewhere, rises a solid elevated attic, forming a severe horizontal outline against the sky. This central mass is buttressed on each side by great consoles, supporting emblematic statues and resting on pedestals, continuous with the clearstory of the nave, and embellished with medallions of Morse and Vail, the American discoverers of the electric telegraph. The most famous and most cherished association of

America with the history of the science of electricity is the discovery of the electric properties of lightning by Franklin. The architects determined, therefore, that a statue of the patriot-philosopher should stand under this great arch, and that to him the main porch on the court should be dedicated. This work was intrusted to the Danish-American sculptor, Mr. Carl Rohl Smith,[16] whose conception of the subject is happily realized in a spirited figure, 15 feet high, representing Franklin as the philosopher, with the historic kite and key, observing the storm-clouds. This noble statue is elevated on a high pedestal in the center of the porch, and behind and over it is formed a colossal niche, of which the triumphal arch is the frame, covered with a half dome or conch, divided by ribs, and profusely enriched with bas-reliefs, recalling, in general aspect, the much admired hemicycle or belvedere in the court of the Vatican palace, and, in detail, the characteristic stucco embellishments in the vaults of the Villa Madama. Around its curved walls is carried the great order of the building, with grouped pilasters. On the main frieze of this niche is written the famous epigram of Turgot in honor of Franklin:

ERIPUIT COELO FULMEN SCEPTRUMQUE TYRANNIS.[17]

In the five bays of the niche are the main doorways, three of which, in the back, open into the central nave; the other two, toward the front, give access to an open ambulatory or portico, which forms the first story of the court frontage of the building. To this portico the subordinate Ionic order of the façades is arranged to form a screen, with two detached columns in each bay. Upon the frieze of this order, where it occurs in the hemicycle, appear the names of the most famous deceased Americans connected with electricity: Henry, Morse, Franklin, Page, and Davenport; while outside, upon the same frieze, in alphabetical order all around the building, are the names of sixty-six great electricians of all ages and countries, whose names have passed into history. The fame of living electricians must rest upon their displays within the structure.

So far as practicable, the decorations of this building are devised to suggest its uses, the conventional embellishments of the orders being varied by the frequent recurrence of the electromagnet and lamp, and the recesses of the hemicycle and porticos being enriched with color. It is intended also to illuminate and emblazon the architectural features at night with an electric display of unprecedented interest and magnitude.

The architectural modeling of this building was done under a contract with the Phillipson Decorative Company of Chicago, the sculpture of the main pediment being from the hand of Mr. Richard Bock of Chicago.

The suggestion which has been made that that part of the Electricity Building toward the lagoon would permit of a freer treatment, by reason of the more natural conditions in the landscape of that region as compared with the artificial character of the court, has a much larger and more important application. All the buildings which we have been considering, because they formed a distinct group, and inclosed an area where art was everything and nature nothing, were for obvious reasons developed according to classic formulas. It seemed proper that, in this entrance-court of the World's Exposition, the world should be received with a formal and stately courtesy, illustrated and made intelligible by an architecture which is the peculiar expression and result of the highest civilizations of history. It was like the use of the Latin language, which, by monumental usage, lends dignity to modern inscriptions, and, by tradition, embalms the liturgical service of the Roman Catholic Church. For reasons equally obvious, the other buildings, which are mainly in charge of the local architects, and which are to be placed in a region where natural conditions are intended to prevail, might receive a development much less restricted in regard to style, and, by following more romantic lines, might be more happily adjusted to their surroundings. These surroundings invite picturesqueness, freedom — qualities peculiarly grateful to American genius, which is naturally impatient of authority and discipline. But we think it will be seen that the architects of Chicago have known how to express these qualities without that license which unhappily is also American; yet with an exuberance, or even joyousness, entirely consistent with refinement of feeling, and in every way appropriate to an occasion of high national festival.

Because of its intermediate position, the Electricity Building may perhaps be considered, in some respects, a transition between these two extremes of architectural thought. At all events, in its sister building, that of Mines and Mining, which occupies a site next west of the Electricity Building, lies parallel with it, and is of nearly the same dimensions, the architect, Mr. S. S. Beman of Chicago, has made a frank departure from the pure-classic tradition, exhibiting an adaptation of form to use, of means to ends, in entire conformity with the practical spirit, without caprice, and without sacrifice of any essential quality of art (Fig. 151). The contrast between these two buildings clearly illustrates how even the conventional forms of architecture may be so handled as to express a fundamental difference of sentiment, corresponding to the difference of occupation.

Mr. Beman's plan for the Mining Building is included within construction-lines giving an extreme length of 700 feet and an extreme width of 350, and he has found it convenient, for reasons hereafter to be explained, to establish 21½ feet as a general module of dimension in laying out his construction. The general scheme of an interior the greater part of which is to be occupied by masses of classified ores, by heavy mining appliances of all kinds, and other bulky exhibits requiring large space and considerable clear height, should provide for a wide, central, open area as little encumbered by columns as possible. Thus the preliminary consideration of this problem seemed to point directly to a study of construction. The roofing of large spaces under similar conditions for the Pullman Company had prepared Mr. Beman to apply a valuable practical experience to the conditions here presented, the result of which was that he was enabled to roof in an area 230 feet wide by 580 feet long (60 feet inside his boundaries all around) by the use of a very light and elegant system of cantilever trusses, supporting a longitudinal central louver with clearstory lights, and bearing upon two rows of steel columns, spaced lengthwise 64½ feet on centers (or three of the modules above noted), and, transversely, 115 feet; the outer ends of these cantilevers being anchored to two corresponding rows of columns 57½ feet outside of the inner rows. It would be difficult to devise a simpler, a more economical, or a more effective distribution of constructive features. The extreme height of this shed-roof is 94 feet in the center and 44 feet at the bottom of the slope.

The main practical object of the building being thus happily attained, it remained for the architect to surround this center shed or nave with a system of two-storied aisles 60 feet wide, covered with a continuous louvered roof provided with clearstories for light. The conjunction of roof-slopes, where the aisles and the central nave are joined, creates a valley from which the water can be conducted in spouts carried down with the outer line of main columns. Nothing could be more workmanlike and more practical than this whole arrangement.

However much or however little of decorative character may be permitted on the envelop or inclosure of a building of this sort, it cannot be elevated into the domain of architecture unless this inclosure is developed rationally from the essential conditions of structure behind it, and is in some way made expressive of its uses. Moreover, in the present case it is essential that it should be brought, as a whole, into the great architectural family of which it is to form a part, by any concession or adjustment that may be found most convenient. At the outset it would seem that the uses of the building, the comparatively coarse and rough character of the exhibit within, require a massive treatment of the exterior, and that the architectural language employed should in general be such as to express this idea, as it is capable of expressing every sentiment, however various, desirable to be conveyed in building as a fine art. It naturally follows that the unusual distribution of the interior supports of the roof structure, 64½ feet on centers, should be expressed in the architectural scheme of the exterior on the sides by a corresponding distribution of piers, and that these piers should be made massive, as if constructed with heavy rusticated masonry laid up in marked horizontal courses. In order to give additional emphasis to these expressive buttresses of strength, the whole entablature or cornice of the building is broken around them, and they are surmounted by decorated pedestals or socles supporting banner-staffs. Considerations of proportion give to these piers a width of 10 feet. It also follows logically that the wide bays between these great piers are divided into three segmentally arched divisions of one module each, corresponding to the spacing of the minor supports of the gallery floor; which, in its turn, compels the establishment of a horizontal paneled division in each of these arched divisions, thus forming the first- and second-story window-openings needed for the proper illumination of the building. In all their divisions and subdivisions,

262

therefore, these bays are developed from the structure by growth, and not forced upon it by caprice.

The necessity of bringing the north and south ends of the design into a common scale of height with the court buildings, at the points where comparison is challenged between them, suggests the raising of the main cornice here to a level 11 feet higher than that established on the long fronts by structural conditions. These ends are thus converted into distinct façades of seven great bays, the two corner bays and the central bay in each becoming marked as pavilions, the former being 60 feet wide, to correspond with the width of the inclosing galleries behind them, and the latter, which, from considerations of proportion, grows into a width of 80 feet, becoming the main portal of the building. In all cases the massive and buttress-like character of the piers is insisted on, and, in order to preserve the unity of the design, each constitutes the pedestal of a banner-staff, thus conferring the conventional holiday aspect on a sky-line which might otherwise appear too serious and severe for association with the other buildings of the group. The larger scale of the north and south fronts and their more monumental character have suggested the occupation of each of these seven bays by a great arch, those on the corner pavilions being closed with windows, and the intermediate arches being open with a two-storied loggia behind; but in the central bay the idea of the portal compels the raising of its cornice, the crowning of it with a highly decorated frontispiece in pedimental form, and a marked increase in width, height, and depth of the arch, which is not divided by the loggia of the second story. The superior height and development of this feature also seems to mask the glazed gable-end of the great roof of the central hall; which, however, may be seen in perspective 60 feet behind the line of frontage. The corner bays are furnished with visible low domical roofs supporting circular lanterns. In order to obtain a necessary amalgamation between the monumental masses which form the ends of the building and the long inferior curtain-wall with its nine bays on the east and west sides, it is found necessary in the central bay of these sides to establish a proportionate distribution of masses by repeating in it the motive of the corner bays with their higher entablature, and by crowning it with a pediment, treating the archway as a subordinate entrance or exit in the middle of the long fronts.

Mr. Beman has not attempted to follow the historical styles with precision. Indeed, the logical development of his façades has necessarily conferred upon them a proper modern character. We, however, may see here the influence of the example of the great modillion cornices of the Italian palaces of the sixteenth century, and much other Italian detail of the best eras, mingled with some of the elegant license of the modern Renaissance of France; and in the treatment of the balconies of his loggia, and of the Doric order which upholds them, we may discover a return to the Rome of the Cæsars. The sculpturesque modeling of this building was executed in the ateliers of the Phillipson Decorative Company of Chicago.

IV.

The site of the Transportation Department lies next west of the Mines and Mining Building, and in necessary and convenient proximity to the railroads. In this case the specific character of the exhibit must dictate even more absolutely the practical plan of the structure which is to accommodate it. A very large and characteristic part of this exhibit must be locomotive engines, and other specimens of railroad rolling-stock. In laying out a system of installation for these, it was found more convenient to arrange the rails at right angles to the length of the building, and to space them 16 feet on centers, in order to allow sufficient room for circulation between them. Two pairs of rails, so spaced, to each bay gave a width of 32 feet, which thus became the constant module of dimension and the common divisor of the plan; indeed, this factor proved the basis of the whole architectural scheme. If it had been a few feet more or less, we should have had a different building (Fig. 152). In fact, as is apparent in the analyses of all these designs, the unit of dimension must exercise an influence over architectural compositions analogous to that of the various terms of *tempo*, from *largo* or *adagio* to *allegro*, in their relation to music. The area at the disposal of the architects, Messrs. Adler & Sullivan of Chicago, permitted this divisor to enter thirty times into the length and eight times into the width of their building, which thus became 960 feet long by 256 feet wide, with a triangular area lying westward between the building and the park boundaries, whereon could be located all such annex buildings as might be required to accommodate the rougher rolling-stock, and such other exhibits as could not find place in the main building.

In studying the roofing and lighting of this space, it was found convenient to set aside three of these modules or divisors for the width of a lofty longitudinal central nave, which should be open to its whole height to accommodate those exhibits requiring considerable vertical space (such as aërial devices and elevators); and two modules and a half on each side for two-storied aisles, where road vehicles, and all other means of light transportation by land or water, could be arranged and classified. Each aisle, as well as the nave, is furnished with double pitched roofs and skylights, and the nave is carried high enough to permit the introduction of two ranges of clearstory windows, of which the lower are circular. It was the purpose of the architects to treat this double clearstory with decorative detail; but considerations of economy have deprived us of much of this interesting interior effect. Studies, however, have been made for the occupation of the triforium wall-space beneath these windows by a broad painted frieze, extending quite around the nave, and setting forth poetically the history of transportation from archaic to modern times. For reasons which will presently appear, it was consistent with their scheme to finish these roofs at the ends with hips, and not with gables.

In considering, in outline, how these great buildings have assumed definite architectural shape, we have been anxious to show that they have grown from practical conditions by logical or reasonable processes, and are not the result of mere personal idiosyncrasies, imposing upon the work favorite formulas of design, which have no essential relations to these conditions. Nevertheless, these buildings, being, in their principles of growth, problems of art and not of mathematics or mere engineering, each has been capable of many widely differing artistic solutions, through equally rational processes, from that which it has actually received, just as the same idea would necessarily be expressed by half a dozen masters of literature in half a dozen different ways, or as the same theme would be treated by several musical composers in several harmonic ways, according to the personal equation or the accident of mood of the master in each case. The architect uses his conventional historic forms as the poet uses his conventional historic words; both forms and words have come down to us, modified and enriched by the generations of mankind through which they have passed, and for this reason there is often a deeper significance in them than is patent to the multitude. Architectural formulas, in their various developments through centuries of usage, have become symbols of the genius of nations; no architect can adapt them intelligently and successfully to his work unless his mind has been saturated with these inner meanings, and unless he has learned to respect the language which he uses. The harmonious combination which he may be able to make of these forms, and his applications of them to his composition, may be simply correct, because free from errors of architectural grammar or rhetoric; or they may be brilliant, because they are also original without caprice; surprising without evidence of effort; poetic, because of his inner light. The degrees of success range from correctness to brilliancy, and the varieties are infinite.

Now the work of Adler & Sullivan in this Transportation Building is widely different from that which they would have produced had they been placed under those restrictions which, for the reasons stated, were voluntarily and properly assumed by the architects of the Court. The former were free to use any language of form fitted to express the purposes of their building, and they were under no other limitations than those furnished by minds educated and trained in art. In endeavoring to show, therefore, how their work took shape, we shall, in this as in other cases, — carefully avoiding the attitude of criticism, which would be premature and improper, — proceed not as if the methods of development were exact and positive in a scientific sense, and recognizing that there cannot be any single, final, and only possible solution to a problem of art. No true artist ever wrote Q.E.D. under his project.

The general plan and method of accommodation being accepted, we are now in position to see how they will affect the architectural expression of the interior. We imagine the architects reasoning as follows:

It is our purpose to confer upon an object of utility an expression of fitness and beauty — to utter truth, not only with correctness, but with the grace of poetic diction. In the first place, therefore, let us inclose the structure which we have developed with a wall having merely functions of usefulness. In piercing this wall for the necessary windows, let us make one large opening to correspond with each of the 32-foot bays established by our module of dimension; but let us not make these openings so wide as to narrow the piers

265

between them and thus to convert what we intend to be a wall into a colonnade or arcade. Let us preserve the idea of a wall-surface by keeping our piers wide, and by finishing our openings with arches so that the spandrel surfaces between may be added to the area of repose. But in making the window-openings high enough for the practical purpose of lighting the interior, we have left only a narrow and weak wall-surface over them. In order to remedy this defect, and to bring our wall to a height which will not be low when compared with that of our neighbors, we venture to build it 10 feet higher than is constructionally necessary, so that it shall reach a total height of 53 feet, thus forming a screen to mask the aisle-roofs behind. Now, for the necessary protection and shadow to the plain surface of our wall, let us place upon it a boldly overhanging coping. To give dignity and apparent stability to the closure which we are considering, we then find it necessary to make our wall thick and massive, and these qualities must be illustrated in the treatment of the jambs of our openings. If the jambs are cut through at right angles, we shall make an inadequate and ineffective use of this quality of thickness or massiveness of wall; on the other hand, we shall increase the apparent depth of wall, and draw attention to it, by splaying the jambs with a series of right-angled returns, thus engendering in each opening a nest of diminishing arches, and, as it were, easing off the wall-surface at these points, as was done by the Romanesque and Gothic builders. We have already arranged that our long front shall be thirty bays long, and our end fronts eight bays long. But one of these bays must occur in the center of each front for the sake of the entrances; this will leave a half-bay at the corners. The result of this is that we have a wider pier at the ends, and by this simple device give a natural pause to the succession of arches on each front at the corners, without resorting for this purpose to the conventional end-pavilions, for which our plan does not offer sufficient excuse.

But the frontage which our wall-surface has thus developed, though entirely reasonable, is low, monotonous, and mechanical in its effect. The first difficulty, in its relation to the architectural composition as a whole, we may readily remedy by exaggerating the height of our central nave, so that, from ordinary points of view, it shall be seen to disengage itself well from the ridges of the aisle-roofs which encompass it, and thus form a part of the exterior architecture. To each bay of the upper part of the clearstory, thus elevated, we give two arches, corresponding in character to the single arch in the façade, though properly smaller in scale, and, by the same reasoning, we find it essential to raise these clearstory walls higher than the eaves of the nave-roof, and to crown them with a second overhanging coping.

We have thus designed a series of wall-surfaces in what seems to us a perfectly logical manner, but, as yet, with no projections whatever to break their monotony, — no pilasters, no string-courses, no base, no moldings of any sort, and no cornice, in the usual sense, — only a blank flat wall, pierced with deep arched openings, and protected by a boldly overhanging coping, square and uncompromising.

266

Now shall we make a concession to convention, and attempt to illustrate structure and use symbolically by applying projecting architectural features to our flat wall-surfaces after academical fashion and according to Renaissance motives, thereby saying what we have to say in diplomatic language, as it were, using forms which have obtained dignity and significance because of their association with the history of civilization, of which, indeed, they are a part; or rather shall we make this flat wall-surface itself the basis of expression, avoiding words and phrases of Latin origin, and, as was done by the Saracens in the Alhambra, who worked, as we are now working, in a plastic substance, which invited molding beneath the surface rather than carving above the surface — shall we decorate these flat surfaces with repeating superficial patterns? By the latter process we may, where we require, make our planes of construction beautiful without losing any of the advantages of simplicity and repose, which we are striving to secure by following rational methods. In treatments of this sort the example of Oriental nations is full of instruction, and we know the rich results obtained in this manner, not only by the Moors of Spain, but by Mohammedan art in the mosques at Cairo, and by Indian art in the tombs of Agra. We shall thus get architectural effects of light and shade, not by delicate playing with the complicated shadows and half-lights of pilasters, porticos, and molded entablatures, as in classic art, nor by the bolder *chiaroscuro* obtained by the buttresses, panels, and corbel-tables of medieval art, but by breaking the broadly staring sunlight on our smooth wall-surfaces with the broad black shadows of our coping, with the sharper and finer shade-lines obtained by recessing the window-reveals in a series of narrow planes, and with the regular spotted effects resulting from our spaces of superficial arabesque or fretwork. These wall-surfaces also invite a treatment by contrasts of color in masses or diapers, after the Oriental manner, thus giving opportunity for effects of festivity, which, however, need not derogate from the massiveness and breadth which seem most consistent with the fundamental character of our building.

It is a recognized principle of composition that a mass may be simplified, or even impoverished, for the sake of emphasizing by contrast a certain highly decorated point of interest. This principle seems especially applicable to our present case, because the purposes of our building do not call for an embellishment which would be appropriate in the zenana of an Indian palace, or in the tomb of an Oriental princess. The architectural virtue to be exercised in our case is self-denial rather than generosity. In the mass of our façades, therefore, we should use our facile means of decoration with great prudence, doing no more than may be necessary to make our wall respected as a work of art.

The west or rear side of our building will be completely occupied and masked by annexes; the north and south ends are so situated as to make the necessary entrances at these points very subordinate: but the center of the east front, toward the Lagoon and opposite the west center of the Liberal Arts Building, must be the main portal of our design. This feature, therefore, may very properly constitute that point of architectural emphasis of which we have spoken, and to which the rest of this façade must be little more than a preparation or foil (Fig. 153). The most majestic feature in the best art of the Mogul emperors, as in the closure of the great mosque at Delhi, or in the Taj-Mehal at Agra, is the porch. It is a flat, square-topped, projecting wall-face, pierced with a lofty pointed arch, forming the opening of a deep square niche, and profusely decorated with borders and spandrel panels of arabesque, and with inscriptions in inlay and superficial sculpture. It has no cornice, and frequently is finished with a parapet of lacework. Instructed by a study of these Oriental masterpieces, we may adjust them to our present use with but few modifications. The rigid, square, projecting mass, with its great arched opening, the profuse superficial decoration, and even the light characteristic kiosks or pagodas which accompanied the original, may all be reproduced here; but in order to amalgamate the whole with the work which we have already developed, it must finish with a similar bold overhanging brow, the arch must be low and round, that it may occupy a proportionate space in the face of our pavilion, and its opening must diminish inward in a succession of lessening arches in the Romanesque manner (Romanesque and Saracenic art having a common parentage at Byzantium), until the opening is reduced to dimensions practicable for a doorway. We may cover the entire superficial area of this pavilion with a delicate embroidery of arabesques and bas-reliefs — its fronts, its returns, its recessed archways, the wall-screen which closes the opening at the back, the face and soffit of its coping, its impost, and its stylobate. We will make the whole fretted mass splendid with gilding, so that this main entrance shall be known as the "Golden Doorway." The pavilion interrupts and discontinues every horizontal line in the edifice, so that we must depend upon a sparse echo of this embroidery on our long wall-faces to bring the composition together and to secure its unity of effect. We will therefore content ourselves with its use on the piers at the point where our arches spring, and on the under side of the coping. Practically the rest is left in repose to offset the splendor of the center. But in order to give a degree of movement to the hard square outlines of the pavilion, and to secure somewhat of a pyramidal effect, we support it on each side with terraces and balconies on a level with the impost of the arch, and accessible by outside stairs, and on each terrace we build a light kiosk against the pavilion in the manner of the Mogul architects. By this somewhat playful device we hope to secure for our building an aspect of festivity more appropriate to the place and occasion than would be obtained if we were content to leave its lines all severely adjusted to rational conditions of design. In like manner, and with the same object of conferring points of interest on the long plain line of frontage, we may venture to open four small exit doors, two on each side of the central portal, with decorated architraves, and flanked by pedestals against the adjoining piers to support groups of typical statuary. The end entrances may be constructed with low, square-topped, projecting pavilions, highly enriched, and flanked by terraces and staircases as in the front. In the center of the nave provision is made for a competitive exhibition of transportation by elevators. These are arranged in a group around a cylindrical core, and give access, by bridges across the nave, to the second floor and to a great terrace over the central portal, and connect with observatory balconies which surround a central lantern. This is the culminating feature of the design; it is highly decorated, and completes the exterior.

We have already stated that the decoration concentrated at various points on the Transportation Building is composed of arabesques. These are mostly foliations, more or less based upon regularly recurring geometrical systems, but following nature in varieties of form and principles of growth. At certain important points these arabesques are frames to figure-subjects in relief, illustrating in allegorical fashion the objects of the building. Properly to complement what we have here supposed the architects themselves might say regarding the genesis of this design, it seems desirable to add a few words of general statement and wider application.

The exact and scholarly conventionalities of the Court buildings recall the most brilliant era in the history of the world — the new birth of the mind, the revival of learning, the reformation in religious, political, and social life, which made modern civilization possible. These conventionalities, based upon ancient example, and highly organized by the discipline of the schools, are the symbols of this civilization. Such work as we see in the architectural system of the building which we have just been studying in outline may, in comparison, be considered romantic or barbaric (using the term in no derogatory sense, but as defining a condition of design outside the pale of classic authority), a product hardly less of invention than of convention, developing from within outward, and taking forms less consciously affected by historical precedent. This assumption of freedom in the hands of uneducated men becomes license and disorder; in the hands of men of training, but without principles, it becomes insubordination, and results in clever work of mere swagger and audacity, a manifestation of personal idiosyncrasy, more or less brilliant and amusing perhaps, but corrupting and unfruitful. With knowledge, but without genius or imagination, it becomes merely archæological: but under favorable circumstances this romanticism may rise into a region of purity, sobriety, and elegance hardly inferior to that occupied for more than twenty centuries (allowing for the medieval interruption) by classic art. Into this region of difficult access the accomplished architects of the Transportation Building are seeking to enter with a fine, courageous spirit of duty, and the evidences of their work, not only on the Exhibition grounds, but more conspicuously in the Auditorium of Chicago, and elsewhere (Figs. 132, 133, 138), are sufficient to indicate that somewhere perhaps in this dangerous field there may be a regeneration for the art of our time and country — not a revival of forms, but an establishing of principles, instructed rather than controlled by a spirit out of the inexhaustible past.

It is eminently fitting that in this exposition of national thought in architecture, our characteristic spirit of eager inquiry, of independent and intelligent experiment, should have the fullest illustration. If our late studies in Byzantine Romanesque and Saracenic art may seem to the foreign critic merely empirical, we may be able to show that in some instances they have been carried far enough to exercise a fructifying influence in the development of style in this country, and to infuse new blood into an art which, in the hands of the graduates of our schools of design, may be in danger of becoming scholastic or exotic, and of developing forms far removed from the uses and sympathies of modern life. In fact, it is not from loyalty to ancient formulas of beauty, not from revivals or correct archæological repetitions, that the true regeneration of modern architecture must come, but from the application to modern necessities and modern structure of the principles which controlled the evolution of the pure historical styles.

Messrs. W. L. B. Jenney & W. B. Mundie of Chicago, architects of the Horticultural Building, have been able to occupy the beautiful site at their disposal with a magnificent frontage of 1000 feet, facing the Lagoon, the ornamental gardens and parterres of the floral department stretching broadly between this long façade and the waterside (Fig. 154). The extreme depth of their building-site is about 250 feet. It was evident to the architects that a building for the cultivation and exposition of growing plants must be based upon what has been found by experience to be the best form for a garden greenhouse or conservatory. The architecture of such a structure must therefore include, as a fundamental feature of design, a series of light one-storied galleries with glazed roofs, from 50 to 70 feet wide, so arranged upon the site as to inclose garden courts, which would have all desirable sunlight, because practical conditions do not permit these surrounding galleries to exceed 22½ feet in height. As this height is only about one third that of the other buildings, and as it is necessary that the architectural mass must in some way be brought into proper relation to them, it became apparent to the architects that from the point of view of composition there should be pavilions at the north and south ends, where they approach nearest to their neighbors, and where comparisons must be instinctively forced upon the beholder, and that these pavilions should hardly be less than 50 feet high. Of course this height suggested two stories, in which could be accommodated not only collections and models illustrative of botany and horticulture, but spacious and attractive restaurants overlooking the gardens. Upon the first story of 21½ feet, therefore, there is constructed in these pavilions another still higher. Thus we have an outline of a building composed of two-storied pavilions at each end of the site, connected by two long, low ranges of one-storied glazed galleries, with an open court between them. But for practical as well as for architectural reasons it is necessary to break this interminable stretch of low galleries with an important and highly decorated central feature. The architects had to accommodate under cover not growing shrubs only, but full tropical tree-growths with grotto effects and fountains. This suggested a much higher but still characteristic feature of greenhouse architecture — a glazed, wide-spreading dome, made as large as the available space would permit, but not so high as to overwhelm the one-storied galleries. This dome naturally took its place in the center, and, as it was to constitute the most imposing feature, interior as well as exterior, it had to be entered as directly as possible from the main porch. A third pavilion was thus introduced in the center of the building. As a matter of convenience as well as of structure, the architects divided their galleries into bays of 24½ feet, which dimension they assumed as the module or unit of their plan. Thirty-one of these modules entered into the length of their building between the end pavilions, leaving for each of these pavilions a width of 118 feet. By experiment they found that the largest dome which architectural considerations would permit must not exceed 180 feet in diameter. They placed, therefore, a glazed domical hall of these dimensions in the center of a two-storied substructure of square plan, of about nine modules, with a projecting frontispiece toward the Lagoon in three parts, of which the central is the portal, the others being crowned by low domes occupying the corners of the square and buttressing the larger central dome.

By a mutual adjustment of the parts thus outlined a definite architectural scheme was obtained, composed of two two-storied end pavilions, 118 feet wide and 250 feet deep, connected in the rear by a continuous one-storied glazed gallery, 50 feet wide and 759½ feet long, against the center of which was placed a great domical pavilion, about 220 feet square, faced with a highly enriched pylon. A second and more important longitudinal gallery, with glazed arched roofs, parallel with the first and 73 feet wide, forming the curtain-walls of the main façade, connected the center with the end pavilions, thus inclosing two garden-courts, 90 feet wide and 270 feet long.

As for the exterior, the architects are committed to a long, low façade, of which the curtain-walls are only 22½ feet high, crowned with a 3-foot balustrade. The expression of their central dome, therefore, must be correspondingly low in proportion to its height; considerations of architectural conformity must be forced into harmony with considerations of practical convenience and use. The vertical section of this dome is accordingly made semicircular, and the center from which the semicircle is struck is on a level with the gallery or second story surrounding the dome, and thus only about 24 feet from the floor, giving a total height of only 114 feet to a dome 180 feet in diameter. So far as the interior is concerned, this proportion is admirable; but the depressed exterior effect of this great glazed dome is partly remedied by a drum or podium, which is established above the flat roof of the square substructure forming the base of the dome, and which is high enough to be seen from ordinary points of view, and also by a highly enriched crown or lantern which surmounts the dome itself. The lower glazed domes, which crowd against its base on the corners, effectually support its outlines, and assist them to spring from the façade with grace and elegance, and without too sudden transitions. The curved sky-lines are also aided by the segmental form of the glazed roofs of the galleries on each hand. The transparent character of this immense ball and the airy lightness of its structure remove it from comparison with

271

the substantial fabrics of the domes that elsewhere in the fields of the Exposition rise with more monumental aspiration. It has a quality of fleeting and iridescent beauty, and seems to be blown like a bubble.

In their decorative scheme the architects preferred to follow Venetian Renaissance models, and they applied to the curtain-walls of their long front galleries a correct Ionic order with pilasters, dividing the frontage into bays corresponding to those of the interior, each being occupied by a glazed arched window, reducing the wall-surfaces to the smallest areas consistent with classic traditions, as in the orangeries of Versailles. This order is continued around the end pavilions; but as the architects were compelled to erect upon this a second story 3 feet higher than that upon which it was placed, to enable their building to compare properly with its neighbors in regard to height, they treated their upper order, which is also Ionic, with an exaggerated frieze 6 feet high, giving an area for decoration, which they richly filled with Cupids, garlands, and festoons, abundantly testifying to the joyous and gentle character of the objects to which the building is dedicated. In these pavilions they were wisely led by the example of Sansovino in the Library of St. Mark on the Piazzetta, Venice, and the arrangement also of crowning balustrades and finials, characteristic of this elegant monument, evidently had a strong influence on the present composition.

The portal is a lofty triumphal arch with a recessed vestibule, decorated with statuary, and in the character of its profuse embellishments of sculpture recalling the work of modern Paris; but in the two square pavilions, crowned with their subordinate domes, flanking the portal, the Venetian motives are again taken up. The Ionic order again appears here, but is on a larger scale than that of the long curtain-walls, and its entablature has a frieze broader even than that of the corner pavilions, and it is enriched with the exuberant but elegant playfulness which the Italian masters knew so well how to employ in the service of their paganized princes.

Seen from whatever point of view, no one can doubt the purposes of this building, and though its architecture has been gaily attuned to a much lighter mood than would be proper to its more serious companions, it does not forget the dignity and grace which belong to it as a work of art.

The decorative modeling and sculpture of this building are the work of Mr. Loredo Taft of Chicago.[18]

The first point of interest connected with the Women's Pavilion resides in the fact that it is the product of a national competition of designs among women. An architectural composition, like any other work of art, is always more or less sensitive to the personal qualities of the designer. Consequently, in examining the works of the successful competitor in this case, there is an irresistible impulse to look for the distinctive characteristics in which the feminine instinct may have betrayed itself. Miss Sophia G. Hayden of Boston is a graduate of the architectural school of the Massachusetts Institute of Technology in that city, and the composition by which she was fortunate enough to win this coveted prize has all the marks of a first-class school problem, intelligently studied according to academical methods, and may fairly stand in this national exposition of architecture as a good example of the sort of training given in our best professional schools. As such, it is proper that it should take its place with the other architectural works in Jackson Park, and it is eminently proper that the exposition of woman's work should be housed in a building in which a certain delicacy and elegance of general treatment, a smaller limit of dimension, a finer scale of detail, and a certain quality of sentiment, which might be designated, in no derogatory sense, as graceful timidity or gentleness, combined however with evident technical knowledge, at once differentiate it from its colossal neighbors, and reveal the sex of its author (Fig. 155).

The manner in which the plan of the Women's Pavilion has been conceived and laid out requires but little concession of criticism in favor of inexperience. In this structure it was intended to accommodate a general exposition of woman's work, whether industrial, artistic, educational, or social. It was to include departments for reform work and charity organizations, a model hospital and kindergarten, a retrospective exhibition, one or more assembly-rooms of various sizes, with libraries, parlors, committee-rooms, and offices. These various services were to be provided for within an area 400 feet long northward by 200 feet wide, lying next north of the Horticultural Building, and in the axis of the Midway Pleasance. These general dimensions, and the comparatively small scale of the building, suggested 10 feet as a module of proportion, and upon this basis it was found convenient to develop the plan and organize the elevations.

The differing and somewhat undefined uses to which the building was to be devoted seemed to require a series of connected rooms of various sizes, all subordinated to a great hall or *salle des pas perdus* of architectural character. Certainly, enough of these subordinate apartments were required to make at least two stories necessary. With reference to lighting, circulation, and economy of space, evidently the most convenient and the simplest way of adjusting the plan was to place the great hall in the middle, to free it from columns, to build it high enough to receive light through clearstory windows, and to envelop it with a lower two-storied structure forming the four façades of the building. From the floor of this hall a convenient communication could be established with the minor halls and offices around it, so that the whole first story could be utilized. In the second story it was apparent that the necessary intercommunication could be effectively provided by surrounding the open central area of the hall by a system of corridors, which should also serve as galleries overlooking the hall, after the manner of an arcade or cloister around an Italian cortile. In order to obtain adequate area for them, this enveloping series of rooms should not exceed 80 feet in depth, and should borrow all the light possible to be obtained from the central hall, or their illumination by daylight would be seriously imperiled.

The exterior expression is evolved from these conditions. The other buildings of the Exposition covering much more extensive areas without any great superiority of mass vertically, their architects have generally found it necessary to emphasize the vertical lines as offsets to the horizontal, and to include two or more stories in one colossal order, thus bringing the architectural scheme into scale with the vastness of the structure. On account of the comparatively small extent and scale of this building, it did not seem to require any such emphasis of vertical lines, and therefore it was proper to permit the two stories to be frankly expressed in its architecture. The architect found that the strong horizontal lines thus created in the façades could be adjusted harmoniously by making the first-story order 21 feet, and the second 23 feet high, the whole resting on a continuous 5-foot stylobate or basement, thus giving about 50 feet as the height of the outer walls. In establishing the general vertical divisions of the main front, Miss Hayden naturally followed the conventional system of a central frontispiece with a pavilion at each end, connected by recessed curtain-walls. The depth of the suites of rooms on the north and south fronts conferred on the end pavilions a width of 80 feet, or eight modules. Over the low roofs of the enveloping suites the clearstory and roof of the lofty central hall should assert themselves as essential features of the exterior. We thus have a frontage fairly blocked out.

In this way the building is massed after the manner of the villas of the Italian Renaissance, and to this school the design is naturally indebted for those details on which the character of the design as a work of art must largely depend. From this point the architect probably developed the work somewhat as follows:

The first story of the curtain-walls between the central and end pavilions must be brought forward nearly to the face of the pavilions to form an exterior portico or ambulatory, its roof serving as a balcony or terrace to the recessed second story. This first story of the curtain-walls she treated as an Italian arcade in 10-foot bays without columns or pilasters, surmounted by a balustrade, while upon the second she imposed a full order of pilasters rather suggested by, than strictly following, Corinthian precedents, with windows between, all adjusted in scale to the almost domestic proportions of the rooms within. The central entrance should take not less than three arches similar to those of the arcade, and should be surmounted by a colonnade of the order adopted for the second story, inclosing a loggia connected with the balcony or terrace to which we have referred, the whole being flanked on each side by a space of solid wall decorated with coupled pilasters on each story, and surmounted by a pediment developed from the main cornice. Practically the same treatment may be repeated on the front face of the two end pavilions, but without the pediment, and also on the side entrances, which, however, should not have a pediment, as that would bring them into competition with the main entrance, and cannot have a loggia, because of the interior conditions of plan. The colonnade must therefore be replaced by a corresponding range of pilasters. But these side entrances may be distinguished by a low attic, constituting, for this part of the building, a third story of small rooms, opening on each side on roof-gardens, which should extend over the end pavilions, surrounded by an open screen formed of an order of light Ionic columns, with caryatids over the loggia below, all after the manner not unusual in the terraced gardens of Italian palaces. The central hall is 67½ feet wide by nearly 200 feet long, and attains an exterior height of 64 feet.

Under the circumstances explained, the design is rather lyric than epic in character, and it takes its proper place on the Exposition grounds with a certain modest grace of manner not inappropriate to its uses and to its authorship.

After an extremely vigorous and hardly contested competition among sculptors of the gentler sex throughout the Union, the sculpture of the main pediment, and of the typical groups surmounting the open screen around the roof-gardens, was awarded to Miss Alice Rideout, of San Francisco. It is needless to say that the subjects are emblematic of woman's great work in the world, and that criticism will be glad to recognize in these compositions all the noble and poetic qualities of art which they aim to set forth.

V.

The visitor, approaching from the south the district which lies between the northern and central divisions of the park, at the point where the apparently capricious and accidental windings of the Lagoon find their northern connection with the lake, will presently catch glimpses of certain long stretches of roof, gaily broken by towers and decorated belvederes, rising above the skirting shrubbery and wood-growth of the shores, and suggesting the hidden luxuries of a "stately pleasure house," decreed by some Kubla Khan of Oriental romance. As he advances nearer, he will discover that this romantic pleasance is accessible from the south by a bridge spanning the waters of the canal, or estuary, connecting the Lagoon with the lake, the architectural masses will become coherent and symmetrical, and finally he will learn from unmistakable characteristics that the Fisheries Pavilion lies before him (Fig. 156). This pavilion is set in the axis of the Liberal Arts Building extended northward, and between the two buildings in the same axis rise the masses of the great structure built by the United States for the Government exposition.

Apparently the architect, Mr. Henry Ives Cobb of Chicago, in preparing his preliminary studies for this interesting exhibit, finally arrived at the conclusion that, in respect to his plan, its general form must be largely controlled by its adjustment to the shape and limited area of the irregular stretch of shore which he was to occupy with his water-front, and, in respect to his elevations, that they should rather affect playfulness than formality in outline, so that they might be in more natural relations with their environment; at the same time, the connection established by the main axial line between his building and those composing the Court, the proper classification and arrangement of the collections which he was to accommodate, and the dignity and importance of the task assigned him, seemed to impose a symmetrical treatment both on plan and elevation. In this case it was the good fortune of the architect to have to deal with a department of the Exposition which invited a treatment almost as characteristic as that of the Horticultural department, which had the type of the glazed conservatory as its point of departure. Marine life seemed to suggest to the architectural mind types of form nearly as marked, while all the other great buildings had to be based more or less on the conventional idea of a palace or office of state, depending rather on their details of decoration than on their general features of structure to indicate the purposes for which they were built. This statement is especially applicable to the formal Renaissance buildings around the Court; but even those outside of the Court, like the Mines and Transportation pavilions, which were more free to adopt forms characteristic of service, could hardly confess their objects so clearly as the two buildings which we have noted.

The architect found that his site would be most conveniently occupied by a compact mass of building hardly larger than 365 feet in length by 165 feet in width; but as this was insufficient for his exhibition, he set aside two distinctive divisions, the aquarial and the angling divisions, to be accommodated in separate pavilions, connected with the ends of the main structure by one-storied corridors, so curved forward in plan that the main frontage should seem to be set back between the two smaller buildings. Thus arranged, the main façade faces southward toward the Government Building, and, being closely connected with the shore-line of the estuary, the whole pile assumes the characteristics of a marine pavilion.

Mr. Cobb found that the most convenient unit of dimension in his construction was 20 feet, and, following the simplest and most obvious arrangement for lighting the interior spaces, he planned to provide for a lofty central hall illuminated by a range of clearstory windows and surrounded by lean-tos, or aisles. To the width of this hall he gave four of his units or modules (80 feet), and to the length fourteen (280 feet), thus leaving for the width of his surrounding aisle, or lean-to, two modules, or 40 feet. The entire area found practicable for the main building was in this way fully occupied. A very characteristic feature was imposed upon his exterior forms by the fact that, unlike the other buildings, two full stories were not required in order to obtain the requisite floor-area. Allowing only one module for the height of his aisle-story, he obtained for the outside walls, including a stylobate, or basement, of 3½ feet, a height limited to 24 feet. This frontage, exceptionally low in comparison with the large area of the building, made it necessary to give to the roofs a pitch sufficiently steep to bring them into the design, and to make them important features in the composition as a whole. A proportionate height for the clearstory walls was found by experiment to be 14 feet, and above this the upper roofs, sloping at the same angle as those below, reached a total height of 65 feet from the floor. In this natural way the exterior expression of the building, distinguishing it from all the other structures of the Exposition, became one of roofs and clearstories. The area in the triforium space under the slope of the aisle roofs being required for exhibition purposes, access to it is obtained by projecting the floor of the triforium, or half second story, into the nave area far enough to form a gallery, or balcony, all around on that level, approached by staircases grouped near the center of the building. The architect thus obtained a mass of building composed of a comparatively low wall, from which roofs sloped steeply to a central ridge, interrupted only by the clearstory of the nave. The conditions clearly demanded an important culminating feature. This he obtained by erecting in the center of his nave a great circular tower, of which the diameter is equal to the whole width of the nave (80 feet), and by providing it with polygonal turrets at the corners to mask the awkwardness occasioned by the passing of a round tower through the slopes of the nave roof. These turrets he arranged to contain staircases, by which access is obtained to an exterior and interior gallery, or balcony, boldly projecting at the level of the apex of the nave roof. Above this he established a high clearstory stage still accompanied by the polygonal towers, and, following the roof-motive of his design, he covered his rounded tower with a steep conical roof, crowned with an upper balcony and a delicate belvedere, which he repeated on a lower level in finishing his four polygonal turrets. The total height thus obtained is 150 feet. To provide for the main entrances it remained to project transepts 80 feet wide from the tower to the center of the long fronts and thence 40 feet outside the walls of the aisles. These transepts preserved the lowness of effect characteristic of the rest of the buildings, by continuing around them the aisle walls, and covering them with pitched roofs without clearstories. The fronts of these transepts are flanked by low polygonal barbican towers belonging to the same family as those already mentioned.

The architectural character of the two separate pavilions is fixed by the results of the study of the unusual conditions involved in providing for the department of aquaria, to which that on the right of the main building is devoted. The fortunate outcome of this study is a polygonal building 60 feet in diameter and 67 feet high, with a windowed clearstory, all arranged in plan and elevation like an Italian baptistery or English chapter-house, with a glass-roofed aisle 37 feet wide, carried around it in the form of a lean-to, exactly as in the main building. A fountain is provided in the circular central hall, which opens into the aisle by an arcade. The aisle is divided into three concentric divisions forming annular spaces encompassing the circular chamber. Of these the middle one is made a vaulted passage, with a groined ceiling supported by columns and arches, corresponding to those separating the central circular chamber from the aisles. The other two annular spaces on each side of this passage are occupied by the aquarial tanks. All these arches on both sides of the passage and in the central chamber are glazed from top to bottom with transparent glass, the lower eight feet, with polished plate, forming the walls of the aquaria, the rest with decorative glass stained with marine tones. In these aquaria the architect has provided for the display of salt-water and freshwater fishes and every form of marine life. The only light which will reach the vaulted passage will pass through the glazed walls of the tanks, and the visitor, in making the circuit of the building through this passage, will seem to be walking dry beneath the water, with all the secrets of the great deep betrayed to him on each hand, according to the systems in use in some of the greater marine museums in the Old World.

The angling pavilion on the other side naturally assumes the same exterior character, and both closely follow the motives of the greater building, which are based very frankly on Southern Romanesque, the outer walls everywhere being formed with a continuous open arcade, the round stilted arches of which are supported on small round columns coupled in the thickness of the wall, as in a cloister. There are three of these arches to each 20-foot bay. Between the coupled columns passes a continuous perforated balustrade, and the building is inclosed by a glazed screen behind this arcade and clear of it. The treatment of the clearstory walls corresponds to this, but with five arches to each bay, and the great clearstory of the tower has a loftier and richer arrangement of arches with grouped jamb-shafts, mullion-shafts, and Romanesque tracery. All the cornices are corbeled according to the style. The Romanesque arcade appears also as the decorative feature of all the belvederes and towers. The only variation made in this arcade treatment to give dignity to the main entrance is to advance slightly from the face of the transept a highly decorated triplet of larger arches covered with a gable, whose outline the architect has enriched with crockets in the form of fishes. The tympanum inclosed by the gable will be occupied by a bas-relief representation of the most heroic business done by fishermen on the great deep — the capture of a whale. Very properly Mr. Cobb has borrowed from marine life the decorative details of his capitals and of the columnar shafts of his porches, and there is nothing in the familiar but inexhaustible range of conventional Romanesque ornament, as applied to this building,

> But doth suffer a sea-change
> Into something rich and strange.[19]

Fishes in every form, crabs, lobsters, water-snakes, frogs, shells, and the infinite algæ of the great deep, are grouped to decorate capital and corbel, but always so massed as to preserve the characteristic outlines and functions of the architectural members. Under the immediate direction of the architect, Mr. Joseph Richter of Chicago has in this way composed from sixty to eighty models of capitals, corbels, and shaft ornaments, each differing from the other in the idea which it conveys, but all loyal to the conventional type. The Romanesque of southern France and northern Spain, even in the religious buildings, is distinguished by a semi-barbaric humor expressed in grotesque and caricature. There is therefore no unnecessary audacity of imagination in the playful treatment of the details of the Fisheries Pavilion; it not only brings it into harmony with the spirit of the style, but serves to make it joyous and festive without loss of dignity, grace, and fitness (Fig. 156).

The whole building shows clearly enough how the modern architect can, on the one hand, use precedent with loyal intelligence, but without being enslaved by it; and on the other, how, when occasion requires, he can be original

278

without going through the superfluous and dangerous process of inventing a new language in which to express himself, as is the custom with the unlettered and the untrained.

After much controversy and many changes of plan and site, the department of Fine Arts found its most appropriate position near the middle of the northern division of the park, surrounded by the smaller pavilions which are to form the headquarters of the several State commissions, and by those to be erected by foreign governments.

This building, the design of which was prepared by Charles B. Atwood,[20] the designer-in-chief in the Bureau of Construction, was practically confined by conditions of site and cost to a frontage of 500 feet, facing north and south, and to a depth of 320 feet, with opportunities for lateral extension by detached wings, connected with the main structure by galleries of communication. It was to be strictly fire-proof, and on this account was carefully isolated. Through this isolation it was freed from the necessity of submitting to concessions for the sake of harmony with neighboring buildings, so that, surrounded by ample grounds dedicated to art, its form and character as a symmetrical monument could be freely developed (Fig. 157).

In formulating the plan, it was found convenient to adopt a decimal module of proportion. In the beginning it was evident that the scheme would be fundamentally affected by the fact that the area was to be occupied, not by one great hall with continuous floor-space, as was the case with all the industrial buildings, but by a series of halls or chambers; and that of these there must be two divisions, one set devoted to the exposition of sculpture and the plastic arts, requiring conditions of area, shape, height, and lighting different from the other set, which had to be arranged for the accommodation of paintings, drawings, and engravings. The former called for ample uninterrupted floor-space, indefinite height, light from above so diffused as to avoid, as far as possible, conflicts of shadows and confusion of reflections, and, in general, a largeness and nobility of aspect entirely consistent with monumental architecture in its highest sense. On the other hand, the galleries of chambers for the exposition of paintings and drawings needed not to be more than 30 feet in width, and demanded clear wall-spaces not more than 20 feet high, with coved ceilings raising the ceiling skylights 10 feet higher, so that the wall-surfaces might have no shadows. A decorative or architectural treatment was not invited. The halls of sculpture, therefore, being the widest, highest, longest, and most architectural, were the arteries of the system, to which all the other members, being lower, smaller, and simpler or more purely utilitarian, had to be distinctly subordinate. The architect, therefore, placed the former in the main axes of his plan, arranging them in the form of a central longitudinal nave, 500 feet long, 100 feet wide, and 64 feet high to the cornice, crossed in the center by a transept 340 feet long, and of the same width and height. These he provided with skylights and clearstory, and with a wide balcony, giving circulation around the entire system at a higher level, and accommodation for bas-reliefs and minor objects of the fictile arts, while the larger works of sculpture and modeling were to occupy the main-floor areas. The outer ends of nave and transept in the center of each façade naturally became porches with vestibules of noble preparation and ceremony. It was also inevitable that the culmination of interest externally and internally should be in the center of the building at the crossing of the great halls. In the hands of the architect this feature took the form of a noble domical chamber, 155 feet high externally and 128 feet high internally, with a diameter of 72 feet. This dome he supported on a massive substructure of octagonal plan, pierced in the axes of the central halls with lofty arched openings, thus dividing the supporting walls into four masses of masonry, so disposed as to give passageway between nave and transepts outside of these piers, to avoid the necessity of making this central hall a thoroughfare. Still further to dignify it as a place which should be not a mere passageway between adjoining halls, but where the more conspicuous objects should be gathered for especial honor, as in the tribune of the Uffizi Palace, he placed two columns of his main order in each opening, supporting an entablature across it on the line of the impost, with statues above, as was often done in the Roman baths and basilicas, so as to form an open screen. By this great central feature the sculpture-halls are divided into two long and two short courts.

Doors on the sides of the longer courts give access to the ends of a series of twenty-four picture-galleries, which are made of the standard height and width of 30 feet, and 60 feet long, thus affording for each gallery about 2500 feet of wall-space available for hanging, this being a convenient unit for dividing the collection into groups according to character or nationality. At the outer ends of these transverse galleries, opposite doors open into larger longitudinal intercepting galleries, about 40 feet wide, forming the envelop of the building. At one end these longitudinal galleries communicate with the shorter or transverse courts of sculpture, and, at the other, with corner pavilions, 50 feet square. In this manner nearly 100,000 square feet of hanging-space are obtained in a series of communicating galleries, so contrived as to facilitate classification, and the parallelogram of the plan is completed, becoming compact, articulate, and orderly, justifiable by considerations of circulation, economy of space, convenience, and construction, and as we shall presently discover, leading directly to a symmetrical disposition of exterior masses, which will compose architecturally with dignity and elegance, and without the necessity of having forced upon them any feature of importance not already suggested by the structure itself.

As regards the exterior, the objects of this building seemed very clearly to invite a monumental expression, set forth in terms connected with the evolution of the highest civilizations in history, associated with the greatest triumphs of art, established by the usages of the greatest masters, and formulated by the schools and academies of all nations. It was necessary that it should be pure, formal, and stately, entirely free from caprice or playfulness, refined by scrupulous elegance of detail, and enriched by every device of decorative sculpture which could be consistently recalled from historic art, so that, when completed, it should be fit to enshrine the figures and groups in marble and bronze, the paintings in oil, water-color, and fresco, the carvings in ivory, wood, and marble, the bas-reliefs, engravings, etchings, and drawings, by which the century is taking its rank in history. It is evident that any design not strictly ordained by academic principles and practice, any design indebted to semibarbaric or romantic precedents, impressed with personal idiosyncrasies, or in any way experimental, would, under the circumstances, be out of harmony with the purposes of the building. Indeed, the building itself should be in sympathy with its contents, and as nearly all dogmas of modern art are more or less directly derived through pagan, Christian, or Renaissance experience from classic models, it was evident that the shrine which was to contain them, if Greek in character, would respond to every mood and principle of artistic expression.

The scheme of this building, as already outlined in plan developed in block-elevation, is an extensive parallelogram of flat-roofed sky-lighted buildings, about 47 feet high, raised upon a continuous basement 9 feet high, and emphasized at the corners by projecting pavilions 50 feet square and of the same height as the rest; while, above this low-lying mass, the clearstories and roofs of the central, longitudinal, and transverse courts clearly detach themselves in long level sky-lines, generating in the middle of each façade some form of boldly projecting entrance-porch, and, at the crossing of the courts in the middle of the plan, culminating in a domical feature, which must be made about 155 feet high from the ground in order to be adequate to its functions.

Of course the arrangement of plan in any building, however utilitarian, when developed in elevation, is capable of some degree of architectural expression, either symmetrical or picturesque, as the conditions may invite; and this expression must be based upon considerations of structure and usage. Thus, even the most uncompromising of structural forms, as a grain elevator, or a block of commercial buildings, by decorative treatment may be elevated into a work of art without impairing any of its characteristic functions of utility. But, in laying out his scheme, the architect cannot but mentally anticipate its ultimate appearance when built, and naturally prefers those alternative arrangements of plan which are most capable of architectural effect. So in the present building, Mr. Atwood, in composing his plan, did not permit himself to be embarrassed by unnecessary difficulties in exterior expression through want of prudent foresight. It was hardly by accident, therefore, that the combination of masses which we have seen taking shape lent themselves to what might be called a Renaissance development of pure Greek forms. In considering the conversion of these prosaic masses of utility into the poetry of art, the architect assumed as his key-note the beautiful Ionic of the portico of Athena Polias in the Erectheum, as suggesting a degree of refinement and elegance of detail less redundant but more exact than the Corinthian of the Choragic monument of Lysicrates, less chaste and severe than the Doric of the Parthenon, but happily combining the qualities of both. Unlike any of the buildings which we have been considering, no light is derived through the outer walls (these being the walls of picture-galleries), which, therefore, structurally must be left plain. To obtain a play of light and shadow upon these windowless surfaces, and to make them interesting, the architect, following the Greek method of placing in front of the plain cella walls of the temples a screen, or peristyle, established an Ionic colonnade about 8 feet from his walls, composed of columns 27 feet high, set 10 feet on centers, and resting on the basement, or stylobate, of which we have spoken. Thus a continuous loggia, or sheltered ambulatory, is formed, extending between the bold projection of the central porch on each front and the slighter projection of the corner pavilions, giving to the long curtain-walls a decoration entirely classic in character.

The main entrance in the center of each long front is architecturally distinguished by what is technically known as a *tetrastyle portico in antis*, that is, a portico of four great Ionic columns, 40½ feet high, set between two three-quarter columns built into the jambs of a great opening pierced in the projecting outer wall of the sculpture-court, thus forming an open screen in front of a deep vestibule. This portico is approached by a noble flight of steps with a statue of Minerva in the center thereof, and over this portico is placed an attic, of which the pilasters, corresponding to the columns below, are faced with caryatid figures or telamones, 14 feet high, like those in the clearstory of the Greek temple at Agrigentum, thus bringing the upper cornice of the portico to a height of 73 feet, the whole attic being continuous with the clearstory of the courts, and securing an important bond of architectural unity for the composition. This portico is finished with an enriched pediment, which serves as the decorative expression on the façade of the pitched roof of the courts. Just above the point where these court-roofs abut against the square substructure of the central dome a simpler form of pediment is repeated, this being the external development of the interior columnar entrances to the central domical hall or tribune, to which we have already referred. Above these pediments the square substructure of the central feature finishes with a cornice and crest, preparatory to the round drum and low dome which crown the whole mass. A corresponding but inferior portico, with only two columns *in antis*, is established for the center of the end façades.

The marked predominance on the principal fronts of a boldly projecting portico 73 feet high (representing the courts), while on each side of the portico are long stretches of colonnades only 56 feet high (representing the picture-galleries), was found to be too great, giving a transition too sudden from high to low. This difficulty of composition the architect ingeniously remedied by flanking the mass of this portico with two pavilions of intermediate projection about 30 feet wide, to correspond with the divisions of the plan. These pavilions he made of the same height as the galleries, and faced them with small caryatid blank porticos, suggested by that of the Erectheum. Behind these pavilions, in the four internal angles formed at the junction of the longitudinal and transverse courts, are circular staircases, giving access to the system of balconies around these courts. The domes covering these staircases are so developed externally as to perform a similar service of preparation at the corners of the square substructure of the great central dome. The corner pavilions the architect decorated with flat pedimented porticos, and the light iron colonnettes supporting the interior balconies and the roofs of the courts are modeled after suggestions in the painted architecture on the walls of Pompeii.

It is a part of the scheme to make the numerous statues, friezes, and other decorations, in the round and in relief, replicas of the greatest masterpieces of Greek and Renaissance art, so that the building itself shall be a museum, not of historical sculpture only, but of painting.

It is fortunate that the opportunity of presenting in this building a monument which internally and externally should be a specimen of serious and elegant academic architecture has been improved in a manner so scholarly and so loyal to traditions. We present this composition in geometrical elevation and plan, so that the eye may at once perceive how exterior and interior have grown together, the former becoming an architectural expression of the latter, and the latter yielding no point of convenience or economy to adjust itself to any preconceived theory of design. The whole is an artistic organism, delicately poised, in which use and beauty find themselves in a condition of perfect harmony.

There is no building on the grounds which we should more regret to see destroyed at the conclusion of the Exposition than this beautiful monument. Its essential structure is, as we have seen, fire-proof; only its porticos, its peristyles, and its exterior decorative details are temporary. These could be so readily replaced by permanent construction in the same form, that the architects of all the buildings hope it may be permitted to remain as the most appropriate and worthy memorial of the Exposition of 1893.

We have seen that the Fisheries Pavilion, with its tentacle-like arms, is closely nested in the indentations of the northern margin of the estuary which connects the waters of the Lagoon with the lake. On the opposite side of this estuary is the northern or water front of the United States Government Pavilion, the longitudinal axis of which, extended northward, passes through the center of the Fisheries Pavilion, and, extended southward, forms also the longitudinal axis of the immense palace of Manufactures and the Liberal Arts.

By this axial system the group of buildings on the lake-side is architecturally allied with the main groups around the great basin and its connecting canals, the Transportation Building, on the shoreward side of the Lagoon, having corresponding relations with them. The largest and most important structures of the Exposition thus have a mutual correspondence, which is of the utmost value in the expression of dignity and purpose. The other great pavilions (the Horticultural, the Women's, the Illinois State, and the Art buildings) are ranged with the lines of city avenues and streets on another axial system. But this divergence of lines is masked by the interposition of the Lagoon, with its wooded and winding shores.

In the Government Building the departments of War, Agriculture, and the Interior, and the National Museum required each a space of about 20,000 feet; while the National Fisheries Commission, the Post-office, and the departments of State, Justice, and the Treasury, with the other public offices, each demanded spaces varying from 18,000 to 1600 feet. These departments combined demanded about 148,000 feet of floor-space, with considerable additional accommodation for offices of administration, and special collections in galleries. These considerations dictated for the building a length of 420 feet on the axial line, to which we have referred, and a width of 350 (Fig. 158). The naval exhibit is to be held in a separate structure, built in the lake, east of the National Building, on the exact model of a first-class modern armored battle-ship, fully equipped and manned, lying alongside a mole extended from the shore. The level area between the building and the lake provides outside accommodation for a model marine hospital, for the apparatus and daily exercise of a life-saving station, for a naval observatory, for the experimental plantation and irrigation exhibit of the Agricultural Department, and for the parade-ground of an encampment of United States troops. The Lighthouse Board has its exhibit at the end of the pier of which we have spoken.

For the main building of the Government exhibit the supervising architect of the Treasury Department, Mr. W. J. Edbrooke, conceived a structure occupying the entire area of which we have spoken in such a manner as to obtain a vast uninterrupted hall, in which whatever subdivisions might be required should be effected by partitions having no structural significance. By six ranges of columns set 25 feet on centers he secured support for seven parallel longitudinal aisles, each 50 feet wide, of which four, including the outer aisles, are high, with pitched or gabled roofs, and the other three, alternating with these, are low with segmentally arched roofs, over which the high aisles obtain a well-distributed light throughout the interior by a range of clearstory windows. These longitudinal aisles are crossed transversely in the center by a higher transept, consisting of a nave, or main hall, 40 feet wide, flanked by double 20-foot aisles.

From a decorative point of view, it was evident that a lofty central, culminating feature must be introduced, of sufficient importance to confer peculiar distinction upon an architectural composition which must stand among the other buildings of the Exposition as an adequate representative of national dignity. The architect, therefore, built in the center of this complex of longitudinal and transverse roofs a dome 120 feet in diameter and 25 feet high from the floor, so that it should dominate the wide-spreading and comparatively low-lying mass of the building from every point of view. Below the roofs this domical structure appears in the middle of the great hall as a central octagonal tribune, or chamber, of which each side, 50 feet wide, is pierced by an arch; above the roof it assumes the form of a sixteen-sided drum, or podium, decorated on each face with an order of coupled arched windows between pilasters, from which spring the ribs of a dome 78 feet high, embellished by lucarnes. A lofty lantern completes the upward movement of the sky-lines, and a corbeled, aërial balcony is introduced as the base of the lantern to give animation and lightness to this most sensitive part of the design.

The architectural character of the inclosing walls of the building must of course depend upon the skill with which the architect has made use of the suggestions of the general plan. The requisite height for a great hall 420 by 350 feet, with galleries across the north and south ends and in the aisles of the transept, gives 45½ feet as the general height of the façades, above which is placed a balustrade to mask the roof-system. We have seen that the loftiest part of this roof-system is in the transept. This feature compels recognition in the central pavilions of the long east and west fronts, which become the principal portals of the building. Each of these pavilions is composed of five members or divisions, corresponding in position and width to the transept and its two aisles on each side. The three central divisions are carried 30½ feet, and the two outer divisions 6 feet, higher than the main cornice. All finish with level sky-lines, but the three middle divisions are crowned, the central one by a typical group of figures, and the other two by national eagles mounted on octagonal pedestals. The idea of the portal is adequately expressed by a central arch, occupying the whole width of the transept, and springing from the level of the main cornice of the building, which is continued across all the pavilions as a string-course.

The structure and dimensions of the outer longitudinal aisles developed in elevation produce a curtain-wall in four 25-foot bays, coincident with the spacing of the columns within, each bay being treated with a great arched window, divided horizontally by a transom or string-course, corresponding with the level of the interior galleries and continued all around the façades. These bays are separated by buttress-piers of slight projection, and on each angle of the building a corner pavilion, 50 feet square, covered with a low square dome, is naturally evolved from the conditions of the plan. Each front of these corner pavilions has a glazed arched opening set between two narrow subordinate pavilions. On the north and south fronts the gable-ends of the longitudinal aisles produce an architectural composition wherein the three central aisles are expressed in a boldly projecting triple entrance-pylon, carefully subordinated to the main entrances on the east and west fronts, the outer aisles in two corner pavilions, and the intermediate lower aisles in a correspondingly depressed frontage 50 feet wide, covered with an ornamented segmental gable, following the roof-lines. Thus it will be seen that the main features of the façades are the direct decorative or architectural expression of the plan, and the design, as a composition of masses, is articulate and reasonable.

The Government architectural office, which designs and constructs more great buildings than any ten private architectural offices in the world, can accomplish its prodigious work only by traditions which are the result of organization and discipline. These traditions have assumed form, more or less definite, under the administration of a succession of supervising architects, who, having found it physically impossible to give to each of the forty or fifty public monuments always simultaneously developing under their charge the study and thought necessary to a work of art, have been constrained to establish formulas of design by which, with the assistance of intelligent and trained subordinates, work might be produced which, if necessarily cold and conventional, should at least be orderly and have the merit of correctness. The characteristics of most of our national buildings may be explained by the conditions under which they have been designed, and therefore no one thinks of regarding them — as the corresponding structures in other civilized nations are regarded — as the highest and most deliberate expressions of national genius in architecture. They are big, costly, and, for the most part, soundly built of the most perfect materials, and with the best workmanship; but with some few exceptions, it has been practically impossible for them to exhibit those qualities of refinement, beauty, and fitness which can come only from special artistic study, and from that sort of inspiration which results from taking pains. They represent our talent for organization, but not our talent for art. The efforts of the American Institute of Architects to obtain legislation whereby the designs for Government buildings may, by direct selection, or by some adequate and just method of competition, be thrown into the hands of the best architects of the country — as is the case among other civilized nations — should, for these reasons, have the warm sympathy and coöperation of all who desire to see this great nation take its proper rank in the history of architecture. Until this is done, our national monuments will continue to be significant rather of our wealth than of our art.

The present architect of the Treasury Department, handicapped, as he is, by prodigious preoccupations and responsibilities, is to be congratulated on what he has been able to accomplish in the architectural outlines of the Government Building. We have seen that its main features are coördinate in plan and elevation; that a well-ordered project has been outlined with every proper regard for symmetry, for lighting, for economical structure, and for the due relation of important to inferior parts; and that as a whole the masses are well balanced. The design is based on Renaissance formulas, but, in respect to detail, when compared with the other buildings of the Exposition in the same style, it will be found to have the true Government stamp. The mind of the master has dictated successfully the general scheme, but the detail, in its facile but crude invention, in its profuse but unimaginative use of conventional phrases and symbols, betrays the fact that it has been developed officially and without the benefit of the master's honest and patient study. The fruits of such study, in the designs of most of the other buildings, which unavoidably challenge comparison with it, are visible in their intelligent respect for historical precedent, and in their knowledge of its proper use in the evolution of modern work, in the refinement and purity of their lines, in the clearness and delicacy of their expression, in their reserve of power, and in the fastidious conscience which has patiently chastened and corrected, has been prodigal of labor in rejecting and amending, and has thus made the work sensitive, elegant, and scholarly. The design of these buildings developed slowly in what Matthew Arnold would call an atmosphere of "sweetness and light." In fact, the organized division of labor in the office of the Government architect must of necessity be fundamentally inimical to the cultivation of true artistic feeling. The work which has resulted, with some few notable exceptions perhaps, constitutes a class by itself, peculiarly mechanical and automatic in character, and, for the most part, destitute of that sort of interest which comes from individuality of expression, and from studious adaptation to conditions of use, site, climate, materials, and environment. This official administration of design, whereby the public work is turned off with the most businesslike expedition, has played no unimportant part in the creation or encouragement of a certain architectural vernacular in our country, through the baneful imitations of untrained architects in private practice. This vernacular will continue to be a reproach to us until the true artist has had opportunity to express himself in our public monuments with the same deliberation which he has shown, and is showing, in his private work, and thus to create a school for a more healthy cultivation of style. Whatever qualities of individuality may have characterized and given interest to the private work of the Government architects, before and after they have taken upon themselves the burden of this office, these qualities have almost invariably disappeared while under the powerful influence of the Government system. These gentlemen have been like the Greek artists, who lost their peculiar and delicate power when they became the servants of Roman masters. They have been compelled to content themselves with the show and not the substance of art, and to acknowledge as their own a succession of cold and formal official monuments, in which the smallest amount of design has to do the largest service by unimaginative but costly repetitions, and which differ one from the other only by reason of the amount of the appropriation in each case, and, to a certain extent, because of the difference in their requirements, not according to the personal quality of the architect who has given to them the respectability of his name. He has laid aside his function as an artist, and has become a creature of politics, of administration, of classifications, and of formalisms.

If our Government could place the designing of its buildings in the hands of architects who have proved their ability to do justice to such great opportunities for professional distinction, the art of architecture would not only receive the encouragement which is due to it from one of the most enlightened nations of the world, but our public monuments would at last adequately express our civilization. In England, in France, in Germany, and, indeed, in all the great European countries, the public buildings are their highest and most characteristic efforts in art. It is the ambition of every architect to make himself worthy to be employed upon them. They constitute the great prizes of the profession. We cross the Atlantic to see the cities which they have made beautiful. In our own country enough of treasure has been appropriated for national buildings, and spent on them, to make our cities equally noble and attractive. But under the present system these opportunities have been worse than lost; for they have encouraged an unnecessary extravagance of expenditure without adequate return, and they offer no higher type to be accepted as the expression of our civilization than respectable conventionality and organized commonplace.

If the suggestive contrasts of quality in the buildings of the Exposition should serve no higher purpose than as an object-lesson to our legislators, teaching them that their responsibilities in respect to our national architecture are not properly discharged by maintaining a costly architectural factory in Washington, the unsubstantial pageant of Jackson Park will not have been in vain.

The Historic Styles and Modern Architecture

(1892–1893)

I.

When an intelligent student, having had no previous practical experience in an active office, graduates from a well-equipped and well-regulated school of architecture, if he has made a proper use of his opportunities with books and practice, he discovers on comparing the condition of his mind when he began his studies with that when he completed them, that he has gained, in some respects, not all that he expected, and in others, much more. On the whole, the result of his self-examination is a surprise.

It has been often observed that an ingenuous and open mind obtains with such an experience most of the advantages of a liberal education. His curriculum has included no Latin or Greek, and perhaps only a reading acquaintance with French, no course of general history or literature, and indeed none of the studies which we are accustomed to consider necessary to the equipment of a man of culture; yet, in his knowledge of the growth and true meaning of civilization and the philosophy of history, in the refinement and acuteness of his mind, in the fastidious delicacy of his perceptions, in the enlargement of his vision, and in the general discipline of his faculties, his friends perceive that he has acquired nearly all that can be acquired by following the more conventional and approved collegiate courses, and, indeed, something more.

The student, if he has been properly trained, has learned the processes by which the historic styles were slowly developed from their rude but poetic stages of archaism to the highest perfection of civilization; he has seen how certain types of form have become fixed in the human mind, and how, by contact with various races and under various political and religious conditions, these types have taken upon themselves various characteristics having evident relation to the spirit or genius of the people and the time. He has seen the early Greeks borrowing their first architectural forms from the Egyptians through their colonies in the delta of the Nile, and he has observed the reciprocal influence exercised by the quick-witted Greeks on the temples and palaces of the Ptolemies; he has seen the most venerable sacerdotal traditions, having their roots in the immemorial past far beyond the reach of recorded history, yielding to the genius of a race of predatory barbarians from the islands of the Ægean; he has seen the growth of Greek art, setting forth in the language of beautiful form the development of the most marvellous civilization in history; he has seen its perfection and its interruption by the conquest of the Romans; he has studied the history of Rome by its monuments, set up in every quarter of the Old World like the standards of conquerors, dominating and immutable, and has followed it to its decline and fall in the villas of the later emperors; he has learned by the same record in brick and marble the changes that came over the Roman spirit at Byzantium; how the genius of the Greek had its turn of triumph over the Roman, made a new civilization under the impulse of a new religion, and built the dome of St. Sophia; in the basilicas of Ravenna and Venice he has read how this new civilization turned to the West, and out of the ruins of pagan splendor developed new and prolific forms of vital beauty; how this Christian impulse travelled far and wide, creating the Romanesque of Milan, Perigeux, Caen, Peterborough, varying with the varying conditions of the races; how on the Isle de France the veritable mediæval spirit, breaking away from the cloisters of the monks and from the bonds of feudalism, began a new exposition of the power of the human mind, and created in two centuries, in the succession of the cathedrals, monuments of the new liberties of the cities; how this marvellous demonstration finally expired in splendor, and was in its turn replaced by the new birth of civilization, by the revival of learning, by the advent of the modern spirit, by the rediscovery of the world and man, as Michelet calls it,[1] all pictured in the palaces and churches of the Renaissance; how every nation and every reign gave to the formulas of the classic orders, which they borrowed from Italy, a new aspect in close sympathy with the spirit of place and time, assuming one general character of forms in Italy, one in France, one in Spain, one in England, one in Germany, each quickly reflecting the growth, character, and feeling of people and courts, every sovereign leaving upon these formulas a record of his reign. He has discovered, in short, that he has studied history from a new standpoint, as yet unattained by the historians. He has obtained, through his technical observation of the growth of styles, an insight into the sources of history denied to those who have obtained their knowledge from literature. He has a wider and more unprejudiced view of the growth of civilization, — a view unimpeded by the personal equation of historians, by their false deductions and literary moods; a view undazzled by personalities, and undisturbed by the immaterial accidents and incidents of the foreground. It has been his privilege to see the story of the development of the human mind under various conditions, written in large characters on the historic monuments, whose inner meanings have unconsciously been opened to him, while he was studying their masks of form, formulating their proportions, and saturating himself with their spirit. He thought he was merely learning the value of lines, colors, and combinations of beautiful or effective detail, when he was also familiarizing himself with the distinctive attitudes of the human mind which gave birth to them. When he was discovering for himself the characteristics of the orders and ornaments of Francis I. and Louis XV., of the Tudors and the Stuarts, he was also unconsciously learning the true spirit of each reign, and all the really essential points in their history. While he was studying the details of the vast façade of Notre Dame of Paris, he was becoming more familiar with the spirit of mediæval history than the students of Guizot or Montalembert.[2] M. Viollet-le-Duc, the only man who has ever written history from an architect's point of view, presents, in his "Dictionnaire Raissoné" (articles "Cathedral" and "Monastic Architecture") a clearer exposition of the mediæval story than any who have given us merely literary expositions of the same theme, without a knowledge of the monuments, which are infallible guides to truth.

This is what is meant when it is said that an exhaustive study of the historic styles is a liberal education, a discipline and refinement of the intellectual faculties, which is often seen reflected in the bearing and general tone of the student. "The conscientious practice of any fine art," says Mr. John Addington Symonds, "directs a man of ordinary talent on the path of real culture." [3]

But it should not be forgotten that, if the effect of this education of mind and hand is to make him a pedant, a precisian, a *doctrinaire*, an archæologist, it fails in its primary object. For an archæologist is not an architect. An archæological architect is a guardian of formulas; he stands isolated from his time, and has no function in advancing contemporary art. A school-project of a mausoleum in Roman Doric, of the house of an artist in the Renaissance of Vignola, of a triumphal bridge, of which the greatest virtue in the mind of the instructor is very properly its indication of the student's intelligent fidelity to ancient types, or even of a tomb or kiosk after the manner of the Caliphs, in which romantic imagination must be justified by technical loyalty to precedent, these are excellent means of discipline; they should be mastered by the student, but if they master him and if, in practice, he does not dare to get away from the letter of these instructions, he is lost.

But the immediate purpose of his exercise in the historic style has been not only in a general way to correct his taste, to sharpen his critical faculties, to teach him to respect the works of the past, and to make his hand the obedient servant of his trained intelligence, but to furnish him with a large vocabulary of conventional forms, to be used, not for their own sakes in quotations and imitations, in revivals and restorations, but, in subordination to the requirements and exactions of the practice of modern building, to express ideas of modern structure with the restrained freedom of a scholar and not with the license of ignorance. "I will walk at liberty," says the Psalmist, "for I seek thy commandments." [4]

The pride of knowledge, which is the comforting and reassuring possession

291

of every graduate of a college or of an architectural school, receives a severe and sometimes a dispiriting check when it comes in contact with the world, which demands that such knowledge must be adjusted to its wants. The architectural graduate, on entering an active office, speedily discovers that prosaic considerations of structure, of economy, of business, of convenience, of mechanical exactness, of adjustment of means to practical ends, seem not only to disregard, but even to insult his school knowledge. There appears at first sight to be but little use for the precepts and formulas which he has with so much pains acquired. Practice appears to have no respect for the doctrines of Vitruvius and Palladio, and demands of him sacrifices of theory which fill him with consternation. The fundamental conditions imposed upon him in the designing of a dwelling, of a commercial building, of a church, of a town hall, of a hotel, are essentially different from and more exacting than those upon which his classic school-projects were based.

The indispensable steel beam by which, in most mercantile buildings, he must cover the open voids of his first story and support the massive superstructure; the slender iron shafts by which he is constrained to uphold the great piers of his frontage; the fireproof envelope of his steel frame which reduces the masses of his masonry and enlarges his openings, — these and innumerable other considerations of structure, convenience, and economy seem to set at defiance those "statics of the eye," [5] as Viollet-le-Duc calls them, which have grown gradually out of the necessities of masonry construction, as practised before the application of modern science to construction, and as exhibited in the works of all the great architects of history.

Thus it seems impossible at first to reconcile theory and practice; but in considering the question what is meant by the preservation of the integrity of styles, we may be able to justify our methods of education and to define the correct relations of the historic styles to modern architecture.

In order to accommodate those conditions of living which must be met by some form of shelter, the various nations of the earth, starting from necessity, constructed buildings out of the most accessible materials, and combined these materials in the most convenient, unaffected, and economical manner. With the growth of civilization and the increasing complexity of requirements to be met by buildings, these original types experienced an enlargement, and in this process the forms originally imposed upon the primitive structure by convenience and necessity gradually became co-ordinate in a definite system. The instinct of mankind is to build beautifully and to ornament construction. The element of art was thus introduced, and the primitive types began to assume grace of proportion and detail, this grace taking its distinctive character from the innate genius of the people. These decorative forms soon became conventional by usage, and, with the increase of wealth, became richer and more complex, without, however, losing sight of the primitive type. The genius or spirit of the people thus became symbolized in their architecture, which, by a series of experiments, developed on certain defined lines, grew towards a perfection exactly indicating and ministering to the increasing prosperity of the race, and an historic style of architecture was at length established, different in general character and in detail from that of other nations, who, starting from different types, under different natural conditions, with a different spirit in each case, developed in different directions.

Now these various harmonious co-ordinations of conventional details, which constitute the historic styles, are all readily accessible to us in books, prints, and photographs; they can be studied, committed to memory, and assimilated. But when these styles are repeated, or imitated and forced into the service of modern work, under a natural impulse to preserve and perpetuate certain beautiful or interesting effects, modern architecture is not advanced a single step. The architect, in quoting these ancient formulas with pedantic exactness, is doing homage to the past, but doing no service to the present. His work is unintelligible to the public; he speaks in a foreign tongue; and from the point of view of art, the highest praise that can be awarded to him is that he is correct in his quotation. He is feigning impressions which he does not feel; he is posing in a masquerade. The more exact and learned is his quotation of forms, the greater is the anachronism. His Venetian Gothic or Renaissance, his Palladian classic, his mediæval English or French, his Northern or Southern Romanesque, precisely recalling in detail and general proportion the original monument which has appealed to his poetic sense, if built upon our city highways, is exotic, not only in form but in sentiment; its associations, whether social or political, belong to another civilization and another habit of thought; its ornaments are inspired by purposes and emotions with which our public can have no possible sympathy; its forms of doors and windows, base and cornice, are, in our effort to repeat their beautiful lines, rendered in a material for which they were not invented, and adjusted to a construction which they do not express.

In adapting the classic formulas to modern uses, however, it will be hereafter set forth in these papers why we must necessarily be restrained by traditions far more powerful, and by lines far more firmly established than those of any romantic styles.

We have seen every architect of a great and powerful nation of the nineteenth century, in the midst of astounding advances in all the sciences, with invention and discovery changing all the aspects of social life, trying to think and act like the builders of the thirteenth century, and uniting in an endeavor to assimilate pointed apertures, stone tracery, cuspidations, buttresses, pinnacles, crockets, grouped shafts, and gargoyles to the age of steel girders, plate glass, electricity, and scientific sanitation!

In the English Gothic revival, archæology reigned supreme for fifty years; architecture piously assumed stained-glass attitudes, and, disguised in a mask of mediæval romance, was happy in ascetic exclusions, while science was building ocean steamers, inventing the electric telegraph and telephone, bridging the Menai Straits, tunnelling the Alps, and laying rails across a continent. The English architects of that time were very precise in the forms of their mouldings; they were studiously solicitous that no detail of the so-called Decorated or Perpendicular subdivisions of the style should find its way into their early English monument; there must be authority for every part, derived from some accepted work of William of Wyckham or Alan de Walsingham.[6] They were, in short, engaged, with almost religious veneration, in the preservation of a style. They were glad to call their work by a strange name, "Victorian Gothic," thinking that while they were forcing their moral dogmas of art on the architecture of a museum of natural history, a town hall, a railway terminus, a London shop front, or a terrace of dwelling-houses, they were succeeding in adapting an old style to new conditions (Figs. 81, 84, 85, 87). They failed, because the art which they revived could not live and grow in the atmosphere into which they had transplanted it with such honest and earnest endeavor. It was inflexible to modern civic uses, and their favorite dogma of truth of material could not be applied to sash windows, steel girders, street fronts of plate glass, fireproof construction of iron and terra-cotta or brick, to all the uses, in short, of an era of unprecedented wealth, ingenuity, and common sense, without an entire surrender of the Gothic formulas, and a complete forgetfulness of their historic and religious associations. A frank acceptance of modern conditions of structure, material, and use entirely smothered both the letter and the spirit of mediævalism. The conservative energy of the English people prolonged the interesting experiment sufficiently to give to the preservation of this style a thorough and comprehensive trial, and when at last Mr. Norman Shaw had the courage to start his Dutch Reform in the revival of the brick pseudo-classic of Queen Anne, the profession was glad to forget its morals and its Gothic for the sake of a new mistress and a less strait-laced theory of architectural design (Fig. 92).

But the Gothic style had the advantage of being a system of interrelated forms evolved directly from a principle of construction, which Mr. Charles Moore,[7] following Viollet-le-Duc, has proved to be a roof vaulted with small stones, and rendered stable by the counter thrusts of buttresses. All the essential characteristics of Gothic architecture were derived directly from this fundamental condition. The structure and the form consequently belong together and constitute a homogeneous system, but one which was proved in the fourteenth century to have exhausted its capacity for progression. It could not go beyond the cathedral of Amiens or Rheims. In these heroic monuments of decorated and economic construction the style was completed and perfected, and the efforts of the modern English architects to preserve the style by endeavoring to correctly repeat some of its less characteristic manifestations in an age when roofs are no longer vaulted with stone, but constructed with steel, iron, terra-cotta, sheet metal, and slate, when we are necessarily controlled by the intensely practical dictates of underwriters and building ordinances, when windows are no longer glazed with leaded quarries, nor mansions built for defence against feudal convulsions, was a wasteful and unprofitable error.

On the other hand, the style (so called) of Queen Anne, which replaced it in England, was rather a subdivision of a style, a quaint and curious phase of the classic Renaissance, an expression of

> The teacup times of hood and hoop,
> And when the patch was worn.[8]

Though it lends itself to modern uses and structure more readily than Gothic, it cannot aid us in the evolution of modern style, which is the proper function of the architect, because, in reviving it and adapting it, we are simply affecting to speak and talk in the language of Addison and Steele, instead of using that more copious vocabulary which has grown out of our new life and our larger experience. Like the Gothic, it cannot be adjusted to our modern uses without losing its essential characteristics, and becoming unrecognizable as the style of Queen Anne (Figs. 49, 56). It becomes a barren hybrid. If we aim to preserve the style in its integrity, we are committing another anachronism. We have hardly yet ceased to be pleased with the novelty of the windows, which, with their reticulation of small panes, carrying the wall surface like tracery across the openings, eliminates from our façades the black and expressionless holes which result from the use of great sheets of polished plate glass; and yet this is a very noble material, and common sense requires us to use it in its own way and make an architecture to conform to it. We still recognize the charm of the stepped gables with their consoles, the carved brick panels, the broken pediments, the tall chimney stacks, the ball-finials, the tortured classic orders, because they remind us perhaps of the Prince of Orange, of Swift, of Mrs. Esmond, and Thackeray's novels. But when we know how to use pure classic, why should we use adulterated and depraved classic for the sake of a fashion which does not express the spirit of our time, but quite another spirit? It is incapable of development; it is not a survival of the fittest; and if we are to be led by duty, which is serious, instead of taste, which is trifling and dilettante, it is useless for us to amuse ourselves and spend our clients' money in preserving the integrity of such a style.

There was a much more serious motive involved in the pseudo-Gothic revival; for the movement never would have held possession of the Anglo-Saxon mind for more than half a century, if it had been a mere matter of fashion. Fashions are proverbially fickle and inconstant, because they do not rest upon principle. But the Gothic revival was not only patriotic, it was moral, almost religious; it was the result of an eloquent appeal from taste and prejudice to reason. The polemics of Pugin, Ruskin, Eastlake, Street, and a score of inferior essayists on the part of the English, and of Victor Hugo[9] and Viollet-le-Duc, on the part of the French, conferred upon the movement the dignity of a reform, of which the watchword was truth. But it was mediæval truth, not abstract truth, which they virtually taught, and the architectural disciples of these literary masters did not succeed in separating the principle from the form, the spirit from the letter. They were, in fact, more concerned with the preservation of the integrity of a style, than with the attempt to elevate modern architecture so that it might fitly express the modern spirit by the application of the principles which had guided the Greeks and the lay architects of the Middle Ages to their distinctive triumphs.

II.

That most thoughtful and suggestive writer, Mr. John Addington Symonds, to whom these papers are indebted for several encouraging confirmations of the views which it seeks to express, observed, in his recent essay on Culture: "No great and spontaneous growths of art have arisen in an age of erudition and assimilation. The Greek drama, the Gothic style of architecture, the romantic drama of Elizabethan England, were products, not of cultivated taste, but of instinctive genius." Again: "Herder taught this fundamental truth to Goethe: really great poetry has always been the product of a national spirit, and not the product of studies confined to the select few." [10]

All educated architects in France, and lately in our own country, have had their taste cultivated, their feeling for proportion refined, their instincts of form purified, and all their artistic capacities enlarged and enlightened by the study and academic practice of the Italian Renaissance. France is the only nation which has consistently followed the classic dogma outside the schools. Indeed, ever since the battle of Marignano, in 1515, the artistic culture of France has been controlled by the Italian Renaissance. It sends the best pupils of its academy to the Villa Medici every year, so that the classic traditions may be constantly refreshed and purified by draughts at their very fountain-head. From the preservation of these traditions in the practice of architecture there have been the Greek defections of Henri Labrouste and Duc (Figs. 94, 96, 96a), the Gothic defections of Lassus and Viollet-le-Duc, and perhaps a Romanesque defection in ecclesiastical work, but the characteristic art of the French nation has been classic for three centuries and a half. But, from the time of Francis I. to the present day, this classic work has not only had a distinctive French character, but it has borrowed from the characteristics of every court traits so marked that we recognize a style of Henry IV., of Louis XIV., XV., and XVI., of the Empire, of Louis Philippe, etc., all of them differing from the Italian Renaissance, which was their model. Thus, with a people of thorough training, artistic genius, and imaginative power, the preservation of a style does not take the form of pedantic archæology, which imitates but which does not create, which, in attempting to recall an ancient spirit, disregards the contemporary spirit, and, in a sort of scholarly inertia of contemplation and study, permits the genius of the current time to go without expression.

It is impossible to say whether the creative genius, even of the French people, if their practice of the national Gothic formulas had not been interrupted at the beginning of the sixteenth century by the irresistible invasion of the Italian Renaissance, would have been able out of this purely native style to develop a style as sensitive and elastic as that which we have been considering. The last expressions of this native art hardly showed marks of fatigue. The wing of Louis XII. at Blois was still Gothic and apparently full of life, and the possibilities of expansion, though erected at the end of the fifteenth century. Yet one cannot study the first French experiment in the Renaissance made fifty years later in the adjoining wing of Francis I., without being satisfied that the time for a change from the old order of things had arrived, and that the new spirit of civilization demanded a new expression far removed from all the associations and limitations of mediævalism, — an expression of joy, relief, triumph, of which the Gothic tongue was incapable. It was a tongue which had long since uttered its most beautiful words under an impulse which could never occur again. The fundamentally changed conditions of life in the sixteenth century required an architecture different from that developed from the structure of the cathedrals.

On the other hand, it is capable of demonstration that the French graduates of the school of Fine Arts, if the course of history had not constrained them to compose with classic materials, would have found, in some historic style which had never exhausted itself, potencies which they could have developed into an architectural scheme quite as elastic. Indeed, the American graduates of this school, unembarrassed by national traditions and stimulated by a free atmosphere, have not found it difficult even in a brief time to make with such a style a beginning more full of life and promise than any so-called revival hitherto attempted (Figs. 101, 106–110b, 129).

But what are the elements in the Italian classic which have made it, in the hands of the French, so much more elastic than the Gothic of the thirteenth century proved itself to be in the hands of the modern English?

We learned among our earliest lessons in architecture that when the Romans, in order to make their empire more splendid, and the symbols of their power more imposing, desired to decorate their massive arched and vaulted constructions of brick or concrete, they seized upon the delicate orders of the Greeks, organized them into a highly artificial system of columns, pilasters, and entablatures, enriched them far beyond the chaste dreams of the builders of the Parthenon and the Erechtheum, and applied them to their work, not as an expression of construction, but as an ornament of pure convention. Vast naked ruins of their vaulted piles still remain in every part of the Old World, but their marble vesture of pseudo-Greek ornament disappeared centuries ago. Although this decorative envelope of their baths, their amphitheatres, palaces, basilicas, forums, bridges, triumphal arches, and aqueducts had no essential relation to the structure which they covered, and although the system of forms, which was thus converted into a mere decoration by the Romans, was a direct development from the structure of the Greeks and a poetic expression of that structure, nevertheless this system, even when merely parasitic to the Roman arch and vault, received at the hands of the Romans a development of its own, which never became entirely capricious and always respected its Greek origin. The elegant Roman used Greek words and Greek phrases in his conversation and in his writings, to enable him to express his growing complications of thought with greater freedom and precision. Every

297

educated Roman could speak Greek and prided himself on his Greek scholarship. Virgil was a Roman Homer; Cicero, a Roman Demosthenes; the Roman dramatists followed Greek lines: but they were always Roman. In like manner, the Roman architects used the Greek formulas in a scholarly manner to confer upon their architecture a degree of elegance and refinement adequate to express their wealth and luxury. But their building enterprises were on a scale so vast and unprecedented that the innate capacity of these formulas to express magnificence was strained to the utmost. From the modest suggestions of the choragic monument of Lysicrates was thus naturally developed the pomp and splendor of the Roman Corinthian; the pure beauty of the Athenian Acropolis was expanded into the imperial opulence of the Palatine mount. But the Romans were too proud of their Greek scholarship to vulgarize what they borrowed from their conquered province. If Greek letters and art had not been imposed upon the Roman mind by their pre-eminent beauty and by their convenient accessibility, what we now call Romanesque art, so far as this art is the expression of the Roman arch, vault, and dome, would have undoubtedly been developed by the Romans themselves, though what forms this pure pagan Romanesque would have assumed it is unprofitable for us now to discuss. The authors of Romanesque art, though they did far more than the Romans themselves to develop the artistic capacities of Roman structure, in rejecting the frank paganism of the Greek orders, gave to this structure a certain spiritual character derived directly from Christian inspiration. The Northern barbarians might have given suggestions to affect the formation of a pagan Romanesque; they certainly would not have refined it.

Thus the Greek orders, in becoming the Roman orders, lost in the main their connection with structure, but they still remained *orders*; that is, each one having grown into definite shape by long usage, and into perfection by the study of the greatest artists in the world, had the force of a dogma; it was associated with, and, indeed, the expression of, an especial political, religious, and social system; it was a creed not to be trifled with so long as the past was respected. But the development which the orders received as decorative formulas was different from that to which they would have submitted if they had remained structural expressions in Rome as they had been in Greece. Yet they are none the less worthy of respect and study on this account. It is true that this development of classic forms under these conditions was not naïve nor strictly logical, as was the case with the mediæval development; on the contrary, it was sophisticated and highly artificial. Their growth was on lines, not of necessity, but of artifice, kept within boundaries defined by certain venerable traditions. The accretions which they received in the course of their progress through history were derived, not from science, but from art, not from economic conditions, but from the creative instincts of mankind. No other set of forms has ever been subjected to an exclusive influence of this sort, none has been used in the service of so many and such various civilizations, and none, therefore, is so closely associated with humanity and the progress of mankind.

Roman civilization was so deeply indebted to that of Greece that its architecture would not have been loyal to its august function to express the essential truths of history if it had failed to be affected by the Greek spirit in just
the same way. The innate genius and strength of the Roman character was
made visible in the concrete massiveness of their great arches and vaults, and
in the ordered complexity of their structures. Its refinement and culture were
rather imposed upon it by Greek influence than a natural development of inborn capacity, just as the Greek orders, which are the symbol of this culture,
were imposed upon the massive Roman arches and vaults as a decoration.
In this service they experienced a certain magnificent sensuous expansion.
They were gradually loaded with expressions of the pride, luxury, and power
of this dominant race. If the original types in this superb growth lost somewhat of their original subtle grace, assumed when they were still expressions
of simple but stately structure, they gained, when used as an ornament, new
qualities, for which they were but slightly, if at all, indebted to structure, and
which, therefore, grew directly and unimpeded out of the spirit of the people.
Hence came a decorative system so large, complicated, magnificent, and peculiar, that notwithstanding the opposition of schools of purists, which from
time to time have arisen to declare that all decoration which is not an expression of structure and use is immoral and depraved, it has exercised and
will continue to exercise a powerful influence upon the architecture of all
peoples who remember and respect the sources of modern civilization.

When the world was, as it were, created anew by the Renaissance, the
Italian masters of the fifteenth century took up these almost forgotten classic
formulas, and, by the power of intelligent experiment, gave to them a refinement and an elegance even greater than they had received at the hands of
the ancient Romans, and a specific character entirely in harmony with the
new civilization. As we have already indicated, the formulas thus modified
have since been used successively by all the nations of Europe, and indeed by
all the civilized races of mankind, and each one has found in the highly organized system of forms a language capable of expressing the noblest thoughts
which can be expressed in architecture, and has so used it that unconsciously
it has ceased to be Italian, and has become French, German, English, Spanish,
Russian, American, and so on. In fact, the Italian Renaissance developed
modern culture.

Now this language, the artful product of so many civilizations, has become
a court language, — a language of formal and stately courtesy and often of
pedantry, — which naturally only people of cultivation can entirely understand and appreciate. To the vast mass of people it is more or less unintelligible, and therefore apparently they take but little interest in it. Moreover,
the artist who speaks in this language finds himself more or less preoccupied
and clogged with classical reminiscences and precedents. His culture super-
sedes his originality. He is thus hampered in two ways. Yet he delights to
design in pure Renaissance, to recall in his work the most delicate and beautiful details which he has seen mellowing in the palaces of Rome, Venice, and

Genoa, to quote from the pages of his Letarouilly,[11] to be exact in his use of classic precedents, to reverence the works of the masters, and thus to be another agent for the preservation of classic style. This practice, like that of virtue, is its own exceeding great reward; but, as in classic music, it requires knowledge to appreciate it. He has no public who can stimulate him with its applause, or correct him with its censure. Self-culture is absolutely indispensable, but it does not in itself create a living art. The scholar, whose mind and heart are so prepossessed by his classicism, is not unlike the euphuist of the fifteenth century, whose affected but copious vocabulary, whose alliterations, consonances, and verbal antitheses, however fine in themselves, and however they may have ultimately contributed to the flexibility and verbal resources of the later English, were quite unintelligible to people of mere common sense.

When the board of architects who were summoned from various parts of the country to assist in the designing of the principal buildings of the World's Columbian Exposition at Chicago, began to consider together in what style the principal buildings, forming the great court of honor at Jackson Park, should be composed, they had no difficulty whatever in reaching a decision. In the entire absence of any distinctively American style capable of giving adequate expression to our position in history, it was evident that the great court wherein the guests of the nation were to be received, and where they should be welcomed with stately ceremony, should be surrounded by buildings of a style most associated with modern civilization, a style so organized and accepted that personal fancy or caprice should have the smallest possible scope in it (Figs. 141–145). It was, therefore, decided that the work should be in classic as pure as our scholarship could command, and on a scale commensurate with the intention of our hospitality. By this decision it was not proposed that the architects of our country were to pose before the world as the conservators of traditions, but to show that the youngest of the nations respects and understands the past and acknowledges its fundamental indebtedness to classic art; in a wider sense perhaps, that the grandeur of the work which America is now doing in the world is in reality based upon a wise conservatism, and that our civilization does not affect to be independent of the experience of mankind in history.

In applying this ordered and established historic style to the great buildings of the Exposition, though it was agreed that, as nearly as possible, a common module of proportion should be used, that the height from the grade line to the top of the cornice should be sixty feet, and that each building should include along its entire frontage an open portico, the result has not been a tedious monotony, but a variety in unity as marked as it is possible to conceive. Such results, so orderly yet so various, could not have been accomplished by the use on a similar scale of any other style known to us. No Romanesque style, no style of the Middle Ages, no Oriental style, whether Indian, Arabic, or Saracenic, has been developed under such conditions as would have made it possible to revive it in the buildings of the Exposition without converting it into a romantic masquerade, in which the personalities of the architects would have inevitably intruded themselves to such an extent as to deprive the *mise en scene* of its unity of effect. We should have procured variety, but the variety would have been capricious and disorderly; it would have represented, not the discipline, but the diversity of our knowledge.

The historic styles are divided by their essential conditions into two great classes, viz., the classic and the romantic. Now, when we are considering the question as to the advisability of preserving the integrity of the styles in modern practice, the fundamental difference between these two classes is forced upon us.

Taking the Romanesque, as perhaps at present the most familiar of the romantic styles, on account of our recent prolonged experiments with it, it must be evident that it can be of no possible use to us if we treat it as archæologists, and attempt to preserve its integrity as an historic style, to repeat with unimaginative fidelity the rude vigor of its undeveloped detail. It can only serve us in our efforts to develop modern style by applying, not its letter, but its spirit to our modern building necessities; and these necessities, both of structure and use, differ so fundamentally from those which existed in the eleventh and twelfth centuries in Normandy and Auvergne that, if we hamper ourselves with the antiquarian conformities of this style, we are simply affecting to be rude when we ought to be refined, to be strict when we ought to be free, to dream in the past when we ought to act in the present, to restrain our inventive powers when we ought to be giving them the largest liberty. With a romantic style we can only progress by testing its remotest possibilities of expansion, while preserving, as far as possible, the spirit which gave to it character and expression. If the style, like the pure Gothic, does not admit of such expansion, it of course cannot be made the medium of progressive architecture. A modern church is as different from a mediæval church as a modern mansion is different from a "moated grange." [12] Mere archæological loyalty to mediævalism cannot satisfy such a problem. At this point our safety is in the discretion and training of the scholar, our danger in the license of ignorant invention.

The value of education in giving discipline and refinement to the mind and in enabling it to appreciate the true spirit of the historic styles, and their proper relations to the civilization of our time, has never been so emphatically vindicated as in the Romanesque revival begun by Mr. Richardson. A survey of the broadening field of effort in this movement will clearly prove that the imitations of the uneducated have been coarse, vulgar, affected, and capricious, and are a drag upon its progress; while the experiments of the trained intelligences of the profession have, so far as we can see, gradually eliminated from the style its archaic elements, which are out of keeping with the modern spirit, and have permitted its finer possibilities to be developed far beyond the apparent promise of the ancient monuments. These experiments have of late been conducted, not with the purpose of preserving the integrity of a certain historic style, but, as the style had never been brought to perfection and thus exhausted, to ascertain whether its hidden potencies could be developed so that it could be used in the service of a progressive and living modern art, without losing its primary virtues of vigor and sincerity. It has been proved that the style was not so entangled with "a creed outworn," [13] and not so indissolubly a part of a superannuated system of building that its desirable qualities could not be used with good effect, and indeed with the promise of a brilliant future in modern work. These desirable qualities are recognizable even in work where modern structure and modern necessities have been most cruel in their exactions and most inconsistent with the preservation of the integrity of any historic style. The style has borne the crucial test of application to a narrow frontage crowded with windows and ten or fifteen stories high with reasonable success (Figs. 121, 124–133, 136, 137). It has been applied to modern churches, dwellings, schoolhouses, libraries, and public buildings of all sorts, and its capacities do not seem to be exhausted. There has been of course plenty of wearisome iteration of familiar motifs; but there has also been a steady progress of development, much more marked than was exhibited in fifty years of experience with the Gothic revival.

Thus the proper treatment of a romantic style in modern work is not to preserve it with the loyalty of the antiquarian, but to develop it with the freedom of the artist. It should be revived, not to control the faculties of designing, but to be controlled by them. On the other hand, classic art presents itself to the modern architect with all the majesty of authority and all the imposing beauty of a perfected language of form. It has expressed the highest civilizations that mankind has achieved, since the Renaissance; it has been formulated outside the restrictions of structure into various purely decorative systems, each representing the most advanced culture of its time. The Gothic purists have stigmatized it as immoral, because, in its modern forms, it is not a growth from mechanical conditions of construction, and consequently does not stand for any idea of truth. They have aimed to prove that to design in this style is not to advance the art of our time by a process of development, but to retard it by superstitious reverence for mere formulas, stiff with traditions, and sophisticated by the pedantry of schools. The obvious answer to these objections is that conformity to classic art and to its historic derivations, with its dogmas of perfect proportion and more or less absolute detail, is to the modern architect a constant service of refinement and purification. In confining his work within certain strict artificial limits, it gives to his study of detail a finer and more discriminating tone and calls for a higher quality of invention. It elevates the composition of ornament into a region of more delicate and more perfect art. The mental effort which this composition compels brings into play springs of human action far more subtle and delicate than those which are touched by the less highly organized styles. If it is our duty to express with our art the civilization of our time, this function could not be fulfilled if we should neglect the style which calls for the exercise of the finest capacities of our culture. Renaissance architecture, in its innumerable manifestations, has been the chosen language in which the greatest architects and most advanced societies of the human race have expressed themselves for more than four centuries. Everything that has been achieved during that spacious era in poetry, in music, in painting, in sculpture, is correlative and coincident with it. In all that it has done it has remained loyal to the formulas of the classic orders, and upon these perfect systems of proportion has been embroidered the essential spirit of all the modern civilizations. By this accumulation it has become the repository of the highest and most beautiful thoughts of mankind which can be expressed in form. We have no doubt that the most cultivated, most learned, and most refined ideas of our race will continue to be expressed in this eloquent language for centuries to come; and though the necessary conditions of these expressions must continue to be the preservation of the integrity of the classic style, we shall see in the future variations upon this august theme at least as marked as those which exist between the Renaissance of Florence, Venice, or Rome, and that of Paris, Madrid, or London (Figs. 178, 179, 183, 188–194).

It is true that the most admirable qualities in the styles of the Renaissance are too technical and artificial to be fully appreciated by the people whose sympathy it should be our effort to win; nevertheless, a great part of what civilized man has to say in architecture can never be said so well in any other style.

The Gothic, the Romanesque, the Saracenic styles all grew out of special conditions of life. Certain races of mankind at certain times have developed these styles, carried them on toward or to perfection, and abandoned them, leaving their monuments along the highways of the world as marks of civilizations outgrown, of political or social systems which had no longer any excuse for existing, or which had been conquered by systems more powerful than themselves. It is certain that more fertile germs of new styles may be found in these than in any of the classic formulas, because the vigor of life is in the primitive types, unconscious of their strength, while in the classic formulas we may discover only its culture and refinement.

No one can predict whether the architecture of our own time is to advance on classic or romantic lines. But it is certain that this advancement can be secured only by preserving the integrity of the former, and by developing the latter with the largest liberty to the utmost limits of their hidden powers. In the former the modern spirit will continue to find expression unconsciously and without intention. The finer elements of this spirit must become visible in the Renaissance of the future, as the corresponding elements of the character of all the nations which have used this most potent art have been revealed in the Renaissance of the past. In the romantic styles, on the other hand, the modern spirit will find its expression by conscious effort to develop them. We may perhaps fairly expect that the most obvious advances toward the establishment of a modern style will be made on romantic lines because of their flexibility to modern structure. Yet classic art will always be with us to elevate and purify our ideal, and to correct the inevitable tendency of the modern mind to wander in regions of unprofitable invention. Will the architecture of the future grow out of some strange amalgam of these conflicting styles, as yet unattempted or unimagined; or will the science of construction, with new materials and new methods, work out at length an architectural fulfilment, independent of precedent? The evolutions of our art are too much involved with unknown conditions of human life to permit us at present even to approach a solution of this problem.

The Columbian Exposition
and American Civilization

(1893)

When a few practical men of affairs, capitalists, bank presidents, manufacturers, merchants, lawyers, were deputed, three years ago, by their fellow-citizens of Chicago, to formulate a scheme for the celebration of the four hundredth anniversary of the landing of Columbus in the western hemisphere by an International Exposition of all the arts and sciences, to be held in that city, it is not probable that they had seriously in mind anything so chimerical as the establishment of a great movement of civilization. Common sense is not apt to work upon any such visionary lines. The elements which gave shape and force to the preliminary consultations were not of a kind to dream of a propaganda of social ideas. And yet, if these gentlemen had deliberately contemplated some such revolutionary proposition as this, their action could not have been more wisely directed to the achievement of this very end.

The progress of civilization is by slow processes of development, in which it is difficult to detect any recognizable points of departure, any definite initial force. These processes are usually growths from seed planted at no especial date, at no easily found place, and by no especial person or persons. They are evolutions out of the dark into the light, and their character is controlled by the genius of races, by influences of environment, and by accidents of history. It may not be difficult, however, to prove that in the age of Pericles, in the Italian Cinquecento, in the defection of Luther, in the court of Queen Elizabeth, may be found four of these points of departure. In the Columbian Exposition we are probably destined to see a fifth, which, for reasons not hard to give, may perhaps be more definite and recognizable than any of the others.

It is now generally conceded that the choice of Chicago, instead of New York, as the seat of this Exposition, has already been fully justified by its results. New York is the commercial metropolis of the country, and, like London, Paris, Vienna, Berlin, and Philadelphia, the seats of previous Expositions, is in the midst of a thickly populated region, enjoying all the fruitions of an elaborate civilization, more or less familiar with and influenced by the best achievements of mankind in every department of human effort, with established institutions of higher culture, with galleries and schools of art, museums, monuments, and all the incitements of a complicated and ordered social life. Under such circumstances, centres like these can hardly be as impressionable as the Western metropolis. The distinction may be clearly drawn that in the former the Exposition was in each case rather emulative than instructive; in the latter it will prove more instructive than emulative.

Chicago is the nucleus of a vast interior country, newly occupied by a prosperous people, who are without local traditions; who have been absorbed in the development of its virgin resources; and who are more abounding in the out-of-door energies of life, more occupied by the practical problems of existence, more determined in their struggle for wealth and knowledge, than any people who ever lived. This nation within a nation is not unconscious of its distance from the long-established centres of the world's highest culture, but it is full of the sleepless enterprise and ambitions of youth; it has organized power, natural ability, quickened apprehensions, and rapidly increasing wealth; it knows its need of those nobler ideals and higher standards which are of such difficult access to a people engaged in the comparatively coarse work of laying the foundations and raising the solid walls of material prosperity. The new nation is now ready to adorn this great fabric, to complete and refine it, and to fit it for a larger life and a wider usefulness. It is like a machine, which requires only those more delicate creative touches necessary to bring its complicated adjustments into perfect working condition, so that it may become effective as a part of the civilizing energy of our time. Books, lectures, and all the apparatus of schools and colleges are meanwhile doing their work in this field.

The most distinctive social feature of Western town life, as compared with that of the East, is the frank earnestness with which these conscious people are seeking for a higher life, and trying to repair the defects of an education less liberal than their present conditions demand. Every town, every village, has its societies for mutual improvement. Grown men and women, in all the grades of social life, go to school again in their clubs, and study history, art, science, literature, with the same energy and enthusiasm which they apply to the accumulation of wealth. University extension is not a diversion, but a most serious occupation. Their organized efforts to realize and comprehend, by literature, prints, and photographs, what is meant by the great achievements in painting, sculpture, and architecture — often with most insufficient means — are pathetic, but most significant of the expectant, awaiting condition of the Western mind. The people of the East and of the Old World can have no comprehension of the eagerness and sincerity with which the West is pursuing, under many difficulties, the study of better culture.

All this slow-working machinery would in due time, of course, unaided, and without the interposition of some such great demonstration of the arts

306

and sciences as will be furnished by the Columbian Exposition, accomplish the work of transition, and the West would presently find itself playing its due part in giving not only grain and cattle, but "sweetness and light," to the rest of the world.

If it were possible to include, in a history of the International Expositions, a correct statement of the influences exerted by them over the industries of the world, it would be found that each furnished a forward impetus of its own to all those elements which make up the civilization of the epoch. When any nation on these great arenas of emulation gave evidence of superior attainments in any art or science, in any production of hand or brain, it gave also to the other nations the most powerful incentive to emulate and to surpass the model. If the great Panhellenic festivals served continually to advance the standard of manly virtues among the Greeks, and to keep in constant and productive tension all their best capacities for moral and mental effort, the modern industrial Expositions have done much more for civilization, and on a much higher scale of human endeavor. The intervals between these Expositions have been Olympiads in the history of our times, in which all the energies of the nations have been exerted to secure the solidarity and progress of the race, and, by a constant advancement of the standards of emulation, to keep the various branches of the human family fairly abreast. The first London Exposition,[1] for example, surprised the English people into a realization of their inferior rank in the fine arts, and in all those industries in which art is an element of production. The whole nation was immediately stimulated by a noble zeal to remedy its proved deficiencies, and subsequent Expositions showed how the wholesome lesson had been taken to heart, and with what success the new standards of achievement were reached.

The Exposition of 1893 will have a similar work to do in this country; but the field over which it has to exert its beneficent influences is a very different field from that of England, France, Austria, Italy, Germany, or even our own Eastern seaboard, of which Philadelphia was the centre in the centennial year. Here it will do far more than merely to supplement the slow but sure and steady function of schools and universities, societies and museums, in the work of civilization; it will not only anticipate this function in time, and give to the progress of the nation, especially of the West, a sudden and mighty forward impulse, which will be felt for generations, but its influence will have an infinitely wider range than could possibly result from the efforts of any number of institutions of liberal or technical training. The Exposition will furnish to our people an object lesson of a magnitude, scope, and significance such as has not been seen elsewhere. They will for the first time be made conscious of the duties, as yet unfulfilled, which they themselves owe to the civilization of the century. They will learn from the lessons of this wonderful pageant that they have not as yet taken their proper place in the world; that there is something far better worth doing than the mere acquiring and spending of wealth; that the works of their hands, their products, their manufactures, are not necessarily the best in the world; that their finer arts are in nearly every

respect deficient in finish and in aim; that, with all their acknowledged ingenuity in the manipulation and manufacture of the coarser staples and products, there are, perhaps, foreign methods more certain, more economical, or
productive of better results; that in various departments of finer manufactures,
in furniture, in the weaving of cottons, linens, silks, woolens, velvets, and in
the designing of the more delicate fabrics, in machinery of all sorts, possibly
in implements, certainly in educational appliances, and wherever science or
art in its best sense has been adapted to industrial uses, there is much to be
learned from the older nations; that tariffs alone and all the other political
devices of protection cannot, in another century of exclusion, bring their productions to a parity with those of countries whose industries are governed only
by the natural laws of supply and demand. They will discover that in painting,
in sculpture, in music, they have scarcely begun to appreciate, much less to
produce, objects of fine art; and that, by cultivating the arts which are not
practically useful, their lives may be made much better worth living, more
fruitful, more full of real enjoyment, and larger in every respect. They will be
suddenly confronted by new ideals and inspired by higher ambitions; they
will find in themselves qualities hitherto unsuspected, capacities for happiness
and powers of production hitherto unknown. They will obtain, in short, a
higher standard by which to measure their own shortcomings and deficiencies;
and if, in some lines of human effort, they are themselves able to set up standards higher than the rest of the world, and find that in these things the world
must come to them to be taught, they will realize that in most other respects
they are in a position of pupilage.

Such a realization by such a people will bear fruit, not in the apathy of mortification and defeat, but in that condition of noble discontent which carries
with it its own speedy correction. Every mechanic who, on visiting the Exposition, discovers that his fellow-workers in England, or France, or Germany,
or Italy, or Turkey, or China, or Japan, have shown, with the same materials,
better workmanship, or accomplished nobler results of beauty or fitness, than
he has yet dreamed of, will no longer be satisfied with his old ideals. Every
workshop, factory, laboratory, and studio in the land will be conscious of a
new impulse. It will be impossible for any man, woman, or child, capable of
receiving impressions, to visit this great treasury of all the industries of hand
and brain without being quickened with new energies. The low routines of
life will be broken by a spirit of reform. New shoots will be grafted on the old
homely but vigorous stock; and the fruitage should have a larger and more
vigorous growth, if there is any virtue left in that native force of character
which is making a family of commonwealths in the wild prairies of the West.

We may, indeed, in the midst of these surprises, comfort ourselves with
the assurance that the most remarkable of all the exhibits to be shown the
foreigner in this year will be the spectacle of the new nation, in the midst of
which is placed its precious but transient jewel, the Columbian Exposition.
And yet, in a vast region of this wild country which it is subjecting to its uses,
— a country already with abundant population, increasing wealth, and vast

resources as yet undeveloped, — there are practically no museums or galleries of art equipped to teach great lessons in a great way, and but few public libraries, none of the higher manufactures, little to stimulate imagination or refine life, no high ideals, no standards of delicate or difficult workmanship in products of art. Daily life here is narrowed and imagination is sterilized by the dreary repetitions of mercantile or agricultural employment. Education, among the greater part of the population, is limited to the elements which may be acquired in the common schools, and to the doubtful influence of newspapers and periodicals. Many lives are begun and finished without seeing a work of good art, in painting, sculpture, or architecture; without being aroused from the apathy of a dull and colorless existence by any object lesson in the higher regions of human effort. The farmers and their families, the ranchmen, the stock-raisers, who form so large a part of the population, are isolated from the centres of moral and intellectual life, and are so engrossed in the occupations of the soil that they are unconscious of their higher capacities, and have absolutely nothing to stimulate their mental energies or awaken their dormant faculties. When they have gathered wealth, they have no idea how to use it to the best advantage. They are hungry for knowledge.

Thus the field is fallow, but full of immense possibilities. In the midst of it, the managers of the Columbian Exposition are gathering together from the wide world examples of the best and noblest results of thought and workmanship in every department of activity and enterprise, and establishing ideals and standards far beyond the dreams of most of their fellow-citizens; they are, in fact, creating a university, open to all, where the courses of instruction cover all the arts and sciences, and are so ordered that to see is to learn. They are installing the objects which are to illustrate these courses, not within mere shelters or sheds, devised only to facilitate classification and arrangement, but in monuments of art, representing in themselves, individually and collectively, the best and highest uses of the art of architecture. No university was ever so majestically housed. The courses relating to mechanics, agriculture, manufactures, and the liberal arts, electricity, mining, transportation, horticulture, the fisheries, the fine arts, the science of government, history, and all the other branches of learning, are each set forth in a palace, in which architecture, sculpture, and painting have combined to make it fit for its high service (Figs. 141–158). In its adornments every artisan will find his own occupation idealized, and will read in its friezes the names of those of his fellow-workmen who have, in the practice of his own art or trade, made themselves illustrious in the history of the world. When the visitor enters the great Court, he will find himself cloistered as never scholar was cloistered before. No philosopher or disciple of the Academy ever walked and meditated in such porches. The great Basin in the midst, with its tributary canals, the terraces and balustrades which surround it, the statues, the monumental fountains, the vases, the bridges, the standards, the rostral columns, the gardens, the kiosks and shelters, are arranged to show that order is heaven's first law (Figs. 142–144). To walk in these grounds will be in itself an education, as well as a pleasure of the most ennobling sort. The whole is on a scale of beauty and magnificence far beyond what the greatest masters of art have provided for emperors and kings. The gateway and vestibule of this university introduce the scholars to a new world.

When Congress settled the question of the location of the World's Fair by preferring Chicago to New York, it was feared that, among a people so little accustomed to demonstrations of high art, the enterprise would take upon itself some of the characteristics of "the greatest show on earth," and that our refined taste would be shocked by a vain display of cheap and vulgar pretense in the buildings. Our reputation as a worthy member of the great community of civilized nations was at stake before the world, and Chicago as yet had done little to give confidence in its ability or desire to make such a use of its great opportunity as would reflect credit and honor upon the republic. Our natural tendency to outdo all other nations by bigness and height rather than by quality of art, to astonish them with novelties of structure and audacities of design rather than to challenge them with carefully studied and scholarly compositions in the academic field, where they had ever been our masters, would here, apparently, have the fullest demonstration. That the Fair would in any respect of art compare with the last Exposition at Paris was hardly to be expected. Of course, it was inevitable that we should have a tower to overtop the masterpiece of Eiffel,[2] a dome to cover a far wider area than that of Vienna, an egg of Columbus bigger and uglier than that of Genoa, and other unspeakable devices of audacious ingenuity, to astonish the vulgar and make the judicious grieve. But the managers of the Exposition, supported by the sympathy and indomitable public spirit of the youngest, most energetic and ambitious of the great capitals of the world, and by the official sanction of a powerful nation, and, more especially, in the use of these aids and of the wealth which was poured into their treasury, being wisely guided by the counsel of the ablest available specialists in the choice and the laying out of the grounds, in the design and construction of the buildings, in their decoration and completion by sculpture and painting, in the innumerable difficulties of engineering presented by the drainage, the water and gas supply, and the distribution of power and light by electricity, in the sanitary and police equipment, and in all the other complicated services of this enterprise, — these putative Philistines of the New World have developed and carried into execution a scheme which, not only in scale, but in those qualities of artistic excellence and refinement which were least expected of them, is acknowledged to surpass even the great triumphs of the Exposition of 1889. The cost of the vast structures of the "White City" has been more than doubled by their architectural form and decorative envelopes. If these forms of art had been called into existence simply as visible manifestations of the wealth, pride, and culture of the country, and as expressions of its noble and lavish hospitality to the nations of the world, it would have been well to count the cost with nicer economy; but, as object lessons to the people, raised to educate them and to arouse their higher consciousness, the managers, without hesitation, considered that they should not withhold their hands until the ideal had been made concrete and palpable in the buildings at Jackson Park, at whatever expenditure of treasure and thought. They have done more: they have successfully resisted the introduction upon the grounds of every device of mere astonishment, — of any feature, indeed, not commended by its practical character or by its quality of art. The irrepressible crank has laid before them a hundred monstrous schemes, but has obtained no foothold within the limits of the Exposition. He must be content to expatiate with his wild vagaries outside the inviolate boundaries.

Possibly, the very best and noblest lesson given to the New World by the Fair is the spectacle presented of the happy results secured through the concert of the fine arts in its great buildings. It is due largely to the indomitable zeal of Mr. D. H. Burnham, the Chief of Construction, to his enthusiastic love of art, to his wide experience in architectural enterprises on a large scale, to the force of his personality, and to his sound judgment, that, setting aside all personal interests and all local prejudices, men of the highest ability in every department of art, summoned from all parts of the country, gladly came to his assistance, and that these men worked together in a spirit of mutual concession, — a spirit never vitiated or weakened by any shadow of jealousy, in all their trying and complicated collaboration, from the beginning to the end. Architects, sculptors, painters, and engineers have all been ready and eager to direct their best efforts to a common end of exalted art; to sacrifice their most cherished ideas, if the development of them was found to conflict with harmony and unity of result. For the first time in our country, architects have enjoyed the inestimable advantage of completing their works by sculpture and painting of a high order, adjusted to the exigencies of the original design. In no single case has a sculptor hesitated to modify the sentiment of his composition so as to conform to the idea of the structure, or to change its outlines so that they might take their proper share, and no more, in the architectural scheme. The best painters in the country have gladly forsaken their easels and their profitable commissions to play a noble but subordinate part in the decoration of the walls and vaulted ceilings of the great peristyles and porches. They have labored, one and all, joyously and sincerely, with eager but most friendly emulation, in this monumental task. Mr. F. D. Millet, the Director of Color,[3] with admirable energy and tact, and with astonishing executive ability, has controlled and harmonized the difficult work of his brother painters; so that over all this department has presided a spirit of *bonhomie* and fellowship which could not fail to have the best results. The necessity for prompt decision and rapid workmanship seemed to spur these artists to their highest endeavor, and to inspire them with a fine enthusiasm. This friendly emulation presented a scene rarely witnessed in the history of art. At the midday rest, painters and sculptors would assemble around their table at the commissariat, compare notes, exchange advice and chaff over the social pipe, after the manner of the studios; and then, with new zeal, each would take his electric boat, and, over the waters of the canals or the Lagoon, find his way to his distant field of operations, disembark at the broad water-stairs of his palace, as if he had been in Venice, climb his rough scaffolding, and resume his difficult and dangerous labors upon the panels of his particular dome or wall surface. In this way they have all lavished their efforts, cheered by the consciousness that they were doing their honest part in this great concert of the arts.

Among the architects this spirit of mutual concession has been especially remarkable. Those concerned in the designing of the buildings surrounding the great Court and Basin, where it was peculiarly necessary that a magnificent unity of sentiment should prevail, and where it was important that each building should assist its neighbors with a sort of high courtesy, avoiding every feature which by rivalry or contrast should bring into the general composition any elements of discord or disproportion, sacrificed themselves to this end with admirable self-denial. If, in any building, a dome was proposed so large as to challenge comparison or suggest rivalry with that of the central Administration Building (Fig. 146), which it was agreed should always be predominant, it was cheerfully suppressed, as was the case in the earlier studies of the Manufacturers' Building (Fig. 149). If, as in the Agricultural Building, a porch was designed, admirably accentuating the centre of the principal façade, but interfering with the continuity of the terrace surrounding the great Basin, it was removed without a murmur of discontent (Fig. 148). If the campaniles of the Electricity Building seemed to introduce an element too lofty in comparison with the element of height in the other designs, they were gladly reduced (Fig. 150). In short, every one of the greater buildings of the Exposition, with the possible exception of the Illinois pavilion and that of the United States (Fig. 158), which were developed independently, has yielded something to the spirit of harmonious conformity, without sacrifice, however, of any essential point of individuality. Thus, wherever the conditions of dignity and unity have required it, each of the great architectural façades has been studied so as to compose well with its neighbors, and give to the dullest comprehension an impression of monumental harmony. In this vast orchestra, no individuality forces itself into undue prominence to disturb the majestic symphony.

No student of architecture who visits the great Court of the Exposition, and sees there how the fundamental principle of variety in unity has been carried into practice on a vast scale, with no unsympathetic censor to check the free developments of art, can fail to take away with him a lesson far more impressive and abiding than can possibly be furnished by examples on any less restricted and less noble field. To the practitioner of this art, who has never enjoyed the advantages of education in the schools, this scene must inevitably prove a revelation of the possibilities of architectural composition in pure style, and an admonition to aim, in his future practice, at the virtues of repose and self-repression, to avoid loading his designs with the conceits of undisciplined invention, and to produce his effects by the careful study and refinement of a few established motifs rather than by crowding his composition with ill-digested novelties. It is sufficiently evident that to architecture, at least, the Exposition will bring a message of civilization which cannot be misunderstood, and which inevitably must have immediate and enduring effects upon the general practice of the art. This practice has always shown itself peculiarly sensitive to the influence of good examples; it is risking little to prophesy that in this country architecture in especial, and the decorative arts in general, will, after this Exposition, be inspired by an irresistible impulse for reform, and for a greater unity of effort in the establishment of style. Certainly, the practical value of thorough training in the art has been amply proved, so that hereafter no aspirant can be content with less.

"There is a solidarity in the arts," said Mr. Norton; "they do not flourish in isolated independence." [4] Painting and sculpture, in the highest sense, cannot flourish when architecture is in a state of depression. Architecture cannot succeed when it is not sustained and completed by its sister arts. To decorate architecture has ever been, and must ever be, the highest function of sculptor or painter. To make architecture fit to receive such decoration is the noblest impulse of that art. Painting, sculpture, and architecture are in their best estate and are enjoying their highest opportunities when they are working together.

But in the monuments of the Exposition still another fine art has played a most conspicuous part in this great concert. There is one man, and, so far as we know, none other, capable of conceiving and carrying out the work of the landscape architects as it has been done at Jackson Park. To Frederick Law Olmsted, assisted in the practical and administrative part of this work by his partner, the late Henry Sargent Codman, is to be credited the brilliant idea of converting the hopeless sand-dunes and intervening marshes of this district into a series of low and broad terraces, intersected by the Basin, the canals, and the Lagoon, which form the most distinguishing and characteristic features of the Exposition. It was mainly by his fine artistic sympathy, in counsel with the advisory architect of the Department of Construction, the late John Wellborn Root, that these terraces were adjusted to receive a great architectural demonstration, illustrated by a series of tentative schemes in block for the locating of the great buildings. This long series finally culminated in one which met all the conditions of architectural arrangement and convenience so completely, and with such fine forethought for all the future exigencies of the Exposition, that the Board of Architects, who were subsequently summoned to distribute among themselves the designing of the buildings, and to whom this final project was submitted, could agree upon no material modifications of it. Never was a combination of monumental buildings, contrived for a specific and monumental purpose, more carefully and ingeniously studied for the production of preconceived effects of order and magnificence. It is with no little astonishment, therefore, that we read in the otherwise most laudatory report of the Marquis Chasseloup-Laubet to the Société des Ingénieurs Civiles that his first and final impression of the group was affected by the absence of a *plan d'ensemble!*[5] This judgment can be accounted for only by the fact that he must have viewed the grounds when they were encumbered by building materials, and must have entered upon the scene at some accidental point, so

313

that the general scheme did not develop to his eye in the proper order, and in the manner provided by the plan. At that time, the monumental railroad entrance at the west end of the Court was hardly accessible. To the visitor entering here, the architectural scheme of the Exposition must necessarily unfold itself with harmonious dignity; the carefully provided vistas cannot fail, as he advances, to have their due effect upon the mind, and leave upon it an indelible impression of unity and order. A glance at the latest plans of the grounds will explain how this impression is produced (Fig. 140). The fine sentiment of fellowship in a common cause, which, as we have seen, marked the relations between the other artists, was especially felt by the architects in working with Messrs. Olmsted and Codman. The architects of building and of landscape were animated by a mutual zeal, and each aided the other with loyalty and enthusiasm. In fact, without the constant exercise of these qualities of brotherhood in art, the general result of harmony, which the French marquis apparently did not see, but which every visitor to the completed grounds will have forced upon him, whatever may be the degree of his susceptibility to emotions of art, would have been impossible. This adjustment of architecture to its environment furnishes still another lesson, which cannot be lost to a people who, by this experience, obtain the highest possible standard of performance in the laying out and adornment of their public parks and pleasure grounds, their boulevards and city squares, and the location of their public buildings.

But if, in the making of the grounds of Jackson Park, and in the location of the palaces of art and industry thereon, there has been achieved a result of conformity and mutual adjustment more admirable than one might see even in the gardens of Versailles or of Marly, and on a scale far more colossal, and if the peristyles, kiosks, fountains, bridges, statues, columns, arches of triumph, and other subordinate features, distributed among the greater buildings, have served to lighten the prevailing effect of majesty and order without disturbing it, it must be frankly admitted that a note of confusion and discordance has been introduced in a comparatively small area at the northern end of the park by the emulation of the States of the Union in their pavilions. The parklike aspect formerly presented in this part of the grounds by the lawns, driveways, and fairly grown trees has quite disappeared, and its avenues, crowded with the ambitious and incongruous structures of the rival commonwealths, have taken upon themselves the heterogeneous characteristics of boulevards in a prosperous town. Here the architects have not been able to enjoy the advantages of concerted action. Several of these structures are beautifully designed, and are contrived with great success to recall the historic memories of the States, respectively, which have erected them. But no attempt at harmony has been made. They are too large for their purposes, and are crowded far too closely for any dignity of effect. Each one, instead of being isolated in its own pleasance, surrounded by trees and shrubbery, where its reminiscences of English colonial dignity, or of the Spanish missions, or of any local quality of Eastern or Western civilization might be independently expressed without challenging comparisons, elbows a neighbor "in contact inconvenient" on either side. Some of them, indeed, are frank examples of our own outworn vernacular architecture, with all its offensive and ungoverned crudities of detail. Perhaps it is well that this element should be expressed somewhere at the World's Fair, for the sake of local color, and that, in comparing these huddled incongruities (which, by the bye, possibly had something to do in affecting the precipitous judgment of the French marquis) with the ordered grandeur and beauty of the main part of the Exposition grounds, the spectator may find the best sort of admonition as to the supreme value of art not only in designing buildings, but in designing combinations of buildings in towns, squares, and streets, so that every structure in them shall have some relation of harmony with its neighbors.

Every block in our large cities is made up of a series of independent, uncompromising individualities, each struggling to distinguish itself by obliterating its neighbors; and if any one of these discordant members succeeds in the greedy emulation, it is generally by virtue of some superior audacity in height or vulgar pretense. True beauty, which loves quiet and peace, is apt to shrink and hide itself for shame at being caught in such quarrelsome company. By this great object lesson at Chicago, any thoughtful mind may learn that order and congruity in the architecture of our city streets are not necessarily monotony and wearisome iteration, but may be obtained by mutual concessions, resulting in an effect of concord without detriment to any desirable quality of individual distinction. To the apprehension of an artist, the earliest existing permanent building in a block, whatever may be its quality as a work of design, has earned its right to give a keynote to those which follow, the observance of which need not embarrass the freedom of their development; for true art is flexible to every local condition. In this way are built the streets of Utopia, perhaps, and the heavenly mansions, but the ideal is not inaccessible even to us in our lower estate. It is simply a question of mutual concession, and

It blesseth him that gives and him that takes.[6]

There is yet another lesson — a lesson of color — which the Exposition will inculcate in a manner not readily forgotten. It has been found, after numerous experiments, that the most effective surface treatment of the large masses, both of the exterior and interior in the greater buildings, is one of nearly pure white, modified, so far as the interiors are concerned, by screens of translucent fabrics, stretched beneath the skylights, in combinations of tints varied to suit the especial conditions of each building. This device furnishes to each an atmosphere of faint rainbow color tones, which is felt as a pervading spirit of refinement throughout the interiors, but is so contrived as in no case to compete with or to influence the stronger local colors of the exhibits. In some of the buildings painted friezes and cartouches have been added, to confer upon them large decorative effects of especial character and significance.

The white marble exterior treatment of the architecture is relieved by a system of awnings, shades, banners, and flags, of fabrics especially woven, and of devices especially contrived, to offset the serious purity of the architectural lines, to supplement the local color embellishments of the painters in the shadows of porches and peristyles, and to confer upon the whole scene a festival aspect, full of joyous animation, but without those harsh contrasts which have hitherto converted our holiday decorations into riotous discords of crude and conflicting colors.

The sudden death of Mr. Root, and later of Mr. Codman, both of them on the threshold of the greatest achievements in their respective fields, is felt not only as a personal bereavement by those comrades in art who were associated with them in the study and execution of this vast enterprise, but as a loss to the whole nation, whose interests they served to the end of their bright careers with entire devotion and unselfish enthusiasm. No story of the Exposition can be complete without an honorable recognition of the great service which they rendered to it.

We are already hearing loud and frequent expressions of regret that, after the brilliant six months of pageantry are over, the vast collections of the Exposition will be scattered to the four winds; the great arches and trusses of steel, and the other merchantable portions of the structures of these palaces of art, will be sold to the highest bidder; the majestic ordonnances of columns and arches, pavilions, domes, and towers, with their statuary, their bas-reliefs and paintings, will disappear from the face of the earth; the fountains will be dried up, the bridges destroyed, the gardens absorbed; the Indians, the Algerians, the Japanese, the Egyptians, and the Esquimaux will "fold their tents like the Arabs, and as silently steal away;" [7] and in a few short months nothing will be left but a vacant area of land, and the memory of the greatest function of the century. The productions of the photographer, the medals of award, and whatever of new life and higher endeavor may follow in the practice of all the arts will perhaps be needed to assure ourselves that the Exposition of 1893 was not a dream.

So far as the architectural designs of the buildings are concerned, as much thought and study have been bestowed upon them as if they were intended for all time. The sculptors and painters have embellished them as they would have embellished permanent monuments. Yet it is not difficult to prove that all this will be no waste of treasure or effort, and that even the ephemeral character of the pageant will make it all the more precious to those who read its purpose aright.

If it is true

> That what we have we prize not to the worth
> Whiles we enjoy it; but being lack'd and lost,
> Why, then we rack the value; then we find
> The virtue that possession would not show us
> Whiles it was ours,[8]

it is equally true that we never value a precious thing so highly as when we know that it will soon pass from our possession forever. The appreciation and enjoyment of such a thing are quickened and magnified by its transiency. The touch of regret in our emotions not only softens, but sweetens our judgment. The "White City" by the lake, which seems to have arisen almost

> like an exhalation, with the sound
> Of dulcet symphonies and voices sweet,[9]

will disappear as it came, like an enchantment, leaving not even a mound, a broken column, or a mouldering capital to mark its place; and every spectator who walks in its porches or gazes upon its mighty fronts will instinctively feel as if, while the unsubstantial pageant lasts, he should make the most of it, and leave no point of its beauty or grandeur unstudied. Every great work of art, whether it presents itself merely as an incident of travel, of whether it is staled by daily contact, has its influence, more or less undefined and unsuspected, upon mind and character. But if the stranger is conscious that to-morrow he must leave it behind forever, it makes upon his intelligence an ineffaceable image. He analyzes it with eager eyes and senses all alert. He instinctively desires to make it his own, a part of himself. The slow work of years is for him done in a day, and for him the conquest of art over the imagination is at once completed. If it is a work of architecture, this conquest is accomplished by the unity of its organism, by its simplicity and wholeness of scheme in general outline, and by the harmonious subordination of its details. This unity impresses the object upon the mind at first view, and engages the attention and interest of the spectator, who is flattered by his ability to comprehend it. Its complications charm him as he is charmed by a strain of music, though in each case the technique may be far beyond his reach. This interest is confirmed if the monument of art is so devised that its finer meanings unfold themselves to his intelligence gradually, its details presenting themselves in the order of their importance to the general scheme. A less harmonious and less symmetrical organism perplexes his mind by the disorder of its composition; its parts are not so subordinated as to appeal to his eye in proper succession. He sees details before he sees the general idea; and the mental impression conveyed to him is blurred and indistinct, if in this way he is constrained to make an effort to understand its motive of design and the message which it brings, — if indeed it has any message except one of warning against false art.

It would seem, therefore, that, in view of the ephemeral character of the Exposition, nothing has been really wasted, and everything has been gained, by that expenditure of means and effort which has been necessary to make it beautiful. Its great function would have been but poorly fulfilled if the spirit of mere utility and common sense had controlled the enterprise, had cheapened it as a demonstration of art, and, because it was to be merely temporary, had made it palpably economical. "A thing of beauty is a joy" not only while you look at it, but "forever." The collections of the Exposition would have been installed as safely and as conveniently in buildings which cost five or six millions as in buildings which cost ten or twelve; but the work of civilization possible to it at the larger price would have been but half done at the lower. The alabaster box of precious ointment was not broken in vain at the feet of our Saviour, though it might have been sold for three hundred pence, and the money given to the poor.[10]

Not only to the practice of all the industrial and liberal arts, but to that of the fine arts, the Exposition will have a bequest of the utmost value; a bequest which could come from no source less exalted; a bequest which, as regards the fine arts in especial, will ever be associated with the assurance of the triumphs to be achieved in the future by their cooperation in a spirit of cordial unity. Whatever may have been the causes which finally culminated in the brilliant solidarity of the arts in the Italian Renaissance of the fifteenth and sixteenth centuries, from which has developed all the best that has been done in art since that time, it can hardly be doubted that, if a new and equally brilliant era shall presently be begun in the New World of Columbus, upon a far larger field, with nobler opportunities and without embarrassment of traditions and prejudices, it will date its initial movement and inspiration in the last decade of the nineteenth century, when the Exposition at Chicago taught its great lessons of civilization.

The Growth of Characteristic Architectural Style in the United States[1]

(1893)

Public opinion concerning modern architecture, so far as it has found any intelligible expression in literature, has been dictated by amateurs, theorists, sentimentalists, and doctrinaires, who, finding in its most characteristic manifestations but little to satisfy the ideals created in their minds by ancient historical monuments, have habitually stigmatized it as vulgar, materialistic, and entirely wanting in all the elements of beautiful design, as they understand it. They are never weary of contrasting, to their obvious disadvantage, the buildings of today with those of classic or romantic times, making no allowance for the fundamental difference in the conditions under which these two classes of structure have been developed. The critical faculties of the laity, familiar only with long-accepted and comparatively primitive ideas, exercised only in archæological studies, have not as yet adapted themselves to the just consideration of that complication of conditions which is slowly molding the art of our time. Our modern masquerades in ancient styles, which, in so far as they have been restrained within the limits of conformity, have apparently contributed little or nothing to the wholesome advancement of this art, have been acceptable to the modern critic in exact proportion to their sterile correctness, and their unimaginative fidelity to the old types. But he has no word or thought of sympathy for those contemporaneous experiments in form, in which the architect of today is more or less ingenuously seeking to adapt the underlying principles of the historical styles to modern materials, modern methods, and modern usage. But it is to these experiments, however crude, however audacious, however much they may differ in their results from the accepted types, that the architecture of our time is indebted for all those elements of life which make consistent progress and development possible.

In this Columbian year of America, when, by an especial manifestation of architecture, we are seeking to present to the world an orderly and deliberate expression of our civilization in its best estate, it seems especially fitting that our unconscious efforts to develop characteristic style should receive respectful consideration instead of contempt, and that the architects themselves should utter a few sane thoughts, while the literary critics are bewailing that art is dead, because we are no longer building classic temples or mediæval cathedrals, and because modern exigencies of construction and usage render it impossible for us to repeat in the New World and in the end of the nineteenth century the mellow beauty of Italian streets of the sixteenth century, or the unconscious poetry of the builders of simpler and less spacious times than our own.

There are many considerations which make it difficult to understand and to trace the lines of modern progress in architecture. We are like soldiers on a field of battle, who are conscious only of the accidents and incidents of their own little foreground, while the great scheme of the combat, its combinations and its larger fortunes, are unintelligible to them. We are, moreover, dealing with far more difficult problems than our predecessors, and, in endeavoring to solve them, we are embarrassed by a knowledge of precedent, which makes it hard for us to be simple and sincere, hard for us not to affect impressions which we do not really feel. Our art has, to a certain extent, become a polyglot, and architecture must now be a learned profession; it must study laws of esthetics; it must evolve theories of design. Instead of floating with the tide of events, undistracted by side issues, and rendering service without effort to the evolution of a style, after the manner of the old builders, we are constrained to exhaust our strength, to become morbid in our self-consciousness, in making comparative analyses of many styles, and in endless experiments with formulas and dogmas.

But in the countries of the Old World the effect of local ancient traditions has, even under these modern conditions, been powerful enough to preserve in each, if not a distinct, certainly a recognizable trait of nationality. The cosmopolitanism engendered by easy intercommunication has not been strong enough entirely to obliterate this tendency to differentiate the contemporaneous styles of our times on national lines. In the modern buildings of Europe we can still detect English, French, German, Russian, Spanish or Italian feeling, legitimately inherited from the past, and, like the languages of these nations, respectively, still bearing ineffaceable traces of their distinctive historical origin.

In the New World we have no patriotic traditions of art, no venerable monuments to assist in the creation and preservation of a sentiment of nationality in our architecture; and yet certain characteristics of style are justly expected of us. Our independent and entirely unprejudiced attitude toward the historical styles is in itself a condition out of which our art should develop a certain quality of distinction. There is a peculiarly American character in our political institutions and in our social ideals, though these institutions and ideals have their roots in ancient civilizations. This distinctive character is recognized in the Old World, and it is evident that the more our especial forms of civilization develop the more they are differentiated from all other contemporary types. In respect to architecture, a large survey of our achievements will indicate that this art has never ceased to perform in America its greatest function as an expression of history, just as it has done elsewhere since history began to record itself in buildings. We have only to compare the condition of architecture here today with that of fifty years ago, disregarding for the moment the incidents of individual caprice, the architectural expressions of personal moods which surround us and distract our judgment, to see a progress on certain distinct lines, a progress in a direction decidedly different from those which at this distance we may trace on the other side of the Atlantic. Indeed, it is not too bold an assumption to say that we are actually achieving characteristic style. If all the ephemeral structures of the last fifty years could be eliminated from our field of vision, and if the few deliberate representative and serious monuments alone remained for our inspection, this achievement, I am persuaded, would be as clearly demonstrated as the style of Pericles, or Augustus, or St. Louis, each of which is expressed to us by a series of great monuments — all the innumerable inferior contemporary buildings, which would have embarrassed our view and disturbed our judgment, having been obliterated by time. The more important buildings are types of contemporary thought; they affect by conscious or unconscious imitation the character of all subsequent inferior structures; they gather to themselves all that is best in the ephemeral experiments of the time; the personal equation of the architect can hardly expatiate in them as in buildings of inferior magnitude and importance, and they stand as milestones, marking the steady development of architectural thought.

By confining our attention to these points, we may possibly discover some of the fundamental principles which have been imposed upon the architects of the New World by the conditions of the civilization which they are unconsciously expressing.

In the old countries, where conservatism is recognized as a virtue, structure and design are adjusted to old formulas, and architectural traditions are thus continued, each country maintaining its own in a spirit of more or less unconscious patriotism. Cosmopolitanism, progress in the science of building, intercommunication, and the influence of the international expositions cannot entirely extinguish the distinctions of race. The accent of localism is everywhere evident, notwithstanding the powerful propaganda of the schools of Paris and the archæological exactions of the academies of Berlin. Here, on the other hand, in the absence of patriotic traditions, the most potent element in the development of form as a fine art is evidently the science of economic building. With us, formulas seem to offer a much less palpable obstacle to the development of structure and to the artistic expression of practical conditions of use.

I think I may venture the proposition that the most distinctive characteristic of our best work in architecture is its hospitality to new materials and new methods of construction, its perfect willingness to attempt to confer architectural character upon the science of the engineer, and to adapt itself without prejudice to the exactions of practical use and occupation.

Before education and the excellent training of our schools began to exercise their wholesome influence upon the art of building here, before principles deduced from the study of ancient art began to refine and purify our architecture and to direct the irresistible force of our progress into more prolific and more healthy channels, this progress was audacious, illiterate and disorderly, with an insolent disregard of all the lessons of the past. In its best estate, it was apt to content itself with imitations of the contemporary work of Europe. These qualities still find abundant expression in every street of every city of our country; they assault us at every turn with evidences of barbaric ignorance or cheap and vulgar pretense. Galvanized iron ornament, cast or stamped, construction concealed behind masks of conventional shape, invention and caprice playing with the noble art of building as if it were furniture — all these still confront us wherever we go. The object seems to have been rather to astonish than to please. But these demonstrations, although they still constitute a large part of our vernacular art, I am persuaded are happily ephemeral. Behind them is an energy which only needs to be properly directed to make a living art possible.

I doubt if the educated architects of the United States realize that their duties in relation to the development of characteristic style are such as have been imposed upon no other architects of ancient or modern time, and that their professional privileges and opportunities are far greater than those which have been enjoyed elsewhere in the history of art. It is needless for me to say that we are surrounded by all that energy and wealth, by all that public spirit, without which the creation of a great era in architecture would be impossible. It is also self-evident that the creation of such an era, that the directing of these great forces of civilization toward an appropriate and adequate expression in architecture, can only be secured by high convictions on the part of the architects; and that these high convictions are only possible to a learned profession — a profession thoroughly versed in the history of art, familiar with precedent, unprejudiced, free, catholic, without national bias in favor of types which are venerable merely because they are national.

But a merely learned architecture can never be a living architecture, because a living architecture has never existed without popular sympathy. The function of education and training in architecture is not to preserve or revive historical styles; much less to corrupt them. Architects are not archæologists but artists, and it has been distinctly proved that mere historical conformity is an obstacle to progress. What did we contribute toward this progress when we were masquerading in Norman, early English, late Decorated, Italian Gothic or the Renaissance of Queen Anne, when the highest praise we could earn from the critics was the phrase, "This is correct"; and when the people disregarded our scholarly performances because they had nothing to do with our times and were not understood?

What, then, should be the education which will enable us to perform these great duties, and to make the best use of these unprecedented opportunities? Is it not clear, in the first place, that the study of the historical styles should be pursued in our schools in a more comprehensive and philosophical manner than they are at present? It should be made evident to the student that these styles are not a succession of isolated and independent phenomena, that they are not accidents of invention, but direct growths out of the history of the human mind, tangible expressions of the development of races in civilization. It is not enough to reduce these styles to formulas and commit them to memory. It is infinitely more important to comprehend the historical conditions which created them and conferred upon each of them its especial spirit and character. If the student were taught to study ancient history in the succession of the styles, and that these styles owe much of their distinctive character and essential value to the political, religious, commercial and ethnological conditions in the midst of which they were respectively developed, he would better understand his own proper functions as an architect in respect to the history of our own times. He would be no more content to limit his efforts to revivals of these styles than the English writers of today would prefer to express their thoughts in the language of Beowulf, or Chaucer, or Spenser, or John Lyly. Architecture would no longer be to him a thing to be played with after the manner of dilettanti, but an art to be treated seriously. The historical styles would no longer be to him a mere dictionary of useful formulas to be quoted or travestied in pedantic or scholastic fashion according to the caprice of the moment, but genuine and unaffected expressions of the effect of various conditions of human life and human knowledge upon the development of decorative forms of building. His own duties toward contemporary art would assume a different character. He would find, indeed, that he could not satisfy modern conditions of design in any given case without considering how his predecessors in the great eras treated similar problems. He must summon to his aid congenial spirits out of the past. His vision must be constantly enlarged and inspired, his thoughts must be continually elevated and purified by their high companionship. He must be compassed round about with a cloud of witnesses. But he cannot produce adequate work if, on the one hand, he falls into mere imitation of precedent, or if, on the other, he depends on his own unaided inventive powers, and works in the solitude of his own fancies. The modern architect, unlike any of his predecessors, must necessarily perform his task by summoning all the past to his assistance. He cannot make for himself a new point of departure without subjecting his designs to all the perils of personal caprice, and all the accidents of temporary mood. He cannot waste his strength and insult his intelligence by inventing a new language in which to express every new thought. Progress is only possible by a certain intelligent unity of effort among the architects; but if this unity of effort confines itself to the adoption of some restricted language of form, some especially favored historical style, we shall once more be placed in complete subjection to archæology, and a succession of unfruitful revivals will again be encouraged, such as has distinguished the history of modern architecture in England and America. The spirit of the artist must be constantly on guard to protect us from affecting impressions which we do not feel.

In the older countries, as I have already ventured to suggest, this necessary unity of effort is in great part secured by the influence of national traditions. The London *Times*, in speaking of the latest book of essays by Mr. Henry James, says that he possesses "an advantage which a cultivated American often enjoys as compared with an equally cultivated Englishman, in that he sees the whole culture of others in Europe in a common perspective, and assimilates all its elements indifferently." [2] In our new country, the architect is constrained to consider equally all the traditions of all the nations. They are all equally interesting to him. His only protection from the embarrassment of such a vast inheritance is that high quality of education which enables him to work rather with the principles than with the formulas furnished by this inheritance, to develop form from structure in the same way and with the same spirit that the architects of antiquity developed the peristyle of the Parthenon from the post and lintel of the Greeks; the Pantheon from the domical structure of the Romans; the halls of the Roman baths and basilicas from the intersections of concrete vaults; the cathedral of Amiens from the establishment of an equilibrium between the thrusts of groined ceilings of small stones and the counterthrusts of buttresses.

The opportunity of the architects of America to develop characteristic modern style lies in the application of these principles to the expression of modern structure by appropriate forms of art, not, on the one hand, by devising new words and phrases, nor, on the other, by forcing historical formulas to perform this difficult service. The wonderful constructional functions of steel girders and posts; the inestimable practical value of immense sheets of plate glass; the braced and riveted frames of light metal, protected by envelopes of porous terra cotta or fire clay; the absolute requirements of modern convenience in commercial buildings; all the difficult conditions of modern economical structure; the exactions of municipal building ordinances; the complicated service of electricity, of the machinery of elevators, of lighting and heating, of plumbing and ventilation; the devices of engineering to meet these conditions; the new materials of structure and decoration; the new and ever-changing practical methods of building; the unprecedented social conditions which are to be accommodated by modern architecture in all its branches; these are the influences which compel the modern architect to frankly abandon the letter of the precepts of Vitruvius, the practice of the monastic and lay builders of the middle ages, the academic systems of the schools, the formulated rules of archæology, and thus unconsciously to develop the elements of style, based upon principles, and but dimly recalling the monuments of historical art. Where the mind of the architect is open and unprejudiced, where his feeling as an artist is sensitive and highly trained, new conditions, such as these, must necessarily generate modified, if not new forms. Of course, these modified or new forms have value only in so far as they emerge unaffectedly and without forcing from these modern complications of structure and use. In this way iron and steel must inevitably impose upon our art new expressions, as marked and as characteristic as were imposed upon it, in the course of history, by the invention, successively, of the arch, the vault, the dome, the groin, and the flying buttress. But it is the natural impulse of the man of education to protest against any innovations which cannot be clothed in those accepted forms of beauty and grace which have become venerable from long usage and from association with the greatest triumphs of art in history. The artist does not readily abandon his ideals; no inspired mechanic or learned engineer will ever appear to overthrow them. The artist alone is now responsible for the present condition of architecture in this country. It is not his disposition to make changes for the sake of change, and he can never forget the historical styles and all that has been done in the past. But if these reminiscences merely serve to confer upon his work an archæological or scholastic character, a great part of his architectural message will be intelligible only to those more or less accomplished in matters of art, and he will continue to utter only pedantic enigmas to the end of time.

I have already intimated that when architecture becomes in this way an aristocratic cult, as it were, it is not a living art. It can only become such when it is addressed to and understood by a much larger public. It does not necessarily follow that architecture must descend from its high ideals in order to become progressive as all other contemporary arts and sciences are progressive. If modern architecture must have qualities to interest the public in order to obtain sympathy, it must also retain possession of those which work for the higher civilization in refining and elevating the common mind, like any other fine art.

Now, in reviewing the broad field of architectural endeavor in this country during the last fifteen or twenty years, or since the time when the trained graduates of our professional schools began to enter upon their labors, the most characteristic developments of architecture in this country have resulted from their honest attempts to express new structure in terms of art without detriment to the highest ideals; and the element of democracy thus introduced into modern style has, I dare to hope, begun to create a sympathetic public, such as our art has not had before within the century which is now closing. For while this public, whose sympathy is so vitally necessary to architecture, are indifferent to points of technical or academical excellence in modern design, and will view without intelligent emotion the clever translation to our modern streets of the façade of a hunting lodge of Francis I, or the archæological travesty of a Verona palace delicately inlaid with colored marbles, within hearing of the roar of the traffic of Broadway in New York, they highly appreciate the difference between the solving of a practical problem of construction or convenient usage by a mechanic or engineer, on the one hand, and by an artist, on the other. They will not submit to inconvenience for the sake of a theory of design, or for the sake of a realization of some exotic ideal, but they will rejoice to see useful things made beautiful, practical ideas elevated into the domain of art, and common sense made consistent with grace and elegance, without being unnecessarily embarrassed or sophisticated in the expression by a pedantic affectation of Greek, Latin, early Christian, or mediæval archaeology. The great object lesson, furnished by the buildings of the Exposition of 1893, cannot fail, I think, to cultivate and refine this natural desire for beautiful expression in form, and to create for the people a more exacting standard of judgment, by which the architecture, which is made for them, may by them be measured, appreciated, and, if necessary, corrected, as it was in the great eras.

When the just but difficult exactions of modern business have been satisfied in a commercial façade; when its piers have been reduced to the smallest, and its glazed openings increased to the largest possible dimensions; and the whole has been built over a gaping void upon a manifest steel girder, thus defying all those beautiful and venerable laws of statics and proportion which were developed from the lintel-construction of the Greeks or the arch-construction of the Romans; when all this has been done without neglect of the conditions necessary to be observed in the creation of a work of art; when, in short, a problem of economic building has been elevated into a sensitive and carefully balanced organism, unaffectedly and obviously fitted for its service, one phase of the proper architecture of our time has been expressed in a manner perfectly reasonable and deserving the respectful consideration of the critic. In this honest performance, so far as it succeeds in being architectural and not merely practical, there is more hope for the future of architecture, a more definite advance has been made toward characteristic style than could be made by any revival undertaken in a mere spirit of archæology. And yet, as I have said, the spirit of our times cannot be duly expressed in architecture without constant reference to the past. When the lantern of Salamanca was so cleverly adjusted as a crown and culmination to a modern religious building in this country as to fascinate more than half the architects of America and set them to studying and adapting the characteristics of the neglected Romanesque in the churches of Auvergne and in the farmsteads of Normandy, another and most valuable contribution was made toward the establishment of characteristic style (Fig. 101);[3] because it was apparently undertaken at a moment when the artistic consciousness seemed to be affected by a certain tendency to effeminacy and over-refinement, and to need an enlargement of its vocabulary, a refreshment of its resources, by an attempt to develop in the modern spirit a primitive and vigorous type of the twelfth century, of which the progress toward perfection or completion had been interrupted, not by its own exhaustion, but by a political event, in which the lay builders of the thirteenth century were constrained to express by new devices of structure a new spirit of religious aspiration and municipal enfranchisement.

But meanwhile the most accomplished architects of this country, loyal to the academical traditions, continue to use in modern work the details and spirit of the classic Renaissance, begun by Brunelleschi and Alberti in the fifteenth century — the most highly organized and most delicately sensitive system of conventional formulas which ever illustrated and adorned the progress of mankind; the only system ever developed entirely independently of structure (Figs. 178, 179, 183, 186, 187). The consummate artifice of this architectural exponent of the modern spirit, whereby civilization has with curious fidelity expressed its various phases without interruption during five of the most active and enlightened centuries of history, cannot be entirely supplanted by any other revival or invention; for it is an essential part of modern history, and has proved by a succession of astonishing variations from the fifteenth to the twentieth centuries that it is a language of form, still elastic and capable of fluently manifesting nearly all that part of the modern spirit which is capable of expression in architecture.

In fact it seems sufficiently evident that, as long as we remember the past and what has been accomplished by the masters of architecture in all the ages, there can never again grow a distinctive style in the sense of what we call Greek, Roman, Christian, Mohammedan or Renaissance; that there never again can come into existence a national style which shall keep strictly within any narrow bounds of architectural expression, excluding all others; but that all the historical demonstrations of art are necessary to constitute that larger and more copious language of form which is necessary to express in terms of art the rapid progress in the science of modern construction, and that many-sided and complicated civilization which it is the obvious destiny of our country to amalgamate, harmonize and justify out of all the civilizations of history.

This statement, I fear, would be too obvious and commonplace to be worth repeating to such an audience as this, if it might not also serve to remind the architects of the new world that the vast privileges of their independence must carry with them a corresponding vastness of responsibility, a corresponding difficulty of adequate performance, and necessitate a constant advance of the standard of professional education, a cosmopolitan enlargement of our field of vision, a constant watchfulness lest we suffer a perfectly practicable progress of triumphant achievement in architecture to be checked either by the pedantry of the scholar or by the graceful caprice of the artist. We have, however, advanced far enough to be reasonably sure that illiterate blundering and vulgar pretense can no longer offer the slightest obstacle to this progress. It is now in your own hands; it is for you to guide its fortunes.

Richard Morris Hunt

(1895)

At the request of those whose wishes I am bound to respect, the honorable duty of formally commemorating the life and professional career of our brother, Richard Morris Hunt, Third President of the American Institute of Architects, has devolved, — unworthily, I fear, — upon me.

But, in fulfilling this duty, there is nothing to be condoned; there are no prejudices in your minds to be laboriously overcome, no facts to be ingeniously suppressed, nothing to be exaggerated or justified by the art of the rhetorician. The career which we are about to celebrate was one so open, so conspicuous, so fortunate and complete, the personality which made it possible was so candid, so vigorous, so gracious, so accomplished, that this Institute, identified with it from the beginning, is eager to welcome all that can be said in its praise. I submit to you, therefore, no perfunctory panegyric, but the unaffected impressions of a man, singularly representative of all the best qualities which can adorn an architect and a gentleman, a man, to whom the profession in this country for its own sake, owes a formal tribute of commemoration and acknowledgment, a man, who not only won our respect and admiration for what he did, but our affection for what he was.

The Angel of Death cannot destroy a full and true life; rather does he preserve it. He confers upon it that symmetry, unity and completeness which remain with us always to quicken and inspire. He purges it of all accidental and unessential elements, and makes a visible and enduring monument of its virtues. The dread Architect has thus rounded off and made beautiful for us forever this large, brilliant and blameless career. But we, brothers in the craft, which this career illustrated and adorned, heavy with a sense of a bereavement which seems irreparable, cannot but grieve that it has closed, and that the living man, whom we admired and loved, we shall no more see or hear. Irreparable, did I say? Not irreparable, so long as we continue to measure ourselves by the high standard of professional conduct which he established, so long as the spirit of serious and tranquil beauty which pervaded his works shall continue to exercise prolific power in the architecture of the new world. For it is the greatest felicity of the masters that what was best in them enjoys blessed immortality in their works and remains to keep alive the divine fire of art.

Those rare qualities in the master whom we now commemorate, which created that peculiar personal affection of which I have spoken, can hardly be made real to those who never came in contact with him; but the genius and training of the man, which expressed themselves in concrete form, can perhaps be so celebrated that those who follow us may, like ourselves, light their torches at his shrine. We, who have been near to Hunt find it difficult to separate the man from his works. To us they together constitute a unity so full of distinction and character, so pervaded and inspired by art, that no history of the development of our architecture in the latter half of the nineteenth century would be possible without a recognition of it as one of its most potent factors.

One of the wisest of men has said that there is something even in the most obscure and humble life, which, if it could be revealed, would be of the utmost interest and value to all mankind.[1] Surely in the noble and conspicuous life which we are now considering it should not be difficult to uncover this precious germ.

I shall not here attempt a detailed biography of Richard Morris Hunt, with all the dates, all the incidents, accidents, honors and accomplishments of his varied career, though the necessity for such a fullness of record is already keenly felt and doubtless will be duly satisfied while the memory of them is yet green and fragrant in the great household of his friends. In the brief time at my disposal I shall only try to account for those qualities in the man which made him dear to us, and which are necessary to be commemorated by this Institute as a part of the history of contemporary architecture.

He was born at Brattleboro, Vermont, October 31st, 1828. He died at Newport, Rhode Island, July 31st, 1895. In three months more the full measure of his life would have been sixty-seven years. He was the fourth of the five children of the Hon. Jonathan Hunt and of his wife, Jane Maria Leavitt, both descended from old New England stock. His father, a gentleman of ample means and high consideration in Vermont, represented that Commonwealth in Congress from 1827 to 1832, and died in Washington while in the public service. The education and training of the young children thus fell into the hands of the maternal grandmother, whose gentle influence was all for sweetness and light, and of the mother, who, fortunately for them, fortunately, indeed, for the future of art in America, was a woman of high spirit, great force of character, and of accomplishments far in advance of her time. She made her own ambitious ideals the standards for them; to their best culture she devoted herself with peculiar energy and sound discretion, and her old age was crowned with their success. She lived to see two of her sons, William and Richard, *par nobile fratrum*,[2] recognized by the civilized world as the most conspicuous and most imposing forces in the development of our national art, the one in painting, the other in architecture, and both as the most lovable and most fascinating of men.

Richard's earliest training was mainly in a private school in New Haven, and in the public schools of Boston. But he was only fifteen years of age when the family moved to Europe and took residence in Geneva, where, following that inborn instinct for art which responds so generously to culture, he studied architecture and drawing for five years in the atelier of Samuel Darier.[3] This experience determined his career and in 1848 Richard confirmed it by entering the Ecole des Beaux Arts of Paris as an élève in the atelier of Hector Martin Lefuel,[4] who thus became his patron. The influence by which he was then surrounded in those happy years of pupilage, the atmosphere of generous emulation which he breathed, the ardent friendships which he formed, apparently converted this spirited American lad into a Frenchman. But beneath the gay and impulsive exterior of the Parisian the solid good sense of his New England stock held him steady and strengthened and confirmed his artistic conscience. This was enlarged and educated by extensive travel in the East and indeed throughout the whole world wherever art had left a mark. Never has travel borne richer fruits or inspired a more receptive or more eager mind.

There were six of these abundant years of study and travel for the brilliant young American, and when his patron, Lefuel, was appointed to succeed Visconti[5] as architect of the new works on the Louvre (Figs. 95, 95a, 95b), by which Napoleon III. desired to make fitting monumental record of his reign, he procured for his favorite pupil a government appointment as inspector of works, and, in that capacity, gave him supervision over the construction of the Pavillon de la Bibliothèque. He was only twenty-six years of age when he entered upon this important duty and he amply justified the singular confidence reposed in him. There is a certain picturesque surprise in the spectacle of a Yankee lad giving form and character to one of the imperial monuments of France. Lefuel, of course, was the responsible architect of this as of all the other new works of the palace, but, while providing for the unity of the masses of buildings composing it and for the proper maintence of the national traditions in this great, historical monument, he knew how to use the abilities of his subordinates to the best advantage in developing the details. In a letter to Mrs. Hunt written in 1867, he said: "My greatest work was done while dear Dick worked with me, and he can justly claim a great share of its success. I do not hide from you those circumstances of which his own modesty does not permit him to speak." This semi-independent position was the opportunity which the ambition of Hunt most needed and most ardently desired. It gave him practical experience in a work illustrating on a great scale just those qualities of academic architecture most congenial to him, and it is a pleasure for us, his pupils, his friends and countrymen, to observe that the part of the new Louvre most remarkable for elegant reserve and temperance of expression in the midst of the most seductive temptations to prodigality which the resources and traditions of the national architecture could present to an enthusiastic nature like that of Hunt, is certainly the Pavillon de la Bibliothèque.

In 1855, in his twenty-seventh year, after an education and training such as no American architect had before or, indeed, has since enjoyed, Hunt returned to his native land, accredited as an ambassador of art from the abounding wealth of the old world to the infinite possibilities of the new. Desiring to become familiar with the methods of work prevailing at home, he immediately sought and obtained employment with Thomas U. Walter, afterwards the second president of this Institute, and then architect of the Capitol extensions at Washington.[6] After six months of this service he returned to New York and began the independent practice of his profession.

This beginning was, as usual with all beginnings, small, uncertain and beset with disappointments. The new world was not then hospitable to such high ideals, such noble enthusiasms, as this first American thoroughbred brought with him from the schools of Paris. He found himself an exile in his own country, and, if he had not been inspired by a patriotic ardor and hopefulness which possessed his whole heart to the end, he would more than once have been tempted to listen to the ardent entreaties of his old comrades in art, who, with sympathetic affection, were eager to welcome him back to the more congenial atmosphere of the old world. There, doubtless, he could have made for himself a great career, for the architecture of France knew that it had lost in this young aspirant one of the most vigorous and brilliant personalities which for many years had appeared in its schools. But his natural loyalty was unshaken, and he stayed because he loved his country and because he modestly believed that, sooner or later, he could do something to direct a part of its crude but tremendous energy to the service of beauty and truth in art.

At this point began my own association with Hunt, and I trust that what I have to reveal concerning this association, and what this association revealed to me, may be the excuse for the personal element which must now enter into this brief narration.

Those of us who were fortunate enough to be placed under the immediate influence of Hunt as his pupils will never forget either the wealth of his resources or the inspiring nature of his instruction. These resources were placed at our disposal with a most lavish hand, and, under the vehement and strenuous manner of the master we quickly discovered the truth and tenderness of his heart. The study of architecture at that time was pursued under the most discouraging conditions. The art was ill understood and indeed hardly respected by the public. There were no schools in which it was recognized as a desirable subject for study. There were but few books available and our traditions were eminently provincial. Examples of good work were so rare that our ideals of perfection were incoherent and doubtful, and were swayed, now in one direction and now in another, by the literary warfare then prevailing between Gothic and classic camps. Mediævalism was

331

sustaining itself by the religious ardor of Pugin and the brilliant rhetoric and poetic imagery of Ruskin. Sentiment was keenly aroused, but discipline was silent. But, though the atmosphere was thick with prejudice and controversy, there was an intellectual movement in the midst of it exceedingly attractive to young men of education and artistic instincts.

In the autumn of 1858, three earnest aspirants for architectural knowledge, applied to Hunt, who had then just completed the Tenth Street Studio Building in New York, to take one of the studios himself and install them there as his pupils (Figs. 167, 168). One of these applicants, our present honored vice-president, George B. Post, had just graduated from the Engineering School of the New York University; the other two were Charles D. Gambrill[7] and myself, who, since their graduation at Harvard four years before, had been pursuing the study of architecture under the somewhat discouraging conditions which then prevailed.

It is due to our dear comrade Gambrill to state here, as a part of this story, that subsequently he entered into two successive partnerships, one with Post and one with Richardson, and that his untimely death, interrupting a career of singular promise, was a loss, not to his friends only, but to the architecture of America.

With the noble generosity of the true artist, Hunt granted our request and equipped one of the studios for our use. Early in the following year we were joined by William R. Ware, now one of the most honored and best beloved names in the history of American architecture, and subsequently by Frank Furness,[8] our comrade from Philadelphia, and by Edmund Quincy and E. L. Hyde, who never practiced our art. Thus we together entered upon an era so rich, so full of surprise and delight that it seems, as we look back upon it, as if once more in the world the joy of the Renaissance, the white light of knowledge had broken in upon the superstitions of romance. To us it was a revelation and an enlargement of vision so sudden and complete that the few years spent by us in that stimulating atmosphere were the most memorable and eventful in life. But if the disciples were glad to learn, the master was generous to teach.

His own studio and home at that time were in the old University Building on Washington Square (Fig. 16). Here he lived as bachelor in spacious and lofty apartments, filled with the spoils of foreign travel. Here were carved antique cabinets, filled with bronzes, medallions, precious glass of Venice and curiosities of fine handiwork in all the arts. The walls were rich with hangings, old panels, sculptured or painted, and modern studies from the studios of Paris. These, together with mediæval missals and embroideries, instruments of music, masterpieces of forged and wrought metal work and of Faience, strange and costly toys of every era of civilization brought into the great chamber the mellow atmosphere of the old world. More than all this to us was Hunt's noble and inexhaustible library, by far the richest, most comprehensive, and most curious collection of books on architecture and the other fine arts which at that time had been brought together in the new world. I doubt if even now this precious library is exceeded in some respects by any of the more modern public collections.

To these treasures the fortunate pupils were welcomed with boundless hospitality. Indeed, Hunt's attitude sometimes made us feel that he considered the labor and cost of bringing them together justified in the light which they shed upon us. For myself I can truly say that the hours spent in the gracious seclusion of that dim chamber were the most fruitful in my life. The aspect of every page, the emotions of every revelation of the world of art come back to my memory clear and distinct as I speak in gratitude and affection.

Our own workshop in the Studio Building was hung with cartoons in colors, and furnished with casts of architectural and decorative detail. Even that working place was not without its ancient carved chimney piece and its cabinets of tarnished gilding (Fig. 4). Here we lived in the midst of a congenial and sympathetic brotherhood of painters and sculptors from the neighboring studios, happy Bohemians, free to come and go as we pleased. Our system of study and practice was based upon that of the Ecole des Beaux Arts, and under the powerful stimulus of the master's criticisms and under the inspiration of the atmosphere which he had created for us, our work was carried on with enthusiastic loyalty. If outside of our boundaries there seemed to be little or no recognition of architecture as a fine art, within it was not only illustrated by all the wealth of the old world but made living to us by the almost tempestuous zeal of the master. In such a place the most unimaginative mind could not fail to be kindled. Whatever latent powers of expression in art we might have were aroused to vigorous action. In that beautiful chamber where he lived we traversed every corner of the world of art and filled our sketch books with the fruits of enchanted travel. But amidst all this excitement and enthusiasm Hunt ever insisted upon the pre-eminent importance of academical discipline and order in design. He was most concerned that the sub-structure of our knowledge should be serious, sane and solid. We were instructed to make our plans on rigidly scholastic lines, and the vertical developments in the elevations we were taught to study in strict classic form according to the method of the French school. Respect for authority and discipline was thus inculcated and we unlearned much of the romantic license which at that time tended to turn the practice of architecture into the hands of amateurs and virtuosos. But while he insisted on the preservation of the classic formulas for the sake of the training of mind and hand, he heartily encouraged the study of every style in which the thought of man had expressed itself in beauty or power. His photographs, books and prints, his own drawings gave us a large view over the whole historical field (Figs. 6–15). Academic prejudices never affected the large catholicity of his mind. His criticisms of our poor attempts were pungent and severe, but so genial and picturesque, that every visit left behind it not only an enduring inspiration, but an atmosphere quickened by his energy and illuminated by his inexhaustible humor. For he was as much a comrade as a master. In short, our experience was a liberal education in the fullest sense, and when we left him with our imaginations no longer sterilized by prejudice and partisanship, but enlarged and enlightened by his influence, his warm interest in our personal and professional welfare never ceased. For myself, at least, in the years that have since gone by, the fine impulse which he first gave to my life has been revived by countless unexpected offices of kindness and solicitude. Through all the vicissitudes of time and space I have felt the warmth of his generous heart.

When, more than thirty years afterwards, in 1893, several of us were summoned to act together again with him on the great national arena at Chicago, the natural dominance of the master again asserted itself without pretension and we once more became his willing and happy pupils. To this instinct of family loyalty in art, through which all the trained intelligences then called together, became close kindred, to this ideal relationship of mutual interest and affection may be attributed in no small measure the majestic unity of the Court of Honor.

When, therefore, the Royal Institute of British Architects gave to Hunt its gold medal of 1893, it honored the man, who, more than any other, had by personal force and high training secured for the architecture of our time and country a standing adequate at last to represent our civilization in terms of art. We recognize the justice of this great distinction less because of any single achievement of his than because we feel and know that our profession has worked upon a higher plane of endeavor and has received from the public a greater respect and consideration since this man began his noble career among us. The American Institute of Architects and, indeed, the whole profession were honored in the honor conferred upon him. For the vitalizing and enchanting personality which impressed itself upon his immediate pupils, and through them upon his pupils' pupils in ever widening circles of beneficent influence, invigorated and enlivened also the first years of this Institute. The battle of the styles was then, as I have already intimated, waged all over the architectural field, and it must be confessed, the earliest discussions of this Institute were ensanguined by the great dispute. Hunt, with all the martial gallantry of his nature inspired the classic camp with ardor. The Gothic side was championed by the strongest and best equipped men in the profession. The whole historic arsenal was ransacked for weapons on both sides, and the controversy was carried on with such heat and was so engrossing that finally a vote was passed (I think it will be found in the archives), excluding this dangerous subject from the discussions of the Institute. It will be readily understood that in these animated disputes the pupils of Hunt, whose names you will see on the first lists of the Institute, where they were written thirty-seven long years ago as associates, followed the white plume of Navarre, and inspired by him with rash zeal, dared to measure their maiden weapons with those of the oldest and most experienced warriors on the other side, men who were doing work, which though our art has since immensely enlarged its scope and exalted its ideals, still holds a high place and has already become, if not venerable, at least historic. But when the smoke of battle cleared away, it would be found that the wounds were not deep and that good fellowship had suffered but little strain.

Indeed, in this respect, it would be difficult to exaggerate the change immediately effected by the establishment of the Institute in the personal and professional relationships of its members; and in this beneficent work Hunt's influence was pre-eminent. Before this establishment, community of thought, mutual friendship hardly existed among architects. The hand of each was turned with jealousy and suspicion against his brother. His processes of design and his business methods were personal secrets. Each concealed his drawings from the rest as if they were pages of a private diary. Even books and prints were carefully secluded from inspection by any rival. Pupils were apprentices, and as in my own case, often looked with eager and unsatisfied eyes through the glass of their master's locked bookcases. There were no ethics of practice, no common ground of mutual protection, no unity of action or thought, no national literature of architecture. The current professional periodicals of England and Germany furnished the sole inspiration of nearly every architectural office in the land. Our work was a dim reflection of the fashions of our British contemporaries, and in our architecture we still remained a dependent province of the mother country. Every conspicuous note which was blown on the other side of the Atlantic had futile and barren echoes in our own land.

When the first American graduate of the French School of Fine Arts appeared upon this scene of narrow architectural subserviency, of professional confusion and doubt, the conditions were ripe for change. The formation of the American Institute of Architects was not intentionally but practically a new Declaration of Independence, in which the ardor of Hunt, crowned as he was with the approval of the highest architectural authority in the old world, played the part of the big signature of John Hancock. I trust I do not underrate whatever other conditions conduced to this most memorable emancipation, but, in my own mind, among them all Hunt's influence was the most potent. I feel sure that the union and brotherhood of professional interests which then manifested itself for the first time on this continent, and the strength which came from that union and brotherhood — the strength with which you now, my brothers, are strong and independent, the strength which has made you Americans in art as in politics, — may in no small degree be attributed to the man, who, at the most critical moment in the development of our national architecture, proved by his example that the most rigid discipline and highest culture which could be furnished by the old world was not inconsistent with the most aggressive and uncompromising patriotism. He brought back from the School of Fine Arts in Paris, not merely a collection of venerable formulas and academic prejudices to make us still more dependent, but a spirit enlarged, enlightened, cosmopolitan. Under this vigorous and wholesome influence, his children in art and his children's children, who in prolific generation have multiplied so as to constitute, I verily believe, the representative majority of this Institute, ceased to be provincial and became national. Thus in respect and affection we are celebrating the career and services of one who, though but little older in years than some of us, has proved his right to be called one of the fathers of American architecture.

It is needless to repeat here the long and brilliant list of his works which include some of the most interesting monuments of our time (Figs. 146, 166–183). We all know them well, and all of us more or less consciously have gathered strength and inspiration from them. But we cannot cease to regret that the noble powers, so admirably fitted for the expression of the grandiose, the magnificent in our art, should have had their principal field, not in our national monuments, which his hand would have made worthy of our civilization, and a quickening impulse in our national art, but in decorating the superb privacies of the Vanderbilts and Goelets, the Marquands and Astors, the Belmonts and the Gerrys (Figs. 174–180, 182, 182a, 182b). Concealed behind the guarded hospitalities of these generous patrons of architecture, the studied proportion, the lovely details, the monumental beauty of Hunt's interior work are doing profitable service in the cause of a higher culture and a nobler civilization. But private work cannot be recognized as expressive of national refinement and national progress. Hunt's latest years, as you all know, when he was suffering from cruel bodily distress, were largely spent in aiding the Institute in its patriotic endeavor to bring our government to a realizing sense of its responsibilities to art. To this noble effort he devoted himself with loyal energy, and much that our cause has already won in Washington, is due to his personal influence and to the magnetic charm of his sincerity and zeal. Hearts, most inaccessible to the silent appeals of beauty and grace in art, were won at last to respect a cause which had for its advocate a man so irresistible in his vitality and so unique and charming in his presence.

But while, with the exception of two buildings at West Point, the Yorktown Monument (Fig. 41) and the National Observatory at Washington, no commissions of national importance and no official honors came to him from the government of his native land, he received from foreign countries recognition such as no other American has enjoyed.

On the 25th of November, 1882, he was made honorary and corresponding member of the Académie des Beaux Arts of the Institute of France.

On the 29th of July, 1884, he was decorated as Chevalier of the Legion of Honor, the "demande" being supported by such great names as Baudry, Bouguereau, Amboise Thomas, Ch. Garnier, Ballu, Bonnat and Falguière.

On the 26th of January, 1886, he was made member of the Société Centrale des Architectes Francaises.

On the 1st of February, 1886, he became honorary and corresponding member of the Royal Institute of British Architects.

On the 12th of April, 1887, he received similar recognition from the Society of Engineers and Architects in Vienna.

On the 29th of June, 1892, he received the degree of LL. D. from Harvard University, the first honor of the kind ever bestowed on an architect, and one which he especially cherished as coming from his native land.

On July 13th, 1892, he became an academician of the Society of St. Luke in Rome, the oldest institution devoted to art in the world.

In 1893 he received the royal gold medal of that year from the Royal Institute of British Architects, the first American thus honored.

In the same year he received perhaps the most distinguished honor of all in his election to fill a vacancy as associate member of the Institute of France, Franklin, I believe, being the only other American so distinguished.

And it is a pleasure to us to remember that in electing him third president of the American Institute of Architects in 1888, we also did him honor, while he, in that capacity, added to the obligations which all architects in this country are glad to acknowledge.

It is not improbable, indeed, that Hunt's professional accomplishments were even more highly appreciated abroad than at home. But the modesty of the man was so sincere, and his heart was so simple that all these honorable distinctions, most of which, perhaps, you now hear for the first time, were received and held by him in trust as recognitions of the progress of our national art. He did not and could not associate them with his own merits. He practiced his art, not for what it would return to him, but because he loved it, and "he blushed to find it fame." [9]

The personal attributes of Hunt gave to his professional character a captivating animation, a frank sincerity, and these qualities, combined with the dignity of his bearing and his manly beauty, made him a notable individuality wherever he moved. His artistic conscience was not a mere instrument of service to be laid aside when not in use, but an active and animating principle of his life. And so he wore it with a peculiar gallantry of manner, not before his professional comrades only, but before the world. But if his manner was sometimes extravagant and impetuous when he was charged with the enthusiasm of his heart, he more often won his audience by a touch of irresistible humor, by a gaiety and bonhomie, which betrayed the fundamental sweetness of his nature. He loved to talk of his art among his friends, and no one was ever so prompt as he to uphold the dignity of his profession, none so generous in protecting and publishing the good work of his brethren, none so gentle and so just in criticism. But he never spared any form of vulgar pretense which threatened to debase that high ideal which he sought to establish for our art in America, and he hated sham. Indeed, in the social world, where because of his accomplishments he was admired, because of his honest and manly heart he was beloved, he was the knight-errant of architecture, turning indifference into respect and doubt into honor for the supreme beauty and dignity of his mistress.

As to Hunt's professional achievements, an architect in the presence of architects cannot indulge in criticism with the freedom and confidence of judgment which are displayed by those without professional responsibilities and convictions. We are all of us too deeply committed by practice, to[o] deeply engrossed in the evolution of our own ideals to judge them without sympathy too warm for truth, or, perhaps, without bias too strong for justice. But the practice of architecture is now no longer a bitter conflict between opposing schools, each striving for preeminence at the expense of the rest, rather a generous emulation carried on upon lines, not parallel indeed, but all tending, as we hope, towards the establishment of a consistent style adequate for our vast and complicated civilization. I venture to say that no one here will question that our late illustrious comrades, Hunt and Richardson, were the most conspicuous leaders in this large and liberal movement. They brought from the French School all its discipline, all its wholesome respect for classic authority and academic principles, but in practice, they expressed themselves with a freedom from classical restraint and scholastic subserviency, which, as it would have been well-nigh impracticable in France, must, it would seem, be accepted as the result of new conditions of life acting upon trained but receptive minds. We can already recognize the service which these minds, so influenced, is exerting in the evolution of those new local types of architecture, which, through much tribulation and infinite errors, must slowly but surely be taking shape among us. The monuments which they left behind them have been powerful agents in preventing the dangerous liberty of our art in America from degenerating into license. Unlike Richardson, Hunt did not leave upon his own work an expression of strong personality, and for that reason his leadership, though far less evident and picturesque, is far safer against the dangers of aberration among his followers. No one can follow Hunt and go far afield. He did not pretend to be inventive, or desire to be original, and the impulsive individuality, so prompt to assert itself under all other conditions, nearly disappeared behind the historic types which he used in design. He respected them too much to use them consciously as a vehicle of his own temporary moods. Only once, when captivated by the phenomenal Graeco-Romantic movement in France under Labrouste, which promised at one time to turn the whole tide of French Renaissance into new channels, did his natural vivacity of temperament betray him (Fig. 171). This was an interesting incident in his career, and, by its singularity, it accentuates his prevailing mood of aristocratic reserve. His pencil in hand was a magic wand, which chastened the buoyancy of his imagination and made him a scholar. Thus he founded no new school. He prevailed, not as an irrepressible genius who breaks traditions, but as a guardian who respects them with the spirit not of an antiquarian but of an artist. His admiration for the great works of the past was based, not upon emotion and sentiment alone, but upon knowledge and solid conviction. He had no ingenious theories concerning the development of modern art; his methods of thought in design were not at all speculative or inventive, as would seem to be most natural to a mind so animated, a spirit so quick and eager; rather were they exact, reserved, business-like. These underlying qualities preserved him from eccentricities or experiments in architectural expression and extended to the conduct of his affairs and the discipline of his office.

He worked with great ease and pleasure to himself in modern French Renaissance, purified and chastened by Greek influence. This, as it were, was his native tongue. In his hands this style was flexible to all the new conditions of material and use in the New World, but his characteristic use of it was rather serious and restrained than playful or expansive. It is in this respect, I believe, that his example is most valuable in the development of national style. But he left behind him also, in proof of the versatility and liberality of his mind, a series of conspicuous works based upon the architectural expressions of an era when the art of the Middle Ages was adjusting itself with astonishing felicity to the exactions of the higher civilization and of the more refined domestic ideals of the sixteenth century. As Richardson found in the vigorous promise of the Romanesque of Auvergne a language of art, agreeable to the robust nature of his genius, and capable of new developments in the service of modern life, Hunt discovered the prolific germs of new life in the lovely domestic Gothic of Touraine, whose progress was checked by the revival of learning in the sixteenth century in France. In the luxurious and flamboyant delicacy of this style, in its elasticity and bright exuberance, in its poetic beauty and cheerfulness, he seemed to find a medium of architectural expression, congenial to his own indomitable youthfulness of heart and not inconsistent with the dignity and order of his cherished ideals (Figs. 174, 176, 177, 180, 182).

Among his latest works the superb house of the Goelets and the interior of the beautiful pavilions of Belcourt at Newport, and, above all, the château of Biltmore in North Carolina, bear witness not only to his profound respect for authority and to his command of precedent, but to a certain pliability of mind, which enabled him to accommodate all the complicated conditions of modern living within the reasonable compass of the Gothic of Chambord or of Pierrefonds. Indeed, in these works he carried the style a step further in natural development without any conscious attempt to express in it his own insistent individuality. No one who studies these beautiful compositions in plan or elevation, without or within, can fail to be impressed by the patient and conscientious elaboration of their delicate detail, and by the constant evidence of wise self-repression and reserved force.

When Hunt began his career in America the English Gothic revival had full possession of the field, and architecture seemed to be in the hands rather of archæological pedants than of creative artists. There was no life in it; it was never happily adjusted to modern conditions and it came to nothing. It now only survives under the protection of the English Church. But the rehabilitations which we are now considering were in the hands of intelligences, disciplined by classical studies yet open to all the inspirations of a new life in a new world. If they were romantic in form they were modern, they were American in feeling. No service of the life of to-day was inconvenienced or embarrassed for the sake of archaeological conformity. Hunt's experiments in romantic style, therefore, promise if rightly used, to serve as enlargements and enrichments of the language of American architecture; they are surely not obstacles to its natural development and will not be set down as barren events in the history of our art.

His ardent solicitude for every detail and process of artisanship which contributed to the architectural symphony brought him into close contact with contractors and skilled mechanics of every calling and grade. Between the master and the workmen there arose a warm feeling of mutual respect and consideration which is the strongest possible testimony of the unaffected simplicity and sincerity of his heart and of his ability to teach without condescension and to correct without offence. It was in affectionate recognition of these rare and gentle qualities of the master that, in completing the W. K. Vanderbilt house in New York (Fig. 174), that delicate casket of precious architecture, the workmen, using a wisely given liberty of design in carving the finial of the highest gable, placed there the life-sized portrait figure of the architect in the garb of a fellow-workman with mallet and chisel in hand. In this way he was elected into a companionship of honorable toil, and, when he died, the family received many touching tributes of respectful sympathy from the master workmen who had enjoyed the privilege of his friendship. Among these expressions there was one from the workmen of Biltmore, embodied on a series of resolutions so significant that I venture to repeat their words:

Whereas, the great Architect of the Universe has in His wisdom removed our fellow laborer, Richard M. Hunt, from this earthly mansion to a building of God, a house not made with hands, eternal in the heavens; and

Whereas, his fame as an artist and his devotion to and his accomplishments in his profession are known to the world, but his generosity, sympathy, and services in behalf of the worthy laboring men of all classes are only known to those whose good fortune it was to be under his immediate supervision;

Therefore we who have worked under him, deeming it fitting that we record our love for and appreciation of him, have

Resolved, that in his death our country has lost its greatest architect, and our skilled workmen, artists and sculptors have lost a kind, considerate and constant friend; for neither his great fame nor his wealth ever caused him to be forgetful, indifferent, or careless of the rights and feelings of his fellowmen and laborers who were aiding in an humbler way in erecting these beautiful buildings, which, only marvellous genius could have imagined and planned;

Resolved, that to him more than any other man of our time all the representative workmen of this country are indebted for the elevation of their trades and arts to the position which they now hold in the ranks of the great army of skilled workmen.

Resolved, that we tender his afflicted family our deepest sympathy and that a copy of these Resolutions be sent to his widow.

Dated at Biltmore, N. C., August 1st, 1895.

B. Worth . . . . . . for the carpenters	J. Miller . . . . for the stone carvers
J. O'Neill . . . . . . bricklayers	J. C. Thompson . . . painters
G. Bartigate . . . . . stone cutters	L. Bowen . . . . . . electricians
S. J. McKeon . . . . plumbers	E. D. Holt . . . . . . tile layers
R. J. Miller . . . . . marble cutters	P. F. Jones . . . . . . coppersmiths
S. C. Gladwyn . . . wood carvers	and slaters
J. Mortimer . . . . . plasterers	P. McNiven . . . . . stone setters

COMMITTEE.

Chairman, George Bartigate,   Secretary, S. C. Gladwyn.

Surely such a testimonial as this is a precious and inspiring inheritance to those who bear the responsibilities of his name, — no less inspiring, no less precious than the tender and loving tributes of the master of that great estate. The principal decorations of the great hall are two life size portraits by Sargent, one of Hunt and the other of Olmsted, who on this splendid field, as elsewhere, worked in most fortunate sympathy to the glory of art in America.

In the opening of this discourse I ventured to intimate that the life which we are commemorating was full, fortunate and complete, beyond the common lot of mankind. I hesitate to speak of the element most essential to this almost ideal condition of felicity and success which was furnished in Hunt's marriage in 1861 to Catherine Howland, daughter of the senior member of the old and famous firm of Howland & Aspinwall of New York. To this alliance he was indebted for a high companionship of the soul, a solace of perfect appreciation, a constant service of sympathy, consecrating all the most productive years of his life. His children, three boys and two girls, surrounded him with respect and devotion, and grandchildren came to make new demands on his inexhaustible capacity of love. Of the two older boys one, as you know, was associated with him in business, and the other has now begun his second year at the Ecole in Paris. May they carry through another generation in triumph the illustrious name they bear!

In this atmosphere of peace and material prosperity, his fame increasing, his opportunities multiplying, compassed by a cloud of witnesses who admired and praised him, the love of his art possessed him with an ever increasing passion. In his last years, when pain and serious disabilities came upon him, this indomitable love was his comfort and consolation. Even in his last and darkest days the desire of creating filled his still active mind with a fair imagery, which, we may truly believe, though here unexpressed in form, was not a vain dreaming. "Even in his ashes live his wonted fires." [10] Upon his deathbed he was seen to raise his hand and, with the fine gesture of the artist, to trace as with a pencil in the air a line of beauty, delicately but firmly fitting the act of grace to the unconscious study of his imagination. And so, a few moments later, with insensible transition, bearing with him the divine creative gift, unsullied, undiminished, immortal, he passed over into the larger life.

> And doubtless unto him is given
> A life that bears immortal fruit,
> In such great offices as suit
> The full-grown energies of Heaven.[11]

Classic Architecture

*From the Point of View of an Architect. A
Discourse Before Johns Hopkins University,
at Baltimore, Md.*[1]

(1895)

Primitive or barbarous nations, being free from the restraints of custom and
highly emotional, express themselves spontaneously in song or ballad. The
effect of culture is to give form and order to these expressions without necessary loss of poetic fire. In like manner architecture gradually developed from
conditions of picturesque liberty among uncivilized races, — a liberty which
often broke into irregular and unconscious expressions of beauty or power,
— into the discipline and ceremonious elegance which distinguish the buildings of races which are advanced in civilization. This discipline of architecture
has been made possible and is still maintained by the remarkable influence
of a certain clearly defined and highly organized system of historical forms,
which though it has by usage become arbitrary, artificial or conventional, has
asserted itself with powerful insistence, and may be recognized not only in
general effects of symmetry and balance of parts, in a certain air of punctilious
formality and self-restraint, but, with infinite variations, in familiar details of
cornice or entablature, of piers or pilasters, and in the decoration of apertures
and wall spaces. This system still prevails in almost every street of every city
of the civilized world.

Though this system of forms has now little or no essential relation to structure, it has been preserved for twenty-two centuries. It has become a sacred
tradition, and schools have been formed to preserve and cultivate it. The
progress and character of civilization among nations and races through this
long historic period is measured by the degree of purity in which this sacred
tradition has been maintained. When civilization declined, it was debased; in
the dark ages it was forgotten; it was revived with the revival of learning; when
civilization has been most highly illuminated, it has become a cult. Every
nation, and, indeed, every reign since the establishment of the Renaissance,
has unconsciously used this tradition in its own way; has enlarged it or modi-

fied it to suit its own material conditions or to express its own characteristic spirit or genius.

This system of forms has thus been subjected to the same formative conditions as language, and it has by these enlargements, become capable of expressing various moods and fashions of thought in terms of architecture. Efforts have been made in modern times to prove by reasoning that this cult is a mere superstition, that it is an arbitrary impediment to the rational development of style, and to replace it with some other system of forms more logical and less arbitrary. The Gothic revival of the earlier half of the Nineteenth century is one of these attempts. This and all the other romantic revivals of the century have thus far only succeeded in enlarging our vocabulary of forms. They have not supplanted, as yet, that older system, which, however conventional, has so grown with the growth of the human mind, is so involved with the history of our race, that it must still be accepted as the basis of architectural speech.

This system of forms, which has survived through such vicissitudes and has had a career so prodigious and so prolific, is classic architecture.

When, through the generosity and public spirit of my professional brother and friend, your fellow citizen, Mr. Wyatt, I had the honor of receiving an invitation to discourse before this university and its friends on this subject of classic architecture, it seemed to me that the time at my disposal, inadequate for the proper discussion of so great a theme, should be used, not in a vain attempt to relate its history or to expound its technique — all this is done in many accessible manuals, — but in an effort to give you, from the point of view of an architect, some reasons for the extraordinary survival which I have referred to, to point out, if possible, some of the qualities in classic architecture which have enabled it to exercise an influence so profound that all the greatest monuments of architecture have been inspired and continue to be inspired, refreshed and purified by constant reference to it as to the highest authority in our art. I desire to show that the survival of classic architecture is not an accident or caprice of fashion, and that it has not been maintained as a living power merely by the prejudice of archæological pedantry or by the insistance of an organized propaganda in the schools, but that it is a logical result from the fact that once in the course of human history, twenty two centuries ago, a gifted people in a remote corner of Europe, surrounded by favorable conditions, achieved for the first and only time in history, a demonstrable perfection in its monuments, and that the ideal, thereby established, could not sleep upon its laurels on the Acropolis of Athens. This perfection, when properly understood, became inspiration, and has been prolific among all subsequent races, in exact proportion to their intelligence and refinement.

As the architecture of the Greeks has been proved to be the highest result of pure creation in the history of mankind, the study of it brings receptive and intelligent minds into immediate and sympathetic contact with the operations of the most subtle and most fastidious intellects ever devoted to the development of form in art. This study sadly misses its aim if it only succeeds in planting the seeds of scholastic prejudice and narrow archæological pedantry. Properly pursued, it not only purifies, inspires and refines the creative instinct, but enlarges the mind and makes it sensitive to every touch of high emotion, not in architecture alone, but in painting, in sculpture, in music, and in literature. In fact it furnishes the most essential elements of a liberal education. Before such an audience as this therefore the serious consideration of what is meant by classic architecture hardly needs an apology.

The simplest element of structure known to man consists in laying a horizontal beam upon two separated upright posts. All the architecture of Egypt, Assyria and Greece was based upon this structural formula, distinctive character or style being conferred upon it in each case by the nature of the building material available, by conditions of climate, by religious and political influences, and, above all, by the spirit or genius of the people expressing itself unconsciously in art. As the systems of architecture, which we call styles, are never inventions, but always growths, the styles of Greece must be considered as developments from those of all the older Oriental nations with which it had any commercial affiliations. But the genius of the Greeks was too original and too powerful to be merely eclectic in its manifestations in art or to be content with any amalgam, however ingenious, of foreign styles. Even in their archaic monuments we cannot discover any direct imitation or repetition of what the wandering Greeks had seen in the cities of the Nile or the Euphrates. On the contrary wherever they went they rather gave than received inspirations. Their earlier structures were naturally in wood, the post and lintel system in its most obvious forms being applied to the closure of their buildings, and when, with the rapid advance of their civilization, they constructed in stone or marble, they reproduced in the nobler material the most characteristic features of wooden construction. The horizontal lintel beam became the architrave or epistyle. The ends of the ceiling beams which crossed the building and rested on the lintel were evident in the triglyphs of the frieze; the spaces between the beams, originally left open for light and air, were closed with slabs, generally sculptured, which we know as the metopes of the frieze; the sheathed ends of the sloping roof beams or rafters, projecting over the frieze for protection, we recognize in the overhanging cornice or corona. All the principal distinctive features of the Doric entablature are thus simply accounted for. Some of the earliest Hellenic monuments in marble, notably certain Lydian tombs, recall the wooden prototypes very frankly. These prototypes however simple and unaffected, belonged to the heroic period of Greece, and having been sanctified by religious associations and by ancient usage, were preserved in their later monuments as an instinctive expression of loyalty to national traditions. No intelligent man has ever found it necessary to invent a new language for the adequate expression of his inspirations, and no true artist ever wasted his energies in a vain attempt to invent a new style of architecture. Indeed, a style of architecture is only the unconscious shaping of traditions to meet new conditions of life and thought.

To this instinct of loyalty to traditions may be attributed also the Hellenic custom of covering the pure white marble of their temples with pigments of contrasting tints in imitation of the color effects produced by the necessary application of preservative coats of paint to the wooden originals. The color effects seemed to them inseparable from the forms of the ancient monuments and were instinctively preserved even when the material used was in itself durable and beautiful and no longer needed such protection. Ingenious attempts have been made in modern times to account for the apparent anomaly of covering Pentelic marble, in part at least, with paint on the ground that this application was primarily intended to enhance by color certain architectural values otherwise dependent on mere contrasts of unassisted light and shade. We find it impossible to believe that the Hellenic mind, accepting color among other consecrated traditions, failed to apply it with the same unerring judgment, the same fastidious taste that they used in adapting wooden forms to constructions in stone or marble. But it is not probable that they used color primarily because it was esthetically necessary to the architectural scheme.

The American school of classical studies at Athens, established under the wise protection of this university and of other similar institutions in our own country, has already, in competition with the schools maintained there by other countries, done signal service in uncovering the precious fragments of tombs, temples, gateways or propylaea, theatres, stoas and choragic monuments in Greece proper, in the Islands of the Ægean, and wherever else on the borders of the Mediterranean restless Hellenic enterprise planted its colonies. Every revelation that is made is a confirmation of the proposition that, though the Greeks in their minor monuments freely experimented with form, as was clearly proved by our own investigations at Assos, in Asia Minor, there can still be traced among these crumbling remains a perfectly reasonable, steady and unaffected development of form from archaic beginnings to a point of achievement, to which the experiments and studies of the greatest artists in the world during all the succeeding centuries have been able to add no new perfection. They have varied but they have never improved the supreme Hellenic type; it still remains to us the ideal of tranquil beauty. During this period of growth Greek civilization remained simple and made no complicated or embarrassing demands upon the ingenuity of the architects. Domestic life required no costly mansions, and palaces, in the modern sense, were not suggested either by the political or social system of the Greeks. The architectural type was not expanded or diverted to meet new and exacting conditions of living, but enjoyed the vast advantage of development on simple lines in the midst of a people becoming more and more fastidious in respect to the expression of pure beauty and aristocratic grace in their public monuments. This expression was rather serious than sumptuous, for the succession of monuments which most clearly marked the progress of architecture was not in the service of civic or secular, but of religious life. Thus we have at first the simple cella or room, containing the image of the god; then a portico was added, formed of two columns standing in a front recess of the temple, like those of the tomb at Beni Hassan on the Nile, generally supposed to be the prototype of the Greek Doric shaft; the type was presently expanded into the prostyle temple, decorated in front with a row of four, six or eight free standing columns; then the interior of the temple was divided into two rooms requiring a corresponding portico in the rear of the temple, which thus became amphiprostyle; finally as wealth increased, the gods were more worthily enshrined in greater and longer temples with various interior subdivisions for a more complicated worship and a higher ceremonial, and these temples began to have columns, not only on the front and rear, but on the sides of the exterior, thus completely enclosing the cella with a peristyle or open screen to protect and make precious the abode of the god. Later there were added for a more majestic approach to the sacred place a double range of columns in front, and thus, finally was evolved the type which expressed in terms of architecture the highest civilization of the Greeks. In this way the Greek artist, undiverted by any such embarrassing complication of requirements as confront us in more modern days, too intent upon the harmonious development of his own style to be attracted by those of other nations, was enabled to concentrate his activity and intelligence on the evolution of detail. The hieratic theme was too sacred to be trifled with and it was maintained to the end in simple and majestic integrity.

In all the temples the columns supported an entablature composed of three elements, which were derived originally, as we have seen, from wooden construction, and which, following the Latin method, we call the architrave, frieze and cornice. Each of these was subdivided into certain minor parts which had definite and recognized relations to the whole. By a process of patient and minute experiments, carried on in successive temples, these major and minor divisions of the entablature were subjected to delicate variations in the efforts to achieve perfection in proportion and in the expression of function. The profile and proportion of every moulding were studied with a fastidious care, and modeled with the utmost subtlety and delicacy of curvature; certain of them began to receive conventional decorations in color or sculpture, or were broken vertically into dentils in order to introduce elements of contrast into the composition and to confer such a degree of elegance and richness upon the composition as it could bear without loss of purity and repose. The extreme fineness and brilliant whiteness of the material in which they worked and the wonderful clearness of the atmosphere of Attica, encouraged this supreme finish of detail. The perceptions of the artists, trained to a high degree of sensitiveness, noted that the broad shadow of the overhanging corona, thrown upon the surface of the frieze beneath, was broken by a series of horizontal half lights and reflections, made by the mouldings which were covered by this shadow. These horizontal contrasts of light and shade, broken by the regular vertical recurrence of dentils and triglyphs, were provided for in the study of profiles with such delicacy that the sun as it touched the marble monument, seemed to extract from it harmonies far more subtle than any evolved from Memphian colossi.

This cultivated sensitiveness of perception was applied to the evolution of the column with remarkable results. The Greek artist observed that the marble shaft, as originally developed from the prototype of the dressed tree trunk, though it was structurally able to perform its functions of support, did not seem to be able to do so with that ease and elegance necessary to the satisfaction of his eye. A cylindrical form diminishing regularly from base to summit appeared, by an instinctive defect of vision, to have a slight inward curve, which weakened its structural expression, and deprived it of energy. This obvious defect he corrected by modeling it with a slight outward curve or swell, which is called the entasis; this curve, like that of a muscle in effort, conferred upon the shaft a certain movement which immediately elevated a mere mechanical feature into the domain of art. He observed also that the light, as it fell upon this shaft of circular section, made a shade upon it of such gentle gradations from light to dark that it still seemed to need an adequate expression of power, which was ingeniously supplied by cutting the smooth surface into a series of vertical channels or flutings, which, not only broke up these too gentle gradations of shade, but repeated the fine curve of the entasis in exquisite variation.

Interposed between the vertical shaft and the horizontal entablature there was originally a plain square block, called the abacus. In the process of this development of structure into architecture, which we are now following, it was early discovered that this transition between supporting and supported members was far too abrupt, too coarse to meet the condition of design at this most important point in the architectural scheme. So the fastidious Greek presently began to interpose between the top of the shaft and the abacus, a moulding of support, developed from the round surface known as the echinus. The experiments made in successive structures in the evolution of this most interesting feature in Greek architecture betray the extreme anxiety of the artist to make it worthy of its position and function. It was a study of curves expressive of various degrees of energy in action, varying infinitely from soft undercut outlines, like those of a crushed cushion, as in the capital of the temple on the Acropolis of Selinus in the Sicilian colony, to the straight rigid lines of the inverted cone which forms the echinus of the capital in the portico of Philip at Delos. Between these extremes the variation in the character of this curve is infinite. As the development of the style approached perfection these curves became so subtle and were so delicately adjusted to the conditions of proportion that they seemed to be foreordained in the base of the shaft, as the potentiality of the flower is in the root of the plant. Indeed, by these refining processes, the architecture became so highly organized, so sensitive, that a variation in the diameter of the shaft, or in its height or its entasis would directly affect the curve of the echinus. This mutual interdependence of parts became so complete that gradually the entire structure grew into an organic unity like that of the human body. Nothing could be added to it or taken away from it without a shock to the entire system. This was not a mechanical unity, like that of a watch or a locomotive, but a living unity or organism, affected by conditions of material, of climate, of surroundings, of size and use. By the operations of these conditions every example, like an individual or a personality, differed reasonably from every other.

In the early part of the present century it was discovered by Penrose, an English architect,[2] after very careful measurements, that the horizontal lines of the stylobate or platform on which the peristyle of the Parthenon rests and those of the entablature which the peristyle supports are all subjected to a slight curvature vertically. It is supposed that this extremely delicate refinement was, like that of the entasis of the column, intended to correct an apparent visual error. In the same service of refinement the axial lines of all the columns of the Parthenon have been found to incline inward slightly, and the diameter of the corner columns was increased so that, when seen from such a point that they were projected against the sky, their outlines might not be so eaten away by the light as to seem inadequate to perform their service with the other members of the peristyle which had the solid cella of the temple for a background.

This organic unity, which I have attempted to describe to you in very brief outline, as a growth out of the physical, social, religious, political and mental conditions of a great people, and not as an accident or an invention, is the Greek Doric style. The decoration of its gables and friezes inspired Phidias to his greatest work in the Parthenon, which must be considered not only the highest and most splendid expression of the Doric style in Greece, but the most perfect ideal of architecture for modern times, and, indeed, for the entire future of the human race, not for imitation, but for inspiration.

In this style the Greeks expressed their native genius most naturally and with the greatest success, for they were a Doric people, and the Doric style prevailed in all their greatest works on the shores of the Mediterranean, not with the tedious iteration of a perfect formula or axiom of architecture, but with an infinite variety of detail and proportion, all loyal to the essential spirit of the style. Its perfection, however, was possible only on Attic ground. The Ionic style, though an Asiatic importation, was so transformed and so elevated by the genius of the Greeks, that it became characteristically Hellenic. The ponderous and heroic majesty of the Doric was not readily adjusted to all the uses of architectural design, and the Greeks, when they desired to use a lighter entablature and more delicate columns were glad to avail themselves of certain suggestions from the coasts of Asia Minor and Syria. The most important of these suggestions was the use of the helix or spiral ornament in certain Persian and Assyrian capitals, from which the Greek artist with a divine creative instinct, developed the Ionic capital. The proportions of the shaft were made more delicate and effeminate than those of the Doric shaft; it was furnished with a moulded base, and the suggestions of the oriental entablature were expanded into the Ionic entablature of three members. The details differed from those of the Doric entablature, and the whole composition, as was the case with the Doric style, gradually assumed its especial proportions and characteristics, and another organism composed of interdependent and mutually balanced parts, was created, lighter and more delicate than the native Doric organism, but capable of even a larger range of expression, from the virginal grace and almost effeminate refinement of the little temple of Wingless Victory before the propylæa of the Acropolis of Athens to the sumptuous splendor of the peristyle of the Mausoleum of Halicarnassus, and the portico of Minerva Polias of the Erectheum.

The growth of these two styles was nearly contemporaneous and both were carried to the highest degree of perfection both in spirit of design and mechanical execution. I have tried to make it clear that this perfection was the result of a very deliberate and thoughtful growth. It was less affected in its development by caprice or by undisciplined emotion, or by personal moods than any other form in the history of art. Like every other style or school of art, the Doric and Ionic of Greece were enriched as they grew, by the creative instinct of great artists. But the Greek artists worked with a sense of high responsibility and in the presence of a people intensely jealous lest their hieratic architecture should receive a stain. With unerring judgment, they rejected every accretion, however poetic or ingenious, which was found not essential to its sublime unity. They strove to make it more beautiful and more perfect by purification and refinement, not, like the ancient and modern barbarians, by intricacy and ornamentation. It was not suffered to grow at will like a wild thing — like the Romantic styles, for instance, — but the two religious and heroic systems of forms which had come to them by tradition, were kept chaste and pure as they developed. None of the creations of man have been subjected to study so continuous and so profound. They are therefore the embodiment of intellectual rather than of spiritual or sensuous beauty, and they represent to the modern mind, *authority*. They have become ideals, from the influence of which civilized man has never been able and probably never will be able to escape. The modern architectural mind has either been overawed by these ideals — has been kept by them in a servile condition of rigid archæological conformity to their technical qualities, and been thus reduced to a state of unprolific pedantry, copying and repeating with unimaginative iteration; or, penetrating beneath the outward form, has been able to extract from Greek art its underlying principles, its fructifying spirit and to apply this spirit as a chastening inspiration to the best and most indigenous work of modern times. This spirit works not for imitation, but for purification, not for conformity or conservatism, but for liberty, for reserve of power, for fastidious care, for noble simplicity, for truth of expression. This is a discovery of our own day, the result of a very modern philosophical method of investigation and study. It is only beginning to bear fruit in an architecture, which, we trust, will in time become not only technically homogeneous, but adequate to express the complicated, many-sided, self conscious civilization of our own day and place. At present only the most illuminated minds have begun to comprehend the subtle Greek spirit and to apply it to modern architectural demonstrations. But even the letter, even the apparent form of Greek architecture was a myth until Stewart and Revett began the revelation of it in the last years of the Eighteenth century, in their famous work on the Antiquities of Athens. Previous to that time it was known to the world only in a very modified form through the mediation of a far more powerful civilization than that of Greece — a civilization which produced another form of classic architecture to which I now ask your attention.

When the Romans forced their political system on all the outlying nations of Europe, Asia and Africa, their architecture was cultivated less for its own sake than to serve as a visible sign to the barbarians of the power and magnificence of the Empire. It was employed less to civilize or refine, than to astonish and overawe. But in the conquest of Greece, they received far more than they gave. The conquerors were themselves conquered by the supreme beauty of Hellenic arts and letters. Among the spoils of war which came to them from this conquest was the fully developed flower of the Doric and Ionic styles. This flower, however, they could not appropriate as a living thing, but only as a symbol; it was far too delicate and sensitive to bear transplanting in a soil so coarse and strong as that of Rome without some very essential changes in its character. The Romans could make the Greek artists their slaves, but they could not control the peculiar creative instinct of their captives; indeed, this instinct could not continue its happy development under these new conditions. The serene atmosphere, the contemplative silence, the simplicity of life, the sympathy of the people, the intellectual exaltation, which had made this growth possible in Attica, which had also made possible the Iliad, the Œdipus Tyrannus, the Panathenaic frieze, were all wanting. The impatient ambition of Rome, her ostentatious splendor, her desire for magnificence rather than beauty, furnished new motives of design. The living organism of the Greek Doric and Ionic styles was little suited to meet these new political and social requirements, and it was found necessary to formulate them and to subject their details and proportions to rules more or less inflexible, so that they could be put to use without inconvenient delay. The delicately studied curves of the Greek mouldings were supplanted by mouldings which could be readily struck with the compass. In this way the Greek styles became Roman *orders* of architecture, and in effect a part of the vast administrative machinery of the Empire. Practically, its buildings were decorated according to official formulas to represent the overwhelming power and wealth of the state.

To these orders the Romans added three more, peculiarly their own, the Tuscan, the Corinthian and the Composite. The Tuscan was a development from the ancient art of Etruria, and was therefore in the main indigenous to the Italian Peninsula. It differed from the Roman Doric mainly in detail only, and the principal features of the two orders were frequently interchanged. It was adapted generally to buildings of severe utility, and received little, if any, decoration. But the Corinthian order had its origin in Greece, where it never passed beyond the experimental stage. In the land of its birth, it was a variation of the Greek Ionic applied mainly to the capital. This feature, in its original form, consisted of a concave calyx or basket shaped cap, borrowed from the Egyptians, but encased not with the lotus or papyrus leaves of the Nile, but with a conventionalized form of the leaf of the wild growing acanthus of Attica, arranged vertically around the calyx. From these sprang four Ionic volutes, like horns, supporting the corners of the square abacus above. Its most highly developed form in Greece appeared in some interior columns of the Temple of Apollo near Miletos, and in the little Choragic monument of Lysicrates at Athens, which latter may perhaps be considered the prototype, of the Roman Corinthian. Following this prototype, a Roman architect, Cossutius, who had been sent to Athens to complete his professional education, designed the capitals of the great Temple of Olympian Zeus at Athens, which was scarcely completed when Sulla transported them to Rome about 84 years B. C., where they were used in the Temple of Jupiter Capitolinus. From this beginning the Corinthian order of Rome speedily developed. Nothing could have been better fitted than this order to express the magnificence and luxury of the Empire. All the other orders contributed to make it sumptuous, and when its various features and proportions had been finally formulated, according to the Roman manner, it represented the very highest and most characteristic expression of Roman art. It appeared, not only in the most splendid monuments of the capital, but, lavishly reproduced in the remotest provinces in great religious and civic buildings, it fascinated the barbarians and confirmed the rule of their conquerors. From the earliest years of the Christian era to the present day the ingenuity of mankind has been spent upon the inexhaustible theme of the Corinthian capital with infinite variation. The carvers of Byzantium and Ravenna, the Gothic sculptors of the middle ages, and all the architects of the Renaissance have worked upon it. It was christianized in the cathedrals; it was restored to paganism in the Renaissance. All the leafage and flora of nature were applied to its bell to express the genius of successive races in history. Possibly, when the capitals of the temple of Capitoline Jove were, in the progress of civilization through the centuries repeated in St. Peters of Rome, in St. Paul's of London, in the Pantheon of Paris, in the capitol of Washington, as they will continue to be repeated in some form or other in the great monuments of the future, either the doctrine of the survival of the fittest or the poverty of the creative powers of man found its most complete demonstration.

As for the Roman Composite order, so called, it was a mere debasement of the Corinthian, it was never distinctly formulated, and it seems to express, not order, but disorder and the license of luxury.

But the most important and most characteristic contribution of the classic architecture of Rome to the artistic resources of the world was not in these five orders, but in the invention of the arch and of its direct derivatives, the vaulted roof and the dome. No invention of men, except, possibly, that of the steel beam and plate glass in modern times, has exercised so great an influence over all subsequent architecture. By virtue of this great discovery, the

Hypostyle Hall of Karnac, on the Nile, filled with the enormous bulk of its columns, the narrow Parthenon with its nave and aisles, and all the ancient roofed monuments, which were necessarily restricted in width by the limitations of a trabeated construction, gave place to the vast open spaces majestically covered by the intersecting vaulting over the halls of the Imperial baths and basilicas, and by the dome of the Roman Pantheon. It made great open interior dimensions possible in architecture. It substituted arcades for colonnades, and gave birth to the science of engineering and to extensive works of public utility until then impossible.

The first development of the principle of the arch in roof construction consisted in the barrel or wagon vault, which was a continuous arch thrown over the space between two parallel walls. Areas of considerable width could thus be covered with permanent curved ceilings, composed of small cut stones fitted together, or with cement concrete laid over a temporary form or centering of wood, which was removed when the work was finished. This was the first substitute for ceilings composed of a series of long transverse stone beams, having a bearing at the ends on opposite columns or walls, as was the case with the ceilings of the peristyles surrounding the Greek temples, and with those covering the narrow aisles in the great halls of Egypt; or for the roofs of wood, which were thrown over the wider central areas of all the pre-Roman buildings. But the primitive barrel vaults of the Romans presented a serious difficulty of construction, as they required a cumbersome and brutal massiveness in the continuous supporting walls, and practically limited the width of the areas to be so covered. The system was thus an obstacle to that free lateral extension which the requirements of the public service in Roman civilization rendered essential in the plans of monumental buildings. It was a political and social necessity therefore, not a sentiment, which inspired the next step in the structural development of architecture. This requirement for indefinite lateral extension suggested the idea of crossing the original longitudinal barrel vault with transverse barrel vaults of the same width, making it practicable to cut great arches through the supporting walls, or, in fact, to reduce them to a series of isolated piers, upon which the great weight of the arched ceiling, or quadripartite vault, as it was called could be concentrated. Heavy continuous walls thus became structurally unnecessary and were only needed in lighter form for closures and partitions.

Architecture was thus emancipated from the strict structural conditions which had confined the development of form in Greece and which had made it necessary for the Greek artist to concentrate his creative energy on the decorative evolution of buildings of the most primitive character, like the cella of their temples. This concentration of power made possible the consummation of the Parthenon, beyond which the Greek evolution could not go in its characteristic national development. A corresponding consummation was not practicable among the Romans, not only because they had rather the practical than the æsthetic sense, but because their creative powers were dissipated over a field of effort which had been indefinitely extended by the consequences of the discovery of the quadri-partite vault. The Greek idea of closure did not go beyond a cell or small room, the plan of which was a parallelogram. The Roman idea embraced an indefinite series of rooms of various dimensions in height, width and length, having definite structural relations one with the other. This indefinite complex of rooms of great horizontal extent, suggested to the Roman builders the provision of vistas and the establishment of centre lines. The plan being thus at length freed from the domination of a structure of limited capacity, assumed for the first time that primary importance in every architectural scheme, which it has maintained to this day. The plan being settled according to conditions of use and convenience, the visible architecture resulted logically and with comparatively little effort. They could surround their lofty central halls with subordinate apartments vaulted at a lower level. By this variation of height they were enabled to secure light for the central halls by high arched windows, thus introducing the clerestory into the architectural scheme. In this way, by a perfectly reasonable process, the Romans developed exterior effects of great variety in height and horizontal extent. In the whole complicated composition they learned how to preserve unity in variety; how to group the various parts so as to provide for a symmetrical balance of masses, with proper culminations. Their work was always done with dignity and order and with a perfection of construction which in many instances has survived, not only the natural vicissitudes of time, but the terrors of political convulsions through more than twenty centuries. Their enormous halls are majestic and imposing even in ruins, and the vast extent and the imperial dignity of their baths and aqueducts, their palaces and villas, their forums and basilicas, their circuses and theatres, their triumphal arches and bridges, their temples and tombs, are still evident not only in Italy, but in the remotest provinces of the Empire, nay, even in the almost inaccessible deserts of North Africa; so that we can readily comprehend how, when these structures were in their glory, the barbarians submitted to a power visibly expressed in monuments so stupendous and overpowering, not only in the massive character of their structures, but in the lavish splendor of their adornments.

The most majestic and architecturally the most imposing and effective development of Roman vaulting was in its adaptation to their circular halls, such as occurred in the baths of Caracalla and Agrippa, the latter being now known as the Rotunda of the Pantheon. If the complex structure of the great Roman monuments permitted any such logical culmination as was achieved by the Greeks in the Parthenon, it would undoubtedly be found in the ingenious construction, in the gracious simplicity, in the overwhelming majesty of this the first and perhaps the most successful of the great domes in the history of architecture. Measured by its influence on all subsequent architecture it must take rank as one of the most important monuments in the world. The conception of it was a great architectural thought and it was entirely Roman. From it was derived another conspicuous feature of Roman architecture, the half-dome or conch, which covered the semi-circular projections of the great chambers of the baths and more especially of the basilicas or courts of justice, in which position they became the prototype of the Christian apse or chevet in the cathedrals.

It must be admitted that Roman vaulting, especially when used on a monumental scale over the great halls of their baths and basilicas, was a development rather from the form than from the construction of the arch. For in such cases it was constructed, not with shaped stones but with a concrete of Roman cement and tufa or pumice stone, filled in solid over the vault which was rarely less than six feet thick in the thinnest part. It was thus a homogenous mass exercising little or no thrust upon the walls and piers, but bearing upon them vertically like a huge hollowed monolith. But, however constructed, we cannot avoid the conclusion that the various forms of vaulting vitally affected or controlled the plans as well as the outward and inward aspects of the Roman building. In fact they imposed upon it fundamental laws of dimension, shape and proportion, before the architects dreamed of decorating it.

This point opens to us a very important and very curious fact in the history of Roman architecture. We have seen that Greek architecture was not something imposed upon structure; it was structure itself, decorated and elevated into a fine art by the genius of a great race. The architecture cannot be removed without destroying the fabric itself. The arch, the vault and the dome of the Roman builders were as capable of characteristic elevation into the domain of high art as the post and lintel of the Greeks. But this construction never received such a development at the hands of the ancient Romans. It was the early Christians who first gave to this structure its own proper decoration at Byzantium, at Ravenna, at Rome, at Venice, at Pisa, at Milan, in Southern France and wherever else that form of art, known in its earlier developments as Byzantine and in its later developments as Romanesque, took shape and prepared the way for Gothic architecture. Indeed, the structural principle of the arch was first developed into true architectural expressions, not by the Greek architects, who worked at Rome under pagan masters, but by the descendents of those Greek architects, the men who worked in Byzantium several centuries afterwards in the perfect freedom of Christianity and under Christian inspirations.

We have seen that the Romans borrowed the forms of Greek art and formulated them into the five orders of Roman architecture. But these orders rarely were applied structurally as in Greece. In Roman temples, which were by no means the most characteristic expressions of Roman art, in the colonnades of the forums, in the porticos of the basilicas and palaces, the Roman orders appeared in their proper functions as decorated construction. But the most characteristic and by far the most common form of Roman structure was dictated by the arch, the vault and the dome. We have seen that these features were invented by the Romans in order to make possible the kind of buildings which were needed by their political and social system. But it was a part of this system that these buildings should not only be orderly in their arrangement, enormous in extent, durable in construction, economical in administration, but also magnificent in adornment. To the Romans, art was necessary to the embellishment of life, but it was to them a secondary, not a primary consideration, and it entered into their ideas of building, not as an integral element but as an afterthought. If it had been an integral element of those ideas, the noblest productions of the Romanesque period would have been anticipated and almost infinitely expanded by the Romans themselves and certainly the whole course of the art of the Renaissance would have been turned into some unknown and unimaginable path of structural beauty and power. Under these conditions the Græco-Roman orders presented themselves as convenient decorative formulas the absolute fitness and propriety of which had been justified by the practice of a race, recognized by the Romans as far more advanced in literature and art than themselves. So, when the question arose how their native system of arches, vaults and piers was to be decorated, they applied to them these ready made formulas as a decoration entirely independent of construction; and all the subsequent developments of the classic orders of architecture down to our own day have in like manner been entirely independent of construction. Against the piers which supported the vaulted roofs of their basilicas and of their great halls in their palaces and public baths, they placed as decorations, fragments of their orders, a column supporting a block with the mouldings of a full entablature, from this sprang the arched construction of the ceiling. They did not think of decorating the pier itself according to its structural functions. They enveloped the whole interior surface of walls with pilasters and entablatures according to the official formulas, executed in the most sumptuous manner with precious marbles and capitals of gilded bronze. They used the exact orders as open screens in the separations of these rooms. All this arbitrary veneering and furnishing was done with great splendor and infinite skill of adaptation. But while the remains of the essential structure of those great vaulted buildings still rear themselves between the hills of Rome, this splendid veneering has long since disappeared.

But by far the most characteristic and important use of the classic orders by the Romans as decorative adjuncts was in their exterior walls. They were so prepossessed by the idea that the Greek styles were necessary to all architectural effects and, in fact, constituted architecture, that they did not think of decorating their own noble and beautiful system of arcuated and vaulted structure, thus creating a legitimate Roman style, but considered that it could not be made architecture without the aid of these styles. They therefore forced their version of them in the form of Roman orders, illogically and without meaning, into the construction of their walls. They either set the full column in front of their walls like a buttress, supporting a block of entablature, but doing no constructive work, as in their triumphal arches; or they built the columns into the structure of the wall for half their diameter — engaged them, as it is called, — in which position they usually supported a continuous entablature, as in the temple of Fortuna Virilis. This latter use of the order was perhaps imitated from an isolated and exceptional example of a similar structure of the Greeks in the great temple of Zeus at Agrigentum, or, more probably, in the little choragic monument of Lysicrates at Athens, before referred to. But as these engaged columns necessitated a costly overhanging entablature, they invented, or adapted from the Greek anta, a flat column or pilaster, which was used most profusely in every Roman monument which had any claim to decorative or architectural character. Between these decorative engaged columns or pilasters occurred the structural arches of the Romans, which alone did the essential work of the walls. In their many-storied buildings, like the theatre of Marcellus or the Flavian amphitheatre, they superimposed these orders or expressions of orders, placing the most robust as the Tuscan or Doric, at the base, the Ionic in the second range, and the Corinthian in the third as the most appropriate decorative culmination of the composition. This superimposition introduced new formulas of proportion applicable to the mutual relations of the orders when so grouped. The successive stories were structurally arcades, the horizontal entablatures or stringcourses between these arcades expressing the floors, and the pilasters or columns standing for the expression of vertical support in the piers between the arches.

This is the Roman system of decorative wall architecture, which was supplanted by a logical and legitimate expression of pure arched construction in Romanesque art without the use of the unnecessary orders, but which, after the Mediæval period, was restored to full power in the architecture of the Renaissance, where it was so refined by the immortal masters of the Fifteenth century in Italy, and so enlarged in its scope by those of the Sixteenth century in France, that modern art has received it as a canonical tradition of architecture, and, in some form or other, repeated the insistant motive in nearly all the Renaissance monuments of the world, but with astonishing variation of detail and ornament. In these variations the genius of every civilized people in the world has expressed itself; even the character of reigning monarchs, as it affected their courts, affected the mixed Roman system of arches and orders which they had inherited from their predecessors; so that, made venerable and precious by these accretions, it has now all the value of a historical record of the various stages of the progress of mankind in civilization; as such, irrespective of its want of structural character, it has become a highly organized and extremely copious language of forms.

It is important to note that in this progress of the mixed Roman system of arches and orders through history the formulas of proportions and details fixed by Rome and confirmed by the Italian masters, have been respected in exact accordance with the degree of culture and artistic feeling existing among the people using it. Wherever these formulas have been disregarded, this system has been debased or travestied, and every such debasement is a sure indication of a corresponding debasement in civilization.

When the Roman Empire was declining to its fall the canonical forms of architecture, established by the best usage of imperial times and requiring a certain virtue of artistic discipline to maintain them in purity, experienced a corresponding decline. Among the changes, more or less capricious and disloyal, which were suffered by these forms, was one of such preeminent importance in its effect upon subsequent architecture that it seems necessary to consider it here.

One of the most conspicuous monuments of this period of decline was the immense palace built by Diocletian, after his retirement from the cares of Empire, at Spalatro, on the Eastern shore of the Adriatic. At this time the authority of official Roman architecture had been so far relaxed that certain free and romantic elements had been permitted to enter into the design of the public monuments. This relaxation of discipline was contemporaneous with and expressive of the failing strength of the Roman state, and affected not only the details, in a certain loss of refinement, but some of the most important and, hitherto most absolute features of the orders. During the period of authority, every Roman arch sprang from an impost or horizontal moulding, very subordinate to the members of the order which was engaged in the wall surface, or, if the arch was very large, from the entablature of the order itself, as in the great arches of the imperial baths and basilicas, or in the interior of the walls of the Pantheon, according to the most authentic restorations. They could not conceive a column without its own entablature. But at Spalatro, among other variations from the official types, the arch was permitted to spring for the first time directly from the capitals of the columns. This change seems very technical and unimportant, but it was enough to indicate the beginning of a revolution, and to serve as a prototype of one of the most distinguishing features of all Romanesque and Gothic art, as compared with classic art. It restored the columns to their proper structural function of direct support, so that they ceased to be mere decorative adjuncts in the architectural scheme, and prepared the way for the final abandonment of the entablature in all the Romantic forms of art. It will be remembered that the Romans of the imperial epoch had used the Greek entablature, with all its delicately studied horizontal lines, to adorn a system of arched structure with which it had no proper affiliations. But in forcing this unnatural adjustment of incongruous features they had used such astonishing skill and ingenuity that when classic architecture was restored to the world with the revival of learning, this ingenious incongruity was retained with all the other features of the revival, as an inseparable and consecrated part of classic art.

In this very brief and inadequate outline of the evolution of Roman architecture in classic times, I have dwelt less upon its history and technique than upon a consideration of those qualities in it which have given it an influence so potent over the intelligence of mankind as expressed in buildings. This architecture would have only a curious archæological interest, were it not that it has had such a prodigious effect on the architecture of the last four centuries and a half. It presents itself to the architects of the present day, FIRST, as a precedent of harmonious organic structure, expressed on a heroic scale and with overwhelming magnificence; and, SECOND, as a precedent of an arbitrary system of decorative forms, exceedingly beautiful and interesting in itself, but applied to a structure which it adorns but does not illustrate. We have

357

seen that from the structural elements of this architecture all the main characteristics of the Romantic styles were directly derived, and that from its decorative and entirely conventional elements have been derived that scientific precision of thought and discipline of the mind, without which modern civilization cannot be expressed adequately in terms of architecture.

Two Interpreters of National Architecture

(1897)

Architecture is not only a demonstration of art, it is also the epigraph of civilization; and the succession of the historical styles is not merely a sequence of independent phenomena, not merely an alphabet of formulas, but visible evidence of the social, religious, and political conditions which have governed the progress of mankind. This fact, so familiar to us now, is one of the latest revelations of the nineteenth century; the knowledge of it is doing more to make architecture intelligible, to restore to it its proper and peculiar function among the fine arts, and to rehabilitate it than any other influence whatever. Indeed, among the architects of to-day, the necessity of such rehabilitation and the way to secure it were not made clearly apparent until the true relationship of the art which they studied and practiced to the time in which they lived had been thus revealed. They discovered that if it was to be once more a living art, they must work in the spirit of their environment; must cease to be merely archæological or eclectic, and learn how to free themselves from the enchantment of their own memories. They discovered that the architects of the great eras succeeded in producing distinction of style by losing their individualities in coöperation, and that the development of a modern style adequate to express modern civilization has been seriously interrupted and delayed by the failure of modern architects to work together in this spirit.

The best that can be said of the architecture of the nineteenth century is that it has been an architecture of exceptionally learned, ingenious, and accomplished individualities. It has been an art of experiments which have failed, and of revivals which have been fruitless. These individualities, with their consciousness highly educated and trained, have been embarrassed rather than aided by their knowledge of the great achievements of the past. It does not seem to have occurred to them to appeal to the sympathies of the people by uttering their inspirations in the vulgar tongue, but they have labored with immense talent and ingenuity to interpret and apply dead languages. Their efforts have been reminiscent, excursive, and experimental. The architects have analyzed, theorized, disputed, and argued. They have formed schools, conserving classic or romantic traditions, — schools which have fallen apart because progress has been found to be impossible on merely archæological lines. Many of the individualities developed under these conditions have been brilliant and powerful, and have had a great following of lesser men. As the century has advanced, certain of these individualities have been inspired by nobler and loftier motives. The architecture of the century, because it has been nourished in the same soil that produced the electric telegraph, the telephone, and all the other triumphs of industrial art, has exhibited a certain sporadic vitality, and, conscious of the universal energy, has occasionally thrown out mighty branches full of the possibilities of a great fruition; but because it has not enjoyed the advantage of concentrated effort, it has not flowered as it flowered in the thirteenth and sixteenth centuries, still less as it flowered in the ages of Pericles and Augustus. In the Court of Honor and in the other official architecture of the World's Columbian Exposition at Chicago, we have seen the best that can be given us by a refined scholarship, by a learned dilettante-ism, and by a skillful virtuosity (Figs. 141–150, 157). But this brilliant demonstration can hardly be accepted as the final consummation of the architectural spirit of the nineteenth century in America. The promise of such a consummation is rather to be found in the later commercial buildings of our great cities, simply because these have been produced under conditions of commercial necessity, and through economical and social forces which were stronger than the conservative scholarship of the architects, and compelled them to enter with doubt and hesitation into a purely modern field of endeavor.

Under these circumstances the history of the architecture of the century is practically a history of individual achievements. In no other era of the art has the personal equation been so insistent. In no other era has the architect been so constrained by the consciousness of his personal moral responsibilities to his art.

Perhaps the genius of John Wellborn Root, of Chicago, which has just been set forth in admirable terms in his Life by Harriet Monroe,[1] is the most conspicuous and interesting as it certainly is the most prolific factor in these Plutarchian annals. The Life reveals the operations of an exceptionally sensitive and active intelligence, trained in the architecture of history, seasoned by the study of the masters, but peculiarly open to the influences of the present. It is especially worth while to consider the career of this man at this moment, because it presents a suggestive contrast to that of another architect, the pioneer of his profession in America, who lived nearly a hundred years before Root, and who practiced under conditions very different from those which inspired and perplexed his brother architect in our own day. This comparison is invited by the fortunate coincidence of the publication of the Life of the elder architect, Charles Bulfinch, of Boston, by his granddaughter.[2]

It is only of late years that the value of the services of this modest gentleman, in interpreting to us in terms of architecture the spirit of the era in which he lived, has begun to be appreciated. He was born in Boston in 1763, practiced architecture in New England and in Washington, and died in 1844. John Wellborn Root was born in Georgia in 1850, practiced mainly in Chicago, and died untimely in 1893. There were thus but eighty-seven years between the beginnings of these two careers, but they were years of such unprecedented activity of development in all the arts of civilization, in the advancement of knowledge, and in the increase of resources that they seemed to bring about a radical change in the point of view of life and duty, and an immense complication and sophistication of ideals, especially in respect to architecture. Bulfinch, working in the midst of a community comparatively poor and provincial, unvexed by theories of art, produced in his long life of eighty-one years but forty-two buildings, principally state-houses, churches, court-houses, colleges, hospitals, and schools. Root, in his fruitful life of forty-three years, under the tremendous impulse of modern wealth and energy, was principally responsible, in the practice of the firm of which he was a member, for a series of buildings unprecedented in number as the productions of a single mind, unprecedented in aggregate value as investments of property, of great variety in style and character, and in several instances of a magnitude until then unattempted. These include forty-four structures of a public character, such as office buildings, hotels, churches, apartment houses, schools, and railway stations, in Chicago; twenty-five of the same class elsewhere; eight buildings to cost from $400,000 to $1,000,000 each, in process of erection at the time of his death; and one hundred and twenty residences. These structures were complicated by conditions of occupation and use unknown in the time of Bulfinch, — sanitary conditions as applied to plumbing and drainage, electrical conditions as applied to lighting, mechanical conditions as applied to elevators and heating, structural conditions as applied to fireproofing, and conditions of new material and methods, the application of which to structure and design involved a fundamental departure from nearly all the ideals handed down in the venerable traditions of architecture.

For reasons which will presently be made apparent, Root's work was often audaciously experimental in character, and, like that of his famous contemporary, Richardson, — a study of whose genius was printed in The Atlantic Monthly of November, 1886, shortly after his death,[3] — was strongly impressed by the personality of the architect. Both of these modern architects, as men of high professional training, respected the traditions of their art, but both were so immersed in the tumultuous tide of life around them that they were but slightly impeded by the prejudices of archæological or scholastic conformity. The modern conditions of architectural expression could not be fairly met by any mere enlargement or combination of the great body of historical precedents which stood ready in their libraries to beguile and ensnare their creative powers.

On the other hand, Bulfinch knew only the formal, inelastic, stately language of the classic school as it was understood in his simpler and less spacious time; and there was nothing in the comparatively narrow and quiet life around him to tempt him from the orthodox lines of this form of art, or to offer any especial stimulus to his inventive faculties (Figs. 160–164). His language of design was based mainly on the formulas furnished in the practice of the followers of Sir Christopher Wren in England. Of these, it is evident that his contemporary, Sir William Chambers, had the most marked influence upon his mind, and that the Somerset House of this master was to him a model of highest achievement. Nothing is more striking in the story of Bulfinch's career than the simplicity of his equipment as an architect. His art was hardly recognized by his fellow citizens as a profession, and outside of Paris there were no schools in which it was inculcated. His father, a physician and man of means, and of unusual breadth of mind, proposed for him a commercial life. But when the young man, after graduating from Harvard, was sent to Europe, in his twenty-second year, to liberalize his education and to enlarge his views, he was far less interested in commercial statistics and methods than in the modern buildings, which he studied with sufficient intelligence to confirm his natural predilections for architecture, to cultivate his instinct for proportions, to correct his judgment, and to furnish him with certain simple ideals of classic form and classic details. His library was limited to two or three standard books on the orders, several contemporary English works, mostly on rural architecture, and a very few archæological collections. During his tour he collected a few picturesque architectural prints and measured a few buildings, among them Wren's beautiful church of St. Stephen's, Walbrook, and his papers give evidence that he made some special studies in perspective.

Untempted and unsophisticated by such affluence of literary resource as besets the modern architect, he was enabled to develop his artistic instincts in peace and prosperity upon the safe and simple lines established by the usage of his time. These instincts, thus guided and confined, were fastidious and correct, but they were not sustained or illustrated by any especial skill in graphic delineation, and, from the modern architect's point of view, the few drawings left to us from his hand are of the most elementary character. But he was a man of sound practical judgment and of recognized probity and prudence; whatever creative powers he possessed were always subjected to the correction of authority and precedent, and were thus protected from the dangers of illiterate aberrations or capricious invention. The letters quoted by his granddaughter and his own fragment of autobiography give few, if any, indications of a habit of architectural thought or speculation, and we look in vain among them for evidences of critical insight or study, or for expressions of enthusiasm or aspiration, such as fill the diaries and correspondence of every modern student of art. He seemed to be essentially a man of reason, cool and self-restrained, rather than a man of sentiment. As such, perhaps, he better commended himself to his fellow citizens as one to be trusted with the conduct of affairs. When he received his commission to build the

State-House of Massachusetts (Fig. 162) he was but thirty-one years of age, but already he had been a member of the board of selectmen of Boston for four years. While practicing as architect, he was chairman of the board continuously for twenty-one years. Indeed, his qualities as a good citizen were held in such high esteem that when, by some unexplained vicissitude of local politics, he failed of reëlection to the board, every elected member immediately resigned, and, on a second trial, he was reinstated by a large majority.

Meanwhile, his architectural work, adjusted to the conditions of a community stable and polite, but without great wealth or exacting standards of taste, was in complete accord with his character as a citizen, and was remarkable for purity, temperance, and an entire freedom from excess or affectation. To the eye of the young student of the present day his constant sense of propriety seems sometimes to border on prudery; but if his play of fancy found abundant scope in an occasional and somewhat reluctant indulgence in the conventional garland or urn of the style which he followed, it must be admitted that he thoroughly understood and respected its formulas of detail and proportion, and never disobeyed its rules.

It is important to observe that in those days the public mind had not been debauched, as is now the case, by a profuse banquet of conflicting styles which it could not assimilate or digest. The true meaning and value of Greek architecture had not been revealed; Gothic architecture had not been analyzed, and as yet it had absolutely no message for the modern mind. There were no theories of the development of the historic styles, and no experiments in reviving them. The wild vagaries which, twenty years after Bulfinch's death, constituted the vernacular architecture of America (Fig. 118) had not begun to disturb the dreams of the builders who, nourished by the simple and wholesome diet of such handbooks as Nicholson's Carpenters' Guide,[4] developed in peace and simplicity of mind that narrow but highly respectable and consistent system of forms which our students are now conscientiously measuring, and our architects carefully imitating with all the respect due to "the Old Colonial." This style, if it may be so called, commends itself to us because it took shape without affectation while adjusting itself to the social requirements of the time. Its highest aim was to be scholastically "correct," and it was "correct" whether applied to the stately mansion of a New England merchant or Virginia planter, or to the porch of the humblest farmhouse.

Bulfinch, having studied modern architecture in England and France, and having observed the works of the Italian masters in northern Italy in his hurried tour, was in position to make a valuable contribution towards the correction of the provincial element in the Old Colonial, and he made this correction with such modesty, discretion, and dignity that in these modern days we cannot witness the desecration or disappearance of any of his few remaining works, so unaffected, so impersonal, so expressive of the spirit of his time, without a pang of regret. For the qualities which were great enough and rare enough to distinguish them above all the other works of his time and country are qualities particularly refreshing to the modern architectural mind, perplexed as it is by a multitude of conflicting ideas, sophisticated as it is by theories of design, and dissatisfied as it is because these theories fail in their application to practice.

Owing to the necessities of rigid economy which he was compelled to observe, nearly all of Bulfinch's works are simple to bareness; and yet no modern attempt to enrich them has made them better works of art, and no attempt has been made to enlarge or extend them, as in the Massachusetts General Hospital, without detriment to their harmony of proportion (Fig. 163). Thus, the modern student, in the midst of his studies of architectural magnificence and luxury, can learn and is learning from these modest buildings what difficult and almost unattainable virtues may be concealed in simplicity. Though these works give evidence of natural taste informed by observation and corrected by study rather than of genius or inspiration, though they are decent and orderly rather than ingenious or original, they contain the essential elements of good architecture, and justify the assumption that Bulfinch needed only the opportunity to produce work equal to the best contemporary monuments of his time in England or America.

When at last in 1818 he was summoned to Washington to complete the work of Thornton and Latrobe on the national Capitol,[5] he accepted the large responsibilities with a reluctance due, not to a want of confidence in his abilities, but to an honorable fear lest, in supplanting Latrobe, he should seem in any way to be interfering with the just rights of his predecessor. Unfortunately, the main architectural features of this great building had been settled before his work began. But to him must be credited the great western central portico, and the steps and terraces which form the monumental approach on that side: and these may be accepted as the best features of the original central building of the Capitol (Fig. 164).

The good taste and discretion which Miss Bulfinch has exhibited in uncovering this modest but honorable and useful career to the light of modern days are what might have been expected from the granddaughter of such a man. We recognize in his life a refreshing aroma of old-fashioned precision and domesticity, and incidentally it is an interesting revelation of the conditions of society in Boston and Washington in the early years of the century. The illustrations of his works are adequate to explain the high esteem in which they are held not only by all who love architecture as an art, but by those who are able to recognize in their characteristic and unconscious variations from the canonical forms of the Old World the promise and potentiality of a new civilization.

Bulfinch's career as an architect had closed when the town of Chicago was thought worthy of incorporation as a city. Twenty-eight years after his death, it was the second city of the Union, and the scene of the beginning of the career of John Wellborn Root. There is a significance in this transition from the respectable tranquillity of Boston when the elder architect, the pioneer of his profession in America, was practicing his art with a serenity born of the simplicity of the conditions around him and of the entire absence of a competitor, to the prosperous confusion of Chicago when the new firm of Burnham & Root were challenging the irrepressible and strenuous world around them for employment. In the intervening years, more full of human experience than cycles of Cathay, new ideals had arisen, and, by a series of vain experiments, architecture, which had fallen behind in the race, was seeking recognition as one of the essential attributes of civilization. But it was no longer an art of formulas, punctilious, academic, absolute; it had thrown off the despotism of classic traditions, and had attempted revivals of every style which had made an impression on the history of architecture. Though the classic formulas still served as the basis of professional training, they were rarely respected in practice; mediæval archæology had tempted the student away from discipline, and he was amusing himself with travesties of every known demonstration of romantic art. He had become either a learned architectural agnostic or an eclectic virtuoso without solid convictions. Meanwhile, technical skill had advanced prodigiously, and the ingenuity and inventive powers of the architects were taxed to the utmost by the exactions of practical requirements which seemed to make the practice of an academic art impossible.

Root found himself in the midst of a conflict of faiths without fixed ideals, and at the mercy of transient fashions and capricious revivals. This was especially true in the tempestuous West, where the stimulus of immense opportunities and the noise of an unprecedented industrial activity were singularly unfavorable to serious thought and scholarly reserve. The architectural demonstrations of this era in the West were for the most part in a condition of illiterate anarchy, forming, however, a recognizable vernacular, of which the only good characteristic was that it adjusted itself without resistance to the fulfillment of practical needs. But this state of things could not last among an ambitious people, anxious to wear all the insignia of high civilization. This vernacular art prevailed only through a time of expectant probation, and there were not wanting certain trained intelligences eager to give to this abundant but disorderly vitality a direction toward a truer and more worthy art. Among these the young firm of Burnham & Root was destined to be preëminent.

It was the good fortune of Root to be dedicated to art even from his birth, and he speedily developed an intelligence singularly alert and warmly sympathetic with every demonstration of beauty in nature and art. The gradual unfolding of the flower of his mind under influences of nature rather than of books is set forth in his Life by Miss Monroe with all the literary skill which we have a right to expect from a poet, and all the affectionate detail which is natural to one so nearly associated with the most active part of Root's career. Yet the narrative is not too redundant, and little is said which is not essential to the proper comprehension of the growth of a vigorous mind from a youth joyous and sunny to a manhood full of sweetness and light. It does not need the success which finally crowned his career to justify even the two hundred and eighty pages of this story. From a psychological point of view alone, it was worth writing as a study of the development of character. But our immediate concern relates only to the professional side of this interesting personality, because it was destined to become a notable force in what we believe will presently be recognized as an important transition in the history at least of American architecture.

His education, unlike that of the very few men in his profession who may dispute preëminence with him, was not academic, and when his instincts first turned him seriously to this art, he did not enjoy the inestimable advantages of education in a properly equipped school of architecture. He was not even studious as a youth. His love of art was inspired by nature; it was kept from going astray by his own strong intelligence; and it was instructed far more by independent observation and experience than by careful preliminary training. Every form of art was welcomed by him with eager instinctive appreciation, and his creative longings found relief and expression in music and painting nearly as happily as in architecture. In mind and body alike he was healthy and powerful, and his physical and mental qualities were in complete accord, one aiding the other.

From his home in Georgia he was sent to school in England during the desolation of the war for the Union, the steamer which conveyed him running the blockade of Wilmington, North Carolina. Here he remained two years, and passed the examinations for Oxford; but he did not matriculate there. On his return to the United States after the war he entered the University of the City of New York, where, as if to counteract the obvious dangers of his innate romantic liberalism, he devoted himself to the most exact of the sciences and took the strict engineering course, graduating with the highest honors in 1869. Here, as elsewhere, his active mind imbibed knowledge by intuition rather than by effort; here, as elsewhere, he was confessed a natural leader, and drew all hearts to him in affection by the ardor of his sympathies, and all minds to him in admiration by the versatility of his genius. While in New York he passed one year as student in the office of Mr. Renwick, where his natural taste for romantic forms of art was stimulated and informed, and another year in the office of Mr. Snook, where he obtained a certain amount of practical experience and some small training, perhaps, in classic art. With this meagre technical outfit, but with a heart of healthy virile ambition, he went to Chicago a few weeks after the great fire, and entered the office of Carter, Drake & Wright [sic]. Here he met Burnham, and in 1873 was prompted to enter with him into that fortunate partnership of mind and heart which was destined to be profitable not to them only, but, in a far larger sense, to the advancement of an architecture adequate to stand for our new civilization.

These four short years of personal contact, as student and draughtsman, with the ordinary practice of the profession do not of course account for Root the architect. In fact, they were comparatively an unimportant incident in the formative part of his career. His natural genius — which, as his biographer says, was "a happy union of invention and facility" [6] — might have made him merely a brilliant dilettante, had it not been combined with a mind of such peculiar sanity and force, such quickness and certainty of apprehension, as in some degree to balance and guide his ebullient enthusiasm without the aid of academic discipline. Indeed, he was one of the very few architects of whom it may be said that they were born, not made; for the education and training essential to qualify his natural inspiration for the service of mankind seemed to come to him more with the growth of his own observant intellect than from ordinary processes of study. But we shall have occasion to note that throughout his life the absence of a systematic grounding in the classics left him too free and unrestrained, too much at the mercy of his own moods. The delicate feeling for proportion and for refinement and precision of detail, which, as he himself acknowledged, can be obtained only from a study of Greek and Roman architecture in the schools, could not come to him as an instinct or as an inspiration.

Another essential element in the development of this man's career was the fortunate influence of his friend and partner, Burnham, whose zeal, no less cordial and fervent than that of Root, was tempered by a personal force and by an administrative capacity which the world had cause later to recognize in the organization of the architecture of the Columbian Exposition. This warm sympathy and strong effectual support gave to Root the opportunity to develop his genius in peace and prosperity, and undoubtedly encouraged, protected, and chastened it. The activity of his inventive powers and the graphic facility with which he gave immediate expression to his quick conceptions often needed just that sort of cool, corrective judgment and discreet restraint outside of himself, which were supplied almost unconsciously by his partner. The fame which justly belongs to him because of the large results which he achieved cannot be diminished by a frank acknowledgment of this noble indebtedness.

Root's work, so controlled, was the most potent influence in the elimination from the American vernacular style of all those characteristic elements of ignorant caprice, of vulgar pretense and lawlessness, which made it so hopeless. "Yet," cried Root bravely, "somewhere in this mass of ungoverned energies lies the principle of life!" [7] This principle he undertook to set free that it might do its work unimpeded, and, by the silent but mighty force of good examples, he succeeded in obliterating all that had given to this vernacular its recognizable external character, and left only the hidden but germinating seed, — its ready adaptability to practical needs. Indeed, it was necessary to destroy this uncouth amalgam of forms, which really constituted the vernacular of America, before he could reform it; and he brought to this new labor of Hercules a spirit far more essentially American than that which had made the vernacular possible. He was, in fact, the most American of all the architects who have impressed themselves upon the history of our national art. His practice, the volume of which, as we have said, was unprecedented, was affected by no academic prejudices, no pride of archæological learning, no stiffness of conformity to conventional formulas or creeds, to prevent him from adjusting himself with the utmost frankness to American conditions as he found them, or from an honest endeavor to express these conditions in terms of architecture. Yet he knew the past thoroughly, and with all the sympathies of his poetic nature had saturated himself with the spirit of the romantic styles, especially of the vigorous Southern Romanesque, which the genius of Richardson had revived to continue its astonishing career of development in the New World (Figs. 101, 106–110b, 129), and of some of the latest demonstrations of the picturesque Gothic of France and the Low Countries. The grammar of these styles he knew as well as their poetry, but he never suffered himself to be controlled by them. Like a skillful writer, he was too sure of his style to be cramped by it. The exotic forms simply enriched and enlarged his vocabulary without making it unintelligible to the people whom he desired to interest. His reformed vernacular was without affectations of learning on the one hand, and without vulgarity or slang on the other. The designs which he made under these convictions of duty were scarcely scholarly in the conventional and academic sense, but they all bore the impress of a deep respect for knowledge and of an insight into the spirit of the styles. They were literary without being pedantic. He aimed also to have them American without that insolent disregard of historical precedent, that affectation of contempt for the great masters, which had been the principal characteristic of the indigenous architecture of the West.

It would have been a miracle if this young man, working in this exalted spirit, in the midst of a community which knew not how to criticise him with discretion, had made no mistakes. He himself admitted that he was "the victim of his own moods, — too facile always carefully to reconsider his designs." [8] Indeed, his ideal was ever far in advance of his works, and in looking back upon them he was accustomed to express his dissatisfaction with the utmost frankness. He seemed to outgrow his own productions as fast as they were executed. Like a true artist, he progressed by his errors, which were a constant spur to higher endeavor (Figs. 120, 125–128, 132, 133, 135–137).

Meanwhile, this rapid sequence of new buildings, each with a clear message of fitness and beauty, began to awaken in the public a new interest. When, for the first time, examples of good art, not speaking in a strange tongue with quotations from the classics, but expressed with elegance and force in terms not entirely unintelligible, appeared upon the streets of the principal city of the West, it became evident that they had no uncertain mission there. The architecture of pretense began forthwith to disappear, with all its bragging assumptions in galvanized iron and jig-sawed wood; façades decorated capriciously, like a bureau or a bedstead, were no longer built. They affronted the aroused intelligence of the people. The tongue-tied language which the builders had been vainly trying to invent to express their inspirations withal gave place to a far more copious vocabulary and a far more grammatical system of forms, the literate product of all the civilizations. The times were ripe for reform, and reform came, not like a fashion to be soon replaced by another, but like a revelation of light. Of course there were many thoughtless imitations and echoes of details and motifs from Root's work, but the most characteristic evidence of a healthy change was not in the copying of his work, but in the observance of the broad principles of design which he urged, publicly and privately, whenever opportunity presented. It should be admitted that change was inevitable with the rapid advance of Western civilization, and with the advent of trained minds into the profession of architecture, and it would probably have taken place in due time had Root never appeared upon the scene; but certainly it was his fortune to hasten it, and to confer upon it the wholesome local character.

The rapidity and completeness of the conquest over the old style, which had grown out of the crude conditions of the frontier towns, have no parallel in the history of architecture, and present a curious contrast to the slow and reluctant transitions of the past. The vital energy in the civilization of the West promptly rejected the lagging vernacular which represented only its least essential characteristics, and gladly recognized in the new types a more competent architectural expression.

The career which was the principal agent in bringing about such a result as this is worthy of careful analysis. Fortunately, the comprehension of the motives which underlay this career, the aspirations which quickened it, the methods and ideals which gave it form and character, need not wait upon the slow, uncertain processes of inference and deduction, for they are revealed with unusual clearness by Root himself in his occasional addresses and essays, and in the frankness and fullness of his conversations.

> Heart affluence of discursive talk,
> From household fountains never dry,[9]

opened his inner life to his friends, and it found unreserved expression in his correspondence.

The contrast between the modest reticence of Bulfinch and Root's freedom of self-revelation is significant of something more than a difference of temperament. The former knew only a sort of orthodox art, bounded by formulas and defined by precepts, which made comparatively small demand upon his moral and intellectual resources. He had but to follow an accepted academic technique with elegant discretion, and his work was over without any strain upon his conscience. But Root, like all of his professional brothers in these modern days, had a vast embarrassing inheritance at his disposal, including all that had been done in the history of the world to express beauty in form under every mood and impulse of creative art. To use this inheritance wisely there were required exhaustive investigation and study, and an appeal not only to reason and taste, but to conscience. There was a right way and a wrong way to use it. The wrong way was that of the indiscriminating eclectic or the fashionable revivalist. The right way was the way of the true artist, and could be discovered only through a final settlement of the question as to how this rich inheritance should affect his creative powers, and how it should be recon-ciled with his obvious duties as an architect of the nineteenth century.

The most active men in the profession — not necessarily the most success-ful, but those who have brought to their work the most illuminated intelli-gence — are not content to let this question settle itself in course of time. They cultivate a sense of duty; they seek for philosophical rather than merely scholastic convictions, and in this quest are ready to face all the perils of bold experiment in design.

Thus, Root, with mind alert and conscience aroused, formulated his im-pressions that he might not be lost in vain speculations, and challenged the sympathies of his friends in open discussion. No architects of any previous century had ever such processes to pass through before making up their minds as to their duties. They had only to float, unquestioning, with the tide of their own civilization. The modern architect has to take into account all the civilizations of the past. If he is ignorant of these civilizations or chooses to neglect them, he finds himself groveling in the crude vernacular of fifteen years ago.

Miss Monroe, with admirable intelligence, enriches forty-seven pages of her book with copious and well-chosen extracts from some of the numerous papers in which Root gave himself lavishly to architectural students or lay-men seeking counsel. These papers are not merely perfunctory essays, but cordial expositions of his professional creed, of his methods of thought and study, of his relations to his clients and his art, and, in short, of all the opera-tions of his mind while engaged in processes of design. No architect ever took the public into his confidence with greater frankness and sincerity, or ever more unconsciously justified himself. "The vigorous modernity of Western life," says his biographer, "appealed to his imagination as a strong artistic motive, as much entitled to respect as any motive of the hallowed past." [10] This was the first article of his professional creed, and the evidences of it appear not only, in various forms, in what he said, but in all that he did as an architect. He studied his environment, he discovered its essential spirit, and he made it the inspiration of his best, most characteristic, and most prolific work. To the layman these pages of extracts are a revelation of the dignity and noble functions of architecture, and to the student of the art they are a liberal education and a vigorous stimulant; to all they reveal a man extraordi-nary in liberality and breadth of view, in adaptability and sincerity, in sweet-ness and strength. Other men in the profession have been more learned, but none have made a better use of what they knew, and surely none have had such an inspiring opportunity to express it.

Many architects of education affect to consider that a conscious effort to assist in the creation of national style is unnecessary; that national style will come, without special effort of theirs, in its own way and in its own time; and that meanwhile, like their great predecessors, they have only to "float with the tide." We have said that Root's example has had a great effect in the

370

West in preparing for an artistic and reasonable, and not a mere accidental differentiation of modern architectural forms in America from all others. That this was not brought about by any process of indifferent or indolent "floating" is evident not only from his professional work, but from the tone of all his literary exposition. We venture to quote passages from various essays and addresses.

"To rightly estimate," he says, "an essentially modern building, therefore, it must not be viewed solely from an archæological standpoint. 'Periods' and 'styles' are all well enough, but you may be sure that whenever in the world there was a period or style of architecture worth preserving, its inner spirit was so closely fitted to the age wherein it flourished that the style could not be fully preserved, either by people who immediately succeeded it or by us after many years." [11]

"We fight our battles behind bulwarks made of stays and ruffs, laces and ribbons, baggy and tight trousers, snuff-boxes and smelling-salts, 'Queen Anne' gables and 'Neo-Jacobean' bays and 'Romanesque' turrets; battlements behind which we risk our professional lives to-day, and which to-morrow we blow into oblivion with a sneer. For our own self-respect, for the dignity of our own position, for the sake of an architecture which shall have within it some vital germ, let us come out from our petticoat fortress and fight our battles in open field. In science and literature, in art, is heard, loudly calling, the voice of reason. For any branch of human knowledge or imagination or aspiration to shut itself from this cry is death." [12]

"It will be seen that this tends directly against the literal use of historic styles. True. But so much the better for the styles as we understand them. A style has never been made by copying with the loving care of a Dryasdust some preceding style. Styles grow by the careful study of all the conditions which lie about each architectural problem; and thus while each will have its distinct differentiation from all others, broad influences of climate, of national habits and institutions, will in time create the type, and this is the only style worth considering. This position is reasonable and is susceptible of rational statement." [13]

"Architecture is so noble a profession that to allow its influence to be swayed by ephemeral fashions, to make its creations things lightly considered and cheaply wrought, is the basest of crimes." [14]

"Architecture is, like every other art, born of its age and environment. So the new type will be found by us, if we do find it, through the frankest possible acceptance of every requirement of modern life in all of its conditions, without regret for the past or idle longing for a future and more fortunate day; this acceptance being accompanied by the intelligent and sympathetic study of the past in the spirit of aspiring emulation, not servile imitation. If the new art is to come, I believe it will be a rational and steady growth from practical conditions outward and upward toward a more or less spiritual expression, and that no man has the right to borrow from another age an architectural idea evolved from the life of that age, unless it fits our life as normally and fully as it fitted the other." [15]

After describing in detail the effect of the new conditions of structure and use developed in the evolution of the modern office building, he says: —

"To other and older types of architecture these new problems are related as the poetry of Darwin's evolution is to other poetry. They destroy, indeed, many of the most admirable and inspiring of architectural forms, but they create forms adapted to the expression of new ideas and new aspects of life. Here vagaries of fashion and temporary fancies should have no influence; here the arbitrary dicta of self-constituted architectural prophets should have no voice. Every one of these problems should be rationally worked out alone, and each should express the character and aims of the people related to it. I do not believe it is possible to exaggerate the importance of the influence which may be exerted for good or evil by these distinctively modern buildings. Hedged about by many unavoidable conditions, they are either gross and self-asserting shams, untrue both in the material realization of their aims and in their art function as expressions of the deeper spirit of the age, or they are sincere, noble, and enduring monuments to the broad and beneficent commerce of the age." [16]

These expressions of noble rebellion against those architectural conventions which, however beautiful and fascinating to the man of education, have no power of progression in the strenuous atmosphere of the New World or of adjustment to its new requirements, and are consequently sterile, are entirely consistent with the character of Root's executed work. This is copiously and on the whole well set forth in his Life by forty-eight text illustrations, and twenty-four full-page etchings, drawings, and gelatine reproductions of his own sketches, which, when considered consecutively in the order of execution, show just that sort of consistent and steady progression which we have a right to expect as the outward expression of an active mind in a continuous state of development. There were, of course, occasional interruptions and aberrations in this series of graphic presentments which indicate how this eager intelligence was experimenting according to the variation of its moods and inspirations. But its essential progress was vindicated by the fact that Root rarely repeated an error, or failed in his subsequent works to make the best use of a success. His last works were his greatest; they were full of his native energy, and gave no suggestion of fatigue or of any desire to rest upon the laurels he had won.

The series of studies for the general architectural scheme of the World's Fair, executed by him while the preliminary projects were taking shape, furnishes a remarkable proof of the fertility of his professional resources, of the exuberance of his poetic temperament, and of his fidelity to his convictions regarding a national architecture. It was at the close of this period of stress and enthusiasm, when the organization for the carrying out of this great work had been completed, that he was overtaken by death.

The sudden and untimely interruption of this really great career has a peculiar pathos to us who remain behind to enjoy the best fruits of it; but to him we may imagine that there has come at last the supreme reward of the artist-soul in a final settlement of all his doubts and a final full realization of his ideal. "Finis coronat opus."

A Letter on the Aesthetics of Bridge Construction

From *De Pontibus: A Pocket-Book for Bridge Engineers*
By *John Alexander Low Waddell* [1]

(1898)

My Dear Mr. Waddell:

After looking over a portion of your instructive treatise on bridges, I find it quite impossible to comply with your request to furnish you with practical suggestions from an architectural point of view as to grace and beauty of design in such structures. As these qualities must be developed from the structure itself, as they must be evolved from its inherent economical and practical conditions, and as they cannot be successfully applied to it as an afterthought, it would be unbecoming for any layman to attempt to show by what process this evolution is to be accomplished. The problem is not an easy one; it is not to be solved by theory, or by any accident of invention or ingenuity. At present, at least, it can only be treated on general lines. Indeed there is no one living, I fear, who can suggest a specific and easily applied remedy for that disease of engineering which is expressed in the curious fact that the most perfect results of science, at least in the art of steel-bridge building as now understood and inculcated, do not recognize any theory of beauty in line or mass.

It is the business of the architect to express structure and purpose with beauty. It is the business of the engineer, as I understand it, to make structures strong, durable, rigid, and economical; to apply pure science, excluding, as a matter of principle, any device of art which, for the sake of mere ornamentation, may add to his fabric a pound of unnecessary weight or a dollar of unnecessary cost.

It cannot be denied that to whatever extent the exercise of this principle may have affected the practice of engineers, they have succeeded, especially as regards bridge-building, in developing a structure which is in every essential respect orderly, consistent, and progressive from a practical point of view. From year to year this development towards mechanical perfection has been plainly visible. The structure of ten years ago has been reasonably and properly superseded by another and better structure, indicating a process of growth without a shadow of caprice; in this process discovery and invention have had their proper influence, uninterrupted by any conservative prejudice or by any theory of design which does not rest directly on practical considerations. But, as I have already observed, this admirable and prolific progress has not carried with it a corresponding progress in grace and beauty of design. In fact, these qualities seem to appear in an inverse proportion to the development of the structural scheme towards the practical idea of strength, stability, and economy. Consequently the stronger, the more rigid, the more economical the structure, the more uncompromising and the more hopeless it seems to be in respect to beauty. The modern steel-girder or cantilever bridge, while, according to our present knowledge, it is perfectly adapted to its uses and functions, is in nearly every case an offence to the landscape in which it occurs. Its lines, since they have ceased to be structural curves, have become hard and ascetic mathematical expressions, and have not been brought into any sympathy whatever with the natural lines of the stream which it crosses, of the opposite banks which it connects, of the meadows, forests, and mountains among which it is placed. All sylvan effects of harmony are shocked by its discordant intrusion. The vast aqueducts of the Romans, the arched bridges of stone, the catenary curves of the modern suspension bridges with their high towers, and some forms of bridges constructed with bowstring girders, are more or less affiliated with the natural conditions, so that they give no shock, save frequently of pleasure at their expression of grace and fitness. But we are assured that these structural forms are obsolete or are becoming obsolete, and that the straight bridge-truss spanning from pier to pier, the cantilever overhanging the perilous abyss, the pivoted draw-span, all constructed with cold geometrical precision, with hard unfeeling lines of tension and compression, have taken their place, to the great advantage of the railroads and the greater security of the public. It is in vain that the conscientious engineer occasionally attempts to compromise with grace by ornamenting his intersections by rosettes or buttons of cast iron, or by rearing a sort of arch or portal of triumph at the entrance to his bridge with a lavish display of metal shell-work, scrolls of forged iron, and tables cast and gilded with names and dates. But the compromise comes too late; the main essential lines cannot be condoned by afterthoughts of this sort; and as far as the eye can see, these lines, though they may satisfy the reason, generally affront the sense of beauty.

Now it seems to me important to note that the methods of nature always culminate in infinite expressions of beauty, and that beauty is an essential part of the principles of natural growth. The Great Creator never makes anything, animate or inanimate, ugly in making it strong or swift or durable, or in fitting it to the economy of nature. Grace is a part of the system of creation. Is it reserved for man in his secondary creation to make things unlovely in proportion to their complete and perfect adaptation to the satisfaction of his practical needs? Is this difference significant of some quality which is wanting in our science?

But, it may be said, if a steel-trussed bridge, economically and wisely constructed according to our present light, offends our ideals of grace and beauty, the fault perhaps is not in the structure, but in the rigidity and immobility of the ideals which have been established by conditions long since outgrown in the progress of science. The attempts of the English bridge-builders in iron in the early part of the century to meet these old ideas resulted in constructions which, though they may satisfy the eye of the artist, and combine more or less gracefully with the landscape, are uneconomical and unscientific. The principles of structure involved are incorrect, and unnecessary expense was incurred in forcing into the design features conventionally acceptable, but which had nothing to do with the structure, and which in fact were a hindrance to it, concealing rather than illustrating it.

The architect will not find it difficult to agree with his brother the engineer, that a mask of ornamental cast iron, covering the essential features of the structure in order to force upon it an effect of grace, is illogical in the extreme. Indeed, a great modern master of architecture has laid down the axiom: "A form which admits of no explanation, or which is mere caprice, cannot be beautiful; and in architecture, certainly, every form which is not inspired by the structure ought therefore to be rejected." [2] The conscientious modern architect aims to shape his design according to this reasonable limitation, and he has been thereby enabled to produce occasional effects of beauty without imposing on his composition a single idea which is not suggested either by the structure or by the use of the building. Even a factory, a gasometer, a railway shed, an elevator, need not challenge the architect in vain to produce effects of fitness not entirely inconsistent with the requirements of art. Indeed, the engineer himself, with axioms or maxims of art, has, in the evolution of the roof-truss, the locomotive, and many industrial machines, succeeded in satisfying ideals of beauty in the very process of making them powerful, compact, and economical of material and space. The modern steel-armored warship has already, in this early stage of its rapid development, substituted for the ideas of maritime beauty, speed, and strength which prevailed in the time of Nelson and the other great historical admirals, and which were celebrated in the songs of Dibdin and Campbell,[3] an entirely different ideal, hardly less imposing, though as yet without poetic recognition. But the evolution of the steel-trussed bridge has as yet satisfied neither old ideals of beauty, nor has it made new ideals. Its essential lines are drawn in apparent disregard or contempt for grace of outline or elegance of detail. The difficulty seems to be inherent in the present approved structural system of designing horizontal, straight, open-trussed girders or cantilevers, resting on rigid vertical piers of masonry or iron, without regard to any other considerations excepting those of statics. The eye requires to be satisfied as well as the trained intelligence, and demands not only grace of proportion, but a certain decorative emphasis expressive of especial functions. The primitive post and lintel structure of stone was as hopeless, apparently, as its modern derivative, the steel-trussed bridge, until the Greeks, with unerring instinct of art, converted it by perfectly rational processes into that ideal expression of beauty which is known as the Doric order. This Doric order is a structure which depends less upon subsidiary decoration than upon proportion for its unparalleled success as a work of art. The Parthenon would still be lovely without the sculptures of its friezes, metopes, and pediments. Its columns, reduced to dimensions which encumber them with no useless brute mass of material, were so treated with entasis, capital, and fluting as to express exactly members in vertical compression; its lintels were so subdivided as to draw attention to, and to illustrate, all their functions in the structural scheme. They contained no features of caprice or fancy. Now the essential qualities of the steel-girder bridge differ from those of the post and lintel of the Greeks because, in the former, the structure of the lintels permits of a wider spacing of the posts, and the posts have assumed the dual function of piers for vertical support and of buttresses to withstand the horizontal pressures of the stream in which they are built; the lintels, in their turn, have lost their quality as compact, solid, homogeneous masses, have been resolved into distinct elements, and have become a complicated and highly artificial openwork contrivance of light steel members, which in their dimensions and articulations have been so combined in tension and compression as to produce a structure capable of sustaining without change of form not only its own weight between bearing points far apart, but that of moving trains, and of bearing without detriment vibrations and wind-pressures, and the expansion and contraction of its material by changes of temperature.

These compound lintels or trusses are in themselves triumphs of mind over matter. At this moment they express a stage of evolution which has been in process for a century, and which doubtless will continue to develop in directions impossible to anticipate. They are structures not dedicated to the immortal gods, like the post and lintel in the Greek temples, the decorative character of which was largely inspired by religious emotions, but devised to meet secular and practical conditions of an exceedingly unpoetic and unimaginative character. The mind of the architect appreciates the fine economy of these sensitive and complicated organisms, but it also recognizes that they are still in active process of development; that they are on trial, and will not reach final results *until they shall have assumed those conditions of grace and beauty which are essential to completion.* It is evident enough that all the features of perfection in animals have been very gradually evolved, by survival of the fittest and by adaptation to use, from the awkward and monstrous shapes of the antediluvian period; that geological erosion and drift have clothed the naked rocks with beauty; and that the whole vegetable creation has been improved by art. Nature herself is not contented with inelastic dogmas. In like manner, the locomotive, the steam-engine, the modern war-ship, have all become objects of awful beauty, not because of the imposition of unnecessary features, but because of the natural and reasonable growth of their essential structure.

If, therefore, the ugly character of the present steel-trussed bridge is in itself a proof of the immaturity of the science which has produced it, the

377

remedy, of course, must reside in the perfecting of the science, and this process of perfecting will be quickened, if beauty is recognized in engineering as it is in architecture, as an aim and not as an accident of growth. The architect guides and hastens this progress towards the perfect type by fundamentally composing his structure with a view to an agreeable proportion of its parts; in detail he studies to emphasize the special and important points of his structure by a decorative treatment which shall indicate conventionally the character of the work accomplished at these points. It is true, perhaps, that the structural forms of materials with which the engineers have to work, especially in bridge-building, are hardly so elastic and manageable as those at the command of the architect even in his simplest and most severely practical problems; but it is none the less true that the training of the engineer leads him too often to an absolute disregard, if not contempt, for those refinements of proportion and outline, and for all those delicate adaptations and adjustments of detail, which, though perhaps separately slight, and apparently of small importance, in combination tend to give distinction and a character of fitness and grace to works otherwise, from the point of view of art, rudely immature, basely mechanical, unnecessarily and insolently ugly.

Mr. Henry James says that the French talk of those who see *en beau* and those who see *en laid*. The performance of the modern steel-bridge designers would certainly seem to place them in the latter category. It is no less certain that this result comes not from temperament, which is natural, but from training, which is artificial. The severe and absolute conditions in which the bridge-builders work do not prevent them either from great differences in manner and method of design, or from frequent and unnecessary extravagances of expenditure; but these extravagances are rarely, if ever, lavished in the services of beauty; because the cold and rarefied atmosphere of science and mechanical utility, in which they are accustomed to labor, has gradually frozen out the finer natural instinct which works for art and elegance in design. Beauty of proportion has often been proved by mathematics; but mathematics, when it has been allowed to be the only element in the development of a problem of construction, has never accomplished beautiful results. Such results do not come by accident in any work of design, but by the liberal and generous observance of natural laws. The education, therefore, which from the beginning does not give some recognition to grace, proportion, elegance, as essential parts of construction, must be misleading and one-sided, and cannot lead to perfection. The recognition of these qualities, I am entirely persuaded, does not necessarily imply any sacrifice of practical accuracy in design or of mechanical precision in workmanship, nor need it affect materially that fine economy which is essential to perfection.

Very sincerely yours,
HENRY VAN BRUNT.

Illustrations

1. Commodore Gershom Jacques Van Brunt, U.S.N., August 28, 1798–December 17, 1863.

2. Fayerweather House, 175 Brattle St., Cambridge, Mass. Home of Henry Van Brunt from 1869 to 1883.

3. Sanford Robinson Gifford in character of the Wandering Jew, by Henry Van Brunt; (right) Henry Van Brunt in character of Verdant Green, West Point, June 24, 1860, by Sanford Robinson Gifford. From Van Brunt's sketchbooks.

4. Chimneypiece in Richard Morris Hunt's atelier on 10th Street, New York, April, 1858.

5. Union gunboats, probably drawn off the North Carolina coast during the Civil War.

6. (Top left) Château de Baumais, drawn from a plate in Victor Petit, *Châteaux de France des xvᵉ et xviᵉ siècles*; (below) basement of the Palace of Charles V in the Alhambra, drawn from a plate in Alexandre de Laborde, *Voyage pittoresque et historique de l'Espagne*.

7. Gable of house in carved wood at Cravan, Yonne; (below) old houses at Rouen. Both drawn from plates in Victor Petit, *Châteaux de France des xvᵉ et xviᵉ siècles*.

8. (Bottom left) Scuola San Rocco, Venice, drawn from a plate in Ludwig Runge, *Beiträge zur Kenntniss der Backstein-Architectur Italiens*.

9. Staircase of Louis XIII; (below) Pavillon de Sully, drawn from *Souvenirs de Fontainebleau* (unidentified).

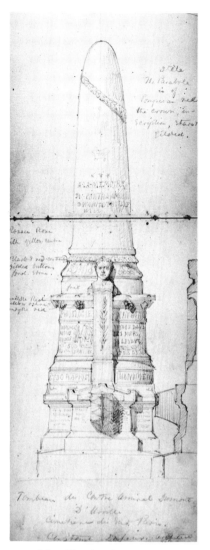

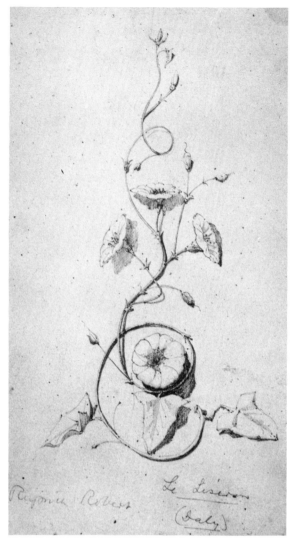

10. Tomb of Contre-Amiral Dumont d'Urville, Paris, drawn from a plate in the *Revue générale d'architecture*, vol. 8.
11. Drawn from a design by Ruprich Robert in the *Revue générale d'architecture*, vol. 10.
12. The *Porte de la Conférence*; (right) the Grotte de Meudon, drawn from engravings by Israel Silvestre.

13. The Royal Stables at Versailles, drawn from an unidentified plate.

14. Drawings from plates in *Oeuvres d'architecture de Jean Le Pautre*.

15. A page from Van Brunt's sketchbook summary of Thomas Rickman, *An Attempt to Discriminate the Styles of Architecture in England from the Conquest to the Reformation.*

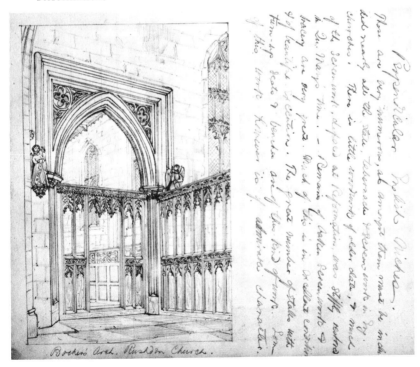

385

16. The New York University Building, Washington Square, New York, where Richard Morris Hunt kept his own apartment and studio from 1856.

17. Peterborough Cathedral and Bishop's Palace, England.

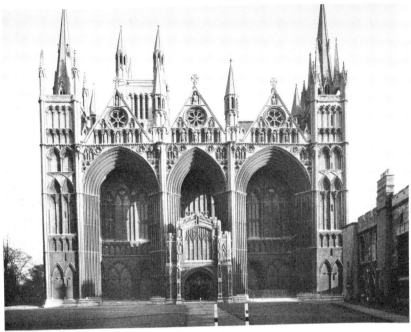

17a.   Peterborough Cathedral, the west front.

17b.   Peterborough Cathedral, from the nave looking into the choir.

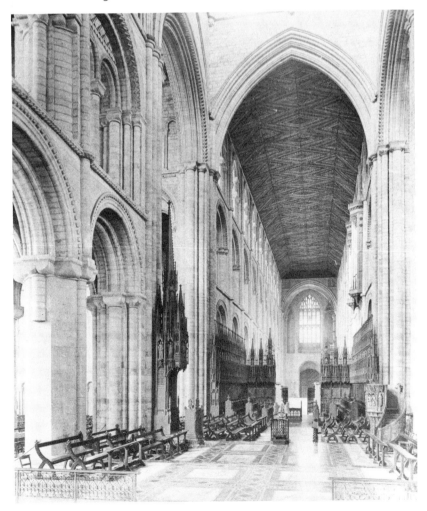

18. Ware and Van Brunt, First Church, Boston, 1865–1867. Photograph 1868–1870.

19. Ware and Van Brunt, church in Nahant, Mass., primarily for summer use, 1868.

20. Ether Monument, Public Garden, Boston, 1868. The statue is by J. Q. A. Ward, but the base has been ascribed to Henry Van Brunt.

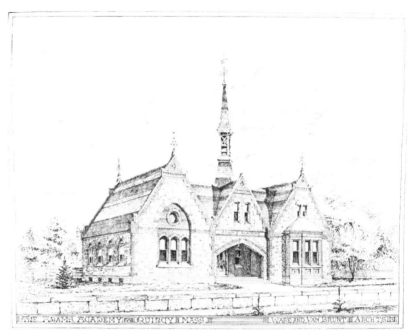

21. Ware and Van Brunt, Adams Academy, Quincy, Mass., 1869, a town library and school building.

22. Ware and Van Brunt, St. John's Chapel, Episcopal Theological School, Cambridge, Mass., 1869–1870.

22a. Ware and Van Brunt, Lawrence Hall, first half, Episcopal Theological School, Cambridge, Mass., 1873.

22b. Ware and Van Brunt, Episcopal Theological School, Cambridge, Mass. Left to right, Lawrence Hall, 1873–1880; Reed Hall, 1875; Burnham Hall, 1879.

23.   Forty-one Brimmer St., Boston, 1869, attributed to Ware and Van Brunt.

24. Ware and Van Brunt, 288 Marlborough St., Boston, 1872, the center house of a row extending from 282 to 292 Marlborough St.

25. Ware and Van Brunt, Weld Hall, Harvard University, 1871–1872.

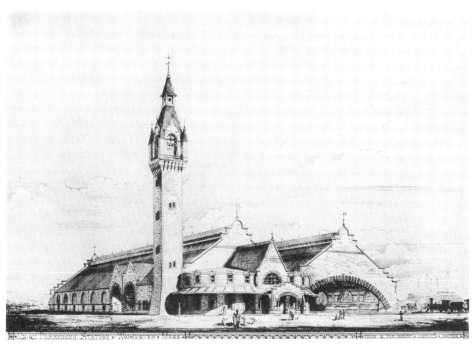

26. Ware and Van Brunt, Union Passenger Station, Worcester, Mass., 1874–1877.

27. Ware and Van Brunt, Third Universalist Church, Cambridge, Mass., 1875.

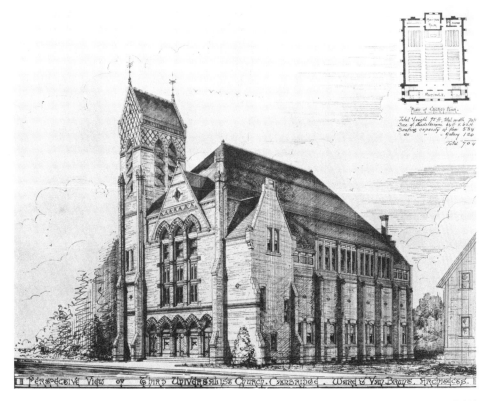

28. Ware and Van Brunt, Memorial Hall, Harvard University. Competition won in 1865. Building, 1874–1878.

29. Ware and Van Brunt, Memorial Hall vestibule, 1876.

30. Gore Hall, Harvard University Library, 1839–1841. Stack addition at right by Ware and Van Brunt, 1876–1877. The tactful blending of new with old is especially noteworthy.

31.   Ware and Van Brunt, the Cass Monument, Detroit, Michigan, 1876.

32.   Ware and Van Brunt, competitive design for the Frazer Institute, Montreal, 1876, a museum and library.

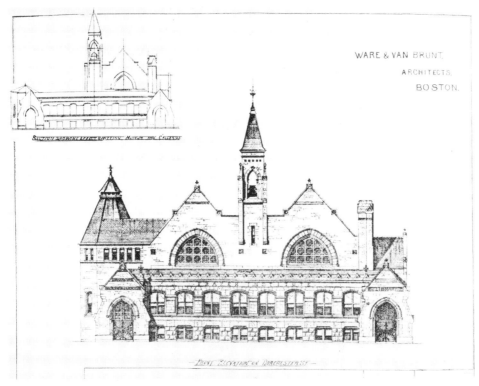

33. Ware and Van Brunt, design for a proposed Cincinnati Music Hall, 1876.

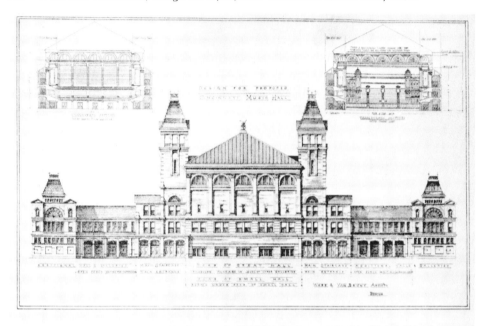

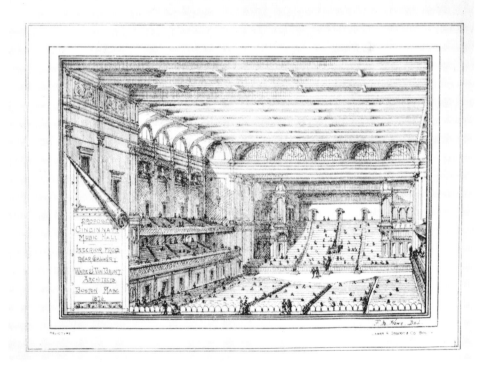

Design of house for E.S. Philbrick Esq — Brookline — Ware & Van Brunt — Archt's

34. Ware and Van Brunt, house for E. S. Philbrick, Brookline, Mass., 1876.
35. Ware and Van Brunt, Hotel Hamilton, Boston, 1876.

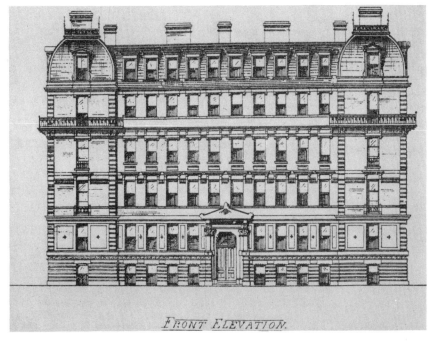

FRONT ELEVATION.

36. Ware and Van Brunt, house of Dr. F. J. Bumstead, New York, 1877.

37.   Ware and Van Brunt, house for A. A. Coburn, Lowell, Mass., 1877.

38. Ware and Van Brunt, competitive design for Milton, Mass., Town Hall, 1878.

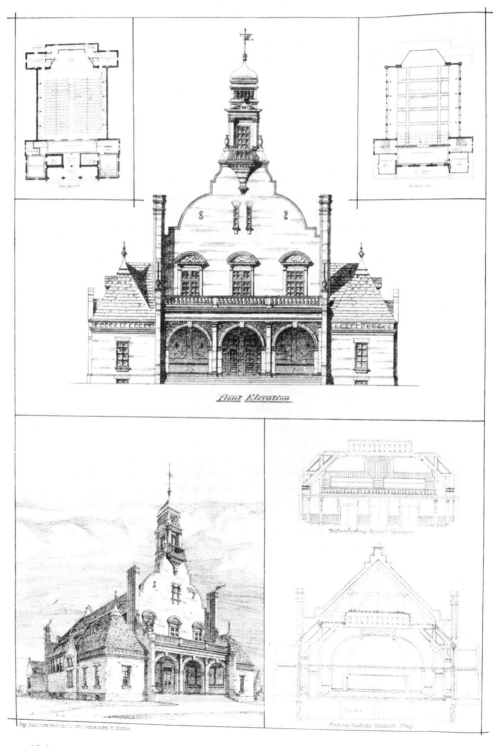

Front Elevation

404

39. Ware and Van Brunt, study for college buildings, 1879. The structure includes laboratories, dormitories, lecture rooms, a theater, library, chapel, and dining halls.

40. Ware and Van Brunt, proposed monument to John C. Calhoun, Charleston, S.C., 1879.

41. Richard Morris Hunt and Henry Van Brunt, design for the Yorktown Monument, 1881.

42.   Ware and Van Brunt, Stone Hall, Wellesley College, Wellesley, Mass., 1880.

43.   Ware and Van Brunt, St. Stephen's Memorial Church, Lynn, Mass., 1881.

43a. Ware and Van Brunt, St. Stephen's Church, Lynn, interior.

Erected by the late Hon. P. R. Midge to the glory of God

and in memory of two of his children · A.D. 1881·

St · Stephen's · Memorial · Church · at Lynn · Mass · · Messrs · Ware · & · Van Brunt · Arch'ts · Boston

43b.   Ware and Van Brunt, St. Stephen's Church, Lynn.

44. Van Brunt and Howe, house for Gilbert Payson, Watertown, Mass., 1882.

45. Henry Van Brunt, the architect's own residence, 167 Brattle St., Cambridge, Mass., 1883. Stable added 1888.

46. Van Brunt and Howe, Library, University of Michigan, Ann Arbor, 1883.

47.   Van Brunt and Howe, Emmanuel Church, Shelburne Falls, Mass., 1883.

EMMANUEL CHURCH, AT SHELBURNE FALLS, MASS.

Messrs. VAN BRUNT & HOWE. Architects. Boston. Mass.

SOUTH WEST VIEW

48. Van Brunt and Howe, Harvard Medical School building, Boston, 1883.

49. Van Brunt and Howe, Hildreth Building, Lowell, Mass., 1883.

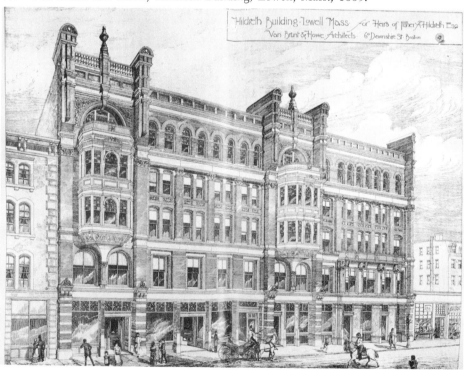

50. Van Brunt and Howe, house at 35 Concord Ave., Cambridge, Mass., 1884.

51. Van Brunt and Howe, unidentified house in Cambridge, Mass.

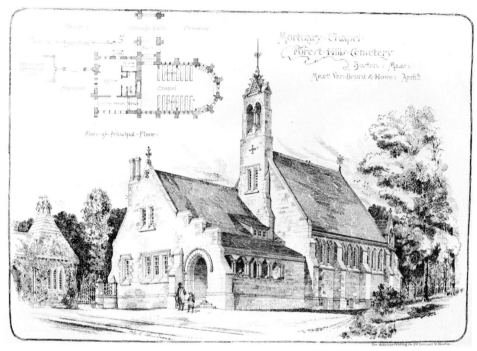

52.   Van Brunt and Howe, Mortuary Chapel, Forest Hills Cemetery, Boston, 1884.

53.   Van Brunt and Howe, Blake Monument, Mount Auburn Cemetery, 1885.

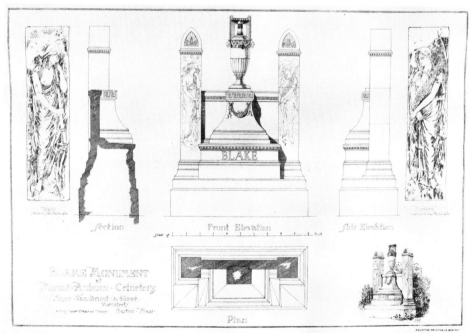

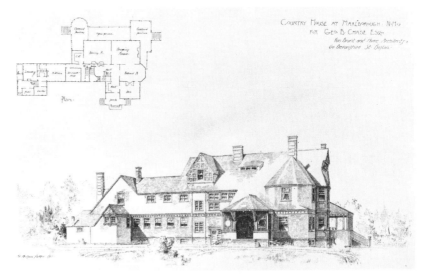

54. Van Brunt and Howe, country house, Marlborough, N.H., for George B. Chase, 1885.

55. Van Brunt and Howe, the Gordon Monument, Savannah, Ga., 1885.

56. Van Brunt and Howe, office building for Nathaniel Thayer, Kansas City, Mo., 1886. A pioneer in modern office requirements in Kansas City, the building included a hydraulic elevator, bells, tubes, electric light, and a marble staircase.

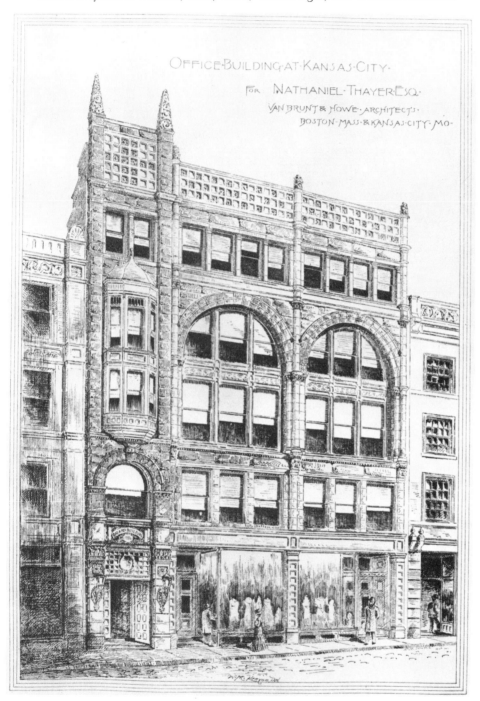

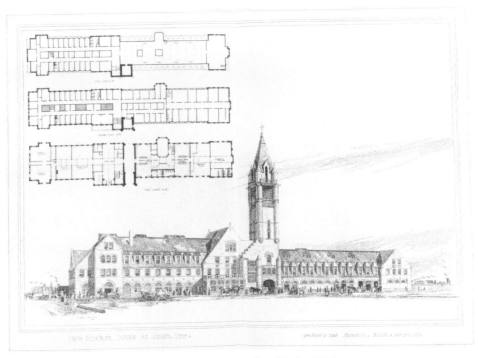

57. Van Brunt and Howe, Union Station, Ogden, Utah, 1886.

58. Van Brunt and Howe, house for J. J. Mastin, Kansas City, Mo., 1887.

59. Van Brunt and Howe, Union Pacific passenger depot, Cheyenne, Wyo., 1887

60. Van Brunt and Howe, Public Library, Dedham, Mass., 1888.

61. Van Brunt and Howe, Public Library, Cambridge, Mass., 1888–1889.

61a. Van Brunt and Howe, entrance portico, Public Library, Cambridge.

62. Van Brunt and Howe, Gibraltar Building, Kansas City, Mo., 1888.

63. Van Brunt and Howe, Kansas City Club, Kansas City, Mo., 1888.

64. Van Brunt and Howe, competitive design for the Cathedral of St. John the Divine, New York, 1889.

65. Van Brunt and Howe, Coates House Hotel, Kansas City, Mo., 1889–1890.

424

66. Van Brunt and Howe, Bullene, Moore, and Emery Store (now Emery, Bird, and Thayer), Kansas City, Mo., 1889–1890. The building is arcaded on three sides to shelter pedestrians.

67. Van Brunt and Howe, Union Station, Portland, Oregon, c. 1893. Stanford White began the design, according to information from the railroad company.

68. Van Brunt and Howe, Old Union Station, Omaha, Neb., c. 1890.

69. Van Brunt and Howe, competitive design for University of Wisconsin Library, Madison, 1896. Second premium design, final competition: a. view in reading room; front elevation; b. (opposite) view in rotunda; side elevation.

VIEW IN READING ROOM.

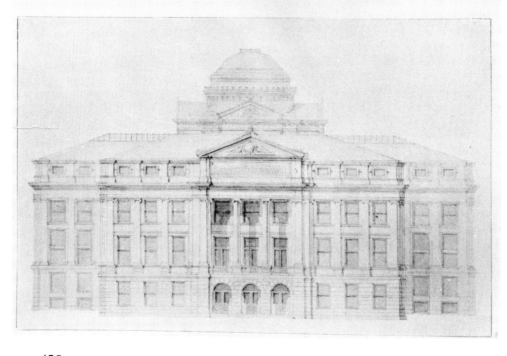

VIEW IN ROTUNDA.

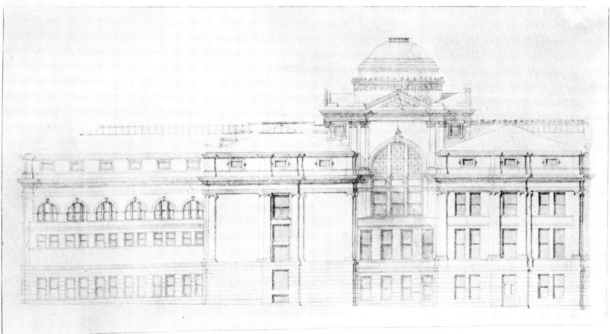

SIDE ELEVATION

70. Van Brunt and Howe, house of K. B. Aman, Kansas City, Mo., c. 1895–1896.

71. Van Brunt and Howe, August R. Meyer house, Kansas City, Mo., 1895–1896.

72. Van Brunt and Howe, house of Mrs. A. W. Armour, Kansas City, Mo., 1903.

73. Van Brunt and Howe, Bryant Building, Kansas City, Mo., 1903.

74. Van Brunt and Howe, house of E. W. Smith, Kansas City, Mo., c. 1903.

75. Van Brunt and Howe, corner of Varied Industries Building,
     Louisiana Purchase Exposition, St. Louis, Mo., 1904.

76. McKim, Mead, and White, New York Life Building, Kansas City, Mo., assisted by Van Brunt and Howe, 1888–1890.

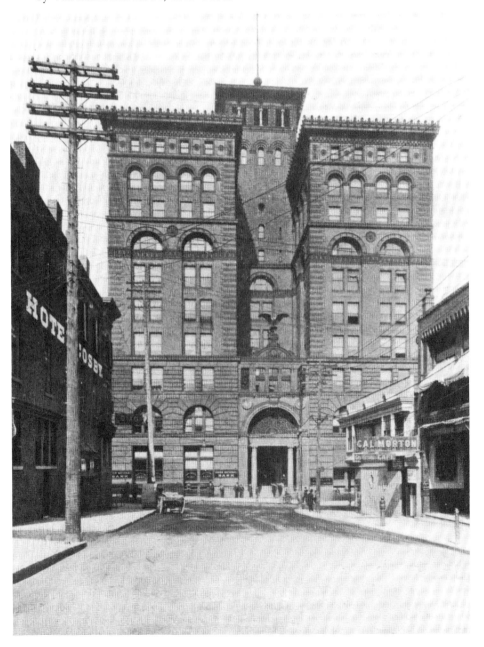

77.   Sir Charles Barry, Houses of Parliament, London, 1840–1865.

78. Augustus Welby Pugin, *An Apology for the Revival of Christian Architecture in England*, Plate VII, 1843. The consistent principles of old domestic architecture applied to modern street buildings.

79. Harvey Lonsdale Elmes, St. George's Hall, Liverpool, 1841–1854.

80. Sir Charles Barry, the Reform Club, London, 1838–1840. The Travellers' Club, 1830–1832, also by Barry, is next on the left.

81. Deane and Woodward, Oxford University Museum, 1855–1859.

82.   Alexander Thomson, Caledonia Road Church, Glasgow, 1856–1857.

83. Alexander Thomson, Moray Place, Glasgow, 1859.

84. Alfred Waterhouse, Manchester Assize Courts, 1859.

85. Alfred Waterhouse, Manchester Town Hall, 1869. Photograph after cleaning and restoration in 1967.

86.   Sir George Gilbert Scott, Albert Memorial, London, 1863–1872.

87.   Sir George Gilbert Scott, St. Pancras Station and Hotel, London, 1865–1875.

88. William Burges, St. Finbarre's Cathedral, Cork, 1865–1876.

89. William Burges, competitive design for the Royal Courts of Justice, Strand, London, 1866.

90. George Edmund Street, Royal Courts of Justice, Strand, London, 1874–1882, designed in 1867.

91. Charles L. Eastlake, *Hints on Household Taste in Furniture, Upholstery, and Other Details,* 1868, Plate XII.

92. Richard Norman Shaw, 185 Queen's Gate, London, 1890.

93. Peter Vischer, the Elder, Shrine of St. Sebald, Nuremberg, 1507–1519. The sarcophagus dates from 1397.

94. Henri Labrouste, Bibliothèque Ste Geneviève, Paris, 1843–1850.

446

94a.   Henri Labrouste, Reading Room, Bibliothèque Ste Geneviève, Paris, 1850.
       The vaulting offers an example of nineteenth-century cast iron decorative work.

447

95. L.- T.- J. Visconti and Hector-Martin Lefuel, Louvre, Paris, north wing on the Place du Carrousel; left to right, Pavillons Turgot, Richelieu, and Colbert, 1850–1857.

95a. Visconti and Lefuel, Louvre, Paris, Pavillon Turgot. In the foreground the Gambetta monument.

95b.   Visconti and Lefuel, Louvre, Paris, Pavillon Richelieu.

96. Louis-Joseph Duc, Palais de Justice, Paris. The pavilions between the towers were built after 1840.

96a. Louis-Joseph Duc, Palais de Justice, Paris, west facade, 1857–1868.

97. Jacques-Félix Duban, Ecole des Beaux Arts, Paris, 1860–1862, facade of the Salle des Sculptures.

98.   Charles Garnier, Opéra, Paris, 1861–1874.

99.   Théodore Ballu and Pierre-Joseph Déperthes, Hôtel de Ville, Paris, 1874–1882.

100.   Exposition Universelle, Paris, 1900, Palais des Mines et Métallurgie.

100a.   Exposition Universelle, Paris. 1900, Palais de l'Esplanade des Invalides.

101. Henry Hobson Richardson, Trinity Church, Boston, 1873–1877.

454

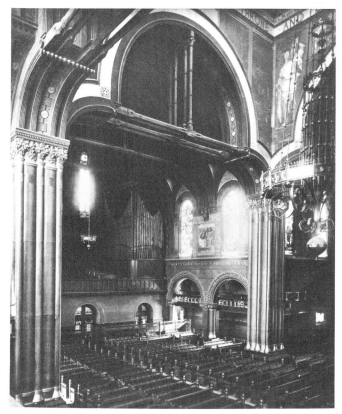

101a.   Henry Hobson Richardson, Trinity Church, interior, looking into the nave. The mural decorations by John LaFarge are visible in the center and at top right.

101b.   Henry Hobson Richardson, Trinity Church, the crossing, looking into the apse. The LaFarge mural paintings are visible at top and at left.

455

102. John LaFarge, mural paintings in Trinity Church, Boston (left) nave.

102a. Prophet in the crossing.

102b. An arch of the crossing.

102c.   Trinity Church, decorations in the tower.

102d.   Trinity Church, lunette in the left transept.

457

103. Henry Hobson Richardson and Leopold Eidlitz, original design for the completion of the New York State Capitol, Albany, 1876. The lower two stories (1867–1876) are in the Italian Renaissance style of Thomas Fuller, the original architect. The third story, beginning the work of Richardson and Eidlitz, makes a transition to the pure Romanesque of the fourth. The central tower was never built.

103a. Henry Hobson Richardson and Leopold Eidlitz, revised design for the State Capitol, Albany. The roof of the building was altered at the behest of the legislature, which specified that the building be completed in its original style. The architects, however, resisted and drew their inspiration from the French, rather than the Italian Renaissance. The advanced terrace was never built.

103b. State Capitol, Albany, eastern front.

459

103c.   State Capitol, Albany, northeast corner.

103d. State Capitol, Albany, north front. The north center, completed in 1879, contains the Assembly Chamber and Staircase.

461

103e. State Capitol, Albany, the Assembly Staircase by Leopold Eidlitz. The round
arched windows are a later addition.

462

103f. (Top left) State Capitol, Albany, the Golden Corridor of the North Pavilion by Leopold Eidlitz. Later the structure cracked, and the corridor was demolished.

103g. (Top right) State Capitol, Albany, the Court of Appeals room, by Leopold Eidlitz, temporary home of the Senate for the first two years after the occupation of the Capitol.

103h. State Capitol, Albany, fireplace in the Assembly Chamber by Leopold Eidlitz.

103i. State Capitol, Albany, the Assembly Chamber by Leopold Eidlitz. The photograph has been much doctored, with faces pasted in. William Morris Hunt's mural, *The Flight of Night*, appears at top right. The pictorial frieze below never existed. The great vaulted ceiling leaked and then cracked and was replaced after ten years by a flat one which covered over Hunt's flaking and discolored murals.

463

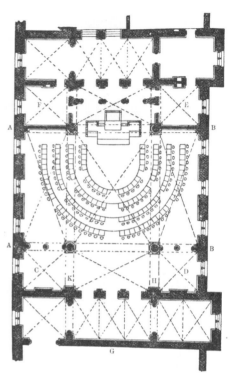

103j. State Capitol, Albany, plan of the Assembly Chamber.

104. William Morris Hunt, sketch for *The Flight of Night* in the Assembly Chamber, Albany.

464

104a. William Morris Hunt, *The Flight of Night*. An old photograph shows the mural painting wedged in between the ceiling vault and an arcade of windows.

104b. William Morris Hunt, *The Discoverer*, mural painting in the Assembly Chamber, Albany.

105. Constantino Brumidi, fresco decoration of the dome in the National Capitol, Washington, D.C.

105a. Constantino Brumidi, fresco decoration in the President's Room, Senate end of the National Capitol, Washington, D.C.

106. Henry Hobson Richardson, Sever Hall, Harvard University, Cambridge, Mass., 1878–1880.

107. Henry Hobson Richardson, Austin Hall, Harvard Law School, Cambridge, Mass., 1881.

108. Henry Hobson Richardson, Crane Library, Quincy, Mass., 1880–1883.

109. Henry Hobson Richardson, railroad station, Auburndale, Mass., 1881.

110. Henry Hobson Richardson, Allegheny County Buildings, Pittsburgh, Courthouse, begun in 1884.

110a. Henry Hobson Richardson, Allegheny County Buildings, Pittsburgh, detail of a doorway in the jail.

110b. Henry Hobson Richardson, Allegheny County Buildings, Pittsburgh, connecting bridge between the courthouse and jail.

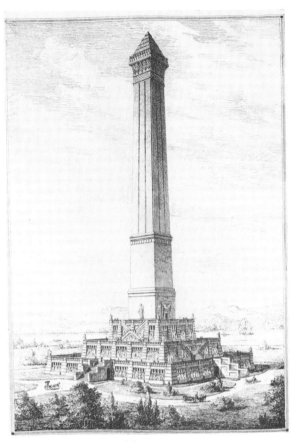

111. (Upper left) Robert Mills, original design for the Washington Monument.
112. H. R. Searle, design for the Washington Monument.
113. (Lower left) John Frazer, design for the Washington Monument.
114. William Story, design for the Washington Monument.

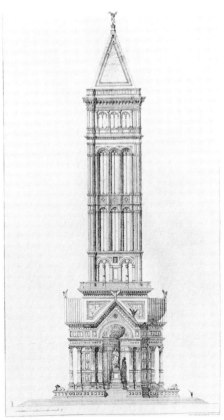

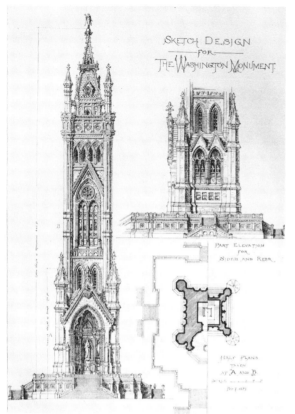

115. M. P. Hapgood, design for the Washington Monument.

116. Paul Schulze, design for the Washington Monument.

117. (Below) Anonymous design for the Washington Monument.

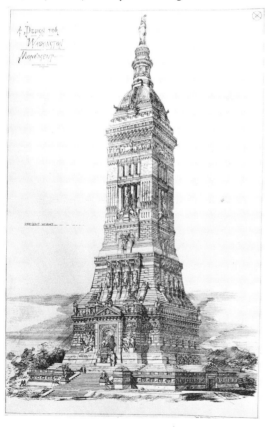

473

118. Crosby's Opera House, Chicago, 1866. An example of the vernacular style of American architecture.

119. Burling and Whitehouse, house of Samuel Nickerson, Chicago, 1883, design 1881.

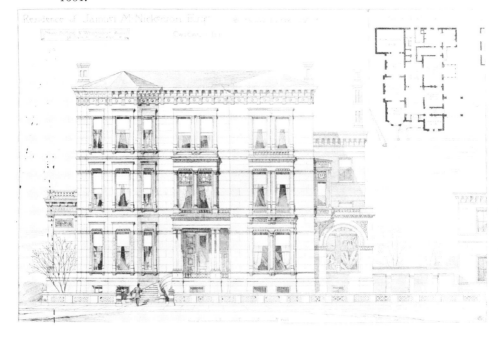

120.   Burnham and Root, Calumet Building, Chicago, 1884.

121. Cobb and Frost, Chicago Opera House block, 1885.

122. Cobb and Frost, Union Club, Chicago, c. 1885.

123. Cobb and Frost, Potter Palmer house, Chicago, 1885.
124. William LeBaron Jenney, Home Insurance Building, Chicago, 1885–1889, before the additions of 1891.

477

125. Burnham and Root, Insurance Exchange Building, later the Continental Bank Building, Chicago, 1885.

126. Burnham and Root, Rookery Building, Chicago, 1886.

127. Burnham and Root, Phoenix Building, Chicago, 1886.

478

128. Burnham and Root, Board of Trade Building, Kansas City, Mo., 1886.

129. Henry Hobson Richardson, Marshall Field Wholesale Store, Chicago, 1887. Richardson's Romanesque here turns Roman and influences Adler and Sullivan's Auditorium Building. Compare also George Post's Produce Exchange.

130. Cobb and Frost, Owings Building, Chicago, 1888.

131. Leroy Buffington, office building, Minneapolis, 1888.

132. Adler and Sullivan, Auditorium Building (center), 1889, with the Studebaker Building and the Art Institute next on Michigan Avenue, Chicago. The photograph, taken just after completion, shows the impact of the scale of the building.

133. Left to right, Adler and Sullivan, Auditorium Building, 1889; Solon S. Beman, Studebaker Building, 1886; Burnham and Root, Art Institute Building, later the Chicago Club, 1885. This photograph, taken two or three years after the preceding, shows the addition to the Art Institute Building.

134. Holabird and Roche, Tacoma Building, Chicago, 1889.

481

135. (Upper left) Burnham and Root, Monadnock Building, Chicago, 1891.

136. Burnham and Root, Masonic Temple, Chicago, 1890–1892.

137. (Below) Burnham and Root, Woman's Temple, Chicago, 1892.

482

138.   Adler and Sullivan, Schiller Building, later the Garrick Theater, Chicago, 1892.

138a.   Louis Sullivan, decorative detail from Garrick Theater Building.

139. Directors of World's Columbian Exposition, Chicago, 1893. Left to right, D. H. Burnham, Director of Works; George B. Post; M. B. Pickett, Secretary of Works; Henry Van Brunt; F. D. Millet, Director of Decoration; Maitland Armstrong, artist; Colonel Edmund Rice, Commandant; Augustus St. Gaudens; Henry Sargent Codman, landscape architect; George D. Maynard, artist; Charles F. McKim; Ernest R. Graham, Assistant Director of Works; Dion Geraldine, General Superintendent.

140. Plan of the grounds, World's Columbian Exposition, Chicago, 1893.

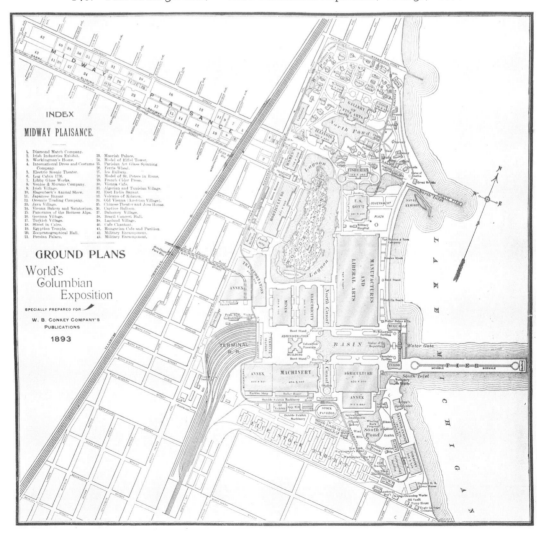

141. World's Columbian Exposition, the Basin, Court of Honor, July 30, 1891, at the start of construction.

142. World's Columbian Exposition, Chicago, 1893, the Court of Honor as completed, looking from the Water Gate to the Administration Building. Daniel Chester French's statue of the Republic is in the foreground. Buildings (left to right) are: Agricultural Building, McKim, Mead, and White; Mechanical Arts Building, Peabody and Stearns; Administration Building, Richard Morris Hunt; Electricity Building, Van Brunt and Howe; and Manufactures Building, George B. Post.

143. World's Columbian Exposition, Court of Honor, from the Administration Building looking to the Water Gate. Frederick MacMonnies' fountain is in the foreground. Left, Manufactures Building, right, Agricultural Building.

144. World's Columbian Exposition, connecting screen between the Agricultural Building and the Mechanical Arts Building. The MacMonnies fountain is in the foreground. Obelisks, rostral columns, and decorative sculpture contribute to the effect of architecture and landscape design.

145. World's Columbian Exposition, Triumphal Arch and Peristyle at the Water Gate, the Court of Honor.

146. Richard Morris Hunt, Administration Building, World's Columbian Exposition.

147.   Peabody and Stearns, Mechanical Arts or Machinery Building, World's Columbian Exposition.

148. McKim, Mead, and White, Agricultural Building, World's Columbian Exposition.

149. George B. Post, Manufactures Building, World's Columbian Exposition, the largest building at the Fair. Compare Post's Produce Exchange, New York.

150. Van Brunt and Howe, Electricity Building, World's Columbian Exposition.

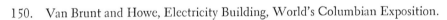

151. Solon S. Beman, Mining Building, World's Columbian Exposition.

152. Adler and Sullivan, Transportation Building, World's Columbian Exposition.

492

153. Adler and Sullivan, Golden Doorway of the Transportation Building, World's Columbian Exposition.

154. Jenney and Mundie, Horticultural Building, World's Columbian Exposition.

155.   Sophia Hayden, Women's Building, World's Columbian Exposition.

156.   Henry Ives Cobb, detail from the Fisheries Building, during construction, World's Columbian Exposition.

157. Charles B. Atwood, Fine Arts Building, World's Columbian Exposition, the only building at the Fair rebuilt in permanent form.

158. W. J. Edbrooke, United States Government Building, World's Columbian Exposition.

159. Massachusetts Hall, Harvard University, Cambridge, Mass., 1718, an example of the modest colonial style of architecture.

160. Charles Bulfinch, north side, Tontine Crescent, Franklin Place, Boston, 1793–1794.

160a.　Charles Bulfinch, Mercantile Library, Tontine Crescent, Franklin Place, Boston, 1793–1794.

161. Charles Bulfinch, University Hall, Harvard University, Cambridge, Mass., 1813–1815.

162. Charles Bulfinch, State House, Boston, designed 1787–1788, built 1795–1798.

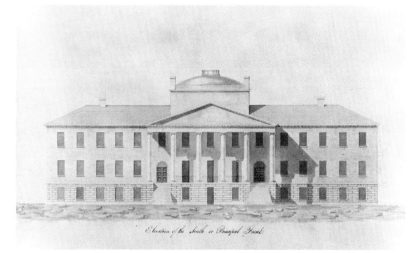

163. Charles Bulfinch, Massachusetts General Hospital, elevation of south or principal front before additions. Designed 1816–1817, executed by Alexander Parris, 1818–1820.

164. Charles Bulfinch, west front of the Old Capitol, Washington, D.C., completed 1827.

165. Peabody and Stearns, Matthews Hall, Harvard University, Cambridge, Mass., 1870–1872.

166.   Richard Morris Hunt, Rossiter house, W. 38th St., New York, 1855–1857.

167. Richard Morris Hunt's studio in the Studio Building, New York.

168. Richard Morris Hunt, Studio Building, W. 10th St., New York, 1857.

169. Richard Morris Hunt, Stuyvesant Apartments, E. 18th St., New York, 1869–1870. Hunt's early debt to French rationalist teaching is here apparent.

502

170. Richard Morris Hunt, Guernsey Building, New York, 1881.

171. Richard Morris Hunt, Lenox Library, New York, 1870–1873, an adaptation of French neo-Grèc style.

172. Richard Morris Hunt, Château-sur-Mer, Newport, R.I., 1872–1873, another example of early rationalist influence on Hunt.

173. Richard Morris Hunt, Tribune Building (center), New York, 1873, another rationalist building and an example of the early tall building in New York.

174. Richard Morris Hunt, W. K. Vanderbilt house, New York, 1879–1881. The first of Hunt's great mansions reflects the rationalist predilection for late French Gothic and early Renaissance style.

175. Richard Morris Hunt, Ogden Mills house, New York, 1885.

176. Richard Morris Hunt, Elbridge T. Gerry house, New York, 1891.

178. Richard Morris Hunt, Marble House, Newport, R.I., 1888–1892,
      home of William K. Vanderbilt.
178a.   Marble House, dining room.

179. Richard Morris Hunt, The Breakers, Newport, R.I., 1892–1895, home of Cornelius Vanderbilt.

179a.   The Breakers, Great Hall.

180. Richard Morris Hunt, Ochre Court, Newport, R.I., 1888–1891, home of Robert Goelet.

181. Richard Morris Hunt, Fogg Art Museum, Harvard University, Cambridge, Mass., 1895, now Hunt Hall.

182. Richard Morris Hunt, Biltmore, Asheville, N.C., 1888–1895,
      home of George Washington Vanderbilt.

182b.   Biltmore, the conservatory.

183.   Richard Morris Hunt and Richard Howland Hunt, Metropolitan Museum of Art, New York, 1895–1904, main entrance.

184. George B. Post, Western Union Building, New York, 1873–1875, an example of the refined and learned eastern style of early office building.

185. George B. Post, Cotton Exchange, New York, 1885, another example of eastern refinement in commercial building.

186. George B. Post, Produce Exchange, New York, 1884, a masterpiece of bold effect and studied detail. Compare Richardson's Marshall Field Wholesale Store and Post's later Manufactures Building at the Chicago Exposition.

187. George B. Post, Cornelius Vanderbilt house, New York. The first half of the house, at Fifth Avenue and 57th Street, was built in 1880. The continuation to 58th Street, shown here, was added in 1894. Some details are attributed to Richard Morris Hunt.

188. McKim, Mead, and White, Municipal Building, New York, 1912–1914, an example of classical architecture employed for effects of civic grandeur after the Chicago Exposition.

188a. Municipal Building, New York, detail.

189. McKim, Mead, and White, apartment building at 998 Fifth Ave., New York, 1910–1911, classical architecture used with urbanity and simple grandeur of effect.

190. Warren and Wetmore, Grand Central Station, New York, 1903–1913. Technology and classical style join after the Chicago Exposition to produce a modern masterpiece. Sculpture by Jules Coutan.

191.   George B. Post, New York Stock Exchange, 1901, American
       classical architecture after the Chicago Exposition.

192. Graham, Anderson, Probst, and White, Continental Illinois National Bank and Trust Company of Chicago, 1924, the main banking hall. D. H. Burnham's successors apply the lessons of the Chicago Exposition for monumental effect.

193. Graham, Burnham and Co., Union Station, Chicago, 1924. Again modern technology and classical grandeur combine to teach a high lesson of civilization.

193a.   Union Station, Chicago, main waiting room. Sculpture later added on right.

194. Arthur Brown, Jr., San Francisco City Hall and Civic Center. Left to right, Veterans Building, 1932; City Hall, 1912; Opera House, 1932, by Brown and G. Albert Lansburgh.

Bibliography of Writings by Henry Van Brunt | Notes | Index

Bibliography of Writings by Henry Van Brunt

The following is a list, in order of publication, of the writings of Van Brunt that I have been able to trace. Starred items are reprinted in this edition. I have not included brief letters and observations printed in *The American Architect and Building News*, nor abridgements there of speeches or articles published in full elsewhere. I have, however, included a few long letters, such as the reply to Charles Eliot Norton on Harvard's architecture, from *The Nation*, when they are, in effect, short articles and have intrinsic importance for an understanding of Van Brunt's thought.

ARTICLES

* "Cast Iron in Decorative Architecture," *The Crayon*, VI (Jan. 1859), 15–20. See also VI (Feb. 1859), 48–49, for Van Brunt's continuation of the argument provoked by his paper, following a reply by Leopold Eidlitz (VI, Jan. 1859, 20–24); see also VI (March 1859), 88–89, for Van Brunt's remarks on domestic architecture.

"About Spires," *Atlantic Monthly*, V (Jan. 1860), 75–88.

"Greek Lines," *Atlantic Monthly*, VII (June 1861), 654–667; VIII (July 1861), 76–88.

* "Architectural Reform," *The Nation*, II (April 5, 1866), 438–439; (April 12, 1866), 469–470. A review of Eugène-Emmanuel Viollet-le-Duc, *Entretiens sur l'architecture* (Paris, 1863).

"Studies of Interior Decoration," *The American Architect and Building News*, II (Feb. 24, 1877), 59–60; (March 10, 1877), 75–76; (March 17, 1877), 84–85; (March 24, 1877), 92–93; (April 14, 1877), 115–116; (April 21, 1877), 123–124; (April 28, 1877), 131–132; (May 5, 1877), 139–140; (May 26, 1877), 163–164; (June 9, 1877), 179–180; (June 23, 1877), 196–197; (June 30, 1877), 204–205; (July 21, 1877), 232–233.

* "Growth of Conscience in the Decorative Arts," *Atlantic Monthly*, XLII (Aug. 1878), 204–215.

"Archaeology and the Vernacular Architecture," *The American Architect and Building News*, IV (Oct. 26, 1878), 143. A letter.

* "The New Architecture at Albany," *The American Architect and Building News*, V (Jan. 8, 1879), 19–21; (Jan. 25, 1879), 28–29.

"New Lives of the Old Masters," *Atlantic Monthly*, XLIII (April 1879), 490–496. A review of M. F. Sweetser, *Artist Biographies* (Boston, 1878).

* "The New Dispensation of Monumental Art," *Atlantic Monthly*, XLIII (May 1879), 633–641.

"The Latest Literature of Art," *Atlantic Monthly*, XLIV (Aug. 1879), 160–170. A review of Eugène Véron, *Aesthetics*, trans. W. H. Armstrong (London and Philadelphia, 1879); Philip G. Hamerton, *The Life of J. M. W. Turner, R.A.* (Boston, 1879); Jacob von Falke, *Art in the House*, ed. Charles C. Perkins (Boston, 1879).

"Harvard Memorial Hall and Sanders Theatre," *Harvard Register*, I (March 1880), 53–55.

* "Eidlitz's Nature of Art," *The Nation*, XXXIII (Dec. 29, 1881), 515–516. A review of Leopold Eidlitz, *The Nature and Function of Art* (New York, 1881).

* "The Personal Equation in Renaissance Architecture," *The American Architect and Building News*, XVII (Jan. 10, 1885), 15–16.

"Grant's Memorial: What Shall It Be?" *The North American Review*, CXLI (Sept. 1885), 282–287.

* "On the Present Condition and Prospects of Architecture," *Atlantic Monthly*, LVII (March 1886), 374–384.

"The Statue of Lief Erikson," *Atlantic Monthly*, LVII (June 1886), 813–815.

* "Henry Hobson Richardson, Architect," *Atlantic Monthly*, LVIII (Nov. 1886), 685–693.

Letter on architectural training, *Technology Architectural Review*, I (April 15, 1888), 11.

* "The Washington Monument," *American Art and American Art Collections*, ed. Walter Montgomery, I (1889), 353–368.

"The Power of Simplicity," *Technology Architectural Review*, II (Oct. 12, 1889), 31–32.

* "Architecture in the West," *Atlantic Monthly*, LXIV (Dec. 1889), 772–784.

"An American Definition of Gothic Architecture," *Atlantic Monthly*, LXVI (July 1890), 126–130. A review of Charles Herbert Moore, *Development and Character of Gothic Architecture* (London and New York, 1890).

* "The Architecture at Harvard," *The Nation*, LI (Sept. 18, 1890), 226.

"The Education of the Architect," *Technology Architectural Review*, III (Oct. 31, 1890), 31–33; (Nov. 29, 1890), 37–39.

* "John Wellborn Root," *The Inland Architect and News Record*, XVI (Jan. 1891), 85–88, reprinted with some excisions as an appendix in Harriet Monroe, *John Wellborn Root* (Park Forest, Ill.: Prairie School Press, 1966), pp. 269–280.

* "Architecture at the World's Columbian Exposition," *Century Magazine*, XLIV (May 1892), 81–99; (July 1892), 385–399; (Aug. 1892), 540–548; (Sept. 1892), 720–731; (Oct. 1892), 897–907, partially reprinted in *Architecture in America: A Battle of Styles*, ed. William A. Coles and Henry Hope Reed, Jr. (New York, Appleton-Century-Crofts, 1961), pp. 151–177.

* "The Historic Styles and Modern Architecture," *The Architectural Review*, I (Aug. 1, 1892), 59–61; II (Jan. 2, 1893), 1–4.

"Architecture among the Poets," *Atlantic Monthly*, LXXI (April 1893), 524–536.

* "The Columbian Exposition and American Civilization," *Atlantic Monthly*, LXXI (May 1893), 577–588, partially reprinted in Coles and Reed, pp. 194–197.

* "The Growth of Characteristic Architectural Style in the United States," *Journal of Proceedings of the American Institute of Architects*, XXVII (1893), 242–253.

"The Development and Prospects of Architecture in the United States," *The United States of America*, ed. Nathaniel Southgate Shaler (New York, 1894), pp. 425–451. This piece is a conflation of passages from other articles, especially "Architecture in the West" and "Henry Hobson Richardson," prefaced by a new short history of the development of architecture in America.

"Architectural Education," *The Inland Architect and News Record*, XXIV (Nov. 1894), 35–36. The paper was originally read as a report of the Standing Committee on Education of the American Institute of Architects at the twenty-eighth annual convention, at New York, October 15, 1894.

* "Richard Morris Hunt," *Journal of Proceedings of the American Institute of Architects*, XXIX (1895), 71–84.

* "Classic Architecture," Baltimore [1895], 32 pp. A lecture given at Johns Hopkins University, printed as a pamphlet.

* "Two Interpreters of National Architecture," *Atlantic Monthly*, LXXIX (1897), 258–269. A review of Harriet Monroe, *The Life of John Wellborn Root* (Boston and New York, 1896); and *Life and Letters of Charles Bulfinch, Architect*, ed. Ellen Susan Bulfinch (Boston and New York, 1896).

* Letter on the aesthetics of bridge construction in J. A. L. Waddell, *De Pontibus: A Pocket-Book for Bridge Engineers*, 2nd ed. (New York, 1906), pp. 40–45. The first edition, which I have not seen, appeared in 1898.

"President's Address before the Convention of 1899," *Journal of Proceedings of the American Institute of Architects*, XXXIII (1899), 12–16.

Contributions to *Dictionary of Architecture and Building*, ed. Russell Sturgis (New York, 1901–1902): Drawing; Eclecticism; Greenhouse; Paint; Painting; Palladian Architecture; Pilaster; Planning; Porch; Proportion; Put Log; Roof; Rosette; Safe; Skylight; Specification; Spire; Stable; Templet; Triglyph; Stellar Vaulting; Wood, Construction in; Woodworking Machinery. Most of these definitions are brief, but a few, like Eclecticism and Proportion, are of interest in terms of Van Brunt's ideas and those of his age.

BOOKS

* A translation of Eugène-Emmanuel Viollet-le-Duc, *Discourses on Architecture*, 2 vols. (Boston, 1875–1881). Van Brunt's introduction to his translation (I, iii–xviii) is reprinted in this edition, and was partially reprinted in Coles and Reed, pp. 23–29.

Greek Lines, and Other Architectural Essays (Boston and New York, 1893). The volume contains the following essays:

"Greek Lines and Their Influence on Modern Architecture." Shortened from its original periodical version.

"The Growth of Conscience in Modern Decoration." Originally published as "Growth of Conscience in the Decorative Arts"; slightly altered.

"Historical Architecture, and the Influence of the Personal Element upon It." A revision of "The Personal Equation in Renaissance Architecture."

"The Royal Château of Blois." The only completely new essay in the collection.

"The Present State of Architecture." Slightly revised from "On the Present Condition and Prospects of Architecture."

"Architecture and Poetry." Revised from "Architecture among the Poets."

Some of the revision of the essays in the book was obviously intended to relate them thematically one to another.

Introduction, Part I: Life and Career

1. X (1903), p. 44 — hereafter cited as AR obituary.

2. *Journal of Proceedings of the American Institute of Architects*, XXXIII (1899), 16.

3. The diaries are in the possession of Mr. Henry Van Brunt, Jr., to whom I am deeply indebted for transcriptions of materials quoted.

4. *New Timon* (1846), 11. 1–2.

5. My own copy of Van Brunt's *Greek Lines and Other Architectural Essays* (Boston and New York, 1893) is dedicated to "Julia Marlowe-Taber with kindest regards of the Author."

6. AR obituary.

7. LXXX (April 11, 1903), 9 — hereafter cited as AABN obituary.

Peter B. Wight, in an important essay, "Henry Van Brunt — Architect, Writer and Philosopher," *The Inland Architect and News Record*, XXIII (April 1894), 29–30, 41–42, 49–50, 60–61, groups Van Brunt with Richard Morris Hunt and Henry H. Richardson as the three most eminent American disciples of the French school of architecture. Of Van Brunt he says that though "less eminent than the other two in the eloquence of the designer and builder, he has always been foremost among the few architectural critics who have had anything to say and been able to give intelligent expression to their ideas" (p. 29). Wight's article is in part a review of Van Brunt's *Greek Lines*, and while he does not fully sympathize with the development of Van Brunt's ideas, he calls the book "the most learned, philosophical and brilliant series of architectural essays that has ever emanated from an American writer" (p. 61). Wight, the architect of the National Academy of Design building in New York, was a leading theoretician of the functionalist school in America.

8. LXXI, 534–536, later reprinted in *Greek Lines*, pp. 267–274.

9. The student pictures by Johann Peter Hasenclever (1810–1853) were a series based on the popular German poem *Jobsiad*; "Falstaff Mustering His Recruits" was by Adolf Schrödter (1805–1875); "Othello and Desdemona" was by Theodor Hildebrandt (1804–1874).

10. Healy's painting of Webster is now in Faneuil Hall, Boston. The portrait of Commodore (then Lieutenant) Van Brunt, 1832, is in the possession of Mr. Henry Van Brunt, Jr.

11. The Astor Library building, subsequently the Hebrew Sheltering and Immigrant Aid Society, is now the home of the New York Shakespeare Theater. Van Brunt would have seen the southern wing of the building.

12. The Spingler Institute was a collegiate seminary for young ladies at Union Square.

13. A bronze medal awarded to Van Brunt by the United States Centennial Commission for his work in the Philadelphia Exhibition is in the possession of Mr. Henry Van Brunt, Jr.

14. III, 33.

15. William Minifie, *A Text Book of Geometrical Drawing* (Baltimore, 1849).

16. Boston, 1854.

17. *AABN* obituary.

18. *AABN* obituary.

19. The classbook, dated 1894, is in the Harvard University Archives.

20. *Boston After Bulfinch* (Cambridge, Mass.: Harvard University Press, 1946), p. 56 — hereafter cited as Kilham.

21. "Richard Morris Hunt." A list of some of the more valuable books in the auction sale of George Snell's library can be found in the *American Architect and Building News*, XLI (July 8, 1893), 28.

22. "Richard Morris Hunt."

23. The Hunt Papers are in the possession of Mr. Alan Burnham, to whom I am indebted for this information and for access to his Hunt materials. See also Alan Burnham, "The New York Architecture of Richard Morris Hunt," *Journal of the Society of Architectural Historians*, XI (May 1952), 11 (hereafter cited as Burnham), and Henry Saylor, *The A.I.A.'s First 100 Years* (Washington, D.C.: American Institute of Architects, 1957), p. 111 (hereafter cited as Saylor), for additional information on Hunt's atelier.

24. Burnham, p. 10.

25. The Rossiter house occasioned a celebrated suit over the client's refusal to pay Hunt's fee. Hunt's success in the case helped to establish the prestige of the architect in America. See Burnham, p. 10.

26. Saylor, p. 4.

27. Saylor, p. 5.

28. Saylor, pp. 4–5.

29. For a fuller discussion of the sketchbooks and what they reveal about Hunt's library, collection, and atelier, see my article, "Richard Morris Hunt and His Library as Revealed in the Studio Sketchbooks of Henry Van Brunt," *The Art Quarterly*, XXX (Fall-Winter 1967), 224–238.

30. The address in the sketchbooks is puzzling, since the usual address given for the Studio Building is 55 W. 10th St.

31. Burnham, p. 12.

32. Burnham, p. 11.

33. For the quotations below dealing with Hunt's atelier and influence see "Richard Morris Hunt."

34. George Post, as a student at the University, would undoubtedly have seen Hunt in the building.

35. See Burnham, p. 11.

36. "The Education of the Architect" (1890), p. 38.

37. The same, p. 33.

38. See my article, cited above, in n. 29, for a complete list of the books in Hunt's library that are drawn upon in Van Brunt's sketchbooks.

39. Richard Morris Hunt Papers.

40. See *The Autobiography of an Idea* (New York: A.I.A. Press, 1924), p. 320.

41. This and the following letter (of Nov. 3, 1861), are in Miscellaneous Manuscripts Rogers, New-York Historical Society. By the time of Rogers' second letter Van Brunt was serving in the Civil War.

42. The sketch alludes to the popular *Adventures of Verdant Green, an Oxford Freshman* (1853–1857) by Edward Bradley (1827–1889).

43. George Templeton Strong mentions meeting Van Brunt on April 11, 1860, at a party. He is listed as one of the "notabilities." See *The Diary of George Templeton Strong, The Civil War, 1860–65*, ed. Allan Nevins and Milton Halsey Thomas (New York: Macmillan, 1952), p. 20. "Cast Iron in Decorative Architecture," though published earlier, was originally a paper delivered at the A.I.A.

44. *AABN* obituary.

45. *AR* obituary. Bainbridge Bunting in *Houses of Boston's Back Bay* (Cambridge, Mass.: The Belknap Press of Harvard University Press, 1967) credits Ware and Van Brunt with houses at 41 Brimmer St. (probably) (Fig. 23), 282–292 Marlborough St. (Fig. 24), and 7–9 Fairfield St.

In addition to works illustrated in this book or just mentioned, the following have been identified as designs of Henry Van Brunt, the firm of Ware and Van Brunt, and its successor, Van Brunt and Howe:

Ware and Van Brunt, church for summer use at Narragansett Pier, R.I., illustrated in *Architectural Sketch Book*, Boston, 1874.

Ware and Van Brunt, Providence, R.I., City Hall, competition design, illustrated in *Architectural Sketch Book*, Boston, 1874.

Ware and Van Brunt, design for a schoolhouse, Providence, R.I., illustrated in *Architectural Sketch Book*, Boston, 1874.

Ware and Van Brunt, design for a drinking fountain, illustrated in *Architectural Sketch Book*, Boston, 1874.

Ware and Van Brunt, Adam Hill house, 12 Reservoir St., Cambridge, Mass., 1877, illustrated in *American Architect and Building News*, II (1877), No. 217.

Ware and Van Brunt, George B. Chase house, 1879, illustrated in *American Architect and Building News*, V (1879), No. 167.

Ware and Van Brunt, Grace Church, New Bedford, Mass., 1880–1881.

Ware and Van Brunt, Deanery, Episcopal Theological School, Cambridge, Mass., illustrated in *American Architect and Building News*, VIII (1880), No. 258.

Ware and Van Brunt, house at Mt. Desert, Maine, illustrated in *American Architect and Building News*, VIII (1880), No. 236.

Ware and Van Brunt (attributed to), 16 Sacramento St., Cambridge, Mass., 1883 and 1893, interior and exterior photos in Cambridge Historical Commission, *Mid-Cambridge Report*, 1967.

Van Brunt and Howe, competition design for Boston Public Library, exhibited at Boston Art Club exhibition, 1886.

Van Brunt and Howe, house at 1705 Massachusetts Avenue, Cambridge, Mass., 1889, photo in Cambridge Historical Commission, *Mid-Cambridge Report*, 1967.

Van Brunt and Howe, house at 10 Channing Place, Cambridge, Mass., 1892, photograph in Cambridge Historical Commission collection.

Van Brunt and Howe, R. Conklin house, Kansas City, Mo., illustrated in *Inland Architect*, XIX (May 1892).

Van Brunt and Howe, Wyoming State Building, World's Columbian Exposition, Chicago, 1893, illustrated in *Inland Architect*, XIX (Feb. 1892).

Van Brunt and Howe, J. D. Griffith house, Kansas City, Mo., 1895–1896.

Van Brunt and Howe, house at 1692 Massachusetts Avenue, Cambridge, Mass., 1896, from Cambridge Historical Commission file.

Van Brunt and Howe, *Kansas City Star* Building, illustrated in *Inland Architect,* XXVIII (Aug. 1896).

Van Brunt and Howe, design for Antlers Hotel competition, Colorado Springs, illustrated in *Inland Architect,* XXXIII (July 1899).

Van Brunt and Howe, Prospect Avenue Christian Church, Kansas City, Mo., 1904.

Van Brunt and Howe, Railroad Station, Sioux City, Iowa.

Van Brunt and Howe, Robert Keith Furniture and Carpet Company, Kansas City, Mo.

Van Brunt and Howe, Kirkland B. Armour house, Kansas City, Mo.

Van Brunt and Howe, extensive additions to Old Federal Building, Kansas City, Mo., for Fidelity Trust Company.

Specific mention is also made in biographical sources of line stations for the Union Pacific Railroad; office, commercial buildings, and dwellings in Omaha, Nebraska; and office buildings in Augusta, Georgia, and Baltimore, Maryland.

46. Miscellaneous Manuscripts J. Q. A. Ward, New-York Historical Society.

47. A letter from Hunt, dated July 26, 1880, in the possession of Henry Van Brunt, Jr., discusses the project.

48. For an account of its construction and a selection of remarks about Memorial Hall see Robert B. Shaffer, "Ruskin, Norton, and Memorial Hall," *Harvard Library Bulletin,* III (Spring 1949), 213–231 — hereafter cited as Shaffer.

49. Kilham, pp. 75–76, writes: "the most resounding example [of Victorian Gothic] is Memorial Hall at Harvard, by Ware and Van Brunt, dedicated in 1874. Harvard has not properly appreciated this monument in recent years, but no matter if it is out of date, I still claim that it has its points. Just prior to the World War I, Harvard imported a French professor of architecture, of the standard type, black-bearded, long-coated, and entirely new to America. It is said that President Lowell invited him for a tour of the college and they started out together through the Yard, Lowell proudly pointing out the cherished square brick boxes, Hollis, Stoughton, and the rest, Duquesne bowing and saying, 'Ah, oui,' 'tres chic,' [sic] 'c'est charmant,' etc., and Lowell dreading the moment when they should come to Memorial Hall. Finally they turned a corner and Memorial appeared, all its pinnacles shining in the sun, and the gilt clock striking like a band coming up the street. Duquesne stopped short, gesticulated, and exclaimed, "Ah, voilá quelque chose' [sic] — 'Ah, there, at last, you have something!' "

50. Shaffer, p. 221.

51. In "Harvard Memorial Hall and Sanders Theatre" (1880) and in no. 12 of the series "Studies of Interior Decoration" (1877), pp. 204–205. The defense quoted in the text is from "Harvard Memorial Hall and Sanders Theatre," p. 53. Van Brunt also replied to an anonymous attack in the New York *World* of January 16, 1876, on the wooden ceiling of the vestibule of Memorial Hall. I suspect the attack was by Leopold Eidlitz. A correspondence ensued. See *The American Architect and Building News,* I (1876), 53–54, 71–72, 87–88.

52. Norton's criticism appeared in "Harvard University in 1890," *Harper's Magazine,* LXXXI (Sept. 1890), 591. Van Brunt replied in the letter entitled "The Architecture at Harvard" reprinted in this edition.

53. Sabine, an assistant professor of Physics at Harvard, had asked for the drawings presumably in connection with accoustical experiments he was then carrying on. Van Brunt's letter is in the Harvard University Archives.

54. See "Architectural Reform."

55. *AABN* obituary.

56. The letter is in the possession of Mr. Henry Van Brunt, Jr.

57. See "Architecture at the World's Columbian Exposition"; "The Columbian Exposition and American Civilization"; and, in part, "The Historic Styles and Modern Architecture," all reprinted in this edition.

58. Kermit Vanderbilt, *Charles Eliot Norton* (Cambridge, Mass.: Harvard University Press, 1959), p. 200. George Woodberry, a disciple of Norton, poet, critic, and later professor of literature at Columbia University, was professor of English at the University of Nebraska from 1877 to 1878 and 1880 to 1882. Note the cultural primitivism and the preoccupation with history and evolution in Norton's remark. The influence of these concepts in nineteenth-century thought is discussed in pt. II, below.

59. Mentions in the *American Architect* of papers he read, of his participation in discussions and as a judge in competitions, and of other doings are too numerous to list. They are in almost every volume, beginning with the first in 1876. For an account of Van Brunt's participation as a central figure in the early years of the Boston Society of Architects, see Walter Muir Whitehill, "Boston Society of Architects, 1867–1967, A Centennial Sketch," *Boston Society of Architects: The First Hundred Years, 1867–1967*, ed: Marvin E. Goody and Robert P. Walsh (Boston: Boston Society of Architects, 1967), pp. 19–47.

60. Van Brunt had always been on close terms with his younger brother, Charles, who had married Agnes Clark of Boston, an aunt of Joseph Clark Grew, former U.S. ambassador to Turkey and Japan and later Undersecretary of State. It was at the house of his sister-in-law that Van Brunt died.

61. Courtlandt Van Brunt attempted to have the A.I.A. publish the journal in 1941, but was unsuccessful. The original manuscript volumes are lost, but a transcript, from which I quote below, was in the possession of the late Mrs. Helen Van Brunt Washburn, who kindly loaned it to me.

62. *AABN* obituary. Letters to William Ware and Frank Howe are specifically mentioned in the diary.

63. See James Fergusson, *A History of Architecture in All Countries* (London, 1874), II, 168. I have not located the remark attributed to Freeman, presumably Edward A. Freeman, whose *History of Architecture* was published in 1849.

64. The European journals record the severe pain Van Brunt experienced on occasion in walking. In spite of this his physical activity, to which the journals readily testify, seems astonishing.

65. *AABN* obituary.

Introduction, Part II: The Writings

1. "Architectural Reform."

2. Eclecticism was the free mingling of motifs taken from various periods and styles.

3. "Architectural Reform."

4. "The Power of Simplicity" (1889), p. 32.

5. See Arthur O. Lovejoy, "On the Discrimination of Romanticisms," *Essays in the History of Ideas* (New York: Capricorn Books, 1960), pp. 245–246.

6. See *The Crayon*, VI (March 1859), 89. Van Brunt did warn against mere copying of the style, though. His suggestion probably reflects the ideas of J.-L. Hittorf as embodied sumptuously by Alfred Normand in the celebrated house of Prince Jérôme Napoléon on the Avenue Montaigne.

7. "Henry Hobson Richardson, Architect."

8. *Histoire de l'architecture classique en France*, VI (Paris: A. Picard, 1955), 254–255.

9. Charles A. Sainte-Beuve, "What Is a Classic?" *Essays by Sainte-Beuve*, trans. Elizabeth Lee (London, 1892), pp. 3–4.

10. The same, p. 9. Tennyson's poem "The Palace of Art" illustrates the same eclecticism of decor and idea, though only to reject it in the end.

11. "The Function of Criticism at the Present Time," *Lectures and Essays in Criticism*, ed. R. H. Super (Ann Arbor: University of Michigan Press, 1962), p. 283.

12. The same, p. 282.

13. "An American Definition of Gothic Architecture" (1890), p. 126; see also "Translator's Introduction to the *Discourses on Architecture* of Eugène-Emmanuel Viollet-le-Duc," p. 103 above.

14. "An American Definition of Gothic Architecture" (1890), p. 127.

15. Reprinted in this edition.

16. "Henry Hobson Richardson, Architect."

17. *Autobiographic Memoirs* (London: Macmillan, 1911), II, 258–259.

18. "Architectural Reform."

19. "The Royal Château of Blois," *Greek Lines and Other Architectural Essays* (Boston and New York, 1893), p. 165.

20. "Architecture in the West."

21. "The Historic Styles and Modern Architecture."

22. "Two Interpreters of National Architecture."

23. "The Historic Styles and Modern Architecture," pt. I. It is worth noting that it is assumed that "abstract" truth is relevant to modern experience.

24. See Introduction, Part I, n. 52.

25. "The Architecture at Harvard."

26. The same.

27. Walter Houghton, *The Victorian Frame of Mind, 1830–1870* (New Haven and London: Yale University Press, 1957), p. 1.

28. "Cast Iron in Decorative Architecture" (italics are mine).

29. "On the Present Condition and Prospects of Architecture."

30. Preface to the second edition of *Lyrical Ballads* (1800), *The Poetical Works of Wordsworth*, ed. Thomas Hutchinson and Ernest de Selincourt (London: Oxford University Press, 1961), p. 735.

31. "The Growth of Conscience in the Decorative Arts."

32. The same.

33. New York, 1899, p. 133.

34. See "Earnestness," chap. 10 in Walter Houghton, *The Victorian Frame of Mind*.

35. The same, p. 234. See also p. 231, n. 30.

36. The same, p. 225.

37. The same, p. 226.

38. See *The Poetical Works of Wordsworth*, p. 750.

39. *Biographia Literaria* (London, 1876), p. 30.

40. The same, p. 43. The parallel between architecture and poetry, each casting aside traditional forms in quest of the concepts of organic form and imaginative innovation, was specifically made by Van Brunt. For him, as for Wordsworth and Coleridge, tradition in poetry was embodied in the neoclassical heroic couplet, just as in architecture it had been represented by eighteenth-century Palladian classical motifs: "Harmonious proportion, metrical form, or, in other words, perfection of technique, though an essential element in both arts, does not in itself make architecture, though there have been in later times historical eras, as in the eighteenth century, when this noble art was so misunderstood that its metre, its technique,

was the only quality which differentiated it from structure; and the public consequently ceased to interest itself in an art which made no deeper appeal to its sympathies. In like manner, the heroic form of versification, which prevailed through the same era, was not infrequently accepted as constituting in itself poetry. But architecture does not reach its highest estate until it is so infused with imagination and fancy — not undisciplined imagination or capricious fancy — that the ordered fabric delights the eye of every intelligent observer and excites emotions like a poem." ("Architecture and Poetry," *Greek Lines*, pp. 234–235.)

41. "The Growth of Conscience in the Decorative Arts."

42. The same.

43. The same (italics mine).

44. Arnold called these principles the "natural truth of Christianity." See Preface to *Last Essays on Church and Religion* (London, 1877).

45. See *The Seven Lamps of Architecture* (London, 1849), pp. 32ff.

46. See *Hints on Household Taste in Furniture, Upholstery, and Other Details* (London, 1878), p. 36.

47. "Architectural Reform."

48. The same.

49. The same.

50. *Discourses on Architecture*, trans. Benjamin Bucknell (New York: Grove Press, 1959), I, 304.

51. The same, I, 448.

52. *The Seven Lamps of Architecture*, pp. 7–8.

53. *Discourses on Architecture*, I, 448.

54. *The Seven Lamps of Architecture*, p. 164.

55. The same, p. 183.

56. The same, p. 17.

57. "The Historic Styles and Modern Architecture," pt. I.

58. Paris, 1854–1868. See especially II, 281, 283, for the argument on cathedrals.

59. P. 6.

60. "Architectural Reform."

61. "J. G. Herder (II)," *Encounter*, XXV (Aug. 1965), 49.

62. Van Brunt's first article, "Cast Iron in Decorative Architecture" (1859), printed in this edition, is a materialistic plea for the use of cast iron in decorative architecture. Nevertheless its argument is most strongly rooted in the idea of the exponent. Architecture should express the character of the age: "they have called this in derision 'a cast iron age.' What if it is? Let us then make a cast iron architecture to express it; and if we set about it earnestly and thoughtfully, it is certainly within the bounds of possibility to ennoble that much reviled material." The sentiments are unlike Ruskin's, but the romantic youthful ardor of the piece is closer to Ruskin than to Viollet-le-Duc. In its defense of the machine, however, the paper shows a flexibility in departing from Ruskin's dogma that is increasingly evident in the later writings. It is also interesting to observe that Van Brunt's view drew a sharply critical retort from Leopold Eidlitz (see Bibliography of Writings by Henry Van Brunt). This may have been Van Brunt's first personal encounter with the rigidity of nineteenth-century architectural theorists, whose severe limitations he tried to expand. As we shall see, Eidlitz becomes a prime example of this type of doctrinaire.

63. "Greek Lines" (July 1861), p. 81.

64. The same, p. 79.

65. Van Brunt, from the beginning to the end of his career, also opposed doctrinaire assertions that geometric figures were the basis of Greek forms or architectural proportion in general. In "Greek Lines" (June 1861), p. 659, he castigates

those who "aim to reduce that magnificent old Hellenic poetry to the cold, hard limitations of Geometry," and in a definition of Proportion for Russell Sturgis' *Dictionary of Architecture and Building* (New York: Macmillan, 1901–1902) he writes cautioningly of Viollet-le-Duc's mathematical speculations on architecture: "while beauty, in line and mass, may sometimes seem to be curiously confirmed by such tests as these, it may be doubtful whether it can be created by them; for elasticity, life, and freedom seem to be the essential qualities of true art."

66. Reprinted in this edition as "Eidlitz's Nature of Art."
67. The same.
68. The same, for this and the following quotations.
69. "The Personal Equation in Renaissance Architecture."
70. The same.
71. The same.
72. The same.
73. The same.
74. This and the following quotation are from "Introduction to the *Discourses*."
75. The same, for this and the following quotation.
76. The same.
77. "On the Present Condition and Prospects of Architecture," for this and the following quotation.
78. The same.
79. See, for instance, *The Seven Lamps of Architecture*, pp. 186–188, and *The Two Paths* (New York, 1859), pp. 115–117.
80. "Henry Hobson Richardson."
81. The same.
82. "Architecture in the West."
83. The same.
84. See the same essay: "Architecture has not kept pace with the advance of science and invention . . . an expression of our civilization."
85. See the same, pp. 188–189 above.
86. See *Autobiography of an Idea* (New York: A.I.A. Press, 1924), pp. 319–325.
87. See "Architecture at the World's Columbian Exposition," pt. IV.
88. See *The Education of Henry Adams. An Autobiography* (Boston and New York: Houghton Mifflin, 1918), p. 343. The idea may have come from Van Brunt's articles.
89. See "The Columbian Exposition and American Civilization."
90. "Architecture at the World's Columbian Exposition," pt. I, for this and the following quotation.
91. The same.
92. "The Columbian Exposition and American Civilization."
93. See "Richard Morris Hunt," reprinted in this edition.
94. "The Columbian Exposition and American Civilization."
95. The same. See especially the concluding paragraph of the essay.
96. See "The Historic Styles and Modern Architecture," pt. II.
97. "Architecture at the World's Columbian Exposition," pt. II.
98. The same, pt. I.
99. The same, pt. I.
100. See "The Biological Fallacy," *The Architecture of Humanism* (Garden City, N. Y.: Doubleday Anchor Books, 1954).
101. "The Royal Château of Blois," *Greek Lines*, p. 176.
102. "Architecture at the World's Columbian Exposition," pt. IV.
103. "Introduction to the *Discourses*."

104. "On the Present Condition and Prospects of Architecture," from which the following quotation is also taken.

105. "The Historic Styles and Modern Architecture," pt. II.

106. *A Son of the Middle Border* (New York: Macmillan, 1917), p. 460.

107. "Architecture at the World's Columbian Exposition," pt. IV.

108. See "The Historic Styles and Modern Architecture," pt. II.

109. "Richard Morris Hunt."

110. "Two Interpreters of National Architecture."

111. "Architecture at the World's Columbian Exposition."

112. The same, pt. I.

113. The influence of the Romantic view of metaphor, as the "functional" expression of feeling, on the organic, functional view of architecture, is the deepest way in which architecture becomes "literary" in the nineteenth century.

114. "Architecture at the World's Columbian Exposition," pt. II.

Van Brunt not only justifies classical unity but reminds us of classical hierarchies in kinds of structures which he elsewhere neglects (see p. 66 above). He correctly points out here that a monumental building has different requirements from an informal domestic or a functional factory building. Today, instead of allowing the highest type of structure to set the ideal of style, we generalize up from the lowest types, which provide the contemporary norm. To a bourgeois mentality a commonplace building seems more "authentic" than a monument. Such a mentality does not grasp that the rarer work demands the more difficult creative effort and is the finest test of artistic capacity. In the same way, we seem ill at ease with the more finished and elaborated "society" portrait and more comfortable with the rough delineation of a peasant or vulgar type.

115. Reprinted in this edition.

116. See, for example, Wallace K. Harrison, "The United Nations Building in New York," *Journal of the Royal Institute of British Architects*, LVIII (March 1951), 171–172.

Cast Iron in Decorative Architecture

1. This essay was originally delivered as a paper before the A.I.A. in New York, Dec. 7, 1858.

2. Mechlin tower: the huge, late Gothic west tower of the Cathedral of St. Rombaut in Mechlin, Belgium; the Chapel of Henry VII was added to the east end of Westminster Abbey between 1502 and 1512. It represents the ultimate development of Gothic style in England.

3. Theodoric's Mausoleum (c. 526) is surmounted by a flat dome hewn out of a single enormous block of stone.

4. William of Wykeham (1324–1404), bishop of Winchester and patron of the rebuilding of Winchester Cathedral, would represent the Gothic style.

5.   "And far across the hills they went
In that new world which is the old,"

Alfred, Lord Tennyson, "The Day Dream" (1842), The Departure, st. 1.

6. For this cardinal tenet of Ruskin's dogma see "Modern Manufacture and Design" (March 1859), *The Two Paths* (New York, 1885), p. 97, and "Changefulness," sec. XXVI in "The Nature of Gothic," *The Stones of Venice* (1851–1853).

7. *The Seven Lamps of Architecture* (London, 1849), p. 161.

8. Adam Kraft (c. 1460–1508), sculptor, and Peter Vischer (c. 1460–1529),

sculptor, were closely associated. The shrine of St. Sebaldus (1508–1519) in the Sebalduskircke, Nuremberg, is Vischer's greatest work. Kraft made the monument of Sebald Schreyer (1492) outside the Sebalduskircke and two other monuments inside the church.

9. Henry Wadsworth Longfellow, "Nuremberg," l. 3.

Architectural Reform

1. [A review of] "Entretiens sur l'Architecture, par M. Viollet-le-Duc, Architecte du Gouvernement et Inspecteur Général des Edifices Diocésains," Paris: A. Morel & Cie. 1863 [VB's note].

2. James Stuart (1713–1788), painter and architect, and Nicholas Revett (1720–1804) published *The Antiquities of Athens* in 1762. The book was the pioneer work of the Greek Revival.

3. Sulpiz Boisserée (1783–1854), scholar of German medieval architecture and especially the cathedral of Cologne, whose history and description (with illustrative drawings) he published in *Geschichte und Beschreibung des Domes von Köln* (1823–1831). He influenced Goethe's interest in the cathedral but was by no means the first serious student of Gothic architecture. A later volume, *Denkmale der Baukunst am Niederrhein von 7–13 Jahrhundert* (1831–1833) surveyed the development of Gothic architecture in Germany before Cologne cathedral.

4. See "Heinrich Heine," *Lectures and Essays in Criticism*, ed. Robert Super (Ann Arbor: University of Michigan Press, 1962), pp. 111ff.

5. The Manchester Assize Courts (1859) are by Alfred Waterhouse (1830–1905). They were modelled on the lines of the Oxford Museum (1855–1859) by Sir Thomas Deane (1792–1871) and Benjamin Woodward (1815–1861).

6. Francesco Primaticcio (1504–1570), painter, sculptor, and architect, was brought to France by François Ier to decorate Fontainebleau. Leonardo da Vinci (1452–1519) was also brought by the same king. In the spring of 1517 he was at Cloux, near Amboise, where he lived till his death as "premier peintre et ingénieur et architecte du roi." Giovanni Lorenzo Bernini (1598–1680) was invited by Louis XIV to design the wing on the east side of the great court of the Louvre, but nothing came of his design, and Claude Perrault's was eventually built.

7. The translator is Van Brunt himself. The anonymity of the review presumably prevented the disclosure. For details of the publication of Van Brunt's translation see the Bibliography of Writings by Henry Van Brunt in this edition.

8. Author's Preface (not included in Van Brunt's translation). For Benjamin Bucknall's version in his translation of the *Discourses on Architecture* (New York: Grove Press, 1959) see p. 6.

9. The same, pp. 6–8.

10. The same, p. 6. Bucknall translates Viollet-le-Duc's phrase as "national genius."

Translator's Introduction to the *Discourses on Architecture* of Eugène-Emmanuel Viollet-le-Duc

1. *Discourses on Architecture*, trans. Henry Van Brunt, I (Boston, 1875), 22.

2. Pierre Lescot (1510–1578), with the sculptor Jean Goujon did the west side of the great court of the Louvre. Philibert Delorme (1515?–1570) was architect of the Château d'Anet and began the Tuileries in 1564 under Catherine de Medici. Jean Bullant (c. 1515–1578) worked on the Château d'Ecouen and followed Delorme as architect of the Tuileries.

3. Henri Labrouste (1801–1875) won the *Premier Grand Prix de Rome* in 1824

and did his official project on the temples of Paestum. He was architect of the Bibliothèque Sainte-Geneviève and leader of the neo-Grèc movement. Louis-Joseph Duc (1802–1879) won the *Grand Prix de Rome* in 1825. The reconstruction of the Palais de Justice was his chief work. Jacques-Félix Duban (1797–1870) won the *Grand Prix de Rome* in 1823. He became chief architect of the Ecole des Beaux Arts. Léon Vaudoyer (1803–1872) won the *Premier Grand Prix de Rome* in 1826. In 1855 he was appointed architect of the cathedral of Marseilles.

4. Jean-Baptiste-Antoine Lassus (1807–1857) was one of the leaders of the modern Gothic school in France. From 1841–1849 he was associated with Duban in the restoration of the Sainte Chapelle, Paris, and after 1849 had charge of that building. In 1845 he was associated with Viollet-le-Duc in the restoration of the cathedral of Nôtre Dame, Paris, and he also restored the spires of Chartres Cathedral.

5. Quatremère de Quincy (1755–1850), professor of archaeology at the Cabinet des Antiquités of the Bibliothèque Nationale, published many works on archaeology and art, among them the *Dictionnaire historique d'architecture* (1832).

6. For the Manchester Assize Courts see "Architectural Reform," n. 5. Alfred Waterhouse also designed the Manchester Town Hall (1869). The new Law Courts in London were by George Edmund Street (1824–1881). Another of the many Gothic designs for the Law Courts was made by William Burges.

7. For Viollet-le-Duc on the architecture of northern Italy see *Discourses* (trans. VB), I, 241; for observations on primitive sources see "Style," *Dictionnaire raisonné de l'architecture française du xie au xvie siècle* (Paris, 1858–1868), VIII, 491.

8. See [J. T. Emmett] "Hope of English Architecture," *Quarterly Review* (American edition), CXXXVII (Oct. 1874), 187–205, esp. p. 189 and the last paragraph of p. 205. The article is a review of James Fergusson, *History of the Modern Styles of Architecture*, 2nd ed. (London, 1873).

9. When the Old Palace of Westminster burned down in 1834, the parliamentary committee in charge of the rebuilding stipulated that the new designs be either Gothic or Elizabethan. Sir Charles Barry (1795–1860), a classicist, won the competition, and medieval details of his building were contributed by Augustus Welby Northmore Pugin (1812–1852).

10. Ralph Waldo Emerson, "The Problem," st. 2.

11. See "Architectural Reform," n. 2.

12. Pugin was an extreme advocate of Gothic architecture in his several writings, such as *Contrasts* (1836), *True Principles of Pointed or Christian Architecture* (1841), and *An Apology for the Revival of Christian Architecture in England* (1843).

13. *Discourses* (trans. VB), I, 57.

14. A misquoting of *coelum non animum mutant*, Horace, *Epistolae*, I, ii, 27.

15. Arnolfo da Lapo, so called erroneously by Vasari. The architect of the rebuilding of the Cathedral of Florence in 1294 or 1298 (to whom Van Brunt refers) was Arnolfo di Cambio (c. 1232–1302).

Growth of Conscience in the Decorative Arts

1. See Thomas Carlyle, "Characteristics," *Critical and Miscellaneous Essays* (London, 1869), p. 350.

2. A misquoting of "Everything by starts and nothing long," John Dryden, "Absalom and Achitophel," ll. 547–548.

3. Jean Le Pautre (1618–1682) was author of *Oeuvres d'architecture*, a principal source book of Renaissance design. André-Charles Boulle (1642–1732) was cabinet maker for Louis XIV at Versailles. Grinling Gibbons (1648–1721), English wood

carver, worked for Sir Christopher Wren in the choir of St. Paul's and in many great houses of England. Thomas Chippendale (c. 1718–1779), English cabinet maker, published *The Gentleman and Cabinet Maker's Directory* (1754), the most influential folio of furniture designs in eighteenth-century England.

4. See "Introduction to the *Discourses*," n. 10.

5. Hermogenes, architect of Alabanda in Caria, invented the pseudodipterus form of temple. His great object was to increase the taste for the Ionic form of temple in preference to the Doric. Callicrates was the architect who in company with Ictinus built the Parthenon on the Acropolis at Athens. Apollodorus of Damascus was employed by the Emperor Trajan to build his Forum, Odeum, and Gymnasium at Rome. Vitruvius (Marcus Vitruvius Pollio), Roman architect and engineer, was author of the treatise *De architectura* (c. 27 B.C.), the principal source of classical architecture and chief authority for architects of the Italian Renaissance. Villard de Honnecourt was a French architect of the first half of the thirteenth century. His sketchbooks give a clear insight into the operations of a medieval workshop and demonstrate how to construct ground plans and elevations of Gothic buildings, church furniture, and ornaments. Robert de Luzarches (d. 1223) in 1220 began work on the reconstruction of the Cathedral of Amiens after the fire of 1218.

6. Erostratus or Herostratus set fire to the Temple of Artemis (Diana) at Ephesus in 356 B.C. on the night of the birth of Alexander the Great. Ctesiphon or Chersiphron, an architect of Cnossus, Crete, in combination with his son Metagenes, had built the temple, considered one of the wonders of the world.

7. Sir George Gilbert Scott (1811–1878), was the restorer of many cathedrals and architect of the Albert Memorial and St. Pancras Station and Hotel, London. William Burges (1827–1881) designed cathedrals in the Gothic style for Lille, Brisbane, and Cork. The work of Alexander Thomson (1817–1875), known as "Greek Thomson," is mainly in Glasgow, where he designed several United Presbyterian churches, including the church of St. Vincent, Egyptian Hall, and almost all the buildings in Gordon St. Richard Norman Shaw (1831–1912), was the founder of the Queen Anne revival, as exemplified in such buildings as Swan House, Chelsea, and the New Zealand Chambers.

8. Viollet-le-Duc [VB's note]. See *Discourses* (trans. VB), I, 314.

9. Charles Locke Eastlake (1833–1906). For his influence see Introduction, Part II.

10. John Ruskin, "Modern Manufacture and Design" (March 1859), *The Two Paths* (New York, 1885), p. 79.

11. "The Deteriorative Power of Conventional Art over Nations," delivered in January, 1858, and printed in *The Two Paths*, p. 25.

12. Ruskin, *The Two Paths*, pp. 46, 47 [VB's note].

13. William Wordsworth, "Elegiac Stanzas, suggested by a picture of Peele Castle, in a storm, painted by Sir George Beaumont," st. 4.

The New Architecture at Albany

1. See Introduction, Part II, and Van Brunt's review "Eidlitz's Nature of Art," for additional commentary on Leopold Eidlitz (1823–1908). See Van Brunt's article on Henry Hobson Richardson reprinted in this edition. Frederick Law Olmsted (1822–1903), America's greatest landscape architect, was the designer of Central Park, Prospect Park, the Boston Park System, the National Capitol grounds, the grounds of Biltmore, near Asheville, N. C., and the landscaping of the World's Columbian Exposition of 1893.

2. John Quincy Adams Ward (1830–1910), sculptor. The bas-reliefs were never executed.

3. William Morris Hunt (1824–1879), painter and brother of Richard Morris Hunt, the architect.

The New Dispensation of Monumental Art

1. Constantino Brumidi (1805–1880), painter of frescoes in the National Capitol.

2. William Cotton, *Sir Joshua Reynolds and His Works* (London, 1856), quoted in Ruskin's "The Unity of Art" (March 1859), *The Two Paths*, p. 72, where Van Brunt may have seen the remark.

3. Eugène Véron, *Aesthetics*, trans. W. H. Armstrong (London and Philadelphia, 1879), p. 288.

4. "No pent-up Utica contracts your powers, / But the whole boundless continent is yours," from Jonathan Mitchell Sewall, Prologue to Addison's *Cato*. Park Benjamin adopted the couplet as the motto of his paper, *The New World*.

Eidlitz's Nature of Art

1. See Introduction, Part II, and "The New Architecture at Albany," reprinted in this edition, for more treatment of Eidlitz.

2. *The Nature and Function of Art*, p. 255.

3. The same, p. 488. See chapter XV, "Science and Art" for some of the ideas following.

4. The same, p. vii.

The Personal Equation in Renaissance Architecture

1. A paper read before the Monday Evening Club [in Boston], by Henry Van Brunt. [VB's note.]

2. "Where Freedom slowly broadens down / From precedent to precedent," Alfred, Lord Tennyson, "You Ask Me Why?" ll. 11–12.

3. Eugène Véron, *Aesthetics*, trans. W. H. Armstrong (London and Philadelphia, 1879), p. 186.

4. Charles Blanc, *Grammaire des arts du dessin* (Paris, 1870), p. 321.

5. François Mansart (1598–1666) reconstructed Blois for Louis XIV's brother, and built the Val-de-Grâce in Paris and the Château de Maisons-Laffitte. Jules Hardouin-Mansart (1646?–1708) designed Versailles for Louis XIV as well as the Dôme des Invalides, the Place Vendôme, and the Place des Victoires.

6. See "Eidlitz's Nature of Art," n. 4.

7. See James Fergusson, *History of the Modern Styles of Architecture* (New York, 1891), I, 179.

On the Present Condition and Prospects of Architecture

1. A review of *Translations of Ancient Arabian Poetry*, ed. Charles James Lyall, *Atheneum* (Oct. 3, 1885), p. 427.

2. Anthemius of Tralles, mathematician and architect from Tralles in Lydia in the sixth century A.D., was one of the architects employed by the Emperor Justinian in building the church of St. Sophia, A.D. 532. Abbot Suger (c. 1081–1151) became abbot of St. Denis and was responsible for the construction of the new abbey church which inaugurated the Gothic style. In his *Libellus de consacratione ecclesiae St. Dionysii* he treats of improvements to St. Denis, describes the treasures of the church, and gives an account of the rebuilding.

3. The Banqueting House is by Inigo Jones (1573–1652); St. George's Hall, Liverpool, is by Harvey Lonsdale Elmes (1814–1849); Sir Charles Barry's influential club houses were the Travellers' Club (1830–1831) and the Reform Club (1838–1840).

4. See "Introduction to the *Discourses*," n. 7.

5. In his novel *Henry Esmond* (1852), William Makepeace Thackeray had used the reign of Queen Anne for background detail and setting and hence had sparked a revived interest in the period.

6. Johann Christoph Friedrich von Schiller, "Das Lied von der Glocke," ll. 19–20.

7. John Milton, *Paradise Lost*, II, 1021.

Henry Hobson Richardson, Architect

1. Thomas Hardy, *Far from the Madding Crowd* (London: Macmillan and Co., Ltd., 1962), p. 271. Sergeant Troy attributes the saying to an old philosopher.

2. See the opening of *Rambler* essay No. 60.

3. The author is the Rev. John Louis Petit. See revised edition (London, 1890), p. xxxiv.

4. Auguste Vaudremer (1829–1914) built the church of St. Pierre de Montrouge.

5. *Hamlet*, II, ii, 457.

Architecture in the West

1. John Keats, *Endymion*, l. 1.

2. Alfred, Lord Tennyson, *In Memoriam*, I.

3. See "Introduction to the *Discourses*," n. 10.

4. James Russell Lowell, "Commemoration Ode," st. VI.

5. John Milton, *Paradise Lost*, I, 711.

6. Daniel Hudson Burnham (1846–1912), partner of John Wellborn Root (1850–1891), was chief of construction of the World's Columbian Exposition of 1893. He was later chairman of the commission for the development of Washington, D. C., and made city plans for Cleveland, San Francisco, and Manila, as well as the Burnham Plan for Chicago. For Root, see Van Brunt's article "John Wellborn Root," below, and his review of Harriet Monroe's biography of the architect. Louis Sullivan (1856–1924) formed a firm with Dankmar Adler (1844–1900) and was a leader in the functionalist movement. His architectural values are contained in *Autobiography of an Idea* (New York: A.I.A. Press, 1924). Henry Ives Cobb (1859–1931) designed buildings for the University of Chicago and the Newberry Library. In 1882 he began practice in Chicago in association with Charles Sumner Frost (1856–1931) and continued the partnership till 1889. William LeBaron Jenney (1832–1907) devised for the Home Insurance Building (1883–1884), Chicago, a method of skeleton construction in which each story was carried independently on columns. This was the first high-rise building to use the method as a basic principle of design and is credited as being the first skyscraper. William Holabird (1854–1923) after 1883 was associated in partnership with Martin Roche (1855–1927). He devised in 1888 the first office building to utilize skeleton construction throughout its facades. Leroy Sunderland Buffington (1847–1931) designed the North Dakota State Capitol at Bismarck, railroad terminals at St. Paul and Minneapolis, and the Pillsbury Flour Mills. He was patentee of the steel frame building, which made possible the erection of the modern skyscraper.

7. *I Henry IV*, I, ii, 101.

The Washington Monument

1. Bertel Thorwaldsen (1768–1844), Danish sculptor; Joseph Andreas Kranner (1801–1871), Bohemian architect. Christian Daniel Rauch (1777–1857), sculptor, did an equestrian monument to Frederick the Great at Berlin in the Unter den Linden (1839–1851). Leo von Klenze (1784–1864) built the Munich Ruhmeshalle (1843–1853), a U-shaped Doric stoa which provides a setting for a giant statue of Bavaria by Schwantaler. Jean-François-Thérèse Chalgrin (1739–1811) began the Arc de Triomphe in 1806. The principal mass and conception of the whole are owing to him. The Scott Monument (1840–1846) is by G. Meikle Kemp (1795–1844). The Wallace Monument (1869) in the Scottish Baronial style, was designed by John Thomas Rochead (1814–1878), architect, of Glasgow.

2. Robert Mills (1781–1855) was one of the chief exponents of the Greek Revival style in the United States. He designed the Washington Monument in Baltimore and was Architect of Public Buildings, Washington, from 1836 to 1851. He built the Treasury, Patent Office, and Post Office buildings there.

3. Erwin von Steinbach (d. 1318) began the west facade of Strasbourg cathedral in 1277 and superintended construction till his death.

4. Robert Charles Winthrop, "National Monument to Washington" (July 4, 1848), *Addresses and Speeches on Various Occasions*, I (Boston, 1852), 88.

5. The design by Henry Robinson Searle, architect, was reproduced as illustration no. 166 in *American Architect and Building News*, vol. V (1879).

6. John Milton, *Paradise Lost*, I, 716.

7. See Robert Dale Owen, *Hints on Public Architecture, Containing, Among Other Illustrations, Views and Plans of the Smithsonian Institution* (New York, 1849), pp. 76, 109. Owen (1801–1877) drafted the bill founding the Smithsonian.

8. William Wetmore Story (1815–1895), whose biography has been written by Henry James. He did statues of Josiah Quincy, Edward Everett, and Colonel Shaw.

9. See illustration no. 202, *American Architect and Building News*, vol. VI (1879).

10. "A grey mountain of marble heaped foursquare, till, built to the skies," Robert Browning, "Saul," l. 178.

The Architecture at Harvard

1. See Introduction, Part I, n. 52.
2. See *The Nation*, LI (Sept. 4, 1890), 192.
3. The Van Brunts sometimes summered at Manitou.

John Wellborn Root

1. *Much Ado about Nothing*, IV, i, 219–224, 226–232.

2. The epitaph of Sir Christopher Wren, composed by his son, is in St. Paul's Cathedral: "Subtus conditur hujus ecclesiae et urbis conditor Christophorus Wren, qui vixit annos ultra nonaginta, non sibi, sed bono publico, Lector, si monumentum requiris, circumspice."

3. James Renwick (1818–1895) was also architect of the Smithsonian Institution, Washington, D. C., and Vassar College Building.

4. John Butler Snook (1815–1901) was architect of the Metropolitan Hotel in New York and the house of William H. Vanderbilt.

5. Carter, Drake, and Wight, the firm of Peter Wight (1838–1925), architect of the National Academy of Design Building, New York, and the Yale School of Fine Arts; famous for Italian Gothic facades in the style popularized by Ruskin.

6. See Harriet Monroe, *John Wellborn Root* (Park Forest, Ill.: Prairie School Press, 1966), p. 126.

7. Edward John Phelps (1822–1900), lawyer and diplomat, made the remark in a speech at the Mansion House, London, on January 24, 1889. It was earlier made by Bishop W. C. Magee in a sermon at Peterborough, England, in 1868.

8. See "The Personal Equation in Renaissance Architecture," n. 7.

9. The opening line of Henry Wadsworth Longfellow's *Kavanaugh* (1849).

Architecture at the World's Columbian Exposition

1. John Milton, *Samson Agonistes*, l. 712.

2. For Richard Morris Hunt, see Van Brunt's eulogy below. George B. Post (1837–1913) was architect of the Western Union Building, the Produce Exchange, the Stock Exchange, and the Cotton Exchange. Charles Follen McKim (1847–1909) joined partnership with William Rutherford Mead (1846–1928) in 1878. They were in turn joined by Stanford White (1853–1906) in 1879. The firm was the leading office during the period of the American Renaissance. McKim designed the Boston Public Library, the campus of Columbia University, the University Club, New York, the Morgan Library, and Pennsylvania Station. White designed the Metropolitan Club, New York, the Washington Arch, New York, and the original Madison Square Garden. Robert Swain Peabody (1845–1917) joined partnership with John Goddard Stearns (1843–1917) in Boston. They designed the statehouse at Concord, N. H., as well as many commercial buildings. Solon S. Beman (1853–1914) designed the buildings of Pullman, Illinois, the Pullman and Studebaker Buildings in Chicago, and the Pabst and Northwest Mutual Life Buildings in Milwaukee. Henry Sargent Codman (1864–1893) was Olmsted's assistant until his early death.

3. Augustus St. Gaudens (1848–1907), sculptor. His chief works are the Shaw Memorial in Boston and the equestrian statue of General William Tecumseh Sherman in New York.

4. Sir Joseph Paxton (1801–1865), gardener and architect, designed the Crystal Palace for the London Exhibition of 1851.

5. Frederic Harrison, "A Few Words about the Nineteenth Century," *Fortnightly Review*, CLXXXIV (April 1882), 426, reprinted in *The Choice of Books and Other Literary Pieces* (London, 1888), pp. 446–447.

6. Karl Bitter (1867–1915), sculptor of the figures in the facade of the Metropolitan Museum and the battle group in Dewey Arch, New York.

7. See "Cast Iron in Decorative Architecture," n. 5.

8. Frederick MacMonnies (1863–1937), sculptor of the statue of Nathan Hale, City Hall Park, New York, the Army and Navy groups and the Quadriga of the Soldiers and Sailors Monument, Brooklyn, and equestrian statues of Theodore Roosevelt and Gen. G. B. McClellan.

9. Daniel Chester French (1850–1931), sculptor of the Minute Man, Concord, Mass., the statue of John Harvard, Cambridge, Mass., and the Lincoln figure in the Lincoln Memorial.

10. Max Bachman (d. 1921), sculptor.

11. Adolph Kraus (1850–1901), sculptor of the Crispus Attucks monument.

12. Alexander Pope, "An Essay on Man," l. 6.

13. The Incantada is the ruins of a late Roman building of the second century, A.D., in Salonica, Greece. It is generally Corinthian in style. Five columns remain with an entablature, above which rises a low attic with engaged figure sculpture. The building is illustrated in Stuart and Revett's *Antiquities of Athens*.

14. Philip Martiny (1858–1927) worked closely with McKim, Mead, and White.

He did the marble carvings in the entrance hall of the Library of Congress, the Soldiers and Sailors Monument, Jersey City, N. J., the south doors of St. Bartholomew's, New York, and the cornice and entrance figures on the New York City Hall of Records.

15. "He either fears his fate too much,
Or his deserts are small
That dares not put it to the touch
To gain or lose it all."

James Graham, First Marquess of Montrose (1612–1650), "My Dear and Only Love," st. 2.

16. Carl Rohl-Smith (1848–1900), designer of the Sherman Monument in front of the Treasury Building, Washington, D. C.

17. Condorcet, in his *Vie de Monsieur* [Anne-Robert] *Turgot* (London, 1786), p. 200, quotes the following inscription on a bust of Franklin: "Eripuit coelo fulmen, mox sceptra tyrannis."

18. Lorado Taft (1860–1936), sculptor of the Columbus Fountain, Washington, D. C., and the Fountain of the Great Lakes and Fountain of Time in Chicago.

19. *The Tempest*, I, ii, 400–401.

20. Charles B. Atwood (1849–1895) was architect of the Hamilton McKown Twombley and William Seward Webb houses on Fifth Avenue, New York. The Fine Arts Building, rebuilt in granite in 1930, is now the Museum of Science and Industry.

The Historic Styles and Modern Architecture

1. Jules Michelet, "Sens et portée de la Renaissance," *Histoire de France*, IX (Paris, 1876), 6.

2. François-Pierre-Guillaume Guizot (1787–1874), French statesman and historian, among whose many works are *Histoire de la civilisation en Europe* (1828) and *Histoire de la civilisation en France* (1830). Charles-Forbes-René de Montalembert (1810–1870) was a historian and academician, among whose works are *Du catholicisme et du vandalisme dans l'art* (1839), praising the architecture and sculpture of the Middle Ages, and *Histoire des moines d'occident depuis saint Benoît jusqu'à saint Bernard* (1860–1867), praising the Middle Ages for their liberty and civilization.

3. John Addington Symonds, "Culture," *In The Key of Blue and Other Prose Essays* (London, 1893), p. 206.

4. Psalms 119:45.

5. See *Discourses* (trans. VB), I, 295 and 298.

6. Alan of Walsingham (d. 1364?), the architect who rebuilt the tower of Ely Cathedral and made other additions, constructing the unique octagonal lantern.

7. Charles Moore, *Development and Character of Gothic Architecture* (London and New York, 1890), chapter I and *passim*. See Van Brunt's review of the book.

8. "In teacup times of hood and hoop,
Or while the patch was worn."

Alfred, Lord Tennyson, "The Talking Oak," 1. 63.

9. Victor Hugo (1802–1885) made Gothic architecture the basis of his novel *Nôtre-Dame de Paris* and stimulated great interest in its beauties.

10. "Culture," pp. 211 and 212, respectively.

11. Paul-Marie Letarouilly (1795–1855), architect and author of *Edifices de Rome moderne* (Paris, 1840).

12. Alfred, Lord Tennyson, "Mariana."
13. William Wordsworth, "The world is too much with us."

The Columbian Exposition and American Civilization

1. Of 1851.
2. The Eiffel Tower, built by Gustave Eiffel (1832–1923) for the Paris Exhibition of 1889.
3. Francis Davis Millet (1846–1912), painter, associated with E. A. Abbey, John Singer Sargent, and Henry James, in a colony of expatriate Americans at Broadway, England.
4. See Charles Eliot Norton, "The Building of the Church of St. Denis," *Harper's Magazine*, LXXIX (1889), 766–767.
5. For the report of the Marquis de Chasseloup-Laubat see *Mémoires et compte rendu des travaux de la société des ingénieurs civils* (Octobre, 1892), p. 653.
6. *The Merchant of Venice*, IV, i, 187.
7. Henry Wadsworth Longfellow, "The Day Is Done," st. 11.
8. See "John Wellborn Root," n. 1.
9. John Milton, *Paradise Lost*, I, 711–712.
10. See John 12:3.

The Growth of Characteristic Architectural Style in the United States

1. Prepared by invitation of the American Institute of Architects, to be read at its annual convention, but by its courtesy made a part of the programme of the Congress of Architects [VB's note].
2. A review of Henry James' *Essays in London and Elsewhere*, London *Times*, June 23, 1893, p. 8.
3. Richardson's adaptation of the tower of the Cathedral of Salamanca for Trinity Church, Boston. The adaptation was probably the work of Stanford White, who was then in Richardson's office.

Richard Morris Hunt

1. Dr. Johnson. See "Henry Hobson Richardson, Architect," n. 2.
2. Horace, *Satires*, 2, 3, 243.
3. Samuel Darier (1808–1884).
4. Hector-Martin Lefuel (1810–1880), chief architect of the new Louvre, succeeding Visconti. He finished the inner fronts of the buildings enclosing the Place du Carrousel and remodelled the Grande Galerie of the Louvre from the Pavillon Lesdiguières to the Pavillon de Flore. Between 1860 and 1870 he remodelled the Pavillon de Flore and between 1871 and 1876 the Pavillon Marsan.
5. Louis-Tullius-Joachim Visconti (1791–1853) built the Fontaine Louvois, Paris, the Fontaine Molière, and the Fontaine of the Place Saint-Sulpice. He made plans for the completion of the Louvre, but his death intervened, and the work was modified and carried out by his successor, Lefuel.
6. Thomas Ustick Walter (1804–1887), architect of Girard College, Philadelphia, as well as the Capitol dome and extensions.
7. In 1867 Gambrill entered into partnership with Henry Hobson Richardson.
8. Frank Furness (1839–1912), the Philadelphia architect in whose office (Furness and Hewitt) the young Louis Sullivan received part of his training. The firm designed the Pennsylvania Academy of Fine Arts (1871–1876).

9.   "Let humble Allen, with an awkward shame,
                Do good by stealth, and blush to call it fame."

Alexander Pope, "Epilogue to the Satires," 11. 135–136.

10.   "E'en in our ashes live their wonted fires,"

Thomas Gray, "Elegy in a Country Churchyard," st. 23.

11. Alfred, Lord Tennyson, *In Memoriam*, XL, 20.

Classic Architecture

1. My copy of this pamphlet, which was Van Brunt's own, contains several corrections of the text in the author's own hand. I have silently altered the printed version to incorporate them.

2. Francis Cranmer Penrose (1817–1903), author of *An Investigation of the Principles of Athenian Architecture* (1851) and architect in charge of St. Paul's Cathedral, London.

Two Interpreters of National Architecture

1. *The Life of John Wellborn Root*, by Harriet Monroe. Boston and New York: Houghton Mifflin & Co., 1896 [VB's note].

2. *Life and Letters of Charles Bulfinch, Architect. With Other Family Papers.* Edited by his Granddaughter, Ellen Susan Bulfinch. With an Introduction by Charles A. Cummings. Boston and New York: Houghton Mifflin & Co., 1896 [VB's note].

3. See Van Brunt's article, "Henry Hobson Richardson," in this edition.

4. Peter Nicholson (1765–1844), *The New Carpenter's Guide*, London, 1792, and many subsequent editions.

5. William Thornton (1759–1828), architect of the Capitol, Washington, D. C., and Octagon House, Washington, D. C. Benjamin Henry Latrobe (1764–1820), architect of the south wing of the Capitol, who designed the "American order" of corncob capitals for the east basement vestibule. He was in charge of the rebuilding of the Capitol after the War of 1812. He also designed the Catholic Cathedral in Baltimore.

6. Harriet Monroe, *John Wellborn Root*, p. 25.

7. The same, p. 192.

8. The same, p. 110.

9. Alfred, Lord Tennyson, *In Memoriam*, CIX, 2.

10. Monroe, *Root*, p. 62.

11. The same, p. 63.

12. The same, p. 65.

13. The same, p. 69.

14. The same, p. 75.

15. The same, p. 95.

16. The same, pp. 107–108.

A Letter on the Aesthetics of Bridge Construction

1. John Alexander Low Waddell (1854–1938), civil engineer. He was in practice in Kansas City from 1886 to 1920, and thereafter in New York. Waddell, one of the best known bridge engineers and consultants of his time, originated the modern vertical-lift bridge, the first of its type being the South Halsted St. Bridge, Chicago, 1893.

2. See "The Growth of Conscience," n. 8.

3. Charles Dibdin (1745–1814), British musician, dramatist, novelist, actor, and songwriter. He introduced many of the sea songs which stimulated the spirit of the Navy during the French War. He wrote " 'Twas in the good ship 'Rover,' " "Saturday Night at Sea," "I sailed from the Downs in the Nancy," and "Tom Bowling." Thomas Campbell (1777–1844), poet, author of "Ye Mariners of England."

Index

Index

6; Back Bay Park bridges, 174; Beacon St., 17, 174; Brattle St. Church, 174; 41 Brimmer St., 533, Fig. 23; B. W. Crowninshield house, 174; Ether Monument, 17, Fig. 20; 7–9 Fairfield St., 533; Faneuil Hall, 6, 532; First Church (Unitarian), 17, Fig. 18; Forest Hills Cemetery, Fig. 52; Great Fire, 20; F. L. Higginson house, 174; Hotel Hamilton, Fig. 35; Little and Brown's, 7, 19; 282–292 Marlborough St., 533, Fig. 24; Massachusetts General Hospital, 364, Fig. 163; Mercantile Library, Fig. 160a; Old Music Hall, 9; Park System, 542; Public Garden, 17; Public Library, 533, 546; Shaw Memorial, 546; State House, 363, Fig. 162; stores, 174, 175; Tontine Crescent, Figs. 160, 160a; Trinity Church, 58, 135, 136, 137–140, 174, 176, 177, 548, Figs. 101–101b, 102–102d; Trinity Church rectory, 174; warehouses, 176
Boston after Bulfinch, see Kilham, Walter
Boston and Albany railroad, 174, 177
Bouguereau, Adolphe-William, 336
Boulle, André-Charles, 114, 541
Bourges: Jacques Cœur, house, 27
Bradley, Edward, *Adventures of Verdant Green*, 15, 533, Fig. 3.
Bramante, Donato, 155
Breuer, Marcel, 17
Bridge-building, steel, 73, 374–378, 549
Brioude, Church of St. Julian, 172
Brisbane, Australia: Cathedral, 542
Brookline, Mass., 173, 174; E. S. Philbrick house, Fig. 34
Brooklyn, N.Y.: Prospect Park, 542; Soldiers and Sailors Monument, 546
Brown, Arthur, Jr., Fig. 194
Browning, Robert, 208, 545
Bruges, 85
Brumidi, Constantino, 135, Figs. 105, 105a
Brunelleschi, Filippo, 326
Buddhist temples, 222
Buffalo, N.Y.: W. Dorsheimer house, 174; W. H. Gratwick house, 175; State Asylum, 174
Buffington, Leroy Sunderland, 194, 544, Fig. 131
Bulfinch, Charles, 360–365, 369; works, 361, 362–363, 364, Figs. 160–164
Bulfinch, E. S. (ed.), *Life and Letters of Charles Bulfinch*, 360, 364
Bullant, Jean, 99
Burges, William, 115, 177, 541, Figs. 88, 89
Burling and Whitehouse, 194, 229, Fig. 119
Burlington, Vt.: Billings Library, 174
Burnham, Alan, 12, 532
Burnham, Daniel H., 215, 366, 367, 544, Fig. 192; partnership with Root, 215, 366–367; work at WCE, 65, 225, 227, 228, 229, 233, 311, 367, 544, Fig. 139. *See also* Burnham and Root
Burnham and Root, 193, 215–216, 218, 220–224, 365, 366, Figs. 120, 125–128, 133, 135–137
Byzantine architecture, 79, 87, 118, 142, 184,

268, 269–270, 290, 351, 354; revival, 67, 90, 100, 171

Caen, 290
Cairo, 267
Callicrates, 114, 159
Cambio, Arnolfo di, 85, 109, 541
Cambridge, Eng., 31; Emmanuel College, 31–32; King's College Chapel, 25, 27
Cambridge, Mass.: Blake Monument, Mt. Auburn Cemetery, Fig 53; Brattle St., 18, Fig. 45; Channing Place, 533; 35 Concord Ave., Fig. 50; Episcopal Theological School, 17, Figs. 22–22b, and deanery, 533; Fayerweather house, 18, Fig. 2; Adam Hill house, 533, 546; Massachusetts Ave., 533, 534; Public Library, Figs. 61, 61a; 16 Sacramento St., 533; Third Universalist Church, Fig. 27. *See also* Harvard University
Capitols, state, 193. *See also* individual places
Caracci, Annibale, 144
Carcassonne, 102
Carlyle, Thomas, 19–20, 46, 111
Carter, Drake and Wight, 215, 366
Cast iron, 79–80, 84, 86, 87, 88, 325; construction, 88, 166, 292, 325, 537
Century Magazine, 70, 72
Chalgrin, Jean-François-Thérèse, 196
Chambers, Sir William, 92, 166, 362; *Civil Architecture* (Gwilt, Joseph, ed.), 7–8
Chambord, château de, 93, 128, 256, 339
Charleston, S.C.: monument to John C. Calhoun, Fig. 40
Chartres: Cathedral, 541
Chasseloup-Laubat, Marquis de, 313–314, 315
Chenonceau, château de, 93
Chestnut Hill, Mass.: Boston and Albany railroad depot, 174
Cheyenne, Wyo.: Union Pacific passenger depot, Fig. 59
Chicago, Ill., 60, 306, 364, 365, 368; as center of reform in West, 60, 185–186, 191–192, 193; American Express Co. Bldg., 174; Art Institute, 193, 221, Figs. 132, 133; Auditorium Bldg., 194, 269, Figs. 129, 132, 133; Board of Trade Bldg., 193; Burnham Plan, 544; Calumet Bldg., 218, 220–221, Fig. 120; Chicago Club, 133; Continental Bank Bldg., Fig. 125; Continental Illinois National Bank, Fig. 192; Crosby's Opera House, Fig. 118; fire, 215; Fountain of the Great Lakes, 547; Garrick Theater Bldg., Figs. 138, 138a; J. J. Glessner house, 175; Grannis Bldg., 220; Home Insurance Bldg., 544, Fig. 124; Insurance Exchange Bldg., 193, 220, 221, Fig. 125; Jackson Park (as site for WCE), 216, 225–227, 231; Franklin MacVeagh house, 175; Marshall Field Wholesale Store, 63, 174, 176, Figs. 129, 186; Masonic Temple, 223, 224, Fig. 136; Michigan Ave., Fig. 132; Monadnock Bldg., Fig. 135; Montauk Bldg., 220; Museum of Science and Industry, 547; Newberry Library, 544; Samuel Nickerson house, Fig. 119; Opera House, 194, Fig. 121; Owings

552

Harper's Magazine, 41, 210
Harrison, Frederic, 39, 235
Hartford, Conn.: Cheney Bldgs., 174; Phoenix Insurance Bldg., 174
Harvard, John, 32, 546
Harvard University, 2, 9, 16, 18, 41–42; Appleton Chapel, 211; Fogg Art Museum (Hunt Hall), Fig. 181; Gore Hall, Fig. 30; Harvard Hall, 210; Hastings Hall, 211; Hemenway Gymnasium, 211; Holden Chapel, 210; Hollis Hall, 210; Holworthy Hall, 210; old library, 16; Massachusetts Hall, 210, Fig. 159; Matthews Hall, Fig. 165; Medical School, 16, Fig. 48; Memorial Hall, 16, 17–18, 211, 534, Figs. 28, 29; Peabody Museum, 211; New Law School (Austin Hall), 174, 178, 211, 212, Fig. 107; Sever Hall, 174, 211, 212, Fig. 106; Stoughton Hall, 210; University Hall, Fig. 161; Weld Hall, 16, Fig. 25
Hasenclever, Johann Peter, 531
Hautecœur, Louis, 36
Hayden, Julia Gorham, 173
Hayden, Sophia G., 272–275, Fig. 155
Healy, G. P. A., 6, 532
Henry, Joseph, 260
Herder, J. G., 54, 296
Herkomer, Prof. Hubert, A.RA., house, 175
Hermogenes, 114
Hildebrandt, Theodor, 531
Hillard, George Stillman, 9
Holabird, William, 544. See also Holabird and Roche
Holabird and Roche, 194, 244, Fig. 134
Holyoke, Mass.: railroad depot, 174
Honnecourt, Villard de, 114
Hopkins, Henry, 20
Horace, 109, 329, 541, 548
Howe, Frank, 16, 20, 236, 535. See also Van Brunt and Howe
Hugo, Victor, 41, 295
Hunt, Catherine Howland, 10, 12, 14, 341
Hunt, Richard Howland, Fig. 183
Hunt, Richard Morris: eulogy, 9, 12, and VB's article; Papers, 10; life, 10–11, 329–330; studio, 12–13, 14, 64, Figs. 4, 16, 167 (see also New York, 10th St. Studio Bldg.); pupils, 10, 11, 12–14, 331, 332; connection with A.I.A., 11, 15, 328, 335, 337; appraisal, 11, 58, 69–70, 328–329, 331, 334, 335–336, 337–338, 340, 341; home and library, 12–13, 14, 332–333; methods, 12, 13, 14, 15, 333–334, 340; practice, 14–15, 331; influences on, 14, 15, 330, 333, 335, 338–339; influence of, 15, 20, 334–339; education and training, 329–330; style, 338–339; thought, 334; honors, 334, 336–337; portrait, 341; death, 341; work, 10, 17, 330–331, 332, 334, 336, 339, 531, Figs. 41, 166–183, 187; at WCE, 69, 229, 236–238, 334, Figs. 142, 146
Hunt, William Morris, 132–133, 135, 140, 141, 142–144, 329–330; work, The Discoverer, 141, 142–144, Fig. 104b; Flight of Night, 141, 142–144, Figs. 103i, 104, 104a

Hyde, E. L., 10, 332

India, architecture of, 113, 124, 147, 195, 202, 219, 222, 267, 268, 300; Taj Mahal, 113, 208, 267, 268
Iron, forged, 79, 85, 123. See also Cast iron
Irving, Washington, 4, 5
Istanbul: St. Sophia, 159, 290, 543

James, Henry, 13, 17, 23, 38, 73, 324, 378, 545, 548
James, Henry, Sr., 19–20
Japan, art of, 114, 122, 123, 124, 139, 147
Jenney, William LeBaron, 194, 229, 270–272, Fig. 124. See also Jenney and Mundie
Jenney and Mundie, 270–272, Fig. 154
Jersey City, N.J.: Soldiers and Sailors Monument, 547
Johnson, Samuel, 56, 548
Jones, Inigo, 152, 544
Justinian, Emperor, 160, 543

Kansas City, Mo., 20–21, 191–192, 193; K. B. Aman house, Fig. 70; American Bank, 222; Mrs. A. W. Armour house, Fig. 72; Kirkland B. Armour house, 46, 534; Art Institute, 21; Board of Trade Bldg., 193, Fig. 128; Bryant Bldg., Fig. 73; Kansas City Star Bldg., 534; R. Conklin house, 387; Eastern architects in, 191; Emery, Bird, and Thayer Bldg., 21, 32, Fig. 66; Kansas City Club, Fig. 63; Coates House Hotel, 21, Fig. 65; Exchange Bldg., 222; Old Federal Bldg. (Fidelity Trust Co.), 534; Gibraltar Bldg., Fig. 62; J. D. Griffith house, 46, 534; Robert Keith Furniture and Carpet Co., 534; J. J. Mastin house, Fig. 58; August R. Meyer house, Fig. 71; New York Life Bldg., 21, Fig. 76; Prospect Ave. Christian Church, 534; E. W. Smith house, Fig. 74; Nathaniel Thayer Bldg., Fig. 56
Karnak, 159, 352
Keats, John, 182, 544
Kemp, G. Meikle, 545
Kilham, Walter, 9, 17; Boston after Bulfinch, 532
Kittery, Maine, 4
Klenze, Leo von, 196
Kraft, Adam, 85
Kranner, Joseph Andreas, 196
Kraus, Adolf, 244, 546

Labrouste, Henri, 15, 16–17, 100, 115, 296, 338, Figs. 94, 94a
La Farge, John, 135, 136–141, Figs. 101a, 101b, 102–102d
Landsburgh, G. Albert, Fig. 194
Landscape architecture, see WCE
Laon: Cathedral, 102
Lapo, Arnolfo da, see Cambio, Arnolfo di
Lassus, Jean-Baptiste-Antoine, 100, 296, 541
Latrobe, Benjamin Henry, 364
Laugier, Marc-Antoine, 49
Lee, Admiral Samuel Phillips, 16
Lefuel, Hector-Martin, 10, 330, Figs. 95–95b

Index

Index